*Japanese Science Fiction,
Fantasy and Horror Films*

ALSO BY STUART GALBRAITH IV
AND FROM MCFARLAND

*The Japanese Filmography: A Complete Reference to 209
Filmmakers and the Over 1250 Films Released in the
United States, 1900 through 1994* (1996)

*Motor City Marquees: A Comprehensive, Illustrated
Reference to Motion Picture Theaters in the Detroit Area,
1906–1992* (1994; paperback 2001)

Japanese Science Fiction, Fantasy and Horror Films

A Critical Analysis of 103 Features Released in the United States, 1950–1992

STUART GALBRAITH IV

Research Associate R. M. HAYES

with a foreword by
BILL WARREN

McFarland & Company, Inc., Publishers
Jefferson, North Carolina, and London

The present work is a reprint of the library bound edition of Japanese Science Fiction, Fantasy and Horror Films: A Critical Analysis and Filmography of 103 Features Released in the United States, 1950–1992, *first published in 1994 by McFarland.*

This book is respectfully dedicated to Toho Company, Ltd.'s team of craftsmen and stock company of actors, especially Tomoyuki Tanaka, Ishiro Honda, Akira Ifukube, and Eiji Tsuburaya

LIBRARY OF CONGRESS CATALOGUING-IN-PUBLICATION DATA

Galbraith, Stuart, 1965–
    Japanese science fiction, fantasy and horror films : a critical analysis and filmography of 103 features released in the United States, 1950–1992 / by Stuart Galbraith IV.
    p.   cm.
    Filmography: p.
    Includes bibliographical references and index.

    ISBN-13: 978-0-7864-2126-8
    softcover : 50# alkaline paper ∞

    1. Science fiction films—Japan—History and criticism.
I. Title.
PN1995.9.S26G26   2007
791.43'615—dc20   92-56645

British Library cataloguing data are available

©1994 Stuart Galbraith IV. All rights reserved

No part of this book may be reproduced or transmitted in any form or by any means, electronic or mechanical, including photocopying or recording, or by any information storage and retrieval system, without permission in writing from the publisher.

On the cover: Artwork for the 1988 film *Tetsuo: The Iron Man* (Original Cinema/Photofest)

Manufactured in the United States of America

McFarland & Company, Inc., Publishers
  Box 611, Jefferson, North Carolina 28640
    www.mcfarlandpub.com

Contents

Acknowledgments xi
Preface xiii
A Note About the Text xxi
"A Wind from the East" by Bill Warren xxiii

The Fifties

Rashomon (1950)	2	Throne of Blood (1957)	32
Tales of Ugetsu (1953)	4	Attack from Space (1958)	34
Godzilla, King of the Monsters!		Evil Brain from Outer Space	
(1954/1956)	7	(1958)	35
Gigantis the Fire Monster (1955)	14	The H-Man (1958)	37
Half Human: The Story of the		Invaders from Space (1958)	39
Abominable Snowman (1955/		Varan the Unbelievable (1958/	
1957)	18	1962)	41
The Mysterious Satellite (1956)	21	Battle in Outer Space (1959)	44
Rodan (1956)	23	The Ghost of Yotsuya (1959)	47
Atomic Rulers (1957)	26	Prince of Space (1959)	49
The Mysterians (1957)	28	The Three Treasures (1959)	51

The Sixties

The Final War (1960)	54	Gorath (1962)	72
The Human Vapor (1960)	55	King Kong vs. Godzilla (1962/	
The Secret of the Telegian (1960)	57	1963)	76
Invasion of the Neptune Men		Atragon (1963)	81
(1961)	60	Attack of the Mushroom People	
The Last War (1961)	63	(1963)	84
The Manster (1961)	66	The Lost World of Sinbad	
Mothra (1961)	68	(1963)	87

Dagora, the Space Monster (1964)	90	War of the Monsters (1966)	138
Godzilla vs. the Thing (1964)	92	King Kong Escapes (1967)	141
Ghidrah: The Three-Headed Monster (1964)	96	Monster from a Prehistoric Planet (1967)	145
Kwaidan (1964)	100	Return of the Giant Monsters (1967)	147
Onibaba (1964)	105	Son of Godzilla (1967)	150
Adventure in Takla Makan (1965) (1965)	108	The X from Outer Space (1967)	153
Frankenstein Conquers the World (1965)	109	You Only Live Twice (1967)	155
		Black Lizard (1968)	157
Gammera the Invincible (1965/1966)	112	Destroy All Monsters (1968)	161
Monster Zero (1965)	115	Destroy All Planets (1968)	165
Ebirah, Horror of the Deep (1966)	120	Goke: Bodysnatcher from Hell (1968)	166
		The Green Slime (1968)	169
The Face of Another (1966)	124	Kaidan Botandoro (1968)	172
The Magic Serpent (1966)	126	Mighty Jack (1968)	173
Majin (1966)	129	100 Monsters (1968)	176
The Return of the Giant Majin (1966)	132	Voyage into Space (1968)	177
		Attack of the Monsters (1969)	181
Majin Strikes Again (1966)	133	The Blind Beast (1969)	183
Terror Beneath the Sea (1966)	134	Godzilla's Revenge (1969)	184
War of the Gargantuas (1966)	136	Latitude Zero (1969)	186

The Seventies

Gamera vs. Monster X (1970)	192	The Last Days of Planet Earth (1974)	220
The Vampire Doll (1970)	194		
Yog: Monster from Space (1970)	196	Space Warriors 2000 (1974)	223
Gamera vs. Zigra (1971)	198	Evil of Dracula (1975)	225
Godzilla vs. the Smog Monster (1971)	201	Terror of Mechagodzilla (1975)	227
		Time of the Apes (1975)	230
Lake of Dracula (1971)	204	The Last Dinosaur (1977)	234
Godzilla on Monster Island (1972)	207	The "Legend of the Dinosaurs" (1977)	236
Godzilla vs. Megalon (1973)	210	The War in Space (1977)	239
Tidal Wave (1973/1975)	213	The Bermuda Depths (1978)	242
Godzilla vs. the Cosmic Monster (1974)	217	Fugitive Alien (1978)	244
		Message from Space (1978)	248

Star Force: Fugitive Alien II (1978)	251	Swords of the Space Ark (1979)	253

The Eighties and Beyond

Gamera Super Monster (1980)	258	Solar Crisis (1990)	279
The Ivory Ape (1980)	261	Twilight of the Cockroaches (1989)	283
Virus (1980)	263		
Godzilla 1985 (1984/1985)	266	Godzilla vs. King Ghidorah (1991)	286
Tetsuo: The Iron Man (1988)	270		
Godzilla vs. Biollante (1989)	272	The Guyver (1991)	291
Akira Kurosawa's Dreams (1990)	276	Godzilla vs. Mothra (1992)	293

Filmography 299
An Introductory Note 299
Daiei Motion Picture Company, Ltd. 300
Nikkatsu Corporation 314
Shintoho Company, Ltd. 315
Shochiku Company, Ltd. 318
Toei Company, Ltd. 325
Toho Company, Ltd. 337
Tsuburaya Enterprises, Inc. 376
Miscellaneous Productions 381

Bibliography 395

Appendix: Additional Godzilla Appearances 399

Index 401

Acknowledgments

R. M. Hayes, David Milner and Horácio Higuchi helped considerably with the filmography and offered immeasurably good advice on just about everything else. Hayes and Higuchi know more about motion picture credits than anyone else I know, while Milner's expertise proved invaluable during editing. Their generous and time-consuming efforts are greatly appreciated.

Many, many thanks also to Bill Warren, who graciously agreed to write a foreword. If you haven't already done so, be sure to pick up his two-volume work *Keep Watching the Skies!* — required reading for anyone seriously interested in science fiction films.

My wife, Anne, courageously endured the noisy destruction of Japan at all hours and probably heard the vocal talents of Paul Frees, Marvin Miller and Les Tremayne more frequently than her own husband's.

Mike Vraney of Something Weird Video helped track down some of the hardest-to-find films ever shown on American television.

I'm also indebted to the following individuals and organizations, who in one way or another contributed to this book: Robert Andrews; Robert E. Carr; Andy Cirinesi at Back to the Past; Daiei Motion Picture Co., Ltd.; Roger Fenton; Kitty Films; the Margaret Herrick Research Library; Nikkatsu Corp.; the very generous Ted Okuda; Rankin-Bass Productions, Inc.; Michael Robichaud; Shochiku Co., Ltd.; Toei Co., Ltd.; Tsuburaya Enterprises, Inc.; United Productions of America; Tom White and AD supreme Charles Ziarko.

Preface

"An incredibly awful film." That was how the *New York Times'* Bosley Crowther described *Godzilla, King of the Monsters!* (1956), the first of a long-running series of giant monster movies released in Japan. The *Times* wasn't alone in its opinion of the picture, and save for selected works of acclaimed filmmakers like Akira Kurosawa and Kenji Mizoguchi, Japanese fantastic cinema has become something of a bad joke in the United States.

And yet it survives, remaining very much alive in the hearts and minds of American popular culture. Japanese monsters are the subject of comedy routines and video games. They're on T-shirts and in greeting cards, comic books, pop music lyrics and all manner of commercial advertising (the very expensive "Godzilla vs. Charles Barkley" campaign to name but one example). Certainly, somebody in this country must have liked these films. I was one of those people. I admit it. I love Japanese monster movies.

I grew up in Livonia, a completely nondescript suburb of Detroit. During the 1970s, the local ABC affiliate, WXYZ-TV (Channel 7), preceded its weekday newscasts with "The Four o'Clock Movie." The program opened with a colorful montage of a silhouetted film crew moving lights, booms, etc., all to the beat of lively theme music I still vividly remember. Normally, I rarely watched the show, partly because the movies were brutally cut to fit a tight time slot (incredibly, the program was trimmed to just sixty minutes in its final months); longer features were often shown over several days.

Several times each year, Channel 7 would schedule a "Godzilla Week," which turned out to be just perfect for kids like me. I'd sit glued to my parents' ludicrously poor color television set (everybody and everything came out olive green), until they got sick of the monstrous grunts and groans and bought me a tiny black and white set of my own. *Godzilla vs. the Sea Monster*, *Destroy All Monsters* and *Attack of the Monsters* (a Gamera movie) stand out in particular in my movie-watching memory. I think what made these films so appealing to me is that I was able to watch them with the innocence of childhood. Tue, I knew what I was seeing was not really happening. Moreover, I knew even then that Godzilla was nothing more than a guy in a rubber suit smashing miniature buildings. But unlike most American adults, I was able to suspend my disbelief and enjoy the films for the epic spectacles they were.

Over the next twenty years my interest in movies would expand far beyond the scope of Japanese monster movies. Indeed, I'm one of the few people I know interested in all kinds of movies: science fiction, Westerns, musicals, silent films, foreign "art house" films, short subjects. I also made films myself and am as much interested in the business of moviemaking and movie theaters as in the pictures themselves. I work very hard at keeping an open mind on all manner of films and genres. The fact is that most movies aren't very good, but unless you keep an open mind, you'll miss out on many of the good (or at least interesting) ones. Most Westerns are like any other Western. Most science fiction and horror movies are too cheap and uninspired to be of much interest. Most musicals have uninspired musical numbers.

So it is with Japanese fantastic films. For every *Ugetsu* or *Mothra* (yes, *Mothra*) there seems to be a dozen *Godzilla vs. Megalon*s. The cream of the crop may not be objets d'art—any more so than Hammer or American International's best pictures—but the best of these things are good films, period.

As a professional film critic, I am paid to watch and evaluate a film objectively, and that is what I have tried to do here. Unfortunately, my fellow critics and scholars haven't been giving these films their due, at least not until now. I hold no grudge against those critics who gave these pictures bad reviews—a lot of them are as bad as they claim. I do, however, hold them responsible for the great amount of misinformation they have dished out when discussing Japanese fantastic cinema.

For instance, Roger Ebert, in his review of *Godzilla 1985*, suggested Japanese fantasy film fans have "treasured the absurd dialogue, the bad lip synching, the unbelievable special effects, the phony profundity.... They have deliberately gone after the same inept feeling in *Godzilla 1985*." This is sheer nonsense. Ebert, like so many American film reviewers, mistook the ineptitude of the slapdash Americanization with the sincerely made (if not entirely successful) original Japanese production. Nobody I know "treasures" bad lip synching; most fans of the genre prefer subtitles to dubbing. Moreover, like nearly every American film magazine and newspaper in the United States, Ebert seems to enjoy lambasting these pictures while writing inaccurately about them (Ebert's review contains several factual errors). In the case of the mammoth but mediocre *Motion Picture Guide* and other "reputable" sources, writers are assigning ratings to films they haven't even seen.

Another complaint is the so-called bad acting found in these films. What many critics fail to notice, however, is that unlike American movie stars of the period, Japan's top performers often had no qualms about appearing in science fiction, fantasy and horror films like *Godzilla* or *Mothra*—these were big, ambitious productions and certainly nothing to be ashamed about. That's why you'll find such surprising faces as Takashi Shimura (*Ikiru, Seven Samurai*) in *Godzilla* and *Frankenstein Conquers the World,* Akira Kubo (*Throne of Blood*) in *Destroy All Monsters* and Eiji Okada (*Hiroshima Mon Amour*) in *Ghidrah:*

The Three-Headed Monster. If one is to find fault with the acting, one must instead blame the English dubbing, rarely handled better than indifferently by the films' American distributors.

Subtitles are *always* preferable to dubbing. Even well-dubbed films (such as *Das Boot/The Boat*) rarely convince audiences they're anything but. (Of course, most non–English language productions, until very recently, were shot silent and dubbed in post-production, but one must remember the actors are still speaking the same language, and the biggest stars usually dubbed their own dialog.) Dubbing, however good, compromises the original actor's performance, and always draws attention to itself. When one thinks of Godzilla movies, two images always and immediately come to mind: guys in rubber suits stomping on miniature buildings and poorly synched dubbing. In the course of writing this book, I've watched a number of Japanese tapes and laser discs. While I can't speak Japanese, I was struck at how normal the actors' voices seemed. They didn't sound like cartoons.

Another problem is that these pictures were always intended to be shown on big screens in movie theaters. A four-hundred-foot monster isn't very menacing on a small television set. When audiences today get to see crisp 35mm prints of good Japanese monster movies (called *kaiju eiga* in Japan), they're usually surprised at the effectiveness of the special effects, even though they aren't any more realistic in a theater than they are on television.

Most of the films included in this volume were photographed in an anamorphic wide screen process akin to Panavision and CinemaScope in the United States (TohoScope, DaieiScope, etc.), which, when properly projected, creates an image 2.35 times wider than it is tall. When shown on current television systems, these same films lose nearly half of the original image unless the picture is letterboxed, which is still relatively rare in this country.

Additionally, companies like Toho released many of their films (including the majority of releases from 1957 to 1964) in stereophonic sound. This greatly added to the atmosphere and overall polish of the production. These same films are rarely released in anything but mono in this country, with U.S. audiences losing yet another important facet of their production.

Americanization is another problem these pictures occasionally suffer. They're often recut and rescored, and occasionally new footage is shot and awkwardly inserted. The appearance of American actors in Japanese-made pictures has led to a great deal of confusion as to a given picture's origins. American involvement falls into one of three categories.

The first of these involves American distributors inserting American stars into the original production. The idea was to fool audiences into thinking they were seeing an American-made film. This was how Raymond Burr got to "star" in *Godzilla, King of the Monsters!* He probably never even met any of the film's real stars, and may not have even known what Godzilla looked like while shooting his scenes. Although used on a few other pictures (notably *Half*

Human and *Varan the Unbelievable*), this format was rare because it cost extra to shoot the added footage, and producers quickly realized it fooled no one and added little if anything to the box office.

Beginning in the mid-sixties, companies in the United States began co-financing a few productions, and the Japanese studios, eager to include an American star thus insuring better box office abroad, happily complied. American involvement ranged from very slight (as with UA's ties to Toei's *Message from Space*) to full-blown co-productions (e.g., the Japanese-Italian-U.S.–made, *The Green Slime*). However, by far the most common explanation for the appearance of Western actors in these productions is that they were simply a part of the original production to begin with. If you had a scene set at the UN, you would have to have Caucasian actors. If Godzilla were to attack a United States air base, you'd get a bunch of American-looking extras. These actors—Peggy Neal, Andrew Hughes, Mike Daning, etc.—were amateur thespians who lived in Japan at the time and hired for Western roles where needed. Many of them weren't American at all, but were German, French, etc. They usually spoke their lines in English (many couldn't speak Japanese), which was dubbed into Japanese or subtitled during post-production. Because of the performers' often thick accents, amateur emoting, or both, their dialog usually had to be re-dubbed here in America to be considered acceptable in the States.

Part of the reason I wanted to write this book was because as a kid—and now as an adult—I've found it very difficult to find any solid information on this subject in English. General references omit the majority of the films included in this volume. Sources like (the otherwise reliable) *The American Film Institute Catalog* and especially *The Motion Picture Guide* make unbelievable errors on the most basic information regarding Japanese fantastic films. It's clear by their mistakes that a few shamelessly unethical people are making judgments on films they haven't even seen. With this book, I hope to change that. The filmography that makes up a large part of this volume contains much information never before published (certainly not in English, anyway), and is by far the most complete credits listing of these films to date.

Every film included in the text received close scrutiny—I watched each picture at least once (and often many more times than that), unless otherwise mentioned.

The reader may notice that entries on several highly regarded masterpieces like *Throne of Blood* and *Ugetsu* tend to be shorter than, say, *War of the Gargantuas* and *Godzilla vs. the Smog Monster*. There's a reason for this: the films of Kurosawa and Mizoguchi have been extensively studied and analyzed—maybe even too much from a theoretical point of view (previously published production information and credits listing on these films remain fairly skimpy, however). On the other hand, nobody has ever examined Japanese monster movies at book length before, and thus there is much more to be said. The only other publications that I'm aware of that ever seriously examined these pictures until recently were Greg Shoemaker's *Japanese Fantasy Film Journal* and Ed Godziszewki's *Japanese Giants*, both of which are now defunct and received limited distribution when they were around. *Cinefantastique* generally reviewed new releases with an even hand, but that publication didn't get started until 1970, just as the genre was falling into decline.

One of the few books to give Japanese fantastic films a fair shake is Bill Warren's examination of science fiction films of the 1950s, *Keep Watching the Skies!* His book covered only those films released in the United States between 1950 and 1962, but several early titles (*Godzilla, King of the Monsters!*, *The H-Man*, etc.) made it into his study. I unabashedly admit that this project was inspired by Warren's tome. *Keep Watching the Skies!* is not only the best book ever written about science fiction films, it's one of the best books written about movies, period. His completeness, fairness, and highly readable style made me want to read a similar book on Japanese science fiction, fantasy and horror movies. This book attempts to cover similar territory, Japanese-style (while rooted in the American versions of these films), and I often make references to Warren's book. If I've accomplished something half as good, I'm satisfied.

Just as Hollywood had M-G-M, Paramount and Warner Bros., so too did Japan have major studios which dominated its industry. During the fifties and sixties, Japan's market for theatrical films was remarkably similar to that in the United States fifteen years earlier. Theater attendance peaked in the United States in 1946, when 90 million Americans went to the movies every week. At the same time, exciting new directors began making their mark, with Orson Welles, Preston Sturges, John Huston, Billy Wilder and Gene Kelly leading the pack.

In Japan, film attendance peaked in 1958, when over 21 million residents made weekly visits to the cinema. Output was huge, with several studios releasing as many as two films a week, and double and even triple features became the norm. It was during this decade that many of Japan's greatest films and filmmakers gained international attention, and Japanese films were released for the first time in the United States. Kurosawa's *Rashomon* and *Seven Samurai*, Mizoguchi's *Tales of Ugetsu* and Kinugasa's *Gate of Hell* were but four pictures which had a tremendous impact on world cinema.

Toho dominated the monster movie field. Their Godzilla series, save for a brief absence in the late 1970s and early 1980s, is still going strong after nearly forty years. Toho was founded in 1932. The studio's earliest monster films, made in the fifties, were produced for general audiences. By the late sixties, however, thanks to competition from television and the other majors, Toho's monster product became increasingly geared for younger viewers. By the seventies the studio began dabbling in other areas, including a very successful series of disaster films (made just prior to their American counterparts) and horror pictures modeled after Britain's Hammer films.

Like the Hollywood majors, Japan's production companies also owned and operated 90 percent of that country's big movie theaters, though unlike Hollywood, Japan's studios never had to give them up. Toho even operated and exhibited its product in a couple of theaters in the United States, notably the Toho LaBrea in Los Angeles, which opened in 1960, and theaters in New York and Hawaii, which opened in 1963 and 1964, respectively (many of the films included in the filmography seem to have played Toho-owned theaters in the United States and nowhere else).

Toho's only real competition on the giant monster circuit was Daiei Motion Picture Company. Formed in 1941, Daiei (meaning "big picture") produced *Rashomon* and *Tales of Ugetsu* before introducing the popular "Gamera" and "Majin" films. A prolific studio which also produced a large number of ghost stories, Daiei went bankrupt in 1970-71. In recent years, Daiei has re-entered production, but only on an extremely limited basis, and has released its product through other distributors.

The Tokyo Motion Picture Distribution Company (Tokyo Eiga), better known as Toei, actively produced fantastic films between its successful, violent "yakuza" releases. Formed in 1932, Toei's genre pictures ran the gamut of ghost stories, space operas, and serials, though it generally avoided the giant monster, or *kaiju eiga* genre. Toei also introduced Japanese audiences to wide screen movies, beginning with *The Lord Takes a Bride* (*Ootori-jo no Hanayome*) in April 1957.

Other companies made less of an impact. The prolific Shochiku, whose origins date back to the turn of the century, made few genre films at first, focusing its attentions instead on such projects as its wildly popular and long-running "Tora-san" series. Recently, however, the studio has actively entered the fantastic film market.

Nikkatsu, another old-timer and founded in 1911, concentrated on action-dramas and later soft-core sex films (very popular in Japan during the 1960s and 1970s), before abandoning production altogether.

Shintoho ("New Toho"), founded by ex–Toho employees following a bitter strike in 1947, produced an impressive number of period ghost stories in the late 1950s, but the studio went bankrupt in 1961 and ceased production that May, just as historical pictures were going into decline and following a period of mismanagement and strikes of its own.

Independents like Kadokawa Publishing (*Virus*) and the Art Theatre Guild bolstered the industry during the 1970s, producing about half of the domestic pictures made in the decade. They were often expensive, Hollywood-type productions (often touting Western stars as well), but more commonly represented cheap, soft-core erotic films the financially ailing majors were compelled to distribute.

Animated features became big business in Japan, even though the animation was often farmed out to Taiwan and South Korea to keep production costs down. The limitlessness of animation proved to be another nail in the coffin of live-action fantastic features.

Just as television and other new recreational activities halved film attendance in the United States by the early fifties, film attendance in Japan after the introduction of commercial television (in August 1953, with color sets arriving in 1960) likewise dropped 50 percent by the early 1960s. By 1987, thanks in part to a booming video cassette market, that number plunged to less than 3 million weekly. Added to this was the rise of imported films, mostly from the United States, whose grosses by 1976 exceeded the take from domestically produced features. Today, it is common to find seven of the top ten box office attractions in Japan to be American made. The number of Japanese-made films is only a tiny fraction of the 547 features that were produced in Japan back in 1960.

A serious examination of Japanese fantastic films is long overdue. If you enjoyed Godzilla and Gamera as a youngster, or *Ugetsu* and *Throne of Blood* as an adult, and want to find out more about these films and their production, this book is for you. If you've avoided these films in the past, consider this book a guide to the good, the bad, and the ugly. And maybe by giving the best of these pictures a chance, you'll realize they're anything but incredibly awful films.

A Note About the Text

Japanese fantastic films, as presented to Japanese audiences, were often quite different from what finally made their way to American movie theaters. These films were often recut (sometimes extensively), retitled and occasionally distributed in the States long after their original release in Japan.

To organize the material in the best way possible and minimize the chance of confusion, the following guidelines have been implemented:

1. Reviews for this book are based upon the American versions of these films, not the original Japanese cut. However, those cases where the United States and Japanese versions differ substantially are noted in the text. The filmography credits participants of the English-language versions separately from their Japanese counterparts. The author has made every effort to see the original version of those films that were changed substantially for release in the United States.

2. Titles given are the original theatrical or television titles used for general release in the United States. Thus, *Godzilla vs. Mothra* is listed as *Godzilla vs. the Thing* and *Gamera vs. Guiron* becomes *Attack of the Monsters*.

3. Although listed by their original U.S. titles, films are presented in the text chronologically, according to their Japanese release dates. This is so the reader can best trace the development of fantastic films in Japan. In the United States, these films were often released wildly out of sequence, creating confusion about when certain films were made and in what order.

4. This book does not include fully animated features, which frankly are so different and so numerous (what seems like hundreds since the first—*White Snake Enchantress/Hakuja-den*—in 1958) as to require a book of their own.

5. The text covers only feature films released theatrically or directly to television in the United States. Those films released only in Japan are not included (although I do from the vantage point of mid-1993 include the most recent Godzilla films and a few other titles likely to reach American shores in the near future). Films whose release was limited to Japanese-speaking theaters in the United States have generally been avoided, even though many of these were exhibited with English subtitles. Also excluded are those titles which were trade-screened but which never found a domestic distributor. Selected features culled from Japanese teleseries are included, as are several American-Japanese

co-productions released in the United States as television movies, but elsewhere as theatrical features.

One final note: While I have tried to see every single film included in this book, some have, unfortunately, slipped through the cracks. Part of the problem is that many of these pictures were shown only in Los Angeles and or New York City, sometimes for just a week (or less), and then disappeared into obscurity.

It has also been very difficult to ascertain whether pictures like *Ghost of a One-Eyed Man* or *House of Terrors* were ever shown outside of Japanese-language theaters to general audiences.

Other films were sold directly to American television. They were frequently shown in the sixties and seventies until local stations began discarding their timeworn 16mm prints in favor of newer movies mastered on three quarter inch or Betamax video tape. (Happily, some cable television networks have newly remastered some of these obscure titles.)

The result of all this is that I've been a bit choosy in the main text, while trying to be all-inclusive with the filmography. Die-hard fans of Japanese fantasy films may be disappointed that I've not included entries on *Gunhed* and *The Man in the Moonlight Mask*, but I think the average reader will be delighted to hear about such (mostly) long-unseen treasures as *The Magic Serpent* and *Warning from Space*.

Reviewers I frequently agree or disagree with are often quoted in the main text, and their publications are not always referred to by their full title. Phil Hardy edited two books extensively used here. They are *The Encyclopedia of Horror Movies* (Harper and Row, 1986) and *The Encyclopedia of Film: Science Fiction* (William Morrow, 1984). For the entries through 1962, I frequently quote Bill Warren from his *Keep Watching the Skies!* (two volumes, McFarland and Co., 1982, 1986). *Psychotronic* refers to *The Psychotronic Encyclopedia of Film* (Ballantine, 1983), edited by Michael Weldon, with additional entries by Charles Beesley, Bob Martin and Akira Fitton. I also quote extensively from *The Japanese Fantasy Film Journal* (Greg Shoemaker, 1968–1983), *Japanese Giants* (Ed Godziszewski, 1974–?), and *Markalite* (Pacific Rim, 1990–present).

"A Wind from the East"
by Bill Warren

Americans are notoriously tunnel-visioned when it comes to understanding and appreciating the pop culture of other countries. Partly this is due to simple cultural jingoism: American pop culture has been so influential worldwide that we as a society have come to believe that it is the *only* viable expression for mass entertainment. We not only expect the rest of the world to follow our example, we demand that they do.

In the 1930s, mild British accents seemed unintelligible to those in the stix who also nixed hix pix. Even those British films that did get some release in the United States were frequently propped up with an American star or with a British actor who'd been established in Hollywood films. Usually, they still received wide distribution infrequently in the United States. It wasn't until the Hammer horror movies of the late 1950s that British movies with no-name casts (who soon became familiar) were widely distributed in America.

And if movies with soundtracks *actually in English* had a hard time getting wide release in the United States, those that required dubbing or subtitles fared even less well; they virtually never played anywhere but the largest cities—and in those cities were confined mostly to "art houses," theaters specializing in foreign-language films. In the thirties, forties and fifties, for the most part, "foreign films" meant "European films." But that changed.

Even before the Hammer movies, a foreign movie (not European)—with a relatively unknown American actor added to the cast *after* production—received wide release in the United States and was an unqualified hit. It established a subgenre of films that eventually became as well known as any in the history of films.

This was, obviously, *Godzilla, King of the Monsters!* who is more or less the hero of this book, since without him, it wouldn't exist. In his initial foray, Godzilla was just a huge, lumbering brute, devoid of personality other than a dogged crankiness, but he was spectacular, and his film had a dark, disturbing power. And he was popular. So popular that though he was as thoroughly destroyed as any menace ever has been (he effervesced into nothingness like Alka-Seltzer), he just had to return. The follow-up movie, initially called

Gigantis the Fire Monster in the United States, simply featured *another* Godzilla, who was the menace—then, interestingly, the *hero*—of what seemed to be an endless parade of Japanese monster movies.

Middle-brow critics paid little attention to these films and their science fictional cousins as they swept across the United States. *Battle in Outer Space, The H-Man, The Mysterians, Mothra, Atragon, Monster Zero, Gammera the Invincible* and other theatrical releases were either dismissed with curt "lousy effects" notices, or ignored altogether. The Japanese fantasy films that went straight to television (or, later, videotape) in this country were even more thoroughly ignored.

Except by kids. Children adore dinosaurs, they love spaceships, they are delighted by flashing rays and explosions, by atomic breath and lightning bolts. Kids sucked these into their memories, and eventually as those kids grew up, their love of these films began to emerge in their own work. There was a Saturday-morning Godzilla TV series; standup comics could refer to Godzilla in passing, and their audiences knew at once what they were referring to; Marvel Comics published a Godzilla title for a while; model kits became popular; sports stars wrestled Godzilla in expensive commercials; there was even a dead-serious (if quirky) novel about Godzilla, *Gojiro* by Mark Jacobson; and now, TriStar Pictures is going to make a big-budget *American* Godzilla movie. (But unless the monster is a guy in a suit, will it even *be* Godzilla?)

The odd thing about all this is that while no one ever seems to take the Japanese monster movies very seriously (and on some levels, they don't need to), they also don't dismiss them as crude abominations. In short, the Japanese thrillers are *not* in the "So bad it's good" category. Perhaps it's because in spite of the weird ramifications the films went through, it's clear that the best—and some of the worst—of them are being made by sophisticated, intelligent filmmakers working in a highly unsophisticated format. (They can be compared, oddly enough, with the movies Roy Rogers made between about 1945 and 1950; they're pretty hip for movies about a singing cowboy.)

As the movies became more outlandish, more directly aimed at children and the undiscriminating, directors like Inoshiro (Ishiro) Honda and Noriaki Yuasa found room for occasional jokes, even satire. (*Mothra* is especially interesting in this regard.) And the films were generally handsomely produced, with lavish effects. For some in the West, these films will always look "fakey," but of course, that's a culturally based objection. It was rarely the intention of the producers of *any* kind of Japanese fantasy film, from the high art of movies like *Kwaidan* down to the lowest of the low-brow, such as *Invasion of the Neptune Men,* to be "realistic" at all. It simply is not a consideration in virtually any form of Japanese art, so directing that complaint at these movies is irrelevant.

And as I said earlier, it was Godzilla, King of the Monsters, who led the way, in both fame and infamy. If it hadn't been for Godzilla, surely Stuart

Galbraith wouldn't have been attracted to the odd realm of Japanese fantasy in the first place. If it hadn't been for Godzilla, the shape of Japanese filmmaking might well have been different. There's also little doubt that *Godzilla*, in its initial release, helped to stimulate the growing interest worldwide in science fiction and monster films in the 1950s, just as *Godzilla* itself was inspired by *King Kong*.

There are few more disreputable genres or subgenres than the Japanese monster movie. Film buffs acknowledge the importance of serious, artistic Japanese fantasy movies such as *Ugetsu*, *Kwaidan*, *Onibaba* and Akira Kurosawa's forays into the area, with his brilliant *Rashomon* and *Throne of Blood*. Struggling with the fact that Japanese monster movies are, for all their admitted absurdities, *popular*, film scholars try to find a reason for them, a justification to examine them from an intellectual standpoint.

Do they represent the Japanese anger over being the target of atomic weapons? Is Godzilla himself, and his playmates, the personification of nuclear fears? Were Honda and his collaborators trying to convey an actual (gasp!) *message* in showing us scenes of an impossibly large, radioactively charged dinosauroid smashing cities and fricasseeing weaponry with his atomic halitosis?

I don't mean to scoff at the efforts of this kind of film research and writing, because I respect it; people are infernally complicated thinking machines, and any reasonable attempt to try to trace the linkages will win my respect, partly because I can't do it myself. Nor is that what Stuart Galbraith is up to in this book.

As I tried to in *Keep Watching the Skies!*, Galbraith is attempting to explore not just these movies, but himself. He fell in love with them because they were *fun*. As he says very simply in his preface, "I love Japanese monster movies." He doesn't try to pry the lid off his head and find out why he loves them in general; instead, he tries—and succeeds—in explaining why this or that film works. Does it, in short, deliver the goods?

He has a daunting task. Strong writers have quailed when confronted with trying to explain to skeptics that *Attack of the Mushroom People* can not only be taken seriously, but is actually an interesting film. For those to whom all Godzilla movies look alike, the differences between, say, *Godzilla vs. the Thing* and *Godzilla vs. the Bionic Monster* are not only irrelevant, they're invisible, but Galbraith pinpoints them and explains them.

This book is both long overdue and timed perfectly. As dinosaur mania heats up around the world with huge movies like *Jurassic Park* and the announced American Godzilla movie, this book is reaching the shelves when it should. And the Japanese movies chronicled in this book are in good hands with Stuart Galbraith IV.

The Fifties

Rashomon *(1950)*

Akira Kurosawa's examination of the relative nature of truth was not the first Japanese feature to be shown in the United States, nor was it even likely the first Japanese film with fantastic elements to be shown in this country. *Rashomon* was, however, the first Japanese feature to gain worldwide attention and acclaim and the first to be picked up for distribution in the United States by a major Hollywood studio, RKO Radio Pictures.

Set on a rainy afternoon sometime in the twelfth century, *Rashomon* is a deceptively simple story told to a commoner (Daisuke Kato) by a woodcutter (Takashi Shimura) and a priest (Minoru Chiaki) at the battered Rashomon gate (a huge, impressive set): A samurai, Takehiro (Masayuki Mori), and his wife, Masago (Machiko Kyo), encounter a bandit, Tajomaru (Toshiro Mifune), while traveling down the Sekiyama-Yashishima Road. Tajomaru ties up Takehiro, rapes his wife, and later the samurai is killed with a dagger, which mysteriously disappears. During an inquest, the events leading up to Takehiro's death are obscured by the three conflicting testimonies of Tajomaru, Masago, and Takehiro, whose spirit speaks through a medium (Fumiko Homma). Tajomaru claims the samurai's wife desired him and convinced him to kill her husband. Masago testifies that after her rape, her husband rejected her in shame. After untying Takehiro, she tells him to kill her. She faints, and when she awakens, Takehiro is dead. She says that, in fact, she may have killed him. Takehiro, speaking through the medium—a tour de force of editing, camera work, sound recording and acting—says that Tajomaru asked Masago to marry him after raping her. When she suggests killing Takehiro, the shocked bandit puts the woman's life in her husband's hands. He spares her but is so shamed by her actions that he commits suicide. Finally, the woodcutter, who found the body, offers his version of events. He says that after the woman's rape, Masago was so outraged by the behavior of the two men that she egged them into an almost comically inept duel, which ends with the bandit killing Takehiro. Soon after the woodcutter and priest have finished telling the story to the commoner, the three men find a baby in a ruined temple. The commoner begins stealing the infant's meager possessions and is chastised by the woodcutter. The commoner then accuses the woodcutter of hypocrisy, and suggests it was the woodcutter who stole the missing dagger. The commoner disappears with the baby's belongings. Overcome with guilt, the woodcutter decides to adopt the infant—he already has six children of his own, and one more will not make any difference, he says. The rain stops and the priest's faith in man has been restored.

Rashomon's premise of relative truth was something of a revolutionary idea in motion pictures. And while nearly all mainstream productions continue to spell out plot points one-two-three, Kurosawa's film did open the gates to more subtle, ambiguous screenplays. The picture itself was remade 14 years later as a Western, *The Outrage*, with Paul Newman in the Toshiro Mifune role, and Claire Bloom and Laurence Harvey as the couple who face him. That forgettable production wasn't the only version of the story, however. Variations of the same idea have popped up countless times since, including a terrible, uncredited remake on the syndicated television series "Star Trek: The Next Generation." If the film's premise has lost a lot of its freshness with viewers, its beautiful structure, direction and performances have not. *Rashomon* not only established director Kurosawa's reputation, but also made international stars of Toshiro Mifune and, to a much lesser extent, Masayuki Mori and Takashi Shimura as well.

Mifune was born in 1920 in China, to Japanese parents. His screen career followed wartime service, beginning with *These Foolish Times* in 1946. Under Kurosawa's direction, Mifune's animal-like performance as the bandit (patterned after a lion in a jungle film Mifune and the director had seen) and tremendous screen presence (his eyes are truly amazing) soon catapulted him to international stardom as Japan's biggest and most recognizable star. Rather amazingly, Mifune appeared in 16 of Kurosawa's 17 films from *Drunken Angel* in 1948 through *Red Beard* in 1965. In these films he was rarely less than brilliant. Of Kurosawa, Mifune has written, "I have never as an actor done anything that I am proud of other than with him." Mifune's other fantastic film credits include *The Three Treasures* (1958), *Samurai Pirate* (1963), and Kurosawa's *Throne of Blood* (1957).

Mifune was popular and powerful enough to direct a film of his own and produce several others, beginning in 1963. He also began appearing in U.S. and international productions, starting with *Grand Prix* in 1966 (unfortunately, when asked to speak English, his voice is usually dubbed, often by Paul Frees). This was followed by roles in *Hell in the Pacific* (1969), *Zatoichi Meets Yojimbo* (1971), *Midway* (1976), *Winter Kills* (1979), the television miniseries *Shōgun* (both 1980) and *Inchon* (1982). He appeared regularly in films through 1982 (*The Challenge*), but his roles became much less demanding after the mid-1960s. He appeared in the Toho's 1987 fantasy *Princess from the Moon*, produced by Tomoyuki Tanaka and directed by Kon Ichikawa, the not-bad *Journey of Honor* (1992, filmed in 1990), and *Shadow of the Wolf* (1993) in which Mifune, cast as an Eskimo, was once again dubbed.

Masayuki Mori was born in 1911, the son of novelist Ikumitsu Arishima. His credits include Kurosawa's *They Who Step on the Tiger's Tail* (1945), *The Idiot* (1951), and especially *The Bad Sleep Well* (1960, with Mori cast as the heartless company president), Mizoguchi's *Ugetsu* (1953), *When a Woman Ascends the Stairs* (1963), and *Gateway to Glory* (1970). He seemed to specialize in playing anguished or corrupt characters. Mori died in 1973.

Information on Kurosawa regular Takashi Shimura, who also appeared in numerous *kaiju eiga* productions, can be found in the entry on *Godzilla*,

King of the Monsters! Minoru Chiaki, another regular of both Kurosawa's films and Toho monster movies, can be found in the entry on *Gigantis the Fire Monster.* Kurosawa himself has been written about so extensively (including his own excellent, if incomplete, autobiography), I will not attempt a detailed biographical sketch here (what could I possibly add that hasn't already been said dozens of times elsewhere?) but instead recommend the reader check out any one of the dozens of books written about this seminal artist, particularly Donald Richie's *The Films of Akira Kurosawa* (University of California Press, 1965). In 1992, Kurosawa was still directing, his most recent credits being *Rhapsody in August,* no less beguiling a film than those which first brought him international fame, and *Madadayo* (1993).

Surprisingly, *Rashomon* received mixed reviews in Japan, though it was, in fact, popular with audiences and eventually became the eighth-highest grossing film in Japan that year. Daiei, the company that produced the film (his regular studio, the very conservative Toho, had turned down the project), reluctantly submitted the picture to the Venice Film Festival, where its Grand Prize win surprised no one more than its producers (Kurosawa himself wasn't even aware the picture had been entered until after it had won). The picture's international acclaim soon washed it to American shores, where it was enthusiastically received. "An artistic achievement of such distinct and exotic manner that it is difficult to estimate it alongside conventional story films," said the *New York Times*' Bosley Crowther. "Much of the power of the picture—and it unquestionably has hypnotic power—derives from the brilliance with which the camera of director Akira Kurosawa has been used. The photography is excellent and the flow of images is expressive beyond words." Kurosawa was chosen the best director by the National Board of Review, and the picture received an honorary Academy Award (the foreign language category had not yet been added). More recently, the late John Kobal's survey of international critics (in *The Top 100 Movies*) ranked *Rashomon* as the tenth greatest film of all time.

Tales of Ugetsu *(1953)*

This classic of the foreign cinema, also known as *Ugetsu Monogatari* and simply *Ugetsu* (though first released in the United States under the above title), is widely regarded as one of Japan's greatest films. The National Board of Review was one of countless organizations which ranked the film among the year's ten best. It won the Grand Prize (the "Silver Lion") at the Venice Film Festival, while John Kobal, polling film critics from 22 countries, rated *Ugetsu* one of the 100 best films of all time. And *Sight and Sound*'s polls of the all-time great motion pictures have continually rated *Tales of Ugetsu* in its top ten, joining the likes of *Citizen Kane, The Bicycle Thief* and *Wild Strawberries*. Its fantasy/horror elements are slight, but they're there, and thus it is included here.

Near Lake Biwa in the sixteenth century, a kindly but poor potter, Genjuro (Masayuki Mori), lives with his wife (Mitsuke Mito) and son. Nearby live his brother-in-law, Tobei (Eitaro Ozawa), who has dreams of becoming a samurai, and his wife (Kinuyo Tanaka). As war rages on, Genjuro learns he can make a great deal of money selling his work in a nearby city. Despite the danger of traveling the war-torn area, he decides to chance it. With the help of his wife, Genjuro creates an impressive inventory to take with him. While most of the ceramics are baking, however, pillaging soldiers approach the small village, and the two young families are forced to flee. Genjuro returns to find his furnace out but his pottery intact. The two families prepare to take a boat across the lake to the city. Passing through a dense fog, they encounter a small skiff containing the body of a man attacked by pirates. A worried Genjuro takes his wife and son back to shore to stay safely behind. In the city, Genjuro is wildly successful selling his pots, sake bottles, etc. Tobei uses his share of the profits to buy some samurai armor, though nearby soldiers promptly reject his offer to join them. Tobei's wife, abandoned by her husband, is raped by wandering soldiers. Genjuro is met by the wealthy Lady Wakasa (Machiko Kyo), who places an order and asks that it be delivered to her estate. Once there, she offers to share her riches if he'll marry her. Basking in her beauty and wealth, Genjuro lets greed get the better of him. In his village, Genjuro's wife is forced to flee when the samurai return. Starving soldiers steal the only food she has.

Tobei discovers the severed head of a warlord who committed suicide. Presenting the head before a general, Tobei claims he beheaded the warrior. Although they don't believe his story, the soldiers are so glad to see their enemy dead, they reward Tobei with armor, a horse and a small command. Tobei leads his men to a brothel, where he is shocked to find his wife now working as a prostitute. Tobei vows to return to his former ways and forget all desires of becoming a soldier of fortune.

Meanwhile, Genjuro travels to the city to buy gifts for Lady Wakasa but is shunned by a merchant when he mentions his new lover's name. Genjuro meets a Buddhist priest, who warns him not to return to the estate. When he protests, the priest talks Genjuro into protecting himself. Genjuro returns to the estate. When he is embraced by the woman, she screams. The priest has painted Buddhist scripture on his body for protection against evil spirits. Lady Wakasa, it is revealed, is the ghost of a lonely woman who in life never enjoyed the pleasures of womanhood. Genjuro flees. He encounters some soldiers who accuse him of stealing. When he explains he has come from the Wakasa estate, the soldiers show him the charred remains of the actual estate, burned to the ground ages ago. Genjuro returns home to his wife and son. He's overjoyed to be reunited with his family. When he awakens, his son is there but his wife is nowhere to be found. A villager explains that while he was away she was killed by soldiers. Genjuro returns to his modest life as a potter. The spirit of his dead wife contentedly watches as Genjuro finds happiness in his work and son.

I saw *Ugetsu* for the first time only days after Akira Kurosawa's similar tale of greed and the supernatural, *Throne of Blood* (1957). It has been written that Kurosawa's film is concerned with man's greed and vanity, while director Kenji Mizoguchi shows how their wives fare even worse.

Mizoguchi (1898–1956) was one of the cinema's leading filmmakers in depicting the role of women—as second-class citizens—in Japanese society. Even though more screen time is devoted to the men than the women, it's the wives who are clearly the focus. Mizoguchi died of leukemia just as Kurosawa was becoming popular and the boom in fantastic films was just getting underway. While Mizoguchi's *The Life of Oharu* (1952) is also widely regarded as a classic, many of his other 31 features, for the most part, go unseen in the United States.

Kinuyo Tanaka and Mitsuko Miura are memorable as the two women who fall victim to their husbands' folly. Although Genjuro has indirectly caused his wife's death, she forgives his sins and remains at his side once he returns and takes care of their son. Tobei's wife becomes a prostitute yet is reunited with her reckless but loving husband. (He did not return in the original script, however; the studio imposed the happy ending.) Less sensitive filmmakers, both in Japan and the United States, most certainly would've killed off the character. The rape of Tobei's wife and the attack on Genjuro's by the starving soldiers are both tensely frightening and surprisingly graphic for the time. Genjuro's homecoming also stands out for its passion and unnervingness. It's just too good to be true—and we know it. Genjuro's inability to understand this earns our sympathy. We care about the leading men and can forgive them because they're three-dimensional human beings, with all of mankind's failings. Although seduced by the ghost of Lady Wakasa, we see Genjuro as a basically kind and sensitive man who clearly loves his wife. Tobei is less defined but is pathetic in a comical sort of way.

The film is vivid and exciting, especially in the first half, when the families must flee the pillaging soldiers, then travel across the spooky, fog-enshrouded lake. Mizoguchi directed *Ugetsu*, like many of his films, in a leisurely style, with Kazuo Miyagawa as his director of photography. The film's visual beauty is apparent even on beat-up 16mm prints like the one I first saw the picture on. The cast is uniformly excellent and thankfully didn't have to endure the kind of ludicrous Americanization most of the films in this volume suffered through. Both Masayuki Mori and Machiko Kyo had starred in Kurosawa's *Rashomon* three years earlier and are at the peak of their powers in *Ugetsu*.

Bosley Crowther of the *New York Times* was perplexed by the production: "It is this particular vagueness and use of symbolism and subterfuge that give to this Oriental fable what it has of a sort of eerie charm. They vex you at first with their confusions, but if you have patience, and hold on, intent upon finding out what's cooking, you'll get flavor from this weird, exotic stew." *Variety*'s "Mosk," in typical Variet-ese, suggested the film was produced with Western distribution in mind. "This, plus the brilliant thesping, direction and technical qualities should make this of curio appeal for arty houses in the U.S." Indeed.

Godzilla, King of the Monsters! *(1954/1956)*

This is the film that started it all. *Gojira*, as it is known in Japan, was a tremendous international success and inspired its studio, Toho, to produce an increasing number of science fiction spectacles, ultimately leading to a genuine sci-fi boom in Japan that lasted through the early 1970s. This film and its many sequels were also tremendously influential to Japanese sci-fi television, still going strong to this day. *Godzilla*'s sequels and genre sisters also account for a wildly successful franchise of T-shirts, video games, dolls, hobby kits, buttons, etc., and the character is as much of a cultural icon in Japan as Mickey Mouse is in the United States.

Tokyo has been reduced to smoldering rubble, and casualties number in the thousands. Among the injured is reporter Steve Martin (Raymond Burr), foreign correspondent for United World News. As he recuperates in a makeshift hospital, he remembers the events that led up to the disaster. En route to Cairo, Martin had been on assignment when he had stopped in Tokyo for a brief layover. He had planned to meet with an old college friend, Dr. Serizawa, but is met instead by Serizawa's assistant, who tells Martin that Serizawa is away. Martin is also met at the airport by Security Officer Tomo Iwanaga (Frank Iwanaga). Iwanaga asks Martin if he noticed anything unusual during his flight. Iwanaga explains that a Japanese ship had been mysteriously obliterated by a strange, unknown force. Martin, representing UWN, tags along during the investigation. Over the next several days, eight ships are destroyed by this mysterious force; the only survivors quickly die of radiation burns. (This was based on a true story. A fishing boat sailed too close to an H-bomb test site, and several sailors died shortly thereafter of radiation poisoning.) Panic spreads, and at a special meeting, paleontologist Dr. Yamane (Takashi Shimura) organizes an investigating team which travels to Odo Island, near where the disasters have been occurring. Martin and Iwanaga also travel to the island, along with Yamane's daughter, Emiko (Momoko Kochi), and her fiance, marine Hideto Ogata (Akira Takarada). The strange force appears one evening during a tremendous storm, causing extensive damage. The following morning, the scientists discover radiation everywhere, as well as recently killed sea creatures, heretofore extinct Trilobites. Natives on the island believe the events to be caused by Godzilla, a monster-god they had sacrificed young women to many years before. Godzilla, a 400-foot-tall, radioactive creature roughly resembling an *Allosaurus* (with dorsal fins similar to a *Stegosaurus*), suddenly appears over a hillside. Everyone flees, but just as quickly, Godzilla disappears. Scientists and reporters race over the hillside to find gigantic footprints on the beach, leading out to sea. At a special meeting at the Diet Building, Yamane concludes that the creature is related to the dinosaurs which disappeared millions of years ago and was resurrected and made radioactive by H-bomb testing. The council decides to use depth charges to kill the monster.

Emiko visits Dr. Serizawa (Akihiko Hirata), who was once her fiance in a pre-arranged marriage before she met Ogata. She has come to tell him of her engagement to Ogata, but before she can do so, Serizawa takes Emiko to his basement laboratory. Serizawa has invented an "oxygen destroyer" and proceeds to give her a demonstration of the device, using some fish in a large glass-enclosed tank. Emiko screams at the result and promises to keep Serizawa's horrible invention a secret. Emiko returns home where she finds her father sitting alone in the dark. "Godzilla should not be destroyed. He should be studied," the paleontologist says.

Godzilla appears in Tokyo harbor. Despite an electrical barrier and a massive military defense, nothing seems to stop the creature. The monster attacks a passenger train and slowly makes his way through the city, setting buildings ablaze with his radioactive breath. Martin, reporting Godzilla's rampage, is injured when the monster topples the building the reporter occupies. At the hospital the following afternoon, Emiko attends to Martin's injuries. She tells Martin of what she saw in Serizawa's laboratory. The scientist had dropped a pellet into the fish tank, and in no time all of the fish were gruesomely dissolved into atoms. Martin urges Emiko and Ogata to convince Serizawa to let the military use the oxygen destroyer against Godzilla. Serizawa refuses on the grounds that if the invention were to become publicly known, it might fall into the wrong hands. He must keep his terrible secret to himself. He has a change of heart, however, when a nearby television shows hundreds of children singing a prayer for those who had died in Godzilla's attack. (In the original Japanese cut, the prayer is a plea for nuclear disarmament.) Serizawa, Ogata, Emiko, Dr. Yamane and Martin, along with many others, take a ship to the region where the amphibious creature rests during the daytime. Serizawa and Ogata, wearing deep-sea diving gear, take the oxygen destroyer to the bottom of the sea. Godzilla awakens and approaches the men. Ogata is pulled to the surface and to safety, but Serizawa surprises everyone by remaining below: The secret to the oxygen destroyer shall die with him. He cuts his line as the oxygen destroyer is ignited. Godzilla shrieks and surfaces briefly, before dissolving into atoms.

As Bill Warren points out in his essential *Keep Watching the Skies!*, the 1952 reissue of RKO's 1933 classic *King Kong* played a significant role in the science fiction boom of the 1950s. Its huge box office returns led Warner Bros. to pick up the independent production *The Beast from 20,000 Fathoms* (produced by Mutual Films, Inc., 1953), which in turn led to dozens of similar "monster-on-the-loose" films, including *Them!* (1954), *Tarantula* (1955), and *20 Million Miles to Earth* (1957). The reissue of *King Kong*, the subsequent release of *The Beast from 20,000 Fathoms* and its success were felt as far away as Japan, where Toho producer Tomoyuki Tanaka envisioned a similar Japanese production.

Tanaka was born in 1910 in Osaka. He was active in the theater (as a manager and director) before entering films in 1940. After a stint in the literary department (where he worked with future Toho star Ryo Ikebe), Tanaka became a producer under Iwao Mori. He later produced films directed by Hiroshi Inagaki and Akira Kurosawa (through the sixties), as well as nearly every big effects film produced at Toho, where he later served as president of its Toho-Eiga production arm. Tanaka essentially retired following the production of *Godzilla vs. King Ghidorah* in 1991. Early in 1954, Tanaka shelved a massive Japanese-Indonesian co-production, *Behind the Glory* (*Eiko Kage-ni*) to concentrate his efforts on a new monster movie, tentatively titled "The Big Monster from 20,000 Miles Beneath the Sea" ("Dai kaiju no kaitei niman maru"); its title obviously inspired by both *Beast* and Disney's *20,000 Leagues Under the Sea*.

Tanaka had the good fortune to have as his special effects director a man by the name of Eiji Tsuburaya (1901–1970), who had worked with Tanaka the year before in *Farewell Rabaul*. Tsuburaya began his career as an assistant cameraman and had graduated to a working cinematographer by the mid to late twenties. He had greatly admired *King Kong* and hoped someday to work on a similar project. Originally, Tsuburaya had hoped to build the film around a gigantic octopus, which at the story's climax would attack a ship. This idea was soon dropped, though similar scenes do turn up in several later Tsuburaya projects, notably *King Kong vs. Godzilla, Frankenstein Conquers the World, War of the Gargantuas*, and in an episode of the Tsuburaya-produced "Ultraman" television series.

Screenwriter Takeo Murata, working with Tanaka and Tsuburaya, fashioned instead a story revolving around an amphibious dinosaur, mutated through radiation. The creature was eventually named "Godzilla," supposedly after the nickname of a Toho technician. The word *gojira* is derived from "gorilla" and the Japanese word for whale, "kujira."

Also making contributions to the script was director Ishiro Honda, who had visited Hiroshima in 1946 and had long wanted to somehow translate the apocalyptic horror of what he had seen to the screen. Born in 1911, Honda (also commonly billed as *Inoshiro* Honda) joined Toho in 1933, known at the time as PCL. His career was interrupted by wartime service in China from 1938 to

1946, but he returned to the studio, where close friend Akira Kurosawa had graduated from assistant to full director. Honda himself worked as an assistant director under Kurosawa and Yamamoto. Of Honda Kurosawa has written, "There are few men as honest and reliable... I'm often told that I captured the atmosphere of post-war Japan very well in *Stray Dog* (1949), and, if so, I owe a great deal of that success to Honda." Ishiro Honda made his feature debut with *Aoi Shinju* (1951) and directed nongenre films through at least 1966's *Oyome in oide* ("Come Marry Me"), but like Tsuburaya, he would best be remembered for his Godzilla entries and its offshoots. He retired from directing in 1975 but worked as a close consultant to Kurosawa, billed as a production coordinator or creative consultant on *Kagemusha* (1980), *Ran* (1985), *Akira Kurosawa's Dreams* (1990), *Rhapsody in August* (1991) and *Madadayo* (1993). Honda was planning a comeback, a new science fiction feature about mankind's threat to the environment, when he died in Tokyo on February 28, 1993.

Early models of Godzilla closely resembled a *Tyrannosaurus Rex*, with a much larger head than what appears finally in the film. Early designs also included scales on the monster's body, to better emphasize the creature's aquatic ties. These were replaced by large, rounded "warts" for the body's texture. However, they too were discarded in favor of linear bumps. Because of time and budget limitations, it was decided to photograph the majority of the monster's scenes using puppets and a man in a rubber costume, rather than stop-motion animation process used in *King Kong* and *The Beast from 20,000 Fathoms*. However, there *are* several stop-motion shots in the film, including one of Godzilla's tail and another of a fire truck careening out of control. Some sources have suggested Tsuburaya didn't know or understand how Kong was brought to life and so couldn't use the stop-motion technique. This is sheer nonsense. Although rarely used for more than a few seconds, some form of stop-motion animation turns up in almost every Toho special effects film.

The rubber costume was constructed by pouring latex into a plaster mold. After the suit was painted a deep charcoal gray (not green—ever), the actor climbed into the 100-pound costume through a small opening along the dorsal fins. The actor, who because of limited access to fresh air and the extremely hot studio lights (brighter than normal to accommodate the slow-motion photography used to suggest the creature's great size) could only stay in the suit for very brief stretches, positioned himself just under the headpiece. The head contained a radio control device which triggered the opening and closing of the lower jaw. A partial costume of Godzilla from the waist down only was also constructed for close-ups of Godzilla's legs and feet. Several puppets were used, including one for the close-ups of Godzilla spewing his fiery breath. The puppets were also used for shots involving more facial expression or animated movements above the chest.

The miniature buildings were constructed at one–twenty-fifth scale and photographed in slow motion so as to crumble realistically. An entire three-block section of Tokyo was built. Amusingly, Honda and Tsuburaya were once stopped by security guards at a department store after someone heard the pair discussing the destruction of Tokyo. *Gojira*'s budget was 60 million yen (approximately $900,000 in 1954) at a time when the average Japanese feature cost just $75,000. (Toho's other big film that year, *Seven Samurai* cost $500,000 by comparison.) A radio dramatization that ran from July to September primed audiences for the film's opening in November, when it was an instant success, seen by almost 10 million people in Japan alone. *Gojira* was to Japan what *King Kong* was to American audiences. The film played the Toho LaBrea theater in Los Angeles in 1955, and allegedly Samuel Z. Arkoff and Alex Gordon were among those interested in the foreign rights. Ultimately, however, the rights to the picture in the United States were sold to Joseph E. Levine, whose eclectic career included such diverse hits and misses as *The Graduate* (1967) and *The Steagle* (1971). Rather than release the film in subtitled format where it would most likely have a limited audience at best, Levine saw the film's greatest potential in an English-dubbed American version, with saturation bookings across the country. Levine rather ingeniously decided to shoot new footage, with American actor Burr substituting various minor roles in the film and intercut segments featuring the original players with the Burr footage. The remaining film would consist of undubbed footage in Japanese, with Burr given lines like, "My Japanese is a little rusty." The dubbing of certain segments of the film may have been a last-minute decision considering the rushed appearance and even amateur nature of the performances. The result is surprisingly effective, and probably many were fooled by the new version. Toho apparently liked the American cut, too, for the Raymond Burr version was later released to Japanese theaters. *Gojira* was photographed in the old 1.33:1 Academy aspect ratio. This footage was cut with the 1.85:1 Burr footage. For reasons that aren't very clear, the original footage appears very bland in American prints, a far cry from the super-crisp black and white version on Japanese laser discs.

Akihiko Hirata, who was originally intended to play the part of Ogata, switched roles with Takarada at the last minute. Hirata would be associated with Toho's monster movies throughout his career. Born Akihiko Onoda in 1927, Hirata made his film debut in Toho's *Embrace (Hou-yo)* opposite Toshiro Mifune. Early in 1954, Hirata was cast as a Zero pilot in the war melodrama *Farewell Rabaul (Saraba Rabauru)*. Ishiro Honda, the film's director, liked his performance, which led to his casting in *Godzilla*. Although the actor would continue to appear in such nongenre titles as *Samurai Part II: Duel at Ichijoji Temple* (1955) and *Sanjuro* (1962), he was quickly typecast in special effects pictures. Over the next 15 years, the actor would appear in virtually every Toho monster movie, including *Rodan* (1956), *The Mysterians* (1957), *The H-Man* (1958), *Atragon* (1963), *Latitude Zero* (1968), *Catastrophe: 1999* (1974), *The War in Space* (1978) — and six of the next 14 Godzilla movies. His last film was Toho's 1983 epic, *Sayonara Jupiter*. The actor was slated to appear in *Godzilla 1985* and even helped announce its production for Toho at a press conference, but he died of cancer in July 1984, as shooting was getting started.

Takashi Shimura's appearance in the film must have startled those who had admired his superb performance as the dying administrator in *Ikiru* (1952) and the intensely wise leader of the *Seven Samurai* (1954). Born in 1905, Shimura was a stage actor in films as early as 1941. Shimura's other nongenre credits include the majority of Kurosawa's films: *Sanshiro Sugata* (1943), *The Most Beautiful* (1944), *The Men Who Tread on the Tiger's Tail* (1945), *Those Who Make Tomorrow* and *No Regrets for Our Youth* (both 1946), *Drunken Angel* (1948), *The Quiet Duel* and *Stray Dog* (1949), *Scandal* and *Rashomon* (1950), *The Idiot* (1951), *Record of a Living Being* (1955), *Throne of Blood* (1957), *The Hidden Fortress* (1958), *The Bad Sleep Well* (1960), *Yojimbo* (1961), *Sanjuro* (1962), *High and Low* (1963) and *Red Beard* (1965). His films for other directors include *The Life of Oharu* (1952), *Last Embrace* (1955), *The Samurai Saga* and *Saga of the Vagabonds* (1959) and *I Bombed Pearl Harbor* (1960). Shimura reprised his role in *Gigantis the Fire Monster* (1955). His other genre credits include *Rodan* (1956), *The Mysterians* (1957), *The Three Treasures* (1958), *The Last War* (1961), *Gorath* (1962), *Frankenstein Conquers the World* (1964) and *Kwaidan* (1965). His last film may have been 1979's *Oginsaga*. Shimura died in 1982, after receiving the Medal of Honor (for performing arts) and Fourth Class Order of the Rising Sun.

Akira Takarada was just 19 when he starred with Hirata and Shimura. Another actor who would become long associated with Toho's *kaiju eiga* series, Takarada also starred in *Half Human* (1955), *The Last War* (1961), *Godzilla vs. the Thing* (1964), *Monster Zero* (1965), *Ebirah, Horror of the Deep* (1966), *King Kong Escapes* (1967), *Latitude Zero* (1969) and *Godzilla vs. King Ghidorah* (1992). According to the *Motion Picture Guide,* Takarada also appeared in *The Dangerous Kiss* and *Night in Hong Kong* (both 1961); *Different Sons, Early Autumn* and *Star of Hong Kong* (All 1962), and many other equally unfamiliar productions save for 1961's *I Bombed Pearl Harbor* through 1967's *Let's Go, Young Guy.*

Raymond Burr's role was allegedly filmed in one day (an unlikely story). He's more than adequate, especially considering he was supposed to be reacting to footage shot thousands of miles away and many months earlier. Burr (born 1917) was becoming familiar to American audiences but was several years away from his "Perry Mason" role on television. He appeared in films beginning in 1946. His big break came when he appeared as the murderous husband in Alfred Hitchcock's *Rear Window* (1954), following cameo roles in minor films like *Bride of the Gorilla* (1951) and *Gorilla at Large* (1954). Burr would reprise his Martin role almost thirty years later for *Godzilla 1985* (1985). He was extensively interviewed at that time and seemed genuinely pleased to have been a part of the Godzilla saga.

Harou Nakajima and Katsumi Tetsuka alternated playing Godzilla. Nakajima, a struggling young actor in his early twenties, would play the part solo in 12 more films through 1972. He also played monsters in several other Toho films. Nakajima added what he could to the role, given the extreme limitations of working inside the heavy, head-to-toe rubber costume. It would be several more films, however, before Nakajima would bring a real personality to the part. (Incidentally, Nakajima can be seen throwing the switch as Godzilla hits the high-tension wires.)

The picture was scored by Akira Ifukube (born 1914), a highly regarded classical composer and professor of musical composition at Tokyo University. Ifukube's ominous, distinctly Eastern score would become as much a staple of Toho's monster films (as well as Daiei's *Majin* series) as Tsuburaya's effects. His other credits include *Children of Hiroshima, Harp of Burma, Night Drum, The Secret Scrolls (Part II), The Great Wall, Buddha* and *Sandakan 8*. Ifukube is one of the great composers of movie music, ranking right up there with Bernard Herrmann and Max Steiner. His scores—influenced by Ainu folksongs as well as Stravinsky and Fauré—don't sound like anyone else's and have a powerfully psychological effect that's not soon forgotten. Besides producer Tanaka, Ifukube is the only major behind-the-scenes player still associated with the series, having written the score for *Godzilla vs. Mothra* (1992).

The film received mixed-to-negative reviews in the United States. Bosley Crowther's pithy review for the *New York Times* called *Godzilla, King of the Monsters!* "an incredibly awful film.... The whole thing is in the category of cheap cinematic horror-stuff, and it is too bad that a respectable theatre has to lure children and gullible grown-ups with such fare." *Newsweek* called Godzilla "a 400-foot-high plucked chicken" who "cannot act his way out of a paper bag." *Variety* hated the acting but liked the "excellently lensed" special effects. In 1982, the original Japanese cut of *Gojira*, sans Burr and with English subtitles, became available for national bookings. For essentially the first time, American audiences go to see chilling moments cut from the Burr version, such as a young widow's assurance to her crying daughter as Godzilla approaches. "In just a moment we're going to join daddy," she says. Also reinstated is talk between bit players of their resignation of having to return to the shelters they had used during the war, and one woman's complaint of having survived Nagasaki only to face Godzilla.

The relationship among Emiko, Ogata and Serizawa is also strengthened, giving Serizawa's heroics an even greater air of tragedy. Carrie Rickey in the *Village Voice* found the original cut "still scary after all these years," adding, "At once mythical, topical, melodramatic, and fantastic, *Godzilla* ... is only a rubberized miniature, yes, but the issues at stake are all too global." The Chicago *Tribune*'s Howard Reich called the original "an eerie metaphor for nuclear war.... The movie is a parable on life and death issues, and therefore its sledgehammer means of communication powerfully underscore the message."

In either form, *Godzilla, King of the Monsters!* is perhaps a bit too much like the American films it was admittedly trying to imitate. Atomic weapons testing giving birth to monsters was already a cliché in U.S. monster movies, though obviously it has a weighty significance here. Still, *Godzilla*, like its title creature, lacks a certain amount of personality. The picture is well produced and interesting, but not as distinctive as Toho's later product. The studio would quickly rectify this, however, developing a series of wholly unique sci-fi films no one in Hollywood or Japan could ever quite match. Toho's golden age was just around the corner.

(Much of my information on the making of *Godzilla* comes from an excellent article by Japanese film expert Ed Godziszewski for the now defunct *Japanese Fantasy Film Journal*. Godziszewski concurrently published a fanzine of his own, *Japanese Giants*, and more recently has written for *Markalite*.)

Gigantis the Fire Monster *(1955)*

Just as RKO followed *King Kong* (1933) with a quickly made sequel (*Son of Kong*, also 1933), so too did Toho with a follow-up to their wildly successful *Gojira*. *Gigantis the Fire Monster*, or *Gojira no gyakushu* ("Godzilla's Counterattack") as it was known in Japan, was released less than six months after the original film, though it would take several years to reach general audiences in the United States.

Shoichi Tsukioka (Hiroshi Koizumi) and Koji Kobayashi (Minoru Chiaki) are pilots at a fishing company. Koji's plane has engine trouble and goes down on a remote island. When Shoichi arrives to rescue him, they spot two giant monsters in mortal combat. One is Godzilla (though he's called Gigantis in this picture, distributor Warner Bros. apparently didn't realize Toho, not Embassy, owned the name "Godzilla"), the other is a four-legged, spiny-backed creature called Angilas (Angirasu in Japan), who roughly resembles an Ankylosaurus. The two monsters duke it out with both falling into the sea. Shoichi and Koji hightail it back to the mainland. Japan's leaders hold a conference to determine how to destroy the beasts. Dr. Yamane (Takashi Shimura, reprising his role from *Godzilla*) shows footage of the futile effort to stop "another such monster" that had previously devastated Japan (footage from *Godzilla, King of the Monsters!*). He explains that the first beast was killed by the oxygen destroyer but the inventor of the device was dead and his plans destroyed. The creatures emerge from Osaka Bay, but before they can inflict much damage, flares are ignited which fill the night sky. The monsters are attracted to the bright light, which the military use to lure the beasts away from the city. Meanwhile, a group of convicts being transferred to another prison use the confusion brought on by the monsters to escape. Several of the men steal a fuel truck, and when the police give chase, the truck goes out of control, blowing up near a refinery. The explosion draws the beasts back on shore, where they destroy much of the city. Gigantis bites Angilas in the neck, killing the four-legged beast. Gigantis completes the kill by setting the dead monster ablaze. With the Osaka fishery destroyed, Shoichi and Koji go to work at another branch, located in northern Japan. Koji spots Gigantis in the valley of icy, snow-covered Shinko Island. Gigantis sets Koji's plane afire with his radioactive breath, and the craft crashes into the side of the mountain. Military jets drop bombs into the mountainside above the creature, creating a massive avalanche of glacier ice which buries Gigantis.

Gigantis' script is oddly constructed. The big battle between Gigantis and Angilas, along with the destruction of Osaka, comes at the mid-point instead of the climax. The film's abrupt change in locations (from burned-out Osaka to the "poor-but-happy" northern fishery) is jarring to say the least. However, the monster scenes are generally impressive. The miniatures are finely detailed and well lit. Larger models (Schoichi's plane, for instance) were used for some scenes, and overall the effects work is vastly superior to later films in the series, though the crisp black and white photography helped to cover any deficiencies. Particularly interesting is the scene where the monsters grapple near Osaka castle, and when Godzilla is attracted to a series of flares which light the night sky.

Although the sudden appearance of convicts clearly serves no other purpose than to get Gigantis and Angilas back on shore, their arrival in the story does result in the film's best effects sequence: Some of the runaway prisoners take refuge in a subway terminal. The tumbling monsters above produce a cave-in, sending thousands of gallons of water cascading into the station, drowning the convicts. This sequence was achieved through superb miniature and matte work and is startlingly effective. Some of the scenes where Angilas and Gigantis grapple were mysteriously undercranked, thus making the action appear in fast motion. Though startling, it seems to add to the overall energy of the sequence, if not its realism. As in *Godzilla*, extensive use was made of puppets for the close-ups of the two monsters, and this is well integrated with the man-sized costumes, even though the facial characteristics of the puppets don't really match the suits. The special effects during the final attack on Gigantis are less successful. The icy island is pretty phoney looking, and when the beast is first trapped by the avalanche, it looks as if Gigantis were being smothered in ice cubes.

Godzilla looks pretty much as he did in the previous film. The rubber costumes would wear out or simply rot between pictures, and a new costume would generally have to be built for each new production. The suit used here is a bit thinner and less sturdy than the one used in the original, but most viewers won't notice the difference (unlike in later films where the costumes changed dramatically from film to film).

Angilas is fairly well designed, simple but reasonably believable. The snout is a bit bulbous, and like all four-legged monsters played by two-legged men, Angilas walks on his knees (this is disguised pretty well, however). The monster (never called Anzilla, as some sources claim) would turn up in *Destroy All Monsters* (1968), *Godzilla on Monster Island* (1972), and *Godzilla vs. the Bionic Monster* (1974), as well as in several other seventies films via stock footage.

Hiroshi Koizumi stars. Born in 1926, Koizumi began his professional career as a radio announcer for the Japan Radio Broadcasting Corp. (NHK). He began his screen career in 1951, and also appeared in *Jyoseini kansuru Jyonisho, Konyaku samba Garasu* and *I Bombed Pearl Harbor*. A staple of Toho's fantastic films, Koizumi starred in *Mothra* (1962), *Atragon* and *Attack of the Mushroom People* (both 1963), *Dagora, the Space Monster, Ghidrah: The Three-Headed Monster* and *Godzilla vs. the Thing* (all 1964). Later, he appeared in *Godzilla vs. the Bionic Monster* (1974) and turned up briefly as a geologist in *Godzilla 1985*.

Minoru Chiaki and Yoshio Tsuchiya (the latter cast as the pilot who leads the attack on Gigantis) were members of Akira Kurosawa's stock company of actors. Chiaki played the Banquo role in *Throne of Blood* (1957) and the cheerful Samurai woodchopper in *Seven Samurai* (1954), as well as the part that inspired the creation of *Star Wars*' C-3PO in *The Hidden Fortress* (1958). His other credits include *Ikiru* (1952), *The Lower Depths* (1957), *The Youth and His Amulet* (1961), and *The Face of Another* (1966).

Yoshio Tsuchiya, later *The Human Vapor*, would also appear in *Seven Samurai* as well as Kurosawa's *Yojimbo* (1961). But like Chiaki, Koizumi and the rest of the cast, Tsuchiya is merely a pawn lost in a badly constructed screenplay which gives him little to do, and I discuss his career at greater length elsewhere.

Although *Gigantis* was shown in this country in Japanese-language theaters shortly after its debut in Japan (under the title *Godzilla Raids Again*), it was a long time in coming to general audiences in the States. AB-PT Pictures Corp. secured the American rights for the film, which was to have been released by Republic. When the former collapsed, the rights (since reverted to Toho) were sold to Warner Bros. At one point, it was decided to utilize only the monster footage and build an entirely new story around it. The result was *The Volcano Monsters*, written by Ib Melchior, whose sci-fi scripts include *The Angry Red Planet* (1959), *Journey to the Seventh Planet* (1961), *Reptilicus* (1962), *Robinson Crusoe on Mars* (1964), and the original story for *Death Race 2000* (1975). The new script had Gigantis and Angilas (now simply a *Tyrannosaurus* and *Ankylosaurus*) discovered in a state of hibernation in a large cavern or volcano. The monsters are brought back to San Francisco, where the confrontation between the beasts was to have taken place. Presumably, the monsters would fight in and around Chinatown and Japan Town, thus explaining the appearance of Japanese characters on billboards, buildings, etc. The script called for additional special effects, and *Markalite* reported that effectsman Bob Burns remembers seeing Gigantis and Angilas suits Toho presumably shipped to the United States for the new effects footage. In any event, *The Volcano Monsters* was never made, and the film was simply dubbed. Keye Luke (best known for his recurring role on TV's "Kung Fu" and as Charlie Chan's number one son in the popular film series) dubbed Koizumi.

The late Paul Frees (died in 1986) was one of the all-time great voice actors. Frees not only provided the voices for countless cartoons and other animated programs (Rankin-Bass, Hanna-Barbera, etc.), but he frequently looped miscellaneous voices in major films as well (for example, his voice played a key role in the epic film *Spartacus*). He frequently turned up in science fiction films as well; he was one of the arctic researchers battling *The Thing (from Another World)*, a doomed scientist in *Space Master X-7* (1958) and a reporter (as well as the prologue narrator) in George Pal's *The War of the Worlds* (1953), among others. He even wrote and directed a feature, *The Beatniks* (1958), and co-wrote the film's songs! Beginning with *Rodan*, Frees began dubbing Japanese science fiction films as well. Because of his vocal range, he often dubbed dozens of voices for these films, and one can frequently find him having conversations with himself! George Takei ("Star Trek") and the late Marvin Miller (the voice of "Robby the Robot") also lent their vocal talents.

The dubbing borders on the absurd: When Shoichi's girlfriend tells him how brave he is, Shoichi responds, "Oh, banana oil!" The actor dubbing Chiaki is Daws Butler, another voice performer associated with cartoons, mostly for Hanna-Barbera. Butler's voice for Chiaki is painfully similar to the voice he later did as Yogi Bear, and is understandably hard to take seriously. Another problem with the Americanization was the decision to have Koizumi's character narrate the film. He never says anything useful to the story, and worse yet, he never stops talking. During the destruction of Osaka he says, "The fire raged on, consuming the city she loved." After the destruction he says, "Now it was a smoking cemetery filled with charred memories," and on and on and on.

There's very little left of the original score. Masaru Sato's music was replaced by notably incongruous themes from *Kronos* and *The Deerslayer*, among others. Although little was cut from the original film, stock footage from a wide range of sources (including *Robot Monster* and the Mexican *Adventuras en el Centro la Tiera*, according to *Markalite*, and *Unknown Island*) was inserted into the U.S. version, mostly at the beginning and during Shimura's unintentionally hilarious lecture on Gigantis. Because the film was made at the dawn of the Space Age, a prologue was inserted, featuring lots of stock footage of various rockets taking off and in flight, for no apparent reason.

Variety's "Powe" liked the special effects but found everything else "inept" and "tedious." "Aside from the entertaining scenes of destruction," said Bill Warren, "*Gigantis the Fire Monster* is the least of the Godzilla films." *The Motion*

Picture Guide agreed, giving the film a *½ rating. *Gigantis the Fire Monster*, running a scant 78 minutes, is never boring, though it's not very involving, either. The special effects work is often very good, but the script is poor and badly organized. Godzilla would eventually escape his icy prison to appear in another sequel, but it would take some seven years.

Half Human: The Story of the Abominable Snowman *(1955/1957)*

Half Human, as this film is generally known, is perhaps the perfect example of how disastrous the Americanization of a Japanese import can be. Originally a 95-minute feature in Japan, this Toho production was released in the United States by DCA (Distributors Corporation of America). They edited the film down to a scant 63 minutes. The picture is nowhere near the 78-minute running time reported in most sources, or even the 70-minute time reported in others. What's more, extensive footage—about 20 minutes worth of new scenes—of American actors was cut in, leaving less than half of the original film intact. Rather than dub or subtitle *Half Human*, DCA (or its contracted producer) opted for no dialog at all during the Japanese footage, and practically no sound effects as well. The original score is also gone, replaced by standard library music. What's left is little more than a glimpse of what appears to have been an interesting production.

Dr. John Rayburn (John Carradine) has returned to the United States after a long sabbatical in Japan. In his rather barren office (well, he *has* been gone a while), Rayburn greets two of his colleagues (Russell Thorsen and Robert Karnes), also his closest friends. He tells the men the story of the scientific discovery of the century—a man-ape creature discovered in the mountainous northern region of Japan. "It was mid-December," Rayburn begins, as the film dissolves to the Japanese-shot footage. Five vacationing skiers (including future Toho star Kenji Sahara) split up for no good reason. Three of the skiers wind up in a remote cabin just as a snowstorm hits, soon followed by an avalanche. The next morning, the three skiers, accompanied by the police, search for their two companions, who turn up dead in another cabin. They are apparently the victims of a monstrous snow creature, who leaves several footprints and a clump of hair behind. Switching back to the U.S. footage, Carradine pulls out a mold taken of the footprint (the mold seems ridiculously deep, suggesting the creature sank about a foot with every step), and shows the men the clump of hair. After much tiresome speculation, we return to the film proper. Professor Tanaka leads an expedition to find the beast. The group, which includes

Half Human: The Story of the Abdominable Snowman (1955/1957) 19

the boy (Akira Takarada) and the girl (Momoko Kochi) camp for the night. A curious snowman appears, touching the face of the girl. The creature is covered with hair, and his face resembles that of a Neanderthal man, except for some rather pointy ears. Although credited by most sources as standing 12 feet, and said to be nine feet in the film, the creature appears only slightly taller than the human characters. In a curious decision by the filmmakers that makes the monster both more human looking and frightening, the creature is balding! The girl stirs, screaming at the sight of the snowman. The boy chases the creature but falls into a ravine. After yet more footage of Carradine et al., we learn that the boy has been rescued by a native woman (Akemi Negishi), who takes him to a Tibetan-like tribe that worships the snowman. The boy's arrival angers the chief, who orders the woman to take a sacrifice of food to the snow creature's cave. She sees not only the snowman, but a little snowboy as well. The snowboy appears to be holding some kind of doll (a bear, perhaps?), era though it's difficult to tell for sure. Meanwhile, the natives, fearing that the boy's appearance might anger the snowman, tie the boy up and dangle him over a cliff, where wild birds are to eat him. The snowman comes to the rescue, however, and silently saves the boy. Back to the States, where Carradine unveils the corpse of the snowboy, which has just been examined by Dr. Carl Jordan (Morris Ankrum). Jordan theorizes that the snow creatures had semi-developed vocal chords and could "bellow like an animal yet cry or whimper like a human being." He tells the scientists he believes that in 10 or 15 generations the snow creatures might develop into a species "that might be able to speak a single sentence. I tell you it's incredible! It is my belief," he states, "that this species is one-half animal and . . . Half Human." How did the animal die? Carradine acknowledges it was shot to death. Back to Japanese footage: Representatives from a circus come looking for the snowman. Using the captured snowboy for bait, they capture the adult beast. They put the snowman into a cage and drive away, strangely leaving the snowboy behind. The snowboy follows the circus trucks. There's a scuffle, and the snowboy is shot. The snowman furiously kills all of the circus people and tosses several vehicles off the side of a cliff. The snowman next destroys the tribal village, killing the entire tribe (offscreen), save for the native woman. The scientific expedition (remember them?), including the boy, track the snowman, who by now has kidnapped the girl. Taking her to his cave, he threatens to drop her in a sulphur pit (this scene closely resembles the conclusion to *Son of Frankenstein*). The native woman lunges at the snowman, and expedition members shoot the creature. Both the creature and the native woman fall to their deaths. The film ends with Carradine speculating about offshoot species of snowmen.

Half Human's Japanese footage is occasionally very interesting. The design of the snowman's face is striking and original. Although a mask, it comes across as more expressive than most movie monsters from the period. The design of the snowboy is downright creepy. Toho sent the costume to the United States for the U.S. version, and its ghostly face figures prominently as Ankrum discusses the creature's anatomy. Probably unintentionally, the American filmmakers give us an eyeful. The snowman's first appearance, through the window of a tent, is jarring, and its rescue of Takarada is unnerving. The film, in its U.S. form anyway, becomes more predictable and hence less interesting after that moment. The circus, the sulphur pit and whatnot are all familiar ideas seen before. Perhaps the Japanese version concentrated more on the snow creatures' daily life, or perhaps on the characters tracking the beast, but who knows? The U.S. version not only grossly edits the film, but silences it as well. The original soundtrack is gone lock, stock and barrel. The subtitling of foreign films for release in this country was still in its infancy, and apparently editor-director Kenneth Crane didn't like the combination dubbed-undubbed version of *Godzilla, King of the Monsters!* Here, the sound is simply missing. Despite the use of library music, which adds nothing to the film, and the occasional sound effect or poorly dubbed scream, watching *Half Human* is very much like watching a silent film, albeit narrated by Carradine. Carradine's narration adds little, however, and is often out of sync with the action onscreen. The added footage, obviously shot in a day or two and in no way matching the original footage as Embassy had done with *Godzilla*, stops the film cold. Crane shoots the film in static medium shots which tend to make it more boring than it already is. Carradine's Dr. Rayburn has really no connection with the Japanese footage at all, and his endless speculating denies us the story, rather than supplementing or clarifying it. The film's chronology is also peculiar. Why did the snowman kill the skiers if he was peaceful until his son was killed? Why does Carradine tell us the snowboy was shot before he's killed?

John Carradine was one of the busiest actors in Hollywood, appearing in well over 100 movies. He appeared in several science fiction films during this time, notably *The Invisible Invaders* and *The Cosmic Man* (both 1959). At least in those pictures he played interesting, if preposterous, characters. Here, he might just as well have played Mr. John Carradine as opposed to Dr. John Rayburn. Morris Ankrum was another staple of American science fiction films of the fifties, appearing in countless films, often cast as a military man or scientist. He gives the role his best shot, but his dialog is worse than Carradine's. As for the Japanese cast, it's impossible to judge their performances in such an abridged, silent form. Still, it seems likely Takarada, Sahara, etc., were up to the level of their other Toho films from this period.

Reviews were scant. The *New York Herald-Tribune*'s Paul V. Beckley found the film "Generally slow and the outcome disappointing." *The Motion Picture Guide* gave the film a *½ rating, calling it a "dull film lacking the inventiveness that made [*Godzilla* and *Rodan*] so enjoyable . . . the new scenes . . . made little improvement." Frankly, I doubt very much that the reviewer had ever even seen the original.

Half Human: The Story of the Abominable Snowman is interesting if somewhat familiar in its original footage, yet what quality it might have had was absolutely destroyed thanks to DCA's shoddy American adaptation. This was the first time this would happen to a Toho film, but not the last.

The Mysterious Satellite (1956)

This surprising and occasionally very inventive science fiction melodrama (released to television as *Warning from Space*) is best remembered for its silly-looking though imaginative aliens—friendly creatures that look like walking starfish with big blue eyes in the center of their bodies.

Flying saucers, resembling shooting stars, begin appearing in the skies above Japan. In Tokyo, several of the starfish-like aliens are spotted, and the island nation begins to panic. The creatures begin turning up in the darndest places, emerging from Tokyo Bay, frightening fishermen, and in the wings of a theater, terrifying the orchestra and performers onstage. Retreating to their saucer, the leader of the mission, No. 1 (listed as Ginko in the credits), suggests assuming human form so as not to scare the people of Earth. One of the starfish opposes the idea, but after hearing No. 1's argument, finally concedes. "Very well, I bow to your logic." Using a captured photograph of a popular stage actress, Hikari Aozora (Toyomi Karita), No. 1 is transformed into the Earth woman's double (also played by Karita). Found floating in a lake, No. 1 is picked up by vacationers, and everyone assumes she has amnesia. They also recognize that she looks exactly like the popular Aozora. She visits a physicist named Dr. Matsuda (Isao Yamagata), who has been working with "Urium 101," a form of energy so powerful, "even the H-Bomb in comparison looks like a toy." She tries to destroy the professor's notes, explaining Urium 101 is simply too dangerous to fool around with. As Dr. Matsuda tries to explain his motives, she disappears. Later, the alien appears again before Matsuda, as well as his colleagues, Dr. Komura (Bontaro Miake) and Dr. Isobe (Shozo Nanbu). She says that she is from the planet Paira, a planet on the other side of the sun, but in an orbit identical to Earth's (a common hiding place for other worlds). She explains that she has come to warn mankind of the dangers of nuclear weaponry and also of a flaming, runaway comet (thereafter referred to as Planet R) on a collision course with Earth. She says that if all of Earth's nuclear weapons were fired at Planet R, the runaway body might be destroyed in time. The "World Congress" (i.e., the United Nations) rejects the plan, however, and as Planet R draws closer, earthquakes and tidal waves (a la *When Worlds Collide*) destroy whole cities, while heat from the flaming planet increases the temperature here on Earth. Meanwhile, Dr. Matsuda is kidnapped by a weapons broker who wants to sell Urium 101 to the highest bidder. The scientist is gagged and tied to a chair in an abandoned building in Tokyo, which has since been evacuated. The World Congress finally comes to its senses, but by now it is too late: the nuclear weapons have almost no effect on Planet R. There is an earthquake in Tokyo, and part of the building where Dr. Matsuda is being held collapses. Matsuda, still tied to the chair, nearly falls to his death. No. 1 and several other aliens (also in human form) appear before the scientist. Using his formula for Urium 101, they construct a rocket to blow up Planet R. This tactic is successful, and everyone emerges from the rubble caused by Planet R's close brush with Earth. No. 1 returns to the Pairan spaceship and assumes her natural, starfish-like state.

Daiei's *The Mysterious Satellite*, Japan's first serious production to revolve around alien visitors, is a curious work. While much of the film's story appears to have been inspired by *When Worlds Collide*, its presentation is singularly Japanese. The friendly starfish aliens, for example, are admirably and distinctly nonhumanoid, even if they do look like nothing more than people trapped in giant pillowcases. The flying saucer's interior is abstractly designed, with no clear doors, windows or controls (there is, however, what looks like a pair of whirling hula-hoops; an identical contraption turns up in the big-budget 1978 film, *Superman*). The picture gets a lot of mileage out of its meager budget through imagination and ingenuity. The scientists begin to suspect No. 1 isn't human when Isobe plays tennis with her: she's able to jump ten feet into the air to return Isobe's serves. Later, when a group of schoolgirls spot No. 1—believing her to be Hikari Aozora—and surround the nervous alien, she simply vanishes, reappearing on the other side of a glass door. This effect was done very simply through clever staging and without opticals, but is very effective nonetheless. Also good is No. 1's transformation into Hikari's double. The creature enters a glass chamber, still in starfish form, and, via lap dissolves and putty-like makeup, slowly becomes human. This effect is so good, in fact, that it's repeated (the same sequence is printed in reverse) at the end of the picture. This little reprise appears to have been added by AIP-TV, possibly to expand the running time, but seems an entirely appropriate ending. While the film's spectacles—and not its characters—are its story, screenwriter Hideo Oguni wisely chose to remain focused on the three middle-aged scientists who first spot and study the UFOs. Despite the threat of global destruction, the story is pretty much contained within the scientists' observatory. Another good idea is seen when Tokyo is evacuated and a group of children come to live in the observatory's basement. The combination of the sometimes playful, sometimes frightened children with the much older scientists makes an interesting contrast. Finally, the idea of having the alien's leader be a smart and attractive woman was an original, even daring, idea for the time. That the alien would be friendly at all is unusual.

Warning from Space is not without its faults. Nothing much happens during the first 30 minutes, before No. 1's transformation, and the introduction of the arms broker goes nowhere. The aliens are helpful but not very bright: Why did they frighten everyone by suddenly appearing on Earth in their starfish form? Why didn't they save Dr. Matsuda earlier?

Variety's "Mosk" liked the film. "Though influenced by Yank efforts, it is done with a candor and simplicity which makes it a good entry of this type." More recently, Phil Hardy followed *Variety* in praising the special effects and color photography, adding "For once, aliens are depicted as friendly, a refreshing change from the usual Cold War mentality suffusing Science Fiction material at the time." *The Motion Picture Guide* gave the film a *½ rating, though didn't quite grasp the film's meaning. "A well-scripted illustration of how atomic weapons can be used to save lives rather than obliterating them." "If you think Japanese science fiction movies are all the same," said *Psychotronic*, "this should be a big surprise."

Daiei's *The Mysterious Satellite* is an interesting little picture and far better than the majority of that studio's science fiction output of the 1960s and 1970s.

Rodan *(1956)*

More than any of Toho's other early monster films, *Rodan* tries to imitate American-made sci-fi, just then hitting its stride in 1956. The first half of the film was obviously inspired by the giant ant film *Them!* (1954), while the climax apes both *Godzilla* and any one of the dozens of similar giant monster movies being made at the same time in the United States. *Rodan* (advertised as *Rodan, The Flying Monster*, but released simply as *Rodan*) was Toho's first monster movie in color, and while the miniature-laden climax is impressive, the story is generally uninspired and only marginally interesting. Although popular among *kaiju eiga* fans on both sides of the Pacific, the genre hadn't quite broken away from the American films that had inspired it, though this would quickly change.

Following American-added stock footage of a pair of H-bomb tests (undeniably dramatic footage that would become greatly overused in sci-fi pictures during this time), we are introduced to the small mining community of Kitamatsu, located in Kyushu, the southernmost province of Japan. Ground water has flooded a mine shaft, and several of the miners begin turning up "slaughtered like animals." We meet Shigeru (Kenji Sahara), a miner in love with Kyo (Yumi Shirakawa), whose brother has disappeared. Some of the miners suspect Kyo's brother may be responsible for the killings. Later, two miners and a police inspector tie themselves together and wade through the flooded mine shaft. Two of the men are pulled underwater, and as the third desperately tries to call for help, he is attacked by a creature that makes unintentionally funny squeaky sounds, like two balloons being rubbed together. The community becomes gripped with fear, and Shigeru tries to talk Kyo into leaving town. Just then, a large larvae-type insect with lobster-like claws crashes through a wall. Several more of the creatures (called Meganuron in Japan), each about 15 feet long, attack some residents. The military are brought in, and with help from the miners, they search for the creatures deep underground, a sequence remarkably similar to the climax of *Them!* During the search, Shigeru is trapped when an earthquake separates him from the others. As the miners try to clear the blocked passageway, a team of scientists, including Dr. Kashiwagi (Akihiko Hirata) and reporter Izeki (Yoshibumi Tajima) visit the earthquake site, near an inactive volcano. A second quake stirs up the countryside, and Shigeru suddenly appears—injured and suffering amnesia. Elsewhere, a jet pilot spots a UFO flying about at incredible speeds, doing loops and other seemingly impossible maneuvers. The jet pursues the flying object, but suddenly the UFO turns and crashes into the jet. This is soon followed by other strange occurrences. A British cargo plane is destroyed (offscreen) by the UFO; the object is sighted in such faraway places as China and the Philippines (its extreme altitude prevents anyone from getting a good look at it); and a young couple and several cows disappear near the volcano.

Kyo, trying to cheer up the recuperating Shigeru, shows her boyfriend a tiny bird's nest occupied by a pair of tiny eggs. This triggers Shigeru's memory of the events in the mine. Realizing he was trapped, Shigeru wandered through the cavern, eventually spotting several more of the big larvae-like insects, along with a tremendous egg, dozens of meters tall. The egg hatched, and out popped a large prehistoric reptile, roughly resembling a *pteranodon*. The creature, spotting the comparatively tiny insect monsters, immediately gulped several down. It was this horrific sight that caused Shigeru's amnesia. The scientists return to the now empty cavern, finding only part of the eggshell. Carbon dating places the creature in the Cretaceous period (though only 20 million years ago according to one scientist, approximately 40 million years *after* the Cretaceous period ended). Kashiwagi says the monster has a 500-foot wingspan and is of the species *rodan* (a mythical creature, needless to say). A helicopter flight over the volcano's crater reveals the bleached bones of the missing persons (another scene copied from *Them!*). The creature rises up and is closely followed by a second rodan (one observer suggests it's a mate). The first rodan flies off into the distance. Rodan attacks the city of Sasebo, causing tremendous damage with its huge, flapping wings, which create a typhoon-strength wind. Kitamatsu is evacuated, and the military bombards the rodans' nesting area when they return. This triggers a volcanic eruption, and both creatures are consumed in the lava and noxious fumes.

Rodan is too standard to be of much interest. Much of the story is lifted from the much better *Them!*, with elements from *Godzilla* thrown in as well. Shigeru is pretty colorless, his relationship with Kyo goes nowhere, and he all but disappears once the star attractions make their appearance. The rodans themselves are pretty dull monsters. Patterned after *pteranodons*, they're pretty awkward when not flying (their wings are too rigid to allow much movement, and today many paleontologists believe these creatures couldn't fly at all, but glided like flying squirrels). They simply lack any real personality. One of the monsters would return in later films (beginning with the *Ghidrah: The Three-Headed Monster*), only to be transformed into a silly, foolish caricature.

Rodan was the first of a dozen genre films, mostly for director Ishiro Honda, written by Takeshi Kimura. Kimura's work was uneven, consisting of some of the studio's best (*The H-Man, Gorath, Destroy All Monsters*) and worst films (*Godzilla vs. the Smog Monster*). Still, Kimura's work was generally more consistent and ambitious than that of Shinichi Sekizawa, who alternated *kaiju eiga* writing duties with Kimura (the latter sometimes wrote under the name Kaoru Mabuchi). *Smog Monster* was apparently Kimura's last feature. He died in 1988. Sekizawa died in 1992. "Sekizawa and... Kimura were completely different," Honda told David Milner in a 1992 interview. "If the story was positive, or even childish, it would go to Sekizawa. If it was negative or involved politics, it would go to Kimura."

The special effects are impressive in the scenes involving Rodan's attack on Sasebo. In one scene the monster flies past a highly detailed miniature of a large bridge, the creature's jet stream ripping it apart. Later, when the monster lumbers through Sasebo's business district, there's an incredible shot of a collapsing building where panic-stricken people can be glimpsed dashing about inside. This effect is extremely effective, and I have no idea why this bit of trickery—using simple miniature projection—hardly ever appears again in other Toho films; maybe it was too expensive and time-consuming to shoot. The tiny, generally less detailed miniature jets are much less convincing, as are the silly larvae-like monsters featured in the film's first half (this was one of the few times Toho constructed full-size costumes for oversized characters). During the finale, when the creatures flap about over the exploding volcano, the monsters look like nothing more than kites on a less than breezy day. Generally though, the effects work is good, much better, in fact, than most American sci-fi films of the period.

Although Kenji Sahara (born 1932) had appeared in the bastardized *Half Human* (q.v.), Rodan remains his earliest starring role available to most U.S. genre fans. The versatile actor has appeared in all manner of roles, from the youthful miner here to slimy villains in later productions. Sahara, billed here as Kenji Sawada, and not to be confused with much younger Japanese superstar Kenji Sawada, played one of the Japanese soldiers Frank Sinatra and other members of a cracked-up plane make peace with on a remote island in *None but the Brave* (1965). After *Rodan*, Sahara starred in *The Mysterians* (1957), *The H-Man* (1958), *King Kong vs. Godzilla* (1962), *Atragon* (1963), *Godzilla vs. the Thing* (cameo, 1964), *Ghidrah: The Three-Headed Monster* (cameo, 1964), *War of the Gargantuas* (1966), *Son of Godzilla* (1967),

Destroy All Monsters (1968), *Godzilla's Revenge* (1969), *Yog: Monster from Space* (1970), *Terror of Mechagodzilla* (1975) and, most recently, *Godzilla vs. King Ghidorah* (1991). Sahara was married to co-star Yumi Shirakawa. Shirakawa was Toho's most frequent leading lady through the early sixties, also appearing in *The Mysterians* and *The H-Man* with Sahara, and alone, in starring roles, in *The Secret of the Telegian* (1960), *The Last War* (1961) and *Gorath* (1962). Her last genre film appears to be *Kiganjo no boken* (1965).

The Americanization of *Rodan* was handled by the same team that did *Gigantis the Fire Monster*. Keye Luke dubbed star Kenji Sahara, and Paul Frees did nearly half of the remaining voices. *The Motion Picture Guide* called the film "One of the cornerstones in Japanese monster movies and called the first monster movie in Eastmancolor," but gave it only a *½ rating. Bill Warren liked the picture, but noted that Rodan "never seems to be anything other than stupid and petulant ... the monster flies, that's all."

Atomic Rulers *(1957)*

This feature, usually misidentified as *Atomic Rulers of the World*, was the first of at least four "Starman" films, re-edited from a Japanese theatrical serial, and issued to American television as separate features. There were at least nine "Starman" episodes produced by Shintoho between 1956 and 1959, generally running about 45 minutes apiece, and probably intended to round out a double or triple bill in Japan. In the United States, these pictures were severely cut, with two episodes combined as one, and edited down to 70 to 85 minutes to better fit 90-minute TV time slots. The first two episodes were supposedly re-edited and released in this country as *The Appearance of Supergiant* or *Supergiant I* (Supergiant was Starman's name in Japan), but I can find no record of this, and it's possible that *Atomic Rulers*, re-edited from chapters three and four, might very well have been the first of these films to make it to the States. In any event, the Starman pictures are rarely shown today, and even then by only the cheapest amd most outdated of television stations. This is unfortunate, because while these films make even Daiei's "Gamera" movies appear lavish by comparison, they are, in fact, occasionally very imaginative and inventive. It wouldn't be fair to compare *Atomic Rulers* to American-made features anyway. This was, after all, a serial. And when compared to similar chapter plays produced in the United States—notably *Adventures of Captain Marvel* (Republic, 1941), *Superman* (Columbia, 1948) and *King of the Rocketmen* (Republic, 1949)—*Atomic Rulers* compares favorably.

The High Council of the Emerald Planet in the Moffitt Galaxy mulls over the nuclear arms race on Earth. The creatures, which sit at a long table in front of an attractive starry backdrop (including a large, ringed planet), are dressed in a variety of costumes, most of which look like cannibalized robots from other serials. Several of the beings resemble the starfish aliens from *The Mysterious Satellite* (q.v.). The council learns that the Earth nation of Magolia (which more or less is supposed to be the good ol' U.S. of A) is plotting to conquer the world with a nuclear device they're building at a secret base. The council dispatches Starman (Ken Utsui), a superhero more or less dressed like Captain Marvel, to Earth. Starman is given a special watch called a "globemeter," which gives him the ability to fly, to detect radiation and to speak every language on Earth. Starman doesn't waste any time, as he puts it, saving all "the gentle people of this great Earth." Before he even lands he saves a passenger jet that has lost control of its rudder. Dressed in a business suit (his alter-ego outfit), Starman locates the briefcase containing the Magolian nuclear device. Several Magolian thugs (played by Western actors) try to shoot the superhero, but bullets merely bounce off him. When they try to tackle him, Starman pushes them aside like dolls. During the scuffle, several kids grab the briefcase. One of the kids, Hiroshi, is kidnapped by a Magolian thug, while at the Magolian embassy, the country's leader, Munta Dee (played by a Western actor whose hammy performance is obvious, even though it's dubbed), details his plans of world domination. (Note: Walter Manley blew the Americanization. The sign on the embassy gate clearly names the sinister nation as Merapolia.) After a series of captures and escapes (including a swordfight and Starman's rescue of a young woman from a Magolian guillotine), Starman locates the secret Magolian base, which looks like a low-budget Japanese version of a Ken Adam–designed hideout from a James Bond movie. Starman rescues Hiroshi, retrieves the nuclear device and captures Munta Dee.

There was a horror movie program in Detroit called "Sir Graves Ghastly Presents," which ran every Saturday on the local CBS affiliate, WJBK, channel 2. Sir Graves (aka Lawson J. Deming), the host, would rise out of a cardboard coffin to introduce movies. He'd also dress in drag as "Tilly Trollhouse," Sir Graves' wife, and lip-synch Spike Jones or Florence Foster Jenkins songs. According to Elena M. Watson's *Television Horror Movie Hosts* (McFarland, 1991), Lawson "Generally disliked all Japanese sci-fi movies. In particular, he despised a series of films called *Starman*, which actually embarrassed him." Embarrassed? A guy in drag (as a female vampire) singing "My Old Flame"?

Atomic Rulers is inarguably silly, but it's also reasonably well paced and often quite inventive. I particularly like how Starman changes from the off-white Starman tights to his dark business suit. He merely jumps into the air, and presto! (These simple, impressive bits were accomplished through nothing more than clever editing.) Ken Utsui's superhero has a warm, friendly (though distinctly alien) demeanor. After hanging up his cape, Utsui appeared in *The Great Wall* (1964), *The Falcon Fighters* and *Getaway Glory* (both 1970) and *Gamera vs. Zigra* (1971). In his starman garb, Utsui is not unlike George Reeves' easy-going, civic-minded Superman, appearing on American television at this same time. And like Superman, Starman seems to have an affinity for children. He dazzles them by bending the barrel of a bad guy's pistol or by flying high into the air (generally done with rear-screen projection and miniatures). The production values appear slightly better than those of American serials (certainly American serials of the 1950s, by then notoriously cheap). The Magolian base is a fairly elaborate set, and a futuristic-looking boat was constructed for the villains' ill-fated getaway. The special effects range from okay to poor but are serviceable for a serial and not really embarrassing as such. As it was sold directly to American television, and since it's rarely revived, *Atomic Rulers* received few notices. However, *Psychotronic* recommended this and the other Starman features, calling them "funny excitement that shouldn't be missed." *Atomic Rulers* was followed by *Attack from Space*, *Invaders from Space* (both 1958) and *Evil Brain from Outer Space* (1958-59), which are also included in this text.

The Mysterians *(1957)*

After three giant monster movies in three years, Toho produced this special effects extravaganza built around an alien invasion without a city-smashing monster—well, almost. Japan's film industry was—and still is—fiercely conservative, Toho in particular. After *Godzilla*, whenever Tomoyuki Tanaka produced a special effects film, he always tried to squeeze in a giant monster to help sell the movie, even when the plot didn't call for one. Such is the case with *The Mysterians*, a generally silly but lively and colorful invasion epic. Early scenes feature a giant bird-like robot with "skin" suggesting a tremendous tank. This intriguing creature has little to do with the rest of the story (in the American edition at least) and is all but forgotten once the main action gets underway.

Troubled physical astronomer Ryochi Shiraishi (Akihiko Hirata), his fiance, Hiroko (Momoko Kochi), sister Etsuke (Yumi Shirakawa) and her boyfriend, Joji (Kenji Sahara), attend a harvest festival. Ryochi seems distracted, and Joji chastises him for ignoring Hiroko. A forest fire appears in the distance, and everyone save Ryochi is surprised the fire is coming from beneath the Earth's surface—the trees are burning from their roots. Ryochi disappears, and Joji meets with the astronomer's associate, Dr. Adachi (Takashi Shimura). Ryochi has sent Adachi a half-written report on the planet Mysteroid, part of "a group of small stars between Mars and Saturn." Adachi scoffs at the report, remarking, "I'm not quite that radical." There's a tremendous landslide in the area where Ryochi was staying—the entire village is destroyed, and there are no known survivors. Everyone presumes the astronomer is dead. Joji and Adachi investigate other strange happenings in the area. Dead fish begin to appear, for instance, and the ground becomes hot with radioactivity. Suddenly, out of the mountainside, the aforementioned giant robot bird appears (Bill Warren suggests it looks like "Godzilla in samurai armor"), which, after blowing up a Jeep (an explosion is superimposed over the vehicle—a supremely poor effect), heads straight for a nearby village. After causing some destruction, the robot is stopped near a bridge, where the military is successful in blowing it up. So much for the robot. In the Japanese cut, other such creatures reappear briefly during the effects-laden climax, emerging briefly from the Mysterians' underground lair.

Later, at the Diet Building, Joji addresses Japan's leaders, warning that the robot's appearance and the other strange occurrences suggest alien visitors. Joji believes there is a link between Ryochi's report and the strange happenings. Joji tells Adachi, who observed flying saucers around the dark side of the moon, of a trio of saucers he and Etsuke spotted during the robot's attack. This news is enough to prompt Adachi into making Ryochi's report public. Scientists return to the area, where a giant dome emerges from beneath the Earth's surface (it screws itself out). A disembodied voice requests the presence of five of the scientists (including Joji and Dr. Adachi). The men enter the dome, where they are greeted by the Mysterians: humanoid aliens wearing cantaloupe-colored motorcycle helmets which obscure their faces (Yoshio Tsuchiya is the alien leader according to David Milner). The aliens destroyed their own world thousands of years before with hydrogen bombs. They migrated to Mars, and have since set up a base on the moon and an orbiting space station over the Earth. They say they have come in peace (the robot was apparently intended merely as a demonstration of their power) and ask for the three kilometers of land they now occupy, as well as five Earth women for breeding purposes (the Mysterians have a high birth defect rate, the scars of their nuclear holocaust). In another *faux pas*, they admit they've already "acquired" three of the women; the other two are Etsuke and Hiroko. The alien spokesman unconvincingly asserts, "We are pacifists to the end." Naturally, the scientists refuse and prepare to attack the alien dome. Tanks and other hardware gather around the site. Meanwhile, Joji gives Etsuke and Hiroko the bad news. Just then, Ryochi appears on their television set, dressed as a Mysterian. The scientist says he joined the aliens because he fears mankind's abuse of science will lead to a nuclear holocaust unless the Mysterians intervene. He believes the aliens' message of peace is genuine. Japanese forces attack the dome but are destroyed by a powerful beam emitted from the alien base. Jet fighters are also unsuccessful, destroyed by similar beams from Mysterian saucers. That evening, the aliens are still trying to convince the Earth they mean its people no harm. "Dear people of Earth," they plead from a hovering saucer, "We are fighting only in self-defense." Adachi warns a group of Western reporters the nations of Earth must band together to defeat the

Mysterians before they get a foothold on the planet. Though they are currently based in Japan, he says, your country may be next. Ryochi, seen once again on a television set, warns a group of scientists that "the Earth cannot be left in charge of man." However, inside the tacky dome, Ryochi soon learns that the Mysterians are building a tremendous underground fortress and that their ultimate aim is to conquer the Earth, not save it. Their lust for power disenchants the astronomer. The nations of the Earth band together, and at the "Defense Force of the Earth Head Quarter" [sic], plans are announced to build a giant laser cannon and, later, a device which looks like a big radar dish (the first of an endless stream of such devices in Japanese films). The device, called a Markalite (later the name of a magazine devoted to Japanese fantastic cinema), reflects the aliens' firepower while shooting back an equally powerful beam of its own. Before the Markalites are built, the Earth Defense Forces take another beating from the Mysterians, destroying one of two huge dirigible-size, jet-shaped aircraft. The Mysterians warn the scientists that their base has been expanded to 120 kilometers ("We put you on notice!"), but the Earth refuses to surrender. Etsuke and Hiroko are kidnapped. The Markalites are dropped from the remaining supersized jet, and move toward the alien dome on tank-like treads. Now close enough to the base and matching its firepower, the Markalites commence the attack. Meanwhile, Joji has discovered a small hole near the Mysterians' base, apparently created during the expansion of their fortress. Through a tunnel, he locates the aliens' power center, as well as the kidnapped women (by now the aliens have taken well beyond the original five they asked for). Joji destroys the aliens' power center, but is captured by several Mysterians. One of them takes Joji and the women to a remote tunnel. The Mysterian soldier turns out to be Ryochi in disguise, trying to reconcile the error of his ways. He gives Joji the rest of his report on the Mysterians (!) and orders everyone to leave, while he returns to the base to make sure it's blown up. Thanks to Joji and Ryochi, along with the Markalites, the aliens' fortress is destroyed, though several saucers escape. The nations of the world must stay united in the event the Mysterians should return.

I had the good fortune to see a newly struck, 35mm TohoScope print (without the Perspecta Stereophonic sound, alas) of *The Mysterians* recently, but unlike most of Toho's early sci-fi spectacles, the picture hasn't worn as well as one might expect. In many ways, *The Mysterians* more closely resembles the "Starman" films and similar superhero adventures produced by other studios during the 1950s and early 1960s than those Toho alien invasion films. The Mysterians themselves would be much more at home fighting Space Chief or Starman than they are here. Their costumes, while colorful, are ridiculous and simply out of place in this otherwise straight-faced adventure. Certainly *The Mysterians* was targeted at a more general audience than the Starman films, and yet its aliens are just as ridiculous. When Shimura, Sahara and the other scientists approach the dome, they are instructed to put on special clothing to protect them from the extreme difference of temperature and atmospheric pressure. Once inside, however, we see that the special clothing they're given is nothing more than Dracula-style black capes! The set design within the alien base is equally unimpressive, with most sets overlit and lacking detail (the lower budgeted superhero films do much better in this regard). Interestingly, some of the effects shots of the base appear clearly inspired by *Forbidden Planet*'s (1956) Krell city. The picture also lacks considerable logic in depicting the aliens' actions. Why did they send the robot to attack the city? Why did they kidnap three Earth women before asking the scientists if they cold have them? Why did they wear those bulky helmets all the time? These and many other questions go unanswered and help bring down the entire film.

The special effects, while technically quite good, come off as cold and uninvolving. Once the robot is destroyed, Eiji Tsuburaya's effects center almost exclusively around the two big (and overlong) battles at the end of the film, which, while cut with Sahara's infiltration of the alien base, are somehow lacking the human element. Everyone, including the Mysterians, sit around television monitors watching the mostly remote-controlled battle between the Markalites and the dome unfold. If it weren't for Akira Ifukube's tremendously rousing score, the final controntation between the Mysterians and the Earth forces would be a big bore. The robot, known as Mogera in Japan, is quite interesting. The name was derived from the Japanese word for "mole." The creature is much less ridiculous onscreen than it may sound here, and was one of the studio's most unique creations.

Variety's "Ron" liked the miniatures, but overall found the picture "as corny as it is furious . . . dedicated to those undiscerning enough to be taken in by its hokum. While Junior may be moved by the arrival of outer-space gremlins, big brother and all like him will laugh their heads off." The *New York Times*' H.H.T. (Howard Thompson), reviewing the film on a double-bill with *Watusi* (1959), called the picture "an ear-splitting Japanese-made fantasy, photographed in runny color and dubbed English. This Metro release is crammed with routine footage of death rays and scrambling civilians, not one of whom can act." (Not even Takashi Shimura?) The *Los Angeles Times*' Charles Stinson liked the film, calling it "science fiction in the grand manner." "Lots of massive destruction and good special effects make this an all-time favorite," said *Psychotronic*, while Phil Hardy's *Science Fiction* had this to say: "The best scenes involve the interaction between the aliens and those with the fabulous metallic bird especially its destruction as it walks across a bridge that collapses, causing the device to short-circuit and the aliens to admit defeat." Bill Warren concluded, "Although the film is as gaudy as costume jewelry . . . it will probably remain the ultimate example of flashy Japanese science fiction."

Throne of Blood *(1957)*

Nearly thirty years before he tackled *King Lear*, director Akira Kurosawa helmed this adaptation of another of Shakespeare's tragic characters. *Macbeth* was the basis for his *Kumonoso-djo* (*Throne of Blood*), and it follows the Bard's short but bloody play even closer than the director's Lear story, *Ran* (1985).

Throne of Blood tells the simple story of a weak-willed samurai. After a long but victorious battle, Taketori (Toshiro Mifune) and his friend and fellow warrior (Minoru Chiaki) encounter a spirit who has three visions that promise Taketori power beyond his wildest dreams. After the first of the three visions comes true (he is awarded command of an important fort), he speaks of his encounter to his equally ambitious (if much less subtly so) wife (Isuzu Yamada), who convinces him to murder his superior, a warlord, so that he may ascend to the throne. The second vision has come to pass. The third prediction is a bit more tricky. According to the spirit, his best friend's son (Akira Kubo) will rule following Taketori's reign. His wife now pregnant, Taketoki orders his best friend and his son murdered. The son escapes, however, and begins building an army with the help of elder statesman Noriyasu Odagura (Takashi Shimura). Meanwhile, Taketori is haunted by the spirit of his dead samurai friend, while his wife gives birth to a stillborn baby and goes mad. With troops closing in on his castle, Taketori revisits the spirit, who promises he shall reign until the nearby forest moves. Now confident in his rule, Taketori gives a speech to his troops, who laugh as he does at the idea of the forest moving. But sure enough, it does, for Odagura's forces have advanced to the castle hidden behind large tree branches and other shrubbery. Hopelessly facing an overwhelming number of troops and certain defeat, Taketori's own men begin shooting arrows at the now crazed leader. (This is the picture's most celebrated sequence, and justly so. It's both exciting and painful to watch.) After being struck many times, he drops to his death. The film ends as it began, at the site of the castle, now a foggy ruin.

Throne of Blood was the second of three major film adaptations of the story. Orson Welles filmed Shakespeare's play for Republic Pictures in 1948, with mixed results. Roman Polanski's superb 1971 film, funded by Hugh Hefner's *Playboy* of all things, was a well-directed, extremely bloody, effective work, but like Welles' film did poorly at the box office and received mixed notices. *Throne of Blood*, however, was almost instantly regarded as a masterpiece and continues to be regarded by most critics as one of Japan's greatest films. Part of this seems to be due to the director's simplicity in adapting the story. The story is Shakespeare, the look Japanese. Costumes, acting styles and other conventions of the Noh and Kubuki theater were incorporated into the film, and this was never more apparent than in the early scene where Mifune and Chiaki encounter the spirit (Chieko Naniwa). Dressed in white, with white hair and white makeup, the spirit speaks in a reed-like voice, sitting quietly in a simple hut, surrounded by eerie piles of dirt and skeletal remains. While Japanese audiences were apparently used to such characters in the Noh plays, American audiences were taken aback at the site of an ashen-white ghost at a spinning wheel! The effect is unsettling, thanks in no small part to the superb reaction shots of Mifune.

Equally fine is Isuzu Yamada's Asian Lady Macbeth, given a stronger hand in the proceedings than in most adaptations of the story. Yamada followed her role here with performances in *The Lower Depths* (1957), *Yojimbo* (1961), and *The Great Wall* (1962).

Akira Kubo, later a leading man in Toho's monster movies (*Destroy All Monsters* and *Yog: Monster from Space*) has one of his first big roles as the Malcolm character. More on him later.

"From a purely cinematic standpoint," said *Variety*'s "Tube," "[*Throne of Blood*] is noteworthy for the remarkable manner in which it explores and extends the possibilities of the medium as an instrument for exciting the nerves, the senses and the emotions of the audience. It is all motion picture, an achievement of mood and photographic invention that deserves to be seen for academic purposes alone by every student of the cinema, from novice through professional. Yet, admiration [for the film] must be tempered by recognition of the enormous loss of lyric poetry suffered in translation from one culture to the other. Something is lost, for example, when Macbeth's opening remark, 'So fair and foul a day I have not seen' becomes, according to the subtitles, 'What weather. I've never seen anything like it.'"

Time heals all wounds, they say. The *New York Times*' Bosley Crowther patronized the film, saying it "hits the occidental funny bone.... The action is grotesquely brutish and barbaric ... with Toshiro Mifune as the warrior grunting and bellowing monstrously and making elaborately wild gestures to convey his passion and greed.... To our western eyes, it looks fantastic and funny ... and the final scene, in which the hero is shot so full of arrows that he looks like a porcupine, is a pictorial extravagance that provides a conclusive howl."

Others disagreed. The *Los Angeles Times* called *Throne of Blood* "a masterpiece," while *Time* magazine found it was "the most brilliant and original attempt to put Shakespeare in pictures."

While perhaps not quite up to that level (Olivier's *Richard III*, and Welles' *Othello* and *Chimes at Midnight* are personal favorites of mine), *Throne of Blood* is a supremely exciting work, a simple but vividly alive film, and a genuine classic.

Attack from Space *(1958)*

The second of four Starman adventures, this one is set almost entirely in outer space. *Attack from Space* is more action- and special effects–oriented than *Atomic Rulers* (q.v.), but in nearly every way is a lesser production.

When an evil alien race known as the Sufferians threaten the Earth with nuclear holocaust, the friendly High Council of the Emerald Planet once again dispatches Starman (Ken Utsui) to save the day. The superhero visits a small, Sufferian space station being used as a stockpile for radioactive material. After a big fistfight with several aliens (the Sufferians are humanoid, overdressed in military garb and looking like extras from the Three Stooges' comedy, *You Nazi Spy!*), Starman blows up the station. He then heads for Earth, looking for a Sufferian spy, a "traitor to mankind."

In Japan, kindly Dr. Yamanaka prepares a rocketship, built for peaceful purposes to study the galaxy. Yamanaka's son, Iwoichi, and teenage daughter, Kyoto, try to run an errand for their father but meet up with a Sufferian spy instead (an unidentified western actor who played a Magolian in *Atomic Rulers*). The kids are taken to a secret Sufferian base, hidden beneath a cemetery. Meanwhile, one of Yamanaka's assistants, Tobashi, also turns out to be a Sufferian spy. The scientist is taken to the underground base and ordered to build a rocket engine for the assault against the Earth. Yamanaka refuses, and he and the children are placed in a "thought eradicator," which compels them to obey the Sufferian leader's commands. Everyone hops aboard a rocketship bound for the Sufferian Supreme Headquarters, a space platform orbiting the Earth. Starman spots the rocket and gives chase. The rocket's commander tries to get rid of his pursuer by passing over the "Death Star" (!), a volcanic, fiery planetoid. Starman survives the intense heat, however, and continues chasing the Sufferian ship.

Everyone arrives at the Sufferian headquarters, where they walk around outside without the benefit of oxygen masks and with complete disregard for the lack of gravity and the vacuum of space in general (it might just as well have been someone's balcony in Indiana, for all the difference it makes). The Sufferians demand the Earth to surrender or be destroyed. To demonstrate their power, they blow up a few mountains in the Himalayas. The Earth adamant in its refusal, the Sufferian leader orders the destruction of "downtown New York, London and the Diet Building in Japan," all of which explode in a series of cheap but amusing miniatures. Starman finally arrives at the platform (what took him so long?) just as the Sufferians' mind control of Yamanaka and the kids begins to wear off. After a wildly overlong battle between Starman and about 200 guards, the friendly superhero gets everyone safely aboard the rocketship and they blast off into space. The platform is destroyed when

Yamanaka's ship rams it several times, and Starman heads back for the Emerald Planet until needed once again.

As detailed in the entry on the first Starman adventure, *Atomic Rulers*, the four feature-length Americanizations produced by Walter Manley were adapted from a Japanese serial. Feature versions of serials generally make no sense whatsoever, but *Atomic Rulers* came off surprisingly well: The story, though silly and juvenile, made sense and was generally interesting. This isn't so with *Attack from Space*. The structure, in which Starman is completely absent during the middle third of the picture (indeed, Starman never actually visits Earth at all), is awkward, and his Big Brawl with the Sufferians at the climax goes on and on and on. Another problem is that it's never really explained why a race as scientifically advanced as the Sufferians would need an Earth scientist to build their rocket engines for them, or why everyone is able to walk around without protection in space. In one sequence, Starman tosses a guard over a railing. Where does he fall? To Earth? To the Moon? And another thing, whatever happened to the Sufferians' underground base? *Attack from Space* relies heavily on its cheap special effects and action sequences, which both help and hurt this adventure. The special effects aren't special, but they are plentiful in number. The stuntwork is also poor, a far cry from the Republic serials of the 1940s and the Japanese superhero teleseries that followed. The sets, however, are fairly impressive and compare favorably to lower-budgeted American science fiction films from the same period. A full-size rocketship exterior was built, along with an evocative (if nonsensical) space platform set. The interior of the rocketship is also impressive, looking cramped and serviceable, unlike those found in similar American films, which tend to be boxy, two-dimensional and lacking in detail. *Attack from Space* was followed by *Invaders from Space*.

Evil Brain from Outer Space *(1958)*

The fourth and seemingly final Starman adventure to reach American shores, *Evil Brain from Outer Space*, is by far the most cryptic. This may be due to the fact that the film was apparently culled from three 45-minute chapters of the Japanese serial "Supergiant" and edited down to about half its original length.

According to the narrator, the planet Zemar's omnipotent ruler, Balazar, has been killed by a runaway robot (not shown). His brain has been kept alive, however, and the Zemarians' plans to conquer Earth continue. The High Council of the Emerald Planet realizes, as usual, that if the Earth were to be destroyed in a nuclear war, radiation would reach their peaceful planet as well. And, as usual, the council once again calls on Starman (Ken Utsui again) and his fantastic globemeter, a powerful wristwatch that gives him the ability to fly, to detect radiation, and to speak every language on Earth. Back on Earth, police chase a man carrying a briefcase believed to contain stolen money. They corner him at a bridge, but the briefcase falls into the river below. "The brain! Catch it," cries the man, "or we'll all die!" The man turns out to be Kuwada, an assistant to Dr. Kurotowa, a Zemarian spy with a pet falcon. Kuwada takes his case to a friendly Dr. Sakurai (who was called Dr. Fukami in *Invaders from Space*), Sakurai's children and Starman himself. Starman agrees to help and gives the children one of his magic crystals (also seen in *Invaders from Space*). "Well children," Starman says matter-of-factly, "now I'll go and stop that brain." The story begins losing its way as the evil aliens trigger a series of disasters while preparing to unleash a deadly virus. A Zemarian mutant, a humanoid creature with fangs, bat-like ears and a big eye in the middle of its veiny torso (and printed as a negative image), derails a train, though it's not quite clear how (by its sheer ugliness, perhaps?). Starman battles the dancing creature, avoiding what the narrator describes as the monster's "solid cobalt fingernails." Meanwhile, other Zemarians (who look as human as you and I), dressed in black with dark hoods and (surely unlicensed) Batman emblems on their chests, await the orders of Balazar's brain. After a series of nearly incomprehensible escapes and recaptures, Starman, Sakurai and the Defense Forces infiltrate the Zemarians' secret base, arrest Dr. Kurotowa, and destroy the rather paltry alien brain.

Evil Brain from Outer Space is very nearly plotless. The film is nothing more than a series of vaguely related incidents tied together with a less-than-reliable knot. The Zemarians are sometimes invisible, sometimes human, and sometimes mutated (where they can divide and multiply as well). Late in the story, a deadly Zemarian witch is created by Dr. Kurotowa, a character which goes unexplained like nearly everything else. The story is filled with detectives, scientists and children, who are introduced, vanish and reappear throughout the story. All this confusion, combined with the film's lack of original ideas (the magic crystal from *Invaders from Space*, for example, which is re-introduced then never used here) quickly becomes tiresome, this despite the wildly designed Zemarian mutant and some surprisingly good production values here and there (such as the Ken Adam-ish Zemarian hideout).

Reviews are scarce. *Psychotronic*, which liked the Starman films, said this one was "funnier than *Godzilla vs. the Smog Monster*."

Ken Utsui's superhero would return in several more adventures, none of which would reach English-speaking audiences in the United States. Though ludicrously cheap and always very silly, the Starman films are, like the best American-made serials, occasionally amusing and exciting for undemanding audiences.

The H-Man *(1958)*

This was the first of a trio of films by Toho dealing with men who transform themselves into other matter. In *The H-Man*, blob-like substances dissolve human beings into liquid. *The Human Vapor* saw a man transformed into a gaseous mist, while *The Secret of the Telegian* saw a man turned into something not unlike a television signal. *The H-Man* is the best of the three, far more subtle and restrained in its storytelling than Toho's *kaiju eiga* series, yet also uninhibited in letting loose with its hauntingly gruesome special effects.

During a daring nighttime robbery, narcotics thief Misaki (Hisaya Ito) is about to make a clean getaway when something touches his leg. He begins screaming and shoots at the ground. Just then, he is struck by an oncoming automobile. When the driver climbs out of the car, Misaki has vanished. Only his clothes remain in the pouring rain. Inspector Tominaga (Akihiko Hirata) and his fellow detectives (including Yoshibumi Tajima and Yoshio Tsuchiya) question Misaki's girlfriend, pretty nightclub singer Chikako Arai (Yumi Shirakawa), about the robbery and Misaki's disappearance. Although she tells the detectives she knows nothing and hasn't seen Misaki in several days, Tominaga orders her followed. Chikako is visited by an underworld figure looking for Misaki. When the police arrive, the man escapes through Chikako's window and into the pouring rain. The woman hears several shots, looks out the window and faints. A scientist, Dr. Masada (Kenji Sahara) shows up at Tominaga's office, claiming to have an explanation for Misaki's disappearance. Masada believes men are being dissolved by a mysterious creature or creatures formed when a ship passed through an H-bomb test site in the Pacific. Tominaga laughs at the suggestion, but Masada says he has evidence to support his claim. He takes the inspector to a hospital where two patients are dying of radiation poisoning. They recount how late one night while at sea, their tramp steamer encountered a seemingly deserted ship.

In flashbacks, we learn how several men, including the two now in the hospital, went aboard the silent and dark vessel. They spot what first looks like a body on deck but turns out to be nothing more than someone's clothes. The men nervously laugh at the sight. In the captain's room, they find the captain's uniform neatly sitting at a table, as if the captain suddenly leaped out of his uniform and disappeared. One of the men (Senkichi Omura) decides to take some of these clothes with him, and begins putting some of them on. However, a gooey substance begins dripping and rolling its way toward the sailor from across the room, eventually reaching his pant leg. The man screams, and in front of the other sailors, begins to dissolve like a leaky balloon (which is just how many of the dissolving effects were done). Everyone panics, and several more men are attacked and dissolve when touched by the blob-like substance.

Only two men make it back to the ship (the men now dying in the hospital). As their vessel pulls away from the other ship, they see ghostly blue-green humanoid figures on the deserted ship's deck. Despite the men's stories, Inspector Tominaga still refuses to take Dr. Masada's theory seriously. Masada takes Tominaga to his laboratory, where he bombards a frog with the same kind of radiation the ship apparently passed through. The frog bubbles up and dissolves. Masada argues that the ghostly figures on the ship are H-men, former human beings turned into vampire-like blob monsters that must dissolve fresh humans in order to survive. Later, when demonstrating his theory for the rest of the authorities, Masada dissolves another frog and places the frog liquid near a second frog. The liquidy H-frog dissolves the other, consuming and melding with it. At the nightclub that evening, several of the H-men appear, devouring (well, dissolving then absorbing) a chorus girl, several gangsters and one detective (Tajima). One of the gangsters unmolested by the H-men, Uchida (Mitsuru Sato), who assisted Misaki in the narcotics robbery, removes his clothes so that the police will think he was dissolved. He kidnaps Chikako for reasons unexplained, though it's hinted that he's in love with her. Chikako, on the other hand, is by now in love with Dr. Masada. Uchida's scheme nearly works, only his clothes fail to leave traces of radiation like those left on the clothes of real H-men victims. Uchida takes Chikako through Tokyo's sewer system, where he has hidden the stolen narcotics (50 million yen worth of heroin), and which is also a favorite hiding place of the H-men. Uchida is dissolved by one of the creatures, just as Masada rescues Chikako, and the sewers are ignited with gasoline. The flames evaporate the half-dozen H-men, and the danger is over.

This grisly, racy, but also restrained and colorful film mixes gangsters and sci-fi. Gangster movies, especially those built around the Yakuza, were a wildly popular genre in Japan, and it's not at all surprising that a few of that country's sci-fi pictures would feature gangster subplots as well (other ganster-related sci-fi films from the studio include *Dagora, the Space Monster* and even *Godzilla's Revenge*). The picture, at least in its American form, doesn't make much sense and is often confusing. The H-men (and there are H-men, despite the title) are seen both as moving blobs and as blue-green ghosts, but neither form is adequately explained. Scenes aboard the ship suggest that when a person is dissolved he or she also becomes an H-man, but this is never really explained, either. Still, the film's effects work, where people dissolve into pools of liquid, is quite unnerving, if tame by today's graphic standards of horror. The scenes aboard the silent ship are fairly creepy (especially a long shot where the misty, blue-green H-men stand up on the deck, all eerily aglow), and the lumps of unoccupied clothes are both humorous and creepy at the same time.

Unlike most of Toho's fantastic films from this period, which are marketed for general audiences, *The H-Man* seems to have been geared more for adults. The showgirls' costumes and their dances were pretty racy for 1958, and most of the picture takes place in the seedier side of Tokyo. Coupled with the film's graphic violence, *The H-Man* was just too lurid and gruesome to be a family picture.

According to Bill Warren, when *The H-Man* played in the States, children — who made up the bulk of a sci-fi picture's audience by that time — had the beejeezes scared out of 'em. Phil Hardy called the picture "Honda's most sensual film," while noting the storyline "appears merely an excuse to string together extraordinary scenes of hallucinatory images." *Variety*'s "Ron" found the film "well-made," and considered it superior to both *The Mysterians* and *Gigantis, the Fire Monster* also in release in the United States that same year. He also liked the performances and said the effects were "skillfully and terrifyingly adept."

Invaders from Space *(1958)*

The third of four Starman features culled from the Japanese serial *Supah Jianto* (*Supergiant*), *Invaders from Space* is the least interesting, despite the appearance of colorful, nightmarish aliens — humanoid salamanders.

The Salamander men from the plant Kuroman plot the destruction of Earth. The High Council of the Emerald Planet, fearing radiation from the Earth's destruction will in turn kill them as well, dispatch the superhero Starman once again to save mankind. On Earth, flying saucers are spotted around the globe, and in Japan thousands of people begin coming down with a deadly virus. The virus leaves tiny black spots on its victims and is reminiscent of the American-made serial *Flash Gordon Conquers the Universe* (1940). Professor Asayama, leader of a team of scientists working to counteract the virus' effects, is visited late one evening by a man in a dark business suit and a surgical mask. When the man removes the mask, he is revealed to be one of the Kuromians, a creature with a very wide mouth (partly painted and suggesting Batman's arch-rival, the Joker) and a short, stubby nose spread well across the creature's cheek bones. The Kuromian sprays the professor with radioactive material from his lungs, which compels the scientist to follow the alien back to the Kuromian headquarters. Starman appears outside the scientist's home, however, and the two alien visitors fight one another, performing an impressive series of backflips and other acrobatic stunts in the process. The salamander man forsakes his business suit for scaly green tights. His fingers have also grown much longer (and rubbery), while his head has become somewhat larger and bulbous, with two antennae sticking out. Starman drives the alien away. Two of Professor Asayama's associates, Dr. Fukami and his assistant, Dr. Shimamura, go to the theater where, as the narrator describes it, "an unusual dance troupe gives a weird performance." Dancers, looking a lot like the salamander man seen earlier, perform various leaps and flips (some of the footage is printed in reverse and or in slow motion). The scientists leave the packed house to talk in the lobby. "Doctor, they were very different," Shimamura notes, "I've never seen anyone fly through the air the way they did." "No one can teach that," Fukami says, "It has to be inherited, that's obvious." He goes on to suggest that the performers are aliens and that the theater is being used to spread the virus. A chuckling, eavesdropping salamander man (quietly clinging to the ceiling) tells Fukami he's only too correct. Alien henchmen kidnap the scientists. As the disease spreads, the scientists' children are evacuated from the city. Starman shows up and gives the kids a crystal sphere the size of a baseball. If they're in trouble, Starman explains, they need only smash the crystal, and he will come to rescue them. This is soon put to the test when the kids go out to look for butterflies and are captured by the salamander men. The Kuromians threaten the children in an attempt to get the scientists to reveal top secret defense information. The cystal is smashed, and Starman comes to the rescue, just as one of the children is being lowered into a bubbling pit of lava. The dozens of salamander men are no match for Starman. The aliens retreat, as the narrator says, "to fight another day."

In what surely must originally have been the beginning of the next chapter, Professor Fukami's son, Yuichi, is brought home wrapped in bandages by a mysterious nurse. She explains that the young man received second-degree burns on his face. Despite his injuries, Yuichi urges his father to return to defense headquarters, a secret arsenal where scientists search for a serum to counteract the Kuromian virus. Fukami leaves, and when the scientists' young daughter, Noriko, becomes suspicious, Yuichi removes his bandages. As it turns out, he is not her brother at all but a Kuromian spy! The nurse, also a spy, turns into a salamander witch, complete with a gnarled staff and black cape. The salamander man follows Dr. Fukami to learn the location of the secret arsenal, while the alien witch deals with the professor's children. A convenient tank of compressed copper sulphate in the house is knocked over (every home should have one), and that spray completely melts the witch. (What a world, what a world!) This discovery and newly developed serum provide the defense forces an opportunity to defeat the invaders. The Kuromians theaten to stop the Earth's rotation or slow it down enough to cause (selective) objects to float in mid-air. This creates a minor setback in the production of copper sulphate rifles. The new rifles are built, however, and a strike force, with the help of Starman, defeats the evil aliens.

Invaders from Space is the same old stuff. Dispatched, as usual, by the High Council of the Emerald Planet, Starman has little to do but rescue determined scientists and their squeaky-voiced children. Like *Attack from Space*, *Invaders* is overloaded with fight sequences. For instance, there is a lengthy scene where Starman fights a hoard of salamander men and women in the theater before the scheduled disease-spreading performance. Though this sequence is often inventive (Starman keeps disappearing and reappearing in all parts of the auditorium, much to the annoyance of the aliens), it simply goes on too long. While such scenes can work quite well within the context of a twenty- or forty-minute serial chapter, when edited into a feature such as this, they can quickly become tiresome. For some reason, the sets and special effects are cheaper than usual, with the Kuromian base consisting of cloth backdrops and obviously recycled sets. The minimal special effects are limited to a few clumsy miniature and double exposure shots of the saucer flying over Japan. The aliens are interesting, however, at least when they are in their semi-human form. The nightmarish face of the first salamander man is effective and probably frightened a lot of Japanese children when the film was new. However, for the most part, *Invaders from Space* wallows in repetition and formula plotting, and except for its mildly interesting aliens, it is very mediocre.

Varan the Unbelievable *(1958/1962)*

This Toho-produced giant monster movie is easily their least interesting special effects film of the 1950s. The studio was busy at the same time producing *The Three Treasures*, Japan's *The Ten Commandments*, so it is not unreasonable to imagine that special effects director Eiji Tsuburaya's services and the studio's finances were being taxed there. Or perhaps the answer lies elsewhere. Shortly before his death, director Ishiro Honda told David Milner that *Varan* was initiated by an American firm wanting to release the picture directly to U.S. television. This is very surprising for several reasons: While telefeatures date back to 1950, they were extremely rare until the mid– to late–sixties. Was a theatrical run considered? How was the project financed? Honda said five or six scenes were shot in the standard 1.37:1 ratio, but when a theatrical run in Japan was decided upon (and, most likely, when American financing fell through) the footage was *Super*Scoped into the final print. To this day, *Varan*'s American origins remain a mystery.

Although *Rodan* (1956) was produced in color, and the studio's last science fiction effort, *The Mysterians* (1957), was both in color and in wide screen (as was *The H-Man*, also released in 1958), *Varan the Unbelievable* was filmed in black and white. Production-wise, the film takes several steps backward. The special effects aren't as good as those found in any of the studio's previous monster films, and there is a hurried, sloppy look to the film. While mediocre, *Varan* was made much worse when the picture was brought to the United States. Crown International/Dallas Productions scrapped almost the entire film save for the monster scenes (omitting some of those as well) and built a new story around that wildly popular American movie star, Myron Healey. Less than 15 of the original 85 minutes remain, and the onscreen credits don't even mention Toho or any of its production people (a rather serious omission).

In the new version, Commander James Bradley (Healey) is heading a Japanese experiment to desalinate water on the densely forested Kunishirashima Island. The choice of a large lake for the experiment will mean the displacement of local villagers, but Bradley considers this a small price to pay. His Japanese wife, Anna (Tsuruko Kobayashi), partly out of sympathy for the villagers and partly out of fear of a legendary monster that's supposed to live in the lake, begs her husband to reconsider, even though "as your wife it's not my place to ask." The military is called out to handle the unruly natives (with "heavier weapons," we're told), and when Bradley begins getting bad press for his handling of the operation, decides to compromise: the natives will stay put, and the army will hunt live game and distribute food rations as long as the lake is contaminated with the desalination solution. The experiment begins, and soon enough, Varan the Unbelievable rises up out of the lake, frightening a Japanese soldier to death. As the monster's existence becomes known, Bradley makes preparations to send his wife away to Tokyo, though she wants to stay. ("Right now I just want you to be a good girl," Bradley says.) Varan (who, incidentally, is called Obachi during the film, and *not* Varan; the monster's name is Baran in Japan) attacks the village. Bradley, Anna and Captain Kishi (Clifford Kawada), Bradley's liaison officer, spend some time waiting around a canyon (Bronson Canyon, in fact), while Varan swims off to greener pastures. The monster repels an air and sea attack (featuring unusually poor miniatures), finally making its way to an ocean-side airfield. Bradley, who comes up with the idea of simply using more of the desalination solution against the monster, fixes a busted radio before transmitting the news to his barely glimpsed Japanese associates. Balloons full of the chemical are dropped from a helicopter, and Varan obligingly gobbles them up. The monster gets a tummy ache and falls into the sea, presumably dead.

The American version of *Varan the Unbelievable* is very nearly unwatchable. The Japanese cut of the film was a very standard monster-on-the-loose story, featuring elements found in any number of other *kaiju eiga* productions: a trio of reporters covering the beast's actions, dedicated scientists (Koreya Senda and Akihiko Hirata) trying to stop the seemingly invulnerable monster and so forth. The American version, however, features Myron Healey, Myron Healey and more Myron Healey. The film's first half hour contains barely one minute from the Japanese version, and consists almost entirely of Healey sitting on his front porch blandly discussing the importance of his experiments while complaining about the natives. Bradley is supposed to be the hero, but even back in 1962, when *Varan* was released in the United States, critics complained about the character's arrogant patronizing of the Japanese villagers. The natives are described as "stubborn" and a "simple, primitive people," even by Captain Kishi. Anna, Bradley's passive Japanese wife, fares no better, constantly deferring to her husband's authority. When Varan destroys the village, she blames herself for the monster's destruction by convincing Bradley to let the people stay. Of course, it was Bradley's none-too-interesting experiments and insistence that they be held at this particular lake that caused all the trouble in the first place. Even the press is a target of Sid Harris' screenplay. When Bradley is criticized for his relocation of villagers in Japan's newspapers, Captain Kishi argues, "They should have laws and regulations governing newspaper reporters!" The film's biggest problem, however, is that it's simply too boring. The original story may not have been much, but it's surely more interesting (and I have seen both versions) than watching Myron Healey gaze at invoices and dirty test tubes.

Healey was a competent actor, not really bad here, though fairly dull and uninteresting. Playing very much the square-jawed, slightly paunchy G.I. Joe, Healey's monotone, even-tempered soldier fails to generate excitement. A welcome scene which finds Bradley losing his cool ("Nothing but sand! All I get is sediment!"), is deflated when he quickly regains his composure. Healey simply lacks the charisma of other actors more closely associated with the genre, notably Kenneth Tobey and John Agar. His other fantastic film credits include the underrated Abbott and Costello comedy *The Time of Their Lives* (1946), *The Unearthly* (1957) and *The Incredible Melting Man* (1977).

Surprisingly, some of the monster footage was cut, significantly a brief sequence where Varan sprouts flying squirrel–like glider vanes and zooms off into the skies over Japan (the sound of a jet's roar accompanies the monster's flight). For some reason, in the Japanese version Varan's very presence creates a hurricane-force wind, even when the monster is standing still. The original footage, what little there is, is badly integrated with the newly shot material, both technically and structurally. Unlike the Raymond Burr scenes added for *Godzilla, King of the Monsters!* which carefully blended Burr with members of the action, Healey is almost always divorced from the monster's movements, particularly once the creature has left the lake for bigger and better things. A ludicrous mismatched sequence edits shots of Bradley, Anna and Captain Kishi riding around rocky Bronson Canyon looking for the monster with original footage of Japanese soldiers moving through a densely forested jungle. This sort of careless cutting is typical of the incredible lack of care shown by its American distributor. The editing back and forth is made all the more obvious by the noticeably poor condition of the Japanese footage. *Varan* was no great picture, but its black and white Tohoscope photography was as good as anything in the Myron Healey sequences; it's just printed badly. Varan, who resembles a spiny, four-legged Godzilla (his rather routine roar in the original version was replaced by what sounds like a very hungry person's stomach growling), is hard to make out as it is, and the dark and grainy printing of the Japanese footage doesn't help any. The monster isn't much, however, basically an amalgam of Godzilla and Angilas, with Rodan's flying ability thrown in.

Unlike Godzilla and Rodan, Varan didn't star in any other features (the character made a very brief cameo in *Destroy All Monsters*, 1968). In fact, *Varan the Unbelievable* would be Toho's last monster movie for three years.

Unquestionably, the picture's biggest loss in the Americanization was Akira Ifukube's excellent score, which introduced several musical motifs (notably a theme which would become closely associated with King Ghidorah) that would be used over and over again in later films, and quickly eclipse anything else about this film. For the U.S. version, nearly all of Ifukube's score was replaced by bland Albert Glasser themes from *The Amazing Colossal Man*, and even this isn't done well. Music swells uncontrollably when Bradley talks to his wife, but is nowhere to be heard when Varan attacks the village.

Bill Warren didn't think much of *Varan*. "Despite occasionally good special effects work by Eiji Tsuburaya and his hardworking crew, *Varan* is a very minor entry in Toho's monster parade. The most entertaining (and outrageous) Japanese monster movies still lay in the future." *The Motion Picture Guide* gave *Varan* a *½ rating, calling the effort "pretty laughable." *Variety*'s "Tube": "It is a hackneyed, uninspired carbon copy [of Godzilla and Gorgo], serviceable only as a supporting filler.... Photography is too dark, editing is jagged."

Battle in Outer Space *(1959)*

Toho closed out the decade with one of the best space operas ever produced. *Battle in Outer Space* expands and ultimately improves upon the story ideas introduced in *The Mysterians*, made two years earlier. The picture tells the story of alien invasion in epic terms. It's a special effects extravaganza along the lines of George Pal's *War of the Worlds* (1953), and Japanese moviegoers in 1959 were treated to a special show indeed, replete with beautiful color TohoScope photography and Perspecta stereophonic sound.

The film is set in 1965, when mankind has built an orbiting space station. Man's entry into the space age has not gone unnoticed on other worlds, for as the picture opens the station is attacked by flying saucers which blow up the orbiting wheel. Elsewhere, saucers lift a rail bridge neatly off the ground and high into the air as a train approaches, sending the speeding locomotive crashing into the chasm below. Similar events happen all over the world. An American freighter is ripped apart by a strange water spout in the Panama Canal. Venice is fraught with surging water which floods the city. Delegates from the world's nations meet in Tokyo at the Space Research Center to combat the problem. Major Ichiro Katsumiya (Ryo Ikebe) demonstrates a new ray gun with 600 "megatherms" of power, while Dr. Adachi (Minoru Takada) shows off a pair of rocketships built by scientists from all over the world. One of the ambassadors suddenly appears stricken with illness then tries to steal the new ray gun. It turns out his brain was implanted with a controlling device by the aliens, who kill him with a death ray once the saucermen realize the jig is up. The rocketships are readied for a reconnaissance mission to the moon, where strange radio transmissions have been detected. The first ship is commanded by Dr. Adachi, the second by American Dr. Richardson (Len Stanford). Katsumiya is assigned to Adachi's crew, along with Katsumiya's girlfriend, Etsuko (Kyoko Anzai), and best friend, Iwamura (Yoshio Tsuchiya). The night before the launch, Iwamura becomes possessed by the aliens, a controlling device implanted in his brain. The astronauts (who wear hats that look like white shower caps) depart with great fanfare, including a ticker-tape parade (the film's American editors deleted the crowd's cries of "Banzai!").

The two ships are launched, and the crews grimace at the tremendous acceleration (a clichéd prediction about space travel in early sci-fi pictures which proved groundless). They come across the wreckage of the space station, including a floating, lifeless body, and bow their heads in prayer. The two ships are soon met by saucers guiding glowing meteors in a sequence similar to one found in Universal-International's 1955 production *This Island Earth*. As the crew attempt to destroy the meteors, Iwamura sneaks off and tries to dismantle the heat ray's generator. He's caught by one of the crew and tied up. The meteors destroyed, the crew next hear the disembodied voice of one of the aliens, who warns them not to approach the moon, "for if you do, you will surely die." Ignoring the warning, the two ships land on the curiously blue moon. Leaving Iwamura tied up aboard Adachi's ship, the crews hop aboard two bus-like all-terrain vehicles. They travel through a mountainous region, finally reaching the aliens' base. The aliens exert their power over Iwamura, who successfully frees himself. He kills the crew member left to guard him, blows up the spaceship, then sets about destroying the other. As the men prepare to demolish the alien base with their new ray guns, Etsuko wanders off into a cave where she's met by a horde of child-size aliens in space suits, their helmets obscuring their faces. (Those helmets look very nearly identical to those used by the Endor stormtroopers in *Return of the Jedi*.) Katsumiya destroys the base with one of the ray guns, its destruction releasing Iwamura from his captor's bidding, and he proceeds to deactivate the time bomb he set aboard the second ship. The crews race back to the rocketship, fighting flying saucers all along the way. Richardson's vehicle becomes disabled on some rocks, and its crew joins Adachi's. They reach the landing site to find Adachi's ship destroyed and Iwamura shooting at the saucers with a laser rifle on a mountainside. He tells the crews he blew up the rocketship while possessed by the aliens, and to make up for his deeds, he will ward off the saucers while the crews depart in the remaining vessel.

Back on Earth, everyone prepares for a massive offensive by the aliens. Nations put aside their differences to defeat this common enemy, building fighters able to leave the Earth's orbit and even more powerful ray guns. The fighters are launched, and while several of the alien ships are destroyed, saucer-guided meteors manage to get through the line of defense. One of these falls on Manhattan (in front of the Chrysler Building, in fact), while another obliterates the Golden Gate Bridge in San Francisco. A mother ship, escorted by several of the saucers, flies over Tokyo. The bottom half of the mother ship begins to spin and glow, creating a beam which uproots whole sections of the city like a tremendous vacuum cleaner. The Earth Defense Forces open fire on the ship with gigantic ray guns many stories high (which once again resemble massive radar dishes). The mother ship and its escorts are destroyed, and the Earth is saved.

Battle in Outer Space is about an alien invasion on a global scale. Few studios have ever attempted such a flashy spectacle, and since it succeeds so well, it's easy to forgive the picture's almost total lack of story (the film is simply one gigantic battle) and characterizations. The special effects work is very impressive, certainly more so than anything found in any of the two dozen American-made sci-fi films released in 1959. The miniature work is highly detailed and often very imaginative, such as the design of the rocketships and lunar landscapes. The alien craft are equally interesting, with their manta-ray design and eerily glowing underbellies. The film's highlight comes with the jaw-droppingly impressive climax where Tokyo is literally sucked up into the sky. The scene with the meteor falling on New York lasts but a few seconds, but special effects director Eiji Tsuburaya's crew managed to recreate a huge and reasonably accurate Manhattan skyline. Ironically, this brief sequence also illustrates the problem with watching wide screen pictures like *Battle in Outer Space* on television. The skyline is seen in a single, immobile shot, with the Statue of Liberty on the far right as the meteor comes in from the left, crashing in the center between the Empire State and Chrysler buildings. On television, we get a good look at the not-so-detailed Lady Liberty but miss the incoming meteor, the pan-and-scanning barely getting the exploding rock at all.

Akira Ifukube contributed another terrific score, one of his very best. The dubbing by Bellucci's team of editors is less awkward than most, though *The Monthly Film Bulletin* hated the "ludicrous overacting of the Westernised Occidental cast" and *Variety*'s "Tube" said "most of the acting is overacting."

Perhaps the picture's only drawback is bland Ryo Ikebe. Ikebe, born in 1918, had entered the film industry in Toho's literary department. He made his debut in *Togyo* (1941), followed by roles in *Gendaijin soshun* and *Byaku Fujinmo yoren*. His first fantasy film was *The Vampire Moth* (1956), and after *Battle in Outer Space* he starred in Toho's disaster epic, *Gorath* (1962). He apparently left the genre for many years but returned for Toho's wretched *The War in Space* (1977).

Most reviewers considered the film hopelessly out of date and compared the picture to the Flash Gordon and Buck Rogers serials of the 1930s. *Variety*'s review paid tribute to some of Tsuburaya's work, while complaining that the screenplay was "aimless [and] witless." *The Motion Picture Guide* gave the film a one star rating, which was even lower than the Americanized Varan. "Lots of errors in plot, dubbing, special effects and looping," it said. The *New York Times*' Howard Thompson called the film "the least painful to watch of several such Japanese imports in recent years.... Far and away the most attractive thing about this Toho production is the decor—the clean, bright color and fetching assortment of obvious, but effective, miniature settings and backgrounds. Some of the artwork is downright nifty ... the Japanese have opened a most amusing and beguiling bag of technical tricks." Bill Warren recognized the picture's charms, finding it "reasonably enjoyable" for those looking for mindless fun, as did Phil Hardy, who said the film was "a playful entertainment which never set out to be realistic anyway."

Battle in Outer Space succeeds in an area where nearly all U.S.-made science fiction films by this time fail—showmanship and an ability to produce something visually exciting. With its pleasant theme of global cooperation and impressive special effects, *Battle in Outer Space* remains one of Japan's best science fiction films.

The Ghost of Yotsuya *(1959)*

This Shintoho-made ghost tale is generally regarded as the best of the many film adaptations of Nanboku Tsuruya's 1825 Kubuki play, *Takaido Yotsuya kaidan*. Most available prints are very badly faded, but the story's drama and chilling second half still shine through.

In ancient Okayama, a poor, masterless samurai, Iuemon Tamiya (Shigeru Amachi), asks a powerful samurai leader for his daughter's hand. When the latter refuses, Iuemon kills him in a violent fit of anger. Iuemon meets with the samurai's daughter, Oiwa (Kazuko Wakasugi), and her sister, Osode (Noriko Kitazawa; the sisters' names are incorrectly transliterated in the film's original English subtitles). Unaware that he has killed their father, the sisters ask Iuemon and his partner, Naosuke (Shuntaro Emi), a commoner in love with Osode, to help the women avenge their father's death. Iuemon has also killed the father of Yomoshichi Hikobei (Ryozaburo Nakamura), Osode's suitor, who stands in the way of Iuemon and Naosuke's happiness. Momentarily separated from the women, Iuemon and Naosuke seize the opportunity to stab Yomoshichi at a cliff overlooking a waterfall. Together, they drop the body into the water and tell the women Yomoshichi was killed by a robber. Osode weds Naosuke, mainly because she does not want him to give up looking for her father's murderer. Naosuke, who knows Iuemon did the deed, does nothing. Iuemon marries Oiwa, but the relationship quickly sours, despite Oiwa's endless patience and kindness. They move to Edo (ancient Tokyo) and have a child, but greedy Iuemon quickly tires of Oiwa and their life of poverty. Iuemon saves a wealthy family from a band of hoodlums, and soon the family's patriarchs urge Iuemon to marry their young daughter, Ume (Junko Ikeuchi). Egged on by the Iago-like Naosuke, Iuemon decides to poison his wife. He arranges for a local masseur who is in love with Oiwa, Takuetsu (Jun Otomo), to appear at Iuemon's home, telling the large, bald man he may have Oiwa as his wife. Shortly after he arrives, Oiwa begins to suffer the effects of Iuemon's poison. She develops hideous sores on her face as the horrified Takuetsu watches. Oiwa slits her throat, thus ending her suffering (apparently taking her baby's life as well). Iuemon enters and kills Takuetsu so that he can claim the two were having an adulterous affair. With the help of Naosuke, Iuemon nails the two bodies to either side of a wooden door, which is then dumped in a nearby swamp. Iuemon marries Ume but is soon haunted by the ghastly, rotting corpse of his murdered wife. Images of Oiwa's dead body appear everywhere, but the frantic Iuemon, vainly trying to run through the ghostly image, succeeds only in stabbing Ume and her parents. Naosuke, meanwhile, returns to the swamp, fishing out Oiwa's valuable tortoise comb and clothes. Returning home, he begins washing his feet when he suddenly sees dozens of snakes crawling about his ankles. Osode recognizes her sister's belongings as the zombie-like (but not deformed) image of Oiwa appears before her and Naosuke. Terrified, Naosuke confesses his crimes. Oiwa's ghost leads Osode to a local hotel where she finds Yomoshichi Hikobei, who didn't die from his stab wounds after all (he tells Osode he was found unconscious by a lumberjack). Yomoshichi tells Osode of a dream in which Oiwa's ghost told him Iuemon had killed her. By this time, Iuemon is haunted almost constantly by images of the deformed Oiwa and Takuetsu (who has a big gash across his face), along with more snakes. He goes mad and kills Naosuke. Yomoshichi and Osode, swords in hand, confront the now-raving Iuemon and kill him while the ghosts of Oiwa and Takuetsu reach up through the ground and hold him down.

The Ghost of Yotsuya is a marvelous, genuinely creepy tale. Just as the picture begins to look like a subtle, melancholy variation of *Tales of Ugetsu* — in which a similarly selfish man fails to appreciate his loving wife — *Yotsuya* suddenly shifts gears, becoming an intense, wildly cinematic horror movie. A kind of Asian Hammer film, *The Ghost of Yotsuya* takes a classic work of Japanese literature and proceeds to tell it with amazing visual flair and surprising explicitness. Oiwa's death is painful to watch. Early in the picture, Iuemon thinks nothing of selling all of poor Oiwa's precious belongings, including her comb (a family heirloom, we're told) and even the baby's mosquito net. The poor woman's husband killed her father, and now he has poisoned her. As she examines her sore-covered face, Oiwa tries to comb her hair, which only falls out, taking part of her scalp with it (now *that's* unsettling). Oiwa's first ghostly appearance comes shortly after her murder, as Iuemon prepares to bed down with Ume. The samurai first sees Oiwa's ghost on their bedroom's ceiling—still nailed to that door. Her angry cries of "Why did you kill me?!" add to the creepiness. Takuetsu, a big scar across his face and looking a bit like Tor Johnson, rises out of the blood-red swamp with Oiwa in another chilling scene. These and other similarly effective moments are a credit to director Nobuo Nakagawa and screenwriter Masayoshi Onuki.

The Ghost of Yotsuya had previously been filmed in 1949 by Shochiku and director Keisuke Kinoshita as the two-part *Shinshaku Yotsuya kaidan*. That film starred the great Ken Uehara (*Mothra*, etc.) as Iuemon and Kinuyo Tanaka, also a favorite of Mizoguchi, as both sisters. The more liberal adaptation was highly lauded but was barely distributed (if at all) in the United States. Other versions include Masaki Mori's *Yotsuya kaidan* (1956); another 1959 production; one in 1965 (both also called *Yotsuya kaidan*) and 1969's *Yotsuya Kaidan—Oiwa no Borei*.

The Encyclopedia of Horror Movies reviewer loved *The Ghost of Yotsuya*, calling it "the classic interpretation of the tale."

Prince of Space *(1959)*

Like Shintoho's Starman series, Toei's *Prince of Space* was a Japanese serial, re-edited to feature length for United States distribution. It is uncertain whether this supremely silly adventure was released theatrically in the U.S. or sold directly to television, but there is some evidence to suggest the former. In any case, the film is as tiresome as it is trivial. Although it boasts better production values than the Starman movies, *Prince of Space* is just as innocuous and juvenile.

Orphans Mickey and Kimmy, more or less adopted by bootblack Wally (Tatsuo Umemiya), visit their friend, Johnny, and his professor-father, Dr. Makin, a rocket scientist who has developed a fantastic new fuel. The kids turn on the television, where they see the image of a submarine-like spaceship (closely resembling Toho's *Atragon*). The picture dissolves to an elf-like alien sitting at a desk. He introduces himself as Ambassador Phantom of the planet Krankor. He has a long, pointy nose, a comical, silent-era mustache, and wears a silly hood with what look like a trio of tiny TV antennae on his head. Phantom announces he will be arriving on Earth the next evening and demands that the Earth surrender to his rule. "You will obey me or die," he snarls, adding cynically, "Have a pleasant night's sleep! Ha-ha-ha-ha-ha-ha-ha!" The next day, Professor Makin, the kids and some soldiers encounter a strange, Krankorian device which resembles one of those telescopes tourists feed quarters to for scenic views. The machine begins firing rays which vaporize a few of the soldiers, while a contingent of Krankorian soldiers, including Phantom, appear. Just then, a flying saucer with a big screw on its hull and two laser cannons (which look like big exhaust pipes) lands in a nearby field, and out pops—Ta Da!—the Prince of Space (also played by Umemiya). The Krankorians fire their laser pistols at the caped crusader, who merely deflects the blasts with a Dirty Harry caliber laser pistol–reflective wand. The aliens retreat into their spaceship which zooms away, but the P.O.S. (who's never named by the way; it seems silly to call him Wally) pursues them in his saucer. Phantom orders some "poisonous fog" dispersed in the saucer's path, and the P.O.S. loses sight of the evil aliens. The Krankorians return, however, and succeed in blowing up Dr. Makin's rocketship and kidnapping the professor, along with four other eminent scientists. The scientists are taken aboard the aliens' flagship, the *Black Dragon*, and when Dr. Makin asks about his chauffeur, also kidnapped, Phantom replies, "We blasted him out of an airlock, so by now he may have fallen into a star! Ha-ha-ha-ha-ha-ha!" Phantom demands the scientists' assistance, but they refuse. Just then, the Prince of Space, aboard his saucer, chases the alien ship once again, and as before, Phantom orders more poisonous fog dispersed to lose the pesky superhero. The *Black Dragon* flies back to headquarters on Krankor, where a giant, bat-eared plug-ugly guards the place. At the same time, Phantom orders two of his underlings to learn the Prince of Space's secret alter-ego. When they register a "reading of 98" on Wally the shoeshine boy, they know they've found their man. A group of Krankorians, including Phantom, ambush the P.O.S. in a graveyard, where the evil aliens foolishly shoot more harmless laser beams at the caped hero. Phantom tries to trick the prince by shooting him up close, but our hero is too smart for him. "The stench of your foul breath is more than I can stand," replies the P.O.S. After more outer space shenanigans and yet more poisonous fog, the P.O.S. shoots the giant guardian in the mouth with his laser cannons (in a manner suggesting stellar dental surgery) and finally reaches the Krankorian base where he rescues the scientists. The Krankorians, apparently slow learners, still try to shoot the prince down with their laser pistols. "When will you ever learn your guns won't work on me?" asks the prince, seemingly as frustrated as the film's audience. The scientists escape aboard the *Black Dragon*, while the Prince of Space merrily blows up the Krankorian base and the evil Krankorians inside.

Although *Prince of Space* appears to have had a slightly larger budget than the Starman films, it's just as silly and much less involving. Part of the problem is the dumb aliens, who never learn that the P.O.S. cannot be killed or even slightly injured by their little laser guns. The Prince of Space is seemingly invincible (just like Starman), and because of this the picture has no tension. And unlike Ken Utsui's fatherly, slightly pudgy Starman, Umemiya is colorless by comparison and is simply unable to carry the picture himself. Another problem is the film's endless repetition, with no less than three sequences where the Krankorians manage to lose the prince's saucer by dispersing that damn poisonous fog. Also bringing the film down are its ludicrous, laughable aliens, among the silliest ever committed to celluloid. Besides their ridiculous costumes, the actor dubbing the Phantom, apparently realizing the foolishness of the character, gives a performance that's way over the top, with every other line consisting of that measured, cynical laugh. A sequence featuring the Phantom was prominently and appropriately featured in *It Came from Hollywood* (1982), a bad movie about bad movies. While the production values are slightly better, if less imaginative, than those in Shintoho's Starman films, the special effects are somewhat more elaborate. Still, the whole picture is so trivial and contrived it makes little impact.

Prince of Space received scant reviews. "[A] cheap superhero picture... made with uncharacteristically crude designs for the spaceships and suits," complained Phil Hardy's *Science Fiction*. "Compared to Kobayashi's *Gekko Kamen* (1958), the comic strip effects are singularly unimaginative."

The Three Treasures *(1959)*

One of the problems with writing a book about Japanese fantastic films is the tremendous difficulty in simply *seeing* many of the films I most wanted to include. Dozens and dozens of Japanese features with science fiction, fantasy and horror elements received extremely limited releases in the U.S. and were sometimes restricted to a single theater. (Oh, to have lived near the Toho LaBrea in the sixties!) Although many of these films are available on home video in Japan, in this country it's as if they never existed. The unavailability of this title in the United States is particularly unfortunate. Released by Toho as *Nippon tanjo* (*The Birth of Japan*), *The Three Treasures* is commonly regarded as that country's equivalent of *The Ten Commandments*. It runs just over three hours, not including an intermission, and toplines Japan's biggest star, Toshiro Mifune. The film's production was likely inspired by the tremendous success of similar epic roadshows being made in the United States at the same time.

The picture chronicles the origins of the Shinto, a Japanese religion rooted in nature and ancestor worship, and while I've generally avoided including religious epics, this particular film is important for several reasons. For one thing, many of Toho's familiar stock company of actors and technicians worked on the project. Tomoyuki Tanaka produced, while Eiji Tsuburaya, as usual, directed the special effects. Kyoko Kagawa (*Mothra*), Akihiko Hirata (*Godzilla*), Jun Tazaki (*Atragon*) and Takashi Shimura (*Rashomon* and *The Mysterians*) all appear in the film. Of particular note is Tsuburaya's creation of a seven-headed dragon which Mifune battles in the film's second act. We don't get much of a look at the creature—it's basically all heads, and its body kept offscreen—but it clearly was the inspiration behind a later, much more familiar, Toho monster: King Ghidorah (or Ghidrah if you prefer).

Hiroshi Inagaki directed the movie. Born in 1905, Inagaki began his career as a child actor and switched to directing at the age of 23. He directed over 100 films, including several trilogies (the *Samurai* series, 1954–56, being the most famous). His other credits include an original version of the same story, also released here as *Samurai* (1940), *Secret Scrolls* (two parts, 1957–58), *Daredevil in the Castle* and *The Youth and His Amulet* (both 1961) and *Whirlwind* (1964).

Toshiro Mifune's leading lady, Kyoko Kagawa, would later star in *Mothra* (1961) and also appeared in Inagaki's *Secret Scrolls (Part I)*. She was a favorite actress of Kurosawa, appearing in *The Lower Depths* (1957), *High and Low* (1962) and *Red Beard* (1965), all opposite Mifune. Twenty-eight years later, Kagawa was reunited with director Kurosawa for *Madaday* (1993).

The Three Treasures was released in the United States in a truncated, though subtitled, version, shown at the newly opened Toho LaBrea in Los Angeles in December 1960. Over an hour was excised: Toho's American distribution arm, Toho International, handled the film, which had a limited release outside the LaBrea at best. Judging from the extreme color shifts and abrupt edits on the Japanese version I saw, it seems likely that this shorter version was released in Japan as well (general release versions of longer roadshows were frequently trimmed to allow additional performances and thus insure quicker box office returns).

Variety's "Tube" had this to say of the shorter edition: "Western audiences ... will have to admire the artistry and painstaking photographic mastery of the craftsmen who designed and manufactured this film. Already noted for their miniature, color and special effects work, these Japanese artisans have set a new standard for themselves with this effort.... Hiroshi Inagaki's direction breathes life and vitality into the drama, particularly scenes of combat and notably in the enthusiasm of crude Oriental swordplay.... Kazuo Yamada's lenswork is agile and alert. But it is Eiji Tsuburaya's special effects that steal the picture."

The Sixties

The Final War *(1960)*

This obscure film from Toei is often confused with Toho's similarly titled and scripted 1961 production, *The Last War*. Both revolve around the threat and later the destruction of the world in a nuclear holocaust, triggered by events outside Japan's control. Both pictures feature personal stories of Japanese citizens, helpless against their country's inevitable destruction. *The Final War* was filmed in black and white; *The Last War* is in color. *The Final War* was supposedly released theatrically in the United States, though definitely not very extensively, and possibly not at all; I have only been able to confirm that the picture received an exhibition license in New York State. Although *The Last War* wasn't released theatrically in the United States and sold directly to television, in recent years it has become by far the easier of the two films to see. I've seen and very much liked *The Last War* but have no idea where an English-dubbed or subtitled print of *The Final War* can be found. What follows is a plot synopsis of the film, from *The American Film Institute Catalog 1960–1969*.

A United States Air Force plane accidentally detonates a nuclear bomb over South Korea. While South Korea insists that North Korea set off the explosion, the North Koreans protest U.S. violation of the 38th Parallel. In Japan, the U.S. 7th Fleet mobilizes at Yokosuko. A broadcast from Peking reports that an American U-3 jet has been shot down over the Soviet Union. As Tokyo mobilizes its civil defense units, newspaperman Shigero (Tatsuo Umemiya) reports on the growing crisis, while his sweetheart, Tomoko, a nurse, prepares to care for casualties. Negotiations between the U.S. and the U.S.S.R. break down, and Moscow warns Tokyo that every Japanese air base will be destroyed by H-Bombs within minutes. At dawn, Tokyo lies in ruins, completely destroyed by nuclear weapons. Shigero returns to the city looking for Tomoko but finds that she has been killed; he then dies from exposure to radiation. In Argentina, the only country to survive total devastation, a memorial service is held for mankind. (According to Phil Hardy's *Science Fiction*, the service is held in pouring rain.)

Like *The Last War*, this film seems to emphasize the helplessness and frustration Japan certainly and understandably felt with its role (or lack thereof) during the cold war. Both the Soviet Union and China were less than 500 miles away, and U.S. military, then as now, played a very visible, even pushy role in post-war Japan. Certainly if a nuclear conflict were to have occurred, it's not at all unlikely that Japan would have endured a nuclear strike and total destruction. And like *The Last War*, *The Final War* attempts to dramatize this by presenting a seemingly disconnected story of a young reporter and his fiancée, a nurse, who normally would have many years of happiness to look forward to, just like the sailor and his bride-to-be in Toho's film. If nothing else, *The Final War* reflects fear in the nuclear age from a people all too experienced in its potential horrors. And it is for this reason alone *The Final War* is undeserving of the obscurity it now has.

The Human Vapor *(1960)*

Combining elements of Toho's 1958 production *The H-Man* with *Phantom of the Opera* (as well as Jun Fukuda's *The Secret of the Telegian*, released earlier that year), *The Human Vapor* has a certain poetry, most of which is lost in Brenco's Americanization. Much of the poetry—and logic—has been edited out, while the film's more conventional elements—bank robberies, invisibility and so forth, have been retained.

Mizuno (Yoshio Tsuchiya) meets with a group of newspaper reporters. He says that while he knows the meeting is a trap, he wants to tell his story. He explains that he's an unhappy librarian recently returned after a long stay in a sanitarium. One afternoon, he meets up with a Dr. Sano, who invites Mizuno to participate in a scientific experiment. Believing he has nothing to lose, Mizuno agrees. At Dr. Sano's laboratory, Mizuno is placed inside an enclosed chamber, and once Sano's equipment is turned on, the troubled librarian falls unconscious. He sleeps for 240 hours (ten days and ten nights). When he wakes, he discovers he has the power to dissolve into vapor at will. Somewhat inexplicably angry, Mizuno attacks the doctor while in mist form, creating a large smoky ring around the scientist's neck which asphyxiates him. Mizuno quickly goes mad, believing himself to be superior to other men. He robs several banks, killing a guard in the process. However, unlike the protagonists of other films of this type, he's not interested in wealth. Mizuno wants to use the stolen money to help finance the comeback of a young, troubled classical dancer, Fujichiyo (Kaoru Yachigusa, one of the stars of the Samurai film series), whom he met while in the sanitarium. The police trace the stolen money to Fujichiyo and arrest her. To protect her innocence, Mizuno confesses to the crime. When the police ask how he could have pulled off the bank robberies undetected, he offers a demonstration. In perhaps the film's best scene, Mizuno vaporizes in front of a dozen officers, all of whom are helpless to prevent him not only from escaping, but from stealing another fortune in cash as well. The police refuse to release Fujichiyo, believing her to be the key in stopping the Vapor Man. Mizuno, in vapor form, easily makes his way to her jail cell, but the dancer refuses to escape with Mizuno. Since Fujichiyo has already spent much of the stolen money preparing a comeback recital (she was told it was from "the sale of land"), the police decide to kill the Vapor Man in the theater where Fujichiyo is set to perform. The police release gas into the theater's auditorium which, when ignited, will blow the Vapor Man to smithereens. Mizuno watches Fujichiyo's performance, as the police scurry to get spectators out before the gas is ignited. A switch is thrown, but the Vapor Man has second-guessed the police and nothing happens. However, Fujichiyo, despite her absolute love for Mizuno, ignites the auditorium, and there is a huge explosion. Fujichiyo is killed instantly, but the Vapor Man survives. He can't be killed. With Fujichiyo gone, however, he has no reason for living.

The Human Vapor isn't very involving, partly because we never get to know just why Mizuno and Fujichiyo spent time in the sanitarium, how they met, or for that matter, why they love each other. In the U.S. version at least, Mizuno is both mad and madly in love, yet the two elements don't work together as presented here. We just don't learn enough about these characters to really care about them. Much of the story follows the investigation of the robbery-killings. Led by Detective Okamoto (Tatsuya Mihashi) for the police, and reporter Kyoko (Keiko Sata) for the press, neither one is very interesting (nor played by interesting actors), nor does either profession, as depicted here, engender much sympathy. The police are depicted as ruthless and cold-hearted, willing to sacrifice innocent lives to get the Vapor Man, while the press appear selfish, even brutish, toward the feelings of others. However, Eiji Tsuburaya's special effects crew does a magnificent job, in the brief but highly effective transformation scenes.

Star Yoshio Tsuchiya had a small role as a fighter pilot in *Gigantis, the Fire Monster* and played the tragic Iwamura in *Battle in Outer Space*, an astronaut helpless under the mind control of an alien race. Tsuchiya, who abandoned a promising career as a doctor, was a member of Kurosawa's stock company of actors; he was the determined farmer in Kurosawa's *Seven Samurai*. The actor also appeared in *Yojimbo* (1961), *Sanjuro* (1962), *High and Low* (1963) and *Red Beard* (1965). *The Human Vapor* was his first starring role, and the actor quickly became typecast playing tortured characters, always on the verge of cracking up or helplessly possessed by aliens. Tsuchiya's other fantastic film credits include *Attack of the Mushroom People* (1963), *Frankenstein Conquers the World* (1965), *Monster Zero* (1965, as the controller of Planet X), *Son of Godzilla* (1967), *Destroy All Monsters* (1968) and *Yog: Monster from Space* (1970). Tsuchiya returned to the genre for a major role in *Godzilla vs. King Ghidorah* (1991).

Tatsuya Mihashi's other credits include *High and Low* (1963) and *Tora! Tora! Tora!* (1970). He also starred in *Kagi no kag* (1964), the film Woody Allen comically redubbed as *What's Up, Tiger Lily?* (1966), with Mihashi cast as "Phil Moskowitz"!

Like its co-feature, *Gorath*, *The Human Vapor* was heavily re-edited for U.S. release, with Tsuchiya's identity now revealed at the beginning instead of the mid-point, and an exciting title sequence robbery edited out entirely. *Variety*'s "Whit" saw both features. "[*The Human Vapor*] is the stronger of the two insofar as story development is concerned and leans heavily on expert special effects for its story premise." The dubbing was another matter. "[The] spectator is always aware that lips and words never match, thus decreasing realism." Greg Shoemaker, reviewing the film as part of an excellent series called "The Toho Legacy," published in his *Japanese Fantasy Film Journal* (issues 12–14), had this to say: "Director Honda and special effects director Eiji Tsuburaya enthrall the viewer each in effective manipulation of his field. Honda slowly introduces the audience to a realization that the film is not what it appears. The picture unfolds with each 'clue' transforming that which seems to be a rather routine melodrama/crime film into a vision of uncontrolled madness. Tsuburaya incredibly brings the unstoppable terror to life in a series of creative tableauxs each time the menace is loosed to provide for his beloved. *The Human Vapor* is a slow film, exacting much from the viewer to maintain his attention, but an unusual story and threatening progression into the bizarre, appended by slices of Japanese mores, prescribes recognition for the film as an excellent fantasy."

The Secret of the Telegian *(1960)*

Film critic Gene Siskel (you know, the bald one) once said, "You can only see a film for the first time once." I very much believe in that statement. Watching *Lawrence of Arabia* on a 70-foot screen in Super Panavision and six-track stereo sound is simply going to affect you differently than seeing it for the first time on commercial television, where it's usually broken up over two nights, on top of everything else. Wide screen fantasy films from Japan are at a particularly notable disadvantage. Not only are they needlessly tampered with by their American distributors, but when seen on American television, nearly half the picture is missing at all times because the wide screen image doesn't match the shape of most TV sets. The films are always presented in mono, even though many were released in stereo in Japan. Distributors and TV station managers alike couldn't care less about the quality of the prints, which are often dark, fuzzy and scratched to high heaven. Case in point: Toho's *The Secret of the Telegian*. The film was purchased by Herts-Lion, whose apparent financial woes promptly squelched plans for a theatrical run. Instead, they (or Toho International, depending on sources) released the film directly to television, though only in some parts of the country. So bad was the company's fiscal problems that although filmed in color, *The Secret of the Telegian* was released to TV in black and white. If seeing a color, widescreen and stereo film in black and white, cropped and mono wasn't bad enough, the video copy I saw was duplicated in the cheapest manner imaginable. Apparently someone found an extremely poor 16mm print (possibly from Great Britain, as it runs several minutes longer than listed running times) and simply photographed the fuzzy picture with a video camera as it was projected against a white wall. The *coupe de grace* came about a half hour into the story when a strange insect flew in front of the projector and promptly sat on co-star Yumi Shirakawa's nose! I mention this to point out how difficult it can be to examine these films objectively when seen under such deplorable circumstances. Many of the films covered in this volume have either fallen into public domain or are currently owned by companies with neither the funds nor ambition to strike new masters. I suppose I could have watched all (or nearly all) the films for this book on crisp, letterboxed videos from Japan, but that simply isn't how most Americans will see them, at least not anytime soon. And so what of *The Secret of the Telegian*? Well, even from the print I saw, it is obviously something less than a masterpiece. But first, the story:

At an amusement park, in the "Cave of Horrors," a man, Tsukamoto, is stabbed to death with a bayonet. Kirioka (Koji Tsuruta), normally a science reporter, investigates the crime. At first the nosy newsman is harassed by one of the detectives (Yoshio Tsuchiya) investigating the murder. However, the detective's partner, Kobayashi (Akihiko Hirata), recognizes Kirioka as an old school chum. The men find a pair of old dog tags, as well as a strange mini-transmitter (identified as a "clariotron") which must be kept at an extremely low temperature to function. The three meet again at a nightclub, operated by the dead man's associates. Takashi (Yoshibumi Tajima), Onishi (Seizaburo Kawazu) and Taki (Takamuru Sasaki?) are wealthy smugglers, concerned that their business partner's death may have something to do with their dark past. The three receive a reel of audiotape—a message from ex-corporal Sudo. Sudo and the three men were all in the Imperial Japanese Army and together the night of the Japanese surrender, August 15, 1945 (August 14 according to the English-dubbed print), transporting an important scientist, Dr. Niki (Sachio Sakai?) who was working on an invention to teleport matter. The scientist's belongings include several gold bars, and all but loyal soldier Sudo want to abandon the mission and steal the gold. When Sudo refuses, both he and Dr. Niki are shot and left for dead. The gold was hidden, but when the greedy men returned, both the gold and the two bodies had disappeared. Sudo, the men learn, is very much alive. Sudo announces over the tape that he plans to kill each one of them. The men have already received dog tags, Sudo's kiss of death.

Using the alias Goro Nakamoto, Sudo inquires about some cooling equipment ordered from a research supplier. He acts strangely before one of the company's employees, Akiko (Yumi Shirakawa). Later, Akiko runs into Kirioka at the woman's apartment building, which also happens to be where the murdered man lives (this unlikely coincidence leads nowhere). Kirioka searches the place with Kobayashi, but finds nothing. When Akiko tells Kirioka about

Nakamoto, the newsman and Kobayashi begin to suspect Sudo and Nakamoto are one and the same. They visit the condemned men, who are reluctant to seek police protection because of their criminal past. Sudo, in vintage military uniform, materializes before Takashi. His body, while three-dimensional, looks like a bad television signal, occasionally fuzzy and in need of a horizontal hold adjustment. Sudo stabs Takashi with a bayonet. The detectives chase Sudo to a building where he disappears. A room, containing strange equipment, is burned beyond all recognition. Later, the killer delivers a note to Taki: he will kill him between 11:30 and midnight. Taki accepts the police department's offer for protection, but it's no use: Sudo materializes (disguised as a policeman) and kills the smuggler. He returns via a portable teleporter hidden aboard a freight train, which he blows up after leaving.

Kirioka and Akiko visit Sudo at his rural home, located near an active volcano. Kirioka poses as an electrical engineer, hoping to get a look at the matter transmitter and Dr. Niki, if either exists. Sudo quickly guesses their plans, however, and nobody learns anything. Onishi and his bodyguards (who include Eisei Amamoto) run off to a remote hideout near a fishing village. When they arrive, Onishi is greeted by a note from Sudo, who promises to kill him in two days. The authorities arrive at Sudo's house, where they find Dr. Niki, now in a wheelchair, happily working on his matter transmitter and unaware that Sudo, hired on as an assistant, has been using the fantastic device for his own nefarious purposes. Sudo, meanwhile, has vanished. The police leave, and Sudo returns to use the transport device. He kills Dr. Niki (at which time it is revealed that Sudo has been wearing a false face — he's really horribly scarred) and transports to Onishi's home, where he kills the smuggler and his bodyguards. The detectives and Kirioka chase Sudo to another hidden teleporter, where he vanishes. At the other end, however, the volcano has erupted, creating an earthquake which destroys the transporter's main controls. The mechanism destroyed in mid-transport, Sudo screams and vanishes into oblivion.

Although Eiji Tsuburaya's briefly seen transporting effects are nice, *The Secret of the Telegian* is bogged down by a mediocre script (by Shinichi Sekizawa), which borrows heavily from the 1958 film *The Fly* (and, to a lesser extent, *Phantom of the Opera* and *The H-Man*) without improving upon them. For such a fantastic device, it seems a shame the teleporter is used for such a mundane purpose as revenge.

Sudo is an especially uninteresting character. He has two (and only two) expressions: glowering menace and maniacal laughter. Star Tadao Nakamura is bland as the former corporal, lacking the depth of co-star Yoshio Tsuchiya, future Human Vapor. Nakamura also appeared in *The Secret Scrolls* and *I Bombed Pearl Harbor*, but this was apparently his only starring role in a Japanese fantasy film. Another problem is Sudo's motivations. Sure, he wants to kill the men that tried to kill him, but why does he strangle Dr. Niki? Why is he so lustful toward Akiko? Why does he send notes to the men before killing them? The awkward script also introduces science reporter Kirioka (why isn't he covering the science beat?) then all but forgets him by the end of the story. Toho star Shirakawa (*The H-Man*) has no reason to be in the film at all.

The Secret of the Telegian marked the inauspicious directorial debut of Jun Fukuda. Fukuda (born 1923) was a kind of second-stringer at Toho. When their Godzilla series went into decline, Ishiro Honda stepped out and Fukuda stepped in, directing *Ebirah, Horror of the Deep* (1966), *Son of Godzilla* (1967), and later *Godzilla on Monster Island* (1972), *Godzilla vs. Megalon* (1973), and *Godzilla vs. the Cosmic Monster* (1974). He also directed the wretched *The War in Space* (1977). His other credits include *The Weed of Crime* (1964), *White Rose of Hong Kong* (1965) and *Young Guy Graduates* (1969). He's not a terrible director, though he's not especially good, either. Fukuda was, however, saddled with generally unimaginative fantasy film projects and desperately low budgets. "Fukuda's direction appears starved for Tsuburaya's garnishes," suggested Greg Shoemaker, though Phil Hardy's *Science Fiction* found the story "interesting," adding, "Tsuburaya's special effects are as good as anything achieved in the world at that time and the cinematography achieves respectable noir-ish overtones."

There is good news for *The Secret of the Telegian*. As this book went to press, an obscure distributor began selling English-dubbed, *color* videocassettes of the picture. While this will not improve the film's major script problems, it'll sure help make this presumably attractive film watchable.

Invasion of the Neptune Men *(1961)*

The last of Japan's early superhero movies to reach American shores was this routine but well-produced serial style adventure, with evil aliens once again threatening Earth. Saving the day this time is Space Chief (called "Iron Sharp" in Japan), played by Shinichi "Sonny" Chiba, who went on to become one of Japan's most popular action stars.

A group of schoolboys, looking through a telescope, spot a big, unidentified rocketship (which looks like a thermos with jet wings) as it lands in a forest. Out of the vessel come Neptune men—humanoids dressed in shiny silver clothing and bullet-shaped helmets suggesting alien welders. The children are surrounded by the invaders and appear doomed. Just then, out of the sky comes Space Chief (Chiba) aboard his futuristic, post-modern strato-coupe. He fires his laser pistol at the aliens who quickly retreat. The Neptune men are gone, but not for long. Soon thereafter, all the Earth's mechanical devices begin running backwards: clocks, 45s in jukeboxes, electrically powered trains, etc. Eminent scientist Dr. Tanawai (also father to one of the boys) and his mild-mannered assistant, Mr. Tabana (Super Chief's alter-ego, also played by Chiba), try to determine the source of the disturbances. Unless they can be stopped, mankind appears doomed. "We're in dire peril," Tabana notes. He then suggests alerting the media. Tanawai is against the idea, believing it will cause a panic. "We're scientists, not prophets," he says. The stakes are soon raised when the Neptunians blow up nuclear reactors both in Japan and in the United States. The aliens' presence is publicly acknowledged, and the kids are even given credit for finding the Neptune men in the first place. (Yay!) Tanawai and Tabana build an "electro-barrier," a force field designed to repel the enemy ship. Soon enough, the aliens appear out of the sky in their flying thermos. Tokyo is blacked out (via impressive second-unit footage) as the invaders hurl numerous missiles at the city. The electro-barrier is successful, however, and the missiles harmlessly explode miles above the metropolis. The ship is equally unsuccessful in penetrating the force field, and the alien vessel is forced to abandon the attack. "Hooray for the electro-barrier!" the kids cheer. One of the scientists gives the schoolboys a short-range radar gun. After first testing it on a toy Robby the Robot, the boys discover a small metal globe with numerous antennae sticking out of it, which also emits an electronic whine. The kids take the strange device to Tanawai and Tabana, who decode the noise as a message from the Neptunians. As might be expected, the Neptunians announce their intention to conquer Earth, warning that the electro-barrier will not stop them. The Neptune men create a tremendous dust storm, accompanied by thunder and lightning, which forces the scientists to temporarily turn off the electro-barrier. This gives the aliens enough time to sneak inside the city.

Disguised as guards, the invaders infiltrate the research base, killing several real guards with ray guns. The aliens' lasers leave ghostly, blackened silhouettes of the disintegrated soldiers. The Neptune men severely injure Dr. Tanawai before the kids recognize the alien imposters and Space Chief drives them off. Their rocketship based at a remote beach, the Neptune men further threaten the Earth by lowering the planet's temperature to the freezing point, creating snow in Tokyo and around the world. Hoping this demonstration of force will convince the Earth to surrender, they just as quickly raise temperatures back to normal. A state of martial law is declared, as Tabana and other scientists design and construct "alpha-electro" rockets—special missiles equipped with homing devices set for the Neptunian rocketship's unique metal hull. The big Neptunian ship flies over the city, releasing several dozen hexagonal flying saucers. The saucers, shooting powerful laser beams, blow up several factories and downtown buildings (as well as Tokyo Tower and the Diet Building). Super Chief, back aboard his flying coupe, destroys the saucers one by one in an impressive dogfight sequence, while the alpha-electro rockets blow up the Neptune men's mother ship. The Earth saved, Tanawai makes a speedy recovery, while the kids tell Mr. Tabana they all want to become astronauts.

Despite a woefully familiar script, *Invasion of the Neptune Men* has a few surprises. The picture's villains aren't nearly as comical and over-the-top as they are in most films of this type, say, *Prince of Space*. Sure, they look silly in those bullet-shaped helmets, but no more so than their counterparts in similarly budgeted American sci-fi films from this period. The filmmakers were also wise in keeping the aliens' dialogue to a minimum. They're heard only when delivering their message of doom to the scientists and lack the kind of Snidely Whiplash inflection so common to these pictures (at least the English-dubbed versions of these pictures). The rest of the time, however, they wander about in complete silence, and while they still look a trifle silly, they at least create a sense of menace, unlike their invading brethren. Like Daiei's *Warning from Space* (1956), *Invasion of the Neptune Men* wisely keeps most of the action confined to the research base, with the kids never far from the scientists and military scurrying to defeat their intended conquerors. The result is a sense of geography and spatial relationships sorely lacking in other such fare, particularly the Shintoho–Walter Manley "Starman" features.

Although it's filmed in black and white, Toei appears to have allotted this production a comparatively sizeable budget. The excellent opticals and miniatures are as good as anything produced by Tsuburaya's unit at Toho, particularly the very fine matte work (Toho's mattes were often terrible). Especially good are several shots of the Neptunian rocketship on Earth, and, during the big attack on Tokyo, scenes of fleeing crowds matted near exploding miniature buildings. The effects are so good, in fact, I suspect the big attack on Tokyo and some of the missile shots may have been lifted from a more prestigious production, most likely Toei's *The Final War* (1961), which I've not seen. Even if this were true, the original effects are still quite good. The battle between the saucers and Super Chief's flying coupe is well staged, looking very much like a precursor to the dogfights in George Lucas' *Star Wars* (1977).

This was Shinichi "Sonny" Chiba's second feature. Born Sadeo Maeda in 1939, the athletic actor got his start appearing in a superhero series on Japanese television in 1960 before branching out into features the following year (mostly for Toei, with whom he is still closely associated). Chiba moved back and forth between television and films (including 1966's *Terror Beneath the Sea*), before finally gaining stardom in a string of very popular television shows in the late sixties. He moved into karate features in the seventies and early eighties, including *The Street Fighter* (1975), *The Executioner* and *The Return of the Street Fighter* (1976), *Sister Street Fighter* (1976), *The Bodyguard* (1976), *Champion of Death* (1977), *The Street Fighter's Last Revenge* (1979), *The Bloody Bushido Blade* (for Rankin-Bass and shot at Toho, 1981), and *Karate Killer* (1981), all of which were distributed in the United States. At the same time, Chiba continued to appear in fantastic films, including *Message from Space* (1978), *Time Slip* and *Virus* (both 1980). *Invasion of the Neptune Men* was never theatrically distributed in the United States, released instead to

American television by Walter Manley in 1964. The picture, like Manley's Starman films, suffers the same undeserving brand of "Gee-whiz!" dubbing sure to turn off most potential viewers. While routinely scripted, the film's imaginative and elaborate effects, if nothing else, generate some interest.

The Last War *(1961)*

Not to be confused with Toei's *The Final War*, this Toho production doesn't appear to have been released theatrically in the United States, though it was frequently shown on American television in the 1960s and 1970s. The TV version is missing all production credits, and the name of its distributor is too tiny to make out on most 16mm television prints (*Psychotronic* credits Medallion-TV). Like most Japanese fantastic films not centered around giant monsters, *The Last War* has faded from view in recent years. The picture's curious Americanization and sober handling of its subject matter by a studio more closely associated with lighter fare (*Mothra, King Kong vs. Godzilla*, etc.) — and by a country which experienced the horrors of nuclear destruction firsthand — make *The Last War* a real curio.

World War III is over. Sailors aboard a freighter, including radio operator Takano (Akira Takarada), are aware that radioactive clouds will soon reach them, and so decide to return to Tokyo even though they know that the city is surely destroyed and that their loved ones are almost certainly dead. Takano, himself orphaned during World War II, recalls visiting his fiancée, Seiko Tomura (Yumi Shirakawa), and her family after spending many months at sea. During his final stay before shipping out, he and Seiko had asked the young woman's parents, Mokichi (Frankie Sakai) and Oyoshi (Nobuo Otowa), permission to marry, which is quickly granted. Soon thereafter, Takano's ship departs. Elsewhere, a mother visits her sickly daughter at a nursery. She promises to return in a few days to celebrate the little girl's recovery. At the school, the children sing "It's a Small World" (yes, the same maddening song heard at the popular ride at Walt Disney theme parks). Meanwhile, tensions between two superpowers flare up and the two armies begin employing nuclear weapons in their war games. Later, a series of mishaps on both sides sends the world spinning ever closer to global-thermonuclear destruction, including a malfunction at a missile silo and an avalanche which nearly triggers the global conflict. In other parts of the world, nuclear weapons are fired from jets at a tank battalion, while at the Arctic Circle, an air battle quickly escalates, as jets from both sites fire their nuclear warheads at one another. The end of the world now seems inevitable, despite pleas from the Japanese government for a cease fire. Tokyo is evacuated, but Seiko's father considers this pointless and his family stays put.

"We haven't done anything wrong," he says. "Why should we try to run?" The family sits down to a luxurious meal, and Mokichi encourages his youngest children, Seiko's brother and younger sister, to eat as much as they want. The mother of the little girl vainly tries to return to her daughter, who has now recovered. Because of the onslaught of crowds hopelessly trying to avoid the imminent destruction, the woman is unable to reach her daughter and collapses. The missiles are finally launched, and Tokyo is instantly obliterated. Everyone is killed. In other parts of the world, we see New York, London, Paris, Moscow, etc., face similar destruction. Back aboard Takano's ship, the opening sequence is replayed, while "It's a Small World" is heard over the soundtrack. As Takano and a Caucasian sailor ponder the fate of their loved ones, the soundtrack abruptly switches to an anti-arms race speech by John F. Kennedy. "Mankind must put an end to war," says the president, "or war will put an end to mankind."

The Last War was made in the wake of several American-made dramas dealing with the same subject, including *The World, the Flesh, and the Devil*, and especially Stanley Kramer's star-studded adaptation of Nevil Shute's *On the Beach* (both 1959). The picture's opening, where sailors decide to return home to Japan, knowing they'll die of radiation poisoning by doing so, is nearly identical to what happens to Gregory Peck's submarine crew in Kramer's film. From there, however, *The Last War* deviates sharply from similarly themed American films. *The Last War* is a Japanese film told from a distinctly Japanese and—tragically—experienced point of view. As a whole, American films about nuclear holocaust, until very recently, have been decidedly sanitized. In *The World, the Flesh, and the Devil*, for instance, no dead bodies are ever seen, and Manhattan, where most of the story takes place, has been left completely intact. Moreover, American films on this subject tend to follow the survivors of nuclear conflict rather than its immediate victims. Though we follow Akira Takarada's sailor through the story, the focus is clearly on his fiancée's family, who don't survive. The film expresses Japan's feeling of complete helplessness during the cold war. Even without the post-destruction prologue, it's clear almost from the very start that nuclear war is inevitable. That most of the film takes place between the time this becomes clear and when the bombs finally drop helps further its frustrated, pessimistic tone. Why and how war finally breaks out are never really made clear, just as its victims would never really know what hit them, anyway. The two superpowers represented are obviously the United States and the Soviet Union, though both nations go unnamed, fly different flags and wear fictionalized military uniforms (the blue army represents the United States, while the Soviets wear tan uniforms).

Toshio Yasumi and Takeshi Kimura wrote the screenplay, which has several interesting ideas and characters. Of special interest is the relationship between Mokichi and Oyoshi, Seiko's parents. Oyoshi is supposed to be ailing, yet even after it's clear death is imminent, her husband expects his wife to continue taking her medicine. Early in the story, the sickly woman plants tulips in the couple's small garden, and as the missiles are launched, they express disappointment that the flowers haven't yet sprouted. Interestingly, Seiko argues that the flowers' only chance of survival is to remain underground. The use of "It's a Small World" in the middle and again at the end of the picture is jarring, but not inappropriate. The song was originally written (by Richard M. and Robert B. Sherman of *Mary Poppins* fame) for a Disney-sponsored exhibit at the New York World's Fair in 1964, and I would be interested to learn how the rights to the song were obtained for its use here. Its use, along with the rather ironic excerpt from President Kennedy's speech, neither of which is in the Japanese cut, is interesting in its reflection of the attitudes of the picture's American distributor.

The special effects, once again directed by Eiji Tsuburaya, are very good. Few films prior to *The Last War* actually attempted to depict the kind of global destruction that a nuclear war would certainly create, and probably no Hollywood studio at the time could have done the job as well as Tsuburaya's unit. While less flashy and colorful than in Tsuburaya's monster movies, *The Last War*'s effects are more realistically executed and no less dramatic. The miniature military hardware has a slightly futuristic slant, and a montage of newspaper headlines at one point hints that the story is set sometime in the near future. Scenes of the instant destruction of the world's major capitals (all done in miniature) are expertly handled.

The film is not without its faults: A lengthy monologue where Takano details Japan's post–World War II success ("Japan was second only to the United States in baseball, and just as happy to see the ball hit out of the park!") comes off like a tacky educational short, and Frankie Sakai, though quite good as Seiko's father (as well as one can judge his dubbed performance) appears much too young to be playing Akira Takarada's intended father-in-law. Sakai was a popular television star (on "I'd Love to See"), and his talents were generally better suited to lighter fare, such as Toho's *Mothra*, made the same year. According to The *Motion Picture Guide*, Sakai also appeared in a spoof of Charlie Chan films starring Zero Mostel, *Mastermind* (1969, release delayed until 1976). The actor also had an important supporting role in the epic miniseries *Shogun* (1981). Sakai's wife was played by Nobuo Otowa. Otowa is barely noticeable here (at least in the English-dubbed version), but she would give an incredible performance just three years later in Kaneto Shindo's *Onibaba* (1964). Nobuo also appeared in *Children of Hiroshima* (1952), *The Youth and His Amulet* (1963) and *Kuroneko* (1968).

Reviews of *The Last War* are scant, and, like *The Final War*, it's not even mentioned in Jack G. Shaheen's *Nuclear War Films* (Southern Illinois University Press, 1978). "Eiji Tsuburaya and his technicians enhance death and destruction with their moving landscapes filled with colorful mushroom clouds and choreographed rocket attacks," notes the *Japanese Fantasy Film Journal*'s

Greg Shoemaker. "Reality is held in check as the viewer acquires an affection for the characters threatened with annihilation. One hopes that, as the screen goes black, it would never happen." Phil Hardy's *Science Fiction* notes: "The film's premise is a totally believable, and even probable, scenario. The effects ... are memorable and the acting makes the relevant points, although it is difficult to assess the performances: what would constitute 'appropriate behaviour' in such circumstances is anybody's guess." *The Motion Picture Guide* gave the film a *** rating, noting, somewhat incorrectly, that "the concentration is on those dying, slowly and painfully.... Special effects by the masterful Tsuburaya are far above average."

The Manster *(1961)*

Don't you just love that title? This film only marginally qualifies for this book, as it was an English-language production co-produced by United Artists, which like many U.S. studios, had money tied up in foreign countries that could only be spent there. United Artists spent their money on *The Manster*, among other things. The film was produced, written, directed and performed by Western personnel, though about half of the cast and crew were Japanese. The film itself is a surprisingly effective chiller, with several truly eerie moments. One can also applaud the general audacity of the film's premise — this was, after all, the first two-headed-person movie.

The film starts out extremely well, with Dr. Robert Suzuki (Satoshi "Tetsu" Nakamura) shooting a strange, vaguely human though hairy creature in his laboratory. We next meet American reporter Larry Stanford (played by British actor Peter Dyneley: "a poor man's Lon Chaney, Jr., if ever there could be such a thing," argues R. M. Hayes). Stanford is a tired-looking veteran reporter (he's paunchy and appears to be in his late forties, unusual for a protagonist in sci-fi films of this era) and seems anxious to return home to his American wife, Linda (Jane Hylton). Stanford visits Dr. Suzuki's laboratory — located on a volcano — on what is supposed to be a routine story assignment. Friendly Dr. Suzuki slips Stanford a Mickey Finn, and offers to show him the "real Japan." The reporter falls unconscious. The scientist injects Stanford with a serum which he had previously used on the hairy creature, which turns out to have once been Suzuki's brother. Suzuki's wife, Emiko (Toyoko Takechi), was also injected, and now is disfigured with mis-matched eyes and no memory and kept in a cell by the doctor. Stanford, believing he simply dozed off, takes Suzuki up on his offer to tour the Tokyo the always-busy reporter never had the opportunity to enjoy. At the same time, Stanford becomes irritable and careless about his appearance. He stops shaving, wears grungy clothes, misses work and breaks his promise to his wife to return home to America. Stanford has an affair with a woman (Terri Zimmern) who works for Suzuki. Soon, Stanford's hand gets hairy, which he tries to hide from his co-worker friend, Ian (Norman Van Hawley). Stanford also begins having shoulder pains, and in the film's most incredible moment, he looks in the mirror and sees a single eye on his shoulder, eerily gazing at nothing in particular. Eventually the eye grows into a crudely formed, full-blown head (which *Psychotronic* accurately describes as looking like a carved coconut), and the tortured Stanford makes his way back to Suzuki's laboratory. By this time, his wife has flown in from the States, and Stanford has committed several murders around Tokyo (the implication is that the mind of the head forced the unwilling Stanford to commit the deeds). At the laboratory, the now remorseful Suzuki puts the creature that was once his wife out of her misery. Suzuki in turn is killed by Stanford. At this point, Stanford writhes in agony, and in the picture's second truly original and audacious moment, splits apart into two separate beings (the equally fine U.K. title, also the working title, was *The Split*). The hairy creature throws Stanford's mistress into the volcano. The creature and Stanford grapple, and the creature is killed. The wounded Stanford is reunited with his wife, but as Bill Warren justly asks in *Keep Watching the Skies!*, how is he going to explain all those murders to the police?

The Manster is a remarkable little picture, extremely effective and unsettling at times, and the best of the generally awful two-headed whatsits movies. After *The Manster* came *The Incredible Two-Headed Transplant* (1971), *The Thing with Two Heads* (1972) and *How to Get Ahead in Advertising* (1989), among others. One of the things that sets *The Manster* apart from the others is that the terror comes not from having two heads, but rather from the concept that something is growing inside you, ready to take you over. That's an idea more recent filmmakers have expanded upon, most notably in *Alien* (1979), its sequels and the underrated *The Thing* (1982). The actual two-headedness is played down in *The Manster*; the second head is kept mostly in the shadows, and there appears to have been a conscious attempt *not* to make it look particularly human. The filmmakers also were wise in not trying to fit a second actor under the wardrobe, as was awkwardly done in *The Thing with Two Heads*. The scene with the eye is truly creepy and very Daliesque. I didn't get to see *The Manster* until very recently, but a still from this sequence I saw in *Famous Monsters of Filmland* as a child was enough to give me nightmares. The split is also nicely handled. It's not at all graphic by today's standards, though Stanford's ripped, dripping clothes are pretty gruesome for the early sixties. The opening expertly sets the mood for the picture, and the subplot involving Suzuki's poor wife—who looks like a feminine, Japanese version of Charles Laughton's Hunchback of Notre Dame—is also interesting.

Another facet of the picture rarely mentioned is the surprising depth of its main character. By 1962, characters in nearly every science fiction film made in the United States and even Japan were standard, perfunctory "types": stoic, by-the-book military men, dedicated scientists, etc. Peter Dyneley's Larry Stanford was different—a tired family man, looking ready to retire, harboring a deep resentment against his wife and frustration regarding his career which only become exposed while in his monster state. While no deep character study, there was clearly more thought put into Walter Sheldon's screenplay (from George Breakston's story) than most writers' efforts in similar films. Peter Dyneley was an undistinguished screen actor in films from the early 1950s through the early 1970s (he died in 1973). He had no other genre credits to speak of, save for his vocal talents in Gerry and Sylvia Anderson's two marionette features, *Thunderbirds Are Go* (1966) and *Thunderbirds 6* (1968). Nakamum and Jerry Ito also appeared in *Mothra* (1961), but the rest of the cast is undistinguished.

Writer–co-director–producer George Breakston was a child actor, appearing in such films as *It Happened One Night* and *Great Expectations* (both 1934; he played Pip in the latter) and later as a regular in M-G-M "Andy Hardy" series. He turned to directing and producing in the late forties, making films in all parts of the world, including Africa and his native France. *The Manster* is apparently his only genre film.

Reviews of the picture, perhaps not surprisingly, were not good. "In every way a thorough waste of effort" complained the *Monthly Film Bulletin*, while *The Motion Picture Guide* gave the film a zero rating. Even Bill Warren didn't think much of the film. He acknowledged the eye-on-the-shoulder scene, but overall found the picture "very bad."

Mothra *(1961)*

A fairy tale–monster movie intended for family audiences in its native Japan, *Mothra* is one of that country's best fantastic films. Toho, the studio that produced the film, was at the peak of its creative powers in 1961. The special effects are detailed and very imaginative, the live action characters are interesting and involving, and the overall production has a level of class rarely accorded *kaiju eiga* productions.

After their ship strikes a reef during a typhoon, four sailors are picked up from Beiru Island, used during the atomic bomb tests. The men should have radiation poisoning but don't. They claim berries provided by natives saved their lives. News of natives living on an island previously thought dead and deserted causes an uproar. An expedition is launched by suspicious Rolisican (i.e., American) businessman Clark Nelson (Jerry Ito). He allows an international group of scientists to tag along, including Dr. Chujo (Hiroshi Koizumi) and Dr. Haradawa (Ken Uehara). A determined but friendly reporter, Tsinchan (Frankie Sakai), also known as "Bulldog," sneaks aboard. The expedition is shocked to discover that a portion of the island is lush with vegetation. Chujo, wandering off on his own, finds an ancient inscription on a stone wall, and is caught in a "vampire plant." Before lapsing into unconsciousness, he sees two tiny Japanese-cum-Polynesian women (Emi and Yumi Ito), each about six inches in height, about to rescue him. Chujo recovers, and everyone goes looking for the girls. They find the friendly twins in some shrubbery. The miniature young women smile at the men, not seeming frightened in the slightest. At least, that is, until Nelson grabs the girls—he wants to take them back to Japan. Full-size natives appear, and Nelson is forced to let the girls go. An armed Nelson sneaks back to the island, however, kills several natives and kidnaps the girls. One of the islanders, mortally wounded by Nelson's bullets, makes his way to a shrine, crying "Mothra!" as he dies. There's a small landslide, which unearths a tremendous egg. Greedy Nelson debuts "The Secret Fairies Show," a theatrical presentation featuring the twin fairies, who ride a tiny coach over the audience's heads and sing a native song about Mothra. Bulldog, news photographer Michi (Kyoko Kagawa) and Chujo are outraged at Nelson's exploitation of the girls. They plead with him to return the girls to their island, but he flatly refuses, citing the tremendous success of his show and his financial investment in it.

Back at the island, the giant egg hatches, and Mothra, a gigantic caterpillar, appears. Chujo, Michi and Bulldog manage to see the girls, who to everyone's surprise can speak English (and simultaneously!). They tell their friends not to worry, for Mothra will come and get them. The girls explain they're telepathic, and that Mothra will know where they are. Their only concern is that innocent people in Mothra's path will get hurt. Soon, that's just what happens. Mothra's determination to reach the girls has the creature heading straight for Tokyo, leading the monster to plow through passenger liners, dams and buildings along the way. Despite the destruction, Nelson steadfastly refuses to give up the twins, even after the Rolisican government, which initially supported Nelson, orders him to return the girls. The Japanese military search for Nelson, but in the confusion of Mothra's appearance, Nelson manages to escape undetected aboard a jet bound for Rolisica. Mothra makes her way to Tokyo Tower, where she builds a tremendous cocoon. Despite the Rolisican government's help in providing the Japanese defense forces with a power "maser," which sets the cocoon afire, Mothra survives, emerging as a giant moth. Airborne, the flying monster heads straight for Rolisica. Bulldog, Chujo and Michi take the next plane out of the country to search for Nelson, who by now has made his way to a Western-style ranch, complete with livestock. Mothra reaches "Newkirk City," an amalgam of New York, San Francisco and Los Angeles, and causes incredible devastation. (Toho may have sent a second unit crew to the states for a few shots.) An angry mob of Rolisicans spots Nelson and attacks him (this segment was clearly shot in Japan). When he pulls a gun and begins firing, police officers shoot him dead. Bulldog, Chujo and Michi take the girls to the airport, where Chujo orders local authorities to paint the runway with the giant Mothra symbol he had seen on the temple wall back at the island. He then orders all churches to ring their bells to attract Mothra. The giant creature lands at the airport. The twins give our heroes warm thanks, climb aboard Mothra and fly away. The twins sing a song as they are reunited with their people.

Mothra, or *Mosura* as the picture was known in Japan, was intended for general audiences in that country. The picture was made at the height of the *kaiju eiga* genre's popularity, while director Ishiro Honda, special effects director Eiji Tsuburaya and screenwriter Shinichi Sekizawa were at their most inventive. Not surprisingly, Mothra was largely dismissed in this country as just another monster movie, critics overlooking the film's many other charms. Howard Thompson, reviewing the picture (on a double bill with *The Three Stooges in Orbit*) for the *New York Times*, seemed to like the picture. "For several seasons now the Tokyo studios have been turning out this kind of diversion with some kind of monstrosity terrorizing the country and rattling the screen in an overpowering blend of scenic effects, ranging from obvious to striking. This one is different, if not exactly superior... Although the direction, acting and dialogue are clumsy and absurd... [It] smites the eye with some genuinely artistic panoramas and decor designs.... Several of the special effects shots are brilliant." Thompson also liked the climax: "As touchingly bizarre ... as we've seen in years." But the review by *Variety*'s "Tube" was much more typical. "A ludicrously-written, haphazardly executed monster movie...too awkward in dramatic construction and crude in histrionic style...even cinemutation buffs should wince at this one." The review concludes with the all-telling wrap, "A pretty embarrassing effort on the part of the Toho people to duplicate a Western screen staple." What Tube, like so many other critics in this country failed to understand is that *Mothra* isn't trying to duplicate Western monster movies. As Bill Warren so rightly points out in his review of the picture (in *Keep Watching the Skies!* volume 2), and as I have stressed throughout the book, Japanese and American moviegoers watch films in different ways. In Japan, the so-called realism of its story and special effects mattered little, so long as the story was one worth telling and the special effects work was visually appealing. As Warren acknowledges, *Mothra* is pretty preposterous, but if one tries to look at films like these with acultural eyes one can get a lot more out of them. And by 1961, Toho had mastered the *kaiju eiga* genre.

Pictures like *Mothra* are full of absurdities—tiny twins, giant moths, etc.— but no more so than many popular American films. I had the good fortune to watch these pictures with the innocence of childhood. I never believed at any time that what I was seeing was actually happening, but when the storytellers said, "Here's our premise," I was happy to accept their launching point, however absurd it might be in the real world. If I wanted the real world, I'd watch a Fredrick Wiseman movie. I was a kid, and I wanted films like *Mothra*. One of the things that makes *Mothra* work so well is that it is a story centered around people. Bulldog, Michi and Chujo are all interesting, right from the beginning when Bulldog and Michi sneak into Dr. Haradawa's lab looking for a scoop. Their friendliness to the twins is also appealing, as is Bulldog's courage when he rescues a baby trapped on a bridge about to be destroyed in a Mothra-created flash flood.

Bulldog was played by Frankie Sakai, a popular Japanese comedian who made a few genre films in the early 1960s. Part Lou Costello, part Hildy Johnson, Sakai's Bulldog is an appealing character, determined but never buffoonish. For more on Sakai, please refer to the entry on *The Last War* (1961).

Conversely, Jerry Ito's Clark Nelson is appropriately slimy and sinister. As Warren also notes, the character is a thinly disguised "ugly American" (the actor has always reminded me of "Wild, Wild West" star Ross Martin) though clearly not a symbolic representation. The son of artist Kisaku Ito and an American model, Ito apparently couldn't speak Japanese. In an interview with Bin Uehara, Honda said Ito's Japanese was "truly terrible. He can read a bit, but he really can't speak it." Nonetheless, Honda regarded the actor as "a very bright man." Ito also appeared as the police superintendent in the English-language production *The Manster* (also 1961).

This was Ken Uehara's first *kaiju eiga* production for Toho. Uehara, born 1909, had starred in the 1949 production of *The Ghost of Yotsuya*, and would also star in *Gorath* (1962) and *Atragon* (1963). Like Takashi Shimura, Uehara displays a quiet intelligence and authority, always bringing an air of respectability to the often outlandish storylines. The story's simplicity also works in the picture's favor. *Mothra* isn't out to cause massive destruction; it just wants to rescue the fairies and take them back home. As Warren points out in his *Mothra* entry, giant monsters generally have one of two motivations, to escape or eat as many people as possible. That *Mothra* is able to put a spin (a wild spin at that) on a very tired genre is to its credit. The twin fairies, Mothra's priestesses, are among the studio's finest creations. Played by the Peanuts (Emi and Yumi Ito), a pair of popular singers who had made their recording debut just two years earlier (they recorded covers of many American songs as well), the fairies are delightful characters. They sing attractive numbers, have infectious smiles and never lose hope that Mothra will come and rescue them. No wonder the Secret Fairies Show is so popular. The film isn't perfect. There's a subplot involving Hiroshi Koizumi's younger brother, who tries to rescue the fairies but is caught by Nelson's guards. This scene was probably designed to appeal to younger moviegoers but adds little to the film.

The special effects are often spectacular. The miniature sets the caterpillar Mothra plows through appear to have been built on a slightly larger scale than in most of Toho's monster movies and thus tend to have more detailing. There are several impressive bird's-eye-view shots, once when jets attack the creature at sea and later as it makes its way across the countryside. Later, when Mothra is attacking the impressive-looking Newkirk City, its huge flapping wings create a tremendous wind storm (a la *Rodan*) sending dozens of automobiles flying about the downtown district. While the effects work here is not realistic in the American sense, it is a vivid and impressive sequence. There is also a lot of military hardware—tanks, the impressive maser vehicles used against the cocoon, etc.—which are photographed almost entirely in miniature. Like the rest of the film, they're photographed with an amount of ingenuity and energy completely absent from Toho's seventies films. The twin fairies were generally photographed against enlarged sets (several of which, such as the one used in the jungle sequence, are fairly elaborate) and matted into the main action. Toho's matte work involving live actors rarely is very good, though certainly better than, say, producer Bert I. Gordon's films from the same period (*Attack of the Puppet People*, *The Magic Sword*, etc.). Six-inch models of the girls were used for several quick shots and are effective given their conservative use.

Mothra was picked up by Columbia in the United States, and the dubbing is one of the more successful uses of this format. The American distributors also wisely left the film more or less intact. As it was thirty years ago, *Mothra* is pretty much lumped together with its other cousins at Toho: *Godzilla*, *Rodan* et al. However, those able to watch the picture with an open, acultural mind may be surprised at the generally high quality of one of the genre's finest entries.

Gorath *(1962)*

Although its title suggests a fire-breathing monster, *Gorath* is actually a runaway star on a collision course with Earth. This was Japan's *When Worlds Collide* (1951), and like George Pal's mini-masterpiece, *Gorath* works wonders with what was certainly an even punier budget and somehow manages to surpass the earlier film's visuals.

In the closing months of 1979 (according to the ominous voice of Paul Frees), the Spaceship J-X *Hawk*, commanded by Captain Sonoda (Jun Tazaki), is ordered to investigate a runaway star, Gorath, which is heading for our solar system. The star is six thousand times the mass of the Earth, and because it is only half the Earth's size, the *Hawk*'s crew don't spot the celestial body until it is caught in its gravitational pull. The ship's engines are fired in an effort to break free, but it is too late, with the *Hawk* drawn ever closer, its crew doomed (at the same time, a British ship, the *Intrepid*, also falls victim to Gorath). Sonoda orders his men to be brave and to relay as much data back to the Earth as possible before they are killed ("We have a job to do."), for their sacrifice just may save the Earth. The data is sent, and the ship crashes into Gorath with a terrific explosion. Back on Earth, space cadet Tatsuo Kanai (Akira Kubo) walks around dressed as a robot. He teases Ari (Kumi Mizuno), whom he loves, but she is already engaged to Dr. Manabe (Hiroo Kirino), a member of the doomed *Hawk*. Ari and her girlfriend, Kiyo Sonoda (Yumi Shirakawa), the captain's daughter, return to the latter's house, where they're met by news of the *Hawk*'s destruction. Data sent by the *Hawk* is grim. Gorath is on a collision course with Earth. Dr. Konno (Ken Uehara) and Dr. Tazawa (Ryo Ikebe) consult Kiyo's grandfather, Kesuke Sonoda (Takashi Shimura), and the three come up with a two-part plan: they will try to destroy Gorath before it reaches the Earth, and if that fails, they will fire huge land jets from the South Pole, which will hurl the Earth safely out of Gorath's path. The scientists travel to the United Nations, proposing a controlled 66 billion megaton blast from 88 different sites in Antarctica. At first, the countries of the world are reluctant because of the expense and requisite manpower. The scientists are also surprised to see most of the population either fatalistic or passive about Gorath's approach. Everyone comes to their senses, however, and the UN orders the completion of the *Hawk*'s twin ship, the *Eagle*, and the construction of the firing installation at the South Pole, despite the great expense.

Meanwhile, Tetsuo visits Ari before his ship's departure. He chastises her for wallowing in her fiancé's death, especially since she has always loved Tetsuo anyway. He rather oafishly throws Ari's picture of Dr. Manabe out her apartment window and leaves. Work on the incredible land-jet complex in Antarctica continues. The armies of the world are disbanded to deliver the required manpower, and workers experience delays from tough bedrock and volcanic activity. Meanwhile, the *Eagle* discovers that because of the star's intense gravitational pull and its ability to assimilate anything in its path (we see it suck up the rings of nearby Saturn), Gorath has increased its mass to 6,100 times that of the Earth. Tetsuo is sent out in a mini rocket to collect data, and his ship is nearly destroyed by all the miscellaneous space rocks and other material caught in Gorath's intense field. The experience is so traumatic, Tetsuo goes into amnesic shock, and it soon becomes clear that Gorath cannot be destroyed. The rockets at the South Pole are fired, and the Earth slowly moves out of orbit. The *Hawk* returns to Earth, and Tetsuo is taken to Kesuke Sonoda's home, where Kiyo and Ari are also staying as Gorath passes overhead. Although the Earth escapes colliding with the runaway star, Gorath passes close enough to cause huge tidal waves, which completely submerge Tokyo. The moon does not escape Gorath's gravity field and is absorbed. Gorath's flyby is not entirely destructive, however. It triggers Tetsuo's memory, and, after all, forced the nations of the Earth to set aside their differences and work together. And together they promise to return the planet to its former orbit and rebuild what was lost in its close brush with Gorath.

Like Toho's *Battle in Outer Space* (1959) and Daiei's *Warning from Space* (1956), which *Gorath* in many ways resembles, this is a story of epic proportions, and its optimistic telling after the studio's excellent though relentlessly downbeat *The Last War* (1961) is very appealing. As this book went to press, *Gorath* was available only on video cassettes mastered from severely battered 16mm television prints. Made at the height of Toho's special effects era, *Gorath* is no less an epic than *Mothra* (1961) or *Battle in Outer Space*, and yet I suspect the picture is generally dismissed in this country partly because of the poor condition of all legally available prints.

Takeshi Kimura's screenplay, from former air force pilot Jojiro Okami's story (Toho also adapted *The Mysterians*, *Battle in Outer Space* and *Dagora, the Space Monster* from his stories) has a number of interesting elements. First there is the excellent sequence in which Jun Tazaki's crew learn they are doomed yet work furiously to transmit data back to Earth before they are killed. This understated vignette is full of tension and immediately puts the epic tale in human terms. I also liked how, at first, the general public is apathetic about Gorath's appearance in deep space, instead of eliciting the kind of panicked response one usually associates with Japanese special effects films. Another interesting aspect is that Gorath itself isn't destroyed — the Earth can only get out of its way. An annoying electronic whine, added during the Americanization, is heard whenever Gorath appears, but the star's unstoppability is otherwise expertly dramatized.

Eiji Tsuburaya's effects are generally quite good. There's a terrific daytime shot of Tokyo underwater after Gorath has passed, and much of the actual tidal wave footage is impressive (although once again, the Americanization works against the original picture: an optically printed fog was added, apparently an attempt to obscure the miniature's origins). The special effects in George Pal's *When Worlds Collide* were centered around the building, launch and flight of a getaway rocket, and featured very little in the way of scenes of destruction. *Gorath*'s plentiful effects are on par with or better than those found in the American film. As usual, Tsuburaya's spacecraft are imaginatively designed, as are the miniature construction sites at the South Pole.

At the insistence of producer Tomoyuki Tanaka, the original Japanese version of the film featured a giant monster, this time a tremendous walrus. In the original cut of the picture, the beast (known as Magma in Japan) is unearthed when heat from the South Pole jets loosen some rock formations, releasing the prehistoric creature (played by Haruo Nakajima; he also played Godzilla through 1972's *Godzilla on Monster Island*) from his icy tomb. The walrus attacks one of the Antarctic bases, threatening the entire operation. Ryo Ikebe, Takashi Shimura and Ken Uehara fly to the site aboard a jet-powered hovercraft (which looks a lot like the *AAB Gamma* seen in Shochiku's 1967 film, *The X from Outer Space*). They shoot and kill the creature with a laser beam. The monster's appearance lasted but a few minutes, though the creature was prominently featured in the original film's advertising and was undoubtedly added to insure its box office success. According to Hideyo Tsuburaya's excellent article on the film in *The Japanese Fantasy Film Journal* (#15), Brenco Pictures, the film's U.S. distributor, decided to eliminate the creature after preview audiences laughed at the buck-toothed mammal (sources at Brenco nicknamed the critter Wally the Walrus). The monster was simply removed, and the scenes with the hovercraft shooting at nothing in particular make little sense (the walrus' fin can be glimpsed crashing through a building). Magma's nonappearance in U.S. prints is no great loss, however. I've seen the monster sequence, and it's most unimpressive, with Magma looking stiff and poorly detailed, unusual for Tsuburaya's work from this period. (Perhaps less time was accorded its creation due to the brevity of its screentime.)

Most of Toho's familiar stock company of *kaiju eiga* performers appear in *Gorath*. Although Akira Kubo had appeared in Kurosawa's *Throne of Blood* (1957), it was his role here and in other Toho monster movies for which he is best known in the United States. Born in 1936, Kubo made his screen debut at age 12, in *Kaneno naru Oka* (1948). As an adult, he was often cast in confident, even boastful roles. Kubo next starred in *Attack of the Mushroom People* (1963), followed by lighter roles in *Monster Zero* (1965), *Son of Godzilla* (1967), *Destroy All Monsters* (1968) and *Yog: Monster from Space* (1970), which appears to be his last genre film to date. Fans of the animated series "Speed Racer" tend to spot Kubo right away—he was usually dubbed by Jack Grimes, the same actor who voiced the popular cartoon show's title character.

Kumi Mizuno appears as Kubo's love interest. Mizuno was one of Toho's most interesting performers, chiefly because she'd tend to play assertive yet feminine roles rarely depicted in these kinds of films. Mizuno projected intelligence as well as sex appeal (in *Gorath*, she's seen taking a bubble bath—hubba hubba!). In films as early as 1961, the actress also appeared in *Attack of the Mushroom People* (1963), followed by featured roles in *The Lost World of Sinbad* (1963), *Frankenstein Conquers the World* and *Monster Zero* (both 1965), *Ebirah, Horror of the Deep* and *War of the Gargantuas* (both 1966), and *Whirlwind* (1968). She also appeared with her *Frankenstein* and *Monster Zero* co-star, Nick Adams, in *The Killing Bottle* (1966)—which remains unreleased in the United States—and Woody Allen's comically redubbed *What's Up, Tiger Lily?* When David Milner asked director Honda which actors he especially enjoyed working with, Honda said simply, "The best actress was Kumi Mizuno. She was very genuine. Once she was involved with a film, she would just step right into her role."

Gorath was released by Brenco on a double bill with *The Human Vapor*. The company altered much of the picture, deleting bits (such as the Hawk's crew cry of "Banzai!" as it crashes into the sun), and rearranging others (in the original version, for example, the moon crashes into Gorath at the very end of the film). Most annoying is the insufficient number of voice actors brought in to dub the film: only four performers were used. Once again, Paul Frees is asked to dub approximately every third voice. And as Tsuburaya points out in his *Gorath* retrospective, "Add a defect in the (John) Lucas script which rarely bestows names upon any of the screen characters, and the sum is a dismal lack of definition."

Variety's "Whit" praised the production. "Japanese producers in the past have displayed great ingenuity along this line of scientific speculation... [The] special effects are particularly interesting, but the story itself is possibly too scientific for popular reception... Names of Japanese thesps are unknown in this country but turn in very credible performances, particularly Ryo Ikebe. Particular credit goes to Eiji Tsuburaya for his spectacular effects, and [Ishiro] Honda's direction captures the spirit of Takeshi Kimura's screenplay." Phil Hardy's *Science Fiction* features a curious capsule review and synopsis. "Gorath is generated by the organic material picked up by a spaceship as it moved through the monster's body," and so forth. Huh? At least he gave the film a positive review. *JFFJ*'s Greg Shoemaker said the film was "notable for its intelligent approach to space and the human lives affected... [the] special effects are numerous and superb."

King Kong vs. Godzilla *(1962/1963)*

It was the tremendous success of *King Kong vs. Godzilla* (*KingKong tai Gojira*), seen by more Japanese moviegoers than any other Godzilla film before or since, that established the Big G as a genuine movie star, with enough box office draw to warrant a film series of his own. It had been seven years since Godzilla had been buried under a mountain of ice (in *Gigantis, the Fire Monster*), but after the tremendous success of this film, Toho knew they had a star. The film's popularity in Japan is all the more surprising considering it had its origins in the United States and that Godzilla's participation in the project came late in the game, almost as an afterthought.

American special effects genius Willis O'Brien ("Obie" to his friends), an undisputed master of stop-motion animation, had brought the original King Kong to life in RKO's 1933 classic. It was one of the highest-grossing films of the 1930s, and its reissue in 1952 helped inspire an entire sub-genre of giant monster films, this time with sci-fi themes, beginning with *The Beast from 20,000 Fathoms* (1953). *Fathoms*, as mentioned earlier, inspired the original Godzilla film. Despite *King Kong*'s tremendous success, Hollywood rarely turned to O'Brien's limitless filmmaking ideas. He was rushed into a quickie sequel, *Son of Kong* (also 1933), a delightful film in its own way, but clearly made without the precision and fine tuning of its predecessor. O'Brien's *Mighty*

Joe Young (1949) featured another giant gorilla brought to a civilization with disastrous results. Yet despite the picture's incredible charm, its grosses were not as high as had been hoped, and plans for a sequel, *Tarzan Meets Mighty Joe Young*, were dropped. O'Brien continued to work in the industry, but after *Mighty Joe Young*, his elaborate special effects extravaganzas never came to fruition, at least not during his lifetime (he died in 1963). Shortly before his death, O'Brien developed a story called *King Kong vs. Frankenstein* (later changed to *King Kong vs. the Ginko*). The tongue-in-cheek tale had showman Carl Denham (played by Robert Armstrong in the RKO films) bringing Kong to San Francisco to face a monster created by the grandson of Dr. Frankenstein, which he built using parts of rhinos, elephants, and other African animals. The climax was set atop the Golden Gate Bridge, where the monsters grappled until both fell to their deaths in the bay. According to Donald Glut's *Classic Movie Monsters*, O'Brien took the project to producer John Beck, who promptly removed Obie from the project and had George Worthing Yates (*Them!* and *Earth vs. The Flying Saucers*) write a new screenplay.

Now called *King Kong vs. Prometheus*, Yates' story eliminated the Denham character and made the Frankenstein monster character more intelligent. However, Beck couldn't get financing for the film in the United States and so took it to Toho in Japan. They liked the basic idea, but threw out almost all of O'Brien's and Yates' concepts, and changed Prometheus to Godzilla. Beck, RKO, and Universal-International's involvement with the film's financing and production in Japan was probably minimal. Michael Hayes suggests Beck approached RKO (for use of the Kong character), and they referred him to Toho (RKO having recently acquired *The Mysterians* would support this), and Toho likely agreed to produce the film in exchange for the Far East rights to it. It then stands to reason that RKO and Beck approached Universal to produce the English-language version, with all three parties claiming a percentage of the film's profits. In any event, *King Kong vs. Godzilla* was drastically altered for release in the United States, but more on that later. First, our story...

United Nations television anchor Eric Carter reads the day's news. A United States Navy submarine, sailing north of Japan, encounters an iceberg with unusually high levels of radiation. The sub is attacked by some strange force, and the doomed crew send off a mayday signal and release a colored dye in the water. A rescue helicopter finds the dye near an iceberg. Suddenly, out of a mountain of ice, the pilots spot Godzilla (a good effects shot here) bursting free from his icy tomb. Concurrently, a pharmaceutical company sponsoring a poorly rated television show is looking for a new angle to draw viewers. They hear of a mysterious creature on remote Farou Island, located in the South Pacific several thousand miles east of New Guinea. The company's president, Mr. Tako (Ichiro Arishima), orders Sakurai (Tadao Takashima) and Kinsaburo (Yu Fujiki) to find the creature and bring him back for the program. Before he leaves, Sakurai has dinner with his sister, Fumiko (Mie Hama), and her boyfriend, Kazuo (Kenji Sahara). Kazuo shows off his latest invention, an indestructible thread-like wire. As reported by the United Nations news, Godzilla attacks a U.S. military base, annihilating the small forces there. Eric Carter introduces scientific "expert" Dr. Arnold Johnson (Harry Holcombe). Johnson displays a children's book, *Dinosaurs and Other Prehistoric Animals*, to explain Godzilla's origins. He says that Godzilla is a cross between a *Tyrannosaurus Rex* and a *stegosaurus* (hence the dorsal fins). Sakurai and Kinsaburo arrive at Farou Island, where they are met by natives. Sakurai eases their suspicions by dispensing free cigarettes and radios. Johnson predicts Godzilla will head for Japan "like a salmon returning to the waters in which he was born." Godzilla thinks he's heading home, Johnson says. The native village on Farou Island is attacked by a massive octopus. Just then, a giant gorilla (grown, we are told, to its huge proportions by eating strange berries native to the island), King Kong to you and me, appears. He kills the monster then eats some more berries which make him sleepy. Sakurai has the ape tied to an immense raft wired with dynamite. The raft is towed by a ship heading back to Tokyo. Mr. Tako arrives to inspect his new television star. Back at the UN, Dr. Johnson now predicts Kong and Godzilla will fight one another as they are "instinctive rivals." He explains that Godzilla's brain is tiny and puzzled by the changes that have taken place over the millions of years he was in hibernation. (U-I's release disregards the two earlier Godzilla films. However, the Japanese version's Godzilla is clearly the same one last seen in *Gigantis, the Fire Monster*.) Godzilla uses brute force alone, Johnson says, while Kong is a "thinking monster." Fumiko is told that Kazuo's plane has crashed near Hokkaido, and she catches the next train out. Kazuo arrives home, having actually missed his plane. He learns of Fumiko's departure and races to save her from Godzilla, now approaching the region. Godzilla stomps toward the speeding train. The passengers evacuate, and Fumiko is reunited with Kazuo. Kong, meanwhile, wakes up while tied to the raft. Tako sets off the explosives aboard the raft, but Kong survives and swims toward Tokyo. Kong and Godzilla meet outside the city. They throw a few boulders at one another before Godzilla gives Kong a taste of his fiery breath. The radioactive spray singes Kong's fur. He scratches his head and walks away. The army, led by General Shinzo (Jun Tazaki) set a trap for Godzilla, using a fence of ignited gasoline and a deep pit loaded with explosive charges. It fails to stop the tremendous lizard. Fumiko boards another train as Tokyo's residents flee. This time Kong gets to pull the train off its tracks and spots Fumiko hanging on for dear life. Kong is attracted to the woman and, girl-in-hand, climbs the Diet Building just as RKO's Kong had scaled the Empire State Building. Sakurai convinces the army to fire explosives filled with the berry substance, thus putting Kong to sleep. It works, and Fumiko and Kazuo are reunited. The young inventor's indestructible wire is used to haul Kong to Mount Fuji, near Godzilla's position, where the military hopes the two beasts will destroy one another. Godzilla stomach-kicks Kong, the latter appearing down for the count. A jolt of lightning revives Kong (presumably a bit of business left over from the Frankenstein/Ginko script), who begins punching Godzilla with his electrically charged fists. The battling titans approach Atami Castle, destroying the newly built tourist attraction. The monsters apparently trigger an earthquake (stock footage from *The Mysterians*), sending the monsters falling into the sea. Godzilla never resurfaces, and Kong calmly swims back to Farou Island. Back to Eric Carter, who says, "Strangely enough, we wish him luck [Why?] on his long, long journey home."

A popular though completely false story persists alleging that two endings were shot: In the U.S. version Kong wins, while in Japanese theaters, Godzilla appears victorious. While two endings were never filmed, the U.S. and original Japanese versions differ sharply in other areas. In Japan, *King Kong vs. Godzilla* was intended as light-hearted, family entertainment, and the picture succeeds quite well on this level. The film's spoof of commercialism hits the mark, with its funniest moment having Sakurai gleefully dispensing the cigarettes to the curious natives, including a young boy. A smile in his heart, Sakurai exclaims, "It's all right, they're all smoking!" The performers' broad gesturing is obvious, but fun. Godzilla is clearly the villain of the piece, but his scenes are much less grim and sober than in the fifties films. Kong's scenes, meanwhile, are broadly played and were always intended to be comical.

For the U.S. version, whole sequences were eliminated, and most of Akira Ifukube's wonderful score was needlessly replaced by woefully obvious stock music from Universal-International's library (the theme from *Creature from the Black Lagoon* is heard several times, and some of the musical cues date back to the early forties). The footage of Michael Keith, Harry Holcombe and James Yagi was filmed in the United States and never part of the Japanese cut, while the scenes aboard the submarine and the helicopter were filmed at Toho studios and part of the Japanese cut. In Japan, these latter scenes were shown in English with Japanese subtitles. However, they were still redubbed for the U.S. version because of the limited acting talents of the English-language performers. The dubbing work is often sloppy. One scene has Kinsaburo wearing a headset and carrying a tape recorder, holding out a microphone to record Kong's rampage. The dubbing, however, has him referring to his microphone as a light meter. Much of the action and character development was replaced by the wholly unnecessary UN television stuff, with Michael Keith and Harry Holcombe pretending to be on TV. They're completely detached from the story-at-large, and are as entertaining as the eleven o'clock news. Holcombe's theories on the monster's appearance are laughable, adding nothing, and the film stops dead whenever he and Keith appear, which is far too often. What's left of the Japanese footage is a mixed bag, but not an unfavorable one. Many complaints are levied at the Kong suit, which is indeed shockingly shabby and unconvincing. The corpse-like face is completely immobile (an only slightly more articulate puppet was intercut with the man-sized suit), and the extra-long arms, seen in some shots, are stiff and outrageously phoney. The gorilla skins used in the cheapest American films look many times better than the one used here. Why Toho's staff would come up so short here is a mystery, especially in light of their many other fine creations during this period. In any event, they didn't do much better when the character was more or less revived in *King Kong Escapes* (1967). Godzilla was redesigned, looking much more stout below the waist, but tiny above the shoulders. Akira Watanabe's suit does look more reptilian than those used in any of the sixties films.

The special effects are also below par, given the elaborate and highly inventive work done on *Mothra* the year before. The matte work is especially bad, with shadows, thick black lines and faded images constantly spoiling the effect. (This is partly due to bad printing, however. Japanese prints look much better.) A real (though obviously smaller) octopus was used for most of the scenes of the attack on the native village, and a crude, stop-motion tentacle was built for a couple of shots where it grabs a native. When Kong attacks the mollusk, Tsuburaya either built a rubber replacement or quite possibly wrapped the dead octopus in cellophane; at least that's what it looks like. Stop motion was also used for the brief shot where Godzilla stomach-kicks Kong. The final fight is well staged, though critics rightly suggest the bout looks more like a wrestling match than giant monsters in mortal combat. The model work is less extensive than that in *Mothra*, with some effects (the ship hauling Kong, the Atami Castle) working better than others. This was the first Godzilla film in Tohoscope and color (and stereo, though U.S. audiences heard it in mono), though after such fine entries as *Battle in Outer Space*, *Mothra* and *Gorath*, *Godzilla*'s widescreen debut must be considered a disappointment.

The picture boasts a good cast, including Kenji Sahara and Mie Hama. Hama (born in 1942) also starred in *King Kong Escapes* and in the James Bond film *You Only Live Twice* (1967). According to S. J. Rubin's *The Complete James Bond Encyclopedia*, Hama remains "a major media star in her native Japan—a kind of Japanese Jane Pauley." This was Tadao Takashima's first *kaiju eiga* production. In films as early as 1961's *Eternity of Love* (1961), Takashima also starred in *Atragon* (1963), *Frankenstein Conquers the World* (1965) and *Son of Godzilla* (1967). His son, Masanobu, is also an actor and played Major Kuroki in *Godzilla vs. Biollante* (1989). Akihiko Hirata, Dr. Serizawa in *Godzilla*, turns up as a government official, and Jun Tazaki appears as a general. The late Ichiro Arishima, seen in Toho's *My Friend Death* (1960), steals several scenes as the flustered Mr. Tako. Arishima was considered one of Japan's great comic performers, though some of his charm and several of his best scenes were cut or lost in the translation.

Eugene Archer's review for the *New York Times*, besides giving away the ending, had this to say: "Viewers who attend this ridiculous melodrama ... should know exactly what to expect and get what they deserve.... The one mild surprise in this cheap reprise of earlier Hollywood and Japanese horror films is the ineptitude of its fakery. When the pair of prehistoric monsters finally get together for the battle royal, the effect is nothing more than a couple of dressed up stuntmen throwing cardboard rocks at each other." *Variety*'s "Tube" disagreed. "The miniature work of the Japanese artisans... is first-rate... The battle that ensues could only be described by Don Dunphy. For the record, let it be noted that poor Kong takes one helluva beating until he gets what for him is the equivalent of Popeye's spinach. Onward and upward the arts." *Psychotronic* was sympathetic: "The man-in-the-suit Kong outraged fans of the original, but after the '76 remake it didn't seem so bad." *The Motion Picture Guide*'s review, which included several big errors, gave the film a *½ rating. Phil Hardy's *Science Fiction*, forever reading way too much into the screenplays, called the film "A fascinating pop-culture representation of U.S./Japanese relations." A sequel, minus Kong, *Godzilla vs. the Thing*, followed in 1964.

Atragon *(1963)*

One of Toho's best sci-fi features, *Atragon* is centered around characters, not special effects. By 1963, the studio was beginning to rely more and more on Eiji Tsuburaya's elaborate miniatures and other optical illusions to carry the increasingly sketchy storylines. *Atragon* was different. In fact, while the film does have several impressive effects sequences, overall the effects here are mildly disappointing. It is *Atragon*'s intriguing characters that help make it the excellent sci-fi spectacle it is.

Commercial photographer Susumu Hatanaka (Tadao Takashima), and his assistant, Yoshito Nishibe (Yu Fujiki), are shooting a layout near Tokyo Bay one evening (with a young woman wearing a rather daring bikini), when they witness an automobile containing both a kidnapper and his intended victim plunge into the water. The following morning, the two men spot a beautiful young woman they think would make a perfect model for their next shoot. She is Makoto Shinguji (Yoko Fujiyama), whose father commanded a submarine force which vanished at the end of World War II. She was raised from that time by shipping company president and former Admiral Kosumi (Ken Uehara). Makoto and her guardian are nearly abducted themselves, but Yoshito and Susumu intervene. The kidnapper (Akihiko Hirata) identifies himself as "Agent Number 23" of the Mu Empire before escaping into the sea. Soon thereafter, Kosumi receives a mysterious package, which contains film of the Mu Empire. An Atlantis-like continent which sank to the bottom of the Pacific Ocean two thousand years ago, the Mu Empire now stands ready to reclaim its domination over the surface world. Their sole opposition, we learn, is Captain Shinguji, who is not only still alive but has built a fantastic undersea battleship (the film's title in Japan transliterates as "Undersea Battleship"). The Mu Empire warns that unless Shinguji is stopped, the world will be punished for his actions.

A series of disasters begins throughout the world, and everyone speculates Shinguji's whereabouts. Admiral Kosumi reveals that Captain Shinguji had actually deserted at the end of the war. Meanwhile, a man whom everyone believes is a Mu agent is arrested. The man turns out to be one of Captain Shinguji's soldiers, sent to guard the captain's daughter. The man (Yoshibumi Tajima) agrees to take Makoto, Admiral Kosumi, the photographers and a journalist (Kenji Sahara) to the captain. The group find Captain Shinguji (Jun Tazaki) and his men on an island base and marvel at his many technical accomplishments. Captain Shinguji apologizes to Kosumi, formerly his superior, for deserting at the end of the war. However, when Kosumi asks the captain to launch his super submarine against the Mus, he is outraged: he wants to use the battleship to restore Japan's honor. So consumed by his determination to renew his country's pride, Shinguji is oblivious to its imminent destruction. There is a trial run for the ship, called *Atragon*. Kosumi, the photographers and the others are amazed by the ship's many wonders: it can bore through the earth, fly through the air like a jet, and freeze objects with its "Zero Cannon." That evening, Makoto speaks to her father, who is surprisingly cold to her, as he continues to wallow in his shame. When her father remains adamant against using *Atragon* to stop the Mus, she rejects him. The journalist turns out to be a Mu agent (no surprise there) and explodes a bomb aboard the *Atragon*, crippling the ship. He also kidnaps Makoto and Susumu, taking them back to Mu, and presents them before the beautiful empress (Tetsuko Kobayashi). The empress orders that the pair be sacrificed to the Mus' god, an undersea dragon called Manda (which means "ten- thousand-meter snake" in Japanese). Meanwhile, Captain Shinguji's men manage to repair the *Atragon* and remove the debris blocking the vessel's path. The captain now realizes the errors of his fierce nationalism, vowing to defend the world with his fantastic submarine. The *Atragon* arrives in Tokyo moments after a Mu submarine has devastated the harbor and most of the city with its powerful rays. Shinguji's ship pursues the Mu sub, which leads it straight to the underwater Mu Empire. *Atragon* drills through the Mu city's outer walls and moves straight through to their power center. Using the Zero Cannon, *Atragon* freezes the Mu generators. Susumu and Matoko escape, taking the empress as a hostage, and make it back to the captain's ship. The Mus launch a last-ditch offensive by unleashing Manda, who briefly grapples with the ship before it too is frozen. Explosive charges planted by Shinguji's strike force result in the final destruction of the Mu Empire in a massive explosion. Captain Shinguji is reunited with his daughter and allows the desperate empress to dive overboard into the sea, so that she may die with her people.

I didn't much care for *Atragon* as a kid, partly because the film's monster, Manda, had so little screen time. Like many a youngster, I expected a monster movie, only here the monster doesn't even show up until the film is nearly over. More recently, however, I had the opportunity to see the original Japanese cut of the picture and was surprised at the adult nature of the storyline. Amid *Atragon*'s visual splendor was an intimate story of a guilt-ridden man, his awkward relationship with his daughter and the personal shame he has carried for nearly twenty years. Shinguji is a man who can never forgive himself, yet he goes to such incredible lengths trying to atone for his family's shame that he builds a submarine worthy of Jules Verne. When it is suggested he use Atragon against the Mus, Shinguji is appalled. He's so concerned with restoring his country's pride he nearly fails to recognize its imminent annihilation. Of course, this can be seen as a parable of what happened to the Japanese military at the end of World War II, when refusing to surrender to the Allied Forces meant the near destruction of Japan itself. Some have argued the film to be pro-nationalistic, based, in part, on the government's rise in militarism at the time, but the picture's message is clear: nationalism can be a dangerous thing.

At the heart of the film is Jun Tazaki, longtime supporting player at Toho, in what is probably the role of his career. Tazaki was Japan's Morris Ankrum, appearing in countless genre films, usually as a high-ranking military officer or department head. Ironically, he rarely played anyone who had even the slightest bit of self-doubt, and Tazaki's performance is especially intriguing for anyone familiar with his other work. Born Minoru Tanaka in 1910, Tazaki was in films as early as 1948. He co-starred with Ryo Ikebe (*Battle in Outer Space*) in Kon Ichikawa's *Akatsuki to tsuiseki* (*Pursuit at Dawn*) (1950) and had a supporting role in Teinosuke Kinugasa's *Gate of Hell* (1953). He had cameo roles in Kurosawa's *Seven Samurai* (1954) and Kobayashi's *Kwaidan* (1965), but quickly became associated with genre films, beginning with Toho's *The Three Treasures* (1959). For the next ten years, Tazaki appeared in virtually every *kaiju eiga* film produced at the studio, including *Gorath* and *King Kong vs. Godzilla* (both 1962), *Godzilla vs. the Thing* (1964), *Monster Zero* and *Frankenstein Conquers the World* (both 1965), *Ebirah, Horror of the Deep* and *War of the Gargantuas* (both 1966) and *Destroy All Monsters* (1968). His final role was as a warlord in Kurosawa's *Ran* (1984), where Tazaki was one of the first actors cast by the great director. Tazaki died in 1985.

Atragon features a bevy of Toho regulars, including Ken Uehara, Kenji Sahara, Akihiko Hirata and Yoshibumi Tajima. However, the supporting player who steals the show from everyone else is Tetsuko Kobayashi, whose beautifully snide and wicked Mu empress ranks as one of the all-time great *kaiju eiga* villains. (As previously mentioned, I've not seen the English-language version in some time, and I'm basing my opinion of her performance on the original Japanese version. I have no idea who dubbed her voice in the States.) Kobayashi made her feature debut in *Atragon* and was only 18 at the time of filming. According to *Japanese Giants*, Kobayashi's career "lasted through the early '70s, at which time she semi-retired. She returned to acting in the 1982 TV film, *Fukisuido*, her ambition now to appear some day in a Broadway play."

Eiji Tsuburaya's special effects are uneven. The destruction of the Mu Empire is a pyrotechnics spectacular, and the Mus' attack on the rest of the world—climaxing with an earthquake which swallows whole cities into the Earth—is jaw-droppingly awesome. However, the film's monster, Manda (which later turned up in *Destroy All Monsters*), looks like a last-minute creation by the studio, always eager to include a monster in its special effects films even where one didn't belong. As the underwater footage was shot "dry" on a soundstage, Manda's movements were manipulated by invisible overhead wires, but the creature's clumsy movements painfully reveal their source, as if the marionette's operator had a case of the hiccups. Still, for a picture that began shooting barely three months before its premiere, *Atragon* is a remarkable achievement.

Akira Ifukube wrote the terrific score, one of the composer's best works, and director Ishiro Honda's live action shooting is lively while never losing sight of its intimate character portrayals.

Variety's "Murf" liked the film. "Good acting, fast-paced direction and editing and contemporary political theme result in stock exploitationer for American International . . . special effects by Eiji Tsuburaya are consistently excellent." *Science Fiction*, on the other hand, argued that the picture was in fact pro-military and nationalistic. "The symbol of Japanese national pride," he argued, "does not surrender but defeats the threat to its country without resorting to nuclear weapons, apparently on humanitarian grounds . . . The acting, dubbing and effects work show signs of carelessness and are disappointing." *Psychotronic* liked the film: "A superior Japanese science-fiction/fantasy film . . . an orgy of great special effects." Ed Godziszewski, in an exhaustive article on the film's production in *Japanese Giants* (#7), said the picture was "one of the best efforts of Toho's creative team. . . . Dramatically, as well as structurally, *Atragon* was one of Honda's finest achievements."

Attack of the Mushroom People *(1963)*

Despite a silly—and much-maligned—title, this Toho production, known in Japan as *Matango*, is one of the studio's most atypical and interesting films. Chiefly, it's a psychological horror film—allegory, although it contains science fiction elements as well. While frequently shown on American television during the sixties and seventies, the picture has all but disappeared today, an undeserving fate for this unique and quietly disturbing little film.

Attack of the Mushroom People (1963)

In a darkened room overlooking the nighttime Tokyo skyline, a man who we can't quite see recounts his story of survival. He was one of five holidaymakers—Kessei (Yoshio Tsuchiya), a wealthy businessman; his girlfriend, singer and television star Meimi Sekeguchi (Kumi Mizuno); an assistant professor in psychology, Kenji Morrei (Akira Kubo); his girlfriend, student Akiko Soma (Miki Yashiro); and a mystery writer, Etsuro Yoshida (Hiroshi Tachikawa)—all vacationing off the coast of Japan aboard a yacht, which was suddenly caught in a terrific storm. Despite the experience of the yacht's skipper, Sakeda (Hiroshi Koizumi), and sailor Koyama (Kenji Sahara), the ship loses its way (along with its mast) and drifts for many days. The food and water are nearly gone when the survivors spot an island somewhere near the equator. They head ashore, find fresh water and discover another ship—a rotting, beached research vessel. They find no bodies aboard, but much of the vessel is covered with a damp, moldy fungus. The ship's mirrors are missing, and an eyeless turtle, along with several other mutated animals, is discovered in the ship's laboratory. They find a couple of weeks' worth of food, and decide to clean the large ship and use it as their temporary home while awaiting rescue. The equipment on board and the captain's log suggest the ship was on a top-secret scientific expedition (its country of origin obscure) to study the island's radioactivity. Men sent ashore to gather food, we learn, never returned. When Kessei tries to steal some of the canned food, he is interrupted by a hideous figure dressed in rags with barnacle-like growths all over his face. Although everyone sees the creature, they dismiss the incident as some kind of hallucination. The food slowly begins to run out, and the relationships between the castaways become strained. The fog-shrouded island becomes wet and miserable, and the seven begin searching the island for other sources of nourishment, but they are only able to find a few turtle eggs and some edible roots. There are mushrooms on the island, but in his log book the captain of the research vessel warned that the mushrooms must not be consumed. Meimi, the more attractive of the two women, uses her femininity to get the men fighting amongst themselves. She eventually has an affair with Yoshida, who is slowly going crazy and by now is eating the mushrooms in spite of the warnings.

Many more sunken vessels are found underwater near the beach where Sakeda tries to repair the yacht. He is approached by Kessei, who wants Sakeda to help him steal all the food and sail off without the others, believing that two would have the best chance of making it back to civilization. Sakeda is outraged at the very suggestion. Yoshida, now completely mad, grabs a rifle and prepares to shoot all the men and take the women. There's a scuffle, and Koyama is shot dead. Yoshida is tackled and disarmed and then banished from the ship along with Meimi, who assisted the mad writer. Sakeda disappears, along with the repaired yacht, and a despondent Kessei asks Morrei to help him commit suicide. While Morrei and Akiko go off to look for food, Meimi returns to the vessel, and to Kessei's arms. Meimi takes Kessei to the mushrooms. Overcome with hunger, Kessei succumbs and begins eating them. Meimi then tells him the mushrooms are relentlessly addictive: once you start consuming them, you can never stop. She also tells the terrified Kessei that those who eat the mushrooms eventually become mushrooms themselves. Several human-size mushroom people, mutated human beings from previous shipwrecks, begin to appear. Kessei sees Yoshida, his face now moldy and mutated, happily eating mushrooms. Kessei screams. The yacht drifts back to the island, and Morrei climbs aboard. On one of the cabin walls, Sakeda has written a message explaining that he tried to get back to civilization but was unable. He died at sea. The unhappy Morrei returns to Akiko and the scientific vessel. By now the canned food has run out and roots on the island are getting harder and harder to find. Akiko suggests that they give up and eat the mushrooms — at least they still would survive — but Morrei refuses. The mushroom people attack the ship and carry off Akiko. Morrei goes after her, but it is too late: she has already succumbed and is eating the mushrooms. "It's delicious," she says, "Really!" Somehow, Morrei makes it to the yacht and sails away. After several days, the ship is found, and Morrei is brought back to Tokyo to tell his fantastic story. Locked up in a psychiatric ward, no one believes him. The doctors ask him how he was able to survive the journey back. Turning around, we see Morrei's face covered with fungus. "I ate them!" he screams.

I hadn't seen *Attack of the Mushroom People* in many years before watching it again for this book, but I remembered much of the film quite vividly, especially the twist ending, which had scared the daylights out of me (and it's *still* unnerving, even today). Similar to W. H. Hodgson's story "The Voice of the Night" (1907), *Attack of the Mushroom People* is brimming with dream-like images and ideas. The picture is also similar to William Golding's story *Lord of the Flies*, itself adapted for the screen that same year (by Peter Brook). Both stories revolve around shipwrecked castaways who eventually turn on one another. In *Lord of the Flies*, young schoolboys became animal-like savages, while here, adult men and women turn into big mushrooms. While not quite up to the level of Golding's story, and while the mushroom people themselves (in their final form) are rubbery and unconvincing, for atmosphere alone, few films are as interesting as *Attack of the Mushroom People*. It's simply one of the most atmospheric horror films ever to come out of Japan. At first, the island appears to be a tropical paradise, but it quickly becomes wet, moldy and dreary. By the final third of the film, it is almost constantly raining — day and night — and fog covers the entire island. The idea of it continually drawing ship after ship to its shores, tempting its crews out of existence, is a fascinating concept. There is a feeling of dread which hangs over the story from the very beginning, and the end, when several characters seem downright happy to surrender to their own desires by eating the mushrooms, seems perfectly logical. The rotting research vessel is an inspired creation. When we first see it, most of the ship's interior is covered with several inches of colorful mold. Parts of the ship are moldier than others (the captain's room is caked with the stuff), but even after it has been cleaned up, it's a wonder that any of the castaways would still want to stay there.

The familiar cast, under the direction of Ishiro Honda, does a fine job with the material, and Yoshio Tsuchiya's tortured Kessei is particularly impressive. At the beginning of the story, Tsuchiya's wealthy Kessei is so pompous he wears a captain's outfit even though Sakeda actually drives the boat. Kessei's wealth and power do him little good on the island, and he quickly becomes a pathetic figure, paying tens of thousands of yen for a single turtle egg.

"Illogical on any level except that of fantasy, where it is glaringly consistent," said *Science Fiction*. "This is a picture that... allows us to glimpse something of the nature of the dream logic that structures the monster movie scenarios." *The Motion Picture Guide* gave the film a one-star rating, saying it was "too much for an intelligent mind to accept," but *Psychotronic* called the picture "a real find for bored late-night TV viewers."

The Lost World of Sinbad *(1963)*

This sometimes colorful but ultimately tepid adventure was released to Japanese-speaking theaters as *Samurai Pirate*. American International, who picked the film up for general release in the United States, changed the film's title to the wildly misleading *The Lost World of Sinbad*. (An even more misleading moniker, *The 7th Wonder of Sinbad* [!] was also considered.) The Toho-produced film stars Toshiro Mifune, Japan's biggest star, and was tailored around his talents and box office stature. Intended as a colorful family entertainment, many of Toho's *kaiju eiga* personnel were involved with the fairly lavish project. The studio must have regarded catching Mifune between Kurosawa films as something of a coup, and likely hoped the film would repeat the success of *The Three Treasures* (1959). Unfortunately, the results are disappointing. The picture has the look of a Sinbad movie minus Ray Harryhausen's stop-motion effects, an omission virtually unthinkable to most American fantasy film fans today. Eiji Tsuburaya oversaw the film's few effects shots, mainly limited to a couple of miniatures and some optical work, none of which is terribly impressive. There's too much palace intrigue and not enoug action and adventure in this juvenile film, and lacks the sense of abandon and energy of Toei's much superior *The Magic Serpent* (1966). Of course, the dubbing doesn't help any, particularly here because several of the performances are interesting.

Sinbad (Mifune, whose character is known as Sukezaemon, alias "Luzon," in the Japanese version) is falsely accused of piracy and sentenced to death. He's rescued at the last minute by his crew, who bribed the guards, and is soon off on a new adventure. However, the journey is cut short when Sinbad's ship is caught in a hurricane and ripped apart on a reef. Only Sinbad and two members of his crew survive. The crew members are soon killed by the real pirates (test pilots and bomb squads seem to have lower mortality rates than Sinbad crews). Sinbad himself manages to escape, though the pirates make off with his treasure chest of rare jewels. Sinbad is rescued by Sennin (Ichiro Arishima), an ancient third-class wizard with a curiously pear-shaped, balding head and egg-like eyes. Sinbad visits the island's castle, ruled by a slimy premier who assumed control when the kind-hearted king became ill. A drunken palace guard, Itaka Tsuzuka (Jun Tazaki), challenges Sinbad to a duel, and the two square off briefly, before Sinbad suddenly says, "We'll pick it up some other time," and walks away. Later, Tsuzuka invites Sinbad to become a guard, but when some of the premier's soldiers arrest a group of young women—"He who has no money gives up his daughter," explains Tsuzaka—Sinbad rejects the invitation. Later, he is asked by Miwa (Kumi Mizuno) to join *her* band of petty thieves, but likewise refuses. That afternoon, Sinbad witnesses a procession for the king's daughter, Princess Yaya (Akiko Wakabayashi). The princess drops her handkerchief, which Sinbad uses to gain entrance to the palace. This really ticks off the premier, who's in love with the princess and is plotting to usurp the throne by getting rid of the princess' fiancé, the Prince of Thailand, and her father, the king. The princess immediately takes a liking to Sinbad, though it's clear she's saving her love for the prince. Sinbad notices that she's wearing a necklace from his stolen treasure chest. The premier consults Granny, a white-haired, fanged witch (Eisei Amamoto in drag), who warns him that Sinbad and Sennin threaten the premier's plans.

Sinbad returns to the palace later that evening and is captured and thrown into the dungeon. The wizard materializes before his old friend and turns himself into a fly to snoop about the palace. The wizard learns the premier's plans to poison then cure the ailing king in return for the princess and his kingdom. One of the premier's aides, Sobei (Mie Hama), helps Sinbad escape because she's secretly in love with the premier and doesn't want him to marry the princess. Granny the witch catches her releasing Sinbad, however, and turns her to stone. The witch confronts the wizard and is about to turn him into a statue as well, but he tricks her by transforming one of his nostril hairs into a fly, which the witch assumes is the wizard. She reduces her size, and Sennin is able to capture her in a gourd. Meanwhile, the premier proposes to the princess and promises to restore her father's health. With the princess and the premier looking on, the witch restores the king's health. As he leaves, the premier quietly orders Granny to kill the ruler (Takashi Shimura, wasted in a trivial role). Granny, however, is actually Sennin in disguise. Elsewhere, Sinbad rescues the prince and convinces Miwa and her merry men to storm the castle. Sinbad ties himself to a big wooden kite and is flown to the princess' tower. Sinbad kills Tsuzuka in a lengthy duel, while the witch, who escaped Sennin's gourd, is turned to stone when she accidentally looks into a mirror (the witch's death breaks previous spells, restoring several previously stoned characters, including Sobei, to their fleshly selves). The premier is crushed under the castle's drawbridge, and the king's throne is restored. The next morning, Sinbad can't be found, for he is already out to sea, ready to face new adventures. "I want something else," he tells a sailor, "I don't know what—it lies ahead." When the sailor asks where they are bound, Sinbad replies, "Everywhere."

The Lost World of Sinbad is a standard costume adventure too stodgy to generate much excitement. The picture's characters are broadly played—too much so. The terrible dubbing only emphasizes this; certainly actors the caliber of Toshiro Mifune, Jun Tazaki and Takashi Shimura don't benefit from the cartoony voices, while the comic performances of Ichiro Arishima (*King Kong vs. Godzilla*) and Eisei Amamoto seem even broader than they originally were (Amamoto's witch cackles "mumbo jumbo" whenever casting a spell), coming off as trite and juvenile. For fans of Toho's effects pictures, *The Lost World of Sinbad*'s best assets are the characters created by the studio's familiar stock company of actors, rather than its special effects. Best among the performances is Jun Tazaki's lusty palace guard, a man so tough he's introduced biting the legs off live frogs. His atypical casting as a kind of Far Eastern Hagar the Horrible is amusing, and his relationship with Sinbad (Tazaki's resemblence to Mifune adds to this) is interesting. Mifune, meanwhile, is his usual, fierce-looking self. His rather comical Sinbad is a man who seems to make his way through life by means of sheer bravado, an interesting variation of the character. Also intriguing is Eisei Amamoto's witch. The actor, who touts what surely must be the worst teeth in film history, was usually cast in supporting roles akin to those played by Peter Lorre in American-made films (indeed, Amamoto appears in Woody Allen's comically dubbed *What's Up Tiger Lily?* where the actor is looped by a man imitating Lorre) and, like Lorre, was almost always distinctive and visually striking. His best role was as the evil Dr. Who (no relation) in Toho's *King Kong Escapes* (1967). Ichiro Arishima's leering wizard, who lists to one side whenever he sees a beautiful girl, is interesting, but like Amamoto's witch is so badly dubbed it's hard to appreciate the comic actor's performance.

The picture's attempt to win a big general audience in Japan is pretty obvious. There are bits of gory violence (Tsuzuka's and the premier's death), sex (in fly form, a leering Sennin lands on a woman's bosom) and silly comedy to appeal to children.

Eiji Tsuburaya's special effects are surprisingly mediocre, especially the poor optical work involving the miniature pirate ship and Sinbad's ride aboard the wooden kite. The kite, incidentally, is not a living starfish-shaped creature as suggested in the film's newspaper ads, and a promised giant is nothing more than a burly, 6½-foot strongman, a kind of second string Tor Johnson.

Reviews were mixed, but the picture did win the Italian Trophy of Five Continents for best specialized film, and was praised by the *Japanese Fantasy Film Journal*'s Greg Shoemaker as "the best of the non-Harryhausen Sinbad films and . . . one of the best Japanese sword films." *The Motion Picture Guide* gave the film a ** rating, saying the "performances are overly stiff, with the script lacking in proper pacing of the action sequences." *Variety*'s "Murf" said the film had "good direction and production values despite moderate pace . . . crowd scenes and spectacular derring-do are lacking . . . special effects . . . are all okay though far from sensational." *Monthly Film Bulletin* said the film could "hardly begin to compete with Harryhausen on his own ground," and that it "provides ample evidence of why [Mifune] opted for independence as an actor a few years later."

Dagora, the Space Monster *(1964)*

Of Toho's giant monster movies, this is one of the hardest to see. *Dagora, the Space Monster* was briefly issued to home video in 1983, using a very poor 16mm television print that hardly does the picture's visuals justice. It rarely appears on television and received an extremely limited theatrical run, if any, in this country when it was new. Despite one outstanding special effects sequence, the film is very minor, a silly gangster movie with an extraterrestrial monster awkwardly thrown in.

Television satellite L1000, monitored by Dr. Kurino (Hiroshi Koizumi), orbits the Earth somewhere over Japan. It collides with a blue, pulsating space amoeba named Dagora (which everyone pronounces *Do*gara). Meanwhile, a gang of jewel thieves (including Yoshibumi Tajima and Eisei Amamoto) are in the midst of cracking a safe when they find themselves lifted several feet off the ground and suspended in mid-air. Elsewhere, crystallographer Dr. Munakata (Nobuo Nakamura) has created a sackful of artificial diamonds, which he believes will revolutionize their industrial use. Munakata is visited by Detective Kommei (Yosuke Natsuki), who arrives just as a mysterious American, Mark Jackson (Robert Dunham), breaks into the doctor's home and makes off with the fake stones. Jackson is caught by the jewel thieves, who have an extensive diamond operation in Japan. Jackson escapes as the crooks plan their next job. Strange events begin occurring throughout the world. Smokestacks are ripped loose from their foundations while coal and diamond deposits are carried off into the sky. Munakata and his assistant, Musiyo (Keiko Sawai)—who is also Dr. Kurino's sister—determine that Dagora is a space cell transformed by a pocket of radioactivity. It replenishes its energy by consuming coal and diamonds, both of which are carbon-based substances. If the monster decides to consume *other* carbon forms found on Earth, Munakata warns, mankind (a carbon-based substance) could be next.

The local authorities (led by Jun Tazaki) find Jackson, who now claims to be an investigator for the World Diamond Insurance Association. "I'm a diamond G-Man," he says. Jackson, Kommei, and the jewel thieves become involved in a tiresome series of escapes and recaptures, with the sack of diamonds changing hands like a hot potato. Dagora continues to make its presence known throughout the world, pulling jewelry stores, coal deposits and diamond mines alike skyward. The creature heads for Kyushu, hotly pursued by Munakata, Musiyo, Kurino and the others. The monster begins sucking up things and, in the picture's best moment, reaches down out of the clouds, and with its tentacles, rips a large suspension bridge apart for no clear reason. The army launches several rockets at the creature, which only multiplies its cells. Munakata determines that Dagora can be defeated by using the toxin from bees and wasps, which will cause the creature to crystallize in mid-air. Meanwhile, the jewel thieves capture Jackson and Kommei. They tie up Kommei and handcuff Jackson, placing sticks of dynamite in their coat pockets. The thieves light the fuse then head for Iwaba Beach, where the group's moll (Mie Hama) has made off with the stolen jewels. Our heroes escape and find the gangsters on the beach just as Munakata's bee toxin is released into the atmosphere (the army uses grade-B versions of the Markalite cannons seen in Toho's *The Mysterians*). Dagora crystallizes, causing a tremendous rock shower. The gangsters shoot their female partner but are themselves crushed by one of the falling boulders. Dagora defeated, Jackson and Munakata (who is to report to the UN) board a jet bound for the United States.

Dagora is really two movies in one—a story of inept gangsters who can't seem to get out of the monster's way, and a monster movie continually interrupted by boring jewel thieves. The thieves themselves are typical Japanese gangsters—as seen by Japanese moviemakers, anyway. With their dark sunglasses, white gloves and fedoras, they're hardly inconspicuous, though often visually striking. Eisei Amamoto in particular, with his white suit and black bowler, certainly *looks* interesting. Gangster films were very popular in Japan during the 1960s. Some critics argue the majority of these pictures were intended as send-ups of similar Hollywood films of the early 1930s and were never really meant to be taken seriously. That may certainly be true here. It seems that whenever these criminals are in the middle of a job—swoosh—here comes Dagora, ready to whisk their take to the sky. When a big boulder falls on the hapless thieves, you almost feel sorry for their incredibly bad luck. As much of the film takes place at night, it's hard to even see the monster in current American home video prints. In its theatrical run, however, and on home video in Japan (where it's available in the letterboxed format), Dagora is an impressive sight. One of Toho's truly unique creations, Dagora is a cross between a jellyfish and a kind of space octopus. The scene where the monster rips the suspension bridge off its foundation was filmed using cel animation and an elaborate marionette. It's an extremely effective little moment—too much so perhaps, because watching it one then realizes how disappointing the rest of the film is. As for the falling rocks, along with much of Dagora's inhalation of coal and diamonds, they're below par for special effects director Eiji Tsuburaya. Except for the bridge scene, there is an air of cheapness to the production all-around, possibly due to Toho's busy production schedule that year (which included two Godzilla films). Many of the effects are nothing more than rocks and other material tossed onto miniature sets and printed in reverse (to create the illusion of Dagora's sucking abilities).

The cast is peppered with many familiar faces, including Jun Tazaki (*Atragon*), Eisei Amamoto (*King Kong Escapes*), and the great Susumu Fujita (*Sanshiro Sugata*) who turns up as a general. Yosuke Natsuki had appeared in *I Bombed Pearl Harbor*, *The Youth and His Amulet* and Kurosawa's *Yojimbo* before appearing in Dagora; he also appeared in *Ghidrah: The Three-Headed Monster* and later in *Whirlwind* (1968), the mini-series *Shōgun*, and *Godzilla 1985*. Both he and Hama appear tired and unenthused in *Dagora*.

The dubbing for this outing is especially bad; mouths move without dialogue, and vice versa. Jackson, surprisingly enough, comes off the worst, with the looped actor occasionally pausing between words, resulting in ridiculous inflecting along the lines of, "Ah!... You're... making... a tremendous mistake!"

Variety's "Mosk," reviewing the picture at the Trieste Sci-Fi Film Festival, said "Good looking girls, westernized gangsters and fine special effects keep this familiar fare racing along its fairly short course... Color is good and 'scope is well-utilized." More recently, *The Japanese Fantasy Film Journal*'s Greg Shoemaker expressed his dislike of the Americanized gangsters and suggested that "due to a storyline that is quite far-fetched, the extremes are the film's undoing."

Godzilla vs. the Thing *(1964)*

Toho's monster makers reached the apex of the *kaiju eiga* genre with *Godzilla vs. the Thing*, a superb blending of monster-on-the-loose spectacle with the epic fairy tale. The picture is a sequel to both *King Kong vs. Godzilla* (1962) and *Mothra* (1961). This was the last film in which Godzilla was a purely evil character (until the series was revived in 1984, that is), and critics and fans alike generally agree that this was the best of the series.

Godzilla vs. the Thing (1964)

Following a violent hurricane, reporter Ichiro Sakai (Akira Takarada) and his fresh young photographer, Yoka (Yuriko Hoshi), investigate an industrial site heavily damaged during the storm. Yoka takes a picture of a strange green-gray object which looks like a moldy pizza. Elsewhere, a gigantic egg, apparently carried to Japan by the hurricane's waves, has run aground, and fishermen bring it ashore. The fishermen sell the egg to Kumayama (Yoshibumi Tajima) for 940,038 yen (fishermen say that amount is equal to 153,000 chicken eggs!). Kumayama announces plans to charge people to see the big egg. A scientist investigating the egg's appearance, Professor Miura (Hiroshi Koizumi), protests the sale, arguing that the egg should be studied, not exploited. Sakai and Yoka concur. Kumayama, we learn, is actually fronting the operation for slimy Torahata (Kenji Sahara), who, according to Sakai, is a man of great influence and "acquainted with all the big politicians in the city." Torahata and Kamayama gloat at the tremendous profits to be made building an amusement park around the mysterious egg. The men hear voices: "Please return the egg to us!" It is the twin fairies (Emi and Yumi Ito, reprising their roles from *Mothra*) from Mothra Island (it was called Beiru in the earlier film). The men not only scoff at the idea of returning the egg, they even capture the girls, who manage to escape from Torahata's hotel room. The fairies run into Sakai, Yoka and professor Miura, and explain that the egg belongs to Mothra (called "the Thing" for most of the picture); it was swept away during the hurricane. The natives on the island have been praying for the egg's return, and the fairies have come to Japan to try to get it back. "It may cause all of you great trouble," they warn, suggesting that, when hatched, the creature inside the egg could unintentionally cause tremendous damage. "That is what we want to save you from," they say. The trio try to convince Torahata to give up the egg. Instead, he makes an offer to buy the fairies. The greatly disappointed twins return to their island. Kumayama builds a gigantic incubator, and sneaky Torahata talks him into using his own money to pay for the operation. Miura calls Sakai and Yoka to his lab and immediately treats them for minor radiation poisoning – the moldy pizza object turned out to be hot. The three return to the industrial site, and Yoka, trying to take a picture, notices the distant ground moving. A tail rises up from the earth. It is Godzilla. The monster causes some damage, and in a scene added for the American release (though filmed by Toho), the U.S. Navy is dispatched to combat the big reptile. One of Sakai's co-workers, an egg-eating reporter, Nakamura (Yu Fujiki), suggests asking Mothra for help in defeating the seemingly indestructible Godzilla. Sakai, Yoka and Miura, ashamed that they were not able to help the fairies earlier, are reluctant to ask, but urged on by Sakai's editor (Jun Tazaki), they agree to try.

Arriving at the island, they are shocked at the devastation left by the atomic testing. The landscape is much bleaker than it appeared in *Mothra*. Bleached skeletons of animals are everywhere, and there is no plant life in sight. (A strange gray turtle is seen in the background; its appearance goes unexplained in the American cut of the picture.) The trio locate the natives, who angrily refuse to offer any assistance. "Your people have offended us," explains the stern tribal chief. Just then, the singing of the twin fairies is heard. The girls are sitting in a lush garden, the only green part of the island left. Surprisingly, the fairies politely but sternly also refuse to help. Yuko humbly pleads their case, arguing that mankind must learn to work and live together, for we are all brothers. The fairies finally agree and sing to Mothra (a reprise of the number first heard in *Mothra*, this time sung *a cappella*). Mothra is persuaded to face Godzilla, even though by doing so she will not be able to return to the island. Mothra is dying and will have to use all her remaining strength to defeat the monster. Godzilla continues to cause massive destruction, and the unhappy Kumayama learns that Torahata has cheated him out of all his money. Frustrated, Kumayama beats his boss and begins taking money from Torahata's safe. Torahata shoots Kumayama then flees his hotel room as Godzilla approaches. Godzilla destroys the building, however, and Torahata is crushed in the collapsing structure. Mothra and Godzilla battle to the death, with the gigantic moth dragging the tremendous reptile by the tail. Godzilla scorches one of Mothra's wings. The giant moth flies to her egg and expires. The army tries using electricity against Godzilla, even dropping a series of electrified nets on the beast. (One of the explosions briefly sets the Godzilla costume on fire. I assume this was unintentional but left in the picture because of its startling visual quality.) The fairies and the natives back on the island pray for the egg to hatch. It does, and two larvae emerge (The *New York Times*' Eugene Archer referred to Mothra's offspring as "big worms"). The larvae follow Godzilla to an island where a group of young schoolgirls are stranded, having missed the evacuation. Yoka, Sakai, Miura and Nakamura take a boat to rescue the girls while the two larvae keep Godzilla busy. The larvae catch Godzilla in a crossfire, spraying the beast with their silky, cocooning substance. Godzilla, quickly covered with the thread-like stuff, is rendered immobile and falls into the sea. The schoolgirls are rescued, and the larvae swim away, back to Mothra Island.

With *Godzilla vs. the Thing*, the series reached its creative peak. Everything clicked, from Shinichi Sekizawa's screenplay, to Ishiro Honda's direction, to Akira Ifukube's score, to Eiji Tsuburaya's special effects. The film maintains the fantasy elements of *Mothra* while deftly integrating them with the cold, unrelenting monstrousness of the early Godzillas. It pits the fairy tale–like Mother against a cold, very animal-like Godzilla. Although produced for family audiences and occasionally humorous (as with Nakamura's obsession with eggs), the film is actually darker than the two which preceded it, *King Kong vs. Godzilla* and *Mothra*. In facing King Kong, the Godzilla character was played tongue-in-cheek, with the monsters' duel staged like an elaborate wrestling match. The duel between Godzilla and Mothra, the picture's highlight and the best monster battle of the *kaiju eiga* genre, is played completely straight.

Unlike later films in the series, the monsters here are choreographed like *real animals*. They're really fighting to the death, and this greatly adds to the picture's excitement. Mothra's death is also a bit surprising, even moving. Akira Ifukube's excellent, pounding score adds tremendously in this regard, giving the picture the feel of a genuine epic.

The special effects are generally quite good. As usual for Toho, the matte work is wildly uneven, with some shots blurry and mismatched. The complaint is minor, however, in light of the excellent work in nearly every other department. Godzilla's design has been changed once again. The costume is less reptilian than it was in *King Kong*, while avoiding the ghastly playful look of later films. With its glassy, inhuman stare, slender body and fleshy cheeks, the design used here (as well as in the next several pictures, with minor alterations) was the best of the series. I even prefer it to the look of Toho's current Godzillas, which, while impressive, lack the personality seen in *Godzilla vs. the Thing*.

One of the film's many delights is its carefully developed human story. The picture is surprisingly political, attacking the government for turning its head from the practices of crooked businessmen like Torahata, America for its shortsighted nuclear testing (whose effects are much more visible than they were in *Mothra*), and even common folk like Yuko and Sakai for expecting help while turning their backs on their own brothers, so to speak. Of course, these elements shouldn't be taken too seriously. This is, after all, primarily an entertainment piece intended for mass audiences, but these elements are there. *Godzilla vs. the Thing* deserves points for trying to be more than it is, instead of merely going though the motions like so many of Toho's later films.

The picture's most interesting performances come not from the nominal stars, Takarada, Hoizumi and Hoshi (though they're certainly competent), but rather from the more flashy supporting roles accorded to Kenji Sahara, Yu Fujiki and especially Yoshibumi Tajima. Tajima was another staple in Toho's monster series, beginning with a small role in *Rodan* (1956) and appearing in films as recently as *Godzilla 1985* (1984/1985). He often played a military leader or government official, and his parts ranged from tiny walk-ons to costarring roles. The guillible, almost tragic Kumayama was probably his best role in a fantastic film, and he's quite good. Yu Fujiki is fun as the egg-obsessed Nakamura, who even takes a frying pan with him while on assignment (I wonder if he ever met Edith Massey?).

American International picked up the film in the United States. Their title was apparently inspired by RKO's classic sci-fi thriller *The Thing* (1951), although there's no connection with that picture other than the name itself. American International hid Mothra's identity in their advertising, covering up the mysterious creature in poster art with a big question mark or box; what was seen suggests a creature more along the lines of Biollante. The picture's title has since been changed to *Godzilla vs. Mothra*, though references to "the Thing" remain.

Their dubbing (done at Titra Studios) was competent as far as that goes, and they more or less left the film intact.

Reviews were mixed. *Variety*'s "Hogg" generally liked the picture, applauding the film's "orgy" of special effects and engaging performances by the Peanuts, but said it had "limited appeal." *The Motion Picture Guide*, forever dismissing Japanese sci-fi, gave the film a *½ rating, calling it "Good camp with the added element of cute little monsters." Greg Shoemaker said "the film moves at a lively pace, due to direction and script, and builds to tense climactic scenes." August Ragone and Guy Tucker, writing in *Markalite*, agreed, calling it "the pinnacle achievement of the Godzilla series and Toho's SF/monster cycle."

Ghidrah: The Three-Headed Monster (1964)

A direct and quickly made sequel to *Godzilla vs. the Thing*, *Ghidrah: The Three-Headed Monster* was released barely nine months after the former film's premiere. The Peanuts were back, while Yuriko Hoshi and Hiroshi Koizumi essentially reprised their roles as well. The story reunited Mothra and Godzilla, revived Rodan the Flying Monster, and gave birth to what was perhaps the studio's most inspired character, Ghidrah (known as King Ghidorah in Japan).

A group of astronomers looking for UFOs in the nighttime sky abandon their search. They blame a reporter from Tokyo Broadcasting, Naoko Shindo (Yuriko Hoshi), who doesn't believe in flying saucers, for their nonappearance. Then, out of the night sky, what at first appears to be a flying saucer flies past. However, it turns out to be a false alarm—just a shooting star. Meanwhile, a beautiful princess (Akiko Wakabayashi) is flying to Japan, trying to elude assassins who have already murdered her father. One of the leaders plotting to overthrow the regime, Malness (Hisaya Ito), has already planted a bomb aboard the plane. Before the bomb goes off, however, a bright light appears just outside the princess' window. A ghostly voice tells her, "Stand up Princess and leave this place. Hurry!" She stands up and out the escape hatch she goes. The plane explodes seconds later. The following morning, geologists, led by Professor Murai (Hiroshi Koizumi), travel to the mountainous region where the shooting star has fallen. When they arrive, their compasses go crazy and their picks and shovels are magnetically drawn toward the meteorite. Elsewhere, a plainly dressed woman who claims to be a prophetess from Mars warns skeptical crowds that doom and destruction are imminent. The crowds scoff at her predictions, but Naoko's editor (Kenji Sahara) feels that the woman, who bears a remarkable resemblance to the princess, would be a perfect subject for their "Mysteries in the Twentieth Century" television show and assigns Naoko to tail the prophetess-princess. Naoko's brother, Detective Shindo (Yosuke Natsuki), also notes the woman's resemblance to the princess. He was assigned to guard the princess in Japan before her plane blew up. Unfortunately, Malness also recognizes the princess when her picture appears in the newspaper. Meanwhile, Mothra's priestesses, the twin fairies (Emi and Yumi Ito) appear on a TV show called "What Are They Doing Now?" (hosted by two fast-talking comedians, one dubbed by an actor imitating Buddy Hackett's Chinese waiter character). A young boy has come to the show wanting to know how Mothra's doing these days. "The old one died, you know," one of the fairies explains. But the larva (what happened to the second one?) is "fine, even though he's just a baby." The fairies sing "Call Happiness," "in their own exotic dialect," as one of the show's hosts explains, and we see natives on Infant Island (changed from Mothra Island in the last film) dancing around Mothra, Jr.

The next day Shindo interviews a fisherman (Ikio Sawamura), who says he fished the princess, very much alive, out of the water several evenings before. She exchanged a royal bracelet for the fisherman's clothes. One of the astronomers seen at the film's opening (a miniature flying saucer left over from *Battle in Outer Space* hangs in his office) offers a rather unlikely explanation as to how the princess might have survived falling out of an airplane thousands of feet in the air—something to do with different dimensions and the curvature of space and time. Anyway, the prophetess-princess next turns up at the base of a volcano, warning that the monster Rodan will soon appear. And indeed he does; that is, at least one of the two monsters thought destroyed in the 1956 film appears at the volcano's base (for some reason Rodan's voice is dubbed with Godzilla's familiar roar in this shot). The fairies board a ship bound, it seems, for Infant Island. A reporter asks the fairies about Rodan's next move (and, inexplicably, Godzilla's as well). The prophetess appears, warning passengers not to sail. She predicts the ship will soon be destroyed. That evening Godzilla, having survived his encounter with Mothra's larvae in *Godzilla vs. the Thing*, rises out of the water and sets the ship afire with his atomic breath. Naoko assumes responsibility for the prophetess, checking her into a hotel. Unfortunately, it happens to be the same hotel where Malness and his henchman are holed up. The gangsters corner the emotionless princess, who seems to be suffering some kind of amnesia. The fairies, heeding the prophetess' warning about the ship, climb out of Naoko's purse. Shindo tells his sister, Naoko, the prophetess' true identity. They take her to Dr. Tsukamoto (Takashi Shimura), who runs a battery of tests. Eventually, the princess-prophetess explains that centuries ago, Mars was invaded by a giant monster named Ghidrah. Though thousands of years ahead of us intellectually, the Martian people were wiped out within a month's time. Now Ghidrah's on earth.

Soon enough, the meteorite that Professor Murai has been studying splits open, and in a spectacular ball of fire, Ghidrah appears. A three-headed, golden flying dragon, Ghidrah takes to the skies, flying over cities and destroying everything in its path, thanks to lightning-like arcs of electricity shooting out of each of its three mouths. Godzilla and Rodan are creating all manner of havoc as well, though they seem to be concentrating more on fighting each other rather than destroying Japan's major cities. The government suggests that since Mothra defeated Godzilla (in the previous film), perhaps the big bug might be able to do the same to Ghidrah. The fairies explain that Mothra is no match for Ghidrah, but suggest that perhaps Mothra could persuade Godzilla and Rodan "to cooperate" and that the three Earth monsters working together might be able to defeat the golden dragon. Mothra arrives in Japan, but Godzilla and Rodan, in monster talk (!), explain they'd rather fight each other than help mankind (the fairies obligingly interpret this for the benefit of their Japanese companions). "Awww, these monsters are as stupid as human beings!" Shindo says. Mothra goes at it alone but is clearly no match for the mighty Ghidrah. Godzilla and Rodan have a change of heart, however, and the Greatest Battle on Earth (as the film was called in Japan) is on. Malness makes another attempt on the princess' life, but the battling monsters create an avalanche which kills the assassin. A fall restores the princess' memory, and Mothra, Rodan and Godzilla defeat Ghidrah, who makes a hasty retreat toward outer space.

Ghidrah: The Three-Headed Monster is an episodic if lively entry in the Godzilla series. Although made quickly, the film doesn't look rushed, except perhaps in Shinichi Sekizawa's uneven, convoluted script, further compromised by Continental's slapdash Americanization. Several ideas are introduced, then forgotten. We're told early on there's a mysterious heat wave in the middle of winter; and although the heat wave is emphasized early in the story, it's forgotten by the picture's end. It's also never really clear how and why the princess became a prophetess from Mars. The general idea seems to be that a handful of Martians fled to the Earth centuries ago, and more or less evolved to human form. The Martian intellect was lost over time, though Martian instinct kicks in in times of trouble. That doesn't explain the bright light that approached the princess' plane, however. Still, this plot device does offer an interesting variation on ideas addressed earlier in the BBC television serial, *Quatermass and the Pit* (1958) and later in Stanley Kubrick's *2001: A Space Odyssey* (1968). The Americanization only serves to break the film up further. Several scenes and individual shots are all too obviously edited out of sequence. A reporter asks the twin fairies about Godzilla before he even appears. When Godzilla finally does emerge, he spots Rodan in the night sky (a simple but extremely effective shot), in footage obviously edited out of a later sequence. Perhaps the most glaring example of this cavalier editing occurs when the king of the monsters is first seen hitting the Japanese mainland, followed inexplicably by a shot of him still in the water, approaching land! People, not monsters, were still the film's stars at this point, though Godzilla and company dominate the film's climax.

Ghidrah: The Three-Headed Monster is really the film where Godzilla begins a transformation from evil menace to Protector of Earth. It's also the first film where he begins to take on decidedly human characteristics. In a moment more akin to Laurel and Hardy than *Godzilla* and *Rodan*, the monsters seem to laugh uproariously at one another when Mothra sprays his silky web material at the monsters to get their attention. That the monsters can also talk to one another is more than a bit absurd. (One of the film's silliest moments occurs when the fairies are shocked by Godzilla's apparent off-color remarks. "Godzilla! What terrible language!" exclaim the fairies.) Godzilla, downright villainous in *Godzilla vs. the Thing*, winds up saving young Mothra, the very creature he tried to destroy in the previous film. And while Godzilla is still seen as a threat early on, he's practically loveable by the grand finale. Rodan's transformation is less subtle. Little more than a flying dinosaur in *Rodan*, Rodan was redesigned with more anthropomorphic features for *Ghidrah*. The face is much more comical, augmented by a wildly springy neck which suggests a monstrous jack-in-the-box. Mothra, seen here in caterpillar form, looks pretty much as he did in the last film, and *Markalite* claims that the same costume-prop was used. Ghidrah makes the first of several appearances in this film. An inspired creation, Ghidrah is a wholly Japanese monster, based on the multi-headed dragon seen in Toho's *The Three Treasures* (1959). The monster's first appearance, in a ball of fire, was so impressive that this footage would be used in all of the monster's subsequent appearances (and subsequently updated for 1991's *Godzilla vs. King Ghidorah*). Other Ghidrah effects footage would be utilized extensively and obviously in later features as well.

Yosuke Natsuki is rather bland as Detective Shindo, especially in early scenes, where he's paired with the much more distinctive Akihiko Hirata, cast as the former's boss. Takashi Shimura's appearance comes very late in the film, and he gets swept up in the story rather than adding anything to it. One curious moment comes when Shimura's Dr. Tsukamoto prepares to give the princess therapeutic shock treatments! This was the Peanuts' last appearance as the twin fairies. The characters would turn up again in *Ebirah, Horror of the Deep* (1966), but the roles would be played by other actresses. The Peanuts are often credited as appearing in *Destroy All Monsters* (1968), but they're not in any version of the film that I've ever seen. It's possible they may have appeared in different roles, but if they are in the film, I'm not aware of it. Kenji Sahara has a cameo as Naoko's editor, while Eiji Okada, best remembered for his performance in *Hiroshima Mon Amour* (1960), appears as a geologist.

The *Psychotronic Encyclopedia of Film* liked *Ghidrah*, calling it "one of the best Japanese monster bashes." Phil Hardy's *Science Fiction* got the order of the films mixed up, believing *Monster Zero* (1965) had preceded this entry. Nonetheless, its reviewer also liked *Ghidrah*, adding that the special effects were "better than usual." *Variety*'s "Robe" said, "When the viewer finds himself cheering on the trio of unlikely allies, it's a tribute to Honda's ability to capture an audience... The dubbing is, as usual, atrocious." The *New York Times*' Vincent Canby, reviewing the film on a double bill with *Harum Scarum* ("The Beat & the Beast make a holiday feast!" screamed the ads), said *Ghidrah* "at least provides a smile or two as it lurches and lunges through a veritable anthology of Japanese monster picture plots... the film... is strictly for the comic book set." *The Motion Picture Guide* rated *Ghidrah* **½ stars and complained about the dubbing. "A blind man could've done better." Greg Shoemaker, in his examination of Toho's films, found *Ghidrah*'s script "confusing," saying it also cheapened the character development in favor of extensive monster footage. *Ghidrah: The Three-Headed Monster* is an entertaining, silly adventure. For better or worse, it also spelled the beginning of tremendous changes in characterization for Japan's supermonsters.

Kwaidan *(1964)*

Of all of Japan's films centered around classic ghost stories, *Kwaidan* (or "weird tales") is by far the best known in the United States. An elaborate, visually stunning production, the picture is an omnibus of four traditional tales (one of which was cut for its initial release in the United States) taken from Lafcadio Hearn's 1904 compilation, *Kwaidan: Stories and Studies of Strange Things*.

In "The Black Hair," a poor, dissatisfied samurai (Rentaro Mikuni) leaves his loving, patient wife (Michiyo Aratama). He marries the daughter of a wealthy, socially respected family, but the second wife (Misako Watanabe) turns out to be selfish and callous, and the samurai quickly realizes how much better off he was before, despite living in poverty. He dreams openly of returning to his first wife, which only strains his current relationship further. After several years, the samurai divorces his second wife and returns to his old village. He finds his former home dilapidated, with rotting wood and overgrown weeds everywhere. He is surprised to discover his first wife sitting quietly at a spinning wheel, unchanged since he last saw her. He begs her forgiveness, decrying his cruelty and selfishness. Surprisingly, the wife does forgive him ("I am the greater to see you again," she says, "if only for a moment"), and the two share an evening of passionate reconciliation. The following morning, the samurai awakens to find himself lying against the skeletal remains of his wife, long since deceased. The horrified man becomes intertwined in her long, black hair and turns white and grotesque with shock.

The second segment, "Woman of the Snow," was originally excised during initial U.S. engagements (ironically, advertisements for the film featured a publicity photo from this cut segment). "Woman of the Snow" has since been restored to most theatrical prints and home video, and so I include it here. Woodcutters Minokichi and Musaku find themselves caught in a terrific blizzard. The nearly frozen men find a small, unheated ferryman's hut. A beautiful snow woman (Keiko Kishi), with long black hair, a white face and blue lips enters. She breathes on Musaku's face, and the woodcutter freezes to death. The woman next approaches Minokichi (Tatsuya Nakadai) and is about to kill him, too, when she has a change of heart and decides to spare him. However, she warns him that if he tells anyone what he has seen, she will know and will return to kill him. Minokichi somehow returns to his village, and his mother (Mariko Okada) nurses him through the winter. Soon it is spring, and Minokichi is back at work. He meets a beautiful woman, Yuki (also played by Keiko Kishi), who says she is passing through the village. The two fall in love, and over the next few years they have three children and their happy marriage is greatly admired by the rest of the village. One evening, as Yuki sews a garment for one of her children and Minokichi finishes making a set of sandals for his family, the woodcutter is reminded of his encounter with the snow woman years before as he gazes upon his wife, who so resembles her. He tells Yuki the story of his encounter with the snow woman—he's not sure if it really happened or if it was all a dream, he says. "It was not a dream," Yuki says. The room becomes blue and frozen, and Yuki becomes cold and white. Yuki is the snow woman. She had fallen in love with Minokichi, but now he has broken the spell by breaking his promise. If it were not for the children, she says, she would have killed him instantly. Instead, Minokichi's beloved wife is forced to leave him, dashing out of their small hut and into the night sky.

"Hoichi-the-Earless" is the third and longest segment. Over seven hundred years ago, the Genji and Heike clans fought their last battle. At Dan-no-ura, unable to return to shore because of the intense waves while Genji ships blocked escape to the sea, the Heike army was horribly defeated. Watching the slaughter from a royal barge, Lady Nii held the infant emperor in her arms. She decided to take her charge into the next world, and along with several other attendants, leaped into the blood-red sea and drowned. The sea became haunted, and thousands of strange crabs, with human faces on their backs, began to appear (they're not referred to again in the story, though they certainly are interesting). Years later, a young blind man, Hoichi (Kazuo Nakamura), lives at a Buddhist temple. Left alone one evening, he is approached by the ghost of a samurai (Rentaro Mikuni) who has come to fetch Hoichi and bring him to the samurai's master. Hoichi, not realizing the samurai is a spirit, reluctantly agrees and is taken to a temple-cemetery built nearby to console the dead Heike spirits. "My present Lord, a person of exceedingly high rank," the spirit tells Hoichi, "is now staying at Akamagahara with his numerous attendants. He wanted to view the scene of the battle." He tells Hoichi that his lord had heard of Hoichi's skill with his voice and biwa at reciting the story of the battle. The ghostly entourage is greatly pleased with Hoichi's abilities and has him return night after night. Because of the young man's blindness, the priests and temple custodians become greatly concerned by Hoichi's nightly absences. The head priest (Takashi Shimura, with shaved head) asks Hoichi where he goes, but Hoichi lies to the priest, claiming his nightly trips are a matter of an unimportant personal nature. Finally, Hoichi departs with the ghostly samurai on a particularly stormy evening, and the priest orders the two temple custodians to follow Hoichi. Hoichi, believing himself to be performing in front of a distinguished audience, is furious when the custodians remove him from the deserted cemetery. Returned to the priest, Hoichi is told of the gathering's true identity. They are, of course, the ghosts of the defeated Heike clan, who have come to listen to Hoichi's telling of the battle. To break the ghosts' spell, the priests paint Hoichi from head to toe with the holy text. He is told that when the spirit of the samurai comes, he is not to answer him or make a sound of any kind. Left alone in the temple, Hoichi sits silently with his biwa. The spirit arrives but cannot see Hoichi because of the painted text. However, the priests forgot to paint Hoichi's ears, which appear disembodied to the ghostly samurai. As he has been ordered to bring Hoichi to the temple, the samurai determines that the ears are better than nothing, and rips them from Hoichi's head! The following morning the priests, mournful at their mistake, attend to the now earless Hoichi. Soon, the story of Hoichi's encounter with the spirits becomes known throughout the land, and Hoichi the Earless becomes quite rich telling his story to wealthy travelers.

The final segment is "In a Cup of Tea." Built around the premise that some stories remain unfinished, the narrator explains that writers may die mid-story, have disputes with their publishers and so forth. On New Year's Day of the fourth Tenwa, Kannai (Kan-Emon Nakamura), a samurai for Lord Nakagawa, becomes thirsty. Pouring himself a cup of water, he is shocked to find the reflection of a smiling man (Noboru Nakaya) looking back up at him. Kannai tries several different cups to no avail, since that smiling face just won't go away. He finally swallows the water and along with, it seems, the man's soul. Late that evening, Kannai is assigned guard duty. The spirit of the smiling man, who calls himself Shikibu Heinai, appears. The frightened Kannai tries to run him through with his sword, but Heinai merely vanishes. Kannai calls out the guards, but his story of a ghostly intruder is scoffed at by the other guards (including their commander, played by Jun Tazaki). The next evening, Kannai is off duty and at home when three men appear. They claim to be retainers for Heinai, and Kannai vainly tries to kill the ghostly trio. This is where the unfinished story concluded, the narrator says, and does not wish to suggest an ending as none would prove satisfactory. A publisher appears at the writer's turn-of-the-century cottage, only to find the writer trapped in a watery reflection.

Kwaidan must certainly rank as one of the most visually attractive films ever made. Most of the picture was shot in an airplane hangar, and the sometimes very elaborate (and obviously expensive) indoor and outdoor sets are usually contrasted against decidedly unreal color backdrops. Indeed, the film's brilliant color and other visual elements are one of its main attractions. During "Woman of the Snow," for instance, the swirling blues of the blizzard are capped by strange, surreal eyes which hauntingly look down on the lost woodcutters. (This sequence concludes with the snow woman running toward one of the eyes, in fact.) The Battle of Dan-no-ura was filmed in an immense indoor water tank, with the bloody battle photographed against a brilliant red and orange backdrop. This was, in turn, integrated with an elaborate painting (by Masayoshi Nakamura), and both the editing and visuals of this sequence make for one of the most eye-popping battle sequences ever filmed.

As nearly all American films attempt to recreate reality, few filmmakers are as boldly unreal as the men and women behind *Kwaidan*. The only major Hollywood production I can think of that attempted such a thoroughly unreal setting (other than dream sequences) was *The Wizard of Oz* (1939), which utilized similar, expansive painted backdrops. I have long argued the technical presentation of a particular film is sometimes as important as the film itself, and my own experience with *Kwaidan* is a perfect example. I first saw the film on a battered 16mm panned-and-scanned print (thus losing the original Toho-Scope photography) whose colors had so faded that nearly everyone and everything was a dull pink. Fortunately, the film is now available through The Voyager Company on laser disc (as part of their Criterion collection) and videotape, both in the letterboxed format, and in colors matching the original presentation. If one is unable to screen an unfaded, anamorphic 35mm print, this is certainly the next best thing. You'll notice that I've emphasized throughout the book how much better these pictures look in their original aspect ratios (and on a large theater screen). And this was never more so than with *Kwaidan*.

The film's use of sound is nearly as impressive as its visuals. Forsaking a conventional score, or conventional sound effects for that matter, director Masaki Kobayashi uses a series of primitive sounds (stones, wood) throughout the picture, most notably during the middle segments. He also omits sound altogether where one would expect to find it. When the snow woman leaves Minokichi in the ferryman's hut after making him promise never to speak of her, she runs out the flimsy wooden door into the roaring blizzard. The door slams shut, quickly reopens with a gust of air and the spirit is gone. This sequence is played without sound effects—no sound of the slamming door, no howling winds, etc., and is the more effective for it. Another use of this technique occurs during the Battle of Dan-no-ura in "Hoichi- the-Earless." As Lady Nii and her attendants jump into the blood-red waters, we hear only the primitive wood and stone score, and no splashing or screams. The result is a sequence that is truly unsettling.

Lafcadio Hearn, who wrote under the alias "Yakumo Koizumi," was born in the Ionian Islands in 1850 of Irish and Greek parents. He rejected his strict Catholic upbringing before sailing to America when he was nineteen. Hearn became a newspaper reporter for the New Orleans *Times Democrat*, and his vivid and gruesome description of a burned corpse (which Hearn had not seen) so impressed his editor (!) that he sent the young writer to the West Indies as a correspondent. In 1890, Hearn traveled to Japan, falling in love with the Japanese culture and landing a job as an English professor at Imperial University. He married a Japanese woman and became a Buddhist. It was during the decade preceding his death that Hearn began his acclaimed interpretation of Japanese culture, philosophy and folk tales. The Pulitzer Prize–winning author died in 1904, the same year his *Kwaidan*, a collection of traditional Japanese supernatural tales, was first published.

Of the four segments, "The Woman of the Snow" and "Hoichi-the-Earless" hold up best. "Woman of the Snow" is a beautifully told, tragic story. Perhaps its most interesting element is that we feel as sorry for Yuki, the Snow Woman, as we do for poor Minokichi. By breaking the spell, Yuki is compelled to surrender everything this poor, sympathetic creature had longed for – to be a normal, human woman. "Hoichi-the-Earless" also works wonderfully well. The Roald Dahl-ish twist about the ears is both clever and exceedingly painful. Writing holy text on a man's body to ward off evil spirits was a convention in Japanese ghost stories (it also played a role in Mizoguchi's *Tales of Ugetsu*, among others), not unlike garlic, silver bullets, and crucifixes in Western tales. Still, a clove of garlic 'round the neck isn't nearly so visually stunning as a man painted head-to-toe with Buddhist text, even if one does forget the ears. "The Black Hair" is interesting, if long in the telling. Some critics have charged that the filmmakers purposely edited the picture at its leisurely pace to appeal to the American audience it hoped to attract: the Japanese believed U.S. viewers liked their films this way. Whether this is true or not, *Kwaidan* is arguably overlong. Director Kobayashi approved of the cutting of "Woman of the Snow" during its initial run in the United States, according to *Variety*, though why he would cut one of the picture's best segments and leave the unfunny "In a Cup of Tea" in (it's supposed to be a comedy) is strange to say the least. Some reports suggest "Woman of the Snow" was released separately as a short, but this seems unlikely, at least in theaters in the United States where *Kwaidan* would most likely have played to Western audiences. The best moments of "The Black Hair" come in the samurai's reconciliation with his wife, a moving and emotionally charged sequence. This segment closely resembles yet another part of *Ugetsu*, and I suspect most Western audiences would regard the samurai's punishment as a bit harsh (even his wife forgives him, for cryin' out loud). Then again, he may have only imagined her forgiveness, and she might have died hating his guts. Director Kobayashi infuriated Toho and the film's other backers by his slow, methodical approach to filmmaking, supposedly averaging only three set-ups a day (unheard of in Japan, where features were shot like American serials). A former assistant to Kinoshita, Kobayashi is perhaps ironically best known for his ultra-realistic nine-hour trilogy, *Ningen no joken* (*The Human Condition*) (1959–61). His other films include *Harakiri* and *The Inheritance* (both 1962).

"The Woman of the Snow" stars Tatsuya Nakadai, one of Japan's biggest stars, and most respected actors. Unlike Toshiro Mifune, whose best films were made in collaboration with one director, Akira Kurosawa, Nakadai's diverse credits include films for Kobayashi, Teshigahara, and Kurosawa, among others. For the latter he debuted as an extra in *Seven Samurai* (as a samurai glimpsed walking down a street early in the picture), before starring opposite Mifune in *Yojimbo* (1961), *Sanjuro* (1962), and *High and Low* (1963); and alone in *Kagemusha* (1980) and *Ran* (as the Lear character, 1985). For Kobayashi, Nakadai starred in *The Human Condition* (1959–61) and *Harakiri* (1962); for Teshigahara he appeared in the dark fantasy *The Face of Another* (1966). Nakadai's other genre credits include *Illusion of Blood* (1966), *Portrait of Hell* (1969) and *Hinotori* (1978).

Kwaidan was an expensive flop in Japan, though a wildly successful artistic triumph on the international market. The picture was awarded the Jury's Special Prize at Cannes and was nominated for an Oscar for best foreign language film (it lost to the Czech-made *The Shop On Main Street*). The *New York Times*' Bosley Crowther, reviewing the short version, called the film "a horror picture with an extraordinarily delicate and sensuous quality... *Kwaidan* is a symphony of color and sound that is truly past compare.... It is a film that commands itself mainly to those viewers who can appreciate rare subtlety and grace." *Variety*'s "Mosk" noted the picture was "done in measured cadence and intense feeling ... a visually impressive tour-de-force." *Psychotronic*, also reviewing the three-segment version, said the film was "fascinating." Dissenting was Phil Hardy's *The Encyclopedia of Horror Movies*, whose reviewer found the picture "overrated," though confessed an admiration for the visuals and the score. *The Motion Picture Guide* gave the film a **** rating.

Onibaba *(1964)*

Onibaba (*The Hole*) is a simple, sexually explicit tale of isolation and survival. Beautifully photographed in black and white, its horror elements are slight, but they're there. The film was distributed to art houses in the United States in the subtitled format by Toho International (for Kindai Movie Company, Ltd.).

In sixteenth-century Japan, a middle-aged peasant woman (Nobuko Otowa) and her fawn-like daughter-in-law (Jitsuko Yoshimura) live in a small thatched hut in the middle of an enormous wetlands area, where reeds and other vegetation grow well above their heads. Because of endless war and rampant famine, the two women find themselves resorting to murdering lost or deserting samurai warriors to sell their armor, weapons and anything else of value to a black market dealer (Taiji Tonomura) in exchange for food. While consuming their evening meal, a neighboring farmer, Hachi (Kei Sato), returns from the war. He had traveled with the daughter-in-law's husband (and the woman's son). Hachi says the husband was killed by a mob of angry farmers and that he barely escaped with his own life. Hachi tries to convince the daughter-in-law to move in with him, and since she's been lonely for quite some time, she doesn't refuse his advances. The peasant woman is against the relationship, however. She fears that since her son is now dead and the daughter-in-law has no obligation to remain with her, she'll be abandoned and left to fend for herself. The daughter-in-law begins sneaking out late at night to begin a highly charged romance with Hachi. The peasant woman is aware of the woman's movements, however, silently watching the young lovers with great anguish. Late one evening, after the young woman has left the hut for a late-night rendezvous with Hachi, the peasant woman is visited by a samurai warrior (Jukichi Uno) who wears a hideous mask. The warrior claims he is lost, and orders the woman to guide him out of the wetlands. She asks him about his mask. He says that he has the most beautiful face in all Japan and that he didn't want it damaged during the war. She asks to see his face as payment for guiding him, but he refuses. The woman jumps over an enormous hole in the ground, which is where she and the daughter-in-law have been dumping the bodies of the warriors they've murdered. The samurai falls to his death. Climbing down the dark hole, she removes the mask to discover the man's face is not handsome, but horribly disfigured. She removes his armor, which she intends to sell to the merchant, but keeps the mask for herself.

The following night, the peasant woman tells the daughter-in-law that she is leaving to sell some of the armor, but she actually hides between her hut and the hut belonging to Hachi, who is waiting for the daughter-in-law to sneak out for a midnight tryst. When she does, the peasant woman dons the mask and terrifies the young woman, who returns to the hut. This works for several nights, but eventually the daughter-in-law and Hachi meet amongst the reeds. The daughter-in-law's fears have only strengthened the bond between the young couple. The daughter-in-law decides to move in with Hachi. Hachi returns to his hut, only to be murdered by a starving wanderer. When she returns to the hut, the daughter-in-law finds the peasant woman—still wearing the mask and paralyzed with fear. She confesses her scheme to the daughter-in-law and begs her to help take off the mask: it's stuck. The daughter-in-law, angry at the peasant woman's scheming, whacks at the mask with a hammer, even though it's still on the screaming woman's face. The mask eventually cracks in two, and once removed, the peasant woman's face is even more disfigured than that of the warrior she murdered. The daughter-in-law runs screaming from the hut, closely followed by the peasant woman. The women leap over the hole, and it's implied that the peasant woman does not survive.

Onibaba is a deliberately paced, fascinating and vivid portrait of the daily suffering of peasants during wartime. The main characters are simple farmers driven to cold-blooded murder in order to survive. They're not so much sympathetic as simply pathetic. The middle-aged woman has lost her only son and has to murder others or starve to death herself. She's cold and mean spirited, though she certainly doesn't seem to deserve the fate she's given in the end. Hachi is something of a coward (the peasant woman suspects he murdered her son, which certainly seems possible) and a bit oafish, but his rather sudden and confusing death near the close seems a bit mean spirited as well, though it certainly fits in with the film's apocalyptic theme. Even the daughter-in-law, who seemed like an innocent pawn for most of the picture, turns mean. She pulls at the mask stuck on the peasant woman's face rather ruthlessly. She's angry, but the peasant woman's cries are hard to ignore, and banging the woman's face with the hammer is more than a bit extreme. *Onibaba* was one of the first modern films released in the United States to feature nudity and oncamera simulated sex. From the mid-thirties through 1967, movies featuring nudity of any kind were strictly forbidden in mainstream theatrical features. "Nudies" and other adults-only films from this period were pretty tame by comparison. *Onibaba* is fairly hot stuff even by today's standards, which probably helped it considerably at the box office, both here and in Japan.

Director-screenwriter–art director Kaneto Shindo paints a vivid and intimate portrait of peasant life. The film's wonderfully atmospheric locations help tremendously in this regard. One really can't see more than a few feet in any direction because of the tall vegetation, which is constantly blowing in the wind. This creates a sense of isolation and uneasiness which the director carefully exploits. Shindo was born in 1912, in Hiroshima. He began his screen career as an art director, and later a screenwriter. He worked at Shochiku beginning in 1944 under Kozaburo Yoshimura. He left the studio in 1950 to help establish Kindai Eiga Kyokai, Ltd., a production company not unlike United Artists in the United States. His early credits for Kindai Eiga, *Children of Hiroshima* (1953), *Lucky Dragon No. 5* (1959) and *The Island* (1960), established his reputation. Four years after *Onibaba*, Shindo would direct another horror film, *Kuroneko* (q.v.), which was also released through Toho.

The mask, which seems both anguished and amused at the same time, is truly creepy. If someone were to jump out of nowhere toward *me* wearing that thing, I'd be running, too. However, the effects makeup on the samurai and the peasant woman is much less imaginative, even bland. Kiyomi Kuroda's black and white TohoScope photography is superb and lends tremendously to the film's atmosphere. The current home video version is letterboxed to about 1.66:1 from the 2.35:1 original but is also slightly squeezed to reveal most of the remaining image. The performances, especially Nobuko Otowa's peasant woman, are right on the mark and can be fully appreciated in the brightly subtitled home video version.

The picture received mostly excellent reviews. Phil Hardy, in his *The Encyclopedia of Horror Movies*, said the film was "staged and photographed with consummate mastery" and admired the film's "tremendously powerful performances." *The Motion Picture Guide* gave the film *½, but didn't explain the poor rating. *Variety*'s "Wear" liked the performances and said the film was "sometimes high adventure and exciting, at other times dull in its so-called symbolism." Like many reviewers of the day, much of the review focused on the amount and degree of the film's explicit sexuality. *Onibaba* won the Sphinx Grand Prix at the 1965 Panamanian Awards, for "best film, best screenplay, and best actor (Kei Sato)."

Adventure in Takla Makan *(1965)*

I have not seen this Japanese-made adventure, which was filmed in Iran (near Isfahan) and stars Toshiro Mifune. If the picture was released in the United States, it was probably limited to Los Angeles, New York and possibly a few other cities, and hasn't been seen much in this country since. A brief clip from this Toho production turns up on the laser disc of *Godzilla Fantasia*, a wonderful audio-video collection of Akira Ifukube's music. Based on this single, brief sequence (vaguely reminiscent of *Lawrence of Arabia*), I would like to see the film someday.

According to *Variety*'s review of the film: In the year 700, a shipwrecked sailor in China, Ohsumi (Toshiro Mifune), meets a priest in search of the Buddha's remains. The pair encounter large birds and wizards. They cross the Takla Makan Desert and discover a castle "full of heavies who try to do the pair in." Ohsumi "makes the king a better man, gives him a Japanese wife (Mie Hama?), and departs."

Variety's "Chie" didn't think much of the picture. "Location stuff is first-rate but [the] rest of the film suffers by comparison... The best bet for this picture in the U.S. would be as a kiddy film. Mifune's name might draw the art crowd but the film itself would send them away."

Frankenstein Conquers the World *(1965)*

The Frankenstein legend was brought to modern-day Japan in *Frankenstein Conquers the World*, originally released as *Fuharankanshutain tai chitei kaiju Baragon* (*Frankenstein Against the Subterranean Monster Baragon*). It was the first Japanese fantastic film to feature an American star (albeit a star in decline), and was one of the first Japanese giant monster films to involve American input early on. Now more than ever, Toho's monster movies were being produced for the international market.

In 1945, just as the war in Europe is drawing to a close, German officers break into a European castle-laboratory where a wild-eyed scientist is mixing chemicals. The officers silently but sternly present orders to remove a mysterious steel-case box. The box is taken by German submarine halfway around the world, where it's then transferred to a Japanese sub and delivered to scientists working in Hiroshima. One of the scientists (Takashi Shimura in an all-too-brief cameo) tells the curious courier that the box contains the heart of the Frankenstein monster which, he explains, can never die. As it happens, the heart has arrived just as Allied forces drop the atomic bomb on the city, thus ending World War II and utterly destroying the industrial metropolis. Years later, Dr. James Bowen (Nick Adams), an American, is working as a radiation specialist in Hiroshima, apparently, in part, out of guilt for what his people did to the city years earlier. He's dating an attractive co-worker, Dr. Sueko Togami (Kumi Mizuno), and the two embark on a kind of personal cultural exchange program. A strange-looking, wild boy with a pronounced brow and crooked teeth is seen in Togami's neighborhood. After breaking into an elementary school (killing and eating a rabbit there) and other such mayhem, the boy is taken to Togami and Bowen's laboratory. It is learned that the boy is somehow connected to the Frankenstein heart, which had been bombarded with radiation during the destruction years earlier. Just what the boy's relation is to the heart is unclear. One source suggests that the young boy, starving to death after the bomb was dropped, finds the radioactive heart and eats it, but Toho expert David Milner insists that the radioactive heart simply grew into a complete body. In any event, the boy continues to grow at an alarming rate, eventually becoming so large he must be kept in a makeshift jail cell. The monster—simply called Frankenstein—escapes, ripping one of his own hands off to do so. The hand turns out to be alive, and Bowen's staff examines the none-too-convincing mechanical prop and debates whether to save or destroy Frankenstein, this apparently to pad out the running time. While authorities search for Frankenstein, another creature, a four-legged reptilian monster called Baragon, appears.

The two monsters clash, with Frankenstein seemingly the winner of the Big Bout. Suddenly and without warning, a tremendous earthquake occurs, and Frankenstein sinks deep into the bowels of the Earth. However, an alternate ending, available on Toho Video's release of the picture continues for several minutes after the defeat of Baragon, and minus the sudden tremor. Immediately after Frankenstein kills the giant reptile, a tremendous octopus-like "Devilfish" (the film was originally announced as *Frankenstein vs. the Giant Devilfish*) crawls out of the sea and grapples with Frankenstein. Both monsters fall into the sea a la *King Kong vs. Godzilla*, only this time neither monster surfaces.

The appearance of the devilfish has been the source of great frustration among Japanese fantasy film buffs in the United States. For years it wasn't clear whether this sequence was a part of the final Japanese cut or shot and abandoned sometime before the picture's release. The story goes that the film originally was supposed to revolve around a battle between Frankenstein and the Devilfish—Baragon wasn't in the picture at all—until the Devilfish prop proved too unconvincing, or something. Effects director Eiji Tsuburaya certainly seemed to have a fondness for this type of creature, as similar monsters turn up in *King Kong vs. Godzilla* and *War of the Gargantuas*, the latter a semi-sequel to *Frankenstein Conquers the World*. It's true that the monster looks pretty much like just what it was—a big rubber marionette, albeit a pretty good one as far as rubber octopi go. It's also true that Baragon looks rather hastily designed and constructed. With its ping-pong-ball eyes, glowing horn and Boston Terrier face (which appears to be smiling, at that!) Baragon is anything but threatening, and its brief scenes are mostly comical. One sequence, for instance, finds Baragon so hungry he literally eats a horse. To its credit this was one of the few Japanese monster films that actually attempt to explain what giant monsters eat. Nonetheless, the big battle between Frankenstein and Baragon is a long time in coming and not very interesting when it does.

So what's the devilfish doing in the Japanese video, but not in the American theatrical release? Did the film's distributor in the United States (AIP) cut the devilfish because it wasn't convincing? Not convincing in a film about a one-hundred-foot Frankenstein monster?! You'd think that the appearance of a giant octopus would have helped market the film in the United States. One can easily imagine AIP's publicity department coming up with lurid poster art of the giant octopus clutching a bikini-clad heroine. Did test audiences in the United States laugh at the rubber marionette? Both versions end abruptly and without warning after a very long, tiresome build-up, with neither ending very satisfying. Interestingly, the American version's wrap-up, with Frankenstein being swallowed up in the earthquake, is clearly Toho-shot. Perhaps the picture's U.S. backers insisted Toho shoot the new ending.

Frankenstein Conquers the World is one of Toho's best and last monster movies to revolve around interesting human characters. Unfortunately, the monster footage is often below par, due in part to the reasons described above. The result is an interesting story with interesting characters undone by disappointing effects work. Of course the story is preposterous, but no more so than nearly every Frankenstein film since Universal's *Frankenstein Meets the Wolfman* (1943). The film rather ingeniously brings the Frankenstein legend to Japan, and the opening sequence, with its Axis submarines, pre-bomb Hiroshima and eerie Akira Ifukube score gets the film off to a good start.

Nick Adams was a rising star in the 1950s, with co-starring roles in films as varied as *Rebel Without a Cause* (1955), which starred Adams' friend, James Dean, *Pillow Talk* (1959) and *The Interns* (1962). His fortunes tumbled sharply in the sixties, this despite a best supporting actor nomination for 1963's *Twilight of Honor*. He began appearing in lower-budgeted monster movies—he was also in the British-made *Die, Monster Die* (1965) and Toho's *Monster Zero* (1965, U.S. release 1970)—just prior to his untimely death (generally considered a suicide) in 1968. He was just 37 years old. His multi-picture stay in Japan (which also included the spy thriller *The Killing Bottle*, which went unreleased in the United States) was apparently a happy one, at least according to the fan magazines which reported Adams' admiration for director Ishiro Honda and his co-stars. Although low-keyed, Adams' performance gives the film a much-needed boost. In the U.S. version, Adams speaks English as usual while all the other performers are dubbed. Although Toho's trailer for the film subtitled Adams' speech in the Japanese version, everyone spoke Japanese— Adams' part was dubbed by another actor. Adams' role, an American immersing himself into Japanese culture, is an interesting one that fans of Japanese cinema can certainly relate to, and his relationship with Kumi Mizuno is one of the most interesting in Toho's giant monster series. Mizuno herself was clearly Toho's best genre actress. She was one of the few actresses in Toho's monster movies given strong, intelligent roles. Her Dr. Togami is both smart and compassionate, and her relationship with Adams is appealing.

Tadao Takashima co-stars as a scientist intent on destroying Frankenstein before the monster gets out of hand. It's not much of a part, though it's his role that accounts for the film's most interesting special effect: After Takashima goes searching for Frankenstein, Adams and Mizuno are seen driving through a dense forest, when suddenly the gigantic legs of Frankenstein step out from behind the trees to block the road. The monster, with Takashima's body in one hand, sets the wounded scientist down and departs. It's an eerie and effective moment. However, scenes like that are few and far between. After a promising start, the film becomes bogged down as the trio of scientists and the military spend far too much time searching for the monster. The final battle is especially uninteresting and only hurts the picture further.

In his highly readable *The Frankenstein Legend*, Donald Glut notes that the miniature work was "showing sloppiness," but "still gave visual excitement to an otherwise non-traditional and mostly ridiculous Frankenstein effort." *Variety's* "Robe" noted "dat ol' debbilfish" had disappeared and considered the script "straight out of the file used by director Ishiro Honda in the past," but considered the film "a good programmer." Predictably, *The Motion Picture Guide* gave the film a zero rating, calling the picture "pitiful... the results are barely laughable... really awful, even for a Japanese monster movie." *Psychotronic* didn't think much of the picture either, calling it "ridiculous" and "a new low in horror," while Greg Shoemaker said "the lead roles receive a goodly portion of the script's attention... and fortunately, the Japanese players have been treated well by their English voices and lines." *Frankenstein Conquers the World* is ridiculous but also very nearly saved by its interesting premise and the fine performances of Adams and Mizuno. Unfortunately, its middle third is deadly dull, and its sloppy and limited special effects bring down the entire show.

Gammera the Invincible *(1965/1966)*

The success of Toho's Godzilla pictures led rival Daiei to create a monster series of its own. The Gamera movies (the second "m" was added for the Americanization and dropped after the first feature) were popular enough to warrant a new production each year, ending only with Daiei's bankruptcy in the early seventies. The Gamera films had significantly lower budgets than Toho's monsteramas and were aimed at a much younger audience. Toho followed suit on its own increasingly less successful genre pictures, resulting in a creative tailspin in the *kaiju eiga* cycle. The stories became less imaginative, more juvenile, and depressingly cheap. Taking a cue from Godzilla's debut in *King of the Monsters!*, *Gammera the Invincible* featured additional footage shot for the American release. Brian Donlevy and Albert Dekker toplined the new footage, set at an Alaskan army base, the Pentagon and UN headquarters. This version was frequently shown on American television in the 1970s, but has since been supplanted by Sandy Frank's television and home video version, more or less the Japanese original (and now called *Gamera*). This new version has been completely redubbed, while Donlevy, Dekker and the rest of the American cast have been excised. What follows is a synopsis of *Gamera*, not *Gammera the Invincible*, but their storylines are very nearly identical.

Dr. Hidaka (Eiji Funakoshi) is part of a scientific expedition in the frozen Arctic. The expedition meets an Eskimo, just as strangely silent, low-flying jets from an unnamed nation (they're Russian in *Gammera the Invincible*) appear overhead. At a nearby U.S. air base (whose commander talks like Buddy Hackett) fighters are dispatched. The American pilots manage to shoot down one of the enemy jets, which, as it turns out, was carrying atomic weapons. The plane crashes, creating a tremendous radioactive explosion. Out of the flames rises a gigantic prehistoric turtle, which the Eskimo calls Gamera. The two-hundred-foot creature has a wrinkly face and oversized, useless tusks on the lower jaw which as Donald Glut suggests, "come dangerously close to impaling the eyes every time Gamera shuts his mouth." The Eskimo says that "strange giant turtles" once lived on the "Arctic continent" (it's not, incidentally). He gives Hidaka an ancient stone and claims that the beast is "the devil's envoy." Gamera lumbers to Hidaka's ship, crushing it and setting it aflame with his fiery breath (Gamera breathes real flames compared to Godzilla's animated spray). Hidaka suggests the creature will soon die of radiation poisoning, and soon the world's attention turns to the appearance of a glowing flying saucer which is spotted in every corner of the world.

Meanwhile, a little boy named Kenny (strangely, several names in the Daiei version have been Anglicized, but remain Japanese in *Gammera the Invicible*) is scolded by his father (his grandfather in the American edition) for becoming too obsessed with turtles. He draws pictures of them all day long and even takes his pet turtle, "Tibby," to school. Kenny's father orders his son to get rid of Tibby. As Kenny takes his pet to the beach, Gamera appears over a ridge and Kenny races to the top of a nearby lighthouse to greet the supersized reptile. The monster clumsily knocks over part of the tower, and Kenny falls. Gamera catches the youngster in the nick of time, however, gently setting him on the ground below. "He knew I liked turtles!" Kenny insists. Gamera next appears at a geothermal power station and consumes the plant's energy. The army tries to stop Gamera with electric power lines, but the monster only seems to like the juice. Dr. Hidaka suggests that electricity "charges it like a battery!" Hidaka and the military consult Dr. Murase (Jun Hamamura), who suggests that since heat-based weapons don't seem to work, why not try using cold against the monster? Military strategists offer a top-secret bomb "that can freeze just about anything." The only problem is that its effects last but ten minutes. The bomb is exploded, and the defense forces work quickly, turning the big turtle on its back, making it helpless. However, just as victory appears to be at hand, Gamera pulls in his head and limbs and flames appear from the creature's sockets (what happened to its head and limbs?). The monster begins spinning like a top and flies away like a gigantic, flaming frisbee. Gamera is the UFO! The monster invades Tokyo, causing massive destruction and killing hundreds of people. Authorities decide to use "Plan Z," which somehow involves a secret base built with Japanese-U.S.-Soviet monies. The military keeps Gamera busy while preparations for "Plan Z" are being made. They release trainloads of petroleum and coal for the titanic turtle to ingest. A smiling Kenny rides one of the cars to meet his monstrous pal but is rescued at the last minute. To attract the monster to the base, the defense forces ignite a line of flames (his favorite food, we're told), leading straight to the island base. Gamera is drawn to a large platform which—surprise—turns out to be the capsule for a rocketship. The big reptile is trapped inside, and the rocket is immediately launched into deep space. The mission is a success, and even little Kenny seems happy. He announces his intention to become an astronaut, so that he can be reunited with his new friend. "Gamera, see you soon!" he says.

One of the problems with *Gamera* is that it's neither a kiddie adventure nor a serious monster movie. The conflict between these two elements takes on ludicrous proportions with Kenny insisting that Gamera "loves children" and is "good and gentle," as the monster roasts fleeing extras. The Eskimo calls the creature nothing less than the "devil's envoy," and yet Gamera happily rescues Kenny at the lighthouse (after conveniently knocking it over in the first place). Kenny's obsession with turtles goes unexplained at the beginning of the film, and is completely unresolved at the end. Judging by his continually foolish and dangerous actions, Kenny doesn't need Gamera so much as a good psychiatrist. The military's efforts to get rid of the monster are predictable and quite tiresome. *Variety*'s "Byro" thought Plan Z "an appropriate idea for *Gamera*, a film which can be rated as Grade Z," while *The Motion Picture Guide*, giving the film a zero rating, suggested Plan Z's rocket "should have smuggled the sequel scripts instead."

Gamera was the only film in the series shot in black and white; indeed, it was the last of Japan's giant monster films released in this format. By 1965, black and white features were fairly rare, even in Japan (Daiei had been a major force in the switch over to color stock in the first place, oddly enough). Maybe they shot the picture this way because *Godzilla* was in black and white. The decision to film in black and white *did help* in one respect—the special effects look less cheap than those in later, color entries. A bit more care seems to have been accorded to this production. There are, for example, several interesting effects. A nice matte shot showing Gamera destroying the arctic ship as sailors flee across an iceberg is impressive, rivaling Toho's best work from the period. A gigantic prehistoric turtle isn't a bad idea for a monster, though Daiei's effects crew has the character up on its hind legs most of the time, when it should be crawling on all fours. Of course, this problem is minor compared to the monster's flying abilities, which add nothing to the story. In later films, Gamera would face creatures even more outlandish than itself. Daiei's monster menagerie never followed even the most basic rules of zoology, and were always a disappointment compared to Toho's giant monsters.

Gammera the Invincible was the only film in the series to see a theatrical release in the United States. Five of the seven sequels were picked up by American International television (AIP-TV); the sixth and seventh were released directly to television in the late 1980s. The Americanized version was in many ways an improvement over the original cut. The dubbing is far superior, and the edits made to accommodate the inserted scenes move the original film along at a better clip. The Buddy Hackett footage was replaced by new scenes set at an Alaskan airbase and featuring Dick O'Neill (*The Taking of Pelham One, Two, Three* and *Wolfen*) as a general. O'Neill is a familiar character actor who specializes in short-tempered military and working man types.

Brian Donlevy and Albert Dekker, both men in the unhappy twilight of their careers, were featured in much more static scenes set at the Pentagon and at a tiny UN conference room. Donlevy was a popular heavy during the thirties and forties, appearing opposite Marlene Dietrich and James Stewart in *Destry Rides Again* and Gary Cooper in *Beau Geste* (both 1939). But he also played surly anti-heroes in films like Preston Sturges' landmark comedy, *The Great McGinty* (1940). In the 1950s Donlevy's career fell into sharp decline, brought on by a devastating bout with alcoholism, but was fine in Hammer's first two Quatermass films, *The Creeping Unknown/The Quatermass Experiment* (1955) and *Enemy from Space/Quatermass II* (1957). By the 1960s, however, Donlevy's drinking problems had obviously affected his screen performances. He continued to act in films, including a starring turn in *Curse of the Fly* (1965), but by then his line readings were notably slurred and clouded. In *Gammera the Invincible*, the actor is acceptable in the UN scenes (surprising, given the absolute gobbledygook he has here) but appears lost during the Pentagon sequence. Donlevy died in 1972. Albert Dekker was an interesting, difficult-to-cast performer, best known to genre fans as *Dr. Cyclops* (1940). Dekker appeared in *Beau Geste* as well, along with *The Man in the Iron Mask* (1939), *Among the Living* (1941), *The Pretender* (1948), *Kiss Me Deadly* (1955), and the posthumously released *The Wild Bunch* (1969), but remains best-known for his notorious accident-suicide in 1968. His role is much less prominent than Donlevy's, though he was probably a better actor. Alan Oppenheimer (*Westworld*, *The Hindenburg*) is hammy in the only other significant American padding, as a scientist debating Gammera's existence on a talk show.

The Gamera movies are slow-moving, slow-witted, and almost unwatchable, little more than expanded kiddie shows touting special effects only marginally better than what was already flooding Japanese television. What appeal these pictures might have had on big screens in Japan in the 1960s is all but lost on American television today.... But we may not have seen the last of Gamera: a remake has been announced.

Monster Zero *(1965)*

Toho's Godzilla entry for 1965 is an enjoyable if structurally flawed film combining elements from the past few entries with, for the first time, the concept of alien invasion, previously dramatized in the studio's *The Mysterians* (1957) and *Battle in Outer Space* (1959). Godzilla's transformation from nuclear-bred reptilian terror to homogenized Savior of Earth continued, and while the film breaks little, if any, new ground, it is an enjoyable picture and perhaps the most representative of the sixties Godzilla films.

When a mysterious planet is discovered beyond Jupiter, the World Space Authority launches an exploratory space ship, the P-1, to investigate. Astronauts Glenn (Nick Adams) and Fuji (Akira Takarada) stay in communication with project leader Dr. Sakurai (Jun Tazaki) back on Earth until the ship passes into Jupiter's shadow. Meanwhile, Fuji's sister, Haruno (Keiko Sawai), meets with her inventor boyfriend, Tetsuo (Akira Kubo, atypically cast in a broadly comic role), of whom her brother does not approve. Tetsuo has invented a compact and very noisy alarm which he sells to a Miss Namikawa (Kumi Mizuno), a representative of World Education Corporation, for $100,000. P-1 lands on Planet X. Fuji eyes a pair of footprints, and when he later plants a flag, lightning appears out of the sky. Fuji returns to the landing site to find that Glenn and the ship have vanished. Just then, a glowing cylinder rises from the ground and a voice orders Fuji to step inside. Taken deep inside an underground alien base, Fuji is reunited with Glenn. The astronauts are greeted by the Controller of Planet X (a completely unrecognizable Yoshio Tsuchiya) and his aides. The ludicrously costumed aliens wear too-tight gray jumpsuits, slit-like sunglasses, black hoods (with antennae), oversized black collars and tiny vests. They also wear curl-up shoes, the kind one might expect to find on the tiny feet of Santa's elves. The X-ites ask the astronauts for Earth's help. A giant creature, which the X-ites call Monster Zero, has forced the citizens of Planet X underground. Suddenly, Monster Zero appears. It is King Ghidorah (called Ghidrah in the previous entry), the flying golden dragon, who sprays the area with electrical bolts from each of its three heads (which explains the lightning Fuji saw earlier) before departing. At the same time, the X-ites' base experiences a "hydrogenoxide" (i.e., water) emergency. Planet X's Controller asks the Earth's assistance in defeating the monster. The X-ites want to borrow Godzilla and Rodan to use as "exterminators" against Ghidorah so that they may live in peace. For Earth's help, the X-ites offer a miracle drug, which the aliens claim will cure all diseases known to man. Glenn and Fuji depart, promising to carry the X-ites' message to the leaders of Earth. As the P-1 flies off, the Controller of Planet X laughs menacingly.

At a meeting in the Diet Building, everyone agrees to help Planet X in exchange for the miracle drug, but Glenn and Fuji begin to get suspicious. The astronauts meet with Haruno and Tetsuo. Fuji still disapproves of his sister's boyfriend, especially when he learns Tetsuo hasn't yet received any money for his invention. Tetsuo has made inquiries at World Education Corporation, which turns out to be a front for X-ites operations. Glenn leaves for a weekend getaway with his girlfriend, who turns out to be Namikawa. Later, Glenn tells Fuji that he saw the Controller in the bungalow where he and Namikawa had slept. They begin to suspect Planet X may be getting short of water and, as

Glenn puts it, "maybe they figured it's time to move." The military gathers at Lake Myojin, looking for Godzilla. The lake bubbles up, and everyone is surprised to see not Godzilla but several pot-bellied X-ite saucers rise from the lake. They were on Earth all along. One of the saucers lands, and several X-ites, including the Controller, meet with officials. Sakurai chastises the aliens for visiting Earth unannounced, but this is soon forgotten. Sakurai, Glenn and Fuji are invited back to Planet X to watch the battle. Glenn says goodbye to Namikawa, promising to marry her when he returns. She leaves, and Tetsuo follows her. Godzilla and Rodan are lifted out of the lake and mountainside, respectively, and carried aloft by the saucers, safely "crated" in transparent spheres (there's a terrific low-angle shot of the three saucers, monsters in tow, flying off into space, whose beautiful wide screen composition is unfortunately cropped for television). The saucers drop the monsters on Planet X, then quickly retreat underground to watch the big battle. Soon enough, King Ghidorah appears, but Godzilla and Rodan quickly drive the monster off. Glenn and Fuji snoop around the base and find a pair of X-ite women who look just like Namikawa.

Back on Earth, Tetsuo has followed Namikawa to a large lakeside cottage, the X-ites' secret headquarters. X-ites quickly throw Tetsuo into a soundproof cell. The seemingly grateful X-ites give Sakurai a tape of the miracle drug's formula, then send them back to Earth in an exact duplicate of the P-1 the X-ites made during the astronauts' previous visit. The tape is played, but—surprise!—not only is there no mention of a miracle drug, but the Controller of Planet X demands the Earth surrender to the aliens. "Double-crossing finks!" yells Glenn. Glenn finds Namikawa, now wearing an X-ite uniform. She pleads with her lover to become a citizen of Planet X so that they can marry, but the astronaut refuses. "We're gonna fight to the last man, baby." More X-ites appear, and Namikawa slips a piece of paper in Glenn's jacket just before she's shot dead by the X-ites. "You rats," explodes Glenn, "You stinkin' rats!" Planet X launches an assault on the Earth, sending Ghidorah to attack the United States in the Western Hemisphere (not shown), while Godzilla and Rodan take care of Japan. Fuji and Sakurai determine that the monsters are being controlled by means of synthetic brain waves (Fuji had seen the X-ites pilot the saucer by mere thought en route to Planet X), and works on a device that will sever the similar waves controlling Godzilla and Rodan. Glenn is taken to the X-ites' island base and thrown into the cell with Tetsuo. They find Namikawa's note, in which she tells Glenn that her love was "beyond all computation," and that "we machines can be destroyed by a certain simple sound." Tetsuo realizes that the sound must be the same as the noise emitted from his invention. He happens to have one in his pocket (didn't they search him?) and begins blaring the alarm, which cripples the guards and allows the pair to escape. Defense forces (led by Yoshibumi Tajima) sever the X-ites' thought control over the monsters, while Tetsuo's deafening invention is blasted through speakers. The saucers begin dropping like flies, and their island base is blown up. Free from the X-ites' control, Godzilla and Rodan square off against Ghidorah, who once again is defeated. Sakurai orders Glenn and Fuji back to Planet X, to serve as ambassadors in their water crisis. Glenn laughs, saying, "Whatever's fair, pal."

Monster Zero (known today as *Godzilla vs. Monster Zero*) is a very enjoyable if silly entry, with Toho's monster unit at the peak of its powers. By now everyone, from directors Honda and Tsuburaya to the familiar ensemble cast, had perfected the genre while having not yet grown tired of it. Shinichi Sekizawa's script is flawed, but interesting. It begs the question, If the aliens were already on Earth and always had the ability to control the monsters (including Ghidorah), why pretend to be peaceful creatures in need of Earth's help? Why offer the miracle drug at all?

Still, the film is full of surprises. The scene where Fuji returns to the P-1's landing site to find that Glenn and the P-1 have vanished is both humorous and eerie. The identity of Monster Zero, while clearly promised in all advertising for the film, is a surprise (I certainly didn't expect to see the creature when I first saw the film), as are Namikawa's duplicates and the second P-1 on Planet X. For this outing, the monsters take a back seat to the human characters. The relationship between Glenn and Namikawa is particularly interesting. Nick Adams and Kumi Mizuno were also paired in *Frankenstein Conquers the World*, and *Monster Zero* takes their relationship one step further, sexually anyway (overtly sexual relationships are unusual for a Toho monster film; I suspect this element would not have been included if Glenn's character were Japanese). As I've stated elsewhere, Mizuno was far and away the most interesting of Toho's *kaiju eiga* actresses, while Adams' culturally diplomatic American was always likeable.

August Ragone and Guy Tucker relate an amusing story about Adams in their excellent examination of Honda's Godzilla pictures, "The Legend of Godzilla: The Honda Years," published in *Markalite* #3.

> Unlike most of the Hollywood actors that followed him, [Adams] was... very popular with the cast and crew, particularly Yoshio Tsuchiya, an inveterate practical joker who started Adams' Japanese lessons by teaching him to say "I'm starving!" for "Good morning," and later, "How's it hanging?" for "Pleased to meet you"—this latter incident reportedly caused a group of wealthy old ladies to shrink from him in horror. Adams quickly learned to dish it back, learning the real Japanese for "You're overacting!" during Tsuchiya's scenes as Controller of Planet X. Adams very much admired Tsuchiya, partly due to his work with Kurosawa, and asked if he could arrange for Toshiro Mifune to dub Adams' voice for the Japanese version. The reply: "Sure, can you get Henry Fonda to do mine?"

Surprisingly, the monsters are given the short shrift here, their scenes confined to two brief battles, the first on Planet X, and the latter on Earth, which unfortunately incorporates extensive footage from *Rodan*, grainily *Super-Scoped* and never matching the newly shot effects footage. The monsters have changed little since *Ghidrah: The Three-Headed Monster* the year before. Ghidorah makes a splashy entrance, flying straight toward the camera over the impressive diorama of Planet X (including a beautifully painted backdrop, dominated by a massive Jupiter). Godzilla continued his transformation from bad guy to superhero; in the picture's most embarrassing moment (or highlight, depending on one's tastes), Godzilla does a little jig on Planet X after driving off Ghidorah, a piece of business apparently inspired by "Ahso Matsu-kun," a Japanese comic Tsuburaya admired. Rodan, silly as ever, has a reduced role. Mothra, who was needed to defeat the three-headed dragon before, isn't even mentioned here. Other effects are variable, but generally workable and sometimes very impressive. For once, the studio's matte work is up to the level of its miniatures. After P-1 has landed on Planet X, there is some nice cutting between the massive three-meters-tall miniature of the rocket and several matte shots of Adams preparing to be lowered down to the surface. Later, there's an almost flawless matte of the X-ites climbing out of their saucers after it has risen from the lake.

Honda's live action direction is crisp and to the point, while Akira Ifukube wrote another fine score for the film. Particularly good are Takeo Kita's unearthly X-ite sets, put to good use early in the film. It's a shame that the aliens' costumes are so silly in comparison. *Monster Zero*, like *Frankenstein Conquers the World*, was made in collaboration with Henry G. Saperstein Enterprises, which for some strange reason waited four and a half years (and some two years after Adams' death) before releasing the picture stateside. Adams' voice was left untouched, while Takarada, Mizuno and especially Kubo and Tsuchiya were dubbed with the usual cartoon-like voices, and certainly not by the likes of Henry Fonda (Marvin Miller dubbed Takarada's voice, according to the *JFFJ*).

Science Fiction, which mistakenly believed *Monster Zero* was made prior to *Ghidrah: The Three-Headed Monster*, read too much into the film's storyline, suggesting that "the monsters that so recently threatened the world have now been changed into the Earth's most powerful weapons, confirming a drastic shift in attitude towards military force, signaled in [*Atragon*] and [*Dagora, the Space Monster*] ... Ghidorah [was] the most vicious of the creatures to populate the genre, possibly because it had no connection with tension within Japan and represented a pure and hostile 'outside.'" *The Motion Picture Guide* called *Monster Zero* "top-flight science fiction, which we've come to expect from Toho and Honda." That doesn't explain, however, why they gave the film just a ** rating, and many Toho/Honda films lower than that. Greg Shoemaker, in his "Toho Legacy" series for the *Japanese Fantasy Film Journal*, liked the film's "unrelenting pace" and particularly admired the sequence where Godzilla and Rodan are transported to Planet X. He did have reservations, though. "The picture's live-action leads are not so intriguing, nor are they well-developed. The film's major drawback, however, is mediocre dubbing of godawful voices and comic book dialogue. In this highly incredulous genre, one of the requirements for audience acceptability is realistic speech. The villains, all graduates of the 'Snidely Whiplash School of Voice,' are an example of failure in this area." *Markalite*, in the aforementioned look at Honda's Godzilla pictures, noted "Sekizawa's scenario, while witty, is laced with heavier drama than in [*Ghidrah: The Three-Headed Monster*], while the treatment of the monsters is loose, and increasingly humorous.... The structure of the film is such that this point is easy to overlook, largely due to the ever-professional hand of Ishiro Honda, whose direction is as speedy and compact as ever, especially with the fluid transitions from scene to scene."

Ebirah, Horror of the Deep *(1966)*

Toho's Godzilla entry for the year, originally released to American television as the above, but better known today as *Godzilla Versus the Sea Monster*, has a noticeably lower budget, a second-string director (Jun Fukuda) and a markedly different musical score (by Masaru Sato), and yet in many ways it's one of the best films in the series. What's lacking in so many Japanese monster movies is a story with enough interest to carry viewers to the Big Payoff: the monster scenes. Godzilla doesn't even show up until about halfway into the film, but the story here is so interesting and well paced, one doesn't have time to get impatient.

Deep in the South Pacific, a fisherman, Yata (Toru Ibuke), watches helplessly as his sailboat is attacked by a gigantic monster. A giant claw rises out of the stormy sea and crushes the comparatively tiny craft. Two months later, his brother, Ruta (Toru Watanabe) believes Yata is still alive somewhere and visits a dance marathon, hoping to win the sailboat that's offered as first prize. He's too late to enter, however, and instead hangs out with friends Ichiro and Mita (Chotaro Togano and Hideo Sunazuka). The three visit a harbor and find a sailboat, the *Yahlen*, perfectly suited to Ruta's needs. (A major gaffe in the editing of the American edition here, as the ship's name can clearly be seen on Yata's boat in the opening sequence as well.) The men are met by the suspicious Yashi (Akira Takarada), who is first angered by their sneaking aboard, then mysteriously allows them to spend the night on the ship. The following morning, Mita, Ichiro and Yashi rise from their slumber shocked to find themselves far out to sea. Ruta has stolen the boat to look for his brother. It's a "gift of the gods," he says. Since nobody seems to be in a hurry to return to port, the men go along with the plan. Over the radio, they hear that the ship they have stolen belonged not to Yashi, but to a retired American businessman. Yashi, we learn, was behind a heist of four million yen. To pass the time, the bored bank robber makes a skeleton key. "You have your hobbies, I have mine," he says. A storm develops, and the *Yahlen* is attacked by the giant lobster-like monster, Ebirah (the critter goes unnamed in the English language version).

The following morning, the men awaken on a nearby tropical island and scale the side of a cliff. Mita finds a sword at the top, and the men see a ship — spraying a strange, yellow liquid — entering the far-off bay. From a distance, the men see Polynesian natives being unloaded by soldiers at a military base and presented to an eyepatch-wearing captain (Akihiko Hirata). "Something stinks," Yashi warns the others. Several natives try to escape and are pursued by the captain's soldiers. Two of the natives find a pontoon and paddle out to sea. Ebirah attacks their tiny craft, however, and eats them. The base commander (Jun Tazaki) tells the captain that a young native, Daiyo (Kumi Mizuno), has also escaped and orders the captain's men after her. Daiyo runs into our heroes, and the group finds refuge in a hidden cave. Daiyo explains that she is from Infant Island and that her people are being kidnapped by the shipload to work as slaves. She prays to Mothra (last seen in *Ghidrah: The Three-Headed Monster*) for help, and says the sword Mita found must have belonged to one of the natives. She also tells Ruta that his brother is alive and well on her island. While in the cave, the group makes another discovery: the sleeping yet very much living body of Godzilla. On Infant Island, the natives, along with the twin fairies (now played by "The Bambi Pair" according to the Japanese credits) pray to Mothra, currently hibernating, for assistance.

Meanwhile, Daiyo and the castaways decide to check out the base. Yashi uses his skeleton key to sneak the group into a laboratory, where they discover that the base is being used to produce heavy water for atomic bombs. (The fictional country goes unnamed in the English language version, but is the Red Bamboo in the Japanese version). The captain suddenly appears, and Mita is captured, while the escaping Ruta gets his foot tangled in a weather balloon and is carried off into the clouds. Yashi, Ichiro and Daiyo return to the cave. Ichiro suggests using the sword as a lightning rod to revive Godzilla, who will then keep the soldiers busy while the group rescues Mita and the native slaves. Mita meanwhile convinces the natives — who are being used to produce the yellow liquid which wards off Ebirah — to produce a phony batch of the stuff. Ruta's balloon finally lands on Infant Island, and he is reunited with Yata. The brothers hop in a pontoon to return to the island to rescue the natives. Lightning strikes the sword, which in turn revives Godzilla. The monster promptly squares off against Ebirah, with the two throwing boulders at one another almost like a father and son playing catch. A wild pitch sends one boulder crashing down on the base, destroying a watchtower. A disgruntled Ebirah retreats. The brothers locate Yashi, Ichiro and Daiyo, and an overzealous Yata leads the group toward the base. Godzilla fights a giant condor before defeating an attack by jets dispatched by the worried Red Bamboo officials. The group makes its way back into the laboratory, just as Godzilla attacks the base. A scientist (Hisaya Ho) confronts the group near a control panel, warning, "Stay where you are! I touch this button, and the whole island will be destroyed in an atomic explosion!" Yashi's reply: "Don't touch it!" The scientist appears hesitant, but just then Godzilla steps on the building, sending debris falling on top of the scientist, who presses the button. Before succumbing, he warns the group that the explosion will occur in just two hours. The base commander and the captain flee the annihilated base, but the phony yellow liquid fails to deter Ebirah, who attacks and destroys their ship, killing everyone aboard. Godzilla and Ebirah face off once again. This time Godzilla defeats the sea creature by tearing off its gigantic claws. Yashi and the others save Mita and the natives, just as Mothra shows up to rescue everybody. Yashi decides to turn over a new leaf, while Godzilla jumps off the island seconds before it explodes (in the Japanese laser disc version, which is letterboxed, overhead studio lights are clearly visible above the exploding island). Godzilla swims away for parts unknown.

Ebirah, Horror of the Deep was an attempt by Toho to break away from the similar storylines of the last several Godzilla entries. Perhaps more importantly, this picture's tropical setting was part of the studio's attempt to reduce production costs — miniature palm trees being less expensive to construct than miniature cityscapes. Toho had hoped to cannibalize and reuse the same props and miniatures from film to film, which explains the shift away from urban settings in the first half of the decade to tropical ones in the second. After *Ebirah*, Toho's *Son of Godzilla* and *King Kong Escapes* (both 1967), *Destroy All Monsters* (1968), *Godzilla's Revenge* and *Latitude Zero* (both 1969) and *Yog: Monster from Space* (1970) would each utilize a tropical setting, in whole or in part. *Ebirah*'s budget is noticeably slimmer, with special effects below director Eiji Tsuburaya's usual standards, though by now Teisho Arikawa and Teruyoshi Nakano had essentially taken over anyway. Scenes of the title monster's giant claw rising out of the sea are quite effective, however. Keeping the monster in the water at all times works well because it not only hides the legs of its human operator, but it creates a sense of lurking menace, an idea best capitalized on in Steven Spielberg's *Jaws*. What then makes *Ebirah* the delightful adventure it is can be traced to Shinichi Sekizawa's script, which combines elements of castaway films like 1961's *Mysterious Island* (which this closely resembles) with the James Bond movies, which had become an international phenomenon by 1966. Certainly the idea of a SPECTRE-like organization operating a hidden base was inspired by the Bond pictures. Godzilla's appearance is important to the story, yet the film is still people-centered. And while Godzilla is still looked upon with fear, by this time it's also with a certain amount of affection as well. When it looks as if Godzilla is about to be destroyed in the film's explosive finale, the castaways yell to the creature to get off the island. He did, after all, destroy the evil base.

Director Jun Fukuda had the misfortune to direct most of the bad Godzilla movies, including several truly awful seventies entries. In his defense, he generally had a much smaller budget to work with than series regular Ishiro Honda, and while Fukuda's style is a bit more haphazard than Honda's (his monster films seem to have many more zoom and hand-held camera shots than Honda's productions), most viewers probably can't see much of a difference between the two directors' styles.

Masaru Sato's music is also quite different from Akira Ifukube's scores from previous films. Like the picture itself, Sato's music suggests a James Bond adventure more than an epic monster movie, although it does have several nice themes. Though his monster motifs aren't as well known in the United States as Akira Ifukubas, Sato wrote nearly as many fantastic film scores; his credits include *Gigantis the Fire Monster* (1955), *The H-Man* (1958), *Samurai Pirate* (1963), *Son of Godzilla* (1967), *Submersion of Japan* (1973), and *Godzilla vs. the Bionic Monster* (1974). Sato was also associated with Akira Kurosawa's work from this period. When the director's regular composer, Fumio Hayasaka, died suddenly during the scoring of *Record of a Living Being* (1955), Sato took over. He went on to score all of the director's films through *Red Beard* (1965), including *Throne of Blood* and *The Lower Depths* (both 1957), *The Hidden Fortress* (1958), *Yojimbo* (1961), *Sanjuro* (1962), and *High and Low* (1963).

The acting in *Ebirah* is mostly undistinguished, although Akihiko Hirata seems to relish his juicy villainous role, as does Akira Takarada, playing against type as the smooth safecracker.

Ebirah, Horror of the Deep was the first of two Godzilla films which bypassed a theatrical run (apparently, though in this picture's case this is unconfirmed) in the United States and were released directly to television. The title was quickly changed to the more exploitable *Godzilla Versus the Sea Monster*, which is what it's known as today. The extremely poor television home video version is horribly panned and scanned: When the American handling the optical conversion cuts from one side of the screen to the other within a single set-up, several frames are often left on the wrong side at the beginning of the shot, creating a momentary blur in the action.

Ebirah received few notices. *Variety*'s "Chie," reviewing the film in Japan, compared the title monster favorably to other Japanese horrors: "He does not fawn like Majin, or simper and brindle like Godzilla, nor flutter about self-importantly like Mothra," Chie said. "He is a really good, old-fashioned, unrepentant monster." More recently, Greg Shoemaker argued that the picture was "a melange of thrusts...a pastiche that is confusing and mismatched." Leonard Maltin's *TV Movies* gave the film a **½ rating, calling it a "particularly colorful and lively entry," though *The Motion Picture Guide* gave it *½. While some audiences were undoubtedly disappointed by the lack of scenes of urban destruction, *Ebirah, Horror of the Deep* is an entirely respectable entry in the Godzilla series, and in fact, one of the best.

The Face of Another *(1966)*

This was director Hiroshi Teshigahara and screenwriter-novelist Kobo Abe's eagerly awaited follow-up to the critically acclaimed art house hit, *Woman in the Dunes* (1964). And like that film, *The Face of Another* is an existential allegory, this time with a science fiction premise.

An industrial accident has left Okuyama (Tatsuya Nakadai) bitter and scarred, both emotionally and physically. Severe facial burns have forced him to wear bandages over almost his entire head, leaving only tiny holes for his eyes and mouth. His wife (Machiko Kyo) remains at his side, but rejects his sexual advances. At work, his employer (Eiji Okada) remains friendly but vague about Okuyama's future with the company. Okuyama considers himself a dead man. Visiting a psychiatrist and plastic surgeon (Mikijiro Hira) who specializes in reconstructing arms, legs and other body parts, Okuyama asks the doctor to construct a new face for him. The doctor finally agrees, even though he considers the procedure unethical. As the doctor begins making preparations, Okuyama tells his wife he's leaving town on a business trip. The men approach a stranger (also played by Nakadai), and give him 10,000 yen to use his face as a model. The doctor constructs a thin latex-like mask, which is then applied to Okuyama's face with an adhesive. While Okuyama is unable to perspire through the mask, making it hard for him to breathe, the mask is a remarkable achievement, though, as Okuyama says, "It's a strange feeling, like someone has taken me over." Armed with a new face – and identity – Okuyama rents an apartment. The mask slowly begins to dictate his personality, however, and when he tries to visit his boss (he pretends to be his brother) the secretary turns him away. Wearing the mask, Okuyama decides to seduce his wife, which he does. After they make love, however, his wife admits she knew it was him all along. In anger, Okuyama begins ripping his mask off, and the woman flees. Okuyama contemplates killing his wife but assaults a young woman instead. The doctor bails Okuyama out of jail and tells him he is free at last. The doctor sees a crowd of faceless men and women before Okuyama stabs him to death.

The Face of Another comes from a period when avant-garde cinema was all the rage, and showy, self-indulgent, stylized direction frequently overwhelmed the films themselves. This is certainly true here, a picture with a large number of startling, haunting images, but which is also needlessly confusing and preachy. Though eagerly awaited, *The Face of Another* failed to light the fire of critics and audiences in the United States, though it was initially screened to enthusiastic crowds at the Venice and New York film festivals.

Born in 1927, director Teshigahara studied art and was a film critic before directing documentary shorts in the early 1950s. He entered features with *The Pitfall* in 1961, but it was his low-budget ($100,000), groundbreaking *Woman in the Dunes* that propelled the director to stardom. According to the late Ephraim Katz's *The Film Encyclopedia*, "Teshigahara's subsequent films, mainly psychological thrillers, have been less daring or innovative." The director has made only a handful of films since *The Face of Another*, his most recent being *Rikyu* (1989) and *Basara: The Princess Goh* (1992). At the time, however, the director stated, "Many motion pictures today terminate on a message of cheap humanity, neighborly love and easy-going humanism. This film begins where others end."

Variety's "Chie" liked the novel, but gave the film a mixed review. "[An] often irritating, sometimes confusing, but at least consistently disturbing film. Abe's screenplay is loose and makes consistent reference to the novel which most viewers will not have read. Further, Teshigahara, always a self-indulgent director, has apparently arbitrarily included scenes which obtrude and irritate with their modish meaninglessness." Like many critics, *Variety*'s reviewer complained about the film's unexplained, seemingly pointless subplot involving a horribly scarred young woman (Bibari Maeda) who sleeps with a man then commits suicide. In Kobo Abe's novel, the woman was a fictional character in a film Okuyama sees, but here the woman is introduced without any explanation at all, and her appearances do nothing but stop the main narrative dead in its tracks. This sort of needless confusion isn't art — it's bad filmmaking. I'm not suggesting that movies need be clear and easy to follow all of the time; indeed, far too many American-made films *are* overly familiar and predictable, while some of the greatest films ever made are abstract and ambiguous. I'm merely suggesting that while dazzling an audience with avant-garde sets and weird camera angles is all well and good, these effects by themselves can no longer impress an audience as they did when avant-garde cinema was new and on the cutting edge. The best avant-garde films are timeless in their universality. *The Face of Another*, in comparison, seems dated and self-indulgent. To its credit, the film is visually and aurally impressive. Toru Takemitsu's electronic score, which generally sounds like chimes ringing underwater, is unsettling, especially when set against footage of otherwise silent crowds.

Hiroshi Segawa's crisp black and white photography is effectively creepy, especially the sequences in the doctor's post-modern laboratory (significantly, neither the lab nor the doctor himself was in the original novel). Abe and Teshigahara's script places such unusual items as transparent anatomical drawings and a gigantic ear sculpture in the room, as well as blowing hair matted in a doorway for no reason in particular. None of this makes any sense, but it's certainly visually spectacular. Tatsuya Nakadai's performance was criticized at the time as being rather wooden, though his measured, resonant voice adds a certain creepiness when his character is wrapped in bandages or is without his mask (the character's scarred face is kept mostly in shadows). Michiko Kyo, who had appeared in Kurosawa's *Rashomon* 16 years earlier, is fine as Okuyama's wife. Her middle-aged, time-worn face makes her an interesting subject for Okuyama's advances, and Kyo's restrained performance adds to the general tension between the two characters. Eiji Okada and Kyoko Kishida (who plays a nurse) had starred in *Woman in the Dunes* for Teshigahara, but their roles are too small to really make much of an impression.

The *Hollywood Reporter*'s John Mahoney liked the film's cryptic turns, noting "Teshigahara is frequently heavy-handed and occasionally indulges in intensely personal obscurities in making his point, but the whole is always brilliantly fascinating, richly styled and distinctly provocative." The *Los Angeles Times*' Kevin Thomas complained that the picture's first hour was all talk, but that "the film's final 40 minutes are so rapid and exciting and culminate in a climax so bizarre that all that has gone before is worth sitting through."

The Magic Serpent (1966)

This amazing little fairy tale cum *kaiju eiga* production from Toei was unknown to me until I began writing this book. It was sold directly to American television, and reviews or anything else written about this nearly forgotten film are extremely scarce. That's a shame, because this lively production is full of imaginative ideas and colorful, if somewhat garish, special effects.

In feudal Japan, the lord Ugata and his wife are overthrown and murdered by Yukidaijo (Bin Amatsu) and his second, Orochimaru (Ryutaro Otomo), the latter bearing a certain resemblance to Olivier's Richard III. Yukidaijo also orders the murder of Ugata's boy prince, Ikazuchimaru, but the lad escapes with the help of royal servants aboard a small boat. The boat is spotted and a giant dragon rises out of the lake and attacks the boat. The servants are killed, and things don't look so hot for Ikazuchimaru, either, when a giant eagle appears out of the sky. The bird scratches the dragon's face (creating a continuous spray of blood in the best Sam Peckinpah tradition) and whisks the boy to safety. After the opening titles (in which the "Produced by Shigeru Okada" credit is followed by "Produced by Shigeru Okada"), ten years have passed, and Ikazuchimaru is now a young man (and played by Hiroki Matsutaka). He has undergone intensive training from an old wizard, who has also taught him the powers of a certain cosmic force. The wizard also had taught another pupil, until that student turned to evil (sound familiar?). Anyway, the prince is still a wanted man and seems to be constantly under attack by Yukidaijo's ninjas. One of the ninjas manages to decapitate the prince, but the severed head only laughs, while the headless body subdues the frightened ninja, who bites off then swallows his tongue. Reattaching his head, the prince sees someone watching the duel from behind some trees and tackles them. When the prince grabs the person's chest, he realizes that the person is a woman (how this racy bit of clumsy discovery ever made it to commercial television is beyond me). The woman, Tsunate (Tomoko Ogawa), is looking for her father, whom she has never met, and whose identity is unknown to her. She explains that when she was just a baby, her father abandoned her late mother.

Meanwhile, Ikazuchimaru's master is visited by a snake, whom the wizard quickly identifies as his former student. Resuming human form, the wizard's former student is none other than Orochimaru! Orochimaru claims to be visiting the wizard out of concern for his former master's health, but the old sorcerer knows better, knowing Orochimaru is still after Ugata's son, the prince. Orochimaru had turned himself into the dragon years earlier (he has a scar on his forehead where the wizard's eagle had scratched him). Orochimaru offers to return some scrolls he had stolen years before. The wizard is skeptical but overjoyed when they are handed to him. It's a trick, however: the paper turns into an asp which bites the wizard. Orochimaru assures the wizard's death by stabbing the old magician as well. When the prince returns with Tsunate, the wizard is near death but hangs on just long enough to recognize the young woman. Hmmmmm. The prince promises to avenge his master's death, as well as Yukidaijo's murder of his parents. The prince heads for the castle, while Tsunate, who believes her father lives at the castle as well, decides to tag along. Before setting out, Tsunate's maternal grandmother warns her grandchild that the girl's father will probably reject her. "You won't find happiness with him," she warns and gives her a magical hairpin with a spider on it, just in case.

Arriving in the village, the prince is quickly recognized by Yukidaijo's soldiers, but a kindly farmer, loyal to the Ugata family, pretends the prince is his son-in-law. Yukidaijo appears, quickly sees through the farmer's story, and kills him. He is about to kill the farmer's daughter, Osaki, and little boy, when the film abruptly switches to black and white and the ghosts of Ugata and his murdered followers appear, frightening Yukidaijo's soldiers. The spirits depart (and the film switches back to color) while Ikazuchimaru, who had conjured the spirits, appears on a rooftop. The prince creates a colorful golden ring which encircles Yukidaijo's men like a rope encircling a lassoed longhorn at a rodeo. The ring is broken and the men are freed when Orochimaru materializes and engages the prince in a lively magical duel. The battle ends in a draw, though Osaki and later the little boy are taken prisoner. Tsunate, who had been sleeping in an abandoned temple, overhears a group of soldiers discussing plans to trap the prince. She's discovered and is about to be killed when a wandering, mysterious bandit, Momobe, comes to the woman's rescue. Momobe turns out to be a spy, and when Tsunate is captured, the bandit tells Orochimaru that the evil wizard is the girl's father. Orochimaru doesn't show much fatherly love, ordering Tsunate to kill Ikazuchimaru. Torn between her now passionate love for the prince and duty to her father (whom Ikazuchimaru has pledged to kill, remember), she reluctantly agrees to comply with her father's orders. The woman is given some poison to drop into the prince's tea, but when she begins to get cold feet, Momobe slips the poison in the prince's drink instead. Ikazuchimaru falls over dead, and when the bandit gives Tsunate a sword to finish the job, she refuses. Touched, Momobe decides, somewhat belatedly, to join the fight against Orochimaru and Yukidaijo. Fortunately, the prince rises, having never died at all. Later, Orochimaru learns of Momobe's defection, and murders him.

Yukidaijo is celebrating at the castle (musicians playing traditional instruments have been ludicrously dubbed with a very sixties orchestration which sounds like the Cha-cha), and is looking most lustfully toward Osaki, the dead farmer's daughter. Just then, a giant horned frog conjured by the prince (himself standing atop the amphibian's head) appears over one of the castle walls and begins smashing everything in sight. The prince jumps aboard a comet and finds Yukidaijo, whom he kills. Orochimaru, who had been plotting to usurp the throne from Yukidaijo anyway, thanks the prince for saving him the trouble and turns into a dragon once again. When it becomes apparent that the prince's big frog is no match for Orochimaru in dragon form, Tsunate remembers the magical spider pin and throws it into the air. "Forgive me, father," she says. The pin becomes a rather disappointing giant spider (a marionette), which, along with the horned frog, is able to defeat Orochimaru the dragon. The evil wizard returns to his human form to face Ikazuchimaru for a brief round of conventional swordplay, with Orochimaru fatally stabbed. The villains defeated, the prince surprisingly renounces his throne (well, the castle *was* reduced to a pile of rubble) and grants his subjects the right to govern themselves. The prince, it seems, is more interested in returning home with Tsunate. The couple hops aboard the giant eagle and flies away.

The Magic Serpent is a silly and highly entertaining film. It makes no pretense to be anything other than what it is—a fairy tale—and succeeds wonderfully. The picture is full of colorful action, barely stopping long enough to catch its breath between its duels and dragons. In recent years, a large number of American film critics have inexplicably gone bananas over violent action films made in Hong Kong (*The Killer*, the *A Better Tomorrow* series, etc.). Critics have lauded the filmmakers' innovative use of editing and non-stop (violent) action. What these critics fail to realize is that these pictures, while often visually interesting, are imitating the very worst kind of Hollywood film—mindless, derivative action pictures. What's more, the very elements these critics go ga-ga over today were already well established in Asian films decades earlier (and were the same films they continually panned). *The Magic Serpent* is a perfect example of this. The picture is replete with imaginative sequences, with attributes similar to the fast-paced stylization so popular in today's Hong Kong–made productions, while genuinely inventive and anything but imitative of American genre films. For instance, the appearance of Ugata's spirit—and the disappearance of all color—was a simple, highly effective idea which adds a great deal of atmosphere. As hinted earlier, I suspect that George Lucas or one of his associates had seen and liked *The Magic Serpent*. Lucas freely admits that his *Star Wars* films were greatly influenced by Japanese period films, and it seems reasonable that the producer-director might have liked the relationships between the doddering wizard and two students: one good, the other (an apprentice gone bad) evil.

Hiroki Matsukata is quite likable as the young prince. The actor also appeared in *Hiken Yaburi* (1969), but I have no other information on him. The dragon and the giant frog (*Froggo and Draggo* is given as one of the film's alternate titles), played by men in rubber suits, aren't remotely realistic but are colorful, and their design is refreshingly different from Toho's more familiar monstrosities (though, in the American version, each creature's roar is dubbed by a Toho monster: the dragon's roar is Godzilla's, the frog is Rodan's, and the eagle is Mothra's). The colorful dragon is a cross between one of King Ghidorah's heads (the monster here has an unusually long neck) and that disastrous dragon from Denmark, *Reptilicus*. But the creature Orochimaru's dragon most resembles is the comical fire breather seen in George Pal's Cinerama fantasy, *The Wonderful World of the Brothers Grimm* (1962). The big frog is less interesting (it's a big frog, that's all) but the battle between the two creatures takes some interesting turns; when the frog begins shooting flames at the dragon from its mouth, the dragon responds by sending a mouthful of *water* back at the frog, thus dousing the flames. The sequence is staged at a castle overlooking a lake, an interesting location, and the miniature art direction is attractively done. The optical work is also quite nice. The astonishing scene where the prince is beheaded, only to laugh at his frightened opponent, is quite good for the period, while the film's other optical work, such as the prince's ride atop the giant frog, is reasonably convincing.

Strangely included in *The Encyclopedia of Horror Movies*, its reviewer said "this crudely acted but colorful fantasy owes much to Seiji Yada's art direction and the inventiveness of Mokuami Kawatake's original story." A great many Japanese fantastic films, once staples of late night and Saturday afternoon television, have all but vanished from local stations in recent years, having been replaced by high-profile syndicated features, idiotic cop shows re-edited to feature length, and bad TV movies. The disappearance of some of these films is no great loss. Not so with *The Magic Serpent*, a delightful action-packed fairy tale.

Majin *(1966)*

This Daiei production, released to American television as *Majin, the Monster of Terror*, was the first of three films starring the Far East's equivalent of the Golem. Unlike the studio's Gamera series, the Majin (pronounced Ma-jeen) films were comparatively elaborate productions. Toho's favorite *kaiju eiga* composer, Akira Ifukube, was brought in to score the picture, and the special effects were far more accomplished than anything found in the flying turtle features. The *Majin* films themselves, all of which are set in eighteenth-century Japan, are pure melodrama, but not without interest, and are generally entertaining.

Shino, a warrior-god's spirit, has been entombed in a forty-foot statue near a mountainside. Nearby, a fair and kindly lord, Hanabusa, is overthrown and killed by Samanosuke (Ryutaro Gomi) and his portly chamberlain, Gunjuro (Tatsuo Endo). Samanosuke orders Hanabusa's son and daughter—the prince and princess—murdered as well, but they escape with the help of one of Hana-busa's loyal servants, Kogenta (Jun Fujimaki), and a middle-aged Shino priestess (the role is unfortunately not credited in available materials). The priestess leads the small band to a cave near the statue hosting Shino's spirit, which is called Majin. Samanosuke orders all public prayer designed to keep Majin locked into the mountainside forbidden. Bad idea, Samanosuke. In the ten years that follow, the cruel leader enslaves the people of the village, forcing them to build a new fort and surrender most of their crops, leaving everyone in a state of near starvation. Prince Tadafumi (Yoshihiko Aoyama), now 19 years old, decides to return to the village to claim his right to rule. After much pleading, Kogenta goes in his place but is quickly captured. Tadafumi tries to rescue him but is also captured (neither man seems very smart in this regard, a serious failing of the picture). The priestess, by now an old woman, visits Samanosuke warning him to surrender the two men or face Majin's wrath. "He will not permit this cruelty to go on," she says. The leader responds by murdering the woman, cutting her down with his sword. Samanosuke orders Gunjuro and his men to tear down the statue. The soldiers climb all over the thing and begin whacking at it with hammers. It's decided they need to use a large chisel, which is lodged into the statue's forehead. Suddenly, the statue's forehead begins to bleed and the statue itself briefly comes to life. There is a tremendous earthquake, and Gunjuro and his men are swallowed up in the Earth, which then seals itself up again. When the princess, Kozasa (Miwa Takada), learns of the priestess' death and the men's capture, she humbly presents herself before Majin, asking for his help. At first nothing happens, but when Kozasa begins to shed tears and even contemplates jumping over a waterfall which overlooks the mountain, Majin comes to life. The stoic stone arrives at the newly built fort just as Tadafumi and Kogenta are being crucified. As the villagers revolt, Majin tears the fort to pieces and kills soldiers loyal to the cruel leader. Majin locates Samanosuke, removes the big chisel in its forehead, squishes Samanosuke, then nails the evil warlord to a wall. Shino's spirit leaves the statue, heads into the clouds, and Majin crumbles into dust.

Obviously, *Majin* attempts to combine elements popular in historical melodramas with those found in the successful *kaiju* genre, which was just then beginning to decline in Japan. The results are mixed, but generally interesting. The picture is a pretty standard melodrama until Majin comes to life, which doesn't happen until the film has nearly ended, and well over an hour into the story. When the Majin films were shown on television in the sixties and seventies as part of "Japanese Monster Weeks," kids were invariably disappointed at the statue's tardiness, like a concert where the star attraction plays only 45 minutes. In all three films, Majin does little more than wake up near the end (when the going gets tough, the tough get going), smashes a few buildings and squishes the bad guys before returning to his statue state. That Daiei was able to squeeze two sequels out of the idea is something of an accomplishment. The films are lavish compared to the studio's Gamera series. The flying turtle films were, after the first entry, centered around one or two individuals, usually a couple of kids, whereas the Majin films tend to have a larger, slightly grandiose air and sense of scale. The scenery is lush, the casts are large (there are more extras, anyway) and the wide screen photography (lost on TV screens) lends a sense of grandeur. Probably the film's best non–Majin moment comes when a young boy, running through the forbidden forest where Majin dwells, panics and begins hallucinating all manner of spirits, eyes and skeletons in the brush. It has nothing really to do with the rest of the film, but perhaps foreshadows director Kimiyoshi Yasuda's excellent 1968 film, *100 Monsters* (which also starred Miwa Takada and was scripted by Tetsuro Yoshida, who also penned *Majin*). Akira Ifukube, heretofore associated with Toho's monster films, jumped studios to write *Majin*'s score, which is capped by a distinctly Ifukubean three-note motif for the statue.

 The special effects, while limited to the last ten to fifteen minutes, are far better than anything in the Gamera films, and at least on a par with Toho's efforts of the mid-sixties. The Majin costume does have several drawbacks, however. Try as they might, Daiei's special effects crew was never quite able to disguise the fact that the Majin suit of armor was, in fact, rubber. Another bad idea was allowing real human eyes to peek out from behind the false face, which only drew further attention to the fakery. Unlike most *kaiju eiga* entries by this time, nearly every shot of Majin was filmed at an extreme low angle, greatly adding to the illusion of height. Majin also walks slowly and ponderously (we hear every footstep), and his actions refreshingly bear little resemblance to the tag-team matches going on at the Toho lot during this period. *Majin* has the distinction of being one of the few Japanese fantastic films released in this country simultaneously dubbed and subtitled. Both versions, released in 1968, were advertised as straight monster movies, with the exploitive (and misleading) catch phrase, "Majin. Terror Monster. He Could Love or Destroy Anything He Wanted!" The film doesn't appear to have been a hit and was soon sold to American International Television. In recent years all three Majin films have virtually disappeared in the United States.

Phil Hardy's *Horror Movies* liked *Majin*: "[Yoshiyuki] Kuroda's special effects... are expertly achieved and generally integrate the rubber-clad Majin well into the sequences." Howard Thompson of the *New York Times*, reviewing the subtitled version, wasn't impressed. "The picture is typical of a kind of Asian movie fare that apparently packs 'em in back home. It thumps forward like an old-fashioned Western, keyed by ominous music and fetching color." *The Motion Picture Guide* gave the film a ** rating, saying "Majin isn't as hokey as Godzilla, but the movie isn't *The Seven Samurai* [sic] either." Majin was followed by two confusingly titled sequels, the first of which was *The Return of the Giant Majin* (1966).

The Return of the Giant Majin *(1966)*

This first sequel to *Majin, the Monster of Terror* (1966) follows the original film's narrative quite closely, with the giant stone statue Majin this time on a small island in the middle of a lake. As in the original, an evil warlord ruthlessly oppresses poor villagers while preparing to execute a group of rebels (this time led by Gamera regular Kojiro Hongo) and a young, virginal priestess, Lady Sayuri (Shiho Fujimura), before Majin comes to life in the final reel. As before, he destroys the warlord's fortress, restores the villagers' freedom and dissolves (this time into water) until called upon again. If *Majin, the Monster of Terror* is extremely difficult to see in most television markets, its sequel is even more obscure. *Return*'s theatrical release in this country, either dubbed or subtitled, is unconfirmed, and it rarely turns up on American television. While writing this book, I was only able to locate a Japanese language print minus English subtitles, and as I've mentioned before, I don't speak Japanese. Even so, it's obvious the picture is basically more of the same, with all of the original's qualities and shortcomings. This isn't necessarily a bad thing, for *The Return of the Giant Majin* is an attractive, visually impressive film. And as with the original *Majin*, Daiei appears to have spent more money on this series than their Gamera films, which gives it an air of respectability.

One of the benefits of watching the Japanese tape of the picture is the lovely DaieiScope photography and attractive locations, preserved in the letterboxed format. This version is also thankfully lacking in the over-the-top voice characterizations AIP-TV, the film's U.S. distributor (according to most sources), was souring these pictures with. While *Return* is quite similar to the original *Majin*, there are some differences. This time, Majin lives on an island in the middle of a lake, and when he finally awakens (which like the first film, isn't until a good hour into the story), he lumbers to the mainland by parting the water just like Charlton Heston in *The Ten Commandments* (1956). The effect, while confined to fewer shots, is actually better than what appears in the Cecil B. DeMille production. The villains are a bit more threatening; they actually blow up the statue near the beginning of the film (the headpiece falls into a lagoon, where it later rises up), rather than just sticking a chisel in its forehead. Later, when Majin attacks the warlord's fortress, they try, albeit unsuccessfully, to bring Majin down by setting charges near the walking statue and grabbing at it with big hooks and chains. Majin, apparently compensating for his opponents' newfound cleverness, now has the ability to shoot fire (strangely, from between its legs). In a bit of poetic justice, the warlord who sentenced Lady Sayuri to be burned on the cross is himself burned alive. Majin sets his fleeing skiff afire, and when the terrified warlord climbs the mast, he becomes entangled in the sail and winds up in the same crucified position as his intended victim. Other production aspects, are on a par with those of the first film (one or two effects shots appear to be stock from *Majin*—otherwise, everything else is new). Akira Ifukube wrote the score again, though this time the picture's musical cues sound more like reworked Godzilla themes. The equally obscure *Majin Strikes Again*, released in Japan late that same year, brought the series to its conclusion.

Majin Strikes Again *(1966)*

The great stone samurai faced yet another evil warlord in this third and final Majin adventure. This time, Majin saves three children, perhaps an effort by Daiei to appeal to the successful kiddie market they so successfully tapped with their Gamera films. In any event, this entry, which also features a very impresssive earthquake and flood, would be the last for the hideous idol.

To the best of my knowledge, the Majin films were shown only once or twice in the Detroit area by the local ABC affiliate, WXYZ (Channel 7), and haven't been seen since. Like the other films in the series, *Majin Strikes Again* isn't legally available on video in English, and I know of no television station that still airs the old prints.

Variety's "Chie" saw the film in Japan in mid–January 1967, and his brief review had this to say: "The special effects, particularly at the beginning (earthquake, fire, flood) are better than usual, but Majin himself is obviously a man in a plastic and rubber suit carefully crunching expensive models. One of the problems is that the camera angle always gives away the trick." In the wake of Toho's successfully revived and revamped Godzilla series, *Markalite* reported (in its fall 1991 issue) that Daiei's president had announced a new Majin film, a co-production between the studio and Golden Harvest (H.K.) Ltd., an international company well known for its Hong Kong–filmed adventures, including several with Bruce Lee. The magazine went on to say that shooting on the new film would begin in 1993.

Terror Beneath the Sea *(1966)*

If this Toei release looks like a serial, part of the reason may lie in the fact that this was originally intended to be shown on U.S. television in three parts, prior to a theatrical release that never happened. The 1992 edition of Leonard Maltin's *Movie and Video Guide* pretty much sums up the film: "The usual." A megalomaniac bent on conquering the earth with a race of Gill Man–like monsters is stopped in the nick of time. Little separates this from U.S.-made productions with similar storylines, and in fact, several equally undistinguished undersea adventures were produced in this country at about the same time (*Around the World Under the Sea* and *Destination Inner Space*, both 1966).

Following what are perhaps the most ineptly edited opening titles in film history, the story begins aboard a U.S. submarine, where a new homing torpedo is being demonstrated for members of the press, including reporter Ken Abe (Shinichi "Sonny" Chiba) and photographer Jennie (Peggy Neal). Something goes wrong, and the silhouette of a figure, more or less resembling a man, appears on a monitor just as the torpedo explodes. Ken and Jennie go diving the next day, hoping to unravel the mystery. Jennie snaps a picture of a strange humanoid creature but drops the camera. The U.S. Navy scoffs at the sighting, but Ken and Jennie go diving again the following morning and discover a passageway leading to a secret underwater base. The two are met by more creatures (which resemble dime store versions of the *Creature from the Black Lagoon*) and sunglass-wearing arch-fiend Dr. Rufus Moore (!). Dr. Moore (Eric Nielsen) gives Ken and Jennie a brief tour of his hidden base, including a demonstration of a laboratory where Dr. Heim (Mike Daning) turns men into the gill creatures, which he calls water cyborgs. The skin is essentially burned off while Heim surgically implants a set of gills (which is just the reverse of what happens to the Creature from the Black Lagoon in the 1956 film *The Creature Walks Among Us*). Heim and Moore explain that once mutated into monsters, the victim's "minds [become] memory banks." He gives a demonstration by flipping an all-purpose dial marked with commands such as "fight" and "work." Moore's cyborgs kidnap a renowned physicist, Professor Howard (Andrew Hughes), and take him back to the base. When Howard refuses to help Moore in his plans to conquer the Earth, he sends Ken and Jennie off to be converted into cyborgs. The navy, meanwhile, has discovered Jennie's camera. They develop the film, finding the picture of that cyborg. They dispatch a sub, which Moore's men fire upon. Moore's base begins to crumble under the sub's arsenal, and a short circuit turns the cyborgs against Moore's human army. Meanwhile, Ken, Jennie and Professor Howard escape just as the base and everyone in it are blown to smithereens.

There's little to recommend *Terror Beneath the Sea*. The no-neck cyborgs, with their black, rubbery eyes and slit mouths, have completely immobile faces and are totally lacking in character. The body suits are even worse, looking more like loose-fitting pajamas than skin. The special effects, limited to shots of the submarine, the base, a few missiles and other hardware, range from poor to reasonably good. The interior sets are cheap but occasionally imaginative. The music is terrible, however, vaguely resembling what one might find in a bad Hanna-Barbera cartoon. The film's one saving grace is the idea of having Neal and Chiba witnessing the creation of the cyborgs, only to later become part cyborg themselves. The idea of losing one's humanity has been explored in surprisingly few films (*Invasion of the Body Snatchers* being the most famous; this film resembles the 1978 *The Island of Dr. Moreau*). The makeup is crude, to say the least (once partially converted, Neal and Chiba look like they have bubble gum smeared on their hands and jowls), but the fact that filmmakers would allow their leading man and woman to become half-monsters is surprising. The film cheats, however, once they've made their escape. Professor Howard, for reasons never explained, "knew the treatment to cure [them]." Still, it's an interesting idea in an otherwise unexceptional story.

Although about 90 percent of the cast speaks English, the entire film was redubbed for U.S. distribution. Like other Japanese productions with international casts, the English-speaking performers are often nonactors, semi-professional at best. Hughes, who turned up in minor roles in many of Toho's sixties films, perhaps most memorably in 1968's *Destroy All Monsters* (he also appeared in the medium-budgeted *Flight from Ashiya*, released in 1964), was a businessman who considered acting a hobby and was a member of the Tokyo Amateur Dramatic Club. Mike Daning, hammy as the villainous Dr. Heim, was an executive at Pacific Television Corporation. Peggy Neal, only 19 at the time of filming, was a college student and model with no acting experience. The attractive though wooden actress also appeared in *The X from Outer Space* (1967), where she appeared much more relaxed and confident in her abilities.

Science Fiction said the film was an "unpretentious but energetically directed mixture of comic strips, science fiction and monster movies." *Psychotronic* was enthusiastic: "Fun to watch and the transformation scenes are incredible!" Toei would fare much better with their not-so-bad U.S.-Japanese-Italian co-production, *The Green Slime* (1968), which had several of the same cast members.

War of the Gargantuas (1966)

This Toho production was intended as a sequel to *Frankenstein Conquers the World* (1965), but alleged last-minute re-editing (and possibly some reshooting) obscures this fact in the U.S. cut. In nearly every way it is a better movie, though American audiences had to wait almost four years to see it.

A giant octopus attacks a ship at sea, its slimy tentacles wrapping around a terrified crew member. Just as all appears lost, another giant monster appears, in the form of a green, hairy *and* scaly man: a Green Gargantua. The gargantua (called Gaira in Japan) kills the giant octopus, then sets about eating sailors vainly trying to swim to shore. The incident is quickly linked to experiments overseen by Dr. Paul Stewart (Russ Tamblyn) and his assistants, Akemi (Kumi Mizuno, more or less reprising her *Frankenstein* role) and Yuzo (Kenji Sahara). Stewart recalls finding a small brown creature (played by a small man or child in a furry suit which resembles an Ewok) which grew to a tremendous size and lost a hand trying to escape. Although the creature's body was never recovered, Stewart dismisses the possible connection to the sailors' story. "Ah, they were probably on a bad LSD trip." The Green Gargantua appears again, however, first caught in some fishermen's nets and later at an airport. Stewart and Akemi decide to check the "Japan Alps," while Yuzo inspects the beaches. Meanwhile, the army (led by reliable Jun Tazaki) tries to stop the man-eating monster with plans of electrifying Tokyo Bay. At a rooftop nightclub, a truly awful singer ("Special Guest Star" Kipp Hamilton) warbles through something called "Feel in My Heart," one of the all-time high-camp songs to be associated with a monster movie. The Green Gargantua interrupts the number, but not soon enough. The army uses a "laser gun" on the Green Gargantua, which nearly kills him. However, out of nowhere, a peaceful Brown Gargantua (Sanda to the Japanese) appears, rescuing his kin. The savage Green Gargantua isn't very grateful to his passive counterpart, however, and the two wrestle after the Green Gargantua eats a couple of passersby. Stewart speculates that a piece of the original creature's flesh tore off at sea and mutated with plankton, resulting in the Green Gargantua: The two gargantuas are half-brothers. One of the scientists likens them to Cain and Abel, while hip Dr. Stewart replies, "Sounds like some countries I know." Stewart and especially Akemi want to save the innocent Brown Gargantua. The more passive monster saved Akemi from a fall, and besides, Akemi argues, "Our gargantua wouldn't help the green one!" Stewart warns the military that blowing up the monsters isn't the answer anyway, as cells from the two creatures could result in the growth of an almost unlimited number of new gargantuas. Green Gargantua attacks Tokyo, closely followed by his brown brother. Despite the presence of the evil green baddy, Akemi still wants to try and save Brown Gargantua. Dr. Stewart agrees to help. "Just remember he's not a toy poodle," Stewart warns. Green Gargantua spots Stewart and Akemi and, in a well-staged shot, reaches down into the subway where they have taken refuge. He grabs Akemi but drops her about twenty feet when Brown Gargantua suddenly appears. Stewart takes Akemi to a hospital as the Green Gargantua spars with the reluctant Brown Gargantua. The two monsters fall into Tokyo Bay and are swept out to sea, where an underwater volcano erupts and presumably destroys the creatures.

It's clear watching *War of the Gargantuas* that the film was intended as a sequel to *Frankenstein Conquers the World*: the reference to a severed hand, the presence of Kumi Mizuno and Green Gargantua's battle with the mollusk are just three of the pictures' overlapping elements. The film was originally released in Japan as *Frankenstein Monsters: Sanda Against Gaira*, but, according to some sources, the film was quickly pulled and re-edited, removing all Frankenstein references. It's also possible that new footage may also have been shot. However, the current home video version in Japan retains these references. Several of Tamblyn's own lines are wildly out of sync, so it's possible that some of his dialog was relooped for the U.S. edition to avoid references to the earlier film. However, Bill Warren says Tamblyn told him that the dialog track had been lost and the actor had to redub his lines without the benefit of the script!

Despite a much less interesting storyline, *War of the Gargantuas* is silly fun and undeserving of the "BOMB" rating given the film in Leonard Maltin's *Movie and Video Guide*. *Frankenstein Conquers the World* had an interesting first half but became bogged down in an overlong search for the monster. The ridiculous and even pointless appearance of the silly-looking Baragon didn't help matters. *War of the Gargantuas* may not be very good, but it's never boring. The special effects aren't convincing, but they're much more plentiful in number than in *Frankenstein*, and occasionally quite imaginative (I particularly enjoyed watching Green Gargantua squish automobiles one-by-one). The monster suits are much more mobile than the rubber reptiles that actors like Harou Nakajima usually have to contend with. The headpieces permitted the actors to see and express themselves with their own eyes, rather than electronically controlled ping pong balls. The result is monsters who can actually run instead of lumber through Eiji Tsuburaya's plentiful miniature sets; the monsters' agility is refreshing. The design of the gargantuas is also an improvement over that of the earlier film. Instead of appearing basically human (as in *Frankenstein*) the gargantuas are plug-ugly monsters—scaly and hairy, with pointed ears and massive teeth (the Green Gargantua's teeth are too massive, with several actually pointing *away* from his mouth—how does he eat?). The faces are immobile, but the actors inside try their best to be expressive via pantomime and their eyes. The matte work, however, is glaringly obvious. The size of the monsters is inconsistent, thanks largely to the sloppy work done here.

Russ Tamblyn was a fairly big star in the late fifties and early sixties—his film credits include several big musicals (*Seven Brides for Seven Brothers*, *West Side Story*) and a couple of fantasies for producer George Pal (*Tom Thumb*, *Wonderful World of the Brothers Grimm*). Born in 1934, Tamblyn was a child performer (billed as "Rusty" Tamblyn, on account of his rust-colored hair) and appeared opposite Dean Stockwell in *The Boy with Green Hair* (1948) at age 13. His career took a rather surprising dip in the sixties; *War of the Gargantuas* was released just four short years after *Grimm*, a big-budget Cinerama/M-G-M production, and shortly after this, Tamblyn appeared in Al Adamson's notoriously dreadful *Dracula vs. Frankenstein* (1969/71). He's made a comeback in recent years, appearing with his *West Side Story* co-star, Richard Beymer, in director David Lynch's teleseries "Twin Peaks." Tamblyn's performance is a bit flip but basically enjoyable. Kumi Mizuno's back, but it's hard to judge her performance here as her dubbing counterpart in the U.S. version is just awful. Another dubbing problem is the almost constant use of the same bit of stock music heard anytime one of the gargantuas appears. Akira Ifukube's score is heard in some scenes but is constantly interrupted in the American version by an annoyingly repetitive stock theme (also used in *Night of the Living Dead*, I believe).

Maltin's book said the film was "strange, even by Japanese monster-movie standards." Phil Hardy's *Science Fiction*, which mistakenly stated the octopus scenes were stock footage from *Frankenstein*, said "the effects are spectacular and extremely well-done." "One of the funniest Japanese monster bashes," said *Psychotronic*, with a "wonderful song...Devo used to do at live performances." Not surprisingly, *The Motion Picture Guide* gave *War of the Gargantuas* a zero rating, calling it a "trashy Japanese giant monster film," while conversely admiring the "very effective special effects." While hardly one of Toho's best efforts, *War of the Gargantuas* is entertaining, and holds up well today.

War of the Monsters *(1966)*

Daiei's second Gamera film was the first of the series in color, but it doesn't help much. Despite the complete absence of children and a rather sober approach, *War of the Monsters* (known today as *Gamera vs. Barugon*) is a dull mess. Too silly to be taken seriously and too dull and uninvolving to have much camp value, it's the least distinguished of the series.

The picture begins with stock footage from *Gammera the Invincible*, the original black and white footage tinted here. Gamera (or Gammera, if you prefer), having been captured in the rocket, is launched into outer space. The black and white stock scenes switch to the newly shot color footage as the rocket strikes a bright red meteor, and Gamera is set free. He immediately returns to Earth for no good reason (revenge perhaps?), taking his anger out against mankind by hurling himself against a large dam. Meanwhile, a trio of crooks travel to New Guinea in search of a giant opal, supposedly hidden in a cave. Once there, the natives give the usual warnings: "You must not go there, believe me!" and "An evil spirit lives there!" but the crooks are only interested in that opal. The men arrive at the cave, and one quickly finds the jewel. He's stung by a scorpion, however, and dies. The greedier of the two survivors, Omura (Akira Natsuki?), sees an opportunity to get the jewel for himself and blows up the cave with the other man, Kasuke (Kojiro Hongo), still inside. Kasuke survives, but by the time he regains consciousness, Omura is long gone. Omura takes a tramp steamer back to Japan but is laid up with a severe case of athlete's foot (certainly a unique plot device, I'll say). The ship's doctor suggests an infrared lamp, which Omura mistakenly leaves on as the ship approaches Tokyo Harbor. The lamp's rays hit the opal, which turns out not to be an opal at all, but an egg containing a monster called Barugon!

Published materials have suggested that Toho loaned out its Baragon costume (from *Frankenstein Conquers the World*) to Daiei for this production. Not so. The monsters are completely different—this a Barugon, Toho's is Baragon—though it's entirely possible that Daiei *did* want to confuse Japanese moviegoers. The four-legged monster has an oversized head, roughly similar to that of a rhino, a spiny back and a long tail. Like most four-legged *maninasuitasauruses* (as coined by SFXman Tom Scherman), Barugon generally walks on his knees, something which the filmmakers here don't seem anxious to hide. Barugon has an extremely long tongue, which looks like nothing more than a long stick covered with red rubber, and which darts out of his mouth like a jack-in-the-box. If that were not enough, on the tip of his tongue is a little orifice which sprays a freezing substance. From the creature's glowing, spiny back comes a colorful killer rainbow. Gamera, nearly forgotten about by this time, shows up but is almost instantly frozen by Barugon. The now reformed Kasuke returns to Japan with a native girl (Kyoko Enami), who has brought with her a 5,000-carat diamond. She explains that every 1,000 years, a monster shows up on her island and the natives have to use a diamond's bright reflection to get rid of the beast. This is the last of their diamonds, but she offers it to the military to help defeat Barugon. (This little story warrants a little reflection of its own: Why do they have to use a super-duper diamond? Why did the natives use up all *their* diamonds? Did they wear out? Did they throw them away? Why do the monsters come every 1,000 years? Are they prompt?) In any event, "Operation Diamond" is launched, and although some tinkering with infrared-red light is required, the monster does indeed become attracted to the light. Kasuke and the military try to lead Barugon out to sea (where he'll supposedly drown), but greedy Omura shows up and steals the massive gem. Barugon grabs Omura with that super tongue (a giant prop tongue was built, though used for only one shot) and eats both Omura and the diamond. Later, Kasuke explores some wreckage caused by Barugon's killer rainbow. He notices that all that remains of a jeep hit by the rainbow were its rearview mirrors. Kasuke determines that a giant mirror could be used to deflect the rainbow back at Barugon, and thus, "Operation Rear View Mirror" is born. Barugon fires off one of the killer rainbows, which is reflected in the military's newly built giant mirror. The ray bounces back, and singes Barugon's butt. The operation is called off, however, when everyone realizes that monsters don't make the same mistake twice (?!). Just then Gamera, having thawed out, appears out of the sky, and the two monsters grapple. The heroic reptilian Frisbee drowns Barugon, and the giant turtle flies back into outer space.

War of the Monsters would be a camp classic if it weren't so dull; at 100 minutes, it's at least a half hour (if not 100 minutes) too long. Gamera is hardly in the story at all, barely three scenes: at the dam and the two encounters with Barugon. The business with the tongue and the killer rainbow are hilariously absurd, even for a giant monster movie. The film is played straight, leaving the cast to read (dubbed) lines like "That monster's tongue cannot possibly be stopped!" The film's *Treasure of Sierra Madre* plotting in the first half becomes incoherent by the end, with Omura searching for the opal long after it's clear it was a monster's egg. Like Gamera, Kasuke is forgotten about for very long stretches, even though it's clear early on that he's the film's hero.

The special effects are cheap and uninspired. A little more attention seems to have been paid to the dam sequence, but it's nothing special. The dubbing and music are mediocre, the performances (including that of Daiei regular Hongo) undistinguished. The special effects were under the direction of Noriyaki Yuasa, Daiei's counterpart to Toho's Eiji Tsuburaya. Yuasa had directed *Gamera* (1965) but focused his attentions on the effects in this entry, letting Shigeo Tanaka (*The Great Wall*) handle the live action sequences. After *War of the Monsters*, however, Yuasa would helm both the live action and effects scenes for the rest of the series, including the pseudo–Gamera feature built almost entirely around stock footage from earlier films, *Gamera Super Monster* (1980).

This was the first Gamera film for Daiei star Kojiro Hongo. Hongo had appeared in the epic *The Great Wall* and starred in *The Return of the Giant Majin* the same year he made this. He went on to do two more Gamera adventures, *The Return of the Giant Monsters* (1967) and *Destroy All Planets* (1968), as well as *Along with Ghosts* and *The Haunted Castle* (both 1969).

War of the Monsters was sold directly to television and received scant reviews. *Variety*'s "Chie" reviewed the film in Japan and felt that Gamera simply "does not have the winning personality of the Toho stable." He also complained about the "poorly chosen" camera angles for the special effects sequences and the length of the picture. *The Motion Picture Guide* called *War of the Monsters* "good Saturday morning hangover material," and gave the picture a *½ rating. *War of the Monsters* may not be the worst Gamera movie, but it is the least interesting.

King Kong Escapes *(1967)*

Neither a sequel to RKO's 1933 classic nor Toho's own *King Kong vs. Godzilla* (1962), this silly adventure was based on the American animated cartoon teleseries, "King Kong," which ran some 78 episodes over three seasons on the American Broadcasting Companies, Inc. (ABC) beginning September 1966. The series was set on Mondo Island, where Professor Bond and his two children, Bobby and Susan, discover Kong and research the island's prehistory. Dr. Who, an evil, megalomaniac scientist (and obviously not based on the popular British television character) wants Kong for his own dastardly purposes, and episodes revolved around the conflict among Who, Professor Bond and the giant gorilla. Rankin-Bass, who created the show, was branching into features in the mid-sixties and produced this live-action adaptation with Toho, with the permission of RKO General, who owned the Kong character. Rankin-Bass is best known for their often charming holiday television specials for children ("Rudolph the Red-Nosed Reindeer," "Santa Claus Is Coming to Town," etc.), usually filmed in "Animagic," a stop-motion puppet animation process. One of the company's first features, *The Daydreamer* (1966), was partly filmed in this process, as was their delightful *Mad Monster Party?* (1967). In the late 1970s, Rankin-Bass would ally themselves to Tsuburaya Enterprises, co-producing a number of live-action features, generally released directly to television in the United States. *King Kong Escapes* was their first venture, and if one understands going into the picture that it's based on a cartoon series, the picture can be reasonably enjoyable, though it is a minor, generally uninvolving film.

At the Arctic Circle, somewhere near the North Pole, Dr. Who (Eisei Amamoto, dubbed by the versatile Paul Frees) proudly shows off his latest creation, a sixty-foot robot version of King Kong, constructed using plans stolen from Kong scholar Carl Nelson. Madame X (Mie Hama), an agent for an unnamed foreign power, is there to witness the Mechani-Kong mine a precious mineral, Element X, needed to build a nuclear arsenal for her country's army. At first the Mechani-Kong appears to be a success, with the steel gorilla digging deep into the frozen terrain. When it reaches the glowing mineral, however, a "magnetic mass" destroys much of its circuitry. Madame X, unhappy with Dr. Who's progress, threatens to cut off her country's funding. Who orders his men to work day and night repairing the robot. Elsewhere, Nelson (Rhodes Reason) is commanding a UN research team aboard the nuclear sub *Explorer*. The submarine is slightly damaged in an underwater rock slide, which Nelson sees as a perfect opportunity to slip out to visit Mondo Island. Nelson invites his lieutenant commander, Jiro Nomura (Akira Takarada) and the pretty ship's nurse, Susan (Linda Miller), ashore. Taking the sub's tiny hydroplane, the three explore the tropical island. Off in the distance, they hear an old native (Ikio Sawamura) warn Nelson (in a Javanese dialect) that they are trespassing on Kong's island. The men leave Susan alone for a minute, and a large dinosaur, resembling a *Tyrannosaurus Rex* (called Gorosaurus in *Destroy All Monsters*, made the following year) heads straight for her. Her screams awaken the sleeping King Kong, who promptly comes to her rescue. In a scene obviously inspired by the 1933 film, Kong and the dinosaur grapple while Susan watches helplessly from a nearby tree. Kong defeats the beast, just as Nomura and Nelson come to Susan's aid. The dinosaur stirs briefly (Kong rips the creature's frothing jaws apart), allowing the three enough time to make their escape. On the way back to the sub, however, they are attacked by a snake-like water serpent. Kong wades through the water to meet the beast, killing it as well. Nelson, Susan and Nomura climb back inside the sub, only the crew hasn't yet finished making repairs. Kong begins shaking the *Explorer*, and Susan volunteers to go topside to try and calm the beast. Infatuated with the attractive blonde, Kong stares glassy-eyed at her, picks her up with his paw, and contemplates taking her back with him to the island. Susan talks Kong out of it, however, and once the sub is ready, she returns to the ship which quickly departs. Nelson reports Kong's existence to a UN committee. He calls Mondo Island "a living museum of the prehistoric age" and announces a second expedition, not to capture but to study Kong. Madame X, disguised as a reporter, radios the news (via secret compartments in her hat and lipstick) to Dr. Who. Casting Mechani-Kong aside, the evil scientist decides the real Kong would be even better to dig for Element X. Dr. Who and his henchmen travel to Mondo Island, where Who shoots the old native and knocks Kong unconscious with ether bombs. The ape's arms and legs are tied to several helicopters, and Kong is flown to the doctor's waiting freighter. When Nelson, Nomura and Susan arrive, they find Kong gone and the old native dying. He tells them Kong was ape-napped by "an oriental skeleton, who lies like a gutter rat." Nelson immediately suspects "my old friend, that international Judas, Dr. Who." Nomura wonders if they'll ever be able to track down Kong. "Sure," Nelson replies, "as long as they haven't taken him to the North Pole." Little does he know. As the *Explorer* heads for the nearest UN station, the sub is met by a transport plane. Nelson, Nomura and Susan climb aboard and quickly realize that the plane is operated by one of Who's men (Yoshibumi Tajima).

Meanwhile, Dr. Who hypnotizes Kong and places little transceivers near each of the ape's ears. Kong begins digging for Element X but, like Mechani-Kong, stops when he finally reaches the brightly glowing mineral. "Kong! What's the matter?" the frustrated Who asks, "You're slowing down! Go on, you idiot ape!" It's no use, however, and soon Kong frees himself from Who's mind control. Nelson, Nomura and Susan are brought before Who, and Nelson refuses to help the mad genius. Madame X tries to seduce Nelson, who asks "What's a nice girl like you doing in a place like this?" Madame X's efforts unsuccessful, Nomura and Susan (who appear infatuated with one another) are taken to a cell, which Who begins freezing. Surprisingly, Nelson ignores Who's threats and appears ready to let his friends freeze. Just as Who is about to press Susan's face against one of the frozen cell walls, Kong breaks out of his cage and jumps into the Arctic sea, with Mechani-Kong in hot pursuit. Dr. Who and Madame X, the latter by now tired of the whole affair, follow Kong to Tokyo in their freighter. Madame X, now in love with Commander Nelson, sets him and his companions free. "I'm sorry my country wasn't right," she says. Trying to head off an attack on the city, Susan runs to Kong's arms (well, paw anyway). "Calm down, Kong," she assures the beast, "we're your friends." Just then, Mechani-Kong crashes through a building, and the two creatures begin a duel to the death. Mechani-Kong grabs Susan, and Who threatens to drop her from the top of Tokyo Tower if the real Kong doesn't return to Who's freighter. Madame X tries to sabotage the doctor's control panel, but the evil scientist shoots her dead. Nomura scales the tower to rescue Susan while Kong and his mechanical counterpart grapple on the tower. Part of the tower collapses, sending Mechani-Kong crashing to the ground below. The next morning, Who's freighter attempts a getaway (why did they wait so long?), but Susan orders Kong after the ship like a dog after the morning newspaper. The ape tears the ship apart, and Dr. Who is crushed under some debris (blood spurts out of his mouth, rather graphic for a G-rated feature). His work done, Kong swims away, presumably back to Mondo Island. As Nelson suggests, "I think he's had enough of civilization."

King Kong Escapes is a silly, juvenile picture though reasonably enjoyable and fairly representative of Toho's late-sixties output. Kong fares slightly better than he did in *King Kong vs. Godzilla*, when Toho's effects artists constructed what was probably the worst ape suit in screen history. This Kong isn't really any better, but at least it's more expressive. With its glassy eyes and oversized, comical head, Kong suggests not so much the Eighth Wonder of the World as Homer Simpson. The head is articulated in a very minimal way, with its blinking eyes (which always seem to be on the verge of tears) and duck-like lips. A second costume was built for some of the more rigorous action sequences, such as Kong's battle with the unimpressive sea snake. The grossly mis-matched head is wide-eyed, larger, and completely lacking in expression. Mechani-Kong is impressive, though one has to wonder why anyone would want to build a robot to look like an ape. The character was obviously the inspiration for the much less interesting Mechagodzilla, which starred in two of Toho's seventies films. Several shots and sequences were virtually duplicated for these later pictures, released as *Godzilla vs. the Cosmic Monster* and *Terror of Mechagodzilla* in the United States. Although the sea serpent appears to have been added as an afterthought, the *Tyrannosaur* was one of the studio's best looking monsters. Although it can't compare with its inspiration (from the 1933 original), Gorosaurus' detail work and restrained design and detail work make it a most impressive creation.

Rhodes Reason was brought in for dubious American marquee value. The lookalike brother of actor Rex Reason (*This Island Earth*), Rhodes had starred in two television series, the syndicated "White Hunter" in 1958, and "Bus Stop" during the 1961-1962 season. (Brother Rex was appearing in "The Roaring Twenties" that same period for the same network, which must have been confusing). Unlike his brother, who had appeared in several sci-fi features during the 1950s, Rhodes was mainly associated with television, including appearances on "Science Fiction Theatre," "Thriller," "The Time Tunnel" and even an episode of "Star Trek." After *King Kong Escapes*, Reason's only other film credits are for *The Delta Factor* (1970) and *Cat Murkil and Her Silks* (1976). Like his brother, Reason was a handsome but fairly wooden actor, his coarse, stoic features best suited for Westerns and undemanding roles such as this.

Linda Miller apparently lived in Japan and was one of a stock company of Western performers called upon by the various studios when needed. She's horrible, but her voice appears to have been dubbed by another actress, so perhaps she really isn't to blame. Miller, who is the daughter of Jackie Gleason, had a minor, nonspeaking role in *The Green Slime*.

Mie Hama, also in *King Kong vs. Godzilla* (in a different role), and fresh from her high-profile co-starring role in the big-budget Bond film *You Only Live Twice* (q.v.), is interesting as Madame X. Considering her glamorous, sexy role in the Bond picture, it seems strange that she would be costumed so frumpily here. Hama was a familiar star at Toho since the early sixties. Besides the *Kong* films, she appeared in *The Youth and His Amulet* (1961) and *The Lost World of Sinbad* (1963) and was one of the characters dubbed by Woody Allen for *What's Up, Tiger Lily?* (1966). Her comparatively restrained performance makes a nice contrast to Eisei Amamoto's deliriously hammy Dr. Who. With his truly awful teeth and Dracula-style black cape, Amamoto's Who is a memorable, if very silly, villain. Akira Ifukube contributed another fine score, though the effects work is uneven and occasionally sloppy.

King Kong Escapes was released in the United States by Universal, who made a big mistake by obscuring the connection to the Rankin-Bass series. They went so far as to claim "The all-new *King Kong Escapes* is far superior in its technique showing the tremendous advances made in cinematic art." (!) With promotion like that, the picture got just the critical reaction it deserved. *Variety*'s "Murf" found the film "dull," the direction and performances "below average" and the dubbing "horrible." Vincent Canby's curious review for the *New York Times* seemed as much a criticism of the Japanese people as their latest movie.

The Japanese, who show the greatest delicacy in arranging flowers and manufacturing transistor radios, are all thumbs when it comes to making monster movies like *King Kong Escapes*.

The Toho moviemakers are quite good at building miniature sets, but much of the process of photography—matching the miniatures with full-scale shots—is just bad. The English-language dialog that comes out of the mouths of the Japanese actors could well be Urdu, and the plotting is hopelessly primitive, although it is littered with found symbols, most of which have to do with a (perhaps Hiroshima inspired) death wish.

More recently, *Science Fiction* found the effects work a mixed bag, liking the staging, but noted that "the model work shows signs of the deadening effects of routine production activities." *Psychotronic* said Mechani-Kong looked like "a giant metal Magilla Gorilla," and that the picture had "maximum laughs and excitement."

Monster from a Prehistoric Planet (1967)

The prehistoric planet in the misleading title is actually good ol' Earth, and despite what the title may imply, the monster is a standard Japanese whatzit, and not a dinosaur.

Magazine writers Hiroshi Kurosaki (Tamio Kawaji) and Sanburo Hayashi (Kokan Katsura) and pretty photographer Itoko Koyanagi (Yoko Yamamoto), along with a group of university scientists, are searching the South Seas looking for exotic animals. Their boss, publishing magnate Funazu (Keisuke Yukioka), is branching out into the tourist trade, announcing to the press his plans to build a gigantic South Seas tourist attraction on mainland Japan: Playmate Land. "A southeast trip without leaving the country," Funazu promises. At sea, the crew is shaken by an undersea earthquake, triggered by an erupting volcano on a nearby island. Everyone goes ashore, where they meet a group of jubilant Polynesian natives who think the expedition is responsible for stopping the eruption and subsequent earthquake. Kurosaki and Itoko investigate a large statue they saw from their ship, despite the warnings of a young native boy, Saki (Masanori Machida, in blackface and wearing an afro wig), not to go anywhere near the gigantic idol. "Ah, it's only a stone statue," Kurosaki says; he apparently hasn't seen the *Majin* movies. Another earthquake topples the idol, revealing an opening to a large cave. They go inside to investigate (where they're soon joined by Sanburo) and discover a five-foot egg along with the bones of a strange creature, which they assume was the long-dead animal that laid the egg. Yet another earthquake gets the egg hatching, and out pops a human-sized bird-reptile, which the natives call Gappa. Everyone thinks that the cuddly critter would be just right for Playmate Land, and they crate the tiny monster up, even though this makes the natives mighty angry.

Shortly after the writers and scientists leave the island, who should appear but a Godzilla-size Mama and Papa Gappa, who storm through the native village and begin pursuing their kidnapped baby monster. Baby Gappa is presented to Funazu, who sends the creature to Toto University to be studied while the park is being built. Gappa begins growing at a tremendous rate, eventually reaching a height of about forty feet. The magazine writers begin having second thoughts about removing Baby Gappa from his natural habitat, though the scientists, led by Dr. Tonooka (Yuji Kotaka?), see the creature as a once-in-a-lifetime scientific opportunity. Meanwhile, a U.S. submarine picks up several natives set adrift after their experience with the monster parents. Young Saki, still begging for Gappa's return, convinces an American scientist, Dr. John McDonald, to take him back to Japan to try to convince Funazu to give the creature up. The publisher refuses, but now even Funazu's young daughter realizes the monster's gotta go. This becomes even more apparent as Mama and Papa Gappa turn up in Sagami Bay and later begin stomping about in the Atami area like grumpy tourists. The triphibian parents (they fly, they swim, they walk on land) hide out in Lake Kawaguchi, but the military, with the assistance of Tonooka, manages to drive the beast away by sinking a quartet of outboards loaded up with huge speakers emitting sound waves. This helps not at all, and the beasts soon head for Tokyo, causing more damage en route. At long last everyone comes to their senses, and Gappa is returned to his parents. In an absurd though strangely touching finale, Baby Gappa is reunited with Mom and Pop, and the three happily fly off into the sunset.

Nikkatsu's single *kaiju eiga* entry, *Monster from a Prehistoric Planet*, is essentially a remake of the 1961 British production *Gorgo*, also about a giant prehistoric baby reptile captured for public display whose even bigger mother shows up, causing a lot of destruction trying to get her kid back. *Monster from a Prehistoric Planet* adds little to this basic concept, borrowing its loose ends from *King Kong* and Toho's *Mothra*—South Sea natives who want their god returned, a happy ending set on an airport runway, etc. The human characters are quickly lost once the monster show gets under way, though they're just stock characters anyway—colorless reporters and scientists—and none of the actors is especially appealing. The film has a curious wrap-up, though, sure to anger many a feminist. Photographer Itoko, presumably inspired by Mama Gappa's motherly love, suddenly announces that she's quitting her job. "I guess I'm just an ordinary woman," she declares, "I should stay home, marry an office worker and wash diapers." Ouch!

The monster effects, by former Toho special effects art director Akira Watanabe, are okay but lack the perfectionistic drive of Eiji Tsuburaya's work.

The camera set-ups are conventional and generally uninteresting, and most of the miniatures look cheap and lacking in detail (check out the electrical towers destroyed by the beasts). Particularly bad is a brief sequence set underwater but filmed on an obviously dry set. The monsters themselves are fairly ridiculous, humanoid bird-reptiles, with both wings and arms, short, stubby beaks and glowing eyes. There was an attempt to make each of the three monsters look slightly different, unlike *Gorgo* which simply recycled the same costume for each of its characters.

The U.S. version is poorly dubbed, and current television and home video versions are poor dupes taken from a 16mm television print. The opening titles cue the viewer of the Americanization's sloppiness: Instead of squeezing or letterboxing the credits, AIP simply positioned the camera in the center of the image, so that most of the titles read along the lines of "lish dialogue by William Ro."

Phil Hardy's *Science Fiction* liked the film, which its reviewer considered an affectionate parody. "The effects are excellent and the script is worthy of a witty children's comedy." *Variety*'s "Chie," reviewing the film in Japan, also liked the picture. "Nikkatsu's creation, Gappa, [is] a real credit to his grandparents, King Kong and Godzilla... a technically superior film which blends horror and hokum, cataclysm and camp in just the right proportions... the Gappa family is completely endearing. These are the only Japanese monsters one might like to see again." While the ending is indeed cute, the rest of the picture is sloppy and derivative. Tongue-in-cheek or no, *Monster from a Prehistoric Planet* is a tiresome retread.

Return of the Giant Monsters *(1967)*

This was the third film in the Gamera series, and it's one of the most tolerable. Although an annoying, pudgy little boy plays a key role in the story, the picture is, if only slightly, more adult than the first two, and the screenplay throws a few twists into what was by now a creatively sapped genre. The film, known today as *Gamera vs. Gaos*, is nonetheless mediocre; the monster scenes are mostly unimaginative and derivative, and the film is too long by at least twenty minutes.

A series of volcanic eruptions and earthquakes halts construction of a new expressway, which is under the supervision of engineer Tsutsumi (Kojiro Hongo). Also delaying completion of the roadway is a group of farmers, led by the elderly Kanamura (Kichijiro Ueda). The government wants to buy the farmers' land, but Kanamura advises them to hold out for a better offer. Elsewhere, members of the media are flown over the site in a large helicopter. Directly below, in a densely forested canyon, someone or something shoots a yellow "supersonic sound beam" at the chopper, which neatly splits it in two. The helicopter crashes to the ground. Although Gamera, the flying, fire-breathing turtle has been seen in the area, the military does not regard him as a suspect. "Gamera doesn't send out destructive rays, to the best of our knowledge," one scientist says. A nosy reporter, hoping to photograph the source of the beam, meets Kanamura's grandson, Eiichi (Hisayuki Abe) in the forest. The chubby kid and the reporter find a cave where the laser beam appears to have originated. There's another tremor, and the cowardly journalist runs out of the cave, leaving the kid to fend for himself. Outside, however, the reporter is lifted high off the ground. Quickly turning around, the reporter finds himself in the hands of a giant bat-Rodan wannabe that gobbles him up like a pistachio. Eiichi looks like the monster's next course when Gamera shows up to rescue the kid from the big bat's clutches. The turtle whisks Eiichi to safety, though Gamera's arm is nearly severed by one of the bat creature's laser beams (no Gamera film would be complete without one of these pseudo-graphic scenes). Eiichi rides aboard the turtle's back (doubtlessly the dream of many Japanese and American children in the late sixties) and is returned to his elders. Gamera swims to the bottom of the sea to tend to his wounds. Questioned by the military and some scientists, Eiichi calls the bat monster Gaos, because it sounds as "if it were screaming 'Gaos!'"

The scientists theorize that Gaos' beams are created by sound waves. The monster, we're told, has "a system of double throats. Sound is generated in one and highly amplified in the other." In an attempt to explain away the rubber costume's stiffness, they add that the two throats restrict the movement of the monster's head. Right. They also say that Gaos was awakened by all of those eruptions and earthquakes. Eiichi suggests that because Gaos comes out only at night, he must be a nocturnal creature, something the scientists never considered. They decide to use extra-bright "AGIL" flares against the monster and put Tsutsumi in charge of the operation, along with a Mutt and Jeff pair of assistants, one of whom (at least the actor dubbing him) seems to be imitating Curly Howard of the Three Stooges. The flares only seem to irritate the beast, who flies through the city, slices apart automobiles and a castle, and eats several city folk. Everyone gathers at a stadium, where the bright lights keep the creature away. Gamera returns, and the monsters battle in mid-air (a poorly staged duel). The big turtle bites one of Gaos' feet, hanging onto it as the sun begins to rise. The monster's head begins to glow red as it frantically tries to get away. The bat creature shoots several laser beams at Gamera's head (more of that squirting blue blood, oh boy!) and breaks free, though losing a couple of toes in the process. The next morning, workers find Gaos' dismembered toes, which quickly begin shrinking before their very eyes. Ultra-violet rays emitted from the sun shrink Gaoses! Back in the bat cave, the creature grows a couple of new digits. In what is perhaps the most preposterous plan to destroy a giant monster, it's decided to trap Gaos by luring him with a big bowl of imitation human blood, placed atop a revolving platform (a modified hotel restaurant, looking like a big record player), which will so disorient the creature that he'll lose track of time and shrink in the morning sun. Everyone prepares for "Operation Whirlybird," and soon enough, the creature is spinning like a top slurping up the pseudo-blood. Unfortunately, a substation blows, and the dizzy creature figures out he's been played for a fool.

Meanwhile, Tsutsumi tells the farmers that the government has canceled further construction on their land and they can forget about selling it. The farmers, now believing they should have sold their parcels when they had the chance, berate Eiichi's grandfather. Eiichi, angered by the greedy farmers' treatment, throws his toys at them. Eiichi tells his grandfather his latest plan to get rid of Gaos: simply burn the surrounding forest so the creature will have to leave his roost. The grandfather takes the idea to the military, and it is quickly implemented. At the same time, Gamera shows up, does the two-step to avoid the monster's deadly beam and prevents Gaos from flying away. The sun begins to rise, but Gamera, not wanting to take any chances, also throws the tremendous bat into an erupting volcano. Tsutsumi tells the farmers construction of the expressway is on again after all, and Eiichi and his grandfather are heroes. (Prints of the film conclude, most inappropriately, with randomly chosen, nonsensical clips from *Gammera the Invincible* and from sequences earlier in this picture, apparently to pad out the running time.)

Return of the Giant Monsters is very slightly better than both *Gammera the Invincible* and *War of the Monsters*. The first film shamelessly aped Toho's first Godzilla film, bringing to it a wildly incongruous subplot about a lonely, turtle-lovin' boy. The second film was just plain boring, and its monster, Barugon, ludicrous beyond belief. By comparison, *Return of the Giant Monsters* seems less forced and more confident in its storytelling, such as it is. While Gaos is clearly patterned after Rodan (when he flaps his big wings, he creates a ferocious, Rodan-force wind), the monster is actually more interesting than Toho's Pterodactyl. A kind of giant vampire bat, Gaos actually eats people (something rare for these critters), and the creature's fear of the sun is something of a novelty. Gaos' unique laser beam mouth, which neatly slices automobiles, helicopters and buildings the way you and I might slice bread, is amusing. The model work for these sequences is generally okay, better in fact than those in any other Gamera film save the original. The matte work is also better than average; there is a nice shot of Gamera flying behind a volcano early in the film, along with an okay matte of the reporters boarding the doomed helicopter. The monster's scenes with Gamera, however, are the same old stuff. Gaos is badly designed, a supremely stiff, expressionless creature with no personality at all. Its movements are extremely limited: it flaps its rigid wings, opens its trap door mouth, and blinks. Eiichi is a pudgy, annoying child, typical of those found in Japanese fantasy films. His adult sister (Reiko Kasahara) seems to serve no other purpose than to try and wrangle the unruly youngster, her dialogue consisting almost entirely of lines like "Eiichi, you're interrupting an important meeting," and "You're disturbing your grandfather, Eiichi." The dubbing, as usual, is terrible. It's amazing how the simple looping of a line like "Yes, all the qualities of human blood. I'm grateful," can be transformed into something so ridiculous.

The Motion Picture Guide, which strangely referred to Gaos as a kind of "scaly flying fox," gave the film a *½ rating, while *Variety*'s "Chie" called Gaos "singularly ill-equipped for a monster. He cannot stand light, hates water and is afraid of fire." However, he noted "the man inside is a born actor. Gaos exhibits a strong sense of timing, a good deal of projection, and consequently generates an amount of empathy—he is obviously a Stanislavsky monster."

Son of Godzilla (1967)

Toho's Godzilla series entered the kiddie market with this, the eighth feature starring the big lizard. Directed once again by Jun Fukuda with music by Masaru Sato, *Son of Godzilla* might've been a good little film if they hadn't bothered to include the title creature. The creation of Minya, as he is commonly known in the U.S. (he's called Minira in Japan, and goes unnamed in American prints), was a big mistake by Toho, and only served to drive away the series' adult audience even further. However, save for the title character the picture's story, by Kazue Shiba and series regular Shinichi Sekizawa, is actually quite interesting.

On remote Solgell Island in the South Pacific, a team of UN-backed scientists, led by Dr. Kusumi (Tadeo Takashima), is conducting top-secret weather experiments. One afternoon, a plane appears overhead and reporter-photographer Goro Masaki (Akira Kubo) parachutes to the island. Goro is looking for a story, and the angry Kusumi orders him to leave. Goro's plane is long gone, however, so Kusumi's second in command, Fujisaki (Akihiko Hirata), suggests that Goro could take over kitchen duty and other menial chores around the tropical island. That evening, the scientists hear strange noises (that sound like "shhirrrp!") and see a large praying mantis, about fifteen feet long, hiding in the bushes. They fire at the beast, which departs. The following afternoon, Goro is looking for native plants to spice up the menu when he sees a beautiful woman (Beverly [Bibari] Maeda) quietly swimming. She sees Goro, and the frightened woman swims away. Back at the camp, nobody believes Goro's story about the girl (the island had been searched), and several members of the research team, especially Furukawa (Yoshio Tsuchiya), have become testy because of the island's humidity and steamy temperature. Kusumi tells Goro that the scientists are trying to control the island's weather. They hope by learning how to control the weather, they can turn deserts and other wastelands into thriving areas. The team launches and explodes a weather balloon, which begins lowering the island's temperature. A second balloon designed to stabilize the former's freezing effects malfunctions, and its radioactive capsule ignites. This causes a radioactive storm, which raises the island's temperature to nearly two hundred degrees Fahrenheit. Furukawa cracks up, and the radio goes dead from the heat. The radiation causes the mantises to grow even larger, several stories larger, in fact. The creatures, which Goro names gimantises (though known as Kamakirasu in Japan), unearth a tremendous egg. The monsters begin smashing the hatching egg, and out pops Minya, a baby Godzilla. Just as the mantises appear ready to eat the baby lizard, the real Godzilla shows up. The proud papa proceeds to thrash the giant insects. Goro stumbles into a cave, the young woman's hiding place. She turns out to be Reiko (Saeko in the Japanese version) Matsumiya. Her late father was an archeologist living on the island, and she remained there after he died. She warns the men of yet another monster, this one named Spiga (pronounced "Spee-ga"). Several of the scientists (including Furukawa) come down with a fever, and Reiko tells Goro of a "red water" which will cure their illness almost instantly. Reiko and Goro travel past Spiga's lair to get the juice and observe Godzilla teaching Minya how to roar and shoot radioactive flames from its mouth (with Minya barely able to register anything more than harmless smoke rings). The King of the Monsters is teaching Minya "just like a papa," Goro says. Reiko becomes cornered by one of the gimantises, and Minya tries to save the girl (she had fed the creature some berries). Instead of warding off the big insect, Minya awakens Spiga, a big, hairy spider who promptly traps Goro and Reiko in its silky web-substance (à la *Mothra*) as well as Minya and the gimantis. Spiga kills the gimantis with its stinger and is about to kill Minya, too, when Godzilla appears. Goro uses his lighter to get himself and Reiko free, and the pair head back to camp. Kusumi and the men, now hiding in a cave because of all the monsters, decide to try the experiment again, which they think might freeze the monsters. Godzilla, like Minya, is quickly caught in Spiga's sticky web, but with Minya's help is able to free himself, and the father-and-son team defeats the deadly arachnid. A second set of balloons is launched, which freezes the island. The temperature drops to ten below zero, and it begins to snow. The researchers, along with Goro and Reiko, head out to sea where they are rescued by a submarine. As snow blankets the island, Minya and Godzilla embrace, hibernating until the island warms up once again.

Like *Ebirah, Horror of the Deep* (1966), *Son of Godzilla* takes place on a tropical island. This was a move by Toho to cut costs (the sets and props could be reused, no expensive miniature cityscapes, etc.), but unlike the Godzilla films of the 1970s, both *Ebirah* and *Son of Godzilla* have decent stories that bely their lower-case budgets. Avoiding the Broadway-ese native chorus lines so common in Ishiro Honda's films (*King Kong vs. Godzilla*, *Mothra*), *Son of Godzilla*'s tropical island is a sweaty, prehistoric gravel pit, with monsters lurking around every palm tree. The gimantises are a welcome departure from the increasingly zany men-in-suit creations Toho was beginning to rely on. The gimantises were elaborate marionettes, operated in a manner similar to the much less menacing Mothra. Their design and manipulation (by Fumio Nakadai) is a significant improvement over Universal-International's title creature in *The Deadly Mantis* (1957), whose behavior and design were anything but logical. The creatures make an interesting foe for Godzilla and are quite impressive when photographed from low angles behind the miniature palms (Sato's National Geographic Special–style score here is also a plus). One of the film's best shots has Goro and Kusumi running from the battle scene as Godzilla sets one of the creatures on fire. As the two men run through a field, one of the creatures' flaming, disembodied limbs sails overhead. Spiga (Kumonga in Japan) is less inspired, basically just a big, hairy spider (with eight eyes). Also a marionette, the creation is largely undistinguished, though it does have a truly disgusting mouth.

Minya was one of Toho's more unfortunate characters. It doesn't look like Godzilla at all, but rather like an unpleasant cross between a tadpole and a badly deformed human fetus. The sounds coming from the creature appear to be a bizarre potpourri of human infants ("Wa-wa!" it shrieks, as if calling for its mother), braying jackasses and whimpering cocker spaniels. Minya was played by actor Little Man Machan for most of the picture, but for its big entrance, a woefully inexpressive prop, roughly resembling a rubber ducky, was used, dragged along the ground by wires. Minya is clumsy and constantly seems to be hit by flying rocks, knocked down by Godzilla's flaying tail or sprayed by Spiga's silky web. I guess this was an attempt to endear the creature to equally awkward children, but it only makes the character look foolish. As Minya bore so little resemblance to Godzilla, Godzilla was altered to resemble Minya. The papa monster's ghastly new face suggests a bug-eyed frog with an oversized mouth. The father-son relationship is decidedly unreptilian, with Godzilla patting Minya on the head when the latter breathes radioactive fire, and so forth. The bizarre, strangely touching ending (possibly inspired by *Monster from a Prehistoric Planet*, released earlier that year), with Godzilla and Minya in each other's arms as they are slowly covered with a blanket of snow, must surely rank as one of the strangest monster finales of all time. The Godzilla movies after *Godzilla vs. the Thing* almost always end with the Big G swimming off into the sunset. This ending deserves points for its gentle audacity.

Kubo, Takashima, Sahara and Tsuchiya are all back in familiar roles. The part of Reiko Matsumiya might have been played by Kumi Mizuno. Instead Bibari Maeda was cast. After Mizuno's similar role in *Ebirah*, Maeda's spunky jungle queen is a bit of a let-down. Masaru Sato's score helps establish the generally light tone of the picture, and several of his monster themes are interesting. *Son of Godzilla*, like *Ebirah*, was sold directly to U.S. television and never shown theatrically in this country, at least not in English. Subsequently, the film received few reviews.

Donald Glut, in his *Classic Movie Monsters*, noted Minya looked like "something out of a medical book of human freaks," but enjoyed the "bizarre and tender" wrap-up. *Science Fiction* enjoyed the picture's "considerable humour," and, incredibly, considered the effects work to be "probably the best... in the series." *The Motion Picture Guide* seemed to agree about the effects, but gave the film a paltry * rating. Minya would make a short cameo in *Destroy All Monsters*, before reaching full-blown stardom in *Godzilla's Revenge* (1969).

The X from Outer Space *(1967)*

It's too bad Shochiku didn't produce more giant monster films, for their only entry into the genre, *The X from Outer Space*, is a lot of fun. Production-wise, the picture is up to the level of Toho's films of the period, and the generally light tone bodes well for this silly but enjoyable monster movie.

Dr. Berman (Franz Gruber) arrives at the Fuji-Astro Flying Center (FAFC) with the fuel needed to launch the space probe *AAB-Gamma* on a hazardous journey to Mars. The previous six expeditions disappeared, apparently attacked by some kind of UFO. The four-man crew consists of stern Captain Sano (Toshiya Kazusaki), biologist Lisa (Peggy Neal), communications officer Miyamoto (Shinichi Yanagisawa) and the ship's doctor, Shioda (Keisuke Sonoi). Once in outer space, Lisa activates a device which looks like a popcorn popper, warning the crew of intense radiation outside the ship. They spot the UFO, which Miyamoto describes as "the world's largest fried egg" (perhaps not an egg, but it *does* look a bit like an Egg McMuffin). Shioda comes down with a case of space sickness, and Lisa, who is in love with Captain Sano, is hurt when Sano brusquely chastises her as she tries to give Shioda first aid. The UFO disappears, and *AAB-Gamma* is ordered to a lunar base, where the stricken Shioda is taken to Dr. Stein (Mike Daning) while Lisa meets Sano's girlfriend, Michiko (Itoko Harada). At the base, the crew members enjoy hot showers (using "man-made water") and giant fruit. Lisa gives Michiko—the women now wearing cocktail dresses—a pair of earrings she smuggled to the moon. With Shioda unable to continue the mission, the reluctant Dr. Stein is pressed into service as the ship's doctor. "Ah, spaceships!" grumbles the portly sawbones. The crew heads for Mars and en route encounters a meteor shower. One of the tiny rocks punctures the ship's hull, which depressurizes the cabin. Miyamoto plugs the hole with his rear end before it's sealed (the hole in the hull, that is) with a piece of metal. The UFO appears once again and discharges small blinking blobs which latch onto the ship. Lisa and Captain Sano remove the radioactive organisms, saving one for further analysis. Michiko shows up in a small craft to refuel the ship, and everybody returns to Earth.

While the crew attend a party at Dr. Berman's, the blob hatches, and later a three-toed footprint is spotted in the lab. "It looks like the claw of a big chicken!" Miyamoto says. The crew members return to their hotel to find the power out, and off in the distance they see a series of explosions. Out of the fire and smoke appears the now super-size Guilala, a reptilian creature that does, in fact, resemble a giant chicken. The strange creature has a beak, Dizzy Gillespie–style cheeks, and a truly bizarre head that makes the creature look like it's wearing some kind of jet-shaped hat. The monster attacks Tokyo, destroying a passenger jet and picking up a freighter and throwing it at some smokestacks, etc. It's determined that the monster can absorb energy, which rules out using an H-bomb. The crew return to outer space and fiddle with guilalium, a substance which they decide could envelope Guilala, preventing the monster from absorbing any further energy. Guilala heads for FAFC headquarters, looking for more energy to consume. Lisa is temporarily pinned down when some debris crushes her foot, and Sano and Miyamoto lure the monster away with a trailer loaded with nuclear fuel. Jets attack Guilala with the guilalium, which looks like shaving cream. The monster shrinks back to its original size and blob shape, and FAFC leaders decide to launch it back out into space. Lisa becomes resigned to losing Sano to Michiko (the monster taught her that "love demands courage"), and Sano and Michiko watch as the rocket carrying the former monster disappears into the clouds.

Despite its preposterous monster and standard second half, which follows the tried-and-true monster on the loose formula, *The X from Outer Space* is nevertheless an enjoyable little picture. The film's tone is immediately established with the sprightly title music, which is a strange cross between Japanese pop and Django Reinhardt, hardly the sort of thing one would expect to hear in a monster movie.

The special effects, while obviously inexpensive, show a level of ingenuity and imagination that was becoming increasingly rare at Shochiku's rival, Toho. The camera angles for some of the miniature shots are interesting (there are a couple of chicken-eye-view shots, low camera angles, etc.), and the miniatures themselves aren't bad. The design of the *AAB-Gamma* is interesting, looking a bit like a futuristic sled. The attractive miniature even has a pair of spinning radar dishes. It's these little details that make *The X from Outer Space* a lot of fun.

Peggy Neal, who also starred in *Terror Beneath the Sea* (1966), is back, and while her performance isn't much better, she does have a winning personality. Shinichi Yanagisawa is interesting in the usual comedy relief spot, and Mike Daning, also in *Terror Beneath the Sea*, is watchable.

Phil Hardy found the monster "well-designed, as are the sets and models, but there is the unfortunate tendency to film the creature frontally with the camera at 'normal' human height, as opposed to the usual low angle shots required to endow the monster with an imposing stature and a sense of menace." *The X from Outer Space* was released directly to television by AIP-TV, though a brief clip appears in the mediocre *It Came from Hollywood* (1982).

You Only Live Twice *(1967)*

This James Bond adventure isn't a Japanese production. However, it *is* science fiction, was (partly) filmed at Toho Studios and around Japan, features several of that country's genre stars and is very accessible in the United States. And so, with some hesitation, I include it here. The picture has already been more than adequately covered in other sources, most notably in two excellent books on the James Bond series: *The James Bond Films*, by Steven Jay Rubin, and especially *The James Bond Bedside Companion*, by Raymond Benson.

In a nutshell, American and Soviet space capsules are being kidnapped while orbiting the Earth, and both countries blame each other. The British government suspects someone else at work, and dispatches James Bond (Sean Connery), secret agent 007, to investigate. The Brits fake his death to make it easier for Bond to move about Japan, and disguise him (rather unconvincingly) as a Japanese fisherman. With the aid of "Tiger" Tanaka (Tetsuro Tamba), head of the Japanese Secret Service, and agents Aki (Akiko Wakabayashi) and Kissy Suzuki (Mie Hama), Bond traces the capsule nappings to an extinct volcano, where agents from SPECTRE (Special Executive for Counterintelligence, Terrorism, Revenge and Extortion) have built a fortress-like base and launch and recovery pad. Behind it all is the cat-loving leader of SPECTRE (and Bond's arch-rival), Ernst Stavro Blofeld (Donald Pleasence). Bond leads a Japanese assault force into the fantastic base, blowing it up. Blofeld escapes, however, and returns in the sequel, *On Her Majesty's Secret Service* (1969).

You Only Live Twice was the fifth Bond movie, following *Dr. No* (1962), *From Russia with Love* (1963), *Goldfinger* (1964) and *Thunderball* (1965). James Bond became an international cultural phenomenon and spawned countless imitative features (including the Bond parody, *Casino Royale*, also released in 1967) and television shows ("The Man from Uncle," etc.) and even influenced Japan's *kaiju eiga* series. However, as the Broccoli-Saltzman films soared in popularity, they also became increasingly complex as each film tried to top the one that had preceded it. Production time became longer and longer, which put a strain on the crew, virtually unchanged since *Dr. No*.

Star Sean Connery, wanting to branch out into other roles, became increasingly unhappy with the long (and apparently disorganized) shooting schedules, which prevented him from accepting several plum assignments. Connery left the series after *You Only Live Twice*, and while the next entry, *On Her Majesty's Secret Service* (1969), was a mostly excellent film on its own, the picture's atypical storyline and Connery's absence doomed it from becoming the breakthrough smash everyone had hoped for. A lucrative contract lured Connery back for *Diamonds Are Forever* (1971), but by then the series had lost its edge and barely resembled the earliest and best films. Critics charged that Connery's unhappiness can be seen in his performance in *You Only Live Twice*, but it's doubtful audiences watching the picture today—unaware of the actor's dispute with the film's producers—would even notice.

A bigger problem is the film's formulaic design and its departure from Ian Fleming's original story. The novel *You Only Live Twice* was the final third of the so-called Blofeld Trilogy, begun in 1961 with *Thunderball*, and continuing with *On Her Majesty's Secret Service*, published in 1963. The story *OHMSS* ends with Bond getting married, only to have his wife suddenly and brutally murdered by Blofeld. *You Only Live Twice*, Fleming's last completed work and published in 1964, was about Bond's revenge. In that novel, Blofeld, now living in a castle on the island of Kyushu, entices Japanese citizens to commit suicide in a deadly botanical garden filled with poisonous plants. Fleming's early novels (*Casino Royale* was the first, published in 1953) were entertaining, but the stuff of pulp fiction. His later works, while undeniably sexist, were actually quite good, and *OHMSS* and *You Only Live Twice* were probably the best of the bunch. The end credits of the film *Thunderball* promised "James Bond Will Return in *On Her Majesty's Secret Service*," but at the last minute the producers decided to do *You Only Live Twice*. This made no chronological sense, and Bond's desire to avenge his wife's death obviously had to be dropped. The producers also found Blofeld's suicide garden too bizarre and downbeat as well and instructed screenwriter Roald Dahl to fashion a new story following the formula established by the last two pictures. The result is an epic sci-fi adventure, not a Bond movie. While very entertaining, the film is far removed from the near gimmickless adventures of *From Russia with Love*.

Visually, the picture is extremely impressive. Freddie Young directed the often stunning Panavision photography (which was very impressive on big theater screens), while Ken Adam designed the knock-out, one-of-a-kind SPECTRE base set inside an extinct volcano (though actually filmed in England). John Barry's music may be the best of the series, while Maurice Binder did his usual fine title design work. Interestingly, the optical effects, depicting the space capsules in orbit and filmed in England, are surprisingly poor. For such a big-budget ($9.5 million), high profile picture, it's ironic that Toho's much-maligned optical effects are better than anything presented here.

Several Toho stars appear in the film. Akiko Wakabayashi stars as Aki, a role which Raymond Benson accurately describes as the entry's requisite "sacrificial lamb," while it is Mie Hama who actually winds up in Bond's arms for the close. Wakabayashi and Hama had appeared together in *King Kong vs. Godzilla* (1962), *The Lost World of Sinbad* (1963) and *What's Up, Tiger Lily?* (1966). Wakabayashi also played Princess Salno in *Ghidrah: The Three-Headed Monster*, and a jewel thief in *Dagora, the Space Monster* (1964), while Hama would appear in Toho's *King Kong Escapes* (1967) shortly after completing her role here. While both actresses appear to have been dubbed, they're appealing and their energy enlivens the occasionally tired look of the film's star. Tetsuro Tamba, who plays the friendly "Tiger," had appeared in *Harakiri* (1962), had been a samurai in *Kwaidan*, would later star in Toho's *Submersion of Japan* (1973) and made a guest appearance in Toei's *Message from Space* (1978).

Variety's "Beau" pretty much summed it up: "A smooth piece of entertainment that wisely doesn't overdo the elbow-nudging, winking self-parody of so many of its imitators." The *New York Times*' Bosley Crowther said, "This noisy and violent picture is pegged with the notion that nothing succeeds like excess. And because it is shamelessly excessive, it is about a half-hour too long... Through it all, Mr. Connery paces with his elegant nonchalance a little more non than usual, but altogether able in the clinches and in tossing off the gags of Roald Dahl." Phil Hardy's *Science Fiction* found the film to be "one of the wittiest Bond movies." Raymond Benson acknowledged the film's pictorial qualities and Barry's score, while complaining that they were "among the few redeemable elements of the film." While perhaps not a James Bond film along the lines of *From Russia with Love* or *Goldfinger*, *You Only Live Twice* is an entertaining spectacle, and few were disappointed with its stunning visuals and exciting action sequences when it was new.

Black Lizard *(1968)*

This gloriously campy film—based on a play by Yukio Mishima—contains several horrific elements near the end of the picture reminiscent of *House of Wax* (1953). The picture was way ahead of its time, and English-speaking audiences in the United States didn't get the opportunity to see it until many years after its initial release in Japan. *Black Lizard* premiered in Los Angeles in February 1985, but, for some reason, the rest of the country had to wait—in some cases six or seven years—before the picture reached them (I didn't get to see a 35mm print of the film until early 1992, nearly twenty-five years after its Japanese premiere!).

Japan's number one detective, Akechi (Isao Kimura), visits a secret, wildly mod nightclub (described by one critic as looking as if it were shot "on the set of 'Playboy After Dark'"), operated by the mysterious beauty Midorigawa

(Akihiro Maruyama in drag). "It's a night made for crime," she tells the detective, "I love nights like this." Later, she confronts an ex-lover, a musician who threatens suicide. Later, Akechi learns of the musician's death and the strange disappearance of his corpse from the morgue. Curious, the detective speaks to the pathologist and finds a tiny black lizard near where the dead man's body was being held. A wealthy jeweler named Iwasa (Junja Usami) receives a letter warning that his daughter, Sanae (Kikko Matsuoka), is in imminent danger and hires Akechi to guard her. Akechi believes criminals are after the jeweler's fabled "Star of Egypt," a diamond worth 120 million yen. Akechi, Iwasa and his daughter travel to Osaka, where they hope to trap the criminal at a hotel. While Akechi and Iwasa discuss their plans, Sanae visits with a woman who turns out to be Midorigawa. She introduces the young woman to Yamakawa, and the three visit one of the hotel rooms, supposedly to look at some art. When they arrive, Sanae is knocked unconscious with ether, her clothes are removed, and she's placed inside a trunk. Soon thereafter, Akechi and Iwasa receive a telegram from the criminals saying they plan to strike at midnight. The jeweler, concerned for his daughter's safety, checks her room where the young woman (actually Midorigawa in disguise) claims to be turning in for the night. Iwasa downs several sleeping pills and goes to sleep in a nearby bed, and Midorigawa slips out of the room. Akechi, awaiting the criminals' midnight strike in an adjoining room, answers a knock at the door. It is Midorigawa, who claims she heard of Iwasa's plight in the lobby. She flirts with Akechi ("I've never met a detective like you," she notes, "one who has such a deep and romantic attachment to crime") while waiting for the midnight hour. "The white sheet of tedium suddenly smoulders to reveal a crime's profile," Akechi says. "[I]t's enjoyable to wait for its sudden appearances."

Waiting for the hour to strike, Midorigawa suggests a wager. She and Akechi will play cards, the stakes being her jewelry for his career as a detective. Surprisingly, Akechi agrees at once. Before the game can be decided, however, midnight passes and nothing happens. Midorigawa suggests that perhaps the villains have *already* struck. Akechi rushes to Sanae's bedside to discover a mannequin in her place. Iwasa chastises Akechi for allowing his daughter to be kidnapped, but at that moment the detective receives a telephone call. Sanae is safe: Akechi had guessed Midorigawa's plans and had had the trunk followed and retrieved (though Yamakawa, using the alias "Amamiya," has escaped). Akechi asserts that Midorigawa is the notorious, if glamorous Black Lizard, a master criminal. Although the jig is up, the Black Lizard, as a precaution, has stolen Akechi's pistol from his jacket and makes a hasty retreat. The detective orders all exits from the hotel blocked, but she escapes disguised as a man (!). Iwasa returns to Tokyo, where he has hired a swarm of bodyguards to protect his daughter and the Star of Egypt. Some men arrive with a living room set the jeweler had ordered, which is then placed inside the house. Meanwhile, Akechi visits Sanae in her bedroom, warning her to be careful.

That night, Iwasa's maid, Hina (Toshiko Kobayashi), actually a Black Lizard spy, delivers a secret message to her associates using a radio device in the sofa ("Monkeys adorn the cow with candles," and other such silly code words). The middle-aged woman is caught by Iwasa's security chief, Matoba, but the maid, whose eyes turn gold, whips a poisonous snake at him, which bites and kills him. Hina, along with a bald brute, Okawa, kidnaps Sanae once again, placing her in a secret compartment inside the sofa. Matoba's hand is cut off and placed on top of the sofa (with a tiny black lizard in the disembodied hand's palm). Hina screams, feigning shock at discovering Matoba's body. Iwasa orders the bloody sofa removed, and the Black Lizard's men (dressed as movers) are only too happy to do so. The Black Lizard demands the Star of Egypt in exchange for Sanae's life. An exchange is arranged at the New Shinonome Pier. Iwasa, alone at the dock per the Black Lizard's instructions, hands over the diamond, while she promises Sanae's return before the evening is over. However, the Black Lizard has other plans for the young woman. The Black Lizard whisks the girl away aboard a ship bound for the villainess' island hideaway and "private art collection." Sanae is angry but confident that Akechi will rescue her. This outrages the Black Lizard, who becomes suspicious that the detective may somehow have gotten on board. She orders the ship searched. Lying on Iwasa's sofa, she hears breathing from beneath the cushions. Akechi is on board! She has the sofa tied up and confesses her love for Akechi as her equal, even though they are on opposite sides of the law and she will have to kill him ("I kill you because I love you so!" she says). She runs the sofa through with a sword, and, after a brief ceremony, has the lot dropped into the ocean. While everyone else is on deck, an elderly hunchback, who calls himself Matsukichi, emerges from a closet in the Black Lizard's cabin.

The party arrives at the island, where the Black Lizard shows Sanae her "art collection": human corpses preserved frozen in erotic and violent poses. The Black Lizard kisses one of the statues (played by Yukio Mishima!) and announces that Sanae is to be the newest addition to the gallery. Amamiya, madly in love with the Black Lizard, becomes so jealous at the attention she accords the Mishima statue, he tries to help Sanae escape. He figures he'll be captured and turned into a statue, too, thus winning back the Black Lizard's attentions. The hunchback, after helping to recapture the young couple, mysteriously slips a newspaper under the Black Lizard's door and kills Okawa. Amamiya confesses to Sanae that he also has feelings for her, and she admits to not being Sanae, but a woman named Yoko Sakurayana, Sanae's double, who agreed to help Akechi. That morning, the Black Lizard reads the newspaper, which has a front page story about Akechi's switch, and becomes enraged. The police appear suddenly, and the hunchback turns out to have been Akechi all along: he had thrown his voice from the closet to the sofa. Hina tries to kill the detective by throwing one of her poisonous snakes, but the Black Lizard chops the reptile in two with a sword, and stabs Hina instead. The Black Lizard retreats to her room, where she takes a fatal dose of poison. Akechi runs to her side, confessing his love for her as she dies.

The Black Lizard is an outrageously funny and very clever little film, and I'm quite pleased it was picked up for distribution here, even if it did take almost fifteen years. The picture is many things. It most closely resembles the films of Baltimore filmmaker John Waters, especially his earlier features starring the late, great Divine (Harris Glenn Milstead), and in particular, Waters' hilariously tasteless *Female Trouble* (1974). Both films address the idea of crime as beauty, Waters' film sending its protagonist to the electric chair for killing audience members during a performance art piece (among other things), while the Black Lizard steals diamonds and makes human statues. Like Waters' best films, *Black Lizard* is very much aware of its flamboyance. It's much less concerned with making Maruyama look like a woman than it is with making the character glamorous. And so she is. The wild collection of wigs and costumes worn by the actor, and his supremely over-the-top, Mae West–Jayne Mansfield–type delivery are just perfect.

Akihiro Maruyama was born in Nagasaki in 1935 and began his career as a French chanson vocalist at age 17. He became a popular performer in radio and on television, this despite the fact that by this time he wore heavy make-up and unisex-style clothes. In 1967, he began a hugely successful series of shows in Tokyo's underground theater with poet Shuji Terayama. Maruyama met Yukio Mishima in 1952, and the two became friends. When Mishima adapted *Black Lizard* for the stage, the writer recommended Maruyama for the lead role. After Mishima's notorious suicide (committing seppuku–hari-kiri–he drove a blade into his abdomen, then signaled a cadet to behead him), Maruyama changed his name to Akihiro Miwa, and began writing an Ann Landers–style advice column, which remains popular to this day. The multi-faceted, still popular actor-singer currently stars in several television shows and appears in commercials and on the stage.

Black Lizard was directed by Kinji Fukasaku. Born in 1930, Fukasaku joined Toei in 1953 and worked as an assistant director before directing his first feature, *Furaibo, Akai Tanima no Sangeki*, in 1961. His genre titles include *The Green Slime* (also 1968), the dreadful but energetic *Message from Space* (1978) and the interesting *Virus* (1980). He replaced Akira Kurosawa as director (with Toshio Masuda) of the Japanese half of *Tora! Tora! Tora!* (1970). With fast-paced films from Hong Kong all the rage among high-brow critics, it's time Fukasaku's breathless style was given a second look. *Black Lizard* moves like Mario Andretti on the Indianapolis Speedway. Fukasaku compensates for the picture's low budget (probably less than $500,000) through involving set-ups and creative blocking of characters. During the card game, for instance, the director quickly cuts between shots taken *beneath* the glass card table looking up at the leads, to close-ups of Maruyama's exaggerated expressions and Isao Kimura's stoic ones. Kimura, by the way, deserves much credit for the film's success, for the more outrageous Maruyama becomes, the more understated Kimura's straight-faced performance is. The straight man is usually critical to a successful comic pairing, and this is true here. Masashige Narusawa's script, based on Mishima's play, is full of witty, outrageous dialogue, particularly between the two leads, and the film's twists are genuinely surprising. The foiled kidnapping at the hotel is a standout, and the picture never quite matches its perfection thereafter.

Reviews were generally positive. "If ever a movie had 'cult picture' written all over it... *Black Lizard* is that movie," said the *San Francisco Examiner*'s David Armstrong. "This is a silly but enjoyable film, virtually uncategorizable and impossible to take seriously." The *New York Post*'s Jami Bernard called the picture "fun and overheated, with secret codes as clumsy as those of 'Get Smart' and just the slightest suggestion of necrophila... *Black Lizard* is a stylishly tacky thrill." "If Jean Cocteau had ever made a garish wide-screen-and-Technicolor pulp crime movie, it might have looked a little bit like *Black Lizard*," suggested the *Los Angeles Herald Examiner*'s David Chute. "This nutball Japanese camp thriller... is a little like a Fu Manchu or Dr. Mabuse story, with a crafty female supercriminal at the hub of its machinations."

Destroy All Monsters *(1968)*

This all-star monster orgy was the last of the classic Toho special effects films. This was their last hurrah, an attempt to return the creatively slipping *kaiju eiga* to its glory days. Director Ishiro Honda, composer Akira Ifukube and others would be back in future projects, but after *Destroy All Monsters*, it just wasn't the same.

The year is 1999. The United Nations Scientific Council (UNSC) has established a base on the moon, and lunar-bound spacecraft are launched almost daily. On Ogasawara Island in the Pacific, an underwater research team studies marine life, including artificially evolved animals. In an area of the island known as Monsterland, all the world's giant monsters have been gathered in the interest of world security. The monsters—Godzilla, Rodan, Mothra (caterpillar form), Manda (last seen in *Atragon*), Minya (the *Son of Godzilla*), Angilas (from *Gigantis, the Fire Monster*), Gorosaurus (from *King Kong Escapes*), Baragon (from *Frankenstein Conquers the World*), Spiga (from *Son of Godzilla*) and Varan (from *Varan the Unbelievable*)—are free to roam the island, but are prevented from leaving thanks to special electronic devices (including an invisible magnetic force field) tailored to each monster's own characteristics. Kyoko Manaba (Yukiko Kobayashi) has come to the island to assist Dr. Otani (Yoshio Tsuchiya) in his study of the creatures. Just as she arrives, Kyoko gets a long long-distance video-telephone call from her boyfriend, Katsuo Yamabe (Akira Kubo), flight captain of the *Moonlight SY-3* rocketship. Their call is interrupted by a power and communications blackout, as noxious fumes enter the island's control center, fumes which soon engulf the entire island, including Monsterland.

Back at the UNSC, reports begin coming in from around the world. Rodan is sighted over Moscow (destroying the Kremlin, in fact). Gorosaurus has emerged from beneath the Arc de Triomphe in Paris, destroying that famous landmark. Elsewhere, Mothra attacks Peking; Manda invades London; and Godzilla suddenly appears in New York, destroying the UN building with a blast of radioactive fire. Dr. Yoshido (Jun Tazaki) orders Captain Yamabe to take the *SY-3* to Ogasawara Island to find out what went wrong. Once there, Captain Yamabe and his men find Dr. Otani and Kyoko in a serene, trance-like state. They explain that the monsters are being guided by remote control and demonstrate this by having Mothra destroy a speeding train, Godzilla ignite a ship at sea and Rodan obliterate a passenger jet. The shocked crew of the *SY-3* is taken before a beautiful woman with a sinister smile (Kyoko Ai), and dressed in shiny silver. She is introduced as the queen of the Kilaaks, and we learn that she is from a tiny planet located between Mars and Jupiter. The Kilaaks have come to conquer Earth and make its people their slaves. Yamabe's men charge the Kilaak queen. Bullets merely bounce off the alien, while one of Yamabe's men receives an electrical jolt when he tries to grab her. The crew members of the *SY-3* grab Dr. Otani and make a hasty retreat, fighting the men of the Ogasawaran base, now under Kilaak mind control. Taken back to the UNSC, Dr. Yoshido and Yamabe try to question Dr. Otani, who is still under the Kilaaks' influence. He says nothing, and when the two men aren't looking, Otani jumps out of a window and falls to his death. When Yamabe and Yoshido run down to retrieve his body, they are met by Kyoko and men from the island base, who desperately want something from Otani's body. Police arrive at the scene, and Kyoko and the others escape. An autopsy reveals a highly sophisticated mini-transceiver planted in Otani's neck, just beneath the ear. A farmer (Ikio Maruyama) discovers a strange stone on his land, which turns out to act as a Kilaak "relay station" in controlling the monsters. A worldwide search turns up similar devices in the Alps, in Dover, in church steeples in Spain, and even one inside a coconut in Guam. Tokyo, heretofore untouched by the monsters, is suddenly attacked by Rodan, Manda, Godzilla and Mothra all at once. As General Sugiyama (Yoshibumi Tajima) tries to save the city, Kyoko appears before the UNSC, acting as an agent of the Kilaaks and ordering the Earth to surrender. A desperate Yamabe grabs Kyoko and rips out her earrings (ouch!), which contain Kilaak transceivers. Kyoko's ears are bleeding like crazy, but she is free from the aliens' mind-control. Yamabe spots a Kilaak flying saucer heading for Mt. Fuji and decides to follow it in the *SY-3*. The rocketship is attacked by Rodan, however, and Yamabe loses track of the saucer. He orders a search of the entire Fuji area.

Later, Yamabe and his men find a cave where an image of the Kilaak queen, along with those of several other aliens, appears on a cave wall (interestingly, all of the Kilaak are women). The queen shows him images of their powerful base, suggesting that any resistance would be futile. The queen and her consorts vanish. It's determined that the main Kilaak controlling transmitter is on the moon, and Yamabe and the *SY-3* crew track the radio waves to a remote lunar crater. Several Kilaaks stationed there try to burn the Earth ship with a bevy of remote control flame throwers, but the *SY-3* crew, escaping in a tank-like "ground car," manages to destroy the Kilaak base. The crew locates the transmitter, along with several Kilaaks who, once exposed to the cold, have returned to their natural state — slug-like living metal. Now in possession of the controlling transmitter, the UNSC decides to turn the tables on the Kilaaks and order the monsters to attack the Kilaaks' Mt. Fuji hideout. As the monsters converge at the base of Mt. Fuji, King Ghidorah, the three-headed, flying dragon, appears out of the sky. Controlled by the Kilaaks, Ghidorah attacks the other monsters. Ghidorah first grapples with Angilas, carrying the monster high into the air then dropping him. The spiky monster's fall creates an avalanche, revealing the Kilaaks' sphere-like base inside Mt. Fuji. It's apparent that Ghidorah is no match for the earth monsters and is soon defeated. Another monster appears, this one a flying ball of fire, which turns out to be nothing more than a Kilaak saucer. The *SY-3* crew gives chase and shoots it down. The Earth is saved. Later, Dr. Yoshido, Captain Yamabe and Kyoko fly over Ogasawara Island, where Earth's monsters have been safely returned to their idyllic existence.

While more than a trifle silly to most, and a disappointment to demanding *kaiju eiga* fans today, few films gave me as much pleasure growing up in suburbia as this all-star monster rally. *Destroy All Monsters* was Toho's attempt to win back the steadily dwindling older audience the studio had so firmly tapped earlier in the decade. The film's budget was higher than any of its special effects films since *Ghidrah*, and the storyline harked back to Toho's earlier pictures. *Destory All Monsters* (not *Destroy All Monsters!* as it is commonly listed) marked the return of Ishiro Honda to the series. Why did the director take a two-picture break? "There were scheduling problems, and also Toho decided that they did not want people to feel that monster films had to be directed by me," Honda told David Milner in 1992. "Frankly, I was having a hard time humanizing Godzilla the way Toho wanted anyway," he added. "I was even hesitant to let Mothra act as a mediator between Godzilla and Rodan in [*Ghidrah: The Three-Headed Monster*]. It certainly would have been difficult for me to direct *Son of Godzilla*." Scenes revolving around Captain Yamabe and the *SY-3*, particularly those that take place on the moon, strongly suggest *Battle in Outer Space*. As in that film, the battle and its spectacle are the story, and while one may find fault with the comparative lack of characterization, few films in the *kaiju eiga* genre are as visually spectacular as *Destroy All Monsters*. Monsters unseen in more than a decade emerged from storage (or were rebuilt) to appear in the film. Minya's comical appearance was, thankfully, limited to the final battle, where he blows a smoke ring around one of Ghidorah's heads. Several new concepts, such as undersea farming and cross-breeding of the monsters were dropped for budgetary reasons.

The poor condition of the original costumes relegated Baragon (it was he and *not* Gorosaurus that was intended to emerge in Paris) and especially Varan to the background (the latter's appearance limited to a few long shots). A new, more anthropomorphic suit was designed for Angilas, while Manda's face was redesigned, probably to look less like a spare head for Ghidorah. The Godzilla suit was changed again—thank goodness—away from the goofy Papa Godzilla look of *Son of...* and more or less reviving its appearance in *Ebirah*. For the first (and so far only) time, Japan's giant monsters have become a genuine global threat, and not limited to Japan alone. And unlike *Son of Godzilla*, *Destroy All Monsters* is played completely straight, as the nations of the world brace themselves for the ultimate alien invasion. Save for Minya's smoke rings, even the big battle with Ghidorah is played without the boulder-tossing, jig-dancing shenanigans of past efforts.

The special effects, while not quite up to the standards of *kaiju eiga* films made early in the decade, are plentiful and generally better than more recent efforts like *Ebirah* and *King Kong Escapes*.

Akira Ifukube wrote one of his finest scores for *Destroy All Monsters*, including an exciting new march, one of the the composer's best and most recognizable themes. The familiar cast includes Jun Tazaki (in his final *kaiju eiga* appearance), Akira Kubo, Yoshio Tsuchiya, Kenji Sahara (as the moon base commander), and Yoshibumi Tajima, among others, all in familiar roles.

Surprisingly, the film is generally looked down on by most critics. Greg Shoemaker, for instance, (cryptically) blasted *Destroy All Monsters* in his Toho retrospective for the *JFFJ*: "The picture fails to better the genre it interprets, choosing to reinforce that which has been immortalized on film since 1954 and surprisingly misrepresenting the best.... From all this, an imaginary source for the production's script, effects, etc. can be hypothesized as an output of computer-fed parameters of earlier films in an effort to seek an ultimate of its kind." *Variety*'s "Tone" also looked at the film with disapproval. "[The] plot is on comic strip level, special effects depend upon obvious miniatures, and acting (human) is from school of *Flash Gordon*.... Score is barely routine and ... Honda's direction of Tanaka production is static." *Science Fiction*, while misidentifying several of the monsters, along with several plot points, said, "By this time Godzilla ... and company have degenerated into vaudeville characters." *Destroy All Monsters* does have its admirers. *Psychotronic* proclaimed it "the ultimate Japanese monster movie!" and the picture, unavailable on home video and not widely aired on commercial television in 1993, remains a popular tape among collectors and bootleg video outlets.

Destroy All Planets *(1968)*

The English-language title of this fourth Gamera adventure was likely an attempt by American International (who sold the film directly to U.S. television) to confuse Japanese fantasy film buffs who had seen the much better *Destroy All Monsters* (also released by AIP) at around that same time. While Daiei's three previous Gamera entries had been bargain basement stuff compared to Toho's monster epics, they seem downright lavish compared to this cheapie. *Destroy All Planets* admirably varies somewhat from the usual formula, but it tests its audience's patience with an inexcusable amount of stock footage from the three previous films: *Gammera the Invincible* (1965), *War of the Monsters* (1966) and *Return of the Giant Monsters* (1967). Rising costs and diminishing box office returns forced both Daiei and Toho to cut corners in their respective effects-laden features. *Destroy All Planets* was the first such film to blatantly incorporate previously seen footage in place of expensive new effects.

Unseen aliens, on board a swirling spaceship that looks like five striped ping pong balls glued together, decide to conquer Earth, "the planet most similar to ours in all the universe." Before they can get underway, however, the ship is attacked by Japan's favorite reptilian frisbee, Gamera. The aliens radio back to their home planet to "send spaceship #2 immediately!" and try to warn their comrades of the prehistoric beast. "It's name is..." Just then, the ship explodes. After a rousing chorus of Gamera's bouncy little theme song, we meet two likeable, if troublesome boy scouts. Masao (Toru Takatsuka) and Jim (Carl Clay) sneak out of camp and find a tiny, boy-sized "pocket submarine" at the nearby International Research Laboratories. Masao, a boy genius, switches two all-purpose cables so that everything will run in reverse (forward means backward, left means right, etc.). Later, when inventor Dr. Dobie (Peter Williams) and scoutmaster Shimada (Kojiro Hongo) try to give the troop a demonstration of the new device, the sabotaged ship runs amok. However, Masao offers to "fix" the tiny craft, and he and Jim gleefully take the submersible to the bottom of the sea, where they meet up with Gamera. Meanwhile, spaceship #2 shows up, and the aliens place both Gamera and the nearby sub in a "Super Catch Ray," a translucent, underwater sphere. The aliens decide to explore the big turtle's "memory waves"—in other words, look at footage from the creature's earlier romps. After a whopping 20 minutes of stock footage, the aliens decide to take advantage of Gamera's one weakness: "his unusual and overpowering kindness to children." The boys are kidnapped and held captive aboard the alien ship. Inserting a control device (also resembling a painted ping pong ball) at the base of the monster's head, the aliens order Gamera to attack Japan, threatening the boys' lives if the monster fails to comply. Gamera smashes his way across the countryside (more stock footage), while the boys wander freely aboard the alien ship. For the first time, we get a good look at the extraterrestrials, who are humanoid with glowing eyes. The boys also find a silly-looking fifteen-foot starfish/squid-like creature whose pushed-in face resembles a parakeet. The UN decides the Earth must surrender to the aliens rather than sacrifice the boys' lives (fat chance!), but fortunately, Masao remembers the little number he did on the submarine and pulls the same switcheroo on the aliens' ship. The boys escape, while Gamera breaks free from the mind control and smashes the aliens' spaceship. In a truly bizarre bit of business, the squid creature beheads the humanoid crew. Then, the humanoid aliens turn into squid creatures themselves, which then meld with their apparent leader, forming one giant, Gamera-sized monster. The creature (called Viras), now looking like a half-peeled banana (and resembling "Beaker" of the Muppets) attacks Gamera. After the usual amount of bloodletting, the monster is defeated, the Earth is saved and the boys are heroes.

Nearly one-third of *Destroy All Planets*' running time is allotted to stock footage. The aliens' scan of Gamera's "memory waves" goes on endlessly, with none-too-impressive flashbacks shamelessly eating up screen time. When Gamera falls under the aliens' mind control and attacks the countryside, we're treated to yet more familiar footage, such as the big turtle's destruction of a dam, lifted from *War of the Monsters* (1966). The picture has few new effects, none of which is the least bit impressive. Especially bad is the pocket submarine, which looks exactly like a bathtub toy. *Destroy All Planets* has several interesting ideas, such as the aliens' ability to move from one part of the spaceship to another by floating through corridors. When Masao and Peter try to do this, they fall flat on their faces. "Why do you suppose they save the good things just for the grown-ups?" one of the boys asks. Also interesting is how the aliens, over-confident in their ship's security system, give the boys free rein of the craft. They can order sandwiches, visit the squid and even radio the UN (via Masao's Dick Tracyesque wristwatch-radio) not to surrender; they just can't leave. Unfortunately, these ideas are all that hold this flimsy production together, and that's not enough.

"To see him making eyes at two kids and wagging his rudimentary tail, is enough to destroy your faith in monster-kind," said *Variety*'s "Chie," who reviewed the film in Japan. "For those who like their monsters fierce, there's something sad about all this." The entry that followed, *Attack of the Monsters* (1969), was no less silly but significantly more entertaining.

Goke, Bodysnatcher from Hell *(1968)*

This Shochiku production, released to home video in 1984 as *Body Snatcher from Hell*, is an intriguing sci-fi–horror–disaster tale which successfully jumbles several genres with the greatest of ease. With the exception of Toho's *Attack of the Mushroom People* (1963), there really isn't a picture quite like it.

During what is supposed to be a routine flight from Tokyo to Itami, strange events appear to spell doom for the passengers and crew aboard an Air Japan commercial jet. The sky is filled with strange, orange-red clouds: "Like flying into a sea of blood," notes the pilot (Hiroyuki Nishimoto). Birds in flight, mysteriously terrified, crash into the windows of the plane with bloody thuds. The jet receives a call over the radio that a note was found warning of a bomb on board the aircraft. The captain orders an immediate search. The co-pilot, Sugisaka (Teruo Yoshida), and stewardess, Kazumi (Tomomi Sato), begin searching the passengers' carry-on bags. One of the passengers, a mildly effeminate man dressed in a white jacket, white shirt and gloves and wearing sunglasses, claims to have brought nothing on board. However, Sugisaka and Kazumi discover a bag belonging to the man containing a rifle and vial of acid, though no bomb. The man, Teraoka (Hideo Ko), apparently assassinated an ambassador (the great Andrew Hughes, seen in stills!) and announces that he's hijacking the plane to Okinawa. During the flight, however, a bright yellow UFO closely passes the jet, knocking out all its controls. The plane makes a spectacular crash landing. The pilot and the gunman are killed, while one of the passengers, apparently an associate of Teraoka (this isn't clear in the English-dubbed version), who, in any event, actually had the bomb, runs off with the device. Sugisaka chases after him and rescues the criminal from a landslide. The survivors have no idea where they are (the terrain is mountainous, rocky and apparently lifeless) and are without food and water. Teraoka, apparently only stunned, wakes up and runs off into the night with Kazumi as a hostage. The two discover a blindingly yellow, translucent UFO, which vaguely resembles a gold pith helmet with four swirling balls underneath. Teraoka is drawn toward the craft. Inside, he stands before a pulsating fluorescent blue blob, which splits the assassin's forehead right down the center. Outside the UFO, Kazumi screams. Sugisaka finds Kazumi in a state of shock and carries her back to the plane, where a psychiatrist, Momotake (Kazuo Kato), hypnotizes her to learn what happened. It seems that after the blob split the assassin's forehead, it crawled inside Teraoka's head.

Meanwhile, the other passengers are having their own problems. A crooked politician, Mano (Eizo Kitamura), fools around with Noriko (Yuko Kunsunoki), the wife of an arms dealer associate, Tokiyasu. Surprisingly, the dealer is more than willing to sacrifice his wife to help close a multi-million yen arms sale. However, Mano and Tokiyasu grow to hate one another, and soon the arms dealer is torturing the weak-willed Mano by giving him a flask of whiskey, which only burns the parched throat of the politician. Elsewhere, Momotake is attacked by Teraoka, now possessed by aliens. He kills the psychiatrist by sucking his blood, vampire style. Later, Teraoka shows up at the wrecked plane, still sporting that giant vertical wound in the middle of his forehead. Although the other passengers are reluctant to help the zombie-like assassin, a sympathetic American, Mrs. Neal (Cathy Horlan), insists he be cared for. Her husband was recently killed in Vietnam by a similar-looking head injury. Inside the wrecked fuselage, Teraoka next murders Tokiyasu and takes the man's wife to the UFO. The next morning, everyone goes looking for Noriko. They find her at the top of a cliff. Through Noriko the aliens, called Gokemidoro, announce their intention to annihilate the Earth. They also say mankind has "already turned Earth into a monstrous battle field" of war and destruction. Noriko collapses, falling off the cliff. Everyone rushes to her body, which has already become mummified by the alien possession.

Back at the crash site, Mano, Mrs. Neal and a scientist, Saga (Masaya Takahashi), decide to learn more about what they're up against by sacrificing one of the passengers to the bloodsucking aliens. The three, by now crazy with fear, settle on the bomber, who is thrown outside. Teraoka shows up almost at once, but before the alien can get at him, the frightened man, standing just outside the plane, blows himself up with his own bomb. The explosion, which makes a small hole in the already twisted fuselage, injures Saga's legs. Mrs. Neal and Mano decide to try and make their way back to civilization, wherever that might be. They don't get very far: Mrs. Neal is soon bitten by Teraoka, while cowardly Mano hightails it back to the plane. Co-pilot Sugisaka and stewardess Kazumi try to help the man back inside the plane, but instead the politician locks the couple out. Sugisaka throws a pail of gasoline on Teraoka, followed by his lighter, which sets the possessed man afire. The alien simply leaves his body, however, the blob dripping back out the man's forehead. Teraoka collapses, turning into a sandy substance which blows away in the wind. The alien goo slimes its way through the blown-out hole of the fuselage and takes over the body of Saga, creating a similar vertical scar on his forehead. The possessed scientist kills Mano, but Sugisaka and Kazumi manage to escape. The alien Saga returns to the UFO, leaving Saga's body to crumble and blow away in the wind like Teraoka. Sugisaka and Kazumi, having abandoned the plane, try to make it back to civilization. As it turns out, they were only a short distance from a toll road entrance, where a line of automobiles waits to enter. They rush up to the first car and are shocked to find only blood-drained bodies inside. They run to the next car—ditto. They run to the next and the next. At the tollbooth, the operator has mummified. Sugisaka and Kazumi find a nearby city. They enter an office building—the lobby is filled with corpses. One of the bodies, possessed by an alien, says "It's too late now to wish you had lived differently ...it's too late to repent." Reconciled to their fate, they watch as a UFO passes overhead. From outer space, we see dozens of saucers approaching the Earth, which soon becomes a lifeless world.

Although the picture's center is a bit familiar, what precedes and follows it is quite remarkable. The opening sequence, where the story's characters are introduced prior to the plane wreck, contains several unsettling ideas whose delicate scripting is apparent even on brutishly dubbed American prints. The birds that mysteriously fling themselves at the plane with crashes of blood and feathers, as if aware that judgment is at hand, are most unsettling. And the red-orange sky and introduction of the *Close Encounters*-like UFO is admirably restrained. The aircraft miniature and its crash are obviously phoney but so dramatically handled one hardly notices. The ending is genuinely surprising. Of course, most films of this type would've had the young couple rescued. Indeed, the very fact that the plane crashed so close to civilization alone is inventive, and the picture could have ended right there. Susumu Takaku's screenplay, however, doesn't let our heroes off that easily, subjecting viewers to a jarring, unsettling and entirely appropriate wrap-up. The writer is less successful with the overly symbolic characters (Mano in particular) and some of their motivations (such as Mrs. Neal's sudden transformation from sympathetic widow to ugly foreigner), and some of the performances are weak. But for the most part, *Goke, Bodysnatcher from Hell* is a reasonably scary, intriguingly atypical example of Japanese fantasy-horror. The production values are quite good. The photography, as usual for the studio at this time, is colorful and makes excellent use of the wide screen (lost, of course, on current English-language prints). Besides the imaginative miniatures, a full-size mock-up of the plane's exterior was constructed, and the art direction of its smashed interior is also nice.

The Motion Picture Guide gave the film a * rating while getting the story wrong, and said, "Coupled with bad acting and sloppy direction, this resembles *Invasion of the Body Snatchers*, though not nearly as well done." *Psychotronic* called the picture "pretty amazing," while Phil Hardy's *Science Fiction* argued that "the film is over-written, awkwardly directed and badly-acted."

The Green Slime *(1968)*

Metro-Goldwyn-Mayer followed the release of its ground-breaking *2001: A Space Odyssey* with this silly space adventure, a Japanese-U.S.-Italian co-production. Occasionally exciting if badly written and flatly lit and directed, *The Green Slime* is ultimately undone by some of the most laughably ridiculous monsters in screen history.

Sometime in the future, asteroid Flora—which closely resembles the title menace from Toho's *Gorath* (1962)—is on a collision course with Earth. In fact, the big rock is spotted just 12 hours before its predicted collision. (It is highly unlikely that such an asteroid would go undetected for so long, even using 1968 technology.) General Jonathan Thompson (Bud Widom) orders retired astronaut Jack Rankin (Robert Horton) to take command of Space Station Gamma 3 and organize a detail to travel to the asteroid and blow it up before it reaches Earth. Stopping off at the space station, Rankin runs into his old girlfriend, Dr. Lisa Benson (Italian actress Luciana Paluzzi), and her new fiancé, Commander Vince Elliot (Richard Jaeckel), who was also Rankin's best friend. The three are cool but courteous to one another as Rankin readies his crew. Dr. Hans Halvorsen (Ted Gunther) worms his way into the mission, as does Commander Elliot. Aboard a rocketship, the asteroid crew quickly reach the out-of-control rock. The men separate and begin laying charges. Halvorsen finds some green, pulsating blobs and places one of the organisms in a container. The blobs also attach themselves to the spacemen's astro-buggies, and they have to pry off the little creatures (which look like drippy, moldy carpet). General Thompson radios the ship, telling Rankin that the asteroid has accelerated (how?) and the detonation will have to be moved up by several minutes, giving the crew precious little time to get away. Halvorsen wants to study the creatures, but Rankin smashes the container and orders him aboard. However, some of the green stuff splatters on one of the crewmen's pantlegs. The fleeing rocketship barely escapes the exploding asteroid (a phony-looking but well-edited and exciting sequence), and the crew returns triumphantly to Gamma 3. Rankin bitches to Lisa about Elliot, saying, "He's too nice to be a commanding officer." On a recent mission, Rankin explains, Elliot "sacrificed ten men to save one." Lisa asks Rankin to be more sympathetic, arguing that the incident "nearly destroyed" the guilt-ridden Elliot. Rankin orders everything decontaminated three times, but as crewman Michaels (Richard Hylland) sets about decontaminating the space suits, the green stuff only seems to grow. When he opens the door to the decontamination chamber, he is suddenly attacked by midget-size monsters—the Green Slime. Michaels lets out a bloodcurdling scream before being burned to a crisp by the electrified creatures.

The ludicrous monsters are a model of bad design. The four-foot-tall, bipedal, bell-shaped creatures have a single red eye in the center of their bodies, set in a lip-shaped socket. Below that are lots of little, less-visible eyes, which sit above a grassy skin which suggests a hula skirt. Some of the creatures have two arm-like tentacles, while others have four or more (controlled by wires). Some also have red, lobster-like pincers. None of the tentacles appears functional in the slightest, and the actors inside the creature suits do little but flail them about as if waving pennants at a pep rally. Rankin wants to kill the monsters immediately, but wimpy Elliot and Dr. Halvorsen think they should be captured alive. After a disastrous effort to throw a net over one of the beasts (many men are killed or wounded) Rankin takes charge. Halvorsen determines that the creatures feed on energy, and later the green slimes (which make noises like high-pitched whoopee cushions) turn up in the infirmary, where they scare some patients and nurses. Rankin and Elliot try to isolate the creatures in one part of the station, but the energy-eating slimes only trigger an explosion that blows up a part of the floating wheel. Most of the creatures survive the blast and move out onto the space station's hull where they attach themselves to a solar generator and begin renewing their energy. Rankin orders the space station evacuated, while Elliot takes command of a detail which dons space suits and keeps the creatures busy as everyone else boards a waiting rocket. Something happens to the wheel's remote self-destruct panel, and Rankin has to go back into the ship—by now swarming with the green critters—to set the timer himself. Returning from outside, Elliot shows Rankin he's a man of action after all by rescuing the latter from the slimes. Just as they make their escape, however, one of the creatures gives Elliot an electrified hug, killing him. Rankin carries Elliot's body back to the rocket ship. The space station's rockets ignite, hurling the wheel into the Earth's atmosphere, where it harmlessly burns on re-entry. The creatures destroyed, Rankin recommends that the late Commander Elliot be awarded the highest possible citation—albeit posthumously.

The Green Slime's storyline—in which monsters lurk about a highly confined area—has turned up in countless science fiction and horror films, perhaps most famously in *The Thing (From Another World)* (1951) and *Aliens* (1986). Needless to say, the picture's ludicrously awful roly-poly monsters aren't frightening in the slightest, and the film's flat, even lighting scheme does little to disguise their hopeless design. The picture isn't bad until the critters show up; the film's first act, where Rankin, Elliot and the others blow up the asteroid, is generally exciting, and the final seconds preceding the rock's destruction are edited for maximum thrills. The triangle of Rankin, Elliot and Lisa is trite in the extreme, the male bonding even more so, and the bland performances by the three leads don't help at all.

Robert Horton is especially colorless as the grouchy Commander Rankin. Horton is best known as Flint McCullough on TV's "Wagon Train" and to genre fans for his many appearances on "Alfred Hitchcock Presents." His rugged features were best suited to Westerns, and the actor seems out of place here. Richard Jaeckel, on the other hand, excelled in military roles, from early supporting parts in pictures like *Sands of Iwo Jima* (1949) to more recent fare, such as the wretched *Delta Force 2* (1990). After his plum supporting role in *The Dirty Dozen* (1967), and that picture's huge box office success, it's surprising that Jaeckel would appear in films as minor as *The Green Slime* and *Latitude Zero* (1969). Maybe leads in minor films were more appealing than character parts in major ones. Maybe he liked Japan. In any event, neither character is very interesting. In fact, their constant bickering and dueling testosterone become quite annoying.

Although beautiful Luciana Paluzzi (born 1931) had been in films (mostly in her native Italy) since the mid-fifties, her big break at international stardom came when she played a coldhearted villainess in the most popular of James Bond films, *Thunderball* (1965), opposite Sean Connery. Although her voice was dubbed by another actress, the role led to similar parts in features—

including the spy adventure *The Venetian Affair* (1967), with Robert Vaughn — and on television. She's pretty but colorless in *The Green Slime*. She continued to star or co-star in a wide range of films, mostly in the United States and Italy, through at least the late 1970s. Most of the rest of the cast was comprised of various amateur and semi-professional Caucasian actors living in Japan. Ted Gunther appeared in *Terror Beneath the Sea* (1966), while Robert Dunham, who plays Jaeckel's second-in-command, played the American diamond investigator in *Dagora, the Space Monster* (1964). Even Linda Miller, who starred with Rhodes Reason in *King Kong Escapes* (1967) turns up, though she has no lines as one of Paluzzi's nurses.

The special effects, by ex–Toho employees Akira Watanabe and Yukio Manoda, are far below their work for Eiji Tsuburaya. The miniatures are badly lit and lacking in detail. There are a few imaginative camera set-ups, and the exciting editing of the asteroid's explosion was probably their doing, but overall the work is sloppy and disappointing. And of course, there are those monsters.

Director Kinji Fukasaku's direction is flat and uninteresting. His *Black Lizard* was fast-paced, funny and exciting, so why is this so bland by comparison? Perhaps the explanation lies in the inherent difficulties of multi-lingual productions.

Predictably, reviews were mostly negative. *Variety*'s "Brad" called it "a poor man's version of *2001*. The special effects are amateurish, the story and script in the same category." Leonard Maltin's *Movie and Video Guide* gave the picture a *½ rating, suggesting that it was "not as much fun as it sounds." Also giving the film a poor review was *The Motion Picture Guide*, who called it "a bargain-basement production." *Psychotronic*'s authors labeled the title creatures "the most laughably unconvincing monsters of any Japanese production in years." They also noted that the picture's title song—a wildly out of place novelty rock number—was released as a single.

Kaidan Botandoro *(1968)*

What kind of release, if any, this Daiei ghost story had in the United States is uncertain. It was reviewed in Japan by *Variety* in June 1968 (the time of year when most ghost stories are released in that country) and may have been exhibited here by Daiei International, most likely with English subtitles.

The film's title, which translates to "A Tale of Peonies and Lanterns," refers to the O-Bon festival, where lanterns, representing dead loved ones, are gently floated on serene ponds and lakes. At one such festival, Shinzaburo (Kojiro Hongo, who starred in *Destroy All Planets* that same year), meets an attractive young woman, Otsuya (Miyoko Akaza), and her companion, Oyone (Michiko

Ohtsuka). Otsuya asks Shinzaburo to "marry" her for the duration of the festival. As he's lonely and she's beautiful, Shinzaburo agrees. He soon learns, however, that the women are ghosts, according to the man's servant, Banzo (Akira Nishimura) and a local teacher (Takashi Shimura). When Shinzaburo refuses to see the women, they confess they're free to walk the Earth for the duration of the festival, but are unable to join the land of the dead until Otsuya finds a lover. After much consideration, Shinzaburo decides to see his Otsuya once again, and visits her grave site. The next morning, Shinzaburo's body is discovered by local villagers—holding a female skeleton in his arms. He has followed the women into the land of the dead.

Kaidan Botandoro's screenplay was written by Yoshitaka Yoda, who also wrote Mizoguchi's *Ugetsu*. This film seems very much in the same mold; like *Ugetsu*, the women are strongly written and sympathetic, even if their actions do result in the man's death.

Variety's "Chie" called the film "one of the most persuasive Japanese ghost stories since Mizoguchi's *Ugetsu*... an extremely beautiful story." Phil Hardy's *The Encyclopedia of Horror Movies* agreed. "One of the enchantingly funereal love poems which were a specialty of Yoda."

Mighty Jack *(1968)*

As Eiji Tsuburaya, Toho's longtime effects director, became less involved with the day-to-day concerns of the studio's Godzilla series (though every effects shot was still subject to his approval), his attentions turned elsewhere. Tsuburaya formed his own production company in the mid-1960s and began shooting several effects-oriented series for Japanese television. Best known among these was "Ultraman" (1966–67), widely syndicated to American television throughout the late 1960s and early 1970s. "Ultraman," which was preceded by another series, "Ultra Q" (1966), begat at least seven more series: "Ultra Seven" (1967–68), "Return of Ultraman" (1971–72), "Ultraman Ace" (1972–73), "Ultraman Taro" (1973–74), "Ultraman Leo" (1974–75), "Ultraman 80" (1980–81) and "Ultraman Great" (1991). A number of episodes were re-edited and released theatrically in Japan, and at least two legitimate features, *Space Warriors 2000* (q.v.) and *The Ultraman Story* (1984) were produced as well. Tsuburaya's company also produced other live-action effects oriented series, including "Mirrorman" (1971), "Fireman" (1973), "Jumborg Ace" (1973), "Pro Wrestling Star Aztecizer" (1976–77), "Dinosaur War–Aizenborg" (1977–78) and "Dinosaur Fighting Team Kosheidon" (1978–79). After the director's death in 1970, Tsuburaya Productions became involved in several telefeatures produced in conjunction with the American firm Rankin-Bass.

One of the best of the Tsuburaya television shows was "Mighty Jack" ("Maitei Jiyaku") which ran 13 one-hour episodes in 1968. The series was wildly derivative, borrowing elements from the James Bond films, "Mission: Impossible," "Voyage to the Bottom of the Sea" and Toho's *Atragon*. Though hardly original, the program's energy and colorful effects made it entertaining enough. The program was never syndicated in the United States. However, Sandy Frank Enterprises, best known for reissuing the Gamera films and re-editing Japanese television shows into features for syndication and home video release, purchased the rights to the series in the mid-eighties. They essentially spliced the first and last episodes ("The Man Who Vanished from Paris" and "The Mysterious Dirigible") together, with bits from other shows to fill in the narrative gaps.

The picture opens with a colorful montage where various Mighty Jack agents dash to their secret hideout, a map shop. The secret squad of men and women was formed by the Japanese government to combat "Q," an organization financed by a fanatical group of terrorists bent on conquering the Earth. As the narrator warns, "Q is near, far—everywhere!" Equipped with an enormous flying supersub, also called *Mighty Jack*, the team investigates the disappearance of Harold Atari, a professional mountaineer and expert in cartography. Mighty Jack's leader, Colonel Yabuki, will not explain why he's so important, just that it's imperative he be rescued. Atari was in Paris when both he and his car were kidnapped and air-lifted to a remote island in the Pacific. Fortunately, just before he left the country, Colonel Yabuki gave Atari a special suit equipped with a hidden transmitter.

As Mighty Jack agent Dr. Hide searches for Atari aboard a freighter, Captain Tenda and Lieutenant Jerry (Masanori Jihei) scan the area with the "electro-scout," a jet-sized flying sub, possibly inspired by the similar craft appearing in Irwin Allen's "Voyage to the Bottom of the Sea" TV show at about this same time. The *Mighty Jack* crew locate Q's island base. Their arrival does not go undetected. Q's cat-loving leader (a rather shameless rip-off of James Bond's chief nemesis, Blofeld) offers the safe return of Atari in exchange for *Mighty Jack*. The offer is naturally refused. Atari, meanwhile, seems impatient about his rescue. "Be quick about it," he says, "unless you're all frightened pigeons." Atari's comments annoy square-jawed Jerry, but the others caution the lieutenant, "He's a V.I.P." Jerry and the captain sneak ashore that evening and rescue Atari. Atari suggests blowing up the island base, and the suggestion is carried out.

Returning to Mighty Jack's base, Colonel Yabuki and Captain Tenda proudly present—surprise!—*Major* Atari to *Mighty Jack*'s crew. Atari takes command of *Mighty Jack* and its mission against the forces of Q. Moving on to the obvious second half of the pseudo-feature, Q's forces attack a Japanese titanium atomic center. Using a device capable of converting molecular energy, Q's forces instantly freeze the research base. Atari and Colonel Yabuki conclude that one of the government scientists studying molecular energy for them must have sold out to Q. Both Dr. Von Mueller and Dr. Takibana claim their records were recently stolen. Meanwhile, Yabuki's assistant is attacked while approaching her car. She's rescued by a writer, Manuel Perez. Meanwhile, another female agent of Mighty Jack befriends yet another writer, Roberto Okumura (Jerry Ito). Both men are Q agents trying to sabotage Mighty Jack. Elsewhere, it's learned that Takibana's half–German son and assistant, Fritz, is the Q agent who stole secret plans. Using a bulky "syncotron unit," a bulky rifle used to freeze things, Q's men infiltrate the supersub, severely damaging the craft. Thanks to Takibana's help, however, Mighty Jack (confusingly) locates Q's base. After a typically impressive pyrotechnics show, Q's leader commits suicide.

Mighty Jack was shot in 16mm, and as its effects were always intended for the small screen, they don't really compare to Tsuburaya's Toho work. The models appear to be much smaller in scale and are less detailed. Nonetheless, they are filmed in an imaginative fashion and are generally appealing. The same is true of the live action shooting. Like "Mission: Impossible" (at least the show's first few seasons), *Mighty Jack* manages to hide its meager budget with a machine gun pace, action-oriented camera angles and movements, and imaginative art direction (I like the idea of how each Mighty Jack agent passes through a numbered door to get to the big sub). Another big plus is Isao Tomita's score, the kind of music that makes you want to run up and down a few flights of stairs.

The cast is largely composed of actors unfamiliar to most Americans (including this writer). Longtime Toho character man Eisei Amamoto (Dr. Who in *King Kong Escapes*) is a Mighty Jack agent, but his role is very minor (at least in the two episodes shown here). It's good, however, to see Jerry Ito (*Mothra*) playing another very theatrical villain. The rest of the cast admirably creates very individualized characters. Even the most minor of Mighty Jack agents or Q villains stand out in some way. It's a shame the dubbing is so terrible.

The first half works much better than the concluding story, partly because it's more character driven and far more coherent (remember, we're missing eleven hours of story here). The introduction of Atari's character is very interesting, and Lieutenant Jerry's overconfidence and annoyance about Atari's rescue are a nice twist. Tsuburaya followed his "Mighty Jack" series with a somewhat campier sequel, "Fight! Mighty Jack," which, like its predécessor, was never syndicated in the United States. As Bob Johnson points out in his review of the feature in *Markalite*, it's unfortunate that Sandy Frank didn't issue both series in their entirety. Mighty Jack's characters are likable, and based on these two episodes, I'd like to see more of them and their adventures.

100 Monsters *(1968)*

Like several other Japanese productions covered in this text, I've only had the opportunity to see *100 Monsters* in Japanese, without English subtitles. The film was released in this country, probably with English subtitles, but hasn't been seen here since the late 1960s, and its availability even then is uncertain. What *is* certain upon seeing the picture is that there is much to like.

According to Phil Hardy's *Encyclopedia of Horror Movies*, the story revolves around a ruthless landowner who turns a religious shrine into a brothel, much to the anger of the poor community in which it's built. The brothel opens with a performance of the "One Hundred Monster Collection," a famous ghost story. An exorcism, required at the conclusion of the performance, isn't carried out, sending the tale's spirits into the world of the living. The often wildly designed ghosts haunt the village, and eventually the property owner commits suicide.

Even without understanding Japanese, it's apparent that this Daiei production is actually quite similar to the studio's Majin films. Both center around a wealthy and powerful outsider who blusters his way into a poor village and sets up camp. His fall is necessitated not by the oppressed peasants but by a supernatural force beyond their control. The film seems to have been targeted for general audiences. There are moments of violence, sex, horror and humor scattered throughout the film, many of which are quite effective. For Western audiences, the most interesting element is the monsters themselves. They're quite strange and spooky and very different from what we're accustomed to.

The film opens with a prologue which finds a frightened man running through a dark forest, only to be confronted by a dark, not quite discernable shape with a big bloodshot eye in its center. Later in the film, two fishermen are haunted by a strange woman who has the ability to stretch her rubbery neck to tremendous lengths, wrapping it around one of the men like a serpent. She laughs most sinisterly, and the well-executed effect is very unsettling. The picture's most unusual spirit appears after one of the human characters (the dimwitted son of the landowner?) continually paints an unopened umbrella with one leg, one eye, two arms and a big long tongue dangling from its mouth. The young man is surprised when one of his drawings comes to life (after first appearing as a cartoon). The happy young man is delighted with the bizarre but friendly creature (played by a Muppet-like marionette), which licks the man's face like a cocker spaniel. The Japanese laser disc *100 Monsters* ends with the trailer for another film, presumably a sequel, which features many of the same ghosts, including the umbrella critter. Apparently, the picture is *Along with Ghosts*, also known as *Journey Along Tokaido Road* [Daiei, 1969]. Moments like these, to say the least, are not the stuff of Western horror films, and it's a shame that this wonderfully atmospheric production—which compares quite favorably to the likes of *Kwaidan*—is today so hard to see.

Voyage into Space *(1968)*

Toei's television series "Jiyaianto Robo" ("Giant Robot," 1967–68) was an amusing if obvious attempt to cash in on the success of Tsuburaya's "Ultraman" series. Syndicated in the United States that same year as "Johnny Sokko and His Flying Robot," the program featured a stoic mechanical man who fought off giant monsters from the Gargoyle Gang, aliens bent on conquering Earth. In 1970, AIP-TV edited several episodes together to feature length and sold it to television stations across the country as a legitimate feature. It wasn't, though no one seemed to mind. Fifteen years later, Sandy Frank Enterprises would release its own collection of pseudo-features (*Mighty Jack*, *Fugitive Alien*, etc.), creating a great deal of confusion among film fans who didn't know what to make of these cheap, episodic, but sometimes beguiling "movies." These programs seriously wounded the already poor image of Japanese fantastic cinema most Americans have. Uninformed viewers naturally assumed these slap-dash features were theatrically exhibited in Japan and were understandably astonished by their almost nonexistent production values, hackneyed editing and ridiculously poor dubbing. No wonder programs like Comedy Central's wrong-headed and contemptible "Mystery Science Theater 3000" jumped on these cheapest-of-cheap compilations.

A manta ray–shaped flying saucer invades Earth, gently landing at the bottom of a lake. Several months later, Johnny Sokko (Mitsunobu Keneko), a young boy, and Jerry Mono (Akio Ito), a secret agent for Unicorn, an international defense organization, meet aboard a passenger liner crossing the lake. The ship is attacked by a giant monster, vaguely resembling the water cyborgs from *Terror Beneath the Sea* (q.v.). Johnny and his new friend jump ship before it's destroyed by the big creature. The next morning, the pair awaken on the beach of a strange island. They're approached by the Gargoyle Gang, men wearing sunglasses, beards and berets (with skull emblems). The two heroes are taken to Gargoyle headquarters, but escape to another part of the complex. They stumble upon a giant robot, as well as its inventor, Dr. Lucius Guardian, a brilliant scientist kidnapped by the Gargoylians. The robot is one hundred feet tall and fairly clunky looking; it wears what I assume is supposed to be a samurai's helmet, but it looks more like an ancient Egyptian headdress. Giant Robot, as everyone calls it (though it's sometimes called Robo as well) is completed but lacks the atomic power it needs to get started. Lucius tells Johnny and Jerry that Giant Robot will obey the commands of the first person who addresses it with the wristwatch transmitter Lucius has built (Johnny puts the watch on). The Gargoylians, Lucius warns, want to use the indestructible tin man to conquer the world. Lucius also says, matter-of-factly, "Well, the Gargoyle Gang is going to lose. I've planted an atomic bomb that will explode in five minutes." With this alarming bit of news, Johnny and Jerry hightail it to another part of the island just as the Gargoylian complex explodes (powerfully, but hardly the force of an atomic explosion). Rather than destroying Giant Robot, the big bomb provides just the power the mechanical man needs. Johnny takes control of the robot using that wristwatch he's wearing. Now its master, Johnny orders the robot to fly him and Jerry back to Tokyo. Johnny's exclusive control over Giant Robot earns him a commission at Unicorn, where he's given the code name U-7 (Jerry is U-3), along with a bright orange costume, which shamelessly apes those worn by Ultraman's Scientific Patrol.

Meanwhile, the leader of the Gargoyles, Emperor Guillotine, a trident-carrying blue humanoid with painted-on eyes, wrinkly face and mop-like beard, dispatches a "rolling meteor," the nucleon, to attack Unicorn forces. The army's efforts to destroy the nucleon, which resembles a runaway undersea mine, prove fruitless. Fruitless, that is, until Johnny Sokko and His Flying Robot show up. Giant Robot destroys the dangerous orb. The emperor's second-in-command, Bottonous, a bald, silver-skinned man with an outrageously extended brow, no eyebrows and a big scar on his forehead worthy of Frankenstein's monster, leads the second assault (or second episode in this case). Bottonous' assistant, Dangor, a colorfully painted man with a bulbous head and a peg leg, fires a bullet at Unicorn Commander Azuma's automobile. Azuma isn't hurt, but the emperor, speaking from a micro-cassette player hidden within the bullet, warns Unicorn not to meddle in his plans of conquest. "Surrender while you still can, and we might let you live," he gloats, "Heh, heh heh!" The Gargoylians try to kidnap Dr. Dorian, a scientist working with a strange space vine. The kidnapping is thwarted by Johnny and Jerry (the latter swings through a doorway and nearly brings down the entire flimsy set with him). The Gargoyle Gang eventually gets hold of the space vine, which grows to gigantic proportions (natch). Dr. Dorian warns the army not to fire missiles at the energy-consuming plant, but they ignore his informed pleas. "They should listen to the scientists," Johnny says. An aerial assault on the monster plant, which shoots projectiles of "burning lava" at the jets, proves to be a disaster. Johnny dispatches Giant Robot to the scene. "Power punch now!" Johnny commands. Giant Robot not only destroys the vicious vine but saves several schoolchildren in the process.

Next episode: Tsuzuki, leader of the Kyoto branch of Unicorn, is on his way to an important conference when his train is literally swallowed up by a huge bipedal, one-horned, fire-breathing monster bull, the Lagorian. Tsuzuki survives and is taken before Bottonous. "You're the only witness to our swallowing the train," the silver-faced villain says. "How do you like that, eh?" "Oh no!" cries Tsuzuki, "You killed all those passengers in order to capture me!? Humans wouldn't do that!" "No they don't," Bottonous acknowledges. "And it's a good thing since Gargoylians do!" Tsuzuki is operated on, "transmodulated" into a Gargoylian spy. Eventually, Johnny and Jerry, only briefly fooled by the brainwashed Tsuzuki, are kidnapped and held somewhere beneath Lake Biwa. Just as quickly, Giant Robot is called to the scene, defeats the monster bull and saves Jerry, Johnny and Tsuzuki. Later (i.e., the next episode), Johnny and Jerry explore an abandoned building. "Gee whiz! It's pretty weird isn't it?" Johnny says. "Sure is!" replies Jerry. Why they should find an empty building so bizarre after blue and silver aliens, a vine monster and a gigantic, train-eating bull is anyone's guess. In any event, a Gargoylian sniper shoots Johnny. The assassin, believing the tiny agent dead, heads back to base, but Johnny, wearing a bulletproof uniform, survived the gunshot and sneaks into the hood of the hit man's car. The Gargoylian leader somehow realizes this and sends a gigantic Daliesque eye monster (no mouth, no ears, no body, just a seventy-five-foot eyeball with lid and lashes) to assassinate the assassin. The eyeball lifts the killer's car off the ground, and the hit man falls to his death. Johnny is saved by the ever-reliable Giant Robot. Commander Azuma, apparently sick of that big eye lookin' at him, radios Johnny, "It'll be dawn soon. Get rid of that eye!" A mega-punch from Giant Robot blows the organ to kingdom come. The increasingly frustrated emperor now sends two monsters at once (creatures from earlier episodes on the TV show), one a kite-like creature, the other a more conventional quadruped with a droopy trunk on either side of its mouth. After defeating the monsters, Giant Robot is completely pooped, just as Guillotine had hoped. The Emperor himself becomes gigantic and laughs at the helpless mechanism, seemingly out of power. When someone suggests firing at the giant fiend, Guillotine warns that he's a mass of atomic energy. A single bullet could cause a chain reaction, he says, igniting his entire body, "and the Earth goes with it!" To demonstrate, he pulls off one of his fingernails, tosses it, and indeed it blows up half the countryside. Thankfully, if unimaginatively, Giant Robot's auxiliary power kicks in, and acting on its own, the robot grabs Guillotine and whisks him into deep space. Together, they crash into a flaming meteor. Guillotine and Giant Robot are no more. A teary-eyed Johnny salutes his brave, selfless robot, as the narrator, in dialogue probably inserted for less emotionally prepared American audiences, suggests, rather awkwardly, "When Johnny needs him again perhaps, like a miracle, he will come back, out of the sky."

Typical of Toei's fantasy shows from the period, *Voyage into Space* is an action-packed, breathlessly paced programmer, whose low budget is compensated by an exciting, imaginative use of camera angles, editing, and frequently ingenious staging. The picture is just as preposterous as the *Gamera* movies, but barely any worse production-wise, and far more energetic and entertaining. The show was clearly meant for kids. There are appealing and singularly childlike (though not really childish) ideas throughout. For instance, members of Unicorn snap their fingers in lieu of saluting, which somehow creates a disarming "woooiiip" sound with each snap. With flying robots at his command and aliens to spy on, who wouldn't want to trade places with Johnny Sokko for a day? As escapist entertainment for children, the picture delivers the goods. For adults, it's all very silly and outrageous, but entertaining enough, and one has to admire the boundless imagination of its creators. However, *Voyage into Space* also suffers in the way that almost all feature compilations do. The film is very episodic (where one show ends and another begins is obvious), and the plot is almost nonexistent. As was the case with the re-edited Supergiant-Starman movies, what was exciting in thirty-minute increments becomes repetitive and tedious in a ninety-minute splurge; it's like trying to watch a fifteen-chapter serial in one sitting.

The special effects are better than I had remembered them. I had not seen Johnny or his Flying Robot in nearly twenty years before watching the film again for this book. I had remembered the show being greatly inferior to "Ultraman," but now see that they work on about the same level. The Robo suit is unimaginative and clunky (a sixth grader with lots of cardboard, masking tape and paint could come up with something better), especially when compared to that nifty Ultraman costume. However, the robot does predate the similarly designed Mechagodzilla, with its rocket-launching fingers, ray-shooting eyes, etc. The other effects are about on a par with the Tsuburaya series—the remote-controlled tanks are pathetically bad, but the miniature jets and their manipulation are impressive. Most of the monsters are highly imaginative. The giant, single eye is particularly beguiling. Though anatomically preposterous, its visual appeal is tremendous. The Gargoyle vine is interesting, even more so today for its embryonic resemblance to Toho's Biollante (*Godzilla vs. Biollante*, 1989). The Lagorian is less successful. It looks a bit like Gabera, the monster from *Godzilla's Revenge*, though it's much less detailed and articulate. The creature's face, like Giant Robot's, is completely immobile, giving the more outlandish, less anthropomorphic monsters a creative edge. Giant Robot's battles with all the monsters are more restrained than those found in Tsuburaya's series, possibly due to the flimsiness of the costumes.

The direction, by Minoru Yamada and possibly others, keeps things moving at a fast clip, but also remains focused on the relationship between the likeable Jerry and Johnny. Takeo Yamahsita's music is lively, inspired perhaps by Ennio Morricone's scores for Sergio Leone's Westerns. The editing of the American edition, supervised by Salvatore Billitteri (who managed to misspell every name in the credits but his own), looks like just what it is—a bunch of thirty-minute episodes slapped together as painlessly as possible. *Voyage into Space* lacks the cohesiveness of a genuine *kaiju eiga* entry but moves well and provides viewers a glimpse at one of the loopiest series ever shown on American television.

Attack of the Monsters *(1969)*

Known today as *Gamera vs. Guiron*, *Attack of the Monsters* was Daiei's Gamera entry for 1969, the fifth film starring the giant fire-breathing, jet-propelled turtle. It's a silly kiddie film, and as such, I enjoyed it very much at the time. Unlike earlier Gamera films, which openly emulated Toho's Godzilla series, *Attack of the Monsters* is unabashedly a film for children. Unlike the best children's films, however, this picture is pretty intolerable for most anyone beyond puberty.

Like *Destroy All Planets*, the film's story centers around two young boys, one Japanese and one American. Akiro (Nobuhiko Kazima) and Tom (Christopher Murphy), along with Akiro's little sister, Tomoko (Miyuki Akiyama), spot a flying saucer land not far from Akiro and Tomoko's house. The next morning, the boys find the spaceship, which is mysteriously empty. Akiro and Tom board the craft, and when they start fooling around with the controls, they accidentally launch the saucer. They travel through space, where they meet up with Gamera. The turtle seems to be warning the kids about something, but they're not exactly sure what. The monster seems to be urging them to avoid an oncoming planet, but as the ship is on remote control, there's little the boys can do. The saucer speeds off, and Gamera cannot keep up. The spaceship crashes on the planet "Tera" near a group of futuristic buildings (unconvincing miniatures). A "space" version of the monster Gaos, last seen in 1967's *Return of the Giant Monsters*, appears out of the sky. (This was presumably the very same monster suit, painted silver.) At the same time, the planet's guardian, a four-legged monster named Guiron, appears. The creature resembles a pit bull with a head shaped like a steak knife. The two monsters square off in a jaw-droppingly graphic, if cartoon-like sequence. One of Gaos' laser beams is deflected off Guiron's blade-like face. The bouncing beam cuts off one of Gaos' legs. Next, Gaos swoops down over Guiron, who slices off one of the flying monster's wings (shades of Monty Python!). Now helpless, Gaos is decapitated by the laughing Guiron, who then slices up the dead monster like a sausage. The kids make their way into one of the buildings, where they meet two female aliens, Barbella and Flobella, who pretend to be friendly but are clearly up to no good. Akiro in particular admires the women's world, which he notes is free of "war and traffic accidents." The aliens want to leave the planet before it freezes over, and they tell Akiro and Tom they'll take them with them. What they don't say is that they want to eat the kids' brains en route! They drug Akiro and Tom, shave the former's head and are about to saw it open when Gamera suddenly arrives. Gamera fights Guiron, who severely injures the giant turtle. Gamera falls into a lake, apparently dead. Meanwhile, the kids wake up and manage to escape the aliens' clutches. The aliens try to take off in their newly repaired flying saucer, but just then Guiron begins running amok and neatly slices the ship in two. One of the alien women survives the crash but is later killed when the kids fire a missile at her. A revived Gamera (whose miraculous recovery, as always, goes unexplained) fights Guiron at the bottom of the alien sea ("Knife in the Water," perhaps?) before slaying the beast on land. Gamera welds the saucer back together with his fiery breath, and with saucer-in-mouth, takes the kids back to Earth. Akiro is happy to be back home, despite the presence of war and traffic accidents.

Attack of the Monsters is a better-than-average entry in the Gamera series. By 1969, Daiei seemed to have effectively identified the series' biggest audience and was prepared to make the series for and about children, in this case ordinary, monster-loving boys. The simplicity of the story—kids take spaceship to weird planet, watch monster battles, escape alien cannibals, return home—is appealing. The film's more ghoulish elements, such as the battle between Guiron and Gaos and the idea of brain-eating alien women, is exciting without appearing threatening. In fact, the kids never seem particularly concerned that they're whisked off into outer space and almost eaten alive. Gamera was, by now, the "friend to all children." To get the point across, footage from *Gammera the Invincible*, *War of the Monsters*, *Return of the Giant Monsters* and *Destroy All Planets* is once again recycled, though not nearly to the extent of the previous film. Unlike Toho's seventies Godzilla films and most of the other Gamera movies, *Attack of the Monsters* boasts an appealing cast of child performers. What drags the film down to the very minor status it has among children's films is its depressingly cheap production values. Although filmed in 35mm and anamorphic widescreen (Daieiscope), *Attack of the Monsters* isn't much more elaborate than the giant monster adventures produced on Japanese television at this same time. This is particularly true of the special effects, which look cheap even for a late-sixties Japanese monster movie. The rubber costumes are very basic with an unfinished look about them, and there seems to be a greater use of marionettes and expressionless puppets than in Toho's productions.

The Americanization of the film is nothing less than atrocious. It's not that the synchronization doesn't come anywhere near matching the lip movements of the actors (though that's certainly true here). Rather, it is the fact that most of the dubbing cast do not seem to be acting at all. While the voices of Paul Frees and Les Tremayne can't take the place of undubbed, subtitled performances, they were at least professional enough actors to make their voice characterizations sound dramatic and reasonably believable. In *Attack of the Monsters*, the unidentified actors are simply reading lines, which might just as well have been read by a cocktail waitress or gas station attendant as a voice specialist. Guiron is a bit more interesting than Gamera's other foes, though he's equally preposterous. His battle with Gaos early in the film lets us know he means business, though his subsequent sparring with Gamera never quite matches the audacious, Grand Guignol style of the earlier confrontation. Gamera would return the following year in *Gamera vs. Monster X*.

The Blind Beast (1969)

A blind sculptor, Michio Sofu (Eiji Funakoshi), with the help of his mother, Shino (Noriko Sengoku), kidnaps a young model, Aki Shima (Mako Midori). The woman is taken to the artist's room in a warehouse, where she is continually degraded and sexually assaulted. She eventually surrenders to the man's desires, hoping it'll give her the opportunity to escape. Instead, she becomes increasingly entranced by the sculptor's weird, violent sexual gaming, and eventually goes blind, too, because of the room's darkness. She goes mad, becoming even more depraved than her captor. They begin cutting and whipping one another, and eventually, Aki demands that her kidnapper-lover cut off her arms and legs (to create the "perfect statue"), which he does. The mother is accidentally killed by her son, and he commits suicide.

By all accounts, *The Blind Beast* is a graphic, sleazy tale of sado-masochism bordering and perhaps crossing the line into indulgent tastelessness, depending on one's taste, that is. *Variety*'s "Robe," for instance, praised the cinematography (by Setsuo Kobayshi) and Shigeo Mano's art direction, but overall found the picture revolting:

> [Director] Yasuzo Masamura is an old hand at making commercial films but they have, in the past, [been] potboilers dealing with spies, gangsters and the more normal aspects of sex. He first showed signs of a fascination with sexual aberrations with his 1964 *Manji* (*All Mixed Up*), which dealt with lesbians, and last year's *Daini no Seo* (*The Sex Check*), which uses the shifting sex of some athletes as story material. But these are kindergarten material compared with *The Blind Beast*... it's a sick film.

Phil Hardy's *Encyclopedia of Horror Movies*, on the other hand, praised the new wave filmmaker's approach:

> It exposes the foundation of scopophilia upon the very impossibility of tactile contact with an object of desire... after the scene has been set and motifs announced in the opening sequences (Midori responds as Funakoshi caresses a statue she modeled for), the narrative virtually comes to a stop as a repetitiously oneiric logic takes over... the only element that spoils this otherwise impeccable nightmarish picture is the superfluous dialogue.

The Blind Beast received a limited run (probably limited to Japanese-language theaters) in the United States in 1969, but apparently was popular enough to be reissued in 1974 (as *Warehouse*). I've not seen it.

Godzilla's Revenge *(1969)*

According to *The Japanese Fantasy Film Journal*'s Greg Shoemaker:

Godzilla's Revenge was originally titled *Minya, Son of Godzilla*, promotional copy forewarning the tone to which the film would adhere: "Every boy needs a friend, even if it's a monster." An east coast release failed to deliver the necessary dollar response, so Maron Films, the U.S. distributor, recalled the picture and set about designing a new approach. To play down the kiddie aspect the distributor retitled the film *Godzilla's Revenge*, with advertising sporting an assortment of giant beasts to attract the audience previous Toho monster films drew. Word of mouth spread, and the motion picture was withdrawn, sold to television, and released occasionally to theaters for "kiddie matinees."

Godzilla's Revenge is a children's fantasy, centering around a latch-key little boy, Ichiro (Tomonori Yazaki), who spends much of the story being kicked around by neighborhood bullies. He daydreams of traveling to Monster Island (on a Pan Am jet), where he meets Minya, Godzilla's son. Minya shrinks himself down to kiddie size and talks to his friend in a voice fiercely imitative of Walt Disney's Goofy, with a dash of Don Knotts. "Hey, c'mere, I won't hurt cha," Minya says. Minya gives Ichiro a tour of Monster Island, and the two sit mostly on the sidelines watching stock footage, mainly *Ebirah, Horror of the Deep* (the two battles between Godzilla and the sea monster, Godzilla's battle with the big bird and Red Bamboo jets) and *Son of Godzilla* (Godzilla's fight with Spiga and giant mantises, along with most of the scenes between the reptilian father and son). Whenever Papa G gets the upper hand, Minya shouts lines of approval like, "How do you like that, weirdo?!" and "Godzilla's the one with the *bad* breath!" The film's few new effects sequences center around Gabarah, a green, bipedal reptile with a face like a Boston terrier and a comical, muppet-like tuft of orange hair on the top of its head. The film is basically a morality play, with Gabarah standing in for the neighborhood bully. Gabarah picks on little Minya, who refuses to face the beast ("Golly, no! I'm chicken!" he declares) until Godzilla teaches the uncuddly critter how to "fight his own battles and not be a coward." This in turn inspires Ichiro (in other words, according to Shinichi Sekizawa's script, the way to confront a bully is by becoming an even *bigger bully*). In the real world, Ichiro is kidnapped by a pair of bumbling bank robbers (Sachio Sakai and Kazuo Suzuki) holed up in an abandoned building with 50 million in stolen yen—a subplot largely disconnected from the rest of the action. Ichiro, no longer a "coward," foils the crooks' plans by biting them and using other monstrous techniques he picked up daydreaming about Monster Island. In the end, Ichiro chases away those nasty little bullies, too.

While unabashedly a children's film, and therefore not really comparable to earlier entries which were intended for more general audiences, *Godzilla's Revenge* is nonetheless a tiresome film and a great disappointment following the much superior *Destroy All Monsters* which had succeeded so well in recapturing the flavor of the series' glory days. Most sources cite effects director Eiji Tsuburaya's ailing health during filming (he died in 1970) as the reason for the picture's heavy reliance upon stock footage. I suspect there is more to the story than that. Tsuburaya had a self-reduced role in Toho's Godzilla series by the late sixties (so that he could concentrate on his own production company's efforts). *Destroy All Monsters* was something of a box office disappointment, while at the same time, Toho incurred unplanned expenditures on *Latitude Zero*, according to star Joseph Cotten. Whatever the cause, the extensive use of stock footage, combined with generally unimpressive footage involving Gabarah, gives the film a singularly cheap look. What's more, the recycled scenes failed to fool anyone since the wildly differing design of the Godzilla costumes was obvious even to me when, as a child, I first saw the film.

The sequences not set on Monster Island, while character driven, are written and directed by hands clearly ill at ease with their material (Honda, in fact, directed most of the monster footage). Ichiro looks stiff and unconvincing. This is only emphasized in the dreadful dubbing, with Ichiro given the kind of squeaky, un-childlike voice English-dubbed productions seem forever cursed with. Not that the Japanese soundtrack is significantly better: Kunio Miyauchi's score, which includes an unbearable song sung by Ichiro ("Go! Go! Go-jir-a, etc."), is easily the worst of the series to date.

But the film does have its defenders. Donald Glut called the film "one of the finest children's monster fantasies ever made," when writing about the picture in his *Classic Movie Monsters*. "[A] thoroughly delightful fantasy for children with enough monster action to please fans of the more traditional Godzilla films. Honda's direction of the boy in the real world is sensitive with an understanding of a child's problems." Phil Hardy's *Science Fiction* disagreed: "The Honda-Tsuburaya team's last Godzilla film is a sad occasion. The genre appeared to have run out of steam at this period, awaiting another 'issue' to take over from the nuclear war/U.S. occupation concerns that had underpinned most of the fantasy scenarios of the previous 15 years' monster movies." *The Motion Picture Guide* gave the film a * rating, calling it "extremely bad, though kids may like it." Kids are inclined to enjoy bad movies? "The problem with the film," complained Greg Shoemaker, "is its simplistic view of the world... Minya waging his own battles against his attackers as Ichiro battles with the crooks, while visually creative for a Toho genre film, increases tension to enforce the violent impact. While the young viewer may revel in the spectacle, and hopefully not adapt violence as a means of solving problems, filmgoers in general will find *Revenge* hard to swallow, requiring plenty of sugar to be spoonfed the lesson it so naively teaches."

Latitude Zero *(1969)*

This loopy, everything-but-the-kitchen-sink–style adventure was the last of Toho's big international productions for many years, and one of the very last with the Honda-Ifukube-Tsuburaya team. It's a silly, ridiculous film, and I like it a lot. *Latitude Zero*, very loosely based on a popular American radio serial, has the kind of bravado and audacity rarely found in American features. It more closely resembles theatrical serials from the 1930s—Universal's Flash Gordon serials and especially Republic's *The Undersea Kingdom* (1936). But that is not all—hardly. The film borrows heavily from Jules Verne, fifties sci-fi films, pulp novels, James Bond and the "Batman" television show, among others.

East of New Guinea, at the International Date Line and the equator—latitude zero—a team of scientists are investigating the "Cromwell Current," an underwater jet stream running east to west across the Pacific. A diving bell is lowered from the *Fuji* containing research leader Dr. Ken Tashiro (Akira Takarada), French scientist Dr. Jules Masson (Masumi Okada) and Perry Lawton (Richard Jaeckel), a reporter for Trans-Globe News. The eruption of an underwater volcano separates the bell from its mother ship, hurling it across the ocean floor. The men are injured and knocked unconscious. Tashiro and Lawton awaken to find themselves aboard the Verne-esque submarine *Alpha*. The men's wounds have completely healed and are attended to by the pretty if wildly dressed Dr. Anne Barton (Linda Haynes), who explains that Masson received more serious injuries but should be up and about soon. (Haynes' revealing costumes are comparable to those worn on TV's "Star Trek" at this time.) Tashiro and Lawton meet Captain Craig McKenzie (Joseph Cotten) who explains that the *Alpha* is a vessel without a nation. The two men eye a plaque nearby stating the ship was launched on June 21, 1805. "This is a put-on, isn't it?" Lawton asks. The *Alpha* is attacked by the *Black Shark*, another submarine, commanded by the pony-tailed, dressed-in-black Kroiga (Hikaru Kuroki). Kroiga is an agent for the evil Malic (Cesar Romero), whom she is in love with. Malic, speaking to Kroiga (whom he calls "little one") from his island base on Blood Rock, orders her to attack McKenzie's ship. Using a device which projects a "ghost image" of the sub elsewhere, McKenzie manages to lose Kroiga's ship. McKenzie returns to his underwater base at latitude zero, a fantastic underwater city protected by a force field the *Black Shark* is unable to penetrate.

Tashiro and Lawton marvel at the underwater metropolis, noting the strange mixture of sexy modern costumes with nineteenth century clothes worn by some of the city's residents. "Some prefer the styles they wore when they arrived." McKenzie claims to be 204 years old and that the evil Malic is just one year younger. He refuses, however, to disclose Dr. Barton's age. "Even in Latitude Zero," he says, "we do not discuss the age of a lady." McKenzie allows Lawton to take pictures of the undersea Utopia, even permitting the reporter to help himself to a sack of diamonds, which McKenzie's people manufacture by the truckload. Lawton exclaims, "Please change my name to Alice . . . I just fell through the looking glass!" Masson recovers at the "rehabilitation center" (aided by a doctor played by Akihiko Hirata) and is reunited with his diving bell buddies. Meanwhile, Malic and his mistress Lucretia (Patricia Medina) have Kroiga kidnap Dr. Ogata (Tetsu Nakamura), a scientist living in Japan who has developed a vaccine effective against radiation poisoning. Ogata and his daughter, Tsuruko (Mari Nakayama), have made arrangements to join McKenzie. Lucretia, jealous of Kroiga's romantic interest in Malic, convinces the mad genius to have her operated on and turned into one of Malic's "creations."

In an audacious sequence, Malic places her brain into the body of a lion (a man in a rather cartoony costume) then dissects the wings of a condor and grafts them onto the mammal ("Child's play!" Malic remarks). In a *coup de grace*, he enlarges the beast three-fold via his "amplification system." Lawton, Tashiro and Masson volunteer to join McKenzie and Dr. Barton to rescue Ogata. McKenzie takes the men to the "Bath of Immunity," which will protect them from gun shots, which now bounce off their clothing. His also gives them platinum suits which are impervious to all temperatures and come equipped with combination flame-thrower, paralyzing-gas and laser-beam gloves. James Bond never had it so good. McKenzie and his men battle over-sized rats (more men in cheesy costumes) and "bat men" (ditto). They arrive at Malic's operating room just as he is about to operate on Ogata's brain. Lucretia tries to stab McKenzie with a syringe but is instead accidentally stabbed by Malic. Lucretia turns to dust. Malic escapes and commands Kroiga, now a gigantic flying lioness, to attack the *Alpha*, but the resentful creature fails to respond. Malic then tries to crash McKenzie's sub into the island's rocky cliff using a magnetic device. McKenzie flips a few switches, and his vessel becomes airborne a la *Atragon*, which draws Malic's sub into the rocks instead. Kroiga seizes the opportunity to maul Malic. There's an explosion, and Blood Rock goes up in flames. After a very brief montage depicting surface man's inhumanity to surface man, Lawton announces his return to civilization – Tashiro and Masson have elected to live forever in Latitude Zero. Lawton is picked up by an American Navy vessel observing a splash down. No one there believes his incredible story. His film is completely blank, and someone switched his sackful of diamonds with black soil. Who should appear next but Captain *Glen* McKenzie (Cotten) and some aides (Romero and Takarada). Was it all a dream? Lawton gets a wire from New York regarding the arrival of a sackful of diamonds. (The ending makes no sense, but anyone watching the entire film and complaining about its conclusion deserves what he or she gets.)

Latitude Zero, for all its sloppy production values and resolute absurdity, is a fast-paced, enjoyable adventure. Of course the film is outrageous; that's part of the fun. The film's sloppy special effects would be a major defect in most films, but are no more of a distraction here than those found in Universal's Flash Gordon serials. The effects are well below par, possibly due to the co-production's shaky American financing. In his autobiography, *Vanity Will Get You Somewhere*, Joseph Cotten claims that American producer Don Sharp sent the American cast to Japan just as his company was going bankrupt, and that Toho picked up most, if not all, of the film's production budget. This may explain, in part, the film's ridiculously cheap costumes. Both the lion and the briefly glimpsed condor are played by men in suits: Couldn't they get a real lion and condor? The lion suit looks jarringly unreal, more like something out of a cartoon or stage play than a real lion. The batmen look even worse, and the less said about the giant rats the better. If the film had centered around these nonhuman characters—as most of Toho's monster movies by this time were now doing—then it might have mattered more. As it is, they serve their function. The film's endless stream of gadgets—the flame-throwing gloves, the flying submarine—is equally ludicrous, but no more so than the dozens of movies and television shows inspired by the James Bond craze that was only now beginning to peter out. As silly as *Latitude Zero* is, it's also innocently naive, less forced and thus still preferable to more high-profile features like *Casino Royale* (1967). The film also has an appealing pro-science, vaguely anti-war side. The *Alpha* has no weapons, just defensive devices like that ghost-image projector. Everyone gets along at Latitude Zero, happily developing fantastic new inventions which it might someday unleash onto the rest of the world. Joseph Cotten was, by far, the most prestigious American actor to appear in a Japanese science fiction picture up to this point.

It was around the period of *Latitude Zero* that Cotten began appearing in lower-budgeted science fiction films. He co-starred with Vincent Price in AIP's *The Abominable Dr. Phibes* (1971) and made a brief but memorable appearance in MGM's slightly more prestigious *Soylent Green* (1973). Probably Cotten's worst role came in *Lady Frankenstein* (1971), a picture so forgettable he was apparently too embarrassed to include it in the filmography of his flimsy but entertaining autobiography.

Cotten's appearance in *Latitude Zero* is better understood when one considers that Patricia Medina, a siren of 1950s American movies, was his wife and so the project was one where the two could travel to Japan and work together. Cotten's character, a kind of friendly Captain Nemo, might have appealed to the actor as well.

Although in his mid-sixties at the time of filming, Cotten's costumes are ridiculously lost in the 1960s, with gold V-necks and chains. In one scene he wears a shirt with what looks like 45s glued to its sleeves.

Patricia Medina, who married Cotten in 1960, is even more out of place. She sits around on leopard-skin sofas mixing cocktails for Romero. This was not her first appearance in fantastic films. In films since 1938, her genre credits include *Phantom of the Rue Morgue* (1954) and *The Beast of Hollow Mountain* (1956). She was, however, more closely associated with costumed adventures like *The Magic Carpet* (1951) and *The Black Knight* (1954). She played the Wicked Queen in *Snow White and the Three Stooges* (1961). *Latitude Zero* appears to have been her last film appearance.

This was not Cesar Romero's first encounter with batmen, having made numerous appearances as the Joker on the wildly (if briefly) popular "Batman" teleseries, as well as the theatrical feature of the same name. (Romero was much more interesting than Jack Nicholson's indulgent portrayal in Warner Bros.' bloated feature.) Romero had been a popular character performer closely associated with 20th Century–Fox. He played the Cisco Kid in a series of theatrical films in the 1940s, and following *Latitude Zero* made a memorable villain in Disney's agreeable Dexter Riley series (*The Computer Wore Tennis Shoes, Now You See Him, Now You Don't* and *The Strongest Man in the World*). Romero's Malic is typical of his villainous performances from the period — delightfully hammy.

Richard Jaeckel is... well, Richard Jaeckel. His character is a bit smarmy, but overall he's more likeable than he was in *The Green Slime* (1968). (Biographical information on the actor can be found under that film's entry.)

Akira Takarada and Akihiko Hirata, among others, also appear, but in reduced roles. Although most Japanese films produced during this period were shot silent and dubbed in post-production, *Latitude Zero* was shot "live," with the English cast speaking their lines to the on-set microphones. What's odd about this is that Takarada, Hirata and the rest of the Japanese cast speak their lines as well — in English. Broken English though it be — the actors probably learned their lines phonetically — it is refreshing (and somewhat strange) to hear their actual voices and not those of Paul Frees or Marvin Miller coming from their lips.

Science Fiction saw the film's charms but felt it was undone by the "inept special effects." John R. Duvoli, reviewing the picture in *Cinefantastique* (May 1970), found *Latitude Zero* to be "fun if taken as camp science fiction." Surprisingly, he said the "special effects are well above the level of Toho product of the last decade." *Variety*'s "Mosk," reviewing the picture at the 1969 Venice Film Festival, also liked the "fine special effects" and its "mixture of monsters and sci-fi moralism that is on a comic-strip level and thus disarming and finally entertaining." Monsters and sci-fi moralism are inherently disarming? Despite its charms *Latitude Zero* failed to set the box office world afire, and Toho thus returned to more typical monster productions.

The Seventies

Gamera vs. Monster X *(1970)*

This is the best of Daiei's rather sorry line of Gamera movies. The studio appears to have spent a little more money on this entry than either the last few that had preceded it (*Destroy All Planets*, *Attack of the Monsters*), or the one that would follow (*Gamera vs. Zigra*, 1971). By now, the series' scripts had comfortably moved away from Toho's Godzilla while developing an identity all their own. *Gamera vs. Monster X* is a children's film, and by now Daiei was keenly attuned to its audience. It worked for me. I had not seen the Gamera films for some fifteen years before watching them again for this book; this film and *Attack of the Monsters* were the two I had remembered, undoubtably because they're the series' best.

Young Hiroshi and his archeologist friend, Kaizuki, visit the newly built Expo '70. Kaizuki gives Hiroshi a little lecture about the big event, which was designed to promote international industrial accomplishments under the banner of "progress and humanity." Several thousand miles away, on Wester Island, Hiroshi's American friend, Tommy Williams, watches as his father supervises the excavation of a thirty-foot-high statue, which is to be shipped to and exhibited at the Expo. A black native warns that removing the idol, which vaguely resembles those found on *East*er Island (get it?), will release Jaiga, an ancient god (Jaiga was Monster X's name in Japan). Of course, nobody listens to the native. As a trio of helicopters attempt to uproot the statue, Gamera appears, seemingly to halt the operation. Tommy and his little sister, Susan, believe Gamera may be trying to warn the archeologists about something, but their father asserts, "We can't trust a creature like that," and the idol is quickly lowered into an awaiting ship. Soon after everyone leaves, Monster X emerges from beneath the excavation site. The four-legged creature roughly resembles a horned dinosaur but with a slight *Dimetrodon*-like fin on its back. Gamera returns to the island to face the beast but is disabled by arrow-like projectiles which Monster X inexplicably shoots from its horns. Meanwhile, the crew of the *Nankai-maru* become ill, apparently due to the statue. The ship's doctor can only speculate. "I'd say it's sort of like a curse," he says. When the ship arrives in Osaka, the crew refuse to unload or go anywhere near the big statue. However, some dock workers (who, bizarrely, speak with Brooklynese accents) gladly unload the troublesome stone. "No statue's gonna scare us," one man says. Elsewhere, Monster X plows his way across the ocean, smashing several ships before arriving in Osaka, where he immediately begins thrashing the city, apparently in search of the idol. (In a moment lifted from *Godzilla*, a group of reporters covering the monster's rampage are killed in the monster's fury.) We also see Monster X dispense a deadly heat-ray, which incinerates whole city blocks and turns fleeing crowds into skeletons.

Back on Wester Island, Gamera manages to free himself from Jaiga's deadly darts and heads for Japan. When the big turtle arrives, Monster X's tail pokes Gamera in the neck, which sends him staggering toward the harbor. Gamera's face and one of his feet turn icy white, and he falls head-first into the water. Believing Gamera to be their only hope, scientists examine the lifeless turtle, hoping he might be revived. A helicopter flies overhead and takes an X-ray, which reveals a tumor-like growth in the creature's lung. At first, Gamera expert Dr. Matsui believes the prehistoric beast had developed cancer (from all that fire-breathing, perhaps?), but he is then reminded of a case in Africa involving a sick elephant. He shows Hiroshi, Tommy and the other scientists a film of an elephant with a bloated trunk, as if the mammal had inhaled a basketball. During surgery, the trunk was cut open, and it was discovered that the animal had been infected with larvae. In a truly disgusting shot (possibly faked), we see veterinarians remove spaghetti-like worms from the elephant's nasal passage. Inspired by the film, Hiroshi and Tommy sneak off to the harbor. Hiroshi's Chaplin-esque father had been building a kiddie-sized sub for the Expo (it is similar to the one seen in Daiei's *Destroy All Planets*), which the boys use to enter the giant critter's internal system a la *Fantastic Voyage* (1966). The boys reach Gamera's lungs with little difficulty, and a pocket of air allows them to leave the sub. They find a man-sized Monster X roaming about (presumably, the same costume was used). Hiroshi accidentally kills the critter when he throws his radio at it, the static proving too much of an annoyance for the beast. Scientists determine the uprooted statue had acted like a whistle, keeping Monster X underground until now. They decide to build several huge speakers to combat the monster. At the harbor, scientists believe Gamera can be revived now that the infectious baby X is dead. Hiroshi and Tommy run an electrical cable to Gamera's heart, and with a 7-million volt charge, Gamera the Invincible is as good as new. After a prolonged battle with Monster X, Gamera gets hold of the Wester Island statue and stabs Monster X with it, right between the eyes. The world (to say nothing of Expo '70) is saved.

Gamera vs. Monster X has several advantages over previous entries. For one thing, Monster X is the least ridiculous of Gamera's foes. He looks more like a dinosaur and less like a cartoon, and he has much more detailing and subtlety of design than previous efforts. Monster X walks on four legs, and, unlike most Japanese four-leggers, the actor portraying the creature admirably avoids walking on his hands and knees. The monster fights are as silly as ever, however, with X's blow gun–like horns and heat ray (he can also suck up objects and fly as well) straining what little credibility these pictures have. The film does earn points for avoiding the heavy doses of stock footage which plagued several earlier films, especially *Destroy All Planets*. Except for a few snippets seen during the opening titles over Gamera's theme song, the film seems composed entirely of new footage. (I am referring here to AIP-TV's version of the film. At the time this book went to press, *Gamera vs. Monster X*, also known as *Gamera vs. Jiger*, was not included in King Features' package released to television and home video [*Destroy All Planets* was also excluded]. When and if the Hearst-owned company ever reissues the title, I assume they'll replace AIP's credits with the same bland title design used for their other Gamera releases.) Although shamelessly inspired by 20th Century–Fox's hugely successful *Fantastic Voyage* (and possibly by an episode of "Lost in Space" as well, which featured a journey inside a giant Robot), Hiroshi and Tommy's trip through Gamera's body is a fun idea, and their antics inside the big reptile and aboard the submarine appealed to children both here and in Japan.

Psychotronic called *Gamera vs. Monster X* the "most outrageous" entry yet, though Phil Hardy's *Science Fiction* called the picture "routine... with mawkish children combining Science Fiction with rather more melodrama than usual, although the idea of introducing one monster into another one is an interesting gimmick." Daiei's last official entry, *Gamera vs. Zigra*, was released the following year.

The Vampire Doll (1970)

This was the first of three vampire films produced by Toho and directed by Michio Yamamoto. Unlike the studio's distinctly Japanese special effects films, Yamamoto's vampire stories were decidedly Western in appearance, save, of course, for their Asian casts. Toho was trying to enter the U.S. and European market for horror films. Pictures like *Kwaidan* and *Onibaba* had limited appeal outside the art house circuit, and it was hoped that more conventional horrors like those found in *The Vampire Doll* would reach a wider audience.

After ten years of relative inactivity, vampire movies had seen a major resurgence in the late 1950s, beginning with Britain's Hammer Studios' *Dracula* (1958, known as *Horror of Dracula* in the United States). That film, along with *The Curse of Frankenstein*, made the year before, did tremendous business worldwide and established Peter Cushing (who starred as Van Helsing) as the genre's newest star (Christopher Lee, who played Dracula, wouldn't reach Cushing's level of stardom for several more years). Although made on a tight budget, *Horror of Dracula* was imaginatively produced (in color) and appealed to audiences unaccustomed to the then-daring amount of sex and graphic violence. By 1970, however, the Hammer cycle was running out of steam. The studio released two more Christopher Lee Dracula films that year, *Taste the Blood of Dracula* and *Scars of Dracula*, neither of which could match their work from the late 1950s and early 1960s. At the same time, Hammer began a series of overrated "lesbian vampire" movies, flooding the market with three such films — *Countess Dracula*, *Lust for a Vampire* and *The Vampire Lovers* — in 1970 alone. Lee also appeared as Dracula that year in a sincere but muddled West German–Italian–Spanish adaptation of Bram Stoker's original story, *El Conde Dracula* (*Count Dracula*). Other vampire films released in 1970 include American International's *Count Yorga, Vampire*, *Curse of the Vampires* (a U.S.-Filipino production), *House of Dark Shadows* (based on the popular television soap opera), "The Haunted Screen" segment from Amicus' *The House That Dripped Blood*, the obscure *Incense for the Damned*, Jacinto Molina's (aka Paul Naschy) *La Noche de Walpurgis*, and two more Spanish productions, *El Vampire de la Autopista* and *Vampyros Lesbos*.

With so many vampire-themed movies released so close together, they soon all began to blend together, and originality within the genre was becoming increasingly rare. By 1975, when Toho released their third and final vampire film in this cycle, *Evil of Dracula*, Hammer had effectively killed its golden goose. The British studio by then was even beginning to imitate *Toho*'s vampire films (*The Legend of the 7 Golden Vampires*). The studio's Dracula series was at an end; in fact not one mainstream, English-language vampire movie was produced that year. As the Japanese rarely had dabbled in the distinctly Western vampire myth, there was a certain novelty to the three Yamamoto films. However, they are also imitative of Hammer's work and other Western productions, which, by this time, weren't so hot anyway.

The story: When a young man, Kazuhiko (Atsuo Nakamura), disappears while visiting his mysterious lover, Yuko (Yukiko Kobayashi, who was possessed by evil aliens in *Destroy All Monsters*), his sister, Keiko (Kayo Matsuo), and her lover (Akira Nakao) travel to the woman's mansion. They learn that the woman is a vampire, the result of a pact with the Devil made when Yuko was a little girl and nearly killed in an accident. Yuko attacks Keiko but succeeds only in killing her father, Dr. Yamaguchi (Junya Usami), who had raped Yuko's mother (which is how the vampire woman was conceived in the first place). The death of Yamaguchi breaks the curse binding Yuko to the underworld, and like all good vampires, she crumbles to dust in the picture's final moments.

According to *The Encyclopedia of Horror Movies*, "Yamamoto manages to achieve a few atmospheric scenes but his attempt at a mixture of Japanese ghost-story elements and the Judeo-Christian vampire myth doesn't really work." The picture received a limited release in New York and Los Angeles in the early seventies, but unlike Yamamoto's other blood-sucking tales (1971's *Lake of Dracula* and the aforementioned *Evil of Dracula*), *The Vampire Doll* doesn't appear to have ever been released to American television, and I have not seen it. Howard Thompson of the *New York Times* praised Yamamoto's direction. "[He] tells his grisly story with a cool taciturn detachment. Don't be fooled by what seems a conventional staging. There is plenty lurking around the bend, some of it hair-raising."

Yog: Monster from Space *(1970)*

This rather sorry monster parade was Toho's last fantastic film produced, more or less, by the same team behind *Godzilla, The H-Man, Battle in Outer Space* and *Mothra*. Director Ishiro Honda, composer Akira Ifukube, art director Takeo Kita and others would, for the most part, leave the series after *Yog*, along with onscreen regulars Akira Kubo, Yoshio Tsuchiya and Kenji Sahara. It is sad that their final film together is such a boring mess. *Yog: Monster from Space* is a childish adventure, with monsters as utterly inept in their design as Ei Ogawa's tired screenplay.

The unmanned *Helio 7* is launched into space, bound for Jupiter, where it is to study the giant planet. During its long journey, however, the craft encounters blue alien spores which enter the vessel and reprogram it on a course back toward Earth. Aboard a Pan-Am jet over the Pacific, commercial photographer Taro Kudo (Akira Kubo, with crumpled hat and five o'clock shadow) spots the craft splashing down near an atoll. No one believes Kudo's story, but he's soon approached by Ayako Hoshino (Atsuko Takahashi) who hires him to photograph the area. Her company, the Asia Promotion Agency, is considering building an exotic resort on the "island paradise." Kudo and Ayako are joined by Dr. Kyoichi Miya (Yoshio Tsuchiya), who had worked with Kudo on a scientific expedition several years before. Dr. Miya is traveling to the atoll, called Selga, looking for prehistoric monsters. Two of the company's representatives already on the island, Yokoyama (Chotaro Togin) and Sakura (Mataru Omae), go fishing, despite warnings from the local natives. Sure enough, out of the water rises a tremendous (in size, if not appearance) squid, which grabs Sakura, pulling him underwater to his death. Meanwhile, on a ship bound for Selga, Dr. Miya, Kudo, and Ayako are met by a man who claims to be a free-lance anthropologist, Makoto Obata (Kenji Sahara, sporting a beard and pencil-thin moustache). When the foursome are dropped off at the island, they are greeted by Rico (Noritake Saito), one of the natives, who tells of the squid's attack. Yokoyama, meanwhile, is nearly mad with fright following his encounter with the rubbery monster. Soon, Yokoyama goes completely mad and drives off on with the group's jeep, closely followed by Rico. Returning to their camp site, Yokoyama begins packing his bags when the great squid reappears. The creature (Gezora in Japan) destroys the camp, crushes Yokoyama with its rubbery tentacles (guided by embarrassingly obvious wires), and severely injures Rico, before it is driven off by a swarm of bats. By the time Kudo, Dr. Miya, Ayako and Obata reach the site, the squid is long gone and Rico is in a state of shock (and curiously cross-eyed as well). Miya notices a series of bruises on Rico which look "like a case of frostbite." He speculates that the monster that attacked Rico must be extremely coldblooded. Rico's girlfriend, Saki (Yukiko Kobayashi), appears and whisks the group to her Polynesian village, where the natives are none too happy at the way the Japanese visitors have stirred up trouble. Obata confesses he's not an anthropologist at all, but rather an industrial spy from a rival company wanting the island for itself. The next morning, Kudo and Dr. Miya go scuba diving to look for the monster. They find the wreckage of the *Helio 7*, and, nearby, the monster as well. Like Yokoyama, Miya and Kudo quickly become tangled in the squid's tentacles. The creature suddenly releases the men, however, when a school of porpoises swim by. The giant squid crawls back on land and destroys the natives' village. Kudo shoots out one of the creature's eyes, while the natives, now working with our heroes, ignite a stockpile of gasoline left over from World War II and burn the monster alive. The creature falls into the sea, and the blue spores we saw earlier begin to pour out of the creature's dead body. The spores next possess the body of a crab, which, like the squid, grows to gigantic proportions. Just then, Obata tries to escape aboard a lifeboat as the crab monster ("Ganime") emerges from the water. The resulting wake flips over the craft, and Obata disappears beneath the waves. In an astonishingly unimaginative bit of scripting, the crab monster follows the squid's path almost scene for scene, heading for the village before it, too, is destroyed by some leftover cans of gasoline. Obata, meanwhile, has somehow made his way back on shore near the dead crab monster and becomes the alien spore's next victim (he does not, however, become gigantic like the previous creature). A disembodied voice tells Obata the spores are "Astroquasars," an alien race intent on conquering the Earth (what else?) and that he's lucky enough to be their first victim. The aliens have also taken over and enlarged another creature, this time a spiny-shelled turtle (dubbed "Kameba" by Toho). Meanwhile, Saki and Rico get married in a traditional native ceremony (set to Akira Ifukube's native chant from *King Kong vs. Godzilla*), this despite the fact that Rico is still in a state of shock and suffering from amnesia (another horrendous bit of scripting no one bothered to fix). When Kudo takes a picture of the sorta-happy newlyweds, the camera's flash bulb snaps Rico back to normalcy. Rico recalls the bats that drove the giant squid away, while Dr. Miya, reminded of those porpoises, is inspired to use "sound pressure" against the monsters. He suggests gathering all the island's bats to rid the island of its monsters. Miya, Ayako, Kudo and the natives visit one of the island's caves but find all of the bats mysteriously burned to death. It soon becomes apparent that Obata, now under the aliens' control, has been destroying all of the bats as a precaution. The group finds one untouched cave just as Obata arrives. Kudo tries to stop Obata from killing the bats, but he's only thrown into the air by the now superstrong host. Ayako pleads with Obata to fight the aliens' mind-control, and he seems inspired by the woman's tears. The giant turtle appears, along with another giant crab, whose appearance goes completely unexplained. The crab and the turtle grapple (which doesn't make sense if they're both under the Astroquasars' control), and the monsters, guided by the unleashed bats, fall into a conveniently located volcano. Obata, willing to sacrifice himself to save the Earth, jumps into the volcano as well.

Yog: Monster from Space is a depressingly aimless picture with almost nothing to recommend it. The monsters are paraded in front of the camera with little inventiveness and even less logic. This was the first Toho monster movie produced after the death of effects director Eiji Tsuburaya, and is clearly the worse for his absence. The nondescript, forgettable monsters are crudely designed and badly manipulated. Guide wires are painfully visible, while the land-lubber squid looks ridiculous walking around the island—the operator's legs occupy two of the squid's tentacles, whose ends curl upward like elf shoes.

The effects, supervised by Tsuburaya's longtime effects cameraman, Teisho Arikawa, and assistant director, Teruyoshi Nakano (the latter heading the department after this film), begin well, opening with the imaginatively staged launch of the *Helio 7* (set against a brilliant, fiery sunrise), but once on the island, everything from the matte work to the monster suits reeks of unenthusiasm and sloppiness. The performances are equally uninspired. Kubo, Tsuchiya and Sahara had appeared in Toho's effects pictures almost constantly for the previous ten years, and their weariness is immediately apparent, though Yu Fujiki, the egg-loving reporter in *Godzilla vs. the Thing*, helps liven things up in a cameo as a promotions manager. Even Akira Ifukube's score is unremarkable, pomping and circumstancing at nothing in particular. AIP's dubbing is particularly bad, its constant evenness of tone adding to the boredom.

Greg Shoemaker liked the optical effects (if not the monsters themselves), but rightly called *Yog* an "anachronism." *Monthly Film Bulletin* called the dubbing "asinine," but glumly noted "the erratic storyline provides excuses for a high enough rate of monsters per minute to hold an average audience of schoolchildren in thrall." *Science Fiction* didn't think much of the film, either. "The genre... had become tired, increasingly repeating the same hollow patterns rather than adapting to the changing preoccupations of its audiences. This film is no exception." *Yog: Monster from Space* is a picture made by a studio out of touch with its changing audience, a picture that marked the sad end of an era, and the beginning of a depressingly unimaginative new one.

Gamera vs. Zigra *(1971)*

The Gamera series ground to a halt with the tiresome *Gamera vs. Zigra*. For some reason, this was the only film in the series not shown on American television during the 1970s. It finally reached American shores in 1987, but by then nobody really seemed to care. It's a terrible picture, with production values below even the similar teleseries that were appearing in Japan at the time.

Two marine biologists who live and work at an oceanside Sea World spot a UFO dropping into the sea. Two of their children, Kenny and Helen (Yasushi Sakagami and Arlene Zoeller?), have tagged along, and the foursome take a small outboard to where the UFO went down. The four are transported aboard the alien craft and are met by a sexy female alien (Eiko Yanami). The dense fathers wonder where they are, and when the children say they must be aboard an alien spaceship, the fathers retort, "You two kids watch too much television!" The alien tells the hapless group that she's from the Planet Zigra (pronounced Zee-gra) in the Romulus Galaxy, some four hundred light years away. She demonstrates her powers by triggering an earthquake "of magnitude 18," in Tokyo (not shown) which levels the metropolis. The alien explains that her people used to live underwater on Zigra, but "Earth science" polluted their seas (on Zigra? How?). Zigra's residents now want to live in Earth's oceans, but mankind's pollution has made this difficult. The two men are hypnotized by the alien's glowing eyes, but Kenny and Helen manage to temporarily freeze the alien and escape with their fathers to the boat. Kenny isn't able to start the boat's engine, but Gamera, the giant flying turtle and "friend of all children," appears out of the sky. The giant reptile gently picks up the boat and drops the foursome off on the beach. "He's wonderful!" says Helen. "I love Gamera!" "Ah, that's all you girls think of," complains Kenny. Back aboard the UFO, a shark-like monster, also called Zigra and covered in cobwebs, orders the alien to kill the children, but spare everyone else so that he can make them his slaves.

Meanwhile, Kenny and Helen are questioned by the army about the UFO. When an officer asks Kenny to describe the UFO's interior, he says it's "just like the ones we see on television." You can say that again, Kenny. The female alien comes ashore and hypnotizes a woman and steals her bikini. She gets a lift to Sea World by the park's dolphin trainer. The trainer has a lengthy fight with a hotel manager over some fish, a desperate attempt by the filmmakers to pad out the running time. As the military discuss then rule out using the H-bomb (ho-hum), Gamera attacks the UFO, still underwater, shooting flames at the craft (underwater?). The ship explodes and turns into a larger version of Zigra. Part shark, part bird, with a touch of Captain Nemo's *Nautilus*, Zigra spars briefly with Gamera before he shoots Gamera with the same ray used against Kenny's and Helen's fathers. Hit by the beam, the flaming frisbee helplessly falls into the ocean and the little light in its eye goes out like a burnt-out bulb. The victorious Zigra, who can also talk, announces to the world his plans to conquer the Earth. The creature also announces that he has had a change of heart, deciding not to spare mankind after all. The two marine biologists, still hypnotized, are examined. The dolphin trainer suggests that, since Zigra is an underwater creature, perhaps the men are being controlled by sonar waves. In a hilarious bit, somebody grabs a walkie-talkie and yells

"Ahhhhhhhhhh! Ahhhhhhhhh! Ahhhhhhhhh!" which brings the men out of their trance. The female alien, who had been chasing Kenny and Helen all over Sea World during this time, also gets the walkie-talkie treatment. She turns out not to be an alien at all but rather a geologist named Laura Lee, who was working at a scientific research base on the moon when her moonbuggy was attacked by the UFO (seen briefly at the beginning of the picture) and her mind taken over by Zigra. With Gamera their last hope for survival, the military and now-revived marine biologists decide to see if Gamera is really dead or just hypnotized by Zigra. The biologists hop aboard a bathosphere (improbably lowered by a helicopter) to see if Gamera will respond to the sonar waves. Kenny and Helen sneak aboard and immediately get on everyone's nerves, sticking out their tongues at video monitors aboard the craft and complaining about the noise the sonar device creates. "Daddy, what is that sooouuuund?!" Helen whines. Zigra attacks the bathosphere, cutting the line to the helicopters, and sending the craft bouncing to the ocean floor. Zigra threatens to kill all aboard unless mankind complies with his demands. The monster shark takes a little nap while the world mulls over his offer. Gamera, revived by the sonar waves, uses the opportunity to sneak off with the bathosphere. As their oxygen was running out, Zigra put the four in a state of suspended animation, and earth scientists decide to revive them with electric shocks (!). When Zigra awakens to find the underwater craft missing, the angry monster confronts Gamera on land. The tired bout ends with Gamera burning the aquatic monster to a crisp. After a final bit of moralizing about man's pollution crisis, the kiddies bid Gamera a fond farewell.

Gamera vs. Zigra is a cheap, depressing little film. Much of the picture is nothing less than a blatant product endorsement, urging kiddies in the audience to visit Sea World, with various sea mammals doing all manner of tricks and stunts for the cameras. The bratty kids quickly get on everyone's nerves, while all the adults are depicted as incompetent dolts. There is almost no logic in Fumi Takahashi's script. Zigra talks of using humans as slaves to gather food then wants to use humans *as* food. Why doesn't Zigra kill Gamera once the turtle is under its power? Where did Zigra get the sexy alien costume for Earthling Laura Lee to wear? The monster suggests other Zigras are on the way, but like nearly everything else in the picture, this is never expanded upon. Zigra's size changes throughout the film, as a result of the "water pressure of the ocean" being very different from that of his own planet, Zigra explains. The monster generally stays in the water (though these scenes were filmed on very dry sets) but comes on land long enough to stand on two legs for the big finale. The special effects are poor, with crude, undetailed miniatures, uninspired set-ups and mismatched shots (for instance, the injured Gamera's feet stick above the waterline in some shots, below in others). The terrible rock score is as bad as the dubbing.

After *Zigra*, Daiei announced production of a new Gamera adventure,

Gamera tai Leoman, which was never completed owing to the studio's bankruptcy. In 1980, the modestly revived studio released (through Shochiku) *Gamera Super Monster*, which featured stock footage of the monster superimposed over newly shot live action and animated footage. Few new effects were filmed. The Gamera pictures were geared for the most undemanding of children in Japan. For American youngsters seeing these films in the late 1960s and early 1970s, they were only mildly entertaining. Even then, most kids realized these films were cut-rate imitations of the Godzilla pictures.

Godzilla vs. the Smog Monster *(1971)*

Godzilla was back in theaters after a two-year absence, during which time Toho's special effects director, Eiji Tsuburaya, had died and director Ishiro Honda, along with many of the studio's familiar onscreen personnel, left the series. *Godzilla vs. the Smog Monster* is an unfortunate pastiche of kiddie fare, clumsy social commentary and standard monster movie shenanigans. Clearly lost in 1971, the studio desperately tried to hold onto the series' younger audience, while trying to appeal to counter-culture teenagers and older crowds who remembered the series when it was in its prime. The results are mostly disastrous, though a tiny contingent of *kaiju eiga* fans argue the picture to be more sophisticated than it actually is. Pollution was a hot topic both in Japan and in the United States in the early 1970s. Exploitation filmmakers picked up on the idea, just as their forerunners had done with radiation twenty years earlier. There were other pollution-themed films in Japan (*Gamera vs. Zigra* for one), while in the United States American International Pictures, who also distributed *Smog Monster*, made the vaguely similar *Frogs* (1972), with which this was sometimes billed. However, pollution was rarely anything more than a gimmick in these pictures, and so it was with *Godzilla vs. the Smog Monster*.

Japan is facing a pollution crisis. During the James Bond–Maurice Binder-style credits, we see sludge engulfing a Japanese shoreline and the view of Mt. Fuji blocked by billowing smokestacks. A disgruntled fisherman visits Dr. Yano (Akira Yamauchi), bringing the scientist a strange, eight-inch black tadpole. Shrimp have all but disappeared, the fisherman says, and only mutated fish and tadpoles like this are turning up. In a bit of shameless self-promotion the filmmakers show Yano's son, Ken (Hiroyuki Kawase), playing with his Godzilla toys. A friend of Dr. Yano's, Miki Fujiyama (Keiko Mari), tells Ken he must really like Godzilla. "Superman beats them all," Ken strangely replies. Ken and Dr. Yano watch a televised news report on the appearance of a giant sludge-like monster with two big red eyes, which attacks two listing ships that had collided at sea (one of which is an oil tanker). "Wow! A monster tadpole!" exclaims Ken. Dr. Yano goes scuba diving, while Ken waits on shore. Ken spots a similar though smaller monster swimming towards him. Ken reaches for a knife and slices the beast as it flies out of the water over his head. The creature's black bean soup–like body burns Ken's hand. The monster returns to the sea and swims past Dr. Yano, leaving gray burns on one side of his face. As he recovers, Dr. Yano decides to examine the tadpole the fisherman had brought him. He is surprised to find the tadpole has turned to ash, like used charcoal. He places a tiny speck into a dish of sea water and is shocked to see the tiny speck become a tiny tadpole, almost instantly (shades of Sea Monkeys!). He places two of the tiny tads in the water together, and the two organisms dissolve into a single, larger one. Dr. Yano suggests the monster, which Ken calls Hedora, grows ever larger as millions of the creatures meld together. There is no limit to how big it might grow, Yano says, "as long as man keeps dumping sludge into the sea." Hedora turns up on land and begins sucking dirty black smoke from a nearby smokestack. In doing so, the monster continues to get bigger. In another part of town, Miki and his girlfriend, Yukio (Toshio Shibaki), party at a counterculture night spot, where psychedelic images are projected onto the walls, and where Yukio sings a bad rock number called "Save the Earth" (also heard over the main credits). The teens are momentarily frightened when some stray Hedora sludge starts splashing down a stairway toward them. The sludge retreats, however, strangely leaving a tiny, very dirty kitten behind.

Elsewhere, Godzilla appears, accompanied by the bleating of horns which forever play the star's musical motif, a ludicrous piece which sounds like "wuuuahhhh wuuuahhhh WUUUUAAHHHHH!!" Played without mercy throughout the picture, it strongly suggests the Big G has had one sake too many. The creatures square off in a lethargic, even boring monster duel, which goes absolutely nowhere and ends in a stalemate. Hedora returns to Tagonoura Bay the next morning, and Miki and Yukio are nearly eaten when Hedora develops a taste for polluting automobiles. The Smog Monster flies around some more, emitting a sulfuric acid mist, which turns everyone in the creature's path to bleached skeletons. Ken suggests drying the creature out somehow, inspiring Dr. Yano to develop a massive electrical field. Miki, Yukio and other young folk hold a massive anti-pollution party at the base of Mt. Fuji. They build a huge bonfire (which I doubt helped the environment any) and sing and dance to more bad rock songs. Hedora appears, and Miki, apparently on a bad acid trip (earlier, he had hallucinated that Yukio and the other teens were fish), stupidly tells everyone to throw torches at the titanic monster. "It's afraid of fire!" Miki yells, as the match-size torches harmlessly fall at the monster's ankles. In response, Hedora merely sprays some of that toxic gas at the teens, who drop like flies. Just then, Godzilla shows up, and the two monsters engage in another tiresome battle. Hedora tries to bury the King of the Monsters in its diarrhea-like discharge and spits mud pies at the lizard (including one that hits him in the eye, as if the big lizard was trying to eat a juicy grapefruit). Hedora, attracted by a line of truck headlights, heads for the electrical field, but the warring monsters knock down the power lines that charge it. However, Godzilla sprays one of the 120-foot electrodes with his fiery breath, causing Hedora to burn to a crisp. Godzilla reaches into the monster's abdomen and pulls out what look like a pair of eggs. Godzilla burns those as well. In a sequence that could only have been added to pad out the film, the heretofore disintegrated Hedora mysteriously revives and flies away. The flustered Godzilla pulls his tail between his legs and begins breathing fire, which propels the beast through the air! Godzilla flies!? Catching up with the Smog Monster, Godzilla once again charges the electrical field and burns the beast to a crisp. His mission accomplished, Godzilla heads out to sea, presumably back to Monster Island. A grateful Ken yells, "Godzilla! Thanks a lot!"

Godzilla vs. the Smog Monster is all over the map, with childish monster shenanigans badly integrated with a sloppy anti-pollution message. While there are a few effective shots involving pollution (a broken mannequin covered in sludge, for instance), the film itself is either too preachy, too inept, or both. It also loses most of what little impact it has by repeating its better ideas (the polluted bay, the animated tadpoles) over and over again. The film features brief, "Sesame Street"–style cartoons that try to teach kids about pollution, while adjacent scenes suggest the very weighty idea that everyone on Earth is doomed to die of asphyxiation. Needless to say, these bi-polar approaches don't blend well at all. The human characters are wildly uninteresting, Hiroyuki Kawase's Ken in particular. This was the first Godzilla feature made without Toho's familiar stock company of actors, and the picture is the poorer without them. The film centers around the monsters, who don't have much to do other than flail their arms about until the big finale. Outside of an uncomfortably long neck, the Godzilla costume looks pretty much as it did in *Godzilla's Revenge*. For this outing, Godzilla was given the ability to fly, an embarrassingly awful idea thankfully dropped in future films (though the studio would continue experimenting with the character in the next few entries). The Hedora costume — part sludge, part dirty mop — is undistinguished, though at least it lacks the zany anything-goes quality of monster designs yet to follow. As with Godzilla, it was a big mistake to give Hedora the ability to fly. In flight the creature transforms into what looks like a dirty frisbee with eyes, emitting a jet-like exhaust from its belly. The music, by Riichiro Manabe, is very poor. Besides the obnoxious Godzilla theme and the bad rock numbers, the score features wildly inappropriate instruments like a jew's harp (boinnng boinnng boinnng), heard as Godzilla makes his big entrance.

Not surprisingly, the picture received generally poor notices. Anitra Earle, writing for the *San Francisco Chronicle*, said, "Twenty minutes could be edited out with no loss to anyone, and we are treated to the same shots of the polluted bay over and over again." *The Monster Times*' Jason Thomas and Joe Kane argued, "The theme song will drive you right up the wall." Phil Hardy's *Science Fiction* noted that "the star has changed beyond recognition: from the death-ray–spewing horror of 1954 to the clownish figure prancing about... for the benefit of undemanding children ...The acting... is very affected, and together with an execrable soundtrack, this makes the picture painful to watch at times." In recent years, some *kaiju eiga* fans have argued that at least this production attempts to address what was (and still is) a genuinely serious problem. (They forget, however, that pollution plays a role, albeit a smaller one, in the other seventies entries as well.) Also, they say, Godzilla is a real character in this one, not the mindless beast of old nor the buffoonish creature of later entries. This, they argue, gives *Godzilla vs. the Smog Monster* a slight edge over the other seventies productions. Still, the series was inarguably in rapid decline and would get even worse before it finally got better.

Lake of Dracula *(1971)*

The second of three vampire movies produced at Toho and directed by Michio Yamamoto, *Lake of Dracula* is perhaps the most Western in appearance. The story is, for the most part, routine, though the present-day Asian setting and a slight attempt at characterization add a touch of interest. It's certainly better than Hammer's vampire films from this period, which Toho's short-lived series were closely modeled after.

A little girl named Akiko is walking along the beach with her dog, Leo, when the leash snaps and the little pooch runs off. Akiko follows the dog to a distinctly European mansion, where a bearded, elderly (but clearly Japanese) old man stares menacingly at her. She follows the dog inside, where she sees a woman with long black hair sitting at a piano, her back to the camera. Akiko is shocked to find the woman pale and dead and is startled by a gaunt vampire (Mori Kishida) snarling at her from a stairway. Like the woman, he is pale, almost purplish, and has bright yellow eyes. His mouth is dripping with fresh blood. After the opening titles, we see Akiko (Midori Fujita) 18 years later and now living near a lake with a larger though different dog, also named Leo. She has been haunted by the incident at the mansion ever since childhood, though by now she has come to believe it was a dream. She works through her nightmares by painting a surrealistic work of a big yellow eye. Akiko visits Kusaku, a portly, middle-aged operator of a local boathouse. Kusaku receives a delivery from a strange-looking truck driver. After Akiko leaves, Kusaku opens the crate and is surprised to find a white coffin inside. He angrily calls the shipping agent, and when he returns, the coffin is empty. Just as he breathes a sigh of relief, he is attacked by the same vampire Akiko saw years earlier. Akiko is visited by her doctor boyfriend, Takashi Saki (Osahide Takahashi), whom her sister, Natsuko (Sanae Emi), is also in love with. Saki is suddenly called to the hospital when a pale, comatose woman is found in the middle of the road. She shows signs of massive bleeding, and, sure enough, there are bite marks on her neck. When Natsuko and Leo disappear, Akiko searches the area around her home and finds the dog's body in a brushy field. She finds Kusaku nearby, now looking ashen and zombie-like (and wearing a scarf around his neck). When Akiko inquires about her dog's death, he attacks her. Akiko hits her head against a tree and is knocked out cold. Kusaku takes her to the boathouse, placing her on a table. When she awakens, she sees the vampire, ready to bite her neck. Just then, two fishermen (looking for a boat) appear. The vampire and his zombie-aide retreat.

Later that evening, Saki's patient is beckoned from her hospital bed by the vampire. She's spotted strolling down the corridor, which sends Saki running after her. However, the woman falls off a stairwell to her death. A pasty-faced and obviously bitten Natsuko returns to Akiko's home, along with the vampire himself. Natsuko harbored bitter feelings toward Akiko for many years and says that Mom always liked Akiko best. "You'll be just like me from now on," she declares. Akiko hides in a closet, while Saki is attacked in his car by Kusaku, who was hiding in the back seat. The car veers all over the road before crashing, and when Kusaku tries to attack Saki with a wrench, he suddenly expires, apparently killed by a bolt of lightning, though this isn't clear. Saki returns to the lakeside house, and the vampire is once again driven off. Natsuko is found on the beach and dies before Akiko and Saki can get her to the hospital. With her final breath she begs Akiko to burn her body. At the hospital, Saki orders an autopsy. Later, as a nurse prepares Natsuko's body in the morgue, the dead woman revives in vampire form and attacks the nurse. Saki, meanwhile, hypnotizes Akiko to remember her incident as a child, which turns out not to be a dream at all. She recalls that when Natsuko was born, the younger sibling began receiving all of the attention. From her encounter with the vampire, Akiko soon learned that being frightened won her parents' attention and affection, which Natsuko grew to resent. She also remembers that it was the bearded old man that whisked her to safety that fateful day. Saki decides they must find the mansion. And indeed they do, along with the body of the truck driver who delivered the coffin in the first place. Akiko and Saki enter the dusty mansion, where they find the old man sitting at a desk, his back to the camera. When Saki touches his shoulder, the old man's fingers, stuck to the desk for no obvious reason, break off at the joint. The old man falls to the floor, apparently dead. Akiko and Saki do find the man's diary, however. The old man's family fled Europe for Japan because they were descendents of a race of vampires (Dracula himself in the Japanese version). The old man was never afflicted, but his son eventually became a vampire, and when the old man saw his son kill his son's lover and drink her blood (the dead woman Akiko saw as a child) he knew the family tree was in trouble. He tried to keep his son away from society, but the vampire eventually broke free from his father's rule and even began drinking his father's blood. Just then, the vampire and Natsuko attack the couple. The vampire corners Saki on a second-story balcony, but the old man, momentarily (and unbelievably) revived, grabs his son's pant leg, which causes the bloodsucker to slip off the balcony and onto a tall steel spike, which presumably goes straight through his heart. Natsuko collapses, falling into a natural death, while the vampire crumbles into dust.

For some perverse reason, the big, grisly payoff of *Lake of Dracula* — where we get to see the vampire literally fall apart before our very eyes — is completely eliminated on current television prints. The vampire falls onto the spike, then the next time we see him he is already a dusty skeleton. The scene is, of course, inspired by similar moments which pop up in nearly every Hammer Dracula film, though never really done better than the first time, in *Horror of Dracula* or *Dracula* (1958). Horrific Hammer sequences are usually shown uncut these days for commercial broadcast, so why UPA, the film's American television distributor, would maddeningly decide to cut this is anyone's guess. As for the film itself, *Lake of Dracula* is mildly interesting, but also clumsy and not really very original. In the scene where Akiko hides in a closet, she slowly steps out to find the vampire waiting for her. She looks in the mirror and sees that he casts no reflection, which terrifies her. Apparently the idea was that she climbed out of the closet only because *she was able to look across the room* and assume, based on nothing being reflected in the mirror, that she was safe. This is so badly handled, however, we only realize the director's intention with hindsight, and similar moments (such as Kusaku's death) are also botched. The business with Akiko's painting of the big, yellow eye in the sky (a tribute to Kobayashi's *Kwaidan* perhaps?) is interesting, but never developed. The same is true of the old man's desire to save his family, cursed with vampirism in its blood.

While Hammer was investing in lesbianism and other more sexually explicit themes in its vampire stories, *Lake of Dracula* seems totally unconcerned with sex and sexual relationships. Akiko's boyfriend does nothing more than further the story along, while Akiko's interesting relationship with her sister is rooted in old-fashioned sibling rivalry. This intriguing idea doesn't go as far as it might have, but it is there. The picture is very Western in appearance, from Akiko's very American vacation cottage to the vampire's demise. Mori Kishida has little to do as bloodsucking monster, but he is menacing and distinctive. In the television version, his few lines were unwisely dubbed with a ludicrously bogus European accent.

Phil Hardy's *The Encyclopedia of Horror Movies* liked the picture. "Good timing and compositions combined with Kishida's fairly restrained acting, for most of the picture, help to make this an interesting movie." The *Los Angeles*

Times' Fredric Milstein called the picture "superficial, unsubtle, humorless yet stylishly horrific, appealingly gruesome and exciting. Rokuro Nishigaki's camera provides lots of atmosphere—loving, as it does, shimmering lakescapes, Martian-like skies and all the things tangled branches can hide." *Lake of Dracula* is an acceptable, if unexceptional film. The story is generally routine, but the Eastern locale and attempt (slight as it is) to add a little dimension to its main characters make this somewhat above average for the genre.

Godzilla on Monster Island *(1972)*

Much like the Big Lizard himself, Toho's Godzilla series lumbered forward, despite increasingly juvenile storylines and decreasing budgets. *Godzilla on Monster Island* (known today as *Godzilla vs. Gigan*) is a particularly depressing entry, in some ways the worst film of the series. The picture relies very heavily on stock special effects footage, while its newly shot effects are embarrassingly bad.

An unemployed cartoonist, Gengo (Hiroshi Ishikawa), is having trouble finding a buyer for his latest characters, "Shukra—Monster of Homework," and "Mamagan—the Monster of Strict Mothers." At the urging of his girlfriend, Tomoko (Yuriko Hishimi), a karate expert, Gengo visits World Children's Land, an amusement park presently under construction, whose attractions include a 150-foot Godzilla Tower, a full-size replica of the famous monster, which is to house a monster museum. Gengo meets Kabota (Toshiaki Nishizawa), secretary of World Children's Land. Kabota surprises Gengo by immediately offering him a job as an idea man. Kabota says he wants the park to give kids "everything they want, including peace." "I mean real peace," he continues. "That's the only way to save the world." Entering the corporate headquarters the following afternoon, Gengo runs smack into a young woman rushing out of the building. She drops a reel of audio tape and flees, hotly pursued by Kabota and some guards. Kabota angrily demands Gengo tell him in which direction the woman has fled. Gengo sends him off in the wrong direction. The cartoonist meets the chairman of the company, Fumio, a 17-year-old mathematical genius. Like the secretary, Fumio goes on about the park's mission of peace. That evening, the cartoonist is confronted by the mystery woman and a portly Japanese hippie, who demand the tape back. Mistaking an ear of corn the hippie is carrying for a pistol, Gengo faints dead away. The cartoonist is taken back to the woman's home, where she introduces herself as Machiko Shima (Tomoko Umeda). Her brother, Takashi, a computer technician, was working at Children's World and has disappeared. When she went to make inquiries, she explains, she was told to mind her own business. She stole the tape trying to get some answers. Gengo explains that he hid the tape in a locker, and the three go off to retrieve the reel.

Back at Godzilla Tower, Machiko's technician brother (Kunio Murai), is locked in a storage room, while an alarm in the tower's control room alerts Kabota and Fumio that the tape is being played. Gengo, Machiko and the hippie, Shosaku (Minoru Takashima), listen to the tape, which appears to be nothing more than a series of high-pitched electronic signals. On Monster Island, Godzilla and Angilas hear the transmission, and in the first of many truly embarrassing moments, Godzilla and Angilas actually talk (cartoon balloons in the Japanese version). "Hey, Angilas!" Godzilla grumbles. "Whattya want?" Angilas asks indignantly. "Somethin' funny's going on. You better check." Angilas swims off. "Hurry up!" demands Godzilla. Meanwhile, Gengo begins snooping around the tower and finds Takashi's lighter. Later, he and Shosaku look up Fumio and Kabota's address, tracing the mysterious pair to a small village. When they make inquiries, they are told Fumio has been dead more than a year, the victim of a mountain climbing accident. Angilas turns up in Sagami Bay, where the military fire upon the spiky-backed monster. The creature turns around and swims back to Monster Island. Gengo snoops around the tower some more and finds Takashi locked up in the storage room. Before he can unlock the door, Kabota shows up and orders the cartoonist to leave but gives him a pack of cigarettes to show there are no hard feelings. "He's stupid, but at the same time cunning," Fumio notes. "A very curious specimen indeed." The cartoonist smokes his way back to Machiko's, closely followed by Kabota's men. The cigarettes, we learn, contain mini-transmitters (this obvious device is especially forced). Kabota demands the tape back, but Gengo's girlfriend shows up in the nick of time to karate-kick the villains into a fast retreat. Kabota returns to Godzilla Tower, just as Fumio launches "Plan 6." Pressing a few buttons, King Ghidorah appears, accompanied by a new monster, Gigan, a ridiculous mishmash—part-robot and part-parrot—with a buzz saw in its stomach. Both monsters head for Japan.

Meanwhile, Godzilla and Angilas have "broken out" of Monster Island, and head toward the island nation. "Hey Angilas, c'mon!" says Godzilla. "There's a lot of trouble ahead." Gengo and his friends sneak back to Children's World. The cartoonist and Tomoko climb the stairs leading to the fake Godzilla's head, where Takashi is being held. Captured by Kabota's men, the secretary explains they are to be used as "uniforms"—in other words, as receptacles or hosts. Fumio and Kabota explain they are the vanguard of an alien invasion from Nebula Spacehunter M, a polluted, dying planet not unlike Earth. Using the tapes to control Gigan and Ghidorah, they plan to lure Godzilla to Children's Land, destroy the King of the Monsters, and take over. "We are a species that can survive under the worst possible conditions," Kabota explains. The lights dim, and we see Kabota and Fumio cast shadows that resemble six-foot cockroaches (a good idea badly done). The guards escort the trio back to the storage room. Godzilla and Angilas finally show up and square off against the tepid space monsters. At the tower's base, Shosaku and Machiko inflate a balloon tied to a long cable, which then rises to the storage room's window. Gengo latches the cable to something, and the trio slide down to safety. They get several boxes of TNT from the military, then return once again to the tower where they place the explosives inside an elevator. The car is then sent to the tower where the guards are greeted by a full-scale cartoon of Gengo, Takashi and company, placed over the boxes of TNT. The guards shoot at the boxes, and the Godzilla Tower is blown to smithereens, along with Fumio, Kabota (both briefly return to their natural, cockroach state) and the tapes controlling the space monsters. Lacking direction from the aliens, Ghidorah and Gigan are no match for Godzilla and Angilas, who drive the monsters away. Machiko sees a tiny cockroach scurry under her shoes, and Takashi suggests, "Perhaps one day the cockroaches *are* going to inherit the Earth." Godzilla and Angilas swim back toward Monster Island, and our heroes wish the creatures a pleasant journey.

Godzilla on Monster Island is a pathetic film, badly written and shamelessly drawing upon stock footage from much better entries. In fact, nearly half of the film's special effects shots were culled from other productions. Most of the Monster Island footage is from *Destroy All Monsters* (1968), while most of the military footage was culled from *War of the Gargantuas* (1966). The brief sequence supposedly set on the polluted, Earth-like "Nebula Spacehunter M" is nothing more than stock from *Godzilla vs. the Smog Monster*. Based on the footage, we can see that the planet's citizens drive Japanese automobiles and drink Coca-Cola. Particularly noticeable is the bevy of recycled Ghidorah footage, lifted mainly from *Ghidrah: The Three-Headed Monster* (1964) and *Monster Zero* (1965). A depressingly immobile Ghidorah was built for a tiny amount of new footage, and the difference between the Ghidorah of old and its nearly immobile, statue-like counterpart is glaringly obvious. Especially painful are several new shots of the dragon in flight. The model's wings don't flap at all, and its three heads are as rigid as No. 2 pencils. Gigan, with its useless arms, single, red visor eye and buzz saw belly, is representative of the creative dead end the studio had reached in its monster creations. (However, Godzilla would again face Gigan in 1973's *Godzilla vs. Megalon*, and on Japanese television that same year.) On land, Godzilla looks no worse than he did in *Smog Monster*, but a second, poorly designed costume was used for the monster's scenes in the water. Just like the "wet" ape suit used in *King Kong Escapes* (1967), the second Godzilla costume has a much larger head with oversized eyes crossed in a manner suggesting silent clown Ben Turpin. Godzilla and Angilas' dialogue was another sheepish attempt by Toho to take the series in a new direction, following the former's airborne antics in *Godzilla vs. the Smog Monster*. The dialog was heavily distorted and rendered almost incomprehensible in the American version, which was perhaps just as well. Thankfully, Godzilla kept his big mouth shut after this. The miniatures are badly lit and lacking in detail. Children's World is especially poor, looking nothing like an amusement park (the miniatures here don't even look like buildings, for crying out loud). Their poor design is combined with a lack of low-angle camera placement (everything seems to have been shot shoulder-height, severely lessening the sense of scale).

Shinichi Sekizawa's screenplay (co-written by director Jun Fukuda) is a mess. Why do the the aliens hire Gengo at all? There's no reason for them to do so, other than to allow him to stroll around their secret base and uncover their invasion plot. Angilas' first appearance and the amusement park setting add nothing to the story, while the script's yo-yo structure has its human characters endlessly going back and forth to the Godzilla Tower. Ishikawa's Gengo smiles and looks embarrassed through most of the picture (he slips on a globe just like Peter Sellers' Inspector Clouseau) but makes little impression and is typical of the uninteresting characters that populate the seventies Godzilla films.

Science Fiction's reviewer actually liked *Godzilla on Monster Island*. "After some decidedly pallid Godzilla films, the monster's twelfth appearance is more worthy of his reputation." *Psychotronic* disagreed, calling it "probably the worst Godzilla movie." Though *Monthly Film Bulletin* found Gigan "an admirable addition to the roster of monsters," it pointedly complained "What the Toho films have lacked, of course, is any solid, credible human focus amid all the special effects pyrotechnics, and *War of the Monsters* [the film's U.K. title] remains true to type by centering on a gaggle of 'youth identification figures' (including a token hippie)." *Godzilla on Monster Island* didn't reach American shores until 1977 and even then was limited to children's matinees and quickly vanished. Unfortunately, the next film in the series would receive a lot more attention.

Godzilla vs. Megalon *(1973)*

Toho's Godzilla series hit rock bottom with this travesty, a terrible film generally even worse than *Godzilla on Monster Island*, which is saying quite a bit. Like *Monster Island*, *Godzilla vs. Megalon* is rife with stock footage and looks even cheaper than the film that preceded it. By now Godzilla has become little more than a reptilian exterminator, ready to take on all monstrous comers. And like *Godzilla vs. the Smog Monster*, the picture is cursed with the presence of an annoying little boy, dubbed by a performer whose voice is anything but childlike, suggesting instead a mildly retarded adult sped-up to 78 rpms. The result will send even the most tolerant *kaiju eiga* fans climbing the walls.

Atomic testing near the Aleutians rattles the Atlantian-like, subterranean kingdom of Seatopia (not the Mu Empire from *Atragon*, as reported in some sources). The angry Seatopian leader (Robert Dunham) dispatches Megalon, a giant cockroach with drill-like arms, to destroy the surface world. The chunky leader also sends a pair of spies to the home of Goro (Katsuhiko Sasaki), an inventor who lives at a post-modern laboratory-home with his kid brother, Rakusan (Hiroyuki Kawase, also in *Smog Monster*). Goro's latest invention is a six-foot robot, Jet Jaguar, a silly-looking cyborg in the Ultraman mold, with colorful rings wrapped around its arms and legs. The spies, who want to use Jet Jaguar for their own nefarious purposes, are at first unsuccessful when they burgle the house, but later take control of the building when they hit Goro and the kid (along with a friend of theirs, played by Yutaka Hayashi) with knock-out gas. Rakusan and Goro wake up to find themselves tied up inside a big crate placed aboard a pickup truck. The truck is driven to the side of the dam, where the drivers prepare to dump their load. Just then, Megalon appears, smashes the dam, and bats the crate hundreds of feet into the air. The wooden box lands in a field, leaving Goro and Rakusan dazed but otherwise alright. (Needless to say, this bit is pure fantasy; both would have died instantly.) Back at Goro's lab, one of the spies controls Jet Jaguar's movements from an instrument panel. He sends the robot (who can fly) to Megalon to guide the big bug to Tokyo, where he destroys much of the city (stock footage from earlier films) and battles the military (ditto). Goro, who carries a mini-transmitter around his neck, soon regains control of Jet Jaguar and orders him to go to Monster Island to enlist Godzilla's help against Megalon. Sensing trouble, the Seatopians place a call to the "Starhunter Universe M." "Tell them we need Gigan's help immediately," the Seatopian leader tells an assistant, "and notify our people on Easter Island!" Jet Jaguar converses with Godzilla, who immediately agrees to help (he does not, however, talk as he did in *Monster Island*). The flying robot returns to the mainland (Godzilla has to wade through the ocean, you see) and suddenly grows to gigantic proportions to face Megalon. "He just programmed himself in some way to increase his own size," Goro explains, none too convincingly. Soon Gigan, the robot bird with the buzzsaw belly, appears, and it looks like curtains for Jet Jaguar. Fortunately, Godzilla shows up as well, and the Big Battle begins. Gigan grazes Godzilla's shoulder, which begins spurting blood just as in Daiei's Gamera films, and both our reptilian hero and the colorful robot are trapped in a ring of fire. They come out swinging, however, and soon Gigan and Megalon retreat, the bird zooming off, back to Starhunter M while Megalon heads underground, presumably back to Seatopia. Jet Jaguar shakes Godzilla's hand, congratulating him on a job well done, then shrinks back to his normal size. Goro speculates whether the robot would ever return to his super-size state. "I reckon he'd do it again, if the need ever rose again," he says. The picture concludes with a silly but likeable song, sung entirely in Japanese, before the film abruptly comes to a thankful end.

With *Godzilla vs. Megalon*, Toho's once grandly entertaining series reached its lowest ebb. The picture is spectacularly unimaginative, even when it comes to incorporating the stock footage into the picture. For instance, one scene finds Megalon ducking behind some trees as a Maser cannon shoots its beam at the creature. This is footage from *War of the Gargantuas*, used here because it's nearly impossible to tell it's a gargantua and not Megalon behind the row of miniature pines. However, this same sequence was already lifted in *Monster Island*, when effects director Teruyoshi Nakano pulled a fast one using Gigan standing in for the gargantua. The only new effects sequences are the blandly directed wrestling match at the end and the okay scene where Megalon destroys the dam. Nearly every other effects shot outside the big bout is from an earlier Toho picture, most of which had already been recycled before. The film's other production credits are equally cheesy. The dreadful music even revives the terrible Godzilla theme from *Smog Monster*. Like *Monster Island*, none of Toho's familiar stable of performers appears in the film. Robert Dunham, who appeared in *Dagora, the Space Monster* (1964) and *The Green Slime* (1968), has a small part as the Seatopian leader, though he looks wildly out of place with his distinctly seventies sideburns (which are pasted on) and mustache. Goro, Rakusan and their friend are singularly uninteresting, and their actions are consistently foolish and juvenile. When the Seatopian spies invade their flat, Goro and Rakusan "borrow" a model jet from a hobby shop for the sole purpose of crashing it into a spy's head. Similar high jinks, including a car chase more appropriate to *It's a Mad, Mad, Mad, Mad World* than a Godzilla movie, are wildly incongruous to the monster scenes and help carry the rest of an already sorry picture further down. Megalon is badly designed, especially the misplaced, star-shaped protrusion on its forehead (*Variety*'s reviewer describes it as a "death-dealing electric daisy") that shoots laser beams. Megalon spends a lot of time jumping from place to place as if practicing for a standing long jump competition, lifted about by very visible wires. Jet Jaguar looks even worse, a dime store Ultraman. The character was played by a man wearing a tight-fitting costume, and because of its anthropomorphic design and the character's change in size, it only serves to emphasize the fakery interacting with the other monsters. Godzilla is plain embarrassing, ready to save the world and looking like a puppy ready to bring in the morning paper. The suit has been redesigned and appallingly simplified. American Robert Short's Godzilla costume, built around the same time and seen in *Hollywood Boulevard* (1976), on "Saturday Night (Live)" and on NBC's campy television premiere of *Megalon* in 1977, is an artistic triumph by comparison.

Shockingly, *Godzilla vs. Megalon* actually received good reviews from several esteemed critics, who clearly hadn't the slightest idea what Japanese fantastic cinema was all about. Many of the same critics who blasted Toho's effects work in the past praised the very same effects shots that are awkwardly inserted here. For instance, Vincent Canby of the *New York Times* actually gave the film the good review that was quoted in the picture's advertising. "[It] would amuse Woody Allen... It's wildly preposterous and funny (often intentionally)

...which is why he's so appealing." Cinema Shares' wildly misleading advertising placed Godzilla and Megalon atop the the World Trade Center, an obvious and apparently effective attempt to cash in on the not-yet-released *King Kong* remake. Perhaps most depressing was the line, "All New! Never Before Seen!" Well, if you haven't seen *War of the Gargantuas, Destroy All Monsters*... Ads also wrongly stated this was the first time Godzilla might be enjoyed "In Widescreen and Color." They couldn't even get Jet Jaguar's name right, billing him as "Robotman." "For the kiddie market," said *Variety*'s "Jac," "*Godzilla vs. Megalon* is a good little tale of conflict... Action is well-paced with lots of fireworks, lightning bolts, shifting land masses and Perils of Pauline escapes by humans and monsters. The miniature and technical effects are superb, reflecting a creative understanding of the camera." Phil Hardy's *Science Fiction*, which, like the *Variety* review, misidentified Gigan as Borodan (the name derived from Cinema Shares' slapdash promotional comic book), concurred: "The effects are expertly done, and it looked as if the series was beginning to revive under the guidance of [director Jun] Fukuda." *The Motion Picture Guide*, while giving the film a *½ rating, called it "Good fun from the 'So Bad It's Good' school."

Saner heads thought differently. *Psychotronic* called the film "laughable," while Greg Shoemaker complained,

> Special effects director Teruyoshi Nakano... is at his best when required to deliver cartoon animated rays and force fields and spectacular pyrotechnics. With few exceptions, he's at his worst when asked to produce miniatures, latex creatures and visual effects photography. This area of weakness, unfortunately, is the heart of the product.
>
> [The human stars] appear lacking in the depth of their acting ability, amateurish, if you will. But the blame may be shared with the scripts for seldom is the viewer allowed to explore the characters on the screen, since the players deliver little except to expound plot action and court disaster.

Gregory V. Feret's review in *Cinefantastique* noted "Those who never forgave Toho for their treatment of King Kong in past films might now find themselves perversely vindicated in this... in which they similarly abuse their own character, Godzilla. Beyond that, the film deals a low blow to confessed Japanese genre fans like myself."

Tidal Wave *(1973/1975)*

Nippon chiubotsu (*Submersion of Japan*) was Toho's biggest and most popular special effects extravaganza of the decade. The epic production cost $3 million, a figure almost unheard of for a Japanese feature; it ran nearly 2½ hours. It dramatized one of the most innate fears among Japanese citizens: the disastrous annihilation, natural or otherwise, of their vulnerable nation. The film was a huge hit in Japan, as much for its commentary on that country's (and the world's) psyche as its lavish special effects. In 1975, Roger Corman's New World Pictures picked up the film for release in the United States. To them, *Submersion of Japan* was just another disaster film. They ruthlessly deleted an entire hour from the original, added a few new scenes with Lorne Greene (he had had a plum supporting role the year before in *Earthquake*) and did the usual poor dubbing job. This heavily compromised version, while keeping the essence of *Submersion*'s story, denied Americans the opportunity to see the longer, much more intelligent and moving original version. Most Americans, that is. Bill Warren saw the subtitled 140-minute cut prior to viewing *Tidal Wave*. New World apparently gave *Submersion* an extremely limited release of its own but quickly pulled it from theaters (possibly due to a conflict with Toho International over its release, or with the Motion Picture Association of America because of the film's rating). In his review of both films in *Cinefantastique* (vol. 4, no. 4), Warren called the bastardized edition "nothing less than [a] desecration."

Tidal Wave opens as scientist Tadokoro Tanaka (Kenji Kobayashi) and bathysphere pilot Onoda (Hiroshi Fujioka) travel to the ocean floor, examining an island that, without warning, suddenly and mysteriously sank beneath the sea. They find the undersea current going in the wrong direction and a strange, continual shift of mud and rock. Later, Onoda and his girlfriend, Reiko (Ayumi Ishida), curl up for a romantic evening. They begin to make love on the beach but are interrupted when a nearby volcano blows its top. Dr. Tanaka meets with ancient Prince Watari (Shogo Shimada), who notes that swallows under his house have abandoned their nest, even though it's the middle of summer. Tanaka says that swallows from all over the country have been leaving Japan. Tanaka, suddenly looking haggard, tells a group of scientists he believes the Earth's core has expanded, causing great continental shifts. These shifts, he predicts, will result in the submersion of Japan within just two years. A tremendous earthquake rocks Tokyo. Most of the city is engulfed in flames, and several million people die. (For Japanese audiences, this sequence undoubtedly recalled the devastating Tokyo and Yokohama earthquake of 1923, which left nearly one hundred thousand people dead.) The prime minister (Tetsuro Tamba) is torn between trying to save what's left of the city and mobilizing his forces to leave everything behind. Convinced Tanaka's theories are accurate, Japan prepares for the biggest exodus in world history. Japan's ambassador to Australia (Nubuo Nakamura) visits that country's prime minister (Andrew Hughes, dubbed with a thick "G'day" accent). He tries to negotiate the emigration of 5 million Japanese to Australia, but the prime minister of Australia rejects the mass relocation. He seems more concerned with salvaging Japan's art treasures. The Japanese ambassador to the United States (John Fujioka) visits his American counterpart, Warren Richards (Lorne Greene), with the same request. Richards is cautious but slightly more open to the proposal. (Fujioka is in the American edition only; the familiar character actor appeared in AIP's *Futureworld* at about this same time.) New estimates show Japan's submersion occurring much more rapidly than first thought. Now, scientists predict Japan will not exist in ten months. On the last day of regularly scheduled flights out of the country, Onoda and Reiko make preparations to fly to Geneva, even though this means leaving many friends and relatives behind. Panic brought on by the eruption of long-dormant Mt. Fuji causes Reiko to miss her train to the airport. Onoda stays behind as well. At the United Nations, it's reported that 8.4 million citizens have been relocated to 21 countries but that 101.6 million remain. Richards makes a plea to the assembly, likening Japan's fate to that of a sinking ship whose passengers await rescue. Osaka disappears under the sea. Soon, 26 million more are saved, but many more die as Japan sinks into oblivion. Prince Watari and Dr. Tanaka decide it's better to die in one's own bed, so to speak, and remain behind. The prime minister is among the last to leave. Reiko and Onoda, though still separated, make it to safety (in Siberia?). A train whisks the Japanese survivors to unfamiliar destinations as they try to rebuild their lives.

From the editing of the American edition it isn't clear what's happening at the end of the picture. We see a train carrying the Japanese refugees and Reiko looking out a window. We see Onoda as well, but it isn't clear if he's in the same car or even aboard the same train. They don't seem to be together, but maybe they are. It certainly makes sense that in the mad mass exodus people would be separated from their loved ones, but the editing here is frustrating. This is just one of the truncated edition's many problems. Once it's discovered that Japan is indeed sinking, the American film's thrust becomes depressingly one-note: getting the hell off. A big part of the original film was the horrible identity struggle its characters faced. Japan's entire history was going up in flames (or rather, going down in water), while its culture was, at best, being scattered to the winds. Because the human story was cut by nearly one-half, characters go through jarring changes with little or no explanation. Dr. Tanaka becomes a distraught zombie. The scenes with Onoda and Reiko are cut to the point that they become clichéd ciphers, not really characters at all. Their dialogue in the American edition ("Show me your ocean," Reiko tells Onoda, "I want to feel it!") becomes hysterically awful.

And then there's the issue of those countries willing or not willing to absorb the influx of millions of refugees. In *Submersion of Japan*, the United States takes in its share of Japanese survivors, even without Lorne Greene's help, but there is much more international conflict. Certainly the sudden introduction of several million souls, mostly poor, into *any* country is bound to have an adverse effect on its economy (as was recently proven in Germany) and, as expected, no country wants to take in any more people than is absolutely necessary. Although this is a major part of the original story, it's barely touched upon here.

Greene's role in the American version is curious. His first onscreen appearance doesn't come until about the halfway point, where he actually seems to be giving Ambassador Narita the brush off in their first meeting; he's cautious at best. Later, Richards predictably makes an impassioned speech about mobilizing the evacuation effort. Although Greene's appearance, as Warren said in his review, "created weird little oases in the surrounding confusion," the actor isn't bad at all. The Canadian-born Greene had spent what seemed like forever as patriarch to the Cartwright family on TV's "Bonanza," but had an undistinguished film career. In *Earthquake*, his first film role in several years, Greene was outrageously cast as Ava Gardner's *father* but was nevertheless memorable as a company president helping employees escape a teetering skyscraper following The Big One. In 1978, Greene headlined the bland cast of the terrible "Battlestar Galactica," followed by another series ("Code Red") before his death in 1987. No one in the Japanese cast—not Kobayashi (later the prime minister in *Godzilla 1985*), not Tamba, not Tetsuro Fujioka—is given enough screentime to make an impression.

The special effects, on the other hand, *are* impressive and represent Teruyoshi Nakano's best work as effects director at Toho. His budget was obviously many times what he was given on the Godzilla series; the miniatures and pyrotechnics are plentiful, the camera work more imaginative. No studio had attempted this scale of destruction-in-miniature since Toho's *The Last War*, and Nakano manages to top that film's visuals. We see bridges collapsing, skyscrapers tumbling, volcanoes erupting, the earth breaking apart and an entire metropolis engulfed in flames (the last of these is extremely well done and superbly edited). The best effects shots are, to my knowledge, completely original—bird's-eye-view, or, more accurately, satellite's-eye-view shots of Japan as it slowly crumbles into the Pacific. Except for the famous shot in Alfred Hitchcock's *The Birds* (1963; literally a bird's-eye-view), I've never seen anything quite like it. The other technical credits are fine inasmuch as one can judge from the awful panned-and-scanned 16mm prints American audiences now have to contend with. Masaru Sato's score is uneven but generally fine. The American dubbing, featuring the talents of Marvin Miller, Paul Frees (I think) and lifelong film fan and future director Joe Dante, is just terrible. The looping of the romantic scenes between Onoda and Reika is among the worst ever.

"It's really too bad that people outside the largest U.S. cities will almost certainly never see *Submersion of Japan*, and will be deceived into thinking the incoherent, confusing bore *Tidal Wave* somehow accurately represents the film," said Bill Warren. "*Submersion of Japan* is one of the genuine epics of science fiction, easily deserving a Hugo and any other appropriate award." Reviewing the 113-minute international version of *Submersion* shown at the Cannes Film Festival, *Variety*'s "Mosk" was less enthused with the human drama and concentrated his review on the "well-done special effects... [The] storyline is mainly solid and instructive without being too much of a drag to the awaited [effects]." One final note: A sequel to *Submersion of Japan* was reported in a number of American publications. *Famous Monsters* called it *After Japan Sinks*, while Warren's review refers to *Submersion of Japan, Part II*. In fact a direct sequel was never made, though *Submersion in Japan* was followed by an unsuccessful teleseries remake of the same name.

Godzilla vs. the Cosmic Monster *(1974)*

Released in Japan as *Gojira tai Mekagojira* (*Godzilla Against Mechagodzilla*), Toho's 20th anniversary Godzilla entry was an improvement over *Godzilla vs. Megalon*, but that's not saying much. In Japan, the picture made a bit more money than the previous entry, but this was still a far cry from Toho's grosses in the early sixties. The cycle was winding down.

The picture opens with a curious Angilas (last seen in *Godzilla on Monster Island*) observing a tremendous explosion; this sequence is never really explained. After the opening titles, brothers Keisuke (Masaaki Daimon) and Masahiko witness an Okinawan Azumi princess (Beru-Bera Lin) perform a traditional dance. The woman faints when she has a vision of a monster (King Ghidorah, who otherwise isn't in the film) which she believes will set fire to the city. Masahiko explores a nearby cave and finds a shiny piece of metal. Keisuke meanwhile uncovers a series of ancient Okinawan cave paintings, along with a small statue of the god King Seesar (pronounced See-zar), guardian of the Azumis. An investigator from the archeology department of a prominent university, Saeko (Reiko Tajima), translates the cave paintings: "When a mountain appears above the clouds, a monster will attempt to destroy the world." What's more, "when a red moon sets and the sun rises in the west, two monsters will appear to save the people." Hmmm, sounds like a Toho monster movie to me. In any event, Keisuke and Saeko fly back to the mainland and along the way spot a dark cloud in the sky shaped like a mountain. They also meet a mysterious man (Mori Kishida) who claims to be a reporter looking for a scoop. Masahiko takes the metal to Professor Miyajima (Akihiko Hirata), who discovers the object to be made of space titanium, a substance heretofore found only in outer space. Keisuke takes the statue to his uncle, Professor Wagura (Hiroshi Koizumi), who examines it with Saeko. A burglar tries to steal the statue, but he is unsuccessful. Godzilla appears and topples an apartment building. Is this the monster of the ancient prophecy? Angilas, apparently having tunneled his way to Japan from Monster Island, tries to stop Godzilla from causing any more damage, but Godzilla fights his former ally. "Something's wrong," Masahiko says. "Godzilla shouldn't attack his friend Angilas!" The spiny, four-legged monster manages to rip a piece of Godzilla's skin off, revealing a shiny substance underneath. Godzilla grabs Angilas' jaws and tries to pry them apart (blood, looking like red paint, squirts out of the monster's mouth). Angilas is defeated. Masahiko finds more space titanium where the monsters grappled and takes it to Professor Miyajima. Miyajima is excited about the find. He proudly shows off his unusual pipe, which when taken apart, "destroys positive and negative electrodes." "It's a powerful pipe!" remarks Masahiko.

Godzilla appears in the city, setting the metropolis afire, when who should appear bursting out of a building like a stripper out of a cake (and without explanation), but another Godzilla! This is clearly *the* Godzilla, for he does a double-take at the sight of his apparent twin. The deception unmasked, the pseudo–Godzilla sheds his fake skin to reveal a robot endoskeleton double of the King of the Monsters, complete with rockets for fingers and toes, and various lethal rays emitting from its eyes and chest plate. The two Godzillas briefly spar. Godzilla is severely wounded, and Mechagodzilla is damaged and flies away. Professor Wagura determines that the statue of King Seesar needs to be placed at a shrine at the Azumi Castle. Saeko and Keisuke take a passenger liner back to Okinawa to return the statue to its rightful place. A thief aboard the ship tries to steal the statue. Keisuke shoots him, and half of the burglar's face develops primate features like something out of *Planet of the Apes* (1968). It looks as if Keisuke is doomed when the man-ape has him cornered on deck, but the "reporter" shoots the creature, who falls overboard. Professor Miyajima, his daughter and Masahiko return to the cave, where they're captured by humanoid aliens "from the third planet of the black hole, outer space." Now dressed in standard shiny silver costumes, the Commander for the Conquest for Earth (Goro Mutsu) explains Mechagodzilla is their ultimate weapon, but they need the Nobel Prize–winning Miyajima to make some repairs. At first he refuses, but surrenders to their demands when the Commander threatens his daughter. Mechagodzilla repaired, the Commander throws Miyajima in a cell with the others, then turns on some steam and hot lights attempting to scald the trio to death. Keisuke and the "reporter," who turns out to be an agent for INTERPOL, find Miyajima's pipe in the cave and infiltrate the hidden base. They rescue Miyajima, his daughter and Masahiko, despite being briefly detained by some guards who warn the group to "reach for the sky." There's another escape, with most of the men staying behind to destroy the base, while the women and Keisuke manage to return the statue, despite the appearance of more space apes. Mechagodzilla appears, just as the princess, a descendent of the Azumi royal family, sings a song beckoning the god King Seesar, who climbs out of the interior of a mountain. Part religious god, part lion (Bert Lahr cowardly lion, that is) King Seesar squares off against Mechagodzilla. The real Godzilla, having been revived by several bolts of lightning, also appears. The Commander is shot (he also turns into an ape, this time with stubby horns on his face), Miyajima is killed (after using that pipe of his to short circuit the aliens' control panel), and the base is destroyed. Mechagodzilla is defeated, with Godzilla beheading the robot, no less. King Seesar goes back to his mountain home.

Godzilla vs. the Cosmic Monster is a bit more lively than *Godzilla vs. Megalon*, the previous entry. While the aliens are obvious rip-offs of *Planet of the Apes* (the fifth and final "Apes" film was released in 1973), they're an improvement over the silly villains in *Megalon*, and no whiny kids are involved (though the film is certainly juvenile). Masaru Sato's score is interesting, and series veterans Akihiko Hirata, Hiroshi Koizumi and Kenji Sahara (as the ship's captain) make welcome appearances. Unlike the previous couple of entries, *Godzilla vs. the Cosmic Monster* is devoid of the extensive stock footage which so marred *Megalon* and *Godzilla on Monster Island* (Greg Shoemaker says there are snippets from *Godzilla vs. the Smog Monster* and *Submersion of Japan* in the picture).

The film is still a complete mess, however, from the poor effects work to the equally poor direction of Jun Fukuda. Godzilla, Angilas, King Seesar and Mechagodzilla all look like cartoons, painfully rubbery cartoons at that. The Godzilla suit has the same puppy dog design seen in *Megalon*, and the miniatures are badly lit and lack detail. As usual, the battling monsters look more like overdressed wrestlers than gigantic beasts. There's an interesting circular dolly shot that pays homage to Sergio Leone, but otherwise the set-ups are the usual stuff. Mechagodzilla, doubtlessly inspired by the "Mechani-Kong" in Toho's *King Kong Escapes*, looks okay, though it's always clear he's hardly made of "Space Titanium," but rather good old-fashioned rubber. One important question: Why do the aliens want it to look like Godzilla?

"There was no way that Toho's twenty-sixth monster frolic could have been anything other tham formulary," said *Monthly Film Bulletin*, "but it could clearly have been much less shambling than it is. . . . Much of the trouble springs from the conception of King Seesar, supposedly leonine but actually rather shaggy-dog–like, whose presence lends the (Leone-inspired) three-way confrontation at the end more than a touch of bathos: the good, the bad, and the cuddly." Despite *Godzilla vs. Megalon*'s apparent success in the United States, Cinema Shares' run of *Godzilla vs. the Cosmic Monster* was limited to Saturday "kiddie" matinees. If anything, the dubbing is even worse than in *Megalon*, with lines constantly read with the same bored tone. The picture was rarely reviewed, but the film did receive notice when Universal Television, producers of the "Six Million Dollar Man" and "The Bionic Woman" teleseries, threatened to sue Cinema Shares over the use of the name "Bionic" in the film's original title, *Godzilla vs. the Bionic Monster*. The film's moniker was quickly changed to *Godzilla vs. the Cosmic Monster*, and *Godzilla vs. Mecha-*

godzilla for home video and television release. Mechagodzilla would return the following year for the direct sequel, *Terror of Mechagodzilla* (1975).

The Last Days of Planet Earth *(1974)*

A follow-up, of sorts, to Toho's wildly successful *Submersion of Japan* (1973), *The Last Days of Planet Earth* in many respects can been seen as an unofficial remake of the studio's anti-nuclear tale, *The Last War* (1961). Both films express the helplessness Japan felt during the cold war, the more recent film adding such topical issues as pollution and the environment with equal measure. And like *The Last War*, *The Last Days* is virtually plotless. The events leading up to the end of the world are its story, though like the earlier film, *The Last Days of Planet Earth* attempts, much less successfully, to focus on a specific family: a middle-aged man and his ailing wife, their adult daughter and her boyfriend, a journalist. The story is *very* loosely based on the writings of Michel de Notredame — Nostradamus (1503-1566) — the French astrologer whose debatably uncanny 1555 book of prophecies, *Centuries*, form the shaky premise of this speculative disaster-science fiction spectacle.

Life in the twentieth century is in a state of utter chaos. Dr. Nishiyama (Tetsuro Tamba), a scientist who subscribes to Nostradamus' predictions about the end of the world, madly attempts to curtail the rampant pollution and military build-up on Earth. We shouldn't ignore "Mother Nature's rules," he warns. In Japan, children are forced to wear surgical masks because of the pollution, while other parts of the world face severe drought and starvation (Nishiyama explains that one person dies of hunger every 46 seconds). Nishiyama and his son-in-law, Akira (Toshio Kurosawa?), investigate the appearance of huge slugs discovered in the bay. Scientists (including Akihiko Hirata and Hiroshi Koizumi, in cameo roles) grimly report on the decaying state of the environment. All sea life is being killed by industrial waste, and thousands of dead fish are being washed ashore. The situation gets worse. Nishiyama visits a doctor (Takashi Shimura), who explains that one-third of all newborn babies in Japan have deformities. In other parts of the country, strange weeds invade Tokyo's subway system, while near an abandoned zinc mine, children who had been drinking the ground water either die or develop amazing mental and physical abilities (we see one little girl jump high into the air, comically lifted by invisible wires). Nishiyama suggests shutting down the country's factories for ten years and putting all Japanese citizens on a strict rationed diet. The government rejects his plans. Pollution in the atmosphere plays havoc on the weather, creating blizzards in Egypt (we see snow-capped pyramids) and freezing the northern Pacific. Near the equator, it only gets hotter, creating more drought and starvation than ever before.

Nishiyama accompanies a UN search party looking for a team of missing scientists who had been studying strange phenomena in New Guinea. Nishiyama and the UN team find strange plants (including a weird tree that eats a parrot), oversized, phony bats and poisonous slugs. They also find what's left of the missing scientists, who have since mutated into pathetic zombie-like horrors. The UN team argue whether to euthanize the men. Elsewhere, an SST jet accidently blows up over Japan, creating a large hole in the ozone layer. Intense ultra-violet light heats up the island nation, and many people die of radiation burns. Muriko, Nishiyama's daughter, informs her ailing mother, Nobuo, that she is pregnant. Despite the risk of the baby being deformed, Nobuo urges her daughter to have the baby anyway. Nobuo tells her daughter to move out of the city to the less chaotic countryside. Soon thereafter, a giant traffic jam leaves all routes in and out of Tokyo gridlocked. A motorist goes crazy and plows his car through the bumper-to-bumper traffic, causing a chain reaction of exploding gasoline tanks (Toho's production department liked this footage so much that it was used in nearly every effects film Toho made through *Godzilla 1985*). Later, the smog gets so bad, sunlight begins refracting in weird ways, acting as a mirror and reflecting an eerie, upside-down image of Tokyo in the sky. Nishiyama returns home, and soon his wife dies. At a special meeting of the country's scientists and government officials, he warns that food shortages around the world may trigger a nuclear war between the superpowers. We see missiles being launched and the great cities of the world are obliterated in H-bomb blasts. The planet is now barren, blasted back to its prehistory—with nothing remaining of civilization. And yet, man himself has survived, though now horribly deformed. We see two of these grotesque creatures fight like animals over a slug each wants to eat. But wait! This isn't the end after all. Suddenly we're back in the Diet Building, as Nishiyama explains, "The world I describe doesn't exist today... only God knows the future, but such a future *could* exist." The picture concludes with a kind of multiple choice quiz, with images of a serene, wonderful world (little girls learning ballet, men playing baseball, couples frolicking on the beach, etc.) intercut with scenes from earlier in the picture. Which is it folks, a.) utopia, or b.) Armageddon?

Although the film contains several haunting sequences, *The Last Days of Planet Earth* is a minor film. Tamba's character, who also narrates, comes across as very preachy and blustery (granted, much of this is due to the bad actor dubbing Tamba's voice), even when we might agree with what he's saying. The bulk of the picture is sloppily done, with its ineffective sequences outnumbering the effective ones at least five to one. The cheat ending is particularly jarring and annoying, especially when one considers how the movie's actual wrap pales compared to the eerie one that had preceded it. The post-apocalyptic pair of mutants, who closely resemble John Merrick, the "Elephant Man," are seen only briefly and yet are quite creepy to look at. The makeup is very imaginative considering the picture's budget, and the actors scurry about in a haunting, not-quite-human manner. Also unsettling is a brief sequence, after the ozone layer rips open, where a family flees their burning house, only to fall to the ground and themselves burn. This sequence (along with several others) intentionally evokes memories of Hiroshima and Nagasaki and is most effective. There's too little of this "world gone wild" sensibility, however, with far too much of the picture consisting of bland newsreel footage (which esthetically never matches the rest of the film, anyway), or badly written vignettes, notably a sequence where a group of fatalistic hippies decide to party till they drop, literally. Other ideas, such as the heretofore mentioned community of superchildren created by the contaminated water, are more funny than frightening.

Takashi Shimura makes his first appearance in a Toho genre film in almost ten years, which also appears to have been his last. It's a small, forgettable role, but the actor's professionalism is apparent, even in this dubbed performance. Teruyoshi Nakano's effects are fewer in number than, say, a Godzilla picture, but they are adequate. The sequence in snow-covered Egypt is amusing, and several shots of Tokyo's destruction are slightly above average. However, many of the picture's visuals are culled from blurry newsreels, and the nuclear holocaust finale is stock footage from *The Last War*.

Greg Shoemaker argued in his "The Toho Legacy" that while the film's plea for a united front against global pollution and the nuclear threat "is warranted and just . . . the picture fails to inject a compelling human drama which could have made the impact that much more agonizingly real." Leonard Maltin's team of reviewers hated the film, giving it a "BOMB" rating, calling it "preachy, laughably staged, atrociously dubbed; presented, perhaps, by the *National Enquirer*."

The picture was released in Great Britain as *Catastrophe: 1999*, but received a limited release in the United States at best. Linda Gross, who reviewed the film for the *Los Angeles Times* under the title *Prophecies of Nostradamus* (it's not clear whether the version she saw was dubbed or subtitled; in any event, it appears to have been marketed for ethnic cinemas rather than a general audience), said, "You may wish the world had ended before this bleak Japanese movie . . . began. "It's not a bad idea, though hardly original, but it's a terrible movie that doesn't seem to have been carried out beyond the concept." Conversely, Phil Hardy's *Science Fiction* had nothing but praise for the film. "The pollution movie to end them all . . . A brilliant array of special effects and a deliriously imaginative concatenation of surreal images make this an impressive fireworks display of all elements of disaster, pollution and monster movies all rolled into one giant spectacle . . . As a fantasy of the end of the world, few are more captivatingly realized."

Space Warriors 2000 (1974)

This abomination originated as a Japanese-Thai co-production, *The Six Ultra Brothers vs. the Monster Army*, an Ultraman movie that was, in fact, really a vehicle for a Thai-based superhero, a giant monkey god named Hanuman. For reasons undetermined, that film wasn't released theatrically in Japan until 1979. The English-language version, *Space Warriors 2000*, deleted much of the Thai footage, while a tiresome "it-was-only-a-dream" opening and close, featuring Occidental actors, was added. This version adopted an embarrassingly campy attitude which, beyond its racist overtures, was both uninspired and unintelligible. Most Americans who have seen the Japanese-Thai film have little good to say of it, but it still must be better than the English-language version, for *Space Warriors 2000* is very nearly unwatchable. It is, simply, the worse Western adaptation of an Asian fantasy feature I've ever seen.

Nicholas' father returns home from a business trip in Vienna and has brought back an Ultraman doll for his son. The boy, who adores Ultraman, is overjoyed. Back in Vienna, however, at the toy shop where the doll was purchased, a worried, elderly toymaker chastises his wife for selling the Ultraman figure. The doll was never meant to be sold, he says; "It was special." Some time ago, the toymaker had been visited by a strange man (unseen to us) who instructed him to take care of the doll, actually an Ultra-being. Back in the United States, Nicholas is about to fall asleep when the Ultra-being reveals its true identity. It explains it has been waiting for just such a boy as Nicholas, one pure of heart. The Ultra-being whisks Nicholas to the garish but inventively designed headquarters on Planet Ultra, where he is invited to join the fight against giant evil aliens bent on destroying the Earth. "Good *must* triumph over evil," everyone says, and Nicholas' spirit assumes the identity of one of the Ultra Brothers. "Through your life force, we will live," the Ultra-beings say. For the next forty minutes we're treated—if that's the word—to an incomprehensible barrage of monster battle footage, culled from various "Ultra" television shows. These forty minutes make absolutely no sense at all, adding nothing to the story but confusion, and, for reasons discussed later, are practically unwatchable. The picture abruptly changes gears as everything shifts to Thailand, where the happy-go-lucky giant monkey god, Hanuman, rescues a religious artifact (the decapitated head of a Buddha statue) stolen by thieves. The giant monkey god frightens the criminals by perilously (but merrily) dancing over their jeep. Later, the world is threatened when the Sun moves out of its orbit and begins roasting the Earth. Hanuman visits the guardian of the sun, politely asking that the star be returned to its original position in the heavens. Possibly taken aback by Hanuman's constant dancing, the guardian complies. However, all that added heat on Earth is enough to awaken "The Monster Army," an indescribable menagerie of giant beasties. Hanuman stands ready but is outmatched until the Ultra Brothers come to lend a hand. "If we win this," Hanuman tells them, "everything is rosy. If we lose, the world is doomed. Makes you kinda humble, doesn't it?" Although much of Thailand is destroyed by tidal waves, earthquakes and an erupting volcano, the monsters are defeated (the rubber "flesh" is peeled off one creature; another has its limbs chopped off). The battle won, Hanuman warmly thanks each Ultra-being. Just then, Nicholas wakes up. It was all a dream! "Too much dessert I think," says Nicholas' father.

The unwatchability of *Space Warriors 2000* ("The Year of the Monkey Wrench," according to the credits) is three-fold. For starters, the original production, according to Japanese fantasy film experts like Ed Godziszewski, wasn't particularly good to begin with. Second, the English-language adaptation is resolutely amateurish, written by talentless hacks with nothing but contempt for their picture's audience. Finally, the sound and picture transfer of the original footage is astonishingly poor. *The Six Ultra Brothers* was originally presented in an anamorphic wide screen format. For the American television edition, this footage was not decompressed, resulting in an extremely distorted, unpleasantly squeezed image — in other words, everyone is as thin as a toothpick. As much of the Westernized film was culled and converted from the standard TV ratio of the Tsuburaya shows to 35mm scope, and thus severely cropped on the top and bottom to begin with, the resultant image is downright headache-inducing. It's like trying to watch a movie through a murky goldfish bowl with one eye closed. And the editing only worsens the problem. The forty minutes of nonstop battle scenes add nothing. There are no normal-sized human beings in the film at all save for the western actors seen at the very beginning and the end. There's no sense of geography or time. There is no story. The banter between the Ultra-beings and the monsters is trite, consisting of Ninja Turtle-esque dialogue along the lines of "Who are these creeps?! I'll have 'em for lunch!" Most of these voices went through a synthesizer but can barely be understood.

As camp, the picture is awful. There's not a single laugh to be had, and much of the so-called humor is as embarrassing as it is insane, such as one end credit, "We wish to thank the Kamikaze Pilots for clearing the airways during the shooting of this picture." What is that supposed to mean? Even the jokes don't make sense. The footage of the "American" family (clearly filmed outside the United States and dubbed with singularly British accents) adds nothing but running time, while the sudden influx of Thai footage near the end makes little sense. The effects during the Thai footage are mediocre but no worse than Toho's giant monster films from the period, and somewhat better than the footage lifted from the later "Ultra" series. The opening titles, featuring a colorful myriad of Ultra-beings, are attractive, but their modest charm is quickly undermined by those "joke" credits. The cast, according to the film, includes Mothra, "Godzelda" and "a whole cast of Japanese stuntmen whose names we could not read." Mothra, needless to say, isn't in the film at all.

Though it is very popular throughout Asia, most Americans have been, as yet, unable to experience the entire "Ultra" saga, which has continued more or less unabated in Japan for over twenty-five years. Only the second series, 1967's "Ultraman" (it followed "Ultra Q," made the previous year), has been widely shown in the United States, though "Ultra Seven" received some airplay in Hawaii. At least ten series (with over four hundred episodes!) and six features have been produced thus far. As Bob Johnson and August Ragone state in their highly recommended article, "The Ultra Series: 25 Years of Science Fantasies from Tsuburaya Productions" (in *Markalite* #2), "There have been spin-offs, imitations, theatrical shorts, commercial endorsements, stage shows, reams of merchandise—the Ultra Series has become deeply entrenched in Japanese pop culture. George Lucas should be green with envy." *The Six Ultra Brothers vs. the Monster Army*, however, is little more than a footnote in the Ultra story; *Space Warriors 2000* is an atrocity and not recommended.

Evil of Dracula *(1975)*

Toho's last vampire movie was more of the same, this time set at a remote girls' school. The picture does have a few good moments, but for the most part, it's very conventional and illogically scripted. By 1975, vampire films in the Hammer mode had run out of steam. The British studio that had been so influential less than twenty years earlier with *The Curse of Frankenstein* and *Horror of Dracula* was now struggling to stay afloat, and the vampire genre fell out of favor before new projects like Universal's big-budgeted *Dracula*, Werner Herzog's *Nosferatu: Phantom der Nacht* and the comedy *Love at First Bite* (all 1979) attempted to lure moviegoers back into the fold.

Toho's film begins with the arrival of psychology professor Shiraki (Toshio Kurosawa) at a lonely, rural train station. Offered a position at a small women's college, Shiraki is met by professor Yoshi, the French literature teacher (Katsuhiko Sasaki, the human star of *Godzilla vs. Megalon*). En route to the school, Shiraki notices an utterly mangled taxicab in a ditch, and Yoshi explains that the vehicle was struck by a drunken driver. Both the cabbie and the wife of the school's principal were killed in the crash. (The version of the film I saw repeated portions of this sequence—and without setting it to any kind of mood; the editing was very poor.) In any event, Shiraki arrives at the school and offers his condolences to the principal (Kunie Tanaka). Oddly (and unbelievably), the principal explains that he's keeping his dead wife's body in the basement, per the local custom, because, he says, "there's always the hope the corpse might come back to life." The principal, who claims to be ill, also surprises Shiraki by telling him that he wants the professor to succeed him. Shiraki spends the night but is awakened by the voice of a woman singing, which he follows to a dark room, where a woman in a white nightgown stands in a trance-like state. Shiraki notices the woman bleeding, just as he is attacked by a female vampire. Shiraki hits his head and blacks out. The next morning the professor, who suspects the previous night's incident was just a nightmare, wanders through the house and finds the coffin of the principal's wife in the basement. When he opens it, he discovers that the dead wife is the vampire that had attacked him earlier. The principal himself appears and expresses outrage that Shiraki opened the coffin. Shiraki's job prospects, however, appear unscathed. The professor meets a trio of students—Kyoko, Kumi and Yukiko—and later the school's doctor, Shimimura. The doctor explains that some time earlier one of the students had vanished "into thin air" and that Shiraki's predecessor, who was also in line to succeed the principal, had been committed to an insane asylum. Kyoko finds a white rose outside her room. Later, she encounters the principal, also a vampire, who bites her on the breast.

The next morning, professor Shiraki is showing slides of Rorschach tests, when Kyoko hallucinates that one of the blotches turns red with blood. She stands up, screams, and promptly faints. Shimimura examines her and finds the bite wounds. Shiraki goes for a drive with the doctor, who tells the story of a European sailor who was shipwrecked in the area some two hundred years earlier. Because Christianity was outlawed in Japan during that time, the man was tortured, renounced his beliefs and became a vampire. Shimimura explains that he has been collecting local tales for several years, and he says, "Although they happened a long time ago, they are, in fact, true." The students leave campus for the holidays, save for Kumi (who by now is in love with Shiraki), Kyoko and Yukiko. At first, Kyoko appears to be getting better but later tries to stab Shiraki, and falls off a balcony to her death. Shiraki obtains his predecessor's diary, which hints that not only are the principal and his wife vampires, but that every principal before him was afflicted with a taste for blood. Yukiko disappears, and Shimimura finds her wandering through a forest, where she embraces the fanged principal. Shimimura takes a few photos as evidence but is discovered. The professor, Kumi, and a guard find Yukiko, along with Shimimura's camera. They develop the film to find Yukiko strangely posed in an embrace—the principal didn't photograph! Meanwhile, the white rose has turned blood red. Yukiko wanders off again, this time to the principal's home, where his vampire wife cuts and removes Yukiko's face, placing it atop her own and assimilating her identity. The principal's wife, as Yukiko, returns to the school, and tells professor Shiraki that Kumi has gone home. The vampire also asks Shiraki to marry her. However, the professor quickly sees through the wife's treachery. The principal and professor Yoshi, the latter essaying a badly sketched Renfield role, explain that the bodies of Shimimura, Kyoko and Yuki have been dumped in a lake. There's a struggle, and Yoshi falls into the lake, where he apparently drowns. Soon thereafter, the principal bites Kumi, which prompts Shiraki to throw an axe at him. When the principal removes the axe from his chest, Shiraki stabs the vampire in the heart with a hot poker, thus warding off any possible vampiric curse on Kumi and sending both the principal and his wife crumbling into bleached skeletons (and unlike *Lake of Dracula*, the disintegration of the vampires is left intact).

Although *Evil of Dracula* starts out well, with Shiraki's arrival at the train station and the intriguing ride past the wrecked taxicab (which in the end has little to do with the story), the picture is mostly derivative of other films, notably Hammer's 1970 production, *Lust for a Vampire*, itself based upon Sheridan LeFanu's "Carmilla." The greater problem is the picture's notable lack of logical characters and storytelling. When all of the school's students leave for the holidays, why do Kumi, Kyoko and Yukiko stay behind? Why doesn't Shiraki get suspicious when the principal gives him all that malarkey about keeping his wife's body around? Why does the poker work but not the axe? When the principal discovers that Shiraki opened his wife's coffin, he accuses him of nothing less than religious sacrilege, yet he allows him to continue teaching and still plans to have the professor succeed him as principal.

Fantastic films already ask their audiences to accept characters and events they're not likely to swallow in the real world, and can work only when they follow their own peculiar logic. There doesn't seem to be any logic governing *Evil of Dracula*. Another problem is Riichiro Manabe's singularly distracting score. Manabe also wrote the dreadful music to Toho's *Godzilla vs. the Smog Monster* (1971), and his work here is nearly as poor, sounding very much like a cat walking across an organ's keyboard while a five-year-old plays with an electric guitar.

"Yamamoto and his scenarists appeared to have run out of interesting ways of treating this subject," complained *The Encyclopedia of Horror Movies*, "This ludicrous anti-authoritarian youth movie sadly spelled the end of a once-promising series." Bill Warren's review in *Cinefantastique* called the film "average" and stated the film was "virtually not Japanese at all. Sone vividly gory scenes, handsome, but cheap."

Terror of Mechagodzilla *(1975)*

Toho's fifteeth Godzilla movie was the last of a very tired line. The series went into hiatus until revived by the comparatively big-budgeted, revisionist sequel-cum-remake, *Gojira* (1984). *Terror of Mechagodzilla*, also known as *Terror of Godzilla*, is a direct sequel to *Godzilla vs. the Cosmic Monster* and a tired-looking retread, although the the return of director Ishiro Honda and Akira Ifukube's musical talents help some.

Picking up where *Godzilla vs. the Cosmic Monster* left off, the submarine *Akatsuki* searches for the remains of Mechagodzilla, as a young woman (Tomoko Ai) watches on a nearby beach. The submarine is attack by a tremendous (though wholly fictional) dinosaur, Titanosaurus, a bipedal sea monster which crushes the sub with its bare hands. Biologist Akira Ichinoshi (Katsuhiko Sasaki) and INTERPOL agent and former college friend Murakoshi (Katsmasu Uchida) meet with INTERPOL leaders to discuss the sub's loss. Elsewhere, humanoid aliens from the Third Planet of the Black Hole discuss their planned conquest of the Earth. They discuss the assistance of human scientist Shizo Mafune (Akihiko Hirata), who twenty years ago was a top scientist, specializing in underwater research. Mafune wanted to farm the seas and planned underwater cities until he was discredited when he claimed to have discovered a dinosaur—the Titanosaurus—and even said he could control the beast. Fired from his research job fifteen years ago, he fell onto hard times and, during this time, his wife died. Now the misanthropic scientist and his daughter, Katsura (who turns out to be the woman seen at the beach), are working for the aliens, led by Project Leader Mugan (Goro Mutsu again). Mugan has recovered and rebuilt Mechagodzilla (complete with the initials "MG2" painted on one arm) and uses Titanosaurus to keep away nosy INTERPOL agents. Normally a peaceful creature, Titanosaurus' mind is controlled by Katsura. Mafune agrees to help the aliens in their conquest and determines that Mechagodzilla needs human brain cells to be most effective. An unnamed INTERPOL agent and prisoner of the aliens tries to flee his captors. Before being recaptured, he hands some space titanium to a sewer worker. Ichinoshi and Murakoshi try to visit Mafune to discuss his dinosaur theory, but Katsura tells the men her father died some years ago. She becomes attracted to Ichinoshi, and when he announces plans for an expedition to search for the Titanosaur, she warns him to steer clear but will not say why. Mafune, like his daughter, begins to have second thoughts about helping the alien invaders. Mugan reminds Mafune that Katsura was killed during Mafune's lean years—she was electrocuted while assisting her scientist father—and that aliens saved her by turning her into a cyborg: part human, part machine. Ichinoshi and the new sub are attacked by Titanosaurus, but manage to escape at the last minute. Ichinoshi decides to build a "giant, supersonic wave oscillator" to combat the beast. Katsura contemplates what the world would be like if all the old monsters were to rise again (brief stock footage from *Destroy All Monsters* and *Ghidrah: The Three-Headed Monster*), as Mugan gloats, "Now they're going to eat their words!" while ordering Titanosaurus to attack Tokyo. "We will build you a beautiful new home out of the desolated ashes of Tokyo!" Mugan tells a now remorseful Mafune. Godzilla intercepts the Titanosaur, and when Katsura is momentarily distracted, the beast peacefully goes back into the water. Ichinoshi is captured by the aliens, just as INTERPOL agents find and destroy the alien base.

Meanwhile, Titanosaurus and Mechagodzilla, controlled through Katsura's robotic parts, attack the heart of the city. The sea creature creates a powerful wind a la Rodan by swishing its fin-like tail about, while Mechagodzilla creates havoc with its rocket-equipped fingers and toes. Godzilla appears and grapples with Titanosaurus again, while Mechagodzilla tangles with a squadron of pesky jets. The King of the Monsters goes down for the count and is even buried when Mechagodzilla causes an avalanche with his rocket fingers. Titanosaurus is so happy at Godzilla's apparent death he even does a little jig on the monster's grave. The oscillator is at long last mounted on a helicopter. Mechagodzilla sees the chopper racing toward Titanosaurus and is about to destroy it with its rockets, when Godzilla leaps out of his intended grave. Brushing the dirt from his bumpy gray body, Godzilla rushes Mechagodzilla, while the chopper, using the supersonic oscillator, keeps Titanosaurus at bay. Ichinoshi frees himself, and Katsura is about to shoot him when Murakoshi appears and shoots the cyborg-woman. Mafune is also shot, though it's unclear by the editing just who did the deed. Ichinoshi tells the dying Katsura, "Even if you're a cyborg, Katsura, I still love you." Godzilla once again rips Mechagodzilla's head off, only this time the monster comes equipped with an electronic brain underneath. Nonetheless, Godzilla manages to defeat his mechanical double. Mugan escapes INTERPOL agents by jumping off a cliff into the sea, where several flying saucers have been hidden. Godzilla destroys the saucers with his fiery breath just as they begin lifting off. Godzilla also defeats Titanosaurus, sending the monster falling backward off the cliff and into the sea. The Earth is saved. Godzilla, now wading in the ocean with a ghastly toothy grin on his face, swims away victorious.

Terror of Mechagodzilla was Ishiro Honda's first monster movie since *Yog* and his first Godzilla picture since *Godzilla's Revenge* six years earlier. Even in this short period of time, it is clear that Toho's monster movie budgets had plummeted to the point where even Honda's skills couldn't really save the film.

The story is basically a retread of the previous entry, with a scientist (played in both films by Akihiko Hirata) forced to work for aliens on a robot Godzilla to save his daughter's life. Titanosaurus is only slightly more interesting than King Seesar, and the aliens, no longer seen in ape makeup but wearing silly helmets, even less so. Akihiko Hirata is the only recognizable member of the cast, and unfortunately he's more than a bit hammy in his final series appearance (he died in 1984). The tragic Mafune character would be interesting if it weren't played so broadly. The character is introduced in an interesting montage of black and white stills, but once Hirata puts on his "old professor" make-up, he overplays the role in a manner that's obvious even in this poorly dubbed version. The relationship between Katsura and Ichinoshi is even less interesting, and the actors playing Ichinoshi and Murakoshi are virtually interchangeable.

The special effects, while no better than in any of the other seventies films, show a bit more imagination. While not very good, the scenes of Mechagodzilla and Titanosaurus attacking Tokyo are welcome after so many monster sequences set against barren, building-less landscapes. One of the more interesting special effects has Mechagodzilla launching his rockets down a car-lined city street. The rockets explode down the street one by one, finally reaching the camera and sending miniature automobiles flying high into the air. Titanosaurus (Chitanozaurusu in Japan) may look rubbery, but at least the creature is designed with a modicum of logic, something sorely lacking in most of Toho's "anything goes" creations of the seventies. Like the rest of the monster cast, Titanosaurus was shot from extreme low angles some of the time, often against the real sky in normal light, giving the creatures an illusion of height also missing for some time. The matte work is often poor, with the monsters always appearing much larger than they should be when matted with fleeing citizens. The wrestling scenes between the monsters is a bit more imaginative than those in the last few pictures, though once again staged with the monsters emoting an embarrassing amount of overly anthropomorphic expressions.

Britain's *Monthly Film Bulletin* complained the special effects not involving the monsters were "glaringly amateurish, and the human drama...stilted to the point of paralysis." According to writer David Milner, *Terror of Mechagodzilla* bypassed a theatrical run, and was first shown on American television in 1978. However, other sources insist it was shown theatrically in some regions of the country, possibly as *Terror of Godzilla* (advertising material featuring this title exists).

The film was the least successful of the series in Japan, and producer Tomoyuki Tanaka seemed to acknowledge that the series was at a creative dead end. If it was to continue, Godzilla would have to undergo a major metamorphosis, which it did some nine years later.

Time of the Apes *(1975)*

The film version of Pierre Boulle's *Planet of the Apes* was the surprise hit of 1968. Producer Arthur P. Jacobs spent three and one half years trying to sell his film project, produced only after he allied himself with star Charlton Heston and agreed to shoot a test reel featuring Heston and Edward G. Robinson, the latter elaborately made up as a talking orangutan. (Robinson soon dropped out, and his role was played by Maurice Evans.) Until the test reel was shown, studio executives just didn't think human actors would be believable as apes. The medium-budget film cost around $5 million but made several times that during its initial release. (By 1993 the film had taken in some $15 million in U.S. and Canadian rentals alone.) The picture also received some very good notices, such as Pauline Kael's review in *The New Yorker*, which proclaimed *Apes* "one of the best science fiction fantasies ever to come out of Hollywood." This critical and commercial success, just as the studio's big films of the period (*Doctor Dolittle* and *Star!* among others) catapulted it precariously close to financial ruin, seems to have caught Fox and even Jacobs off guard. A sequel, *Beneath the Planet of the Apes* (1970), was rushed into production. Heston was understandably dissatisfied with the script and agreed to appear only in an extended cameo. Despite its many inadequacies, *Beneath* proved successful as well and led to three more films: *Escape from the Planet of the Apes* (1971), *Conquest of the Planet of the Apes* (1972) and *Battle for the Planet of the Apes* (1973). The middle entries were full of interesting concepts, but the budgets were too low and much of the talent both in front of and behind the camera was second rate. The final film and the two teleseries that followed (one animated, the other live action) were badly written and cheaply made.

Although the popularity of the Apes films lasted only a few years, they were nevertheless a genuine cultural phenomenon, and it's surprising that few producers tried to cash in on their success. In fact, the only American film that seemed to, ahem, "ape" it was Universal's bizarre *Skullduggery* (1970). Fox's series was, presumably, popular in Japan as well. *Godzilla vs. the Bionic Monster* (1974) featured alien apes disguised as human beings, and a character named "Space Apeman Gori" turned up in "Spectralman" (aka "Spectreman"), a 1971 Japanese teleseries. An even more blatant rip-off, however, came when Tsuburaya Enterprises created a TV show built entirely around talking primates: "Ape Corps." That series was re-edited to feature length in the United States and released under the title *Time of the Apes*.

In the adaptation, young Johnny and his older sister, Caroline, visit their Uncle Charlie (as absurd an Anglicization as I've ever heard), a scientist conducting "cold sleep experiments." Aided by his assistant, Kathryn, the scientist defrosts and successfully revives a frozen monkey he had held in a state of suspended animation. (This sequence virtually duplicates the opening to the 1954 sci-fi thriller *Gog*.) An earthquake and a volcanic eruption nearby rock the installation, sending Johnny, Caroline and Kathryn seeking shelter in nearby metal capsules, which resemble tiny diving bells. Falling debris activates the capsules, instantly freezing our hapless trio.

They awaken to find themselves in an unfamiliar, drab office building. They are met by talking, men-like apes. A brutish gorilla, Gaybor (sometimes pronounced Gay-Bar!) orders the humans shot, but luckily (for them if not for us) they manage to escape. Making their way to a typical Japanese house, the trio are spotted by a frightened ape-child who screams, "Naked apes!" A second ape-kid, Pepe (a girl), isn't frightened by the humans. Helped along by the ape-girl, the humans make their way to Green Mountain, counterpart to the rocky "Forbidden Zone" seen in the American film. The band encounter a series of traps, laid by Godo, a bearded, solitary human who has managed to avoid the apes most of his life. Shortly after Godo sheds his beard, everyone save Pepe is recaptured. Gaybor hates the elusive Godo and is about to have him shot when the apes' leader, "His Excellency" (a hulking, gray-haired gorilla) drives up and orders the execution halted. Claiming to be sympathetic to humans, he takes the foursome back to his base. Pepe sneaks onto the base and rescues Johnny and Godo; the humans disguise themselves as apes and hop aboard a military truck and, later, a passenger train. The three return to the base to rescue the women. Kathryn, convinced that the ape leader is sincere about wanting to help them, is reluctant to leave, but all make their way back to the rocky terrain beyond Green Mountain. En route Pepe is returned to her frantic mother. In the mountains, the four are once again confronted by Gaybor, who we learn blames Godo for the death of his wife and son. A flying saucer, which had been appearing periodically throughout the story for no apparent reason, shows up to reveal how Gaybor's wife and son really died, via a big video monitor on the UFO's belly. It seems that Gaybor's wife and son somehow found themselves dangling off the side of a cliff, and Godo tried to rescue them. He managed to save the ape boy, but Gaybor, watching from a distance, assumed the human was trying to kill the child, fired at Godo, and fatally shot his own son instead. His Excellency appears once again as Gaybor wanders off, whimpering, into the distance. The ape leader allows the humans to leave, which they do.

The four decide to take their chances with the UFO, which had acted as a kind of guardian angel for them, deactivating the apes' guns at opportune moments. Inside the saucer they find a "U.E.C. computer," a control-all ecosystem device and self-proclaimed "master of the entire universe." The computer explains that it's 2030 and that the quartet are all that remain of the human race. The computer figures it wouldn't be a good idea to send them back to the apes and forces them to choose to (a) hop back into the capsules for a few more millennia, or (b) allow the computer to whisk them to another planet. Kathryn and the kids opt for the former, but Godo will have none of it. He attacks the computer and disappears. Shaken, Kathryn, Caroline and Johnny climb back into their capsules. Caroline awakens to find herself, Johnny and Kathryn back in a laboratory. She spots more apes, but these are only hallucinations, for now the trio are back in the present, safe in the arms of good ol' Uncle Charlie, who explains that they have been buried in the earthquake and it has taken a week to dig them out. Just how and why did everyone make it back to the present? The preposterous and nearly incomprehensible explanation is worth quoting: "You've had an incredible adventure, I know," Uncle Charlie says, "But time is relative...I noticed certain deviations in the time scale. It shows 3,714 years, and the temperature shows an incredibly low temperature. We thought 273 degrees below zero was the lowest temperature, but these readings indicate an even more extreme temperature, and that could have elongated the time scale... It's all very clear! Instead of progressing into the future, you reverted into the past. But there was another factor, the extremely low temperature, which caused the time scale to warp, and therefore the deep freeze capsule acted as a time converter!" "It sounds simple, doesn't it?" exclaims the relieved Kathryn. We next see Godo, apparently trapped in the far future, as he wanders through a sandy desert. Where he is no one can say, but as Kathryn says, "he'll always be in our hearts."

I have not seen the series from which *Time of the Apes* was derived and have no idea as to whether it makes any more sense than this nonsensical pseudo-feature does. The film's last fifteen minutes are absolute gobbledygook, defying the most basic rules of logic and storytelling. Why does the all-powerful computer force the band to choose between two completely undesirable options? If it could banish them into the future, why not send them back to the past? How did the man-made computer come to dominate mankind? What'll happen to Godo? Another curious aspect to this feature adaptation is how Kathryn, Johnny and Caroline never seem to wonder where (or when) they are. The astronauts in the Apes films were horrified to learn that everyone they ever knew had died hundreds of years earlier, and when Heston discovered the planet of the apes is really Earth, he was shocked and utterly devastated at mankind's fate. Neither of these implications ever seems to have occurred to the characters here. From the way they talk, in fact, it's suggested they almost think that they were whisked away to some distant nation, like Scotland or Bulgaria. At least they keep telling the apes that they're from "another country." Our heroes don't seem much interested in the UFO, either (also not believable), reacting to it as if it were as commonplace as a helicopter or pickup truck.

Unlike *Planet of the Apes*, intended as a social commentary as much as anything else, *Time of the Apes* seems interested in action and little else. There's none of the apes' social structure so carefully and cleverly laid out in *Planet*, where orangutans represented religion and science, gorillas the military and champanzees the general populace. There is a greater variety of primates in *Time of the Apes*—baboons, gibbons, even a proboscis monkey—but they appear to have been chosen more for their visual appeal than any kind of symbolic reasoning. Their makeup is crude and not very articulate, but passable and colorful. (Certainly better than the hideously inadequate masks worn by extras in the American films.) Despite their variety, the apes themselves are dull and uninteresting. The only apes given anything like characterization are Pepe, Gaybor and the sympathetic leader, referred to only as His Excellency. Gaybor is cursed with that funny name, while his superior's motives in helping the humans never become clear. Spunky Pepe, sporting a white ring of hair around her gibbon-like face, is appealing, though like everyone else, she is held captive in the picture's escape-recapture formula. The human characters are one-dimensional. The constant whining of Kathryn, Caroline and Johnny wears mightily on the viewer (Sandy Frank's typically atrocious dubbing doesn't help matters). Godo is a bland hero. Once again, the richness of the characters found in the first Apes film (especially those played by Heston and Evans) is completely absent here. The similarities the film has to its still-popular American counterpart are undoubtedly what brought it to Western shores. But *Time of the Apes* lacks the intelligence and ingenuity of the American film, opting instead for routinely packaged, mindless thrills.

The Last Dinosaur *(1977)*

Ten years after they allied themselves with Toho for *King Kong Escapes* (1967), the American company Rankin-Bass returned to the giant monster genre—and Japan—for this highly entertaining adventure. Produced in cooperation with Tsuburaya Enterprises (which did the special effects), *The Last Dinosaur* was scheduled to open theatrically in New York City, but was pulled at the last minute and instead made its U.S. debut as a TV movie for ABC.

Researchers drilling near the Arctic Circle have made an amazing discovery. An active volcano has kept a tiny, hopelessly remote area of the frozen north a tropical oasis, unchanged since the prehistoric age. A group of explorers were sent to check out the area, but only one man, scientist Chuck Wade (Steven Keats) made it back. The other five men were killed by what appeared to be a Tyrannosaurus Rex. As the picture opens, big-game hunter and oil baron Masten Thrust (Richard Boone) decides to lead a second expedition. There is much speculation that Thrust wants to add a dinosaur to his collection of mounted heads, but he promises he intends to study the creature, not hunt it down. Thrust asks scientist Wade, Dr. Kawamoto (Tetsu Nakamura, the same actor who created *The Manster*) and Thrust's gaunt and silent manservant, Bunta (Luther Rackley), to join him. In the interest of public relations, Thrust has also agreed to allow the press pool to select one of their own to document the journey. They choose Francesca "Frankie" Banks (Joan Van Ark), a tough-as-nails photographer. Thrust doesn't want a woman on the trip but relents when she mocks him with a striptease, a reference to his revolving door of mistresses. The *Polar Borer*, a tiny craft with a drill-like nose, makes its way through the rock and ice (using a powerful, remote-controlled laser at its bow), finally reaching the prehistoric jungle. The volcanic activity has kept the area near ninety degrees Fahrenheit, though in the distance icy mountains are visible in every direction. A horned dinosaur lumbers its way along the beach and everyone scatters. Everyone but gutsy Frankie, that is. She's determined to get a good shot of the giant beast. Thrust pulls her to safety at the last minute. The two fall into a big puddle of mud, but Frankie's chutzpah clearly impresses Thrust.

Later, everyone goes exploring while Kawamoto sets up camp. Frankie accidentally steps on a large prehistoric turtle (she also loses her purse, which is picked up by a curious, prehistoric woman whom the others don't see). Elsewhere, Kawamoto is squished and presumably eaten by the Tyrannosaur. The dinosaur also begins fooling around with the capsule, eventually taking it back to his lair where he buries it as a dog would a bone. A Triceratops appears and briefly spars with the carnivore. The horned beast is no match for the powerful meat-eater, however, and is killed. The party returns to the camp site to find Kawamoto and the capsule gone and Tyrannosaur footprints everywhere. Thrust then explains he left orders forbidding a rescue attempt should something go wrong: they're on their own. Four months pass. The group moves into a cave, and the men hunt game. Neanderthals (played by Asian actors), initially frightened by the outsiders, become a bit more cocky and begin taunting the explorers. Thrust constructs a crossbow out of what's left of the camping supplies and shoots the leader of the cavemen. The natives retreat, but later the primitive woman seen earlier (Masumi Sekiya) appears, begging for food. She's adopted by the others and given the name "Hazel."

Later, Frankie and Hazel are washing their hair near a small river when suddenly the Tyrannosaur appears. Hazel runs away, and Frankie angers the beast by escaping between the monster's legs. She makes it back to the cave, but the dinosaur will not give up. Meanwhile, the men return from the hunt and find the photographer trapped inside the cave. They tie the end of a rope around a boulder and the other end to the dinosaur's tail. They then dislodge the sphere-shaped rock, sending it with the Tyrannosaur in tow tumbling down a large hill. Thrust is now determined to kill the beast. With everyone's help, a massive catapult is constructed. During this time and for no reason in particular, Bunta wanders off and tries to kill the Tyrannosaur with his spear. Like Nakamura, he's squished and eaten. Just as the catapult is being readied, Chuck accidentally stumbles upon the capsule. With Frankie's help, he manages to haul the light craft back to the lake. They can now go home. Thrust, however, is obsessed with getting that dinosaur and refuses to go back. "First we get the dinosaur," he says, "then we talk about leaving." Frankie, initially attracted to Chuck but now in love with the obsessed hunter, begs him to reconsider. He suggests that she remain behind with him. She reluctantly refuses. Just then the dinosaur appears, and a medicine ball–sized boulder is fired. It lands smack on the monster's head, but the dinosaur recovers almost at once. Thrust still refuses to leave. Frankie is exasperated. "Let it be," she screams, "It's the last one!" "So am I," Thrust says. Frankie and Chuck climb into the capsule and return to civilization, while Thrust is left to hunt the last dinosaur (the last Tyrannosaur anyway). At least he has Hazel to keep him company.

The Last Dinosaur was made at the same time as Dino De Laurentiis' big-budgeted but vaguely similar *King Kong* remake. If this production had had *Kong*'s budget, it might really have been something. As is, it's still better than De Laurentiis' tritely campy, sloppily produced misfire.

The film has an appealing naiveté (something sorely missing from De Laurentiis' film) and a solid, involving story. However, it's difficult to swallow that such a large land mass wouldn't have been spotted before (from a satellite or the like), nor is it believable that some kind of aircraft wouldn't be able to reach the prehistoric oasis. *The Last Dinosaur* is really a throwback to films like *King Kong* and *The Lost World*, which is part of its appeal. Particularly interesting and surprising is the relationship between the three principals, something quite removed from the standard romantic triangle you might suspect. On one hand Frankie is attracted to the handsome, stable and very conventional Chuck Wade, yet she's also drawn toward the craggy, sad-faced Masten Thrust, the last of the great white hunters. Thrust isn't handsome in the conventional sense, and he's clearly far too old for Frankie, yet this gutsy, adventurous photographer is beguiled by Thrust's live-life-to-its-fullest attitude. Well-written is his almost childlike response to Frankie's plea that he return to civilization: "I've got a better idea. You stay with me. [Laughs] I like that idea—Adam and Eve. Now you tell me the truth: What's back there for you? Confusion? Frustration? Here's where life is. Pure. Simple. We could make love... and hunt... and what the hell else is there?" It's a nice monologue strangely but appealingly delivered by Boone. His misanthropic hunter either seems to be barking at someone or pouting in a manner suggesting Wallace Beery's Professor Challenger in *The Lost World*. Some felt Boone, primarily associated with Westerns, was miscast, but his coarse features and intimidating demeanor only make him a more intriguing, complex character than was probably initially intended.

For some reason, men-in-suit dinosaurs became quite popular in non–Japanese productions after the British company Amicus used them in the not-bad *The Land That Time Forgot* (1975), which this closely resembles, and its sequel, *The People That Time Forgot* (1977). Big creatures also appear in *At the Earth's Core* (1976, also by Amicus). The effect isn't particularly convincing, and Tsuburaya's effects, mostly shot in-studio, stand out like a sore thumb when edited with the location footage. The Tyrannosaur is lacking in detail as well, but overall the work is passable, especially on television screens. While much of *The Last Dinosaur* is sloppy and uninspired, it's also engrossing and likeable, and the best of the Rankin-Bass–Tsuburaya co-productions.

The "Legend of the Dinosaurs" *(1977)*

This ghastly film is among the very worst Japanese fantasy films ever produced for theatrical release. It is badly written and directed, and the two prehistoric beasts of the title, a Plesiosaur and a Pterodactyl, are exceedingly inept and unimaginative in their design and manipulation. *The "Legend of the Dinosaurs"* (that's how the title is given onscreen) takes place near the picturesque base of Mt. Fuji, an interesting and unusual locale that the filmmakers fail to exploit. Although much of this interminable film consists of recycled clichés from earlier monster-on-the-loose films, it borrows most liberally from *Jaws*, and the results are dismal.

At the densely forested base of Mt. Fuji, a woman falls through an *Alice in Wonderland*–like wind hole, into the depths of an icy cave, where she sees a six-foot, prehistoric egg crack open. Through the cracks of the eggshell, a slimy eye gazes placidly at her. Although word of the monstrous egg quickly spreads, no one bothers to investigate the matter, save for greedy Ashizawa (Tsunchiko Watase), a pushy geologist (he's the hero, though hardly likeable or interesting). His scientist father believed a dinosaur lived in the nearby lake, but his theory wasn't accepted in the scientific community because such notions would "throw the whole world into total panic." For no reason in particular, a colleague of Ashizawa recounts how Benjamin Franklin had supposedly found a prehistoric toad that had been hibernating for millions of years. "He brought it back to life again!" the scientist insists. He goes on to suggest that dinosaurs create earthquakes. Ashizawa finds the wind hole and is about to climb in when he's interrupted by an earthquake. Elsewhere, a young couple in a paddle boat disappear, and later someone finds the body of a headless horse up in a tree. Despite these mysterious events, a big summer festival is held at the lake, featuring "Beau Yatani and His the Last Longhorn Band." The band is in the middle of an innocuous number when their floating stage is attacked by some unseen force. A big fin is spotted, but this turns out to be nothing more than a pair of pranksters with a cardboard fin (the film's most blatant plagiarism of *Jaws*). The two teens get their comeuppance, however; they're attacked and eaten by the *real* sea monster, described by cast members as a plesiosaur, but looking more like Cecil the friendly sea serpent. A woman aboard a small boat is also attacked and killed while her scuba-diving partner, Cheiko (also Ashizawa's girlfriend), is underwater. When she surfaces, Cheiko finds no one in the boat, as if her friend has vanished into thin air (a faintly unsettling idea). Just then, what's left of the woman's corpse pops up out of the water. Ashizawa forbids Cheiko to go diving. To show her that he's serious, he empties her tank of oxygen and slaps her silly. Ashizawa decides to look for the sea beast on his own but fails to learn about the depth charges being dropped in the lake that day. A forgiving Cheiko learns about the blasting and rescues Ashizawa, pulling him through a passageway leading to the ice cave. Just then (and there are a lot of "just thens" in this picture) the egg hatches completely (what took it so long?) and out pops a pterodactyl, sporting a strange beak which resembles the jaws of a Venus fly trap and so rigid as to resemble an over-starched shirt. The stiff prop flies around the lake before encountering the plesiosaur, improbably deep inside the dense forest and away from any significant water. Just then (what did I tell you?) Mt. Fuji heats up, sending the dinosaurs tumbling into the bowels of the Earth (darn good timing for our heroes, considering that the extinct volcano last erupted in 1707). Cheiko is about to fall into one of the newly created chasms herself, before she's pulled to safety by Ashizawa in the contrived wrap-up.

The "Legend of the Dinosaurs" is dismal. Nothing about the picture works, not the main characters, not the storyline, not the dinosaurs—nothing. The film is so thoroughly contrived, inept, obvious, and boring, it is very difficult to sit through. Ashizawa is neither likeable nor interesting. He appears to want the dinosaur egg solely for its monetary value, though the film's script is so badly written that his motives, like practically everything else in the film, are never very clear. The picture's characters are so vaguely sketched (in the American edition anyway) that they barely seem to exist at all. Usually in cheap films of this type the major players are stereotypes painted in the broadest of strokes (dedicated scientist, oafish rival, love interest, etc.). They're obvious, but at least we know who they are and what they're after, and good actors, such as those found in Toho's stock company during its prime, were able to bring a great deal of charm and interest to their roles. We have no idea who Ashizawa is or just what his relationship to Cheiko is all about. The actors are colorless. They're less than ciphers.

The film has almost no story. Monsters in a lake, that's all. That's where the imagination of the film's producers seems to have ended. Elements found in other pictures of ths type—the ancient legend, the strange clues, the big appearance—all play a role here but are so badly integrated into the film's action as to take on an almost surreal quality. The film is, in many ways, like a dream; one action dissolves into another, without any particular rhyme or reason; ideas are introduced, then forgotten. We're told, for instance, that it has been snowing in Hokaido, even though it's summer. What does this mean? We'll never know, for the subject is never mentioned again. There's an ancient legend about a dragon living in the lake, but its relationship to the plesiosaur is as cryptic as everything else. And there are other questions left unanswered. How did the plesiosaur get enough to eat in such a small lake? (We're told the lake covers an area of only two miles.) Why did the pterodactyl egg take millions of years to hatch, and why did the creature wait so long to climb out? How can the egg, as described in the film, be both petrified *and* hatchable?

The lame and desperate attempt to recapture some of the excitement of *Jaws* fails miserably. The scene with the fake fin was a truly bad idea, only demonstrating how superior Steven Spielberg's film was, and is positively embarrassing. The dinosaurs are badly designed. They're semi-realistic anatomically, but they never seem alive; they're cartoony enough to suggest the Japanese giants of the sixties, but they have no personality. A full-size prop of the plesiosaur's head and neck was built, but the filmmakers must have been dissatisfied with the end result (it looks like a float in a parade). As in Bert I.

Gordon's *Empire of the Ants* (1977), whenever the creature makes an appearance, the director switches to shaky hand-held shots, an obvious effort to hide the monster's inarticulation. The pterodactyl is even worse. For its big battle with the plesiosaur, the prop bounces about on what would appear to be a single wire, making aeronautically preposterous maneuvers, suggesting a ball of yarn dangled before an ornery pussycat. 'Nuff said.

The War in Space *(1977)*

A tedious retread of both *Battle in Outer Space* (1959) and *Atragon* (1963), this dreadful Toho production has not a thing to recommend it. It's a tiresome rehash quickly produced to capitalize on the success of *Star Wars* (also 1977, though this awful feature beat Lucas' film to Japanese theaters), though the picture is more closely derived from earlier—and much better—Toho efforts.

It is autumn 1988. At the Japanese branch of the United Nations Space Bureau, UFO sightings come in from all over the world. At the same time, astronauts aboard the UN's orbiting space station, the *Terra*, report sighting an invading craft just as their communications go dead. Radio waves suggest the UFOs are coming from Venus. The alien ships, which look like incense censers, cause all manner of destruction (stock footage from *Submersion of Japan* and *The Last Days of Planet Earth*). The capital cities of the Earth are destroyed (more stock, this time from Toho's 16-year-old *The Last War*). Miyoshi (Kensaku Morita), a member of the UN team, visits esteemed Professor Takigawa (Ryo Ikebe), whose daughter, June (Yuko Asano?), is in love with Miyoshi but engaged to Miyoshi's co-worker, Murrei. Miyoshi asks Takigawa to complete an aborted space cruiser, the *Gohten*, to send against the invaders. Takigawa refuses. Just why the ship was never completed and why the scientist now refuses to complete it is never satisfactorily explained. Miyoshi leaves, and Takigawa is next visited by Dr. Schmidt (William Ross), who everyone thought had been killed while investigating the UFOs. Schmidt also urges Takigawa to complete the *Gohten*. "If you don't complete it with your own two hands," Schmidt warns, "the United Nations will!" Takigawa recognizes Schmidt as an alien imposter who apparently wants the ship's blueprints to prevent its completion (though his strategy of urging Takigawa to finish it is surely puzzling). Miyoshi returns suddenly, there's a struggle, and the alien commits suicide (by blowing himself up). Miyoshi discovers the green-faced imposter was wearing a latex mask of the dead scientist. The alien's visit is apparently enough to convince Takigawa to resume construction of the *Gohten*, while Commander Oshi (Akihiko Hirata) is chosen to lead Earth's defense. As Miyoshi and the UN team prepare the ship, Jimmy (David Perin), a former team member who had recently worked with NASA, parachutes into Japan to join the special crew. With Takigawa in command, the *Gohten* is launched and is soon attacked by several dozen UFOs, which are quickly annihilated by the Earth ship's superior firepower. The *Gohten* leaves Earth's orbit and heads toward the alien's base on Venus.

During the voyage, Jimmy receives a message that his entire family was killed when the UFOs attacked New York. He remembers (via flashbacks) happier days with the wife and kids, in a montage closely resembling a beer commercial ("It's Miller time..."). Meanwhile, Murrei asks Miyoshi to take care of his fiancée, June, if he is killed in the big battle on Venus. The crew encounters wreckage from the space station, apparently blown up by an alien ship. A member of the *Gohten*'s crew visits what's left of the space wheel (wearing a pressure suit obviously pattered after those worn in *2001: A Space Odyssey*) and finds the body of a fallen comrade, Mikasa. The body, brought aboard the *Gohten*, turns out to be one of the aliens, very much alive. The creature kidnaps June, whisking her away aboard a waiting UFO. Soon Takigawa receives a message from "the Supreme Commander of the Empire of Galaxies" that his daughter (who has inexplicably been dressed in a racy leather outfit by the aliens) will be killed unless he surrenders. Takigawa refuses, and the *Gohten* lands on Venus, several kilometers from the alien base. Using a shoebox-like tank, Miyoshi and a team of soldiers infiltrate the aliens' vessel, the *Daimakan*, which resembles a Portuguese galleon with big solar panel sails. Meanwhile, Murrei, Jimmy and a team of fighter pilots fend off attacking UFOs. Miyoshi sneaks aboard the *Daimakan* and rescues June, though the pair have to contend with a hairy and horned creature resembling Chewbacca from *Star Wars*, this beastie brandishing a gaudy battle axe. Murrei and Jimmy are killed during the battle, while Miyoshi and June return to the *Gohten*. The *Daimakan* and the *Gohten* engage in a rather boring mid-air joust before Takigawa hops aboard the ship's drill-like bow ("inspired" by the *Atragon*), which contains a bomb the scientist has been working on. "If you make a lot of them," Takigawa explains, "you can even blast the whole galaxy apart." The *Gohten*, minus its bow, departs, while the drill bit rams the *Daimakan*, killing the scientist and setting off a chain reaction that blows Venus and the evil invaders to smithereens.

The War in Space is a terrible film. As Greg Shoemaker points out in his Toho retrospective for the *Japanese Fantasy Film Journal*, the film "was to emulate *Star Wars*' blend of entertainment, action and spectacle...a point conceded by Tomoyuki Tanaka, executive producer at Toho. Yet, *The War in Space* looks like an old Toho [science fiction] picture with Japanese 1954 state-of-the-art effects, mediocre acting and score, unconvincing sets and a story right out of *Battle in Outer Space*." Just as that picture had a team of scientists searching and destroying an alien base on the moon, *The War in Space* finds a very similar team of astronauts doing the very same thing on Venus.

As in *Battle in Outer Space*, alien ships attack the major cities of Earth, and some of the stock footage even appears to be from that picture.

The War in Space also bears more than a passing resemblance to the much better *Atragon*. The *Gohten* looks a lot like Captain Shinguji's supersub, even to the point of having a drill as its bow. Like Shinguji, *Gohten*'s inventor, Professor Takigawa, first refuses to send the ship against the invaders. There's no reason for him to do so—it was probably scripted this way simply because *Atragon*'s inventor had done the same, and the writers didn't want to deviate from a proven story, even though as presented here the professor's actions don't make any sense. The picture's similarities to *Atragon* are many: the ship's departure from a debris-filled hangar, the kidnapping of the inventor's daughter and the destruction of the *Daimakan* are all shamelessly aped. The film's similarities to *Star Wars* are less apparent, probably because the filmmakers didn't seem to understand what made the American picture work in the first place. Besides the Chewbacca-inspired monster, the squadron of fighters— which fly through caves inspired by the *Death Star*'s "canyon" — comes closest to emulating (if badly) George Lucas' fantasy. However, Toei's 1978 film, *Message from Space*, is much more clearly a rip-off than *The War in Space* ever is. The picture's wholesale lifting of story ideas from earlier productions wouldn't be so bad if new twists on old clichés had been introduced, but they aren't. *The War in Space* is a half-hearted update, and that's not enough. While derivative itself, *Star Wars* rewrote a genre and made it seem new again.

Quoting Greg Shoemaker again, "Hardware had always been a staple of Toho's genre films, and they were generally criticised because of it. It took *Star Wars* to make it legitimate, at the same time rendering Japanese model construction and photography obsolete." Indeed, *Star Wars*' imperial destroyers and X-wings are to *The War in Space*'s Christmas ornament–like UFOs and Terran fighters what computers are to the abacus.

Worse still, the special effects department, under the supervision of Teruyoshi Nakano and falling ever further into mediocrity, relied more and more on stock footage. The movie attempts nothing less than the near-destruction of Earth, yet barely any new footage of this destruction was shot. The *Gohten* was nothing more than a redressed miniature of the *Alpha* from *Latitude Zero*, and other previously seen props and costumes were also cannibalized from other films. Miniatures constructed specifically for the film, such as the shoe box-like tank vehicle used on Venus, are inadequate and uninteresting.

Toshiaki Tsushima's music, like nearly everything else in the film, is very poor. The consistently inappropriate score overflows with harps, bleating horns and dated seventies rock 'n' roll. The costumes and art direction are especially unimaginative. For instance, the "Supreme Commander of the Empire of Galaxies" is inexplicably dressed like a Roman centurion, a costume apparently left over from a sword and sandal picture. The set design is similarly uninspired. The film is set in the future (which by now has become the past), though except for a mildly futuristic car and the various pieces of space hardware, everyone and everything is as locked in the seventies as pet rocks, *Saturday Night Fever* and Miyoshi's wing-tipped collar. Ryo Ikebe, himself one of the stars of *Battle in Outer Space*, returns to the genre after many years, but his stoic emoting adds little interest. William Ross, who co-produced *Terror Beneath the Sea* (1966) and *The Green Slime* (1968, in which he also appeared), has a small role as the bogus Dr. Schmidt. Akihiko Hirata's role as Earth's Defense commander is abruptly short, little more than an extended cameo. The rest of the cast is amateurish.

The War in Space was sold directly to American television, where it received little attention. Phil Hardy's *Science Fiction* said, "[Director Jun] Fukuda's effort remains a pale, though entertaining, secondhand version of the Lucas film rather than an enjoyable elaboration of the Japanese teleserials which are said to have partly inspired Lucas' film in the first place."

The Bermuda Depths *(1978)*

This Rankin-Bass–Tsuburaya Enterprises co-production is a real mishmash, its story centering around a giant prehistoric turtle and its eighteenth-century guardian, both of whom live in the Bermuda Triangle. Sorely lacking in even the most basic logic, the picture is far from satisfying and leaves too many questions unanswered.

Handsome but troubled Magnus Dens (Leigh McCloskey) returns home to Bermuda after years of psychological care and soul-searching following the mysterious death of his father. He joins a pair of old friends studying gigantism in marine life. Dr. Paulis (Burl Ives) was a colleague of Magnus' father, and his assistant, Eric (Carl Weathers), knows Magnus' family as well. Aware of the young man's tough breaks and mental fragility, they take him under their wing. Paulis and Eric seem to be on the verge of discovering a giant creature living in the Triangle. Unfortunately, none of their nets prove strong enough to capture the beast. Meanwhile, Magnus meets a young woman named Jennie Haniver (Connie Selleca). When he nearly drowns, she pulls him out of the water, saving his life. He recalls playing with her as a child, along with a turtle they helped raise from birth. Magnus had a crush on her even then, and he scratched their initials on the sea turtle's shell. Before his father's death, however, both she and the turtle disappeared into the sea. Now adults, the two fall in love again, though the woman remains a mystery. When Magnus speaks of the woman to Eric and Dr. Paulis, they don't believe him. Paulis explains that "Jennie Haniver" is a term used by islanders referring to phony sea monsters sold to tourists. Paulis worries that Magnus is still mentally ill and seeing things. However, Paulis' superstitious cleaning lady, Delia (Ruth Attaway), believes Magnus' story. She claims Jennie was an eighteenth-century woman aboard a doomed ship at sea. She gave her soul to some kind of sea devil in exchange for immortality. Though she remains beautiful, she's forced to live in the sea and, apparently, tend to the needs of this unseen benefactor. Naturally, Magnus scoffs at the tale. Jennie and Magnus visit his late father's deserted home, which was partially torn apart by some mysterious force. Dr. Paulis shows up looking for Magnus, and Jennie disappears. Magnus presses Dr. Paulis for details of his father's death. Paulis remains vague but finally admits that Magnus' father was eaten. By what or just how Dr. Paulis knows this is never explained.

Elsewhere, Eric examines huge flipper prints that are found on a nearby beach. The length of the tracks suggests a whale-sized beast. Paulis suggests that "these were creatures that could swallow two dinosaurs in one gulp." Paulis begins having doubts about taking the sea creature alive and prepares to return to the United States. Eric, on the other hand, is determined to get the animal — alive if possible, dead if necessary. He gets a silly-looking bazooka-like speargun nicknamed "The Horror." Eric and Magnus take their research ship out to sea once again. Paulis, learning of Eric's plans, cancels his flight and tries to contact the men from shore. At sea, something gets caught in the ship's net. Convinced it's a shark and not the elusive sea beast, Eric goes diving to scare it off. In the dark, murky water, he fires a regular-sized speargun at what turns out to be Jennie, though Eric is unable to see that it's her. Later, the sea creature, a giant *archelon*-like prehistoric turtle, is caught in the net, and Eric shoots it with The Horror. He and Magnus wait for the beast to tire before hauling it back to the mainland. That evening, Jennie climbs aboard the ship and asks Magnus to let the creature go. Vaguely, she explains that she had made it "a promise I regret forever." Paulis, unable to communicate with Eric's ship, hires a helicopter and goes out looking for the men. He and the pilot spot the giant turtle, which rises out of the water and smashes the helicopter, sending it crashing into the water and exploding upon impact. Magnus and Jennie, who apparently didn't hear the chopper's approach, look out to see the fiery blast. Eric rushes out, and Jennie's eyes begin to glow. Just then, the big turtle rises from the water once again, this time crushing the ship. Eric's leg is caught in The Horror's cables and, à la *Moby Dick*, he's dragged and drowned. That morning, Jennie manages to get the unconscious Magnus ashore and gives him one last kiss. Magnus recovers but is now mentally worse off than ever. He visits his parents' graves, and nearby we see a tombstone for Jennie, lost at sea more than two centuries earlier. Magnus declares, "I never want to be near the sea again — ëver," and drops a necklace Jennie made for him into the ocean. Underwater, we see the giant turtle swimming in the distance — with Magnus and Jennie's initials still carved on its back.

The Bermuda Depths is a mess. Although reasonably involving, the picture clearly has no idea what it's about. On one hand, the big turtle is supposed to be a survivor from the dinosaur age, while at other times, the creature is depicted as something altogether different. Delia, for instance, believes the creature is some kind of sea devil, or maybe the Devil himself. Obviously, no prehistoric animal could have granted Jennie immortality, or given her those glowing eyes. Just what exactly this creature is all about remains a mystery. Another problem is the flashbacks of young Magnus and Jennie watching the turtle egg hatch and Magnus carving their initials on it. If Jennie became immortal as an adult, what's she doing as a child here? Delia's dialogue hints that Jennie might appear to mortals as a child, but I don't buy that. More troublesome is the turtle's appearance. How could the creature grant her immortality if it wouldn't be born for another 150 years? Its birth (which presumably occurs sometime in the early sixties) would suggest that Eric and Dr. Paulis were wrong: it's not prehistoric at all, just a big turtle. And, by the way, who killed Magnus' father? *The Bermuda Depths* also places far too much emphasis on the relationship between Magnus and Jennie, which besides being needlessly confusing and frustrating, is acted out by two very bland actors.

Leigh McCloskey appeared in the short-lived teleseries "Executive Suite" and the Italian film *Inferno* (1980). There is little to be said for his acting. Connie Selleca (TV's "Flying High") is pretty but bland as Jennie and never looks anything like an eighteenth century maiden.

Burl Ives is wasted here, and I suspect his few interesting bits of business (e.g., barking at a blowfish) were thought up by the actor himself. His character's sudden and rather pointless death (while giving Tsuburaya's effects crew something to do) adds nothing to the film.

The special effects themselves are not impressive. The turtle monster is much more realistic than Daiei's Gamera, but because the film is more concerned with the relationship between Magnus and Jennie, we hardly get to see the creature. There are a number of bad shots of a miniature of Eric and Dr. Paulis' ship, which are crudely cut with the full-sized vessel.

Although released theatrically in Japan, *The Bermuda Depths* was sold in the United States as a television movie. Leonard Maltin, in *TV Movies*, gave the film a below average rating, appropriately calling the picture "crummy sci-fi."

Fugitive Alien *(1978)*

Yet another pseudo-feature culled from episodes of a Japanese television show, *Fugitive Alien* is somewhat more tolerable than other similarly unfortunate patchworks. The series it was based upon, Tsuburaya Enterprises' "Sutaurufu" ("Starwolf") had a shorter run than most fantastic teleseries produced in Japan at this time and was thus easier to edit down to an acceptable running time. In fact, *Fugitive Alien* and its direct "sequel," *Star Force: Fugitive Alien II*, seem to constitute, in essence, the entire series. *Fugitive Alien* is more coherent and character-driven than *Time of the Apes* or *Mighty Jack*, but like those films, it would have been better served if simply released in the original format, series television. Taken in half-hour chunks, the picture is reasonably paced and has a few decent characters, but as a 102-minute "movie," *Fugitive Alien* appears cheap and tiresome.

Sometime in the future, humanoid raiders from Valnastar launch an attack on the Earth. One of their soldiers, Ken (Tatsuya Azuma), enjoys the excitement of the battle until he spots a little boy, also coincidentally named Ken, followed by the boy's frantic mother, fleeing in terror. Taken aback at the thought of killing his namesake, Ken is unable to shoot the mother and child. When Ken's partner attempts to do so, Ken grabs him, and in the scuffle, Ken accidentally shoots his partner dead. This is witnessed by other Valna raiders (known as Starwolf warriors), who pursue the "traitor." Ken steals one of their spaceships, which is quickly pursued by other fighters. After a brief aerial battle, where everyone zooms between (and sometimes crash into) glassy skyscrapers, Ken escapes to another part of the galaxy. However, his ship is met by more fighters which severely disable it, and Ken is forced to abandon ship. Meanwhile, aboard the Earth ship *Bakkus III*, Captain Joe (Joe Shishido?), a middle-aged, hard-drinking member of Space Command, discusses his impending retirement with the crew. "It's ridiculous to go flying around the stars at my age," he says. The crew—pilot Rocky, computer expert Tami, navigator Dan, and promising young recruit Billy—spot Ken floating in space and decide to pick him up. Just as he's brought aboard, the crew also learn of Valnastar's invasion of Earth. More enemy ships surround the *Bakkus III*, but Ken grabs the controls and outmaneuvers the villain's vessels through a congested asteroid belt. The *Bakkus III* returns to Earth, where Space Command forces have temporarily driven back the intruders. Ken is taken to an infirmary, but, fearing what might happen once his identity is discovered, the wanted alien heads for the hills. Meanwhile, Captain Joe learns that his only daughter has died in the raid, and his wife expires soon thereafter. Ken sneaks aboard the *Bakkus III*, hoping to steal her, but his plans are thwarted by the sudden appearance of Captain Joe. Ken explains his plight, which the fatherly Joe instantly believes. "Ken, you did the right thing," he says. Having changed his mind about retiring, Joe invites Ken to join Space Command, promising to keep his true identity a secret. His options limited, Ken agrees. Rocky is suspicious about Ken, however, rightly believing him to be from Valnastar. Rocky attacks Ken with a forklift in the *Bakkus*' hangar. Only Ken's super strength (ten times that of mortal men) prevents him from getting skewered. Joe intercedes and orders Rocky to cool it.

Back on Valanastar, the evil Lord Halcon, a bald, pasty-faced baddie with dark eye shadow and cape, meets with Ken's former sweetheart (and sister to Ken's dead partner), Rita. In keeping with Valnastaran law, Rita must avenge her brother's death by killing Ken. Halcon orders her to bring back her ex-lover's head. Moving into a new episode, Captain Joe meets with a Space Command official (Akihiko Hirata), who orders Joe and his crew to Karrara (?), a mineral-rich planet besieged by both Valnastar raiders and aliens from Sissar. Earth has agreed to assist the wealthy planet. Our band of heroes land on Karrara and are met by none-too-friendly officials who treat their new allies like dirt. Captain Joe and Rocky are driven to a meeting (aboard a singularly Earth-like jeep) with the Karrarian ruler; everyone else is ordered to stay aboard the ship. Ken disobeys Captain Joe's orders, however, and explores the Karrarian capitol, which looks more Middle Eastern than other-worldly. In a bar, Ken accidentally kills (what, again?) an unruly patron bent on fighting the ex–Starwolf. Ken is arrested and charged with murder, which doesn't exactly help relations with the Karrarians. The ruler asks Joe's permission to execute Ken. "Not at all, suit yourself," Joe says matter-of-factly. Joe returns to his ship, while Ken languishes in a Karrarian prison awaiting execution. Joe contacts Ken via a hidden radio, alerting the ex–Starwolf to buttons on his new Space Command jacket which contain mini-nuclear grenades. Ken uses these to escape, taking with him Yurulin, a Sissarian colonel. The two men are hotly pursued by Karrarian guards, and Yurulin is wounded. Rita, who learned of Ken's capture and escape over Karrarian airways, lands her spaceship nearby. She tells Ken that he is not a legitimate Valnastaran, but rather an earthling, the son of missionaries (this doesn't explain his super strength, however). Rita prepares to shoot Ken, but just can't bring herself to commit the deed. Karrarian guards turn up, and Rita, caught in the crossfire, is fatally shot. Thinking Ken has shot her instead, Rita dies believing her ex-lover to be a traitor. Ken and Colonel Yurulin make their way to the *Bakkus III*, as a title card abruptly informs us the story is "To Be Continued."

Fugitive Alien starts reasonably well, with poor Ken deemed a traitor by the Valnastarans, while uncomfortably trying to hide his identity on Earth. He can't go back to Valnastar, and in light of the deadly raid, he's not in Earth's good graces, either. Even quirky Captain Joe dislikes Ken at first; he blames Ken for the death of his wife and daughter. When the action shifts to Karrara, however, the picture becomes a confusing bore. The Karrarians are supposed to be allies—they requested the Earth's assistance, after all—yet they act like ungrateful bullies. Captain Joe apparently wants Colonel Yurulin's assistance in the fight against the Valnastarans and Sissarians, but the Karrarian lord refuses to even let Joe speak to him. Why? And why doesn't Ken obey Joe's orders to stay aboard the ship? True, it is hinted that Ken left Joe's ship because he's irresistibly drawn to danger and excitement, but this makes Ken look foolish instead of heroic. He's downright manic when he leaves the *Bakkus III*, woo-wooing across the countryside like Daffy Duck. Still, Joe and Ken are a bit more interesting as central characters than those found in similarly Americanized Sandy Frank specials. Ken's encounter with the other Ken is a neat twist, as is his apparent lust for killing up to that point.

With his round face and ever-present flask of booze, Captain Joe, despite the utterly ridiculous name, is one of the more interesting characters to turn up in films of this type; his sort of role is usually filled by the square-jawed, no-nonsense military type. Joe's relationship with Ken is also unusual. Their uneasy alliance isn't quite a friendship; Joe threatens to expose Ken and turn him over to Space Command if he misbehaves ("You'll only continue to live as long as I shut up [sic!]," he says) but also seems to want to help the alien fugitive ("You've got a good chance of turning into a *man*, not just a Starwolf!").

The bulk of *Figutive Alien* is mindless escapist action, however, working on a level akin to American chapterplays of the thirties and forties, though the distinctly Middle Eastern look of Karrara might reflect certain Japanese attitudes about that region of the world (or an American perspective on Kuwait during the Gulf War). The film seems partly inspired by "The Six Million Dollar Man," as Ken, for no particular reason, is able to jump high into the air, bend metal bars, etc., just like Lee Majors. The scene where Ken, aboard the stolen fighter, flies between skyscrapers hotly pursued by Valnastar raiders was obviously inspired by *Star Wars*' trench chase finale; even Ken's ship looks like Luke Skywalker's X-wing.

The special effects are plentiful but cheap and generally unacceptable. There are numerous shots of zooming spacecraft, swirling asteroids, and the like, but the optical work is poor and almost always jittery. The ship Ken steals at the beginning is transparent most of the time, and later, when the *Bakkus III* flies behind the Earth, the scale is all wrong, making the ship look as big as Brazil. Like all filmed TV shows in Japan, "Starwolf" was shot in 16mm, and most of the optical effects were probably done in-camera. Of course, the images are meant to be visually appealing, not realistic per se, but they're also distractingly cheap, especially for what's being fobbed off to American audiences as a legitimate feature.

The costumes are poor. The crew of the *Bakkus III* wear shimmery orange and white jackets that look more like raincoats than spacesuits. But the most bizarre concept, hands down, is the design of the helmets worn by the Starwolf raiders. Inexplicably, each helmet comes with its own curly blond wig, giving the opening raid a surreal, Ed Woodian flavor.

The dubbing is awful. It's also slipshod. For instance, when Karrarian officials come aboard the *Bakkus III*, one of Rocky's lines is dubbed over Joe's lip movements. The English-language dialogue is very awkward, probably a direct translation from the Japanese, and often makes little sense. The appearance of genre veteran Akihiko Hirata is welcome, but his one scene is the worst dubbed in the film and is unintentionally hilarious. If nothing else, Hirata's appearance demonstrates the wide range in dubbing quality over the years; the looping of the actor here makes the voice work in *The Mysterians* appear greatly respectful, even artful by comparison.

Fugitive Alien deserves some credit. Its script is better than those of *The War in Space* and *Message from Space*, and those were legitimate movies. It's much more lively than "Battlestar Galactica," the expensive but dreadful science fiction teleseries that debuted in the United States that same year. When seen in small doses and viewed with the knowledge of its television roots, *Fugitive Alien* is reasonably entertaining. But as a feature, it is poor.

Message from Space *(1978)*

The down side of the phenomenal success of George Lucas' *Star Wars* (1977) was the explosion of cheap, tacky imitations that flooded the market in the years that followed. Lucas freely admitted Japanese films, particularly the work of Akira Kurosawa (the 1958 film *The Hidden Fortress* in particular), and perhaps even Japanese fantastic television helped inspire his nostalgic space opera. From the lively swordplay to the samurai-like "stormtroopers," *Star Wars* looked Japanese. Inspired, in turn, by Lucas' film, the Japanese tried to duplicate its success with this energetic but garish and derivative, if distinctly Japanese, imitation.

The peaceful planet of Jillucia has been brutally conquered by the evil Gavanas, who have turned the tiny world into a desert. Desperately wanting to reclaim their planet, Princess Emeralida (Sue Shiomi) releases eight glowing, holy seeds (which look like walnuts) into the air. These seeds are to find eight chosen warriors who will save her people from the dreaded steel-skinned Gavanas. Emeralida and her burly aide, Urocco (Makoto Sato), hop aboard a Karel Zeman–like combo spaceship–Spanish galleon (complete with sails) and follow the seeds through deep space to see where they land. Two of the chosen turn out to be sprightly teenage "roughriders" Shiro (Hiroyuki Sanada) and Aaron (Philip Casnoff), who both dress like Evel Knievel and take delight in playing "chicken" with the local space patrol officers. The teens fly their small spaceships nose-first toward planets and meteorites, pulling up at the last minute. Shiro and Aaron are quickly joined by rich but ultra-spunky Meia (rhymes with...?) and soon thereafter by hyperactive Jack (Masazumi Okabe), who wears a straw hat and loud sports jacket and looks and acts like a sleazy, cheesy nightclub entertainer. Back on Earth, General Garuda (Vic Morrow) takes heat for giving his deactivated robot, Beba 1, a burial in space, launching an expensive, government-owned rocket in the process. Garuda, dressed like a renegade member of Earth, Wind & Fire, retires to a *Star Wars*–inspired cantina with

Beba's replacement, tiny Beba 2 (Isamu Shimuzu). In his martini, Garuda finds one of those glowing walnuts. Shiro, Aaron and Meia walk in space (bare-fisted and without suits), looking for "space fireflies." They spot the Jillucian ship and find Emeralida and Urocco, who are asleep for no reason in particular. Just then, a Gavanian ship enters the quadrant, and everyone makes a hasty getaway. Emeralida explains the Jillucian plight to Shiro, Aaron, Meia and Jack, as well as General Garuda, but the Earthlings consider the fight to be hopeless and refuse to help. Emeralida is kidnapped by the Gavanas, while plucky Meia has a change of heart and races her spaceship toward Jillucia. Shiro, Jack and Aaron (the latter by now in love with the princess) have bad dreams, and soon they too are on their way. The Gavanian ruler of Jillucia, Rockseia XII (Mikio Narita), a Darth Vader wannabe with a silver face and samurai armor, picks the rich, green Earth as his next conquest. Via huge rockets on the planet's surface, Jillucia moves through the solar system toward our planet. Earth's Federation of Nations launches an attack on the Gavanas, but is horribly defeated. The Gavanas, in turn, give Earth three days to surrender. (It's interesting how intended conquerers always give their opponents plenty of time to think it over).

Elsewhere, the four teens latch Aaron and Shiro's tiny fighters onto Meia's larger ship. Cowardly Jack is kidnapped by the Gavanas, while the others are met by Prince Hans (Shinichi "Sonny" Chiba), who was overthrown by Rockseia. Earth Chairman Noguchi (Tetsuro Tamba) goes to General Garuda, pleading for his help. Inspired by the glowing walnut in his drink, Garuda agrees. Acting as an envoy in the Earth-Gavana negotiations, Garuda, now dressed liked the Scarlet Pimpernel, tries to buy the Earth more time to build a defense. Rockseia anticipates this but lets Jack and the general go free. Everyone heads for a remote section of Jillucia, where six of the chosen ones prepare an air attack on the Gavanas' reactor furnace. Although blowing up the reactor will mean the destruction of Jillucia, its people prefer that to the Gavanas' continued domination. Meanwhile, Beba 2 (who talks just like Tony Randall in *Seven Faces of Dr. Lao*) is overjoyed when he finds one of the holy seeds, making him the seventh of Jillucia's saviors. Before the attack can begin, however, the entire band is captured by a Gavanian ship. They're taken before a large, projected image of Rockseia, and the silvery dictator gleefully informs the band that one member has betrayed them. It turns out to be Urocco, who was opposed to the Jillucians' sacrifice of their world. Rockseia orders Urocco to execute the magnificent seven, but Urocco has a change of heart and pointlessly shoots at the projected image of Rockseia instead. A huge battle erupts, with everyone escaping save Urocco, who dies just before finding a holy seed — he is the eighth chosen one. Prince Hans corners the real Rockseia and challenges him to a duel. Hans wins easily, stabbing the evil dictator in the forehead. Meia, Shiro and Aaron fly their ships to the Gavanian base. Shiro and Aaron's ships split off from Meia's and fly through a Death Star–inspired chasm and blow up the reactor. The planet begins to rip apart, and everyone climbs aboard the space galleon. The Gavanas launch one final, desperate assault, but Meia, Shiro and Aaron, now back in Meia's mother ship, send the entire craft hurling at the Gavanian base, ejecting to safety at the last second. The base explodes, along with the rest of the planet. Free from the Gavanas' rule, the surviving Jillucians are invited to live out their days on Earth, but they politely refuse, preferring instead to find a new world of their own. Meia, Aaron, Shiro and Jack, and even General Garuda and Beba 2 decide to join them.

If imitation is indeed the sincerest form of flattery, the men and women behind *Star Wars* should feel mighty flattered. Wholesale rip-offs, from the cuddly little robot to the feisty heroine named Meia, abound. The film's holy seed musical motif is perhaps the most audacious example, an almost note-for-note copy of John Williams' "Princess Leia" theme from *Star Wars*. When I first saw ads for the film on television, I wondered how the producers had acquired the rights to Williams' score. (They hadn't.) Shiro and Aaron's flight through the tunnel leading to the reactor was obviously inspired by the run fighter pilots made over the surface of the *Death Star*. Interestingly, *Return of the Jedi*, made five years after *Message from Space*, features a sequence almost identical to this one. Of course, the picture's basic storyline borrows heavily from *The Seven Samurai* and *The Magnificent Seven*. Roger Corman's *Battle Beyond the Stars* (1980) also had a similar storyline (and Robert Vaughn, one of the Magnificent Seven himself), but was just as cheesy.

Message from Space cost $5-6 million (one-half *Star Wars*' budget), making it the most expensive Japanese film to that time. Typical of non-Hollywood productions, the money shows on the screen. There are plenty of special effects, impressively large sets and elaborate costumes. It's as gaudy as costume jewelry, but it's there on the screen. What separates a film like *Star Wars* from *Message from Space* is the former's timelessness. Perhaps less apparent in 1977 than it is today, *Message from Space* is very much a product of its time. The costumes, makeup and much of the incidental disco-style score are very dated, even embarrassing. *Star Wars* will probably seem fresh fifty years from now. *Message from Space* was dated almost before it was released. The special effects, clearly meant to be the picture's big attraction, aren't really any more sophisticated than they were when director Kinji Fukasaku made *The Green Slime* ten years earlier. Whereas *Star Wars* revolutionized the use of traveling mattes, computer-controlled cameras and the blue screen process, here's *Message from Space*, still using miniature rocketships dangling from piano wire. Admittedly, they are *good-looking* rocketships on wires (save for the awful Spanish galleon) and manipulated as well as might be expected, but they're simply no match for those found in the film its producers so desperately wanted to compete with. Also spoiling the fun are the four teenagers—especially Meia—and their relentless spunkiness. Their constant "thumbs up" and cries of "Aw, right!" and "Hey, lookin' good!" quickly become tiresome.

Variety's "Robe" said the Japanese "have brought forth an illegitimate baby that is so good it will not shame its unacknowledged parent. The special effects are spectacular, and the action is everything one could wish." *Science Fiction*, whose team of reviewers disliked *Star Wars*, calling it "shallow," "naive" and "a self-consciously manufactured fairy tale," liked *Message from Space*: "A superior space opera-fantasy picture." "Any resemblance between... *Message from Space* and *Star Wars* is purely intentional," noted the *Los Angeles Times*' Kevin Thomas. "The largely adult audience that watched *Message from Space* at the first show Wednesday... laughed it off the screen, but small children will probably be entertained by it — if they can figure out what's going on." The Washington *Star*'s Tom Dowling: "*Message from Space* even permits 'Battlestar Galactica' to make an American hold his head up high with pride." "The fallout from *Star Wars* space garbage continues to litter [the] motion picture screen," complained Michael Blowen of the *Boston Globe*. "The robot isn't as funny as R2D2, the villains couldn't hold a laser beam to the original Darth [Vader], and the effects aren't special. The plot is so diffuse that even Buckminster Fuller couldn't decipher it."

Star Force: Fugitive Alien II *(1978)*

Picking up as abruptly as its predecessor, *Fugitive Alien* (q.v.), left off, *Star Force* begins with the crew of the *Bakkus III* hotly pursued by Karrarian fighters. You'll remember ex–Starwolf Ken (Tatsuya Azuma), the fugitive alien, and a Sissarian, Colonel Yurulin, had escaped from a Karrarian prison, much to the annoyance of that planet's vaguely Middle Eastern leaders. Yurulin, whose loyalties are confused (to say the least), complicates matters by hijacking the *Bakkus III* away from fatherly Captain Joe (Joe Shishido?), pilot Rocky, navigator Dan, computer expert Tami and new recruit Billy. Fortunately, Ken takes charge, and our heroes escape by darting through a black hole. Yurulin is locked up. On the other side of the black hole (which everyone refers to as the "white hole"), Yurulin and the crew come down with an illness akin to acute back pain. Yurulin tells Ken this is due to the ship's proximity to a dying star; with Yurulin's help, Ken guides the ship safely away. As the star explodes (to Bach's *Toccata and Fugue in D Minor*), Captain Joe nods approvingly at the two heroes. Ken's actions also win Rocky over; he tried to kill Ken in the previous film. The *Bakkus III* reaches the planet Sissar, Yurulin's home. Joe's orders are to locate and destroy a none-too-secret planet-destroying weapon now threatening the universe. Over the ship's radio, Yurulin learns he's been kicked out of the army;

he gave the Karrarians information about the weapon (or something) while in their prison. The Space Command ship is attacked by Sissarian fighters, which resemble the friendly, bright and colorful UFOs from *Close Encounters of the Third Kind*. Ken and the others fight off Sissarian ships in a sequence shamelessly patterned after the *Millennium Falcon*'s battle with TIE fighters near the end of *Star Wars*. The *Bakkus III* makes a hasty retreat to the "Devil's Desert," crash landing in some dunes. With the ship covered with hot sand, no one, not even super-strong Ken, is able to open the top hatch. Things look hopeless, and everyone complains. "I said it was the *Devil*'s Desert!" Yurulin says indignantly. He tells everyone to sit tight, insisting that an Old Faithful–like sandstorm will unearth the spaceship in no time. And so it does. Captain Joe readies his crew for the dangerous mission. Rocky warns Joe not to go—the captain is too old for the treacherous journey through the desert, he says. When Joe insists on going, Rocky shoots him with a "knock-out dart." Ken, Rocky, Dan, and Billy disguise themselves as Sissarian soldiers, with Yurulian, still in uniform, leading the way. The band make their way to the secret base, and in an amusing bit, Ken tosses everyone over a tall fence like rag dolls. Our heroes reach the planet-destroying weapon and carefully plant a time bomb. Yurulin has a last-minute change of heart upon hearing the Sissarian national anthem ("My country needs me!" he cries) and tries to deactivate the bomb. A Sissarian guard quite understandably mistakes him for a lunatic and shoots him dead. The bomb goes off and everyone makes it back to the ship.

Although it's nearly one half-hour shorter than its predecessor, *Star Force: Fugitive Alien II* is considerably duller. The previous entry had slightly more character development than most features (pseudo or otherwise) from this period. This one's just an action film. Captain Joe, whose interestingly off-key character was the best thing about *Fugitive Alien*, is in the background here, along with ex–Starwolf Ken's identity crisis. The first film implied some kind of eventual resolution regarding Ken's roots, but the Valnastarans are nowhere to be found here. The other characters are colorless, with the exception of Colonel Yurulin, whose schizophrenic loyalties make little sense. *Fugitive Alien* and its sequel were lifted from the same TV program, and the technical credits are on the same level: competent for Japanese television, inadequate for a feature. The visuals involving the black hole and exploding star are inventive but cheap. The crash landing of the *Bakkus III* on Sissar is a little more elaborate, about average for a Japanese theatrical feature of this sort from this period.

One amusing note: Whenever the crew looks at a television monitor, the film cuts to a real-life but totally unrelated English-language computer program. Most Japanese audiences wouldn't have given these shots a second thought, but they leave American viewers nonplussed. For instance, when Lieutenant Tami looks at her monitor and reports "There's an unidentified spacecraft approaching," we see, in English, what appears to be an order for

$50 worth of goods from a company in Blue Bell, Pennsylvania. The folks behind the Americanization could've simply edited these shots out for all the difference it would've made, but they probably didn't care.

Star Force: Fugitive Alien II is mediocre, though marginally better than most legitimate fantastic features produced in Japan at this time. *Fugitive Alien* is frequently shown on television, but for some reason its sequel rarely follows it. As abruptly and inconclusively as *Fugitive Alien* ends, television programmers probably feel few who have managed to sit through the first film are aching to know what became of Ken, Captain Joe and the rest of the crew of the *Bakkus III*. They're probably right.

Swords of the Space Ark *(1979)*

"Uchu-kara no messeji: ginga taisen" ("Message from Space: Galactic Battle") was a Toei television show loosely based on that studio's successful theatrical feature *Message from Space* (1978). Toei must have worked fast, for the TV show premiered in early July, just as the theatrical feature was being released to theaters. The program ran for 27 episodes through early 1979; New Hope Entertainment boiled the series down to feature length for American consumption. As such, *Swords of the Space Ark* has nothing new to offer. It's not significantly worse than the feature on which it was based; on the other hand, it isn't any better, either.

It is the year 2090. In the fifteenth solar system, aboard a nondescript space freighter, young Hiato (Hiroyuki Sanada), a student at Space Pilot's School on Welsa, hurries home to the planet Kendal, where his father, a high-ranking government official, anxiously awaits his son's arrival. In the cockpit, Drew, the colorless pilot, and his partner, a cigar-smoking, cape-wearing orangutan, Barin, look forward to landing. "We can be back in time for happy hour," the amiable ape says (he talks just like Phil Harris). "Love those banana daiquiris! Heh heh heh." The ape's plans are interrupted, however, when a Gavanas ship, under the command of unseen Emperor Rockseia (despite the name, this is a different character from the film), attacks a Kendal Defense Corps vessel. After destroying the Kendal ship, the invading Gavanas quickly (much too quickly, in fact) conquer the peaceful world. Hiato convinces Drew and Barin to land near the village of Shima, where his father owns Kendal's sole interplanetary radio. Meanwhile, Chief Kogar, leader of the invasion force and clad in a red and black samurai-like uniform, intercepts a distress signal sent by Hiato's father to the Earth asking for help. Kogar orders the entire village of Shima destroyed. Hiato quickly reaches his family's modest home but is too late. His mother and sister have already been murdered, and his father lies fatally stabbed. In his dying breath, Hiato's father tells his son to "look for the lady of the ark." Hiato, Drew and Barin are soon back in outer space, but the freighter is just as quickly attacked by Gavanian fighters (attractive little things that look like six-branch candelabras flying on their sides). Things look hopeless, and Hiato orders Drew and Barin into tiny escape pods. Hiato stays behind, and the ship is blown to smithereens. But Hiato is not dead. He awakens to find himself aboard a new ship, the *Liberty,* and in the presence of the blond-haired, fairy-like Sophia. Impressed by his bravery and goodness, Sophia gives Hiato the *Liberty* to use in the fight against the Gavanas. She also tells him that Rockseia can only be killed with "the heart of. . . three planets": Welsa, Kendal and Kylon. She departs aboard a white Spanish galleon spaceship like the one in *Message from Space.* On Welsa, Hiato is reunited with Barin and Drew.

Elsewhere, Rockseia diverts a comet, "Satan," from its orbit to a collision course with Welsa. The emperor's Majin-like ship (it looks like a giant skull-encrusted statue with rockets where its feet should be) blasts off. Hiato, Barin and Drew, battling Gavanian fighters out in space, are unable to prevent the disaster; Satan and Welsa collide, and there is a tremendous explosion. Welsa is obliterated. However, Sophia, the lady of the ark, has come through again. She rescued the people of Welsa at the last minute by taking them aboard her white ship ("I'll be a monkey's uncle," says Barin). A Welsian princess gives Hiato the "heart of the planet," a green, egg-shaped gem. Hiato, Barin and Drew move on to Kylon, where they locate the second gem at the Temple of Fire. Looking into the second gem, they learn that the third jewel is back on Kendal, hidden inside a gold deity near Inca Island. Eventually, Rockseia captures the first two gems and orders Kogar to search for the third. Hiato is captured and taken before Rockseia who, as it turns out, happens to be Sophia's evil twin sister. Sophia suddenly appears to explain that Rockseia was "born with the Devil's heart beating within her breast." Sophia magically transports Hiato to safety. Kogar finds the third gem and takes it to Rockseia. As he is about to hand it to her, however, Kogar (surprise!) grabs the other two jewels from Rockseia instead, leaving the empress helpless against Kogar's triumvirate of stones. Being evil, however, the villain is unable to activate the gems' powers and mulls this over back on Kendal. Hiato, Barin and Drew find him there, and after a singularly dull battle (Kogar starts a very phony-looking avalanche, shoots flames from his fingertips, etc.), Kogar blows himself up. The gems survive the blast, however, and the trio roar back out into space to put them to good use. Sophia informs the trio that Rockseia can be destroyed by arranging the gems in a triangle around the evil empress. They do so, but nothing happens. Sophia then reveals that she, too, must be within the triangle for the gems to work. Sophia must die to save the universe. Rockseia's and Sophia's ships are blown to bits. Back on Kendal, Sophia's sacrifice is solemnly remembered.

Swords of the Space Ark is more of the same: space apes, cape-wearing villains, a beautiful princess, powerful gems. Like the *Fugitive Alien* films, the production values are acceptable for a television show but not a feature. And like virtually every Japanese teleseries and feature with fantastic elements from this period, *Swords of the Space Ark* was filmed in the hand-held, zoom-crazy style which had become a cliché in Asian filmmaking by this time and only accentuated the picture's cheapness and lack of originality. Like nearly every outer space adventure produced in Japan during this period, *Swords of the Space Ark* is extremely superficial. It's all frosting. The script is on the most basic level imaginable, while the art department, rather than the script or the actors, fleshes out what little identity the picture has. The film holds no suspense and few surprises. Because Sophia has seemingly limitless powers, no one ever seems to be in any danger. She effortlessly rescues Hiato from Rockseia and saves the entire population of Welsa before it's destroyed by the runaway comet. This latter concept is especially hard to take; how could she fit the entire planet's population aboard her tiny ship?

Events unfold at a furious pace in the Americanization. The Gavanas conquest of Kendal lasts all of two minutes. Characters move from one planet to another in seconds. A robot (Beba III?) suddenly turns up in a cockpit of the *Liberty*, but no one has time to even refer to it. The English-language adaptation pointlessly replaced the original music with a new but thoroughly unimpressive score. At least the people behind the Americanization admitted (in the end credits) this was adapted from a TV show. *Swords of the Space Ark* turned up briefly on the Family Channel (then called CBN, the Christian Broadcasting Network) in the mid–1980s but has all but disappeared since. It is not a great loss.

The Eighties and Beyond

Gamera Super Monster *(1980)*

Daiei's fantastic film output hit the gutter with this abysmal production. It's a Gamera movie without Gamera; the big turtle's appearance consists almost entirely of stock footage from six of the seven previous entries. Of course, Daiei (and Toho for that matter) had liberally borrowed clips from earlier glories during the late sixties and especially the lean seventies. But here the practice is taken to its ultimate degree. It's more akin to Columbia's shameless policy throughout the fifties to release "new" two-reelers built almost entirely around previously seen footage, or Blake Edwards' attempt to create a new Pink Panther movie using outtakes of the late Peter Sellers from earlier films (in *Trail of the Pink Panther*, 1982). Daiei would have been better off releasing a compilation film, but they seem to have thought they could pull one off on the audience. It didn't work. The integration of the old clips with the new material is sloppily done. Stock footage of Gamera is matted into a couple of shots, but for the most part he appears woefully detached from the picture's new material.

A huge triangular spaceship from the planet Zanon ("inspired" by the similarly shaped Star Destroyer seen at the beginning of *Star Wars*), has been assigned to attack Earth. Sensing trouble, Kilara (Mach Fumiake), Marsha (Yaeko Kojima), and Mitan (Yoko Komatsu), the three sole survivors from the "peaceful star" M88, spring into action. Abandoning their alter-egos as pet shop owner, teacher and Mazda car saleswoman, they climb aboard Kilara's van, actually a sophisticated flying craft, and transform themselves into superheroes garbed in white tights, red boots and gloves, and requisite cape. The ship's captain, sounding like a surly Cary Grant, warns the women not to interfere. When the trio decide to help the Earth, the captain sends the sexy but evil alien Gilage (Keiko Kudo) to bump them off. We next meet young Keiichi (Koichi Maeda), an obsessive Gamera fan, practicing (of all things) "Camptown Races" on his mother's electric organ. He visits Kilara's pet shop, where she gives the boy a turtle free of charge. Keiichi enjoys the woman's friendliness, but notes "You sound like a space woman." Smart boy, that Keiichi. Meanwhile the Earth is "visited by a chain of major disasters." Beginning the steady stream of stock footage, Gaos from *Return of the Giant Monsters* appears, slicing a helicopter in two and destroying several jets. Keiichi believes Gamera could save everyone and even writes a song, "The Gamera March," in honor of the prehistoric turtle. Keiichi's mother (Toshie Takada) thinks the boy should set his own turtle free, which he does. Somewhat despondent over the loss of his new friend, Keiichi visits Kilara, Marsha and Mitan, where he reprises his "Gamera March" on *their* organ (actually a souped-up master control panel the alien women use). Just then, Gamera shows up to do battle with Gaos. In a curious twist from past films, it's implied that this creature was formerly Keiichi's pet turtle and that Gamera appeared out of the boy's love for his pet, or something. And as in *Godzilla's Revenge, Gamera vs. Zigra* and other tyke-oriented Japanese fantasy films, it's implied that all this hoopla is merely the product of Keiichi's imagination. Gaos' attack goes unreported in the newspapers, for instance, and Keiichi's mother keeps telling her son to "stop talking nonsense." However, this aspect of the film is in no way consistent, so the intent of the screenwriters remains peculiarly enigmatic. Gamera defeats Gaos, so the evil aliens send the shark-like Zigra to combat the big reptile. Gilage befriends Keiichi and instantly transports them both to the beach to watch the battle. The impressed Keiichi rightly guesses that she, too, is from outer space. After Gamera wins his bout with the Zigra, Gilage offers to take Keiichi to Gamera (she actually plans on kidnapping him). Surprisingly, Keiichi isn't too fond of Gilage's transporting ability: "It makes me feel sick," Keiichi complaints. "Besides, it's much easier to go by train." When Gilage pulls on Keiichi's arm, he becomes suspicious. "You're a *bad* spacewoman! You don't even look happy when Gamera wins each time!" Keiichi flees, while Kilara, watching these latest events from her control monitor, rescues the boy. Kilara shows Keiichi her magical van and her home, a small box which resembles a cat carrier. She shrinks to about a foot in height and climbs inside the modest abode.

The monster parade continues with the arrival of Viras (from *Destroy All Planets*) soon followed by Jiger (*Gamera vs. Monster X*), neither of whom lasts very long against Keiichi's super monster. Meanwhile, Gilage blows up Kilara's van, but the trio of spacewomen survive; the box, Kilara tells Keiichi, was protected by "invisible energy." Gilage's failure with both Gamera and the spacewomen does not sit well with the Zanon Captain. He threatens to execute her following each monster's defeat, but each time she convinces him to give her one last chance (this becomes increasingly comical, something I doubt was intentional). She suggests placing a (drably named) "control machine" on Gamera's neck, which the Zanon obligingly beams down. "Go and destroy the Earth!" Gilage commands. This is followed by footage from *War of the Monsters*, with Gamera himself attacking the populace and destroying a dam. (This footage had already been used extensively before in *Destroy All Planets*.) In a bit apparently omitted from the American edition of that film, Gamera's giant feet stomp past a comparatively tiny poster of Godzilla. Kilara flies to the top of Gamera's neck and the control device. Her presence is detected by the Zanon ship, which stupidly fires at her, misses, and knocks out the control machine instead. Gilage attacks Kilara, but she only succeeds in shooting herself in the leg. Later, Keiichi brings the injured space woman home to mother, where the boy expresses his desire that Gilage become his sister. Gilage is touched but worried that when her boss finds out she screwed up again, she'll be executed. Meanwhile, Gamera is challenged by Guiron of *Attack of the Monsters* fame. But wait, you say, that film's monster scenes take place on another planet. "This is the planet where the monsters are held, ready to be sent to the attack," the narrator explains. After dispatching Guiron, and following a boring bout with Barugon (more *War of the Monsters* stock), Gamera eyes the spaceship-train from the animated feature *Galaxy Express 999*. What it's doing here is anyone's guess. Gilage learns the powerful Zanon captain prepares to attack the Earth itself; even the trio of spacewomen are powerless to stop him. (Why did he wait until now to attack?) In an ultimately pointless bit of self-sacrifice, Gilage radios the ship and gives her own coordinates as the location of the superwomen. The ship's ray kills Gilage. Gamera and the Zanon ship commence a game of space "chicken." They collide, and there is a huge explosion. Kilara tells the stunned Keiichi that Gamera sacrificed himself to save the Earth: the flaming frisbee is no more. In an effort to cheer up the boy, who, after all, has just lost not only Gamera, "friend to all children," but a potential sister as well, Kilara tells him, "You're a spaceman now. I shall show you the world." Holding his hand, she whisks him off high into the sky.

Considering that *Gamera Super Monster* was released nearly ten years after the last genuine entry, it's surprising how little the series had changed in style or tone. According to *The Japanese Fantasy Film Journal* (#14), "The producers, aware of the influence of older film material in *Jaws*, *Star Wars* and post–*Star Wars* fantasy movies, intended to parody those [films]." I see no evidence of this, however, for the picture plays like a straight, if hopelessly inept, Gamera movie.

The spacewomen seem more appropriate to Japanese fantastic television than to a live-action feature. Perhaps the filmmakers were hoping to duplicate some of the gentle humor handled so deftly in *Superman* two years earlier (the flying scene at the end seems inspired by the aerial tour of "Metropolis" the Man of Steel gave Lois Lane), but the flying effects, save for the moderately effective take-offs, are more on par with the George Reeves teleseries than the 1978 feature. Mach Fumiake's unusual appearance is partly explained by her career as a female wrestler in Japan, where she apparently gained something of a cult following. With her short, slicked-back hair and masculine wardrobe, she's unlike most any other Japanese screen heroine. Her gesturing is obvious, but her unique appearance is mildly interesting. Her useless companions, on the other hand, have absolutely no purpose in the story—they're there to react to events as they unfold, and nothing more. Their pointless and forced inclusion stands out like a sore thumb.

The Gamera footage is cut into the action with little imagination. The monster's scenes are simply spliced together, with only an occasional reaction shot or two edited in. There's almost no attempt to matte Gamera into the new scenes, and except when Kilara acts as a decoy on the creature's neck (a full-size mock-up), the human characters and Gamera are never seen together. Even the turtle's fatal collision with the Zanon ship is comprised of straight cuts; they're never in the same shot. The original effects (the Zanon ship, the flying van) are inadequate, even amateurish. Gamera's origin (springing forth from

Keiichi's pet) and demise are unusual and go against the grain of the rest of the series. But these anomalies serve no purpose—they're just more dead weight.

There is much in the film that contradicts itself, or appears without explanation. There are many inconsistencies over whether Keiichi is simply imagining the monster battles and the spacewomen. His mother's reaction and the fact that no newspapers are reporting the attacks seem to indicate this is so, and yet later there are scenes like the one between the wounded Gilage and Keiichi's mother. The appearance of the space train gives one pause. Footage from the animated feature *Space Cruiser Yamato* appeared in the Japanese cut as well but wasn't part of the American edition, at least the version I saw. Their puzzling appearance seems to be nothing more than a clumsy and rather shameless cameo intent on boosting ticket sales in Japan (where these films were extremely popular) with an utter disregard for storytelling and logic.

Gamera Super Monster is a hopelessly cheap and unimaginative film. Despite a few twists (clumsy and pointless as they are) the new footage is ineptly handled, and the older clips are overly familiar—the studio already having gone to the stock footage well too many times before. Even the film's title is awkward and unimaginative.

The Ivory Ape *(1980)*

This very minor Rankin-Bass–Tsuburaya Enterprises production was released theatrically in Japan but sold to network television in the States. Like *The Bermuda Depths* (1978), *The Ivory Ape* was filmed in the Caribbean with a Japanese effects crew. The story, built around a seven-foot albino gorilla, barely qualifies for this book, and the picture itself is mediocre.

The title creature is captured in Zaire by Congo natives, who are mad because the big ape has been eating their crops. Greedy bounty hunter Aubrey Range (Derek Partridge) offers to buy the beast, embarrassingly trying to trade a variety of trinkets (including a TV playing Rankin-Bass'· own "Frosty the Snowman" special) before shooting the tribal leader and making off with the beast anyway. The red-eyed ape is loaded aboard a freighter bound for Cuba, where it is to be auctioned off on the black market. The ship is caught in a storm ('scope footage from another production, title unknown), and makes for Bermuda. Meanwhile, spunky animal behavior expert Lil Tyler (Cindy Pickett) has tracked down the ape and makes arrangements to confiscate the animal when the ship reaches port. She calls her former lover and fellow animal expert, Baxter Mapes (Steven Keats), in the United States, and has him meet her there. Abused by a vicious seaman, the ape goes mad, kills the sailor (shades of Dwight Frye!) and jumps ship just as it docks. The ape kills a Bermuda police officer and later scares a woman who spots the white gorilla while driving down a lonely road. Her car flips over, knocking the woman out cold. The ape makes off with the woman's daughter, but when the woman becomes conscious, the white gorilla surrenders the child. News spreads, and an outraged community demands that the creature be killed. A swarm of angry citizens are deputized, but only succeed in shooting a cow. The inspector leading the ape hunt (Earle Hayman) goes to big game hunter and millionaire Marc Kazarian (Jack Palance), a moody, reclusive figure. He hasn't been hunting since his eight-year-old son was eaten by a crocodile on the boy's first big-game shoot. Kazarian also has ties to Range, but just what they might be isn't made clear. Kazarian has a change of heart, however, apparently brought on by the child's near kidnapping, and leads the expedition to hunt down the animal. Meanwhile, Range is strangled by the white gorilla, while Tyler and Mapes try to convince the inspector the primate is really harmless. When the beast is cornered in a church steeple, the kindly inspector gives the pair three hours to sedate the ape. Mapes tries giving the creature some oranges, but the ape only takes a swipe at him. The gorilla sticks its head near a window, and Kazarian, who's having flashbacks of that man-eating croc, decides to shoot the ape anyway. At the last minute, the millionaire hunter sees something in the ape's arms and yells at the other deputies not to shoot. One of the men doesn't listen, however, and the ape is shot dead. Tyler and Mapes rush to the dead ape's side and find a newborn (and black-haired) gorilla. The Ivory Ape was a she.

Albino gorillas are a curiously popular sub-sub-genre in movies. Similar creatures turn up in several films, including *White Pongo* (1945) and *The White Gorilla* (1947), among others. Despite an earnest, pro-environmental storyline (Pickett even wears the picture's message—a T-shirt proclaiming "The Most Dangerous Animal: Man"), *The Ivory Ape* is pretty mediocre stuff. The film's characters are either broad stereotypes (Tyler and Mapes are militant animal lovers, Range the Simon Legree–like hunter) or vague and confusing (Kazarian and his wife, played by Celine Lomez). Until the big payoff, the animal's attacks go unexplained, and the rather dopey experts (who scare the ape into moving toward the open window and fail to realize it's pregnant) don't win much sympathy with their pleas that the animal is really harmless.

Top-billed Jack Palance doesn't make his first appearance until nearly halfway through the film and barely shows up at all after that. The moody, passive millionaire (described as a cross between Hemingway, Howard Hughes and King Kong—Ha!) agrees to hunt the ape because he believes it will cure the demons which have plagued him since his son's death. Why? And why is Kazarian all smiles after the ape is tragically killed? He wanted to save it, after all. Why does he deal with slimy Aubrey Range? Jack Palance is pretty embarrassing in *The Ivory Ape*. His big scene, where he reveals the circumstances surrounding his son's death, is unintentionally hilarious, with Palance acting up a storm, followed by the inspector's solemn, "That was... the worst thing I ever heard."

Steven Keats essays a role similar to the one he played in Rankin-Bass' *The Last Dinosaur*. The ape itself is a significant improvement over Toho's Kong costumes of the sixties. Although a bit bulky and cursed with extra-long arms that aren't convincing, the suit is credible, sort of a B version of Rick Baker's Kong suit for Dino De Laurentiis' 1976 remake. The other technical credits are fair, with nothing really outstanding.

Leonard Maltin's *Movie and Video Guide* gave *The Ivory Ape* an "average" rating saying, "This one resemble(s) a tacky Saturday matinee serial." If only it moved like one.

Virus *(1980)*

With a production cost estimated at $10.5 to $16 million, *Virus* was Japan's most expensive feature to date. Produced by publisher Haruki Kadokawa in association with Japan's TBS television network, *Virus* was an ill-fated attempt to enter the international market—a disaster film released just as the once popular genre was dying. An apocalyptic tale filmed around the world with an international cast of familiar if not stellar performers, most of its budget appears to have been spent shooting on location and hiring English-speaking actors whom the filmmakers mistakenly thought would draw customers in the United States. The resulting film lacked the tacky showmanship of American Irwin Allen's all-star holocausts, but more than made up for it with an intriguing, clever story and sober approach.

East German spies have stolen a man-made virus, "MM88," from a laboratory at the University of Maryland. American agents try to retrieve the deadly vial in Europe, but a plane carrying the bacteria crashes in the Italian Alps, and the vial breaks, exposing the virus to the mountain air. The virus soon spreads throughout Italy, Eastern Europe and the Soviet Union, becoming known as the "Italian Flu." Like the AIDS virus, MM88 is an immune deficiency syndrome; anyone infected with it who develops any kind of illness, even the common cold, dies within a few days. Dr. Meyer (Stuart Gillard), the scientist who developed MM88, tries to tell government officials the source of the plague but is committed to a mental hospital by the military, who want to hide their secret development of the virus from the president. Meyer is released by a senator (Robert Vaughn) who learns of the cover-up, which has been led by the president's own chief of staff, Garland (Henry Silva), without the president's knowledge. Garland believes the virus is a Soviet plot. A call on the hotline from Soviet officials reporting the death of the Russian premiere doesn't shake Garland in his belief. Dr. Meyer tells the president (Glenn Ford) that there's no known vaccine (the military has been giving officials and other public employees a placebo) and that the disease will probably kill everyone on Earth. Around the world, hospitals are inundated with patients, and people are now dying in such great numbers that bodies must be burned in the streets. The president's wife and Dr. Meyer die. The president and the senator realize that the virus cannot spread in extremely cold temperatures and telephone the U.S. base in Antarctica. The president warns Antarctica's inhabitants not to leave the continent, even during the summer months. The senator and the president die. Garland, still believing the Soviets are to blame, turns the nation's nuclear missiles in the ready position, before he too dies. Members from the Japanese base in Antarctica, including Yoshizumi (Masao Kusakari), investigate the nearby Norwegian outpost. Everyone there went crazy after the global virus and either committed suicide or was killed by others. The only survivor is Marit (Olivia Hussey), a pregnant woman whose husband tried to kill her before shooting himself. The tiny communities in Antarctica, representing the United States, the U.S.S.R., Japan and others, discuss the future. The continent's survivors number 855 men, eight women, and enough supplies to last two years. They hope that by the time the food runs out, the virus will also have run its course. A Soviet submarine approaches Antarctica, its crew infected with the virus. The commander of the U.S. team (George Kennedy) regretfully refuses their request to land, and the Soviet leader in Antarctica concurs. The desperate crew says they're landing anyway. Just then, a British submarine appears, lead by Captain MacCloud (American actor Chuck Connors). He destroys the Soviet sub. He tells the Antarctic base his crew is not infected, as they were aboard the submarine since before the spread of the virus began. It's decided that one-to-one relationships between men and women are no longer possible, and the women are ordered to accommodate the men's sex drives. Despite this, Marit and Yoshizumi fall in love. Marit has her late husband's baby. The British sub travels to Japan, looking for survivors. They send out a probe, which finds only rotting skeletons. The probe collects an air sample, which scientists hope to use to develop a vaccine. Yoshizumi determines that a massive earthquake will occur shortly, centered around the North American East Coast. The American leaders realize that the quake could set off the nuclear missiles, which would in turn launch the Soviets' strike force. The Soviets admit one of their missiles is targeted for Antarctica. The British sub heads for Washington. Yoshizumi and U.S. Major Carter (Bo Svenson) volunteer to expose themselves to the virus and deactivate the missile launch control panel. A French scientist believes he has developed a vaccine and gives it to them just before they depart. For safety's sake, the women and children and a small number of men are taken out of range of the targeted base, to a small deserted freighter. Yoshizumi and Major Carter arrive at the White House, now overgrown with grass and littered with yet more skeletons. Before they reach the mission control, deep beneath the White House, the earthquake begins, and Major Carter is killed. Yoshizumi is not able to reach the control panel in time, and the missiles are launched.

Everyone at the Antarctic base is killed. The British sub is destroyed. Because he was underground, Yoshizumi survives. Four years later, a haggard Yoshizumi has made his way south. He comes across a church filled with dessicated skeletons and a crucifix. He hears voices from the Christ figure and skeletons asking about what has happened. The women and children and handful of men have survived – just barely – the four years since most of their co-workers and friends were killed in the nuclear blast. Marit spots Yoshizumi in the distance. He has returned to her.

Though made at about the same time as such dreadful flops as *Beyond the Poseidon Adventure* (1979), *The Concorde: Airport '79* (1979) and *When Time Ran Out...* (1980), *Virus* is in every way a better film, and much closer in spirit to earlier end-of-the-world stories, especially Stanley Kramer's *On The Beach* (1959). The scenes with the British sub exploring Tokyo and later Washington were obviously inspired by a similar trip to San Francisco in Kramer's film, where a desperate American submarine crew investigates a strange radio signal in an otherwise decimated metropolis. And unlike most American disaster films, *Virus* is short on special effects and stunt work. Not that it needs any. The psychological implications of *Virus* are horrifying enough. The brief but frightening scenes of everyday people flooding hospitals, dying in the streets, etc., are most disturbing. The idea of nuclear missiles hitting targets where everybody's already dead is original and eerie.

While the picture's cold war subplot is dated, the idea of chemical warfare isn't. The similarities to the AIDS virus (just beginning to take its toll in 1980, though essentially still unknown by the general public) are also frighteningly real. Most end-of-the-world films made up to this point dodged the issue of rotting corpses, as if they had simply vanished. Not so here. Piles upon piles of dead bodies are only briefly seen, but not easily forgotten. Yoshizumi's conversation with the crucifix and skeletons, though short, is probably the film's best scene, a haunting, intelligently written moment. The film's weakest ideas center around the fate of the world's surviving women, who are forced into sanctioned prostitution. The Antarctic leaders (all but one are men) say they're not happy about the idea but figure they have no choice if they want to keep the peace. That this is so quickly accepted by both the men and the women is surprising and simply not believable. The film is weaker because of it.

The film's Washington scenes are shaky. One source says that Glenn Ford had trouble remembering his lines, but a more likely explanation would be the inherent difficulties of a Japanese director and English-language-speaking actors trying to communicate via interpreters. The problems of shooting on location and using a multi-language crew added considerably to the film's budget. The locations are occasionally impressive. A scene between Svenson and Kusakari is set against an incredible frozen vista, but most of the film could probably have been shot in northern Japan or Tokyo for all the difference it would've ultimately made. Despite the language barrier, the English-language cast deliver competent performances. Ford, problems or no, is fine as the president. Silva was grossly miscast, but his character was overwritten anyway. George Kennedy, by 1980 a staple in disaster movies (the *Airport* series, *Earthquake*) is good in his brief role.

The late Chuck Connors ("The Rifleman") doesn't even attempt a British accent but is otherwise acceptable. Bo Svenson, in one of his best roles, is generally fine. But the film belongs to Masao Kusakari, whose story the picture becomes during the last half. Unfortunately, the actor brings little to the role, though his part appears to have been greatly reduced for the version currently available.

Virus was previewed as a "work-in-progress" in May 1980 at the Cannes Film Festival, running 155 minutes. The film was cut considerably for international release (its Japanese sequences were presumably longer in the home market version, and the U.S. scenes may have been trimmed). Running 108 minutes on home video, *Virus* doesn't appear the worse for the cutting, though the death of all the Norwegians goes unexplained, and some of the footage set in Japan was trimmed. Incredibly, the television version lost another fifteen minutes, and the picture ends with everyone dying in the blast in Washington. Unfortunately, *Virus* was never released theatrically in the United States, and instead was sold directly to cable television, where it soon disappeared. That's too bad, because *Virus* is an intelligent, sober and still potent speculation film, far better than its American counterparts in the disaster film genre.

Godzilla 1985 *(1984/1985)*

After several false starts, Godzilla returned to the big screen in 1985 – December 1984 in Japan – with a big budget (by Japanese filmmaking standards, anyway) remake cum sequel to the 1954 original.

During a storm in the Sea of Japan, the crew of the fishing boat *Yahatamaru* struggle to keep the ship afloat. One of its passengers, Hiroshi Okumura (Shin Takuma), a marine biology student, eyes a nearby rocky island seemingly rise out of the ocean and flash with light. Several days later, newspaper reporter Ken (Goro in the Japanese version) Maki (Ken Tanaka) spots the ship while sailing. He boards the craft only to find the entire crew dead with horrified expressions on their faces and Hiroshi hiding in a locker in a state of shock.

Suddenly, a large insect-creature attacks Ken. He is about to be stung by the creature when Hiroshi kills it with a meat cleaver. The prime minister (Keiji Kobayashi) concludes that the crew were murdered by Godzilla. (This is different from the original version, where the insect creature, an overgrown parasite somehow connected with Godzilla, is what killed the crew. In the U.S. version, the parasite is never explained and quickly forgotten). Worried that news of Godzilla's return would cause a nationwide panic, the prime minister orders a news blackout. When Ken tries to report the story, his editor refuses to run it. He suggests that Ken follow the story by interviewing Professor Hayashida (Yosuke Natsuki). Hayashida tells Ken that Godzilla is "a living nuclear weapon, destined to walk the Earth forever – indestructible – a victim of the modern nuclear age." Ken notices that Hiroshi's sister, Naoko (Yosuko Sawaguchi), works for the professor and tells her of Hiroshi's whereabouts. Meanwhile, Godzilla attacks and destroys a Soviet nuclear sub. The Soviets accuse the United States, which escalates the tensions between the two superpowers. To prevent an international crisis, the prime minister holds a press conference revealing the true culprit behind the sub's destruction. He reveals that not only is Godzilla alive and well, but thanks to the radiation on board the sub he's now bigger than ever. Both the Americans and the Soviets want to use nuclear weapons to destroy Godzilla, but the prime minister refuses. Despite this, a Soviet agent readies a satellite-based nuclear missile, to be launched from a freighter docked in Tokyo Harbor.

Reporter Steve Martin (Raymond Burr), the only American survivor of Godzilla's attack on Tokyo thirty years earlier, is brought to the Pentagon as a consultant. He's met by General Goodhue (Warren Kemmerling) and a smarmy major (Travis Swords), among others. Godzilla comes ashore to attack a nuclear power plant and consume its radioactive core. A flock of birds seems to distract the beast, and he soon departs. Professor Hayashida surmises that Godzilla was attracted to the cry of the birds and believes he might be able to trap and destroy Godzilla. Godzilla next appears in Tokyo Bay and quickly obliterates the first line of defense. The creature's mighty wake severely damages the Soviet freighter, but the fatally injured Russian agent manages to launch the missile anyway. As Martin and the staff at the Pentagon observe from Washington, Godzilla attacks the Shinjuku business district of Tokyo, causing extensive damage. Japan's secret weapon, a flying battle tank, *Super-X*, appears. It fires several poisonous Cadium bombs into Godzilla's mouth as he roars, then he collapses. All celebration comes to a screeching halt, however, as Japan's leaders learn of the incoming Soviet missile. With the help of General Goodhue and the Pentagon, the missile is destroyed en route, exploding in the atmosphere above the metropolis. But the explosion causes a radioactive storm, which revives Godzilla. Taking advantage of a city-wide power failure caused by the explosion, Godzilla destroys *Super-X* and begins his destruction anew. Professor Hayashida, Ken, Naoko and Hiroshi make their way to an island volcano, where their sonar equipment has been set up. Their electronic imitation of the birds' cries attracts Godzilla away from Tokyo to the rim of the volcano. Explosive charges set inside the volcano are detonated, and Godzilla falls into the crater. As the volcano erupts, Martin says, "The reckless ambitions of man are often dwarfed by their dangerous consequences. For now, Godzilla, that strangely innocent and tragic monster, has gone to Earth. Whether he returns or not or is ever seen again by human eyes, the things he has taught remain."

Godzilla 1985 (*Gojira*) was Toho's first giant monster film in nearly ten years. The box office returns on the last few Godzilla films hadn't been so hot, and the series was at a creative dead end. After *Terror of Mechagodzilla*, several new films had been announced. According to an article by August Ragone, in an article which appeared in *Markalite* #1, the first of these was "The Resurrection of Godzilla" (*Gojira futsukatsu*), a remake of the original film, intended as a co-production between Toho and Benedict Pictures Corp.–United Productions of America (UPA), who also had a hand in the last film. Next came "Godzilla Against the Devil" (*Gojira tai Deberu*), and "Godzilla Against Gargantua" (presumably Green Gargantua?), also intended as co-productions with UPA. Later Toho toyed with "Space Godzilla" (*Supesu Gojira*), and later UPA announced an animated feature (they had co-produced an animated Saturday morning series with Hanna-Barbera), but like the other projects, nothing happened. American backers promised a 3-D remake, "Godzilla, King of the Monsters!" as well as "Godzilla vs. Cleveland," but these, too, were shelved. By the mid-1980s, it was clear to producer Tomoyuki Tanaka that the series needed to return to its roots, with Godzilla the bad guy once more. Like Philip Kaufman's *Invasion of the Body Snatchers* (1978), *Godzilla 1985* is both a sequel and a remake, roughly following the original's storyline (Godzilla eats a train, attacks Tokyo, etc.) while incorporating decidedly eighties elements (the threat of nuclear war). Burr reprises his Steve Martin character from the 1956 version (with the "Steve" dropped for obvious reasons). That Godzilla was completely disintegrated in the original was completely forgotten, as were the monster's 14 other film appearances.

Godzilla 1985 isn't quite the triumphant return of the Big G fans of the series might have hoped for. The film has a lot of problems, though many of these are forgivable considering that Toho was completely revamping the series, and, in many ways, starting from scratch. The story, more than the special effects, is the basic problem with *Godzilla 1985*. The film's oddball structure lets us know how Godzilla will be gotten rid of less than forty minutes into the picture and just after the monster's first appearance. The volcano finale is, to say the least, anticlimactic, and the idea of luring a monster with animal sounds was used by Bert I. Gordon in his mediocre giant grasshopper movie, *Beginning of the End* (1957). Meanwhile, there's almost no build-up to the *Super-X* craft's appearance. Its odd shape was supposedly an in-joke reference by the special effects unit to the Smog Monster. Whether this is true or not, *Super-X*'s design is thunderously uninspired and seems detached from and incongruous with the film at large. The film borrows elements from other films besides *Beginning of the End*. The climax apes that of *Rodan*. A lengthy sequence where Ken and Naoko try to escape a skyscraper half-destroyed by Godzilla recalls a similar sequence in *Earthquake* (1974).

Godzilla looks a lot meaner and much more realistic than his seventies film appearances, though the suit's designers made one big mistake: they gave him ping-pong-ball eyes, which makes him resemble a kind of demented muppet. The monster's size was increased to better compete with Tokyo's newer, taller skyscrapers. In doing so, the miniature crew had to build on a smaller scale thus reducing the believability of the finer model work that exemplified Tsuburaya's films. Tanks and other military vehicles seem to bear the brunt of this problem. Here, they really do look like toys. The skyscrapers, however, look impressive, and the scenes of destruction are, for the most part, well done. Less successful is the attack on the nuclear power plant, and Godzilla's defeat at the rim of the volcano. These sequences have a rushed look about them and aren't very convincing or dramatic.

This was the first Godzilla film in nearly twenty years in stereophonic sound, and the picture is much more involving as a result. The Japanese home video version put you right in the middle of the action. Unfortunately, the American stereo tracking pales by comparison; its separations are barely noticeable.

As with the seventies Godzilla entries, the lead characters aren't very involving. The performances are adequate, though not much beyond that. Keiju Kobayashi as the prime minister comes off best, though some of his best scenes were cut for the American version. Yosuko Sawaguchi is impressively awful as Naoko. Her stiff performance and almost total lack of expression transcend the language barrier. A few familiar faces turn up, besides Natsuki (*Ghidrah: The Three-Headed Monster*), Hiroshi Koizumi (*Mothra*) and Yoshibumi Tajima (*Godzilla vs. the Thing*) appear in minor roles.

New World picked up the film for U.S. release. They severely cut the film and added the Raymond Burr footage. They also preceded the feature with Marv Newland's infamous one-joke short, *Bambi Meets Godzilla* (1969), a crudely animated, black and white comedy in which Bambi is crushed by Godzilla's giant foot. While amusing (though it doesn't hold up to multiple viewings), the short seemed to cue audiences to laugh at the feature proper. The Japanese footage in *Godzilla 1985* is generally treated seriously (the film even features subtitles identifying major characters and locales, a la *Tora! Tora! Tora!*), but the scenes with Burr at the Pentagon are constantly undermined by the smart-alecky remarks of Travis Swords' glib major. Godzilla attacks Tokyo, causing an untold number of deaths and injuries, and Swords jokes, "That's quite an urban renewal program they've got over there!" If he doesn't take Godzilla seriously, why should we?

Burr's reprisal of the role he played nearly thirty years earlier was a nice idea, but he's given little to do other than rebuke the major's snide remarks. The American scenes look ridiculously cheap, and the obvious product placement of Dr. Pepper machines at every turn is very annoying and distracting.

While something like thirty minutes of the original film was cut, it doesn't suffer as much as you might suspect. The film's criticism of the arms race was trimmed (including the U.S. ambassador's remark, "This is no time to be discussing principles!"), and the scenes set aboard the freighter were re-edited so that the Russian agent actually launches the missile rather than trying to stop it as in the Japanese cut. A few special effects shots (notably Godzilla's reflection against a mirrored glass skyscraper) were removed for some strange reason, others re-edited out of order. Ernest D. Farino, Jr., did the impressive title design, an improvement over the surprisingly unimaginative Japanese credits work.

The film's tremendous build-up in Japan assured its financial success. In the United States, many of the same critics who had praised, even raved about, Dino De Laurentiis' notorious remake of *King Kong* unmercifully panned Toho's film, with critics making fun of the dubbing (which wasn't Toho's fault) and the special effects.

The *Washington Post*'s Rita Kempley, besides giving away the ending, called the film "a trashy Japanese production... Burr, who looks very much like an Orson Welles balloon for the Macy's Day parade, is actually scarier than the other big guy." A few days later, the *Post*'s Tom Shales noted "New World Pictures has been promoting the film not so much as a fright show, but more as a campy romp... unfortunately, it doesn't work very well on either level. Scarier things have been known to come hopping down the bunny trail." The *Detroit News*' Peter Ross found the film "every bit as bad as the 1955 [sic] classic, and every bit as wonderful." Part of the fun, he said, was "the intentionally bad dubbing." It was?

Despite some severe scripting problems and uneven effects work, *Godzilla 1985* was a step in the right direction for Toho. Unfortunately, its successes were undermined by the campy promotion given it by its distributors in the United States.

Tetsuo: The Iron Man *(1988)*

This atmospheric, violent and largely incoherent picture marked the feature debut of 28-year-old Shinya Tsukamoto, who not only wrote, produced and directed the film, but did the art direction, lighting, editing, special effects and much of the cinematography as well. He also co-stars.

Before the opening titles, a young metal fetishist (Tsukamoto) painfully shoves some scrap metal into his leg through an open, self-inflicted gash. Soon thereafter he's injured in a hit-and-run accident. The driver of the car, a "salaryman" (Tomoroh Taguchi), and his girlfriend (Kei Fujiwara) go on with their lives, making love, apparently unconcerned with life in general until strange things begin happening. While shaving, the salaryman notices a metal thorn growing out of his cheek. Later, he's chased through an empty subway terminal by a strange, haggard young woman with pieces of scrap metal growing out of her body. After making love with his girlfriend, the salaryman dreams he is sodomized by a person (his girlfriend? the makeup and costume obscure this) with a long metal and plastic hose. He awakens to find himself transforming into a creature part man, part scrap metal. When his girlfriend tries to help him, he rapes her with a large, drill-like device that has replaced his penis. Later the pair seem to make love willingly, even though she has stabbed him in the neck, and in the process he apparently kills her (though the film's press materials contradict this, and by now the film's narrative makes little sense). The fetishist, recalling his accident through video-like memories and also becoming increasingly less human, begins stalking the salaryman, and the two confront one another in a warehouse, where they ultimately meld into a two-headed metal beast (an unconvincing and rather uninspired design compared to everything that precedes it), which zooms through Tokyo.

Though visually attractive, impressively repulsive and humorously creepy at times, *Tetsuo: The Iron Man* quickly grows tiresome. The picture is only 67 minutes, yet one quickly becomes anesthetized to its frenetic, industrial techno-pop visuals. Part *Eraserhead*, part community access music video, *Tetsuo* is very much the work of a talented filmmaker making his first feature—and, for good or bad, left to his own devices.

Shinya Tsukamoto was born in Tokyo on January 1, 1960. He began making short films (in Super-8) in 1974 and took up acting four years later. He publicly screened his productions at mobile "cinemas" he devised, and several were shown on television while the director was still in his teens. He earned a degree in fine arts and began directing television commercials, but quit after only two years to concentrate on his films and acting career, and founded a drama company, Kaiju Theatre, to this end. *Tetsuo: The Iron Man*, filmed in 16mm and black and white, was his first feature and was popular enough on the cult movie circuit to warrant a sequel, *Tetsuo II: Body Hammer* (1992, filmed in 35mm and color). According to Derek Elley's review in *Variety*, however, that picture is a sequel in name only.

Tetsuo sharply divided the critics. Glenn Lovell of the San Jose (California) *Mercury News* said the film was "as bizarre, violent and antic as they come—a brilliant scrap-heap of parts of Sam Raimi's *Evil Dead*, David Cronenberg's *The Fly* and, of course, the ultimate midnight attraction, David Lynch's *Eraserhead* ... If possible, the manic and purposely nauseating *Tetsuo* is tougher to cut through than Lynch at his most impenetrable. It's a singular creation that whales away at the subconscious and—through animation, martial-arts buffoonery and time-lapse photography—rubs our noses in everything about the dehumanized '90s we dread most." The Los Angeles *Daily News*' Bob Strauss called the film a "hyperventillating, black-and-white freakout... among the most grotesque cinematic experiences ever filmed. It's also close to brilliant, a *tour de force* of special effects, ingenuity and dank, techno-erotic hysteria." The *San Francisco Examiner*'s Scott Rosenberg, on the other hand, said the picture was "an example of a common avant-garde practice," accusing Tsukamoto of "stealing from the mainstream, injecting stronger doses of sadism and then pretending to offer something strange, wonderful and new." The *New York Post*'s Matthew Flamm preferred *Drum Struck*, the Western-made short with which *Tetsuo* was often paired. Although he praised the film's "truly impressive stop-motion animation," Flamm noted, "*Tetsuo* [has] plenty of weirdness, [but] doesn't know when to stop. Its vision may be bold and original, but it repeats its tricks so often in the course of its 67 minutes that by the end I didn't care." And neither did I.

Godzilla vs. Biollante *(1989)*

This mostly successful effort by Toho to appeal to a new generation of Godzilla fans unfortunately bypassed a theatrical release in the United States and went straight to home video in the final days of 1992. In this, the 17th and most poetic Godzilla film, the fire-breathing lizard faces a decidedly modern monstrosity — a genetically engineered monster plant.

Picking up where 1984's *Gojira* left off, the film opens with Tokyo in ruins, utterly destroyed by Godzilla. The city's Shinjuku district remains closed to the public as crews arrive to salvage the remains of *Super X*, and to check for any lingering radiation. A U.S. commando team, sent by "Bio-Major," a conglomerate of American-owned companies that want to hold a monopoly on the genetic market, slip into the area and retrieve a piece of Godzilla skin. They want to use Godzilla's nearly impervious cells to create an anti-nuclear energy bacteria, which they can use against the other superpowers. But the team is ambushed by SSS9 (Manjhat Beti), an agent for the (fictional) Saradian government, which wants to use the Godzilla cells to help turn their arid country into "a vast granary." After shooting the Americans, SSS9 brings the precious Godzilla cells back to the Middle Eastern nation. The Saradians have invested their oil export profits in genetic research and have engaged Japanese scientist Dr. Genichiro Shiragami (Koji Takahashi) to create a strain of wheat that will grow in the desert. Combining the DNA information of wheat, cacti and the Godzilla cell, Shiragami is on the verge of creating a robust new food source when American Bio-Major agents blow up his lab, killing his young daughter, Erika (Yasuko Sawaguchi), in the process.

Five years later, in 1989, Shiragami returns to Japan, founding a laboratory where he can continue his research. His daughter's death has been a tremendous blow to the scientist, who cultivates his daughter's favorite flowers, roses. Erika's friend, Asuka Okouchi (Yoshiko Tanaka), visits the doctor then returns to her job at the Japan Psyonic Center, where scientists study clairvoyant children. Asuka is shocked when the children all have visions of Godzilla's resurrection. In an amusing shot reminiscent of *Close Encounters of the Third Kind*, children thrust paintings and drawings of Godzilla into the air. Major Sho Kuroki (Masanobu Takashima) and Colonel Goro Gondo (Toru Negishi) of Japan's Self Defense Forces investigate Mount Mihara, where Godzilla had been defeated in 1984. They bring along 17-year-old Miki Saegusa (Megumi Odaka), the strongest of the clairvoyants from the Psyonic Center. She strongly senses Godzilla's return. Asuka's boyfriend, scientist Kazuto Kirishima (Kunihiko Mitamura), persuades the defense forces to use a Godzilla cell of their own to create the anti-nuclear energy bacteria and use it against the monster. Kirishima convinces Shiragami to use his knowledge in genetic engineering to create the anti-nuclear bacteria, under the condition Shiragami be allowed to keep the Godzilla cells at his laboratory. American agents break into the doctor's lab but are surprised by both SSS9 and the appearance of strange vines which attack the men, preventing them from stealing the Godzilla cells. Soon thereafter, the American agents threaten to blow up Mt. Mihara—thus releasing Godzilla from his volcanic tomb—if the Japanese government does not surrender the bacteria. Meanwhile, at Lake Ashino near the doctor's laboratory, a gigantic plant, resembling a tremendous rosebush (complete with a big rosebud for a head), rises out of the lake. Dr. Shiragami explains that he created the creature by using the anti-nuclear bacteria, Godzilla cells, cells from Erika's roses . . . and his late daughter's DNA molecules. Shiragami calls the creature Biollante. It becomes clear that Erika's soul lives through the creature, which horrifies Asuka and Kirishima. They recognize the monster's cries as Erika's.

Elsewhere, the Japanese government is about to hand over the anti-nuclear bacteria when SSS9 ambushes both the Americans and the Japanese and steals the bacteria. The gunplay and confusion result in Mt. Mihara being blown up, and Godzilla is revived. Major Kuroki launches a massive sea offensive against the monster. Several ships are destroyed before Kuroki launches *Super X2*, a newly constructed weapon, now operated by remote control. *Super X2* comes equipped with a deflecting mirror, and when Godzilla tries to blast the airborne ship out of the sky with his fiery spray, *Super X2* merely deflects the radioactive spray back at the monster. Godzilla retreats underwater and heads for Lake Ashino, where he's met by Biollante. Godzilla begins spraying the giant rosebush with his radioactive fire while the monster's vines turn into dozens of Ghidorah-like long-necked, fanged maws which bite Godzilla and spray him with a yellow, acidy vomit-like sap. The big lizard finally destroys Biollante, setting the monster plant afire. However, brightly colored particles (spores?) rise into the sky as the giant bush burns out of control. Godzilla heads toward

Osaka. Miki tries to stop the monster in a telepathic duel but fails. The monster attacks the Nakanoshima district, just as Gondo and Kirishima recover the antinuclear bacteria from a Saradian office there. When SSS9 reports the loss, the Saradian president (Iden Yamanrahl) orders Shiragami assassinated. *Super X2* fires on Godzilla, but the ship has a meltdown and is destroyed. Gondo, leading a strike force armed with anti-nuclear bacteria rockets, fires them at the monster.

The lethal doses do not immediately affect the creature, however, who topples the skyscraper Gondo occupies. The Self Defense Forces determine that in order for the bacteria to kill Godzilla, it must be triggered by an electrical charge, so they set about laying electrical mines. They also create an artificial electrical storm to further their chances against Godzilla. Godzilla is drawn to the minefield, yet despite the many electrical charges he receives from both the lightning and the exploding mines, the indomitable beast still stands.

Just then, the Biollante spores fall to the ground, as Godzilla watches. Suddenly, a new, even larger Biollante, now sporting a crocodile-like snout full of teeth, erupts to the surface. The monsters square off once again, Biollante rumbling like a massive earthquake toward the King of the Monsters. Godzilla, using all his energy battling Biollante, falls into the water, the lethal anti-nuclear bacteria finally taking effect. Biollante dissolves into the same spore-like material seen earlier, and Miki senses that Erika's soul has been freed. Suddenly, SSS9 shoots Dr. Shiragami dead. Kirishima pursues the assassin but is cornered by the agent, who stands ready to shoot the scientist. Kuroki, watching the attack from afar, charges an electrical mine the agent happens to be standing on, and SSS9 is instantly disintegrated. In a disappointing coda, Godzilla mysteriously revives, and heads back out to sea.

Godzilla vs. Biollante is the most poetic film of the series to date. Instead of three-headed dragons or monster lobsters, the Big G comes up against a markedly different opponent—a monster rose with the soul of an innocent girl. And it's the picture's melancholy, wistful tone (even the sky is gray in this one) that probably prevented its theatrical distribution in the United States. But the film isn't perfect. For one thing, there are simply too many characters with similar motives to keep track of. American agents, SSS9, and Dr. Shiragami are all after the Godzilla cells, and each one has a slightly different (and inadequately explained) reason for wanting it.

The picture is also overloaded with stalwart heroes. Sharing screen time with Masanobu Takashima's Major Kuriko and Toru Negishi's Colonel Gondo, top-billed Kunihiko Mitamura seems to barely be in the film at all. There's also a preoccupation with military hardware that tends to bog the picture down. The poorly designed *Super X* wasn't very exciting (or popular with fans) in *Godzilla 1985*, so one wonders why the ship was revived—albeit with improvements—here.

Biollante is an inspired, even scary creation: a Japanese "Audrey II" (the monster plant from *The Little Shop of Horrors*). Godzilla's assault on Osaka is another visual feast, an orgy of mostly excellent miniature effects. Sporting what looks like hundreds of teeth, numerous, serpent-like tendrils and acid, green vomit (an attribute of another king-size monster, *Reptilicus*), the giant plant—Godzilla's first opponent in 14 years—is a big improvement over the monsters the studio created for the 1970s entries (though Biollante's numerous fang-filled tendrils never look like anything but wire-controlled marionettes). The Godzilla costume has been changed again. The head is much smaller and more animal-like in this outing. The cartoon-like eyes of *Godzilla 1985* have been replaced by sinister, dark brown, almost black ones. The shoulders are more muscular, and, except for the head, the creature looks more like a prehistoric *Tyrannosaur* than before.

Godzilla's attack on Osaka is really the film's highlight, an improvement over the similar sequence in *Godzilla 1985*. Special effects director Koichi Kawakita, taking over the reins from Teruyoshi Nakano, uses a wider and much more imaginative range of camera angles. There's an impressive low-angle tracking shot, for instance, looking up at Godzilla from street level, as the monster crushes one building after another. Another impressive shot appears to have been filmed from inside one of the miniature sets, as if looking out of one of the skyscraper's windows as Godzilla passes. The sea battle is also neatly done. Both this and the Osaka scenes are greatly helped by several bird's-eye-view shots of the monster in action. This gives the viewer a sense of geography lacking in other entries.

The acting is unremarkable. Koji Takahashi's Shiragami is too aloof to make much of an impression, and the rest of the male actors are nearly indistinguishable. Incidentally, Masanobu Takashima is the son of Tadeo Takashima (*King Kong vs. Godzilla*, *Atragon*, etc.), making Masanobu a second-generation Godzilla actor. Yasuko Sawaguchi was terrible (in another role) in *Godzilla 1985*. As Shiragami's daughter, her screen time is too brief to allow much of a judgment on her performance here.

Much of *Godzilla vs. Biollante* uses Akira Ifukube's magnificent, if familiar, Godzilla themes, and Koichi Sugiyama's original scoring of other parts of the picture seems bland by comparison. Producer Tomoyuki Tanaka wisely brought in Ifukube himself for the next few pictures.

Godzilla vs. Biollante was directed by 37-year-old Kazuki Omori, an independent-minded young filmmaker, in films since 1977, but with no previous genre experience. His live-action footage is livelier than Kohji Hashimoto's work in *Godzilla 1985* but is otherwise unremarkable.

Despite these complaints, *Godzilla vs. Biollante* is basically a good film and a more than worthy entry in the series. Its unique monster plant combined with some of the best Godzilla destruction scenes yet filmed more than make up for its uninteresting and overcrowded list of human characters.

Akira Kurosawa's Dreams *(1990)*

Director Kurosawa's career appeared to be winding down following his unsuccessful *Dodes' ka-den* (1970). The film's rejection in Japan as well as other personal problems led the filmmaker to attempt suicide the following year. Like his brother before him, he slashed his arms and neck in some twenty-one places. Unlike his brother, however, Kurosawa survived. It took the backing of the Soviet Union's film industry for the director to complete his next work, *Dersu Uzala* (1975). Though it won the Academy Award for best foreign language film that year, Kurosawa was still largely considered a has-been in his own country. His next films, *Kagemusha* (1980) and *Ran* (1985), both samurai epics, had U.S. backing (the latter with French monies as well), including the support of George Lucas, Francis Ford Coppola, Steven Spielberg and Martin Scorsese, each of whom greatly admired the director's work. It was this much-publicized mutual admiration as much as the fine quality of these later films that re-established Kurosawa in the public eye, both in the United States and in Japan.

Following *Kagemusha* and especially *Ran*, *Akira Kurosawa's Dreams* is a disappointment. Despite its promising title, *Dreams* is a pedestrian effort — overlong and often unintentionally funny. There are several good moments, but they are few and far between. The film received mostly good reviews in the United States, but even the most favorable notices barely hid their disappointment, suggesting that even bad Kurosawa was better than no Kurosawa.

The film is broken into eight segments, each supposedly based on a dream or series of dreams actually experienced by the director.

In "Sunshine through the Rain," a little boy known as "I" in Donald Richie's credits (and played by Toshihiko Nakano) and his mother (Mitsuko Baisho) watch the rain fall, this despite the fact it is a bright, sunny day. The mother explains that foxes hold their wedding processions in this weather and that they do not like to be seen. Naturally, the curious little boy sneaks out of the house, and hiding behind a tree, witnesses the wedding ceremony of the foxes (played by men and women in kimonos and painted faces). The foxes spot the boy, and when he returns home, the boy's mother isn't allowed to let the kid back inside the house. The foxes left a *hara kiri* knife for the boy to commit suicide, but the mother suggests going to the foxes' home to apologize. The boy asks where to find the animals, and the mother suggests looking at the end of a rainbow. The boy travels across the countryside, finally spotting a beautiful rainbow in the distance (this gorgeous shot was adapted for the film's poster art).

"The Peach Orchard" begins with a slightly older "I" (Mitsunori Isaki) following a mysterious woman to a stepped hillside, where he sees dozens of human figures, which resemble his sister's collection of dolls, though larger, of course. The dolls explain that they personify the peach trees that used to blossom here but were cut down by the boy's family. The dolls will no longer visit, they explain, to celebrate the blossoming of the trees. The boy explains that the cutting of the trees wasn't his fault, as he liked the peach trees. "Yes, because he likes peaches!" one of the dolls tells the others. The boy begins to cry. His tears convince the dolls of his sincerity, and they decide to let him see the orchard and the blossoming of the trees one last time. The sky fills with falling blossoms, and soon the boy sees the trees everywhere. All too soon, however, the vision is over. The trees disappear, replaced by tree stumps where the dolls once stood.

Next is "The Blizzard." A quartet of mountaineers are lost in a tremendous snowstorm. After endless walking through ice and knee-deep snow, three of the men collapse. The fourth man finds himself covered by a warm fabric, placed over his shivering body by a beautiful woman (Mieko Harada) who calmly says, "The snow is warm. The ice is hot." The figure turns into a blue-faced snow fairy and the man regains consciousness as the figure disappears. He orders his men to their feet, the blizzard ends, and the men locate their camp.

A Japanese soldier returning from the front lines is the subject of "The Tunnel." Following the road back home, the soldier must pass through an ominous tunnel. A military dog (wearing a grenade pack) comes out of the tunnel and growls at him. He proceeds through the tunnel. Once though, the soldier hears footsteps. The ghost of a dead private who had been in the soldier's charge emerges from the tunnel. The private asks the soldier if he's really dead. The soldier apologizes, but says that indeed he is. The private sadly returns into the tunnel. Then, the ghosts of the soldier's entire platoon march out of the tunnel, requesting orders and reporting "no casualties." The soldier again apologizes, saying it was his carelessness that led to their deaths. He speaks of being held in a POW camp after the battle and says he wishes he too had died with his men. He salutes the ghosts then orders them back into the tunnel. They disappear into the blackness. The dog returns and growls at the disgraced soldier.

In "Crows," the narrator, now an adult (Akira Terao), is in a museum admiring several paintings by Vincent Van Gogh. He is drawn into one of the paintings, finding himself in an expressionistic France. He tracks down Van Gogh himself (director-actor Martin Scorsese) in a field. Van Gogh mutters something about having so little time left and vanishes. The young painter wanders through various Van Gogh works, winding up in a field where hundreds of crows appear out of nowhere. The man is back in the museum.

Next up is "Mount Fuji in Red." Six reactors at a nuclear power plant behind Mount Fuji explode. Eventually, Mount Fuji itself becomes red hot (Industrial Light and Magic's effects work here is shaky at best). The narrator finds himself with a young woman (Toshie Negishi), her children and a power station executive (Hisashi Igawa) at a seaside cliff. It seems that everyone else jumped off the cliff into the sea. Clouds of different colors swirl about them. The red one, the executive explains, is plutonium-239, a 10,000,000th of a gram of which causes cancer. The yellow is strontium-90, which causes leukemia. The purple is cesium-137, which affects the reproductive system, causing mutations. The executive says he is partly responsible for the holocaust and jumps to his death. The woman screams "Liars!" and the painter and young woman vainly try to fan away the approaching clouds.

"The Weeping Demon" finds "I" wandering through a post-apocalyptic Japan that has been destroyed in a nuclear attack. The man finds a "demon" (Chosuke Ikariya), a man dressed in tatters and sporting a horn on the top of his head, caused by the radioactivity. The demon shows "I" a field of dandelions the size of trees and a regular-size rose with a stem growing out of the flower. He also speaks of (though we do not see) a two-faced hare and a "hairy fish." "Stupid mankind did this," he explains. He shows "I" a crowd of multi-horned, cannibalistic demons and tells the man that his horn hurts. "Do you want to become a demon?" he asks. The man runs away.

The final segment is "Village of the Waterfalls." "I" enters a quaint village where nearly every building has a small waterfall. There is no electricity, no automobiles, no modern conveniences. He sees some children put flowers on a large stone near a bridge. "I" meets an old man (Chishu Ryu). He asks why there is no electricity. "Why should night be day?" the old man responds, saying that a simpler life is more rewarding. Scientists may be smart, but they're not wise, he says. "I" asks about the flowers placed on the rock. The old man explains that years ago, another traveler died on that spot and that ever since people have placed flowers there whenever they passed. The tradition has been going on for so long, many do not even know why they do this. A lively, gay procession makes its way down a dirt road. The old man explains that it is "a nice, happy funeral" for a woman who died at the age of 99. "To tell the truth," the old man says, "she was my first love, but left me for another." The old man says he's 103 and informs "I" that "life is exciting" before leaving him to join the happy procession. As "I" leaves the village, he places flowers on the memorial stone.

Except for this last segment, based on a real-life incident from the director's youth, *Dreams* is a creative disaster. "The Blizzard" ends well, with the Snow Demon eerily photographed (her long black hair blowing madly in the bitterly cold wind, much like "The Woman of the Snow" segment of Kobayashi's *Kwaidan*), and complemented by some effective sound effects work. Unfortunately, it's preceded by one of the most ridiculously overlong prologues in movie history: The mountaineers slog through the snow and ice in slow motion, while on the soundtrack we hear the heavy breathing of the men. This goes on without relief for nearly six minutes (it seems more like a half-hour). As the heavy breathing filled the theater I saw the film in, several bemused audience members' thoughts turned to what one might expect—an obscene phone call.

"Mount Fuji in Red" and "The Weeping Demon"—the picture's worst segments—are outrageously pretentious, with characters bleating the stories' messages with reckless abandon. The giant dandelions were a bad idea (one can't help but think of TV lawn care ads), and the sight of the man and woman madly fanning the colorful but deadly clouds is unintentionally hilarious and anything but horrifying.

"Crows" makes little sense, especially Van Gogh's mad ravings. Scorsese effectively cast himself in his own film *Taxi Driver* (as a perverted customer of Robert De Niro's title character) and probably did the role as a favor to his idol. Scorsese is seen only briefly here, and he's badly made up (his hair and beard look like they were colored with orange Kool-Aid). The scenes of the artist roaming through Van Gogh's work were accomplished using video technology, painfully obvious in theatrical screenings. Like nearly everything else, it has a slightly comical air probably not intended by the director. "The Tunnel," like so much of the film, has an interesting premise but it's hampered with overly theatrical makeup (the soldiers have deep blue faces) and silly dialog ("No casualties!").

The film's saving grace is "Village of the Windmills." Like the rest of the film, it wears its message on its sleeve but is so utterly charming it transcends its problems. The music used in the segment is very engaging, and the two lead performances are interesting and sympathetic. The other segments carry little weight. "Sunshine through the Rain" ends abruptly while "The Peach Orchard" is undermined by a very poor child actor, though at least the humor in both segments is intended.

In a *Washington Post* review titled *"Dreams* Never Wakes Up," Hal Hinson said that "'Pontifications' might better have served as a more accurate header. Or better yet, 'Sermons'. . . . *Dreams* seems to emerge more out of the superego than from the id." However, Janet Maslin's preview of the film in the *New York Times* argued, "But to view it this way, in the shadow of Mr. Kurosawa's past, is to miss the distillation and purity of his present vision. That vision could as easily be that of a young child as an octogenarian master."

Maybe so, but despite several good ideas, *Akira Kurosawa's Dreams* must be considered a minor film in the great director's career. Fortunately, his next production, the much-underrated *Rhapsody in August*, would be much better.

Solar Crisis *(1990)*

This expensive ($25-40 million) Japanese-American co-production was a big deal in Japan, where advance ticket sales and a lot of hype guaranteed sizable returns in that country—at least for its opening week. In the United States, however, the picture never had a general release; it went straight to video in March 1993. What happened? It had fairly big stars — Charlton Heston, Jack Palance (both Oscar-winners), Peter Boyle and Tim Matheson, among others. Its hefty budget was not wasted; the film certainly looks expensive. Its special effects are plentiful and generally impressive. Chalk it up to the changing economics of film exhibition. *Solar Crisis*, as far as Hollywood was concerned, had "B-Movie" written all over it, and B-movies, in the United States at least, rarely make it to movie theaters anymore. They go straight to video, which is exactly where most Americans first learned the film even existed.

In the year 2050, scientists predict that a colossal mega-flare will burst from the sun and strike the Earth within 48 hours. Dubbed "Starfire," the flare would destroy the Earth's atmosphere, thus destroying all life. The United Command prepares to launch the globe-shaped spaceship *Helois* and its crew of 16 on a desperate mission to save the Earth. They hope to get close enough to launch "Freddy," an anti-matter bomb designed to trigger the flare while on the sun's far side, thus missing the earth completely. Meanwhile, at IXL headquarters in Las Vegas, super-rich industrialist Arnold Teague (Peter Boyle) confers with his staff over the likelihood of the flare-up. Dr. Gunther Haas (Paul Koslo) believes the "Starfire" a certainty, but he's overruled by the beautiful but treacherous Dr. Claire Beeson (Brenda Bakke). Teague's financial interests seem to rest on the hopes that the *Helois*' mission proves unsuccessful. Just what he would hope to gain by this isn't made clear, but he gives the go-ahead to sabotage the operation. Meanwhile, mission commander Captain Steve Kelso (Tim Matheson) prepares his crew for what appears to be a suicide mission. The crew includes stalwart Borg (Dorian Harewood), brave Ken Minami (Japanese-American actor Tetsuya Bessho, curiously the sole Asian in the cast; his role appears to have been beefed up in the Japanese cut, however) and beautiful scientist and psychologist Alex Noffe (Annabel Schofield), a biogenetically enhanced woman with exceptional mental and physical prowess. Aboard *Skytown*, the United Command space station orbiting Earth, Steve meets with his father, Admiral "Skeet" Kelso (Charlton Heston), who is worried about grandson Mike — Steve's son — who, back on Earth, has disappeared from military school and into the desert. Admiral Kelso decides to look for Mike while Steve continues with the mission. Steve tells his crew that the remote guidance system on the probe carrying Freddy (a HAL–like contraption voiced by Paul Williams) isn't ready yet; someone will have to pilot the craft (a dead ringer for Charlton Heston's ship in *Planet of the Apes*) into the sun. Only five crew members are capable of flying the craft, including Alex, Ken and Steve. Ken volunteers for the deadly mission. One of the Teague's men gets aboard the space station and programs the unwilling Alex to sabotage the ship. She seems to have no memory of her assault, nor is she able to stop herself from sabotaging the mission.

Back on Earth, AWOL Mike Kelso's training fighter has crashed; he wanders through the desert until he comes upon a crazy hermit (Jack Palance). Elsewhere,

Teague and his men abandon the dissenting Dr. Haas in the desert so he'll be unable to reveal Teague's plans. Mike and the hermit make their way through the *Road Warrior*-inspired countryside (the extreme conditions having been brought on by all the solar activity) to a run-down bar. Dr. Haas, after walking miles through the desert with no water, makes it to the bar as well and collapses. Teague's men arrive to make sure Haas hasn't spilled the beans, but it is already too late: he has told Mike Kelso everything. Mike is nowhere to be found. Teague's men kill the hermit while trying to extract information on the boy's whereabouts, and Teague's white-haired assassin (who also screwed up Alex's mind) is sent after Mike. Meanwhile, Admiral Kelso has mobilized his forces to locate Mike before Teague's men do. The *Helios* is fast approaching the sun but beset by increasingly deadlier mishaps created by Alex. Ken is pulled off as pilot of the probe when he, not Alex, is suspected of all the sabotage. He's later killed, and the *Helios* is nearly blown up when Alex programs Freddy to blow itself up while still docked in the shuttle bay. Using all her willpower, Alex breaks free of the mind-control and prevents Freddy's detonation, though in so doing she also reveals herself to be the saboteur. Admiral Kelso's men surround Teague's office, but Teague himself is escaping via a private "helijet." The admiral's men shoot the aircraft out of the sky. Mike avoids the assassin's bullets, and is reunited with his grandfather. The *Helios* reaches the sun. With Ken dead and Alex under arrest, Steve prepares to pilot the probe himself. However, Alex, trying to make up for the death and destruction she has caused, knocks Steve unconscious and flies into the sun herself. The flare is ignited and the crisis is over.

It would be easy to dismiss *Solar Crisis* as a bloated special effects extravaganza put together by inexperienced producers working with a derivative script. But it's not that simple, for there is much to like about the picture, problems and all. *Solar Crisis* has a grandeur missing from the genre both in the United States and abroad since the early 1980s, when most producers seemed to give up on outer space stories. After 1983 or so, most big-budget science fiction films either took place on other planets, usually indoors (*Aliens*), or, more frequently, on Earth (the Terminator movies). Visually, *Solar Crisis* is very impressive. The optical effects are plentiful and work most of the time. The picture opted for a look somewhere between *2001* (the *Helios* closely resembles the *Aries IB* from Kubrick's film) and the *Star Trek* movies (*Skytown*). The ships, costumes, etc., are reasonably believable yet evocative.

The production design (by George Jenson) of the scenes in space is erratic but often outstanding. Especially good is the design of the "Drop Ship Bay" where Admiral Kelso leaves son Steve to search for grandson Mike. The shimmery, smooth tubes and irises Heston climbs through are actually more appealing than the overly familiar command areas, overloaded with the usual plethora of blinking lights and video monitors. Less successful are the desert scenes, clearly inspired by the *Mad Max* movies and the endless imitations that followed (though I suppose the look of *Mad Max* was itself inspired by the likes of *A Boy and His Dog*, *Damnation Alley*, and others). However, the Las Vegas footage is well done, boasting good photography, decent matte work, interesting costumes and a neat vacuum cleaner–like taxi. The "robotrucks," automated semis which barrel down freeways like bats out of hell, are also interesting creations.

One good scene finds a speeding robotruck obliterating Jack Palance's motorcycle which was parked in the big semi's path. They try to stop other trucks in the convoy but are understandably nervous about getting in the trucks' way. Palance finally stands firm in the middle of the road, hoping the vehicle's sensors will cause it to stop. It does stop, and he and Corky Nemec's Mike sneak aboard the vehicle and hitch a ride. However, the relationship between Mike and the hermit, along with the admiral's search for his grandson, is extra baggage the picture could've done without. In the end it doesn't have anything to do with Steve's mission, and the chance meeting between Teague's scientist and Mike is too unlikely a coincidence to be believed. Yet unlike other effects-driven films (*The Guyver*, for instance), Joe Gannon and Ted Sarafian's script, from Takeshi Kawata's novel, makes a decent stab at humanizing its characters and genuinely tries to make them interesting. Their talents are not up to the task, however. As a whole, the characters are flat and overly familiar. Heston's admiral, for instance, is cliched; he loves his son, but his devotion to military life has left him something of an emotional cripple. Heston himself had already played this role at least once before, as Edward Albert's dad in the mostly terrible *Midway* (1976). Although he's a bit hammy here, Heston's return to the genre is most welcomed.

Tim Matheson is miscast though he isn't bad. I suspect he was chosen as the heroic mission leader by the Japanese producers, unaware that most Americans identify him as a comic actor, best remembered as one of the stars of *National Lampoon's Animal House* (1978).

Peter Boyle, mistakenly listed as deceased in Danny Peary's *Cult Movie Stars*, appears uncomfortable as Teague, the greedy industrialist with the overly symbolic name. His stoic readings bring much less to the role than his unusual and striking features; he's not a character here, just a presence. His character's motives make no sense whatsoever. Why does he want the mission to fail? He seems convinced the flare-up will not occur, so why stop the mission? "I don't think it's right to mess around with nature," he says.

Jack Palance's scraggly hermit is amusing, but it's a peripheral character to the story proper. The rest of the cast is adequate, but nothing special. Corky Nemec's Mike Kelso is all right, but seems so far removed from the main story it's hard to become involved with the character. Annabel Schofield is beautiful, but she spends most of the time simply looking anguished over the (inadequately explained) mind-control that has taken her over. H. M. Wyant, whom genre fans will recall as the crazed traveler in "The Howling Man" episode of *The Twilight Zone*, has a small role as one of Teague's advisors.

Richard Sarafian's (*Vanishing Point, The Man Who Loved Cat Dancing*) direction keeps things moving but is otherwise anonymous. In fact, he chose to remain anonymous for his work here; for reasons unknown, he used the all-purpose Hollywood pseudonym, "Alan Smithee," in place of his own name in the credits. Composer Maurice Jarre (*Lawrence of Arabia, Doctor Zhivago*) is a cult figure in Japan, but his music here doesn't come alive until the film is almost over, and by then it's too late to make much of an impression.

Reviews were not favorable. *Variety*'s "Sege" saw the Japanese cut.

> As the latest example of nineties-style international film finance, *Solar Crisis* is exceptionally interesting. As a movie, it's an unmitigated stiff... Directed... in a confusingly eclectic style, [it] borrows openly from a range of relatively recent pics, from *Star Wars*–type spaceships to *Mad Max*–type desert inhabitants to a cut-rate *2001: A Space Odyssey* finale. The background noise generated in production designer George Jenson's elaborately technological sets is overmiked, drowning chunks of the dialog. What comes through convinces that the clutter is just as well. ...[The picture] has the feel of those geographically amorphous pan-European outings that Lew Grade came up with in the 1970s.

Guy Tucker's review in *Markalite* (#3) said, "The first Japanese-American science fiction collaboration since *Message from Space* is equally poorly planned, but twenty times as expensive and nowhere near as entertaining. *Message* was a wild, colorful takeoff on *Star Wars* and Japanese costume pictures; *Solar Crisis* is an indifferently-crafted, uncredited remake of *Gorath*."

While it's true that both *Solar Crisis* and Toho's *Gorath* revolve around astronauts trying to prevent an astronomical disaster, to call this film an uncredited remake of *Gorath* is unfair, and no more true than suggesting Toho's film is nothing more than a rip-off of *When Worlds Collide*. Much of *Solar Crisis* falls flat, and it uncomfortably mixes the design and sensibilities of several subgenres which do not naturally come together. It isn't terribly original, and the performances (and some of the casting) are awkward. And yet there's a sense of wonder and spectacle to the film missing from most science fiction films of the last decade. Despite the complaints of its detractors, the film isn't nearly as cold and technology-driven as many recent high-profile spectacles (*Terminator 2*, the *Batman* films, etc.). Though it lacks the warmth and self-assuredness of *Gorath*, there's a glimmer of that film's spirit, and that ain't all bad.

Twilight of the Cockroaches *(1990)*

As I've explained in "A Note about the Text," animated features have been excluded from this book because there are simply so many of these pictures produced in Japan that by all rights they deserve a volume of their own. However, the mostly animated *Twilight of the Cockroaches* has a couple of wholly live action sequences, and much of the film uses live backdrops rather than painted ones. By some strange coincidence, I first saw this exciting and unique epic tragedy right after rewatching Walt Disney's *Bambi* (1942), which made a surprisingly appropriate double bill. Both are animated features dealing with such weighty issues as life and death and survival of the fittest.

Naomi is a young female cockroach (the bugs in this film have human features and are not at all repulsive). She and her boyfriend, Ichiro, enjoy life in the apartment of the curiously passive Saito, a human who lets the bugs eat table scraps and wander freely without so much as a can of Raid in sight. The carefree life of the roaches is interrupted when a bug-warrior from another tribe, Hans, appears. Hans, having fought humans his entire life, cannot believe the happy co-existence with humankind his brother bugs enjoy. Naomi falls in love with Hans and tells her girlfriend that she has second thoughts about her pre-arranged marriage with Ichiro. When the duty-bound Hans decides to return to his own tribe across the courtyard, Naomi follows him. She faces great hardship as she makes her way across the jungle-like field (which is only about 50 feet in human terms). She nearly drowns in a rainstorm and meets a talking turd. Naomi finally reaches the apartment across the way and enters an immense kitchen. Just then, a human female enters, and disgusted by the tiny cockroach, she tries to squish Naomi and later, swat her with a newspaper. Naomi is shocked. She has never experienced such cruelty from humans before. Discovered by the militant roaches of Hans' tribe, Naomi is reunited with her lover. Life is no bed of roses for these roaches, however, and the terrified Naomi watches helplessly as Hans and the other roaches make costly, almost suicidal attacks on the human woman (who clearly can't stand the insects, spraying and stomping the critters at every opportunity). The woman makes a date with Saito, and Naomi hides in the woman's purse. No longer able to watch Hans face death daily, she returns to Ichiro and safety in Saito's apartment. The roach-hating woman moves in from across the courtyard. Saito, we learn, was so depressed after his wife left him he let the roaches eat and wander about because he was too depressed and lonely to do anything about it. Spurred on by his new girlfriend, all that is about to change. Naomi, now pregnant, is uncertain whether the father is Ichiro or Hans. Reunited with Ichiro, the two are wed. The ceremony is interrupted, however, when the human couple arrive with a sackful of roach bombs and bug spray. Hundreds of the roaches die. Hans and his tribe stage an all-out attack on the humans. It is a losing battle, however, and one by one all of the roaches die. Naomi's grandfather tells her that as humans poison each generation of roaches, the insects continue to build up their immunity and will survive long after the human race becomes extinct. Hans is killed, and soon Ichiro and Naomi are the only roaches left. Ichiro and Naomi try to leave the apartment, but Naomi is gassed by bug spray, and Ichiro is blown to pieces when Saito shoots him with a bug gun. Naomi survives, however, and in a closing painting we see her aged and surrounded by a new generation of poison-resistant cockroaches.

Humans-as-roaches is an exciting, original concept. Except for Art Spiegelman's landmark Holocaust parable, *Maus*, in which Jews and Nazis are replaced by mice and cats, I cannot think of a film or story quite like *Twilight of the Cockroaches*. The film opens with Naomi entering the human woman's apartment. All is silent until the human woman walks through the door. Naomi, believing the woman to be friendly, begins to ask for Hans' whereabouts, but is suddenly and shockingly attacked by the woman, who tries to squish her with her shoe. Although a bit confusing by its odd placement at the beginning of the picture instead of where it occurs in the story proper, this sequence is quite unnerving, even distressing, and obviously not for very small children. Although the animation itself is only average, its often ingenious incorporation into the live action adds tremendously to the film's tension. An animated human foot trying to squish little Naomi wouldn't have been half as effective. The cloudburst that turns into a flash flood is done with real water. A cartoon storm just wouldn't have worked.

The filmmakers were wise in telling the picture's story from the roaches' point of view, with the live action camera almost always at ground level. They also resisted the temptation to build larger-than-life sets that might have have had better depth-of-field but most likely would have had a "fakey" look. For instance, water droplets are the size water droplets would be for the tiny bugs. Sound is handled with equal inventiveness. Footsteps become thunderclaps, and in one funny sequence, the woman's innocent gargling becomes the roar of a horrifying monster. *Twilight of the Cockroaches* also has the good sense to poke fun at its basic absurdity, while never abandoning its ingenious roaches-as-people premise. There are lines about "toilet roaches on the make" and pregnant roach women discussing their "litters." Ichiro plays a roach variation of tennis while slurping on a mammoth bottle of Gatorade, for instance, and the bizarre talking turd (a stop-motion creation) is astonishing and outrageous. Some ideas, such as the roaches dancing to fifties rock 'n' roll and a send-up to morning talk shows, fall flat, but most are funny and inventive.

At its heart though, *Twilight of the Cockroaches* is an unnerving and unrelenting tale of horror. Thanks to that opening sequence, we know that even as the cockroaches play their days are numbered, and the final assault on them is truly frightening. Perhaps the picture's scariest moment comes when Naomi finds a tiny building on the floor and steps inside. It turns out to be a roach motel, and doomed roaches trapped inside save her life by lifting her through the deadly trap. The three main characters, Naomi, Ichiro and particularly Hans are pretty bland, though it's nice that the picture revolves around a female character who turns out to be the only one strong enough to survive.

Christopher Potter, reviewing the film for the *Ann Arbor News*, perceptively noted that "such gloomy eulogizing simply isn't part of the Hollywood mindset," and the picture would never have been made in the United States. He said the film was "the most hauntingly sober animated feature ever made, enthralling in its ambiguous action . . . and tragic in its mode of wistful farewell." *The Motion Picture Guide* didn't agree. "Somebody please get that rolled-up newspaper and smack Japanese writer-director Hiroaki Yoshida in the head with it. *Cockroaches* doesn't even qualify as a camp classic. Besides being thoroughly deranged, it's also slow, dull, and numbingly mediocre . . . . *Who Framed Roger Rabbit?* it ain't. Indeed, it isn't even 'Astro Boy.'" However, Vincent Canby of the *New York Times* found the film "a nervy satire" whose animation was technically excellent."

Godzilla vs. King Ghidorah *(1991)*

This very entertaining entry in the long-running Godzilla series was without a U.S. distributor as this book was going to press. *Godzilla vs. King Ghidorah* makes an engaging companion piece to *Biollante*. Whereas the previous film was more poetic and quietly disturbing, *King Ghidorah* is a slam-bang epic and a nostalgic monster movie. Whereas *Biollante* might be considered Lovecraftian, *King Ghidorah* is Wellsian, with its story of time travel and "War of the Worlds"–like scenes of destruction.

In 1992, a UFO appears in the skies above Tokyo and lands near Mt. Fuji. The military quickly surround the craft. Meanwhile, writer Kenichiro Terasawa (Isao [Kohsuke] Toyohara) and his editor, Chiaki Morimura (Kiwako Harada), investigate stories of a dinosaur spotted by a Japanese battalion on Lagos Island (one of the Marshall Islands) near the end of World War II. They visit successful businessman Yasuaki Shindo (Yoshio Tsuchiya), who produces a yellowing photograph of the men from his former unit standing next to a large *Tyrannosaur*–like dinosaur. Terasawa believes the creature is Godzilla before Lagos was exposed to intense radiation during the H-bomb tests on nearby Bikini Island. Terasawa contemplates a book based on his theories. Officials arrive at the UFO site as three human beings emerge. They are Grenchiko (Richard Berger), Wilson (Chuck Wilson) and Emi (aka Emmy) Kano (Anna Nakagawa), representatives from the Earth of the future, the year 2204 to be exact. They say they've come to warn Japan that in the future their country no longer exists. Godzilla returned after his battle with Biollante and destroyed many cities and nuclear power plants, sending radiation and pollution all over the island nation, eventually rendering it uninhabitable. The people from the future offer to lend their assistance, however. Using their time machine, they propose to remove Godzilla from Lagos Island *before* the H-bomb tests mutated the prehistoric animal into the giant, radioactive monster. Emi and an android named M11 (Robert Scottfield) lead the expedition into the past, inviting Terasawa (because of his book, not even written in 1992, but well-known to Emi in the future), Self Defense Forces psychic Miki Saegusa (Megumi Odaka, also seen in *Godzilla vs. Biollante*) and a paleontologist, Masaki (Katsuhiko Sasaki of *Megalon* fame). Emi is unable to invite Shindo or any of the other soldiers who originally saw the dinosaur because only one individual can exist within the same time frame. Aboard a time-warp jet, docked inside the mother UFO and called "KIDS," the four humans and M11 travel back to the past, along with three cuddly bat-cat creatures (which look like pre-mutated gremlins), biogenetically engineered pets of the future, according to Emi.

They arrive on Lagos Island on February 6, 1944. The island is occupied by a small band of Japanese soldiers, including a young Shindo (also played by Tsuchiya). Heavily bombarded by a U.S. Navy destroyer, a ground force descends on the island the following morning. The tiny Japanese force seems doomed to defeat when out of the dense, tropical forest appears the pre-mutated Godzilla—a *Gojirasaur* if you prefer—looking pretty much like a larger version of a *Tyrannosaurus Rex*, with minor variations. The U.S. troops fire at the beast, which only makes it mad. The dinosaur begins swinging its tail about and squishing the soldiers under its feet. The American force is soon wiped out, though a commander aboard a destroyer manages to have the beast shot in the chest. The *Gojirasaurus* falls over, apparently dying. The American ship departs, its commander concluding the island is best explored by a scientific research team, not the Navy. The Japanese soldiers regard the *Gojirasaur* as their savior and are saddened that they are not able to assist the dying animal. They salute the *Gojirasaurus* and depart. The beast continues breathing but is otherwise still, perfect for teleportation, it seems. It's dropped into the Bering Sea. The crew return to the present, but before they leave 1944 behind, Emi quietly lets the three bat-cat creatures called "drats" loose on the island. Returning to 1992, Godzilla vanishes, but suddenly King Ghidorah appears.

Now the trio from the future reveal their true motive: Japan was not destroyed by Godzilla as the aliens had said. In fact, by 2204, Japan has become *the* world power, buying Africa and South America and dominating even China and the United States. Wilson and Grenchiko are renegades from the future who stole the time travel device; they want to inflict damage on Japan to destabilize it and help tip the balance of power back in their countries' favor. The part–Japanese Emi, who originally went along with their scheme, begins to have second thoughts. She tells Terasawa (as they begin to fall for one another) about the creatures she left on Lagos Island in 1944—creatures which were exposed to the H-bomb tests and became King Ghidorah. Now in the present, the flying three-headed monster devastates the city of Fukuoka, and later destroys the Seto Bridge. The Self Defense Forces stage an aerial attack against

Ghidorah using F-15s, but they are no match for the powerful dragon. Miki senses Godzilla is still alive in the Bering Sea, and the Self Defense Forces decide to expose the *Gojirasaurus* to intense radiation, hoping it will mutate into Godzilla and defeat King Ghidorah. The plan works only too well. A nuclear submarine is sent to the site, but Godzilla, already post-mutated thanks to nuclear waste in the existing ocean, destroys the nuclear sub as well and becomes even larger than before. Godzilla confronts Ghidorah near Abashiri. Controlled by Wilson and Grenchiko, Ghidorah clearly has the upper hand. However, Emi, Terasawa and M11 sabotage the UFO, and the men from the future lose control of King Ghidorah. Godzilla's fiery breath blasts Ghidorah's middle head clean off. He burns large holes in its wings as it tries to fly away. The monster falls helplessly into Ohotsuku Sea. Emi and M11 are also successful in teleporting the UFO (minus the KIDS) to a field right in front of Godzilla, who destroys it (with Wilson and Grenchiko inside) with his radioactive fire.

Japan still has a problem, however, namely a 22-story-tall fire-breathing lizard. Unopposed, Godzilla continues to devastate Japan, making his way to Sapporo. Shindo sees his life come full circle and remains behind as Godzilla attacks (Godzilla gives, he takes away). Godzilla and Shindo gaze into each other's eyes for a few moments before Godzilla vaporizes the former soldier. The monster heads for Tokyo as Emi travels forward to her own time (2204, that is). With the help of M11 and the approval of the World Government, she salvages the still living King Ghidorah to use against Godzilla in a final showdown. She turns Ghidorah into a cyborg, replacing its wings and the middle head with mechanical parts. Emi controls the new creature from a tiny cockpit at the base of the middle head. She returns to 1992 just as Godzilla is pummeling the Shinjuku district of Tokyo. The monsters battle, with Godzilla inflicting heavy damage on the cyborg. Emi latches onto the giant lizard with tentacle-like cables and a vise-like chest-piece and carries the lizard high into the air over Tokyo Bay.

In one last, desperate effort, Godzilla sprays the Ghidorah cyborg in midair, sending both monsters crashing to the water below. All is silent, but at long last, the KIDS with Emi on board emerges from the sea. Emi likes this time period, but must return, for she is one of Terasawa's descendants. Meanwhile, at the bottom of the sea, Godzilla's eyelids flutter and the creature roars. Godzilla lives!

Godzilla vs. King Ghidorah must surely rank among the series' finest. While much of the picture liberally borrows elements from the *Terminator* films (M11) and *Aliens* (Emi's battle with Godzilla), not to mention the 17 Godzilla titles which preceded it, the filmmakers explore them on their own terms (those of Japan in the 1990s) and with confident intelligence. Word of the picture's anti–Americanism became a hot topic briefly in this country in the months following the picture's release in Japan. Actually, its America bashing is fairly slight compared to its fierce nationalism—an about-face by the studio that had produced the cautionary *Atragon* thirty years earlier. Of course, Wilson and Grenchiko are supposed to be renegades from the future and not representative Americans and Soviets (Russians?). After all, there are good Caucasian characters in the story—M11 and the world leader who accompanies Emi to look for Ghidorah to name but two. Instead, the film expresses Japan's uneasiness with its continued success in the world market (which ironically went into decline just as the film went into release) and its perception by the rest of the world. Just as *The Submersion of Japan* reflected that country's freedom and fear of isolation from the West, *Godzilla vs. King Ghidorah* puts that same idea into economic terms.

I've always loved time travel stories, and this film plays fast and loose with its almost infinite possibilities. Godzilla's origins have never really been explained, and that this film is able to do that within the context of an already interesting story is a plus. There are other interesting ideas as well, such as when the three representatives from the future first appear before Japanese officials outside of the UFO. We are surprised when they explain they're not real, but 3-D projections, and that they are actually still inside the ship. I also liked the idea that even though the destruction of the nuclear sub presumably increases Godzilla's size, he's mutated before the sub arrives, thanks to radioactive waste already at the site. Because of nuclear dumping, Godzilla was simply *destined* to be born, no matter where the people from the future might have dumped him. Of course, the picture is primarily an epic sci-fi spectacle and it delivers the goods. *King Ghidorah* was supposedly made in response to *Biollante*'s comparatively esoteric, subtler story, which failed to bring in the audiences producer Tomoyuki Tanaka had expected. *King Ghidorah* is a general audience film more in line with the studio's '60s films—the action and spectacle to appeal to children and teenagers, the film's nostalgic and nationalistic underbelly for more mature audiences.

The picture's bountiful special effects sequences are among the finest in the series. They're a significant improvement over Teruyoshi Nakano's work for *Godzilla 1985*, largely thanks to special effects director Koichi Kawakita's continued confidence in using inventive and dramatic camera angles, camera movements and monster poses. For example, as the Ghidorah cyborg flies over Shinjuku toward Godzilla, Kawakita has opted to photograph this sequence from Ghidorah's point of view: we get a look at the geography of the district, and spotting Godzilla from behind the buildings, looking down at the monster, works extremely well. While Godzilla's size (and Ghidorah's too, for that matter) has once again been increased to about 100 meters tall to better compete with Tokyo's increasingly taller skyscrapers, the miniatures don't suffer the way they did in *Godzilla 1985*, another testament to Kawakita's craftsmanship.

The film gets off to a tremendous start, actually beginning with the brief scene in 2204, where Emi and the world leader examine the remains of King

Ghidorah at the bottom of the Ohotsuku Sea. The sinister dragon-like heads lie silently as the two discuss the creature. The leader marvels at the creature's two heads. Emi explains that it originally had three—before it fought Godzilla in the 20th century. To the strains of Akira Ifukube's delightfully nostalgic score (the main title music is a re-orchestrated theme first heard in *King Kong vs. Godzilla*), we next see the UFO appear above Japan in a series of exciting and dramatically staged shots. The scenes on Lagos Island involving the *Gojirasaurus* are handled in a manner similar to the Rankin-Bass–Tsuburaya production of *The Last Dinosaur*. Although not quite a *Tyranosaurus Rex*, the pre-mutated Godzilla is convincingly prehistoric, almost unrecognizable as Godzilla.

Godzilla himself looks even meaner than he did in *Biollante* but is otherwise unchanged. Ghidorah, practically immobile when last seen in the wretched *Godzilla on Monster Island* (1972), once again looks splendidly wicked. Ghidorah's thrilling attack on Fukuoka can be seen as a tribute to the late Eiji Tsuburaya, for it mirrors Tsuburaya's perfectionistic work in *Ghidrah: The Three-Headed Monster* (1964), while updating the miniatures for the '90s. Anyone fearing a "Mecha-Ghidorah" along the lines of the the 1970s films or *King Kong Escapes* needn't have worried.

The Ghidorah cyborg is an inspired, even scary creation. And that the monster would be used by the Japanese against Godzilla is a delightfully unexpected twist. There are other surprises as well. When the KIDS zooms over the destroyer, one of the sailors asks an officer, "Shall we report it, sir?" The officer responds "No," adding, "You can tell your son about it when he's born, Major Spielberg."

Besides Akira Ifukube's return, Yoshio Tsuchiya (*Battle in Outer Space*, *The Human Vapor*) and Kenji Sahara (*Rodan*, *The Mysterians*) resurface to add to the nostalgia, with the latter cast as a government official. Tsuchiya is particularly memorable. His tribute to Godzilla is well acted and strangely touching. But there are problems. Much of the time travel business contradicts itself, failing to follow its own rules. Several scenes shamelessly—and needlessly—ape the *Terminator* films. The cuddly gremlin-like creatures Emi takes with her back to 1944 to be transformed into Ghidorah look like something one might pick up at Toys R Us. And some of Kawakita's effects work involving the UFO and KIDS lack the confidence that clearly shows in the monster footage.

Despite these minor drawbacks, *Godzilla vs. King Ghidorah* remains an exciting, epic entry. And so the series continued with a renewed energy, at long last honoring the classic entries of the 50s and early 60s, while injecting imaginative new twists that reflect Japan today. If the film does ever find a theatrical release in the United States, it will doubtlessly be ridiculed for what critics will cite as poor effects work and probably the picture's derivative elements. You and I will know better.

The Guyver *(1991)*

Except for some mildly interesting monster costumes, *The Guyver* is a cold, creatively barren film. As William Winkler noted in his review in *Markalite* (# 3), this English-language production was made by hands whose expertise was monster suits, and while the suits themselves are occasionally impressive, the rest of the film is, in fact, very bad.

Loosely based on Yoshiki Takaya's serialized *Bio-Booster Armored Guyver*, the picture opens as a Japanese scientist, Dr. Tetsu Segawa (Greg Paik), dashes through the Los Angeles wash (an oft-used location to say the least), carrying an ominous-looking briefcase. The scientist switches cases just before being confronted by a motley gang of villains: bald leader Lisker (Michael Berryman of *The Hills Have Eyes* fame), hulking Ramsey (Peter Spellos), jive-talking Striker (Jimmy Walker) and red-headed musclewoman Weber (Spice Williams). Defending himself, Segawa transforms himself into a fish-like creature, while Lisker turns into another monstrosity. The brief battle ends when Lisker crushes Segawa's head like a melon. The fish-faced scientist dissolves into a pile of goo. Elsewhere, colorless Sean Barker (Jack Armstrong) is studying Aikido, apparently to impress Segawa's daughter, Mizuki (billed as Mizsky in the credits; at any rate, she's played by Vivian Wu). A CIA agent, Max Reed (Mark Hamill, sporting a beard and unconvincing New York accent), arrives to inform Mizuki of her father's death, which pretty much ruins Sean's plans to ask her out that evening. Nonetheless, he follows her and Max to the murder scene. Sean stumbles upon the hidden case, and when *he's* faced by an unrelated gang of hoodlums soon thereafter, a shiny steel ball inside the case suddenly turns wimpy Sean into "The Guyver." Resembling an insect in football gear, super-strong Sean now dispatches the evil gang with the greatest of ease. When it's all over, Sean returns to his natural, human state. Once Lisker realizes he grabbed the wrong briefcase, Mizuki is kidnapped. Max and Sean catch up with the baddies, however, who all turn into monsters. Sean turns into the Guyver, and Max and Mizuki do little but watch the poorly staged fisticuffs from the sidelines. Sean is knocked out and eventually dissolves when Lisker discovers the Guyver's weakness, the silver ball embedded in the superhero's head. Max and Mizuki are whisked away to a warehouse laboratory. There, Fulton Bakus (also referred to as Vaulkus, and played by *Re-Animator*'s David Gale) explains that his company, Kronos, is genetically engineering Zoanoids, monster warriors. An army of creatures the likes of Lisker and Striker could rule the world, he says. The only thing standing in his way is Segawa's bio-boosted armor, the Guyver. Max is placed in a tube to be transformed (why?), while Bakus lusts after Mizuki. The Guyver inexplicably turns up alive and well and somehow manages to best Lisker and company in another tiresome battle. Max is freed from the transformation tube, but the metamorphosis has already begun. Max turns into a pathetic spider creature but dies because "he wasn't in the soup long enough." Just then, Bakus becomes a Zoanoid himself. A dragon-like creature with antlers, many times larger than the other monsters (a company perk?), Bakus battles the Guyver for the big showdown. The Bakus creature is defeated, but, almost perversely, a Kronos agent and Striker survive, hoping to appear in a sequel. "Dy-no-mite!"

The Guyver's story harks back to the outrageous, nearly plotless Japanese serials of the 1950s, but whereas those films were exciting and inventive, *The Guyver* is thunderously dull and appalling in its lack of imagination. The articulated creature costumes are nice, but that's where everything—and I mean everything—stops. The acting, direction, set design, editing, lighting and especially the script are no better than mediocre, and often considerably worse than that. Considering the monsters are the film's only assets, one would think the filmmakers would have at least used some creativity in their presentation. Instead, the costumes are systematically marched in front of the camera like floats at a Macy's Thanksgiving Day parade. In fact, Michael Berryman, Jimmy Walker and Spice Williams aren't even *in* the film's final third, having been completely replaced by their creature counterparts (and played by others). According to Winkler's article, the film's producers didn't want to pay the trio an extra week's salary and simply had them loop their dialogue over the monster footage. Mouthing trite though campy lines in monster form, these characters manage to be neither scary nor funny. Although fairly elaborate, the costumes themselves are nothing special, though Mark Hamill's transformation scene is somewhat better. The giant Bakus monster, apparently a combination of full-size props and stop-motion animation, is also nice, but neither sequence is handled well within the context of the film—they just sit there.

The entire picture is directed in a flat, dull style. Everything takes place at night or in darkly-lit interiors, and the bland, even lighting brings a flatness to every scene, as if the actors were working on a very shallow stage. The performances are equally dim. Top-billed Hamill provides some interest, chiefly because his character is so different from his Luke Skywalker role in George Lucas' *Star Wars* trilogy, the part that catapulted him to limited stardom. The main characters, however, are dull-as-dishwater Jack Armstrong and Vivian Wu (*The Last Emperor*), neither of whom generates much interest. Conversely, David Gale and Jimmy Walker are way over the top as Bakus and Striker. The former is at least entertaining; the latter is simply embarrassing.

Frequently, untalented directors and screenwriters of cheap horror and science fiction films turn to low-brow humor when their talents aren't up to more ambitious screenplays. This seems to be true here. While the story is as bad as everything else, it might have worked a little bit better had it been played straight. The comedy is witless and incredibly contrived, particularly in the dubious talent of Jimmy Walker, still playing his "J. J." role from television.

Several in-jokes, notably the appearance at the Kronos laboratory of a Dr. East (Jeffrey Combs, briefly spoofing his Herbert West role from *Re-Animator*, which was produced by the same hands), go nowhere. Especially painful is the film-within-the-film, wherein Walker's Striker, in monster form, stumbles onto the set of a monster movie (Linnea Quigley has a cameo as the picture's scream queen) and is mistaken for that film's star. In a shameless self-congratulatory bit, the "director" (Michael Deak) tells Striker that "the suit looks great! You look terrific!" Predictably, the director does a big double take when the real monster shows up.

The Guyver was released in Japan by Shochiku-Fuji but bypassed theatrical distribution in the United States, going directly to home video and cable television.

Godzilla vs. Mothra *(1992)*

Toho continued its reworking of the Godzilla myth in its 19th entry, a film more distinctly Japanese than any of the previous post-rebirth entries. *Godzilla vs. King Ghidorah* had been a big hit in Japan, and Toho apparently felt confident enough in the series' domestic success to allow a more ambitious story less geared toward furthering international sales. Like *Godzilla vs. King Ghidorah*, *Gojira vs. Mosura* (*Godzilla vs. Mothra*) was without an American distributor as this book went to press.

A huge meteor crashes into the Ogasawara Sea, which does several things at once. The force of the impact creates a tremendous storm, which unearths a mammoth egg on far-off Infant Island, located near Indonesia. The meteor also awakens a dark, caterpillar-like creature called Battra, heretofore hibernating in Siberia, as well as the sleeping Godzilla, the monster having survived its battle with Mecha-King Ghidorah in the previous film. Meanwhile, in Thailand, an Indiana Jones–type treasure hunter, Takuya Fujita (Tetsuya Bessho), attempts to steal a small statue from an ancient temple. He's nearly killed when the temple's walls and steps begin to collapse à la *Raiders of the Lost Ark*. Fujita barely makes it out alive and is taken into custody by Thai officials. In a Thai jail, Fujita is visited by his ex-wife, Masako Tezuka (Satomi Kobayashi), Japanese security chief Ruzo Dobashi (Shoji Kobayashi), and Kenji Ando (Takehiro Murata), an executive representing Marumoto Corporation, a land development firm. The three spring Fujita from jail because the Marumoto Corporation is planning to develop Infant Island and can use Fujita's expertise in an exploratory mission. Fujita, Masako and Ando arrive at Infant Island, and in another bit shamelessly lifted from an Indiana Jones adventure (this time *Temple of Doom*), the hapless trio attempt to cross a rickety bridge which soon collapses, sending the explorers to one cliffside, where they hang on for dear life. They survive, however, and eventually stumble upon the unearthed egg, along with a nearby cave holding centuries-old drawings of a cross symbol (also seen in *Mothra*) and a rendering of the winged insect itself. Back outside, the trio are greeted by Mothra's six-inch priestesses (Keiko Imamura and Sayaka Osawa), now called the Cosmos. The tiny pair explain they were part of a race which came to Earth long before the evolution of modern man. Twelve thousand years ago, they say, their race tried unsuccessfully to control the weather. This disrupted the planet's environmental balance and unleashed the monster Battra, guardian of the Earth's environmental essence. The alien race, in turn, sent Mothra, their god and protector, to combat Battra near Siberia; the ancient battle concluded with Battra trapped in the Siberian ice. The recent meteor, combined with mankind's own destruction of the environment, has unleashed Battra once again. The giant egg, they add, is Mothra's offspring. Undaunted by this weighty news, Marutomo's president, Takeshi Tomokane (Makoto Otake), orders the egg brought back to Japan for study and exploitation. Battra, meanwhile, appears in Japan and devastates the city of Nagoya, with powerful rays from its horn and eyes doing most of the damage.

At sea, the ship carrying Mothra's egg is met by Godzilla. Just then the egg hatches and a baby Mothra (in caterpillar form) emerges. As the two creatures commence a fierce duel, Battra also appears, joining the confusing battle. Mothra departs, and Godzilla and Battra are eventually trapped when an underwater volcano erupts nearby. Fujita, Masako and the Cosmos arrive in Japan, where they're met by the couple's young daughter, Midori (Shiori Yonezawa). The little girl has not seen her father in some time, and does not approve of his temple desecrations and robberies. Elsewhere, Tomokane and Ando discuss selling the Cosmos and meet with an American businessman to this end. The Cosmos, perhaps feeling threatened, begin singing for their guardian, who heads for Tokyo. Like the original *Mothra*, the big caterpillar just cannot be stopped; it plows its way through the city to where the tiny twins are being held. After it becomes clear to the creature that the Cosmos are unharmed, Mothra begins cocooning itself to the Diet Building. Mt. Fuji suddenly erupts. The seemingly indestructible Godzilla appears, having made its way to Japan through the continental plate. At the Diet Building, Mothra, now in winged form, emerges from the cocoon. Battra also appears, transforming itself to a winged monster as well (it becomes a darker version of Mothra, sort of a Mothra-meets-Batman creation). The three creatures battle one another on land and in the skies over Yokohama. Battra severely disables Mothra and moves on to Godzilla. Godzilla cripples Battra, but Mothra obligingly rejuvenates his former enemy by giving the creature some of its own energy.

At a Yokohaman amusement part, Mothra continues the attack on Godzilla, but the fight proves too much for the weakened insect. A blast of Godzilla's radioactive breath sends a giant Ferris Wheel crashing down toward

Mothra, but Battra suddenly appears, preventing the ride from crushing the insect brother. Mothra and Battra join forces in the battle against Godzilla. Together, they lift the king of the Monsters high into the night sky. The big bugs appear victorious, but in a last-ditch effort, Godzilla sprays Battra with his fiery breath, sending both creatures crashing into the sea below. Mothra, the sole survivor, creates a curtain-like circle around the area, complete with the cross-like image seen on Infant Island. The film closes with Midori's parents reunited (and Fujita swearing off temple robbing). The Cosmos reveal that Battra was supposed to awaken in the distant future to intercept an even bigger meteor presently on a collision course with Earth. Mothra will carry out Battra's mission, they say, and after spiritually joining with the creature, fly out into space.

Kazuki Omori's screenplay for *Godzilla vs. Mothra* is a real mess, though so filled with interesting ideas that its many failings can largely be forgiven. Moreover, the picture's other qualities, especialy Koichi Kawakita's awesome special effects and Akira Ifukube's beautiful score, help tremendously to create one of the series' most satisfying (if wildly uneven) entries yet. One problem is the motivations of the monsters, which are ill-defined at best. Battra is supposed to be the protector of the Earth and has mystical overtones, but its confusing sparring with the other monsters, especially Mothra (who appears to want nothing more than the safe return of the Cosmos), is confusing. And why does the creature attack Japan? It may be due to mankind's own neglect of the environment, but this is never made clear. Other ideas, such as the exploitation of Infant Island, the giant egg and the tiny twins, are left equally underdeveloped. Clearly Toho wanted to rework elements from *Mothra* and *Godzilla vs. The Thing*, two of the studio's most popular films, without actually remaking them, while adding a new monster to insure the picture's box office success. Godzilla in fact has very little to do. Though he impressively smashes buildings and whatnot, he is in no way the picture's center. The picture *has* no center, and that's its biggest problem.

Just as *Godzilla vs. King Ghidorah* shamelessly lifted elements from the *Terminator* films, so too does *Godzilla vs. Mothra* "borrow" ideas from proven American productions, this time from the "Indiana Jones" trilogy. These scenes are effectively filmed, and almost work as a kind of satire of the genre, but ultimately come off as nothing more than an embarrassing rip-off. But there is much to like and much that is unique in *Godzilla vs. Mothra*. The symbolic nature of Battra and Mothra and the film's distinctly Japanese, almost mystical tone are pleasantly and distinctly dissimilar to any monster movie ever made in the West. Omori's decision to change Mothra from Polynesian-esque deity to one-third of a global environmental conflict (while protecting its basic character of guardian to the twins) was a good one. And while the constantly-changing relationships the monsters have to one another is pointlessly confusing, their actions become downright touching toward the end, as Mothra rescues Battra and vice versa.

Akira Ifukube's score is nothing less than superb. His arrangements of familiar themes, as well as a new motif written for Battra, work wonderfully well, especially his adaptation of the several songs sung by the Cosmos. Ifukube's arrangement of "The Song of Mothra," first heard in *Godzilla vs. The Thing*, and used here over the end titles, is just lovely.

Special effects director Koichi Kawakita has done another superlative job. Though Battra isn't particularly impressive in and of itself, the pyrotechnical effects and optical work, spurred by the creature's ray-shooting horn and eyes, are outstanding. Mothra's journey from Infant Island to Japan compares favorably to the same sequence in the original *Mothra*, and the scenes of destruction once the monster hits urban Japan are awesome. In one shot, the creature looks like nothing less than a runaway monster train, plowing through building after building with jaw-dropping unstoppability. Though the monsters' scenes are, thanks to the script, confusingly plotted, the monster battles themselves—at sea and in Yokohama—are equally spectacular. Kawakita's work has clearly matured over the last 10 years; his work here even bests Eiji Tsuburaya's effects for *Mothra* and *Godzilla vs. The Thing*—no small compliment.

Tetsuya Bessho and especially Satomi Kobayashi add a certain depth that had been missing from the series' human characters of late. Their relationship is an interesting one, though like nearly everything else, seems disjointed and out of synch with the rest of the film. Keiko Imamura and Sayaka Osawa fit the Peanuts' old role nicely, and the young performers have notably more charisma than their counterparts in the characters' last appearance, in *Godzilla Versus the Sea Monster*. In keeping with the studio's practice of bringing back series regulars from the fifties and sixties films, Akira Takarada returns in a supporting role, as Environmental Planning Board Chief Joji Minamino. The film marks Takarada's first *kaiju eiga* appearance since 1969's *Latitude Zero*. As with Yosuke Natsuki, Yoshibumi Tajima and Hiroshi Koizumi in *Godzilla 1985*, and Yoshio Tsuchiya and Kenji Sahara in *Godzilla vs. King Ghidorah*, it's great fun to see them again.

Ultimately, while *Godzilla vs. Mothra*'s tone is in keeping with the 1961 *Mothra* and *Godzilla vs. the Thing*, the picture most closely resembles *Ghidrahi: The Three-Headed Monster* in terms of its structure. The story's characters— both monster and human—are disjointed and frequently confusing, but like *Ghidrah*, the film's escapist nature and singularly Japanese approach to monsterdom make *Godzilla vs. Mothra* a vivid and most enjoyable monster epic.

* * *

And so we bid farewell to the Godzilla series for now. As the original *Gojira* approaches its 40th anniversary, the star power of the King of the Monsters remains unabated. As this book was going to press a 20th film, *Gojira vs.*

Mekagojira (*Godzilla vs. Mechagodzilla*) was in production at Toho and slated for a December 1993 release. Takao Okawara will direct once again, Koichi Kawakita will handle the special effects, and Akira Ifukube has agreed to write one last score. This time Mechagodzilla has been reworked as the creation of the Japanese Defense Forces to fight Godzilla, and a (thankfully) revamped Rodan and Minya are slated to appear as well. *Gojira vs. Mekagojira* is rumored to be the last Japanese-made Godzilla film, owing to Columbia-Tri-Star's big-budget remake of the 1954 original, which may be released as early as December 1994. Will the essence of what made the original series so memorable be retained, or will Godzilla simply be transformed into a lumbering, city-smashing brute? Whatever the answer, Godzillaphiles can rest easy in the knowledge that no matter what indignities might befall him, Godzilla, like all good monsters, will rise again.

Filmography

An Introductory Note

What follows is the most extensive listing of cast, credit and release information on Japanese fantastic cinema ever compiled in English. However, new information—an assistant director here, a release date there—kept turning up right until this book went to press, and some data were certainly passed over. Nonetheless, there is much here that has never appeared in print in this part of the world before, and to this end I am indebted to R. M. Hayes and David Milner and Horacio Higuchi for their invaluable, tireless assistance.

There has been a considerable effort made to correct errors that keep popping up in other references, such as actors billed for roles they didn't play. For instance, Kyoko Kagawa, who played the female lead in Toho's *Mothra*, has often been credited with the role of "Clark Nelson," that film's very male villain. Kagawa is a well-known, widely respected actress; she starred opposite Toshiro Mifune in several Kurosawa films from that same period, yet virtually every film reference until now has mis-billed her.

With the help of Milner, Higuchi and Hayes, I've also tried to standardize names and crew positions as much as possible. Japanese names are written with Chinese ideographs and can frequently be interpreted several different ways; this can be confusing even for lifelong natives of Japan. That's why the director Honda is sometimes billed as Ishiro and sometimes as Inoshiro (I'm told he called himself Ishiro, so that's the spelling used in this book), why special effects director Nakano has been billed as Teruyoshi, Akiyoshi and Shokei, etc. It is difficult at times to nail down just who did what.

It should also be noted that I've adopted the family-name-last system common in the West, rather than the patronymic-first format used in Japan (i.e., we say Akira Kurosawa while in Japan the acclaimed filmmaker would be called Kurosawa Akira). This seemed to make more sense for an American-oriented book, despite the move in recent years toward the patronymic-first system now used in most English-language books on Japanese subjects. (But not in films—the only English-language film I'm aware of to do this was Sydney Pollack's *The Yakuza*, which created a lot of confusion for reviewers.)

The Hepburn method of transliteration, favored in international business, literature, the press and films, is used in this book. Credits occasionally list a name or two in an alternate transliteration system, such as the Kunrei, and all others in the Hepburn system. I have standardized these whenever possible.

Films are listed in alphabetical order by studio. As with the text entries, the pictures here are listed by their original English-language title. Those unreleased in the United States are listed by their Japanese title.

Daiei Motion Picture Company, Ltd.

Along with Ghosts. Producer, Masaichi Nagata; Director, Kimiyoshi Yasuda; Screenplay, Tetsuo Yoshida; Directory of Photography, Hiroshi Imai; Music, Hiroshi Watanabe; Sound, Daiei Recording Studio; Special Effects, Daiei Special Effects Department.

Cast: Kojiro Hongo (Hyakutaro), Pepe Hozumi (Shinta), Masami Rurukido (Miyo), Mutsushiro (Toura Saikichi), Yoshito Yamaji (Higuruma), Bokuzen Hidari (Jinbei).

A Daiei Motion Picture Co., Ltd., Production. A Masaichi Nagata Presentation. Westrex Recording System. Daieicolor. DaieiScope. Running time undetermined. Released 1969.

U.S. Version: Released by Daiei International Films, Inc., in subtitled format. Shown in Los Angeles, other playdates undetermined. Also known as *Journey along Tokaido Road*. A sequel (?) to *100 Monsters* (Daiei, 1968). No MPAA rating. Released 1969.

Attack of the Monsters/Gamera tai daiaku Guiron (*Gamera Against the Giant Evil Beast Guiron*). Executive Producer, Masaichi Nagata; Producer, Hidemasa [Hideo] Nagata; Director, Noriaki Yuasa; Planning, Kazumasa Nakano; Screenplay, Fumi Takahashi; Music, Shunsuke Kituchi; Director of Photography, Akira Kitazaki; Sound, Daiei Recording Studio; Special Effects Director, Kazufumi [Kazafumi] Fujii; Special Effects, Daiei Special Effects Department; Monster Design, Ryosaku Takayama.

Cast: Nobuhiro Kazima [Najima] (Akiro), Christopher Murphy (Tom), Miyuki Akiyama (Tomoko), Yuko Hamada (Koniko), Eiji Funakoshi (Dr. Shiga), Kon Omura (Kondo).

A Daiei Motion Picture Co., Ltd., Production. Westrex recording system. Eastman Color (processed by Daiei Laboratory). DaieiScope. 88 minutes. Released March 21, 1969.

U.S. Version: Never released theatrically in the United States. Released directly to television by American International Television (AIP-TV) in 1969. A James H. Nicholson and Samuel Z. Arkoff Presentation; Prints by Perfect. The fifth in the "Gamera" series. Home video and television reissue title: *Gamera vs Guiron*, and minus AIP-TV's credits. Home video version (which claims to be recorded in LP mode, though my copy, at least, is really in cheap EP mode) released by King Features Entertainment, Inc., a subsidiary of the Hearst Corp., and as a Sandy Frank Syndication, Inc., Presentation. Copyright 1969 by Daiei International Films, Inc. No MPAA rating. 82 minutes.

(*Note:* This film and several others listed here are presumed to have been released directly to television. However, many of these titles *did* receive an extremely limited theatrical distribution in subtitled format by Daiei International Films, Inc. The author stresses, however, that their theatrical release, if any, would have been limited to ethnic theaters only.)

The Blind Beast/Moju (*The Blind Beast*). Executive Producer, Masaichi Nagata; Producer, Kazumasa Nakano; Director, Yasuzo Masamura; Screenplay, Yoshio Shirasoka, based on the story "Moju," by Rampo Edogawa; Director of Photography, Setsuo Kobayashi; Art Director, Shigeo Mano; Sound Recording Supervisor, Takeo Sudo; Sound, Daiei Recording Studio; Music, Hikari Hayashi.

Cast: Eiji Funakoshi (Michio Sofu), Mako Midori (Aki Shima), Noriko Sengoku (Shino, Michio's Mother).

A Daiei Motion Picture Co., Ltd., Production. A Masaichi Nagata Presentation. Daieicolor. Daieiscope. Westrex recording system. 86 minutes. Released January 1969.

U.S. Version: Released by Daiei International Films, Inc., in subtitled format. Reissued by Roninfilm as *Warehouse*, and running 86 minutes in February 1974. Running time 84–90 minutes (sources vary). No MPAA rating. Released April 1969.

Buddha/Shaka. Producer, Masaichi Nagata; Associate Producer, Akinari Suzuki; Director, Kenji Misumi; Screenplay, Fuji Yahiro; Production Manager, Masatsugu Hashimoto; Assistant Directors, Akira Inoue, Yoshiyuki Kuroda; Director of Photography, Hiroshi Imai; Lighting, Kenichi Okamotot; Music, Akira Ifukube, performed by the Tokyo Symphony Orchestra, Conducted by Jin Ueda; Editor, Kaji Suganuma; Color Consultant, Yoshiaki Kiura; Technical Advisers, Gakuro Nakamura, Takio Namamura; Choreography, Kitsu Sakakibata; Art Director, Kisaku Ito; Art, Akira Naito; Set Decorator, Teruo Kajitani; Decoration Consultant, Toshiharu Takatsu; Costume Designer, Hachiro Nakajima; Costume Consultant, Yoshio Ueno; Animation, Tomio Sagisu; Sound Recording Supervisor, Masao Osumi; Sound, Daiei Recording Studio; Special Effects, Tatsuyuki, So-Ichi Aisaka; Special Photographic Effects, Tooru Matooba, Chishi Makiura, Daiei Special Effects Department.

Cast: Kojiro Hongo (Prince Siddhartha), Charito Solis (Princess Yashodhara), Shintaro Katsu (Devadatta), Machiko Kyo (Nandabala), Raizo Ichikawa (Kunala), Fujiko Yamamoto (Usha), Hiroshi Kawaguchi (Ajatashatru), Katsuhiko Kobayashi (Ananda), Tamao Nakamura (Auttami), Junko Kano (Matangi), Mieko Kondo (Amana), Tokiko Mita (Sari), Hiromi Ichida (Naccha), Michiko Ai (Kilika), Matasaburo Niwa (Sonna), Keizo Kawasaki (Upali), Reiko Fujiwara (Child's Mother), Gen Mitamura (Shariputra), Ryuzo Shimada (Bhutika), Joji Tsurumi (Arama), Shiro Otsuji (Kalodayi), Yoshiro Kitahara (Kaundinya), Jun Negami (Mahakashyapa), Ganjiro Nakamura (Ashoka), Tohsio Chiba (Graha), Ryuichi Ishii (Bandhu), Yoichi Funaki (Maudgaliputra), Sanemon Arashi (Rayana), Osamu Maryuama (Jivaka), Gen Shimizu (Kisaka), Isuzu Yamada (Kalidevi), Yumeji Tsukioka (Takshakara), Tanie Kitabayashi (Sumi), Chikako Hosokawa (Maya), Haruko Sugimura (Vaidehi), Koreya Senda (Shuddhodana), Ryonosuke Azuma (Bashpa), Shintaro Nanjyo (Mahanaman), Kinya Ichikawa (Chunda), Seishiro Hara (Bhadrika), Saburo Date (Ashvajit), Kongo Reiko (Subhaya), Kimiko Tachibana (Amita).

A Daiei Motion Picture Co., Ltd., Production. A Masaichi Negata Presentation. Filmed at Daiei-Kyoto Studios. Westrex Recording System. Stereophonic Sound. Eastman Color (processsed by Daiei Laboratory). Super 70 Technirama (i.e. modified VistaVision). 156 minutes. Released 1963.

U.S. Version: Released by United Artists Corporation. A Lopert Pictures Corporation Release; Prints by Technicolor. Super 70 Technirama. *Note:* Contains some footage filmed in DaieiScope and converted to 70mm. 139 minutes. No MPAA rating. Released July 2, 1963.

The Curse of the Ghosts/Yotsuya kaidan: Oiwa no borei Producer, Masaichi Nagata; Director, Issei Mori; Screenplay, Kinya Naoi, based on the play, *Yotsuda kaidan* by Nanboku Tsuruya; Director of Photography, Senkichiro Takeda; Art Director, Seiichi Ota; Music, Ishiro Saito; Sound, Daiei Recording Studio; Special Effects, Daiei Special Effects Department.

Cast: Kei Sato (Iemon), Kazuko Inano (Oiwa), Yoshihiko Aoyama (Samurai), Kyoko Mikage (Osode), Shoji Kobayashi, Sonosuke Sawamura.

A Daiei Motion Picture Co., Ltd., Production. A Masaichi Nagata Presentation. Westrex recording system. Daieicolor. Daieiscope. Westrex recording system. 94 minutes. Released 1969.

U.S. Version: Released by Daiei International Films, Inc., in subtitled format. Other versions include *Shinchaku kaidan* (1949), *Tokaido Yotsuya kaidan* (1959) and *Yotsuya kaidan* (1965). 94 minutes. No MPAA rating. Released 1969.

Destroy All Planets/Gamera tai uchu kaiju Bairusu. (*Gamera Against the Space Monster Bairusu*; aka *Gamera tai Viras*). Executive Producer, Masaichi Nagata; Producer, Hidemasa Nagata; Director, Noriyaki Yuasa; Screenplay, Fumi Taka-hashi; Director of Photography, Akira Kitazaki; Music, Kenjiro Hirose; Editor, Shoji

Sekiguchi; Sound Recording Supervisor, Kimio Hida; Sound, Daiei Recording Studio; Special Effects Directors, Kazafumi Fujii, Yuso [Yuzo] Kaneko; Monster Design, Ryosaku Takayama; Special Effects, Daiei Special Effects Department.

Cast: Kojiro Hongo (Nobuhiko Shimada), Toru Takatsuka (Masao Nakaya), Peter Williams (Dr. Dobie), Carl Clay [Kurl Crane, Craig] (Jim Morgan), Michiko Yaegaki (Mariko Nakaya), Mari Atsumi (Junko Aoki), Junko Yashiro [Yatsushiro] (Masako Shibata), Koji Fujiyama (Commander of Jietat), Genzo Wakayama (Boss' Voice), Chikara Hashimoto, Kenichiro Yamane, Kenji Go, Akira Natsuki, Ken Nakehara (Men Like the Doctor [?!]), Mary Horris [Merry Murus].

A Daiei Motion Picture Co., Ltd., Production. A Masaichi Nagata Presentation. Eastman Color (processed by Daiei Laboratory). Daieiscope. Filmed at Daiei-Tokyo Studios. 89 minutes. Released March 20, 1968.

U.S. Version. Never released theatrically in the United States. Released directly to television by American International Television (AIP-TV) in 1969. A James H. Nicholson and Samuel Z. Arkoff Presentation; Post Production Supervisor, Salvatore Billitteri; Director, Bret Morrison; Editors, Eli Haviv, Emil Haviv; Prints by Perfect. Copyright 1969 by AIP-TV. International title: *Gamera vs. Viras*. Also known as (U.K. title?) *Gamera vs. the Outer Space Monster Virus*. The film is often listed at 72–75 minutes, which may have been a reissue running time. Fourth in the "Gamera" series. Includes extensive stock footage from *Gammera the Invincible* (1965), *War of the Monsters* (1966) and *Return of the Giant Monsters* (1967). Copyright 1968 by Daiei International Films, Inc. 89 minutes. No MPAA rating.

Enchanted Princess/Hatsuharu tanuki goten. Executive Producer, Masaishi Nagata; Writer-Director, Keigo Kimura; Director of Photography, Hiroshi Imai; Sound, Daiei Recording Studio.

Cast: Raizo Ichikawa, Ayako Wakao, Shintaro Katsu, Tamao Nakamura, Atsuko Kindaichi, Yoshie Mizutani.

A Daiei Motion Picture Co., Ltd., Production. A Masaichi Nagata Presentation. Western Electric Mirrophonic recording. Daieicolor. Academy Ratio. 85 minutes. Released 1960.

U.S. Version: U.S. distributor, if any, is undetermined.

Gamera vs. Monster X/Gamera taimaju Jaiga (*Gamera Against the Demon Beast Jaiga*). Executive Producer, Masaichi Nagata; Producer, Hidemasa Nagata; Director, Noriyaki Yuasa; Screenplay, Fumi Takahashi; Director of Photography, Akira Kitazaki; Sound, Daiei Recording Studio; Music, Shunsuke Kikuchi; Special Effects Director, Kazafumi Fujii; Special Effects, Daiei Special Effects Department; Monster Design, Ryosaku Takayama.

Cast: Tsutomu Takakuwa, Kelly Varis, Katherine Murphy, Kon Omura, Junko Yashiro.

A Daiei Motion Picture Co., Ltd., Production. A Masaichi Nagata Presentation. Eastman Color (processed by Daiei Laboratory). Daieiscope. 83 minutes. Released March 21, 1970.

U.S. Version: Never released theatrically in the United States. Released directly to television by American International Television (AIP-TV) in 1970. A James H. Nicholson and Samuel Z. Arkoff Presentation. American version by Titra Productions, Inc. Post Production Supervisor, Salvatore Billitteri; Director, Bret Morrison; Editors, Eli Haviv, Emil Haviv. Prints by Perfect. Sixth film in the "Gamera" series. Copyright 1970 by Daiei International Films, Inc. U.K. title (?): *Monsters Invade Expo 70*. Includes stock footage from *War of the Monsters* (1966) and *Attack of the Monsters* (1969). No MPAA rating. 83 minutes.

Gamera vs. Zigra/Gamera tai shinkai kaiju jigura (*Gamera Against the Deep Sea Monster Jigura*). Executive Producer, Masaichi Nagata; Producers, Yoshihiko Manabe, Hidemasa [Hideo] Nagata; Director, Noriyaki Yuasa; Screenplay, Fumi Takahashi; Director of Photography, Akira Uehara; Editor, Zenko Miyazaki; Sound, Hideo Okuyama, Daiei Recording Studio; Music, Shunsuke Kikuchi; Special Effects Director, Kozufumi [Kazufumi, Kazuo] Fujii; Special Effects, Daiei Special Effects Department; Monster Design, Ryosaku Takayama.

Cast: Eiko Yanami (Woman X), Reiko Kasahara (Maid), Mikiko Tsubouchi (Hiroko), Koji Fujiyama (Tom), Isamu Saeki (Yosuke Ishikawa), Yasushi Sakagami (Ken-ichi), Arlene Zoellner, Gloria Zoellner, Shin Minatsu.

A Daiei Motion Picture Co., Ltd., Production. Daieicolor. Daieiscope. Copyright 1971 by Daiei International Films, Inc. 87 minutes. Released July 17, 1971.

U.S. Version: Never released theatrically in the United States. Released directly to television by King Features Entertainment, a subsidiary of the Hearst Corporation, in 1987; A Sandy Frank Film Syndication, Inc., Presentation. Seventh film in the "Gamera" series. No MPAA rating. 87 minutes.

Gammera the Invincible/Daikaiju Gamera (*Giant Monster Gamera*). Director, Noriaki Yuasa; Executive Producer, Masaichi Nagata; Producer, Hidemasa Nagata; Planner (i.e., Production Manager?), Yonejiro Saito; Screenplay, Nizo [Fumi] Takahashi (based on an idea by Yonejiro Saito); Director of Photography, Nobuo Nakashizu [Munekawa]; Editor, Tatsuji Nakashizu; Sound Recording Supervisor, Masao Osumi; Sound, Daiei Recording Studio; Special Effects Director, Yonesaburo [Yonesaburg] Tsukiji, Daiei Special Effects Department; Monster Design, Ryosaku Takayama.

Cast: Eiji Funakoshi (Dr. Hidaka), Harumi (Kiritachi (Kyoko), Junichiro Yamashiko (Aoyaki), Yoshiro Uchida (Toschio), Michiko Sugata (Nobuyo), Yoshiro Kitahara (Sakurai), Jun Hamamura (Dr. Maurase), George Hirose (Japanese Ambassador).

A Daiei Motion Picture Co., Ltd., Production; black and white (processed by Daiei Laboratory); DaieiScope. 86 minutes. Released November 27, 1965.

U.S. Version: Released by World Entertainment Corp. A Harris Associates Presentation. Executive Producer, Ken Barnett; Additional Dialog, Richard Kraft; Director of Photography, Julian Townsend; Editing, Ross-Gaffney, Inc.; Art Director, Hank Aldrich; Assistant Director (Director of U.S. Version?), Sidney Cooperschmidt; Theme Song, Wes Ferrell (performed by the Moons); U.S. version filmed in Totalscope. International Title (?): *The Monster Gamera*. Home Video and television reissue version title: *Gamera*. Distributed by King Features Entertainment, a subsidiary of Hearst Corp.; A Sandy Frank Film Syndication, Inc., Presentation. Copyright 1965 by Daiei International Films, Inc. Reissued to television and home video in 1987 in the original Japanese version (minus the added footage), and the entire film is redubbed. Cast names Anglicized for television and home video version. 86 minutes. No MPAA rating. Released December 15, 1966.

Additional Cast for U.S. Version: Brian Donlevy (General Terry Arnold), Albert Dekker (Secretary of Defense), Diane Findlay (Sergeant Susan Embers), John Baragrey (Captain Lovell), Dick O'Neill (General O' Neill), Mort Marshall (Jules Manning), Alan Oppenheimer (Dr. Emeric Contrare), Stephen Zacharias (Senator Billings), Bob Caraway (Lieutenant Simson), Gene Nua (Lieutenant Clark), John McCurry (Airman First Class Hopkins), Walter Arnold (American Ambassador), Louis Zorich (Russian Ambassador), Robin Craven (British Ambassador), Marvin Miller, Jack Grimes (Dubbing Cast).

The Ghostly Trap/Kaidan otoshiana. Producer, Kazuo Tsukaguchi; Executive Producer, Masaichi Nagata; Director, Koji Shima; Screenplay, Kazui Funabashi; Art Director, Atsuji Shibata; Director of Photography, Joji Ohara; Editor, Toyo Suzuki; Music, Seitaro Ohmori; Sound Recording Supervisor, Tsuchitaro Hayashi; Sound, Daiei Recording Studio.

Cast: Mikio Narita (Haruo Kuramoto), Eiji

Funakoshi (Fumio Nishino), Mayumi Nagisa (Etsuko Nishino), Mako Sanjo (Midori Yukawa), Bontaro Miake (President Yukawa), Kiyoko Hirai (Michiko Yukawa), Mitsuko Tanaka (Natsuko Fukuhara), Mariko Fukuhara (Hanako), Yukiko Tsuyama (Namiko), Yuzo Hayakawa (Sakabe), Chikara Hashimoto (Udegawa), Isamu Saeki (Fujioka), Kenichi Tani (Chief of Satomi Section), Yasuhei Endo (Head of Department), Kenji Ohyama (Managing Director), Nobuo Namikata (Executive Director), Mari Atsumi (Usher), Akira Natsuki (Doctor), Shinsuke Kijima (First Official), Naomasa Kawashima (Second Official), Ken Nakahara (Ikegami).

A Daiei Motion Picture Co., Ltd., Production. A Masaichi Nagata Presentation. Filmed at Daiei-Kyoto Studios. Westrex recording system. Black and white (processed by Daiei Laboratory). DaieiScope. 78 minutes. Released 1968.

U.S. Version: Released by Daiei International Films, Inc., in subtitled format. Also known as *Ghost Story of Booby Trap*. International title: *The Pit of Death*. No MPAA rating. Released 1968.

Ghosts on Parade/Yokai dai senso. Executive Producer, Masaichi Nagata; Producer, Yamato Yashiro; Director, Yoshiyuki Kuroda; Screenplay, Tetsuro Yoshida; Director of Photography, Hiroshi Imai; Art Directors, Seiichi Ohta, Shigeru Kato; Editor, Toshio Taniguchi; Special Effects, Daiei Special Effects Department; Sound Recording Supervisor, Tsuchitaro Hayashi; Sound, Daiei Recording Studio; Music, Shigeru Ikeno.

Cast: Yoshihiko Aoyama (Shinhachiro Mayama), Akane Kawasaki (Chie), Osamu Okawa (Iori Ohdate), Tomoo Uchida (Dainichibo), Gen [Hajime?] Kimura (Saheiji Kawano), Takashi Kanda (Hyogo Isobe), Hanji Wakai, Kenji Wakai (Gate Guards), Hinode Nishikawa (Lower Officer), Ikuko Mori (Long-necked Monster), Chikara Hashimoto (Daimon), Gen Kuroki (River Monster), Hideki Hanamura (Nebula Monster), Keiko Yukitomo (Two-headed Woman), Tokio Oki (Yasuzo), Hiromi Inoue (Shinobu), Yukiyasu Watanabe (Moichi), Mari Kanda (Osaki).

A Daiei Motion Picture Co., Ltd., Production. A Masaichi Nagata Presentation. Fujicolor (processed by Daiei Laboratory). Daieiscope. Westrex recording system. Filmed at Daiei-Kyoto Studios. 79 minutes. Released 1968.

U.S. Version: Released by Daiei International Films, Inc., presumably in subtitled format. No MPAA rating. 79 minutes. Released 1968.

The Girl with Bamboo Leaves/Sasable omon. Producer, Masaichi Nagata; Director, Tokuzo Tanaka; Sound, Daiei Recording Studio; Special Effects, Daiei Special Effects Department.

Cast: (unavailable)

A Daiei Motion Picture Co., Ltd., Production. A Masaichi Negata Presentation. Westrex recording system. Daieicolor. DaieiScope. Running time undetermined. Released 1969.

U.S. Version: Released by Daiei International Films, Inc., in subtitled format. No MPAA rating. Released 1969.

The Haunted Castle/Hiroku kaibyoden. Producer, Masaiachi Nagata; Director, Tokuzo Tanaka; Screenplay, Shozaburo Asai; Director of Photography, Hiroshi Imai; Assistant Director, Rikio Endo; Art Director, Seiichi Ota; Editor, Hiroshi Imai; Sound, Daiei Recording Studio; Music, Hiroshi Mima.

Cast: Kojiro Hongo (Komori), Naomi Kobayashi (Lady Toyo Nabeshima), Mitsuya Kamei (Saya), Matsuhiro [Mutsuhiro] Toura (Chamberlain), Koichi Uenoyama (Lord Nabeshima), Akihisa Toda (Monk Matashichiro), Akane Kawasaki, Natsuke Oka, Ikuko Mori, Yasude Terajima, Shozo Naribu, Shintaro Nanjo, Kazuo Tamaki, Shosaku Sugiyama, Seishiro Hara.

A Daiei Motion Picture Co., Ltd., Production. A Masaichi Nagata Presentation. Fujicolor (processed by Daiei Laboratory). Daieiscope. Westrex recording system. 83 minutes. Released 1969.

U.S. Version: Released by Daiei International Films, Inc. in subtitled format. International title: *Mystery of the Cat-Woman*. No MPAA rating. 83 minutes. Released December 20, 1969.

Hiroku onna ro. Producer, Masaichi Nagata; Director, Akira Inoue; Screenplay, Shozaburo Asai; Art Director, Akira Naito; Director of Photography, Yasukazu Takemura; Editor, Hiroshi Yamada; Music, Takeo Watanabe; Sound Recording Supervisor, Masachiro Okumura; Sound, Daiei Recording Studio.
Cast: Michiyo Yasuda (Oshino), Sanae Nakahara (Otaki), Shigako Shimegi (Myonen), Mayumi Nigisa (Osaki), Machiko Hasegawa (Omatsu), Sei Hiraizumi (Shinpachi Murase), Fumio Watanabe (Tatewaki Ishizu), Jotaro Sennami (Inokichi), Akifumi Inoue (Masugoro), Saburo Date (Kishino), Jun Hamamura (Gihei), Masako Mizuki (Otane), Naomi Kobayashi (Namie), Yusaku Terashima (Old Man in Gambling Den), Kazue Tamaki (Echizen-ya), Jun Katsumura (Tagawa), Ikuko Mori (Okane), Teruko Konoe (Inn Proprietess), Gen Kuroki (Detective), Sumao Ishihara (Stallowner).
A Daiei Motion Picture Co., Ltd., Production. A Masaichi Nagata Presentation. Filmed at Daiei-Kyoto Studios. Westrex recording system. Black and white (processed by Daiei Laboratory). DaieiScope. 96 minutes. Released 1968.
U.S. Version: Distributor undetermined. International title: *Women's Prison*. Sequel: Zoku hiroku onna ro (Daiei, 1968).

The Invisible Swordsman/Tomei Kenshi. Producer, Hidemasa Nagata; Director, Yoshiyuki Kuroda; Sound, Daiei Recording Studio.
Cast: (unavailable)
A Daiei Motion Picture Co., Ltd., Production. Daieicolor. DaieiScope. 79 minutes. Released 1970.
U.S. Version: Distributor undetermined.

Kaibyo Arima goten. Executive Producer, Masaichi Nagata; Director, Ryohei Arai; Sound, Daiei Recording Studio.
Cast: Takako Irie, Kotaro Bando.
A Daiei Motion Picture Co., Ltd., Production. A Masaichi Nagata Presentation. Western Electric Mirrophonic recording. Black and white (processed by Daiei Laboratory). Academy ratio. Running time undetermined. Released 1953.
U.S. Version: Distributor, if any, is undetermined. International title: *Ghost-Cat of Arima Place*.

Kaibyo Gojusan-tsugi. Executive Producer, Masaichi Nagata; Director, Bin Kado; Sound, Daiei Recording Studio.
Cast: Shintaro Katsu, Tokiko Mita.
A Daiei Motion Picture Co., Ltd., Production. A Masaichi Nagata Presentation. Western Electric Mirrophonic recording. Black and white (processed by Daiei Laboratory). Academy ratio. Running time undetermined. Released 1956.
U.S. Version: Distributor, if any, is undetermined. International title: *Ghost-Cat of Gojusan-Tsugi*.

Kaibyo noroi no kabe. Executive Producer, Masaichi Nagata; Director, Kenji Misumi; Sound, Daiei Recording Studio.
Cast: Shintaro Katsu, Yoko Uraji.
A Daiei Motion Picture Co., Ltd., Production. A Masaichi Nagata Presentation. Western Electric Mirrophonic recording. Black and white (processed by Daiei Laboratory). Academy ratio. Running time undetermined. Released 1958.
U.S. Version: Distributor undetermined. International title: *Ghost-Cat Wall of Hatred*.

Kaibyo Okazaki sodo. Executive Producer, Masaichi Nagata; Director, Bin Kado; Sound, Daiei Recording Studio.
Cast: Takako Irie, Kotaro Bando.
A Daiei Motion Picture Co., Ltd., Production. A Masaichi Nagata Presentation. Western Electric Mirrophonic recording. Black and white (processed by Daiei Laboratory). Academy ratio. Running time undetermined. Released 1954.
U.S. Version: Distributor, if any, is undetermined. International title: *Terrible Ghost-Cat of Okazaki*.

Kaibyo Oma-ga-tsuji. Executive Producer, Masaichi Nagata; Director, Bin Kado; Sound, Daiei Recording Studio.

Cast: Takako Irie, Shintaro Katsu.

A Daiei Motion Picture Co., Ltd., Production. A Masaichi Nagata Presentation. Western Electric Mirrophonic recording. Black and white (processed by Daiei Laboratory). Academy ratio. Running time undetermined. Released 1954.

U.S. Version: Distributor, if any, is undetermined. International title: *Ghost-Cat of Oma-Ga-Tsuji*

Kaidan botandoro. Executive Producer, Masaichi Nagata; Director, Satsuo Yamamoto; Screenplay, Yoshitaka [Yoshikata] Yoda; Director of Photography, Chishi Makiura [Makuira]; Art Director, Yoshinobu Nishioka; Editor, Kanji Suganume; Music, Shigeru Ikeno; Sound Recording Supervisor, Tsuchitaro Hayashi; Sound, Daiei Recording Studio.

Cast: Kojiro Hongo (Shinzaburo), Miyoko Akaza (Otsuyu), Michiko Ohtsuka (Oyone), Mayumi Ogawa (Omine), Ko [Akira] Nishimura (Banzo), Takashi Shimura (Hakuodo), Atsumi Uda (Kiku), Takamaru Sasaki (Zenzaemon), Koichi Mizahara (First Relative), Saburo Date (Rokusuke), Norio Shiozaki (Elder Brother), Kazuo Tamamoto (First Man), Gen Kimura (Priest), Shinobu Araki (Priest Ryoseki), Shozo Nanbu (Old Man), Kimiko Tachibana (Mother Nao), Teruko Ohmi (First Wife), Yuko Mori (Second Wife).

A Daiei Motion Picture Co., Ltd., Production. A Masaichi Nagata Presentation. Fujicolor (processed by Daiei Laboratory). Daieiscope. Westrex recording system. 89 minutes. Filmed at Daiei-Kyoto Studios. Released June 15, 1968.

U.S. Version: Released by Daiei International Films, Inc. (?). International titles: *The Bride from Hades* and *A Tale of Peonies and Lanterns*. Also known as *Bride from Hell*, *Ghost Beauty* and *My Bride Is a Ghost*. Daiei currently lists title as *Botandoro*.

Kaidan Fukagawa jowa. Executive Producer, Masaichi Nagata; Director, Minoru Imuzuka; Sound, Daiei Recording Studio.

Cast: Mitsuko Mito, Yuji Hori.

A Daiei Motion Picture Co., Ltd., Production. A Masaichi Nagata Presentation. Western Electric Mirrophonic recording. Black and white (processed by Daiei Laboratory). Academy ratio. Running time undetermined. Released 1952.

U.S. Version: Distributor, if any, is undetermined. International title: *Tragic Ghost Story of Fukagawa*.

Kaidan Kakuidori. Executive Producer, Masaichi Nagata; Director, Issei Mori; Sound, Daiei Recording Studio.

Cast: Eiji Funakoshi, Katsuhiko Kobayashi.

A Daiei Motion Picture Co., Ltd., Production. A Masaichi Nagata Presentation. Western Electric Mirrophonic recording. Black and white (processed by Daiei Laboratory). Academy ratio (?). Running time undetermined. Released 1961.

U.S. Version: Distributor, if any, is undetermined. International title: *Ghost Story of Kakui Street*.

Kaidan Kasanegafuchi. Executive Producer, Masaichi Nagata; Director, Kimiyoshi Yasuda; Based on the story "Shinkei Kasanegufuchi" by Encho Sanyutei; Sound Recording Supervisor, Masao Osumi; Sound, Daiei Recording Studio; Special Effects, Daiei Special Effects Department.

Cast: Ganjiro Nakamura, Yataro Kitagami.

A Daiei Motion Picture Co., Ltd., Production. A Masaichi Nagata Presentation. Western Electric Mirrophonic recording. Black and white (processed by Daiei Laboratory). Academy ratio (?). Running time undetermined. Released 1960

U.S. Version: Never released theatrically in the United States. A remake of *The Depths* (Shintoho, 1957), and remade as *The Masseur's Curse* (Daiei, 1970).

Kaidan onibi no numa. Executive Producer, Masaichi Nagata; Director, Bin Kado; Sound, Daiei Recording Studio.

Cast: Kenzaburo Jo, Meiko Kondo.

A Daiei Motion Picture Co., Ltd., Production. A Masaichi Nagata Presentation. Western Electric Mirrophonic recording.

Black and white (processed by Daiei Laboratory). Academy ratio (?). Running time undetermined. Released 1963.

U.S. Version: Distributor, if any, is undetermined. International title: *Ghost Story of Devil's Fire Swamp.*

Kaidan Saga yashiki. Executive Producer, Masaichi Nagata; Director, Ryohei Arai; Sound, Daiei Recording Studio.

Cast: Takako Irie, Kotaro Bando.

A Daiei Motion Picture Co., Ltd., Production. A Masaichi Nagata Presentation. Western Electric Mirrophonic recording. Black and white (processed by Daiei Laboratory). Academy ratio (?). Running time undetermined. Released 1953.

U.S. Version: Distributor, if any, is undetermined. International title: *Ghost of Saga Mansion.*

Kaidan yonaki-doro. Executive Producer, Masaichi Nagata; Director, Katuhiko Tasaka; Sound, Daiei Recording Studio.

Cast: Ganjiro Nakamura, Katsuhiro.

A Daiei Motion Picture Co., Ltd., Production. A Masaichi Nagata Presentation. Western Electric Mirrophonic recording. Black and white (processed by Daiei Laboratory). Academy ratio (?). Running time undetermined. Released 1962.

U.S. Version: Distributor, if any, is undetermined. International title: *Ghost Story of Stone Lanterns and Crying in the Night.*

Majin/DaiMajin (*Giant Devil*). Producer, Masaichi Nagata; Director, Kimiyoshi Yasuda; Screenplay, Tetsuro Yoshida; Director of Photography, Yoshiyuki Kuroda (Fujio Morita according to some sources); Art Director, Hisashi Okuda; Editor, Hiroshi Yamada [Okuda?]; Music, Akira Ifukube; Sound Recordist Supervisor, Masao Osumi; Sound, Daiei Recording Studio; Special Effects Director, Yoshiyuki Kuroda; Majin Design, Ryosaku Takayama; Special Effects, Daiei Special Effects Department.

Cast: Miwa Takada (Korasa [Kozasa] Hanabusa), Yoshihiko Aoyama (Tadafumi Hanabusa), Jun Fujimaki (Kogenta), Ryutaro Gomi (Lord Samanosuke Odate), Tatsuo Endo (Gunjuro).

A Daiei Motion Picture Co., Ltd., Production. A Masaichi Nagata Presentation. Eastman Color (processed by Daiei Laboratory). DaieiScope. 84 minutes. Released April 17, 1966.

U.S. Version: Simultaneously released in English subtitled version by Daiei International Films, Inc., and in English-dubbed version by Bernard Lewis. Prints by Pathe. Reissued as *Majin the Hideous Idol.* Alternate titles: *The Devil Got Angry* and *The Vengeance of the Monster.* Released to television by American International Television (AIP-TV) as *Majin, the Monster of Terror.* A James H. Nicholson and Samuel Z. Arkoff Presentation. Copyright 1967 by American International Pictures. The first of three "Majin" films. 86 minutes. No MPAA rating. Released August 9, 1968.

Majin Strikes Again/DaiMajin gyakushu (*The Giant Devil's Counterattack*). Producer, Masaichi Nagata; Director, Issei Mori; Screenplay, Tetsuo Yoshida; Directors of Photography, Fujio Morita, Hiroshi Imai; Music, Akira Ifukube; Art Director, Hisashi Okuda; Editor, Hiroshi Yamada; Sound Recording Supervisor, Masao Osumi; Sound, Daiei Recording Studio; Special Effects Director, Yoshiyuki Kuroda; Majin Design, Ryosaku Takayama; Special Effects, Daiei Special Effects Department.

Cast: Hideki Ninomiya, Masahide Kizuka, Shinji Hori, Shiei Iizuka, Muneyuki Nagatomo, Junichiro Yamashita.

A Daiei Motion Picture Co., Ltd., Production. Eastman Color (processed by Daiei Laboratory). Daieiscope. 80 minutes. Released December 10, 1966.

U.S. Version: Never released theatrically in the United States. Released directly to television by American International Television (AIP-TV) in 1968. A James H. Nicholson and Samuel Z. Arkoff Presentation. Director, Lee Kressel; Editors, Eli Haviv and Emil Haviv; Lip Sync, Film-Rite, Inc.; Rerecording, Titan Productions, Inc.; Postproduction Supervisor, Salvatore Billiteri;

Prints by Pathe. The third Majin film. International title: *The Return of Majin*, but not to be confused with *The Return of the Giant Majin*, also 1966.

The Masseur's Curse/Kaidan kasanegafuchi. Producer, Masaichi Nagata; Director, Kimiyoshi Yasuda; Screenplay, Shozaburo Asai, based on the story "Shinkei Kasanegafuchi" by Encho Sanyuti; Director of Photography, Tsuchimoto [Tsuchitaro] Hayashi; Art Director, Akira Naito; Music, Hajime Kaburagi; Sound, Daiei Recording Studio; Special Effects, Daiei Special Effects Department.

Cast: Kenjiro Ishiyama (Soetsu), Matsuko Oka (Osono), Saburo Date (Fukami), Mitsuki Tanaka (Sawano), Ritsu Ishiyama, Maya Kitajima, Reiko Kasahara, Ryuko Minagami, Takumi Shinjo.

A Daiei Motion Picture Co., Ltd., Production. A Masaichi Nagata Presentation. Daieicolor. DaieiScope. Westrex recording system. 82 minutes. Released June 20, 1970.

U.S. Version: Distributed by Daiei International Films, Inc. Also known as *Horror of an Ugly Woman*. Previously filmed as *The Depth* and *Kaidan Kasanegafuchi*. 82 minutes. No MPAA rating. Released 1970.

The Mysterious Satellite/Uchujin Tokyo ni arawaru (*Unknown Satellite Over Tokyo*). Producer, Masaichi Nagata; Director, Koji Shima; Screenplay, Hideo Oguni, based on the novel by Gentaro Nakajima; Director of Photography, Kimio Watanabe; Art Director, Shigeo Muno; Color Design, Taro Okamoto; Editor, Toyo Suzuki; Special Effects Director, Kenmei [Noriaki?] Yuasa; Sound Recording Supervisor, Masao Osumi; Music, Gentaro Nakajima; Special Effects, Daiei Special Effects Department; Sound, Daiei Recording Studio.

Cast: Toyomi Karita (Hikari Aozora, Space-Man Ginko), Keizo Kawasaki (Toru [Isobe]), Isao Yamagata (Dr. Matsuda), Bontaro Miake (Dr. Komura), Shozo Nanbu (Dr. Isobe), Mieko Nagai (Taeko Komura), Kiyoko Hirai (Mrs. Matusuda), Bin Yagasawa (No. 2 Pairan).

A Daiei Motion Picture Co., Ltd., Production. A Masaichi Nagata Presentation. DaieiScope. Eastman Color (processed by Daiei Laboratory). Western Electric Mirrophonic recording. 87 minutes. Released 1956.

U.S. Version: Released in the United States by Daiei International Films, Inc. (?). Released to U.S. television as *Warning from Space* by American International Television. English-language version produced at Titra Sound Studios by Jay H. Cipes and Edward Palmer; Prints by Pathe. Released internationally as *Unknown Satellite over Tokyo* by Daiei International in December 1956. Alternate titles: *The Cosmic Man Appears in Tokyo* and *Space Men [Spacemen] Appear over [in] Tokyo*. Top-billed Karita portrays a female alien, though character's name is given as above. 81 minutes. No MPAA rating. Released 1960–62 (?).

Necromancy/Kaibyo Yonaki numa. Executive Producer, Masaichi Nagata; Director, Katsuhiko Tasaki; Screenplay, Toshio Tamikado; Director of Photography, Senkichiro Takada; Sound, Daiei Recording Studio.

Cast: Shintaro Katsu, Toshio Chiba, Toshio Hosokawa, Tokiko Mita, Michiko Ai.

A Daiei Motion Picture Co., Ltd., Production. A Masaichi Nagata Presentation. Western Electric Mirrophonic recording. Black and white (processed by Daiei Laboratory). Academy ratio. 89 minutes. Released 1957.

U.S. Version: Distributor undetermined. International title: *Ghost-Cat of Yonaki Swamp*..

The Ogre of Mont Oe/Oeyama shuten doji. Executive Producer, Masaichi Nagata; Director, Tokuzo Tanaka; Screenplay, Fuji Yahiro; Director of Photography, Hiroshi Imai; Sound Recording Supervisor, Masao Osumi; Sond, Daiei Recording Studio; Special Effects, Daiei Special Effects Department.

Cast: Kazuo Hasegawa, Raizo Ichikawa, Shintaro Katsu, Kojiro Hongo, Fujiko Yamamoto, Tamao Nakamura.

A Daiei Motion Picture Co., Ltd., Production. A Masaichi Nagata Presentation. Western Electric Mirrophonic recording. Eastman Color (processed by Daiei Laboratory). Academy ratio. 114 minutes. Released 1960.

U.S. Version: Released by Daiei International Films in subtitled format. No MPAA rating. 114 minutes. Released 1960.

100 Monsters/Yokai hyaku monogatari (*100 Ghost Stories*). Executive Producer, Masaichi Nagata; Producer, Yamato Yatsuhiro; Director, Kimiyoshi Yasuda; Screenplay, Tetsuo Yoshida; Director of Photography, Yasukazu Takemura; Art Directors, Yoshinobu Nishioka, Shigeru Kato; Special Effects, Daiei Special Effects Department; Editor, Kanji Suganuma; Sound Recording Supervisor, Masao Osumi; Sound, Daiei Recording Studio; Music, Chumei Watanabe.

Cast: Jun Fujimaki (Yasutaro), Miwa Takada (Okiku), Mikiko Tsubouchi (Osen), Takashi Kanda (Riemon Tajimaya), Ryutaro Gomi (Hotta-Buzennokami), Yoshio Yoshida (Jusuke), Masaru Hiraizumi (Takichi), Rookie Shin-ichi (Shinkichi), Shozo Hayashiya (Storyteller), Koichi Ogura (Tobee), Jun Hamamura (Gohei), Shosaku Sugiyama (Bannai Ibaragi), Tatsuo Hananuno (Jinbee), Saburo (First Ronin), Kazuo Yamamoto (Second Ronin), Shozo Nanbu (Old Town Counselor), Shinobu Araki (Old Priest), Kazue Tamachi (Village Headman), Teruko Oumi (Otora), Ikuko Mori (Ronin's Wife).

A Daiei Motion Picture Co., Ltd., Production. A Masaichi Nagata Presentation. Eastman Color (processed by Daiei Laboratory). Daieiscope. Westrex recording system. 79 minutes. Released 1968.

U.S. Version: Released by Daiei International Films, Inc., in subtitled format (?). International title: *The Hundred Monsters*. Also known as *The Hundred Ghost Stories*. 79 minutes. No MPAA rating. Released 1968.

Rashomon. Executive Producer, Masaichi Nagata; Producer, Jingo Minoru; Director, Akira Kurosawa; Screenplay, Shinobu Hashimoto, Akira Kurosawa, based on the stories "Rashomon" and "Yabu no naka" ("In a Grove") by Ryunosuke Akutagawa; Art Director, So Matsuyama; Set Decorator, H. Motsumoto; Director of Photography, Kazuo Miyagawa; Lighting, Kenichi Okamoto; Editor, Akira Kurosawa; Music, Fumio Hayasaka; Sound, Daiei Recording Studio.

Cast: Toshiro Mifune (Tajomaru, the bandit), Masayuki Mori (Takehiro, the samurai), Machiko Kyo (Masago, the samurai's wife), Takashi Shimura (Woodcutter), Minoru Chiaki (Priest), Kichijiro Ueda (Commoner), Daisuke Kato (Policeman), Fumiko Homma (Witch).

A Daiei Film Production picture. A Masaichi Nagata Presentation. Black and white (processed by Daiei Laboratory). Academy ratio. Western Electric Mirrophonic recording. 88 minutes. Released August 25, 1950.

U.S. Version: Released by RKO Radio Pictures, Inc., in subtitled format. Prints by Pathe. 88 minutes. Remade as *The Outrage* (Metro-Goldwyn-Mayer, 1964). No MPAA rating. Released December 26, 1951.

The Return of the Giant Majin/Dai Majin ikaru (*The Giant Devil Grows Angry*). Producer, Masaichi Nagata; Director, Kenji Misumi; Screenplay, Tetsuo [Tetsuro] Yoshida; Director of Photography, Fujio Morita; Art Director, Hisashi Okuda; Editor, Hiroshi Yamada; Sound, Daiei Recording Studio; Special Effects Director, Yoshiyuki Kuroda; Majin Design, Ryosaku Takayama; Special Effects, Daiei Special Effects Department.

Cast: Kojiro Hongo (Juro Chigusa), Shiho Fujimura (Sayuri), Taro Murui (Todohei), Takashi Kanda (Danjo Mikoshiba), Tara Fujimura, Jutaro Hojo.

A Daiei Motion Picture Co., Ltd., Production. Eastman Color (processed by Daiei Laboratory). DaieiScope. 79 minutes. Released August 13, 1966.

U.S. Version: Never released theatrically in the United States. Released directly to television by American International Television (AIP-TV) in 1968. A James H. Nicholson and Samuel Z. Arkoff Presentation. Director, Lee Kressel; Postproduction Supervisor, Salvatore Billiteri; Editors, Eli Haviv and Emil Haviv; Lip Sync, Film-Rite, Inc.; Rerecording, Titan Productions, Inc.; Prints by Perfect. The second film in the "Majin" trilogy. 79 minutes. No MPAA rating

Return of the Giant Monsters/Daikaiju kuchusen Gamera tai Gyaosu (*Giant Monster Air Battle: Gamera Against Gyaosu*). Executive Producer, Masaichi Nagata; Producer, Hidemasa Nagata; Director, Noriyaki Yuasa; Planning, Kazutada Nakano; Screenplay, Fumi Takahashi; Director of Photography, Akira Uehara; Music, Tadashi Yamaguchi; Editor, Tatsuji Nakashizu; Sound Recording Supervisor, Yukio Okumura; Sound, Daiei Recording Studio; Special Effects, Kazufumi Fujii, Yuzo Kaneko; Monster Design, Ryosaku Takayama.

Cast: Naoyuki [Hisayuki] Abe (Eiichi Kanamura), Kojiro Hongo (Shiro Tsutsumi), Kichijiro Ueda (Tatsuemon Kanamura), Reiko [Reino] Kasahara (Sumiko Kanamura), Taro Marui (Mite no Kuma), Yukitaro Hotaru (Hachiko), Yoshio Kitahara (Dr. Aoki), Shin Minatsu (Okabe), Jun Osanai (Stock Farm Owner), Osamu Maruyama (Chief of Seismological Observatory), Yuju Moriya (Announcer), Akira Natsuki (Commander in Chief), Kenji Oyama (Chief of Police Headquarters), Koichi Ito (Chief of Road Development Section), Teppei Endo (Local Chief of Road Development Section), Joe Ohara (Hotel Manager), Fujio Murakami (Scholar), Takashi Nakamura (Reporter), Naomasa Kawahima (Cowboy), Daigo Inoue (Assistant at Defense Headquarters), Kisao Hida (Policeman), Eiko Yanami, Isamu Saeki, Mikio Tsubouchi, Yasushi Sakagami, Koji Fugiyama.

A Daiei Motion Picture Co., Ltd., Production. Eastman Color (processed by Daiei Laboratory). DaieiScope. Filmed at Daiei-Tokyo Studios. 86 minutes. Released March 15, 1967.

U.S. Version: Never released theatrically in the United States. Released directly to television by American International Television (AIP-TV) in 1967. A James H. Nicholson and Samuel Z. Arkoff Presentation. Postproduction Supervisor, Salvatore Billitteri; Prints by Perfect; Dubbing cast, Mel Wells, others undetermined. Released to home video and reissued to television in 1987 as *Gamera vs. Gaos*, a Sandy Frank Film Syndication, Inc., Presentation, and distributed by King Features Entertainment, a subsidiary of the Hearst Corporation. Copyright 1967 by Daiei International Films, Inc. Current version is minus AIP's credits. Alternate titles: *Dai kaiju kuchusen* and *Boyichi and the Supermonster*. The third film in the "Gamera" series. 86 minutes. No MPAA rating.

Return to Manhood/Nanbanji no Semushi-Otoko. Executive Producer, Masaichi Nagata; Producer, Atsushi Sakai; Director, Torajiro Sato; Screenplay, Akira Fushimi; Story, Katsumi Mizoguchi, based on the novel *Notre Dame de Paris* by Victor Hugo; Director of Photography, Hiroshi Imai; Sound, Daiei Recording Studio.

Cast: Achako Hanabishi, Naitoshi Hayashi, Shunji Sakai, Kyu Sazanka, Tamao Nakamura.

A Daiei Motion Picture Co., Ltd., Production. A Masaichi Nagata Presentation. Western Electric Mirrophonic recording. Black and white (processed by Daiei Laboratory). Academy ratio. 78 minutes. Released 1957.

U.S. Version: Released by Daiei International Films, Inc., in subtitled format. No MPAA rating. 78 minutes. Released 197.

The Snake Girl and the Silver-Haired Witch/Hebimusume to Hakuhatsuki. Executive Producer, Masaichi Nagata; Producer, Kazumasa Nakano; Director, Noriaki Yuasa; Screenplay, Kimiyuki Hasegawa, based on the story "Hebimusune to hakuhatsuki" by Kazuo Kozu; Art Director, Tomohisa Yano; Director of Photography, Akira Uehara; Editor, Yoshiyuki Miyazaki; Music, Shunsuke Kikuchi; Sound Recording Supervisor, Kimio Iida; Sound, Daiei Recording

Studio; Special Effects, Daiei Special Effects Department.
Cast: Yachie Matsui (Sayuri Nanjo), Mayumi Takahashi (Tamami Nanjo), Yoshoi Kitahara (Goro Nanjo), Yuko Hamada (Yuko Nanjo), Sachiko Meguro (Shige Kito), Sei Hiraizumi (Tatsuya Hayashi), Kuniko Miyake (Jamakawa), Saburo Ishiguro (Teacher Sasaki), Tadashi Date (School Servant), Osamu Maruyama (Doctor), Mariko Fukuhara (Doll).
A Daiei Motion Picture Co., Ltd., Production. A Masaichi Nagata Presentation. Westrex recording system. Black and white (processed by Daiei Laboratory). DaieiScope. 82 minutes. Released 1968.
U.S. Version: Released by Daiei International Films, Inc., in subtitled format. 82 minutes. No MPAA rating. Released 1969.

The Snow Woman/Kaidan yukijoro.
Executive Producer, Masaichi Nagata; Producer, Ikuo Kubodera; Director, Tokuzo Tanaka; Screenplay, Fuji [Yahiro, Yahoro] Yakiro, based on the story "Yukioona" ("Snow Woman") by Lafcadio Hearn from his collection *Kwaidan: Stories and Studies of Strange Things*; Director of Photography, Chishi Makiura; Art Director, Akira Naito; Editor, Hiroshi Yamada; Sound Recording Supervisor, Yukio Kaihara; Sound, Daiei Recording Studio; Music, Akira Ifukube; Special Effects, Daiei Special Effects Department.
Cast: Shino Fujimura (Yukioona/Yuki), Akira Ishihama (Yosaku), Machiko Hasegawa (Lady Mino), Taketoshi Naito (Lord Mino), Mizuho Susuki (Gyokei), Fujio Suga (Soju), Sachiko Murase (Soyo), Yoshio Kitshara (Seiju), Masao Shimizu (Jiun), Hisataro Hojo (Matsukawa), Izumi Hara (Virgin in Service of Shrine), Tatsuo Hananuno (Shigetomo), Tokio Oki (First Doctor), Jun Fujikawa (Second Doctor), Yukio Horikita (Sentinel), Hajime Koshikite (Porter), Shinya Saito (Taro).
A Daiei Motion Picture Co., Ltd., Production. A Masaichi Nagata Presentation. Eastman Color (processed by Daiei Laboratory). DaieiScope. Westrex recording system. Filmed at Daiei-Tokyo Studios. 80 minutes. Released 1968.

U.S. Version: Released by Daiei International Films, Inc. Advertised as *Snow Ghost*. International title: *Yukioona*. Also known as *Woman of the Snow*, and *Ghost of the Snow Girl Prostitute*. Previously filmed as a segment in *Kwaidan* (q.v.), and later as *Aido*. No MPAA rating. 80 minutes. Released 1968.

Super Monster/Uchu kaiju Gamera (Space Monster Gamera). Producers, Masaya Tokuyama, Shigeru Shinohara, Hirokazu Ohba; Director, Noriaki Yuasa; Planner, Masaya Tokuyama; Screenplay, Niisan [Nizo, Fumi, etc.] Takahashi; Director of Photography, Michio Takashi, Akira Uehara; Lighting, Tadaaki Shimada; Art Directors, Tomohisa Yano, Akira Inoue; Set Decoration, Nobuhisa Iwata; Editors (stock footage), Shoji Sekiguchi, Tasuji Nakashizu, Zenko Miyazaki; Assistant Director, Hiromi Munemoto; Animated scenes courtesy of Office Academy, Toei Animation Studios; Makeup, Chie Tsuchiya; Script Girl, Midori Kobayashi; Music, Shunsuke Kikuchi; Song, "Love for Future," sung by Mach Fumiake; Sound Recording, Kimio Tobita. Special Effects Unit: Directors, Noriaki Yuasa, Kazufumi Fujii, Yuzo Kaneko, and the Daiei Special Effects Department.
Cast: Mach Fumiake (Kilara), Yaeko Kojima (Marsha), Yoko Komatsu (Mitan), Keiko Dudo (Gilage), Koichi Maeda (Keiichi), Toshie Takada (Keiichi's Mother), Osamu Kobayashi (Voice of *Zanon* Captain), Hiroji Hayashi, Tetsuaki Toyosumi, Hideaki Kobayashi, Makato Ikeda, Kisao Hida.
A Daiei Film Distribution Co., Ltd., Production. Distributed by New Daiei Co., Ltd. Daieicolor. DaieiScope and Panavision. Westrex recording system. 92 minutes. Released March 20, 1980.
U.S. Version: Released by Shochiku Films of America, Inc. in subtitled format (?), presumably on an extremely limited basis. Released to television dubbed in English. A Filmways Pictures Release. Television title: *Gamera Super Monster*. Includes extensive stock footage from *Gammera*

the Invincible (1965), *War of the Monsters* (1966), *Return of the Giant Monsters* (1967), *Destroy All Planets* (1968), *Attack of the Monsters* (1969), *Gamera vs. Monster X* (1970), and *Gamera vs. Zigra* (1971). Additional stock footage lifted from *Space Cruiser Yamato* and *Galaxy Express 999*. 92 minutes. No MPAA rating. Released May 7, 1980.

Tales of Ugetsu/Ugetsu monogatari (*Tales after the Rain*). Producer, Masaichi Nagata; Associate Producer, Kyuichi Tsuji; Director, Kenji Mizoguchi; Screenplay, Matsutaro Kawaguchi, Giken [Yoshikata] Yoda, adapted from the stories "Asaji ga yado" ("The Inn at Asaji"; English title is "The House of Wild Gramineons") and "Jasei no in" ("Serpent of Desire"; English title, "The Maliciousness of the Snake's Evil") by Akinari [Shusei] Ueda, from the collection *Ugetsu monogatari*, and on the story "Le decoration" by Guy de Maupassant; Director of Photography, Kazuo Miyagawa; Choreography, Kinshichi Kodera; Art Direction, Kisau Itoh [Kisaku Ito]; Documentation of the Costumes (Costume Design), Kusune Kainosho; Pottery Consultant, Zengoro Eiraku; Lighting, Kenichi Okamoto; Recording, Iwao Otani; Sound, Daiei Recording Studio; Music, Fumio Hayasaka, Ichiro Saito; Musical Direction, Fumio Hayasaka; Editor, Mitsuji Miyata.

Cast: Masayuki Mori (Genjuro), Eitaro [Sakae] Ozawa (Tobei Nakanogo), Machiko Kyo (Lady Wakasa Kitsuki), Kinuyo Tanaka (Miyagi), Mitsuke Mito [Mitsuko Miura] (Ohama), Sugisaku Aoyama (Old Priest), Ryosuke Kagawa (Village Master), Kichijiro Tsuchida (Silk Merchant), Mitsusaburo Ramon (Tamba Captain), Ichiisaburo Sawamura (Genichi), Kikue Mori (Ukan), Syozo Nambu (Shinto Priest).

A Daiei Motion Picture Company, Ltd., Production. Black and white (processed by Daiei Laboratory). Academy ratio. Western Electric Mirrophonic recording. 96 minutes. Released 1953.

U.S. Version: Released by Edward Harrison Releasing in subtitled format. A Harrison and Davidson Presentation. Originally advertised as the above, but reissued by Janus Films as *Ugetsu*. International title: *Tales after the Rain*. 96 minutes. No MPAA rating. Released September 20, 1954.

Tomei ningen arawaru. Executive Producer, Masaichi Nagata; Director, Shinsei Adachi; Sound, Daiei Recording Studio.

Cast: Chizuru Kitagawa, Takiko Mizunoe.

A Daiei Motion Picture Co., Ltd., Production. Western Electric Mirrophonic recording. Black and white (processed by Daiei Laboratory). Academy ratio. Running time undetermined. Released 1949.

U.S. Version: Never released theatrically in the United States. International title: *The Transparent Man*. Sequel: *The Transparent Man vs. the Fly Man* (Daiei, 1957).

The Transparent Man vs. The Fly Man/ Tomei ningen to Hai-Otoko. Producer, Hidemasa Nagata; Executive Producer, Masaichi Nagata; Director, Mitsuo Murayama; Screenplay, Hajime Takaiwa; Director of Photography, Hiroshi Murai; Sound, Daiei Recording Studio; Special Effects, Daiei Special Effects Department.

Cast: Ryuji Shinagawa, Yoshiro Kitahara, Joji Tsurumi, Yoshihiro Hamaguchi, Junko Kano.

A Daiei Motion Picture Co., Ltd., Production. A Masaichi Nagata Presentation. Western Electric Mirrophonic recording. Black and white (processed by Daiei Laboratory). Academy ratio. Running time undetermined. Released 1957.

U.S. Version: Released by Daiei International Films, Inc. Also advertised as *The Murdering Mite*. A sequel to *Tomei ningen arawaru* (Daiei, 1949).

War of the Monsters/Daikaiju ketto Gamera tai Barugon (*Great Monster Duel: Gamera Against Barugon*). Executive Producer, Masaichi Nagata; Producer, Hidemasa [Hideo] Nagata; Director, Shigeo Tanaka; Planning, Yunejiro [Yonehiro] Saito; Screenplay, Fumi [Nizo] Takahashi; Director of Photography, Michio Takahashi; Special Effects Directors, Noriaki Yuasa, Kazufumi Fujii (*Variety* lists Fumi Takahashi); Monster Design, Ryosaku Takayama; Special

Effects, Daiei Special Effects Department; Sound, Daiei Recording Studio.

Cast: Kyoko Enami [Enama] (Karen), Kojiro Hongo, Akira Natsuki, Koji Fujiyama, Yuzo Hayakawa, Ichiro Sugai.

A Daiei Motion Picture Co., Ltd., Production. Eastman Color (processed by Daiei Laboratory). DaieiScope. 100 minutes. Released April 17, 1966.

U.S. Version: Never released theatrically in the United States. Released directly to television by American International Television (AIP-TV). Postproduction Supervisor, Salvatore Billitteri; Prints by Pathe. Reissued to television and released to home video by King Features Entertainment, a division of the Hearst Corporation, in 1987, as *Gamera vs. Barugon*; A Sandy Frank Syndication, Inc., Presentation. Copyright 1966 by Daiei International Films, Inc. U.K. title: *The War of the Monsters.* Released in West Germany as *Godzilla: der drache aus dem deschungel,* a misleading title to say the least! Second film in the "Gamera" series. Includes footage from *Gammera the Invincible.* 100 minutes. No MPAA rating.

The Whale God/Kuhira-gami. Producer, Masaichi Nagata; Director, Tokuzo Tanaka; Sound Recording Supervisor, Masao Osumi; Sound, Daiei Recording Studio; Special Effects, Daiei Special Effects Department.

Cast: (unavailable)

A Daiei Motion Picture Co., Ltd., Production. A Masaichi Nagata Presentation. Western Electric Mirrophonic recording. Daieicolor. DaieiScope. Running time undetermined. Released 1962.

U.S. Version: Released by Daiei International Films, Inc., in subtitled format. No MPAA rating. Released 1962.

Yoba. Executive Producer, Masichi Negata; Producer, Yasuyoshi Tokuma; Director, Tadashi Imai; Planning, Masumi Kanamaru; Screenplay, Yoko Mizuki, based on the 1918 short story "Yoba," by Ryunosuke Akutagawa; Director of Photography, Kazuo Miyagawa; Music, Riichiro Manabe.

Cast: Machiko Kyo (Oshima), Kazuko Inano (Sawa), Shinjiro Ebara (Shinzo, Oshima's Husband), Rentaro Mikuni (Unryu), Kiyoshi Kodama (Ihara), Tanie Kitabayashi (Midwife), Miki Jinbo (Otoshi), Taro Shigaki (Shinzo, Otoshi's Fiancé)

A Nagata Productions and Daiei Motion Picture Co., Ltd., Production. A Shockiku Co., Ltd., Release. Fujicolor. Panavision. 96 minutes. Released October 16, 1976.

U.S. Version: Distributor, if any, is undetermined. International title (?): *The Possessed.* Alternate title (?): *The Witch.*

Zatoichi Meets His Equal/Zatoichi: "Yabure! Tojin-ken." Executive producers, Masaichi Nagata and Sir Run Run Shaw; Director, Yasuda Kimiyoshi; Director of Photography, Fuji Morita.

Cast: Shintaro Katsu (Zatoichi), Wang Eu (Wang Kong), Yuko Hamaki (Osen).

A Daiei Motion Picture Co., Ltd./Shaw Brothers (H.K.), Ltd., Production. A Japanese-Hong Kong co-production. Filmed in Japan. Daieicolor. DaieiScope. Running time undetermined. Released 1969 (1971 in Hong Kong).

U.S. Version: Released by Toho International Co., Ltd. Advertised as *Zatoichi Meets the One-Armed Swordsman.* A sequel to the Shaw Brothers' *The One-Armed Swordsman* and part of the "Zatoichi" series (1962–1973) which later became a teleseries, all of which starred Katsu. Toho took over the series after 1971. No MPAA rating (?). Released 1973.

Zoku hiroku onna ro. Executive Producer, Masaichi Nagata; Producer, Sadao Zaizen; Director, Kimiyoshi Yasuda; Screenplay, Shozaburo Asai; Art Director, Yoshinobu Nishioka; Director of Photography, Chishi Makuira; Editor, Hiroshi Yamada; Music, Takeo Watanabe; Sound Recording Supervisor, Masao Osumi; Sound, Daiei Recording Studio.

Cast: Michiyo Yasuda (Onami), Sanae Nakahara (Okuma), Kayo Mikimoto (Oseki), Mutsuhiro Toura (Senzo Takeuchi), Mayumi Katsuyama (Otama), Yasuyo Masumura (Okichi), Gen Kimura (Saeki), Tomoo Nagai (Tatewaki Ishide), Saburo Date (Officer of the Law), Kazue Tamachi (Yomin Chiga), Keiko Koyanagi (Otaka), Junko Toyama (Oroku), Hiroko Yashiro (Otoshi), Hiromi

Inoue (Newcomer), Hajime Koshikawa (Jailer), Chikara Hashimoto (Superintendent Officer in the Feudal Age).
A Daiei Motion Picture Co., Ltd., Production. A Masaichi Nagata Presentation. Westrex recording system. Black and white (processed by Daiei Laboratory). DaieiScope. 84 minutes. Released 1968.
U.S. Version: Distributor, if any, is undetermined. International title: *Women's Cell*. A sequel to *Hiroku onna ro* (Daiei, 1968).

Nikkatsu Corporation

Koshoki tomei ningen. Director, Shinya Yamamoto.
Cast: (unavailable)
A Nikkatsu Corp. Production. Nikkatsucolor. NikkatsuScope. Running time undetermined. Released 1979.
U.S. Version: Distributor, if any, is undetermined. A sequel to *Lusty Transparent Man* (Nikkatsu, 1979).

Kyoren no onna shisho. Director, Kenji Mizoguchi; Screenplay, Kawaguchi Matsutaro; Director of Photography, Tatsuysuki Yokota.
Cast: Yoneko Sakai (Daughter), Eiji Nakano (Lover), Yoshiko Okada (Student).
A Nikkatsu Shingekibu Production. Silent. Black and white. Academy ratio. 85 minutes. Released 1926.
U.S. Version: Distributor, if any, is undetermined. International title: *Passion of a Woman Teacher*.

Lusty Transparent Man/Tomei ningen-okase. Producer, Akihiko Yameki; Director, Isao "Ko" Hayashi; Screenplay, Chiko Katsura.
Cast: Izumi Shima, Maria Mari.
A Nikkatsu Corp. Production. Nikkatsucolor. Panavision (?). Running time undetermined. Released 1979.
U.S. Version: Distributor undetermined. A sequel to *Lusty Transparent Human* (Nikkatsu, 1979). Released 1979.

Monster from a Prehistoric Planet/Daikyoju Gappa (*Gigantic Beast Gappa*). Producer, Hideo Koi; Director, Haruyasu Noguchi; Screenplay, Iwao Yamazaki, Ryuzo Nakaishi, based on a story by Akira Watanabe; Director of Photography, Muneo Ueda; Art Director, Kazumi Koike; Music, Saitaro Omori; Editor, Masanori Tsujii; Sound, Saburo Takahashi; Sound Recording, Nikkatsu Sound Studio. Special Effects Unit: Director, Akira Watanabe; Photography, Isamu Kakita, Kenji Kaneda, Yoshiyuki Nakano.
Cast: Tamio Kawaji [Kawachi] (Hiroshi Kurosaki), Yoko Yamamoto (Itoko Koyanagi), Kokan Katsura (Sanburo Hayashi), Keisuke Yukioka (President Funazu), Saburo Hiromatsu (Hosoda), Shiro Oshimi (Oyama), Yuji Kotaka (Daizo Tonooka), Tatsuya [Tatsunari] Fuji (Dr. George Inoue), Koji Wada (Dr. Machida), Yuji Odaka [Oyagi] (Dr. Aihara), Bumon Kahara (A Superior), Masanori ·Machida (Saki), Zenji Yamada (Kamomemaru Shipmaster), Hiroshi Kawano (Head of Defense Department), Toshinosuke Nahao (Commander), Masaru Kamiyama (Professor), Hiroshi Sugie (First Reporter), Hiroshi Ito (Second Reporter), Takashi Koshiba (Third Reporter), Sanpei Mine (First Islander), Kiyoshi Matsue (Second Islander), Kensuke Tamai (Third Islander), Mike Daning (Sailor).
A Nikkatsu Corp. Production. Eastman Color (processed by Nikkatsu Laboratory). NikkatsuScope. 81 minutes. Released April 1967.
U.S. Version: Never released theatrically in the United States. Released to television by American International Television (AIP-TV) in 1968. A James H. Nicholson and Samuel Z. Arkoff Presentation; Dialogue, William Ross; Postproduction Supervisor, Salvatore Billitteri; Prints by Pathe. Copyright 1967 by American International Productions. International Title: *Gappa*. Also known as *Gappa: Triphibian Monster*.

Note: This film is essentially an unauthorized remake of *Gorgo* (Metro-Goldwyn-Mayer, 1961). 81 minutes. No MPAA rating.

Tattooed Swordsman/Kaidan noboriryu. Producers, Hideo Koi, Shiro Sasaki; Director, Teruo Ishii; Screenplay, Teruo Ishii, Yoshida Sone; Director of Photography, Shigeru Kitazumi; Art Director, Akinori Satani; Editor, Osamu Ionuye; Music, Hajime Kaburagi; Sound Recording, Nikkatsu Sound Studio.

Cast: Mieko Kaji (Akemi), Hoki Tokuda (Aiko), Makoto Sato (Samurai), Yoko Tagaki, Hideo Sunazuka, Toru Abe, Yuzo Halumi, Yoshi Kato, Bumon Kahara.

A Nikkatsu Corp. Production. Nikkatsuolor. NikkatsuScope. 84 minutes. Released 1970.

U.S. Version: Released by Toho International Co., Ltd. (most likely). Alternate titles: *The Blind Woman's Curse*, *The Haunted Life of a Dragon-Tattooed Lass* and *Tattooed Swordswoman*. No MPAA rating. Released 1970 (?)

The Temptress/Byokuya no yojo (*The Temptress and the Monk*). Producer, Masayuki Takaki; Director, Eisuki Takizawa; Screenplay, Toshio Yasumi, Kyoka Izumi, based on the novel *Koya hijiri* by Kyoka Izumi; Art Director, Takashi Maysuyama; Director of Photography, Minoru Yokoyama; Nikkatsu Sound Studio.

Cast: Yumeji Tsukioka (Wife), Ryoji Hayama (Monk Socho), Tadashi Kobayashi (Husband), Ichijiro Oya (Grandfather), Jun Hamamura (Outlaw), Akitake Kono.

A Nikkastsu Corp. Production. Eastman Color (processed by Nikkatsu Laboratory). NikkatsuScope. 88 minutes. Released 1958.

U.S. Version: Released by Gaston Hakim Productions International in subtitled format. Subsequently advertised as *The Temptress and the Monk*. Wide screen format advertised as CinemaScope. 88 minutes. No MPAA rating. Released May 27, 1963.

Shintoho Company, Ltd.

Black Cat Mansion/Borei kaibyo yashiki. Producer, Mitsugu Okura; Director, Nobuo Nakagawa; Screenplay, Jiro Fujishima, Yoshihiro Ishikawa; Director of Photography, Tadashi Nishimoto.

Cast: Toshio Hosokawa, Midori Chikuma, Fujii Satsuki, Shin Shibata, Keinosuke Wada, Ryuzburo Nakamura, Fumiko Migata.

A Shintoho Co., Ltd., Production. Western Electric Mirrophonic recording. Black and white. Shintoho-Scope. 69 minutes. Released 1958.

U.S. Version: Distributor, if any, is undetermined. No MPAA rating.

The Bloody Sword of the 99th Virgin/Kyuju-kyuhonme no kimusume. Producer, Mitsugu Okura; Director, Morihei Magatani; Screenplay, Sususmu Takahira, Jiro Fujishima; Director of Photography, Kagai Okado.

Cast: Bunta Sugawara, Namiji Matsuura.

A Shintoho Co., Ltd., Production. Western Electric Mirrophonic recording. Black and white. Shintoho-Scope. 82 minutes. Released 1959.

U.S. Version: Distributor, if any, is undetermined. Also known as *Blood Sword of the 99th Virgin*. No MPAA rating.

The Depths/Kaidan kasanegafuchi. Producer, Mitsugu Okura; Director, Nobuo Nakagawa; Screenplay, Yasunori Kawauchi, based on the story "Shinkei Kasanegufuchi" by Encho Sanyutei; Director of Photography, Yoshimi Hirano.

Cast: Katsuko Wakasugi, Takashi Wada, Tetsuro Tamba, Noriko Kitazawa, Kikuko Hanaoka.

A Shintoho Co., Ltd., Production. Western Electric Mirrophonic recording. Eastman Color. Shintoho-Scope. 57 minutes. Released 1957.

U.S. Version: Distributor undetermined. Also known as *The Ghost of Kasane* and

Ghost Story: The Kanane Swamp. Remade by Daiei in 1960 and 1970 as *Kaidan Kasanegafuchi.* No MPAA rating.

Ghost of Otamange-Ike/Kaibyo Otamange-Ike. Producer, Mitsugu Okura; Director, Yoshihiro Ishikawa; Screenplay, Jiro Fujishima, Yoshihiro Ishikawa; Director of Photography, Kikuzo Kawasaki.
Cast: Shozaburo Date, Noriko Kitazawa, Yoichi Numata, Namiji Matsura.
A Shintoho Co., Ltd., Production. Western Electric Mirrophonic recording. Eastman Color. Shintoho-Scope. 75 minutes. Released 1960.
U.S. Version: Distributor, if any, is undetermined. International title: *The Ghost Cat of Otam-ag-Ike.* No MPAA rating.

The Ghost of Yotsuya/Tokaido Yotsuya kaidan (*Ghost Story of Yotsuda in Tokaido*). Producer, Mitsugu Okura; Director, Nobuo Nakagawa; Screenplay, Masayoshi Onuki, Yoshihiro Ishikawa (the latter not billed on current screen credits), based on the Kabuki play, "Tokaido Yotsuya kaidan" by Nanboku Tsuruya; Director of Photography, Tadashi Nishimoto; Art Director, Haryasu Kurosawa.
Cast: Shigeru Amachi (Iuemon Tamiya), Noriko Kitazawa (Osode Samon), Kazuko Wakasugi (Oiwa Samon), Shuntaro Emi (Naosuke), Junko Ikeuchi (Ume Ito), Ryzoaburo Nakamura (Yomoshichi Hikobei), Jun Otomo (Takuetsu).
A Shintoho Co., Ltd., Production. Western Electric Mirrophonic recording. Eastman Color. Shintoho-Scope. 96 minutes. Released July 11, 1959.
U.S. Version: Released by Shimoto Enterprises in the subtitled format. Also known as *Ghost Story of Yotsuda in Tokaido.* Running time is given as above, though the subtitled print I saw clocked in at 76 minutes. This same print also mis-transliterated the women's names. Oiwa became Iwa, Osode became Sode. No MPAA rating. Release date undetermined.

Girl Diver of Spook Mansion/Ama no bakemono yashiki. Producer, Mitsugu Okura; Director, Morihei Magatani; Screenplay, Akira Sugimoto, Nao Akatsukasa; Director of Photography, Kagai Okado.
Cast: Yoko Mihara (Yumi), Bunta Sugawara, Reiko Sato, Masayo Banri, Yoichi Numata.
A Shintoho Co., Ltd., Production. Western Electric Mirrophonic recording. Black and white. Shintoho-Scope. 82 minutes. Released 1959.
U.S. Version: Distributor, if any, is undetermined. Advertised as *The Haunted Cave.* Sequel: *Ghost of the Girl Diver/Kaidan ama yurei* (1960). No MPAA rating.

He Had to Die/Onryo sakura dai-sodo. Producer, Mitsugi Okura; Director, Kunio Watanabe; Screenplay, Kunio Watanabe, based on an orginal story by Yoshihiro Takenaka; Director of Photography, Takashi Watanabe.
Cast: Kanjuro Arashi, Shoji Nakayama, Joji Oka, Minoru Takada, Ranko Hanai.
A Shintoho Co., Ltd., Production. Western Electric Mirrophonic recording. Black and white. Shintoho-Scope (?). 103 minutes. Released 1957.
U.S. Version: Distributor, if any, is undetermined.

Kaidan Chibusa Enoki. Director, Goro Katano.
Cast: Katsuko Wakasugi, Keiko Hasegawa.
A Shintoho Co., Ltd., Production. Western Electric Mirrophonic recording. Black and white. Academy aspect ratio. Running time undetermined. Released 1958.
U.S. Version: Distributor, if any, is undetermined. International title: *Ghost of Chibusa Enoki.*

Kaidan Kagami-ga-fuchi. Director, Masaki Mori.
Cast: Noriko Kitazawa, Fumiko Miyata.
A Shintoho Co., Ltd., Production. Western Electric Mirrophonic recording. Black and white. Academy ratio. Running time undetermined. Released 1959.
U.S. Version: Distributor, if any, is undetermined. International title: Ghost of Kagami-Ga-Fuchi.

Kaii Utsunomiya tsuritenjo. Director, Nobuo Nakagawa.
Cast: Ryuzaburo Ogasawara, Akemi Tsukuchi.
A Shintoho Co., Ltd., Production. Western Electric Mirrophonic recording. Black and white. Academy ratio. Running time undetermined. Released 1956.
U.S. Version: Distributor, if any, is undetermined.

Sennin Buraku. Director, Morihei Magutani; Screenplay, Isao Matsuki; Director of Photography, Shingenari Yoshida.
Cast: Yoichi Numata, Mayumi Ozora, Mako Sanjo, Akiro Hitomi.
A Shintoho Co., Ltd., Production. Western Electric Mirrophonic recording. Black and white. Shintoho-Scope. 82 minutes. Released 1960.
U.S. Version: Never released theatrically in the United States. International title: *Invitation to the Enchanged Town.*

Seven Mysteries/Kaidan Honjo nanfushigi. Director, Goro Katono; Screenplay, Otoya Hayashi, Nagayoshi Akasada; Story, Akira Sagawa; Director of Photography, Hiroshi Suzuki.
Cast: Juzaburo Akechi, Shigeru Amachi, Hiroshi Hayashi, Uraji Matsuura, Akiko Tamashita, Michiko Tachibana.
A Shintoho Co., Ltd., Production. Western Electric Mirrophonic recording. Black and white. Academy ratio. Running time undetermined. Released 1957.
U.S. Version: Distributor undetermined. Also known as *Ghost Story of Wanderer at Honjo.*

The Sinners of Hell/Jigoku (*Hell*). Producer, Mitsugu Okura; Director, Nobuo Nakagawa; Screenplay, Ichiro Miyagawa, Nobuo Nakagawa; Director of Photography, Mamoru Morita; Art Director, Haryasu Kurosawa.
Cast: Shigeru Amachi (Shiro), Yoichi Numata (Tamura), Ukato Mitsuya (Sachiko), Torahiko Nakamura, Fumiko Miyata, Hiroshi Hayashi, Kimie Tokudaiji, Akiko Yamashita, Jun Otomo.
A Shintoho Co., Ltd., Production. Western Electric Mirrophonic recording. Eastman Color. Shintoho-Scope. 100 minutes. Released July 30, 1960.
U.S. Version: Distributor, if any, is undetermined. Also known as *The Sinners to Hell* and *Hell*. Remade by Toei in 1979. An adults-only feature in Japan, according to Something Weird Video's Mike Vraney. No MPAA rating.

Supergiant/Supa Jyaiantsu. ("Man of Steel"?). Producer, Mitsugi Okura; Directors, Teruo Ishii [chapters 1–6], Akira Mitsuwa [co-director, chapter 3], Koreyoshi Akasaka [co-director, chapter 3], Akira Miwa [chapter 7], Chogi Akasaka [chapters 8–9]; Screenplay, Ichiro Miyagawa, Shinsuke Niegishi, Ishiro Miyagawa; Directors of Photography, Takashi Watanabe, Akira Watanabe, Hiroshi Suzuki, Nobu Boshi. Kiminobu Okada [chapters 8–9]; Music, Chumei Watanabe, Sadao Nagase [chapters 8–9].
Cast: Ken Utsui (Starman [Super Giant]), Junko Ikeuchi [chapters 1–2 only], Minako Yamada [chapters 3–4], Utako Mitsuya [chapters 5–6], Chisako Tahara [chapter 7], Reiko Seto [chapter 8], Terumi Hoshi [chapter 9], Minoru Takada, Ryo Iwashita, Kan Hayashi, Akira Tamura, Hiroshi Asami, Teruhisha Ikeda, Junko Ikeuchi, Shoji Nakayama, Sachihiro Ohsawa, Fumiko Miyata, Kami Ashita, Reiko Seto, Tomohiko Ohtani, Johji Ohara, Shinsuke Mikimoto.
A Shintoho Co., Ltd., Production. Western Electric Mirrorphonic recording. Some chapters filmed in Shintoho-Scope (?). Black and white (chapters 1–7, 9) and Eastman Color (chapter 8). A multi-chapter serial/series. Original films are as follows:

1. *Kotetso no kyojin – Supa Jyaiantsu* ("The Steel Giant – Super Giant"). 49 minutes. Released July 30, 1957.

2. *Zoku kotetsu no kyojin – Supa Jyaiantsu* ("Follow-up to the Adventures of the Steel Giant"). 52 minutes. Released August 16, 1957.

3. *Kotetsu no Kyojin – Supa Jyaiantsu: Kaiseijin no mayo* ("The Steel Giant – Super

Giant: The Evil Castle of the Mysterious Planet People"). 48 minutes. Released October 1957.

4. *Kotetsu no kyojin—Supa Jyaiantsu: chikyu metsubo sunzen* ("The Steel Giant—Super Giant: The Earth Will Be Annihilated Soon"). 39 minutes. Released October 8, 1957.

5. *Supa Jyaiantsu: jinko eisei to jinrui no hametsu* ("Super Giant: Satellites and the Destruction of Mankind"). 39 minutes. Released December 28, 1957.

6. *Supa Jyaiantsu: uchusen to jinko eisei no gekitotsu* ("Super Giant: The Spaceships and Satellites Duel"). 39 minutes. Released January 3, 1958.

7. *Supa Jyaiantsu: uchu kaijin shutsugen* ("Super Giant: Mysterious Spacemen Appear"). 45 minutes. Released April 28, 1958.

8. *Zoku Supa Jyaiantsu (dai hachibu): akuma no keshin* ("Further Adventures of Super Giant [chapter 8]: Devil Incarnate"). 57 minutes. Released March 27, 1959.

9. *Zoku Supa Jyaiantsu (dai kyubu): dokunga ookoku* ("Further Adventures of Super Giant [chapter 9]: Kingdom of the Venomous Moth"). 57 minutes. Released April 24, 1959.

U.S. Version: Never released theatrically in the United States. Selected chapters released directly to television by Medallion TV (i.e. Walter H. Manley Enterprises, Inc.). Copyright 1965 by Walter Manley Enterprises, Inc. Unlike American serials, these films did not form one continuous narrative. Chapters 1–2, 3–4 and 5–6 were two-part stories; chapters 7, 8, and 9 were independent entities. Chapters were recut for U.S. television in 1964–65. Sources differ as to corresponding chapters; an approximation follows:

Chapters 1–2 were recut as *Atomic Rulers* (aka *Atomic Rulers of the World*), running 74 minutes.

Chapters 3–4 became *Invaders from Space*, running 79 minutes.

Chapters 5–6 became *Attack from Space*, running 74 minutes.

Chapter 7 was recut as *Evil Brain from Outer Space*, running 78 minutes.

Chapters 8–9 were apparently never issued in the United States.

Alternate titles: (Chapter 1) *The Steelman from Outer Space*, (2) *Rescue from Outers space*, (3) *Invaders from the Planets*, (4) *The Earth in Danger*, (5) *The Sinister Space-Ships*, (6) *The Destruction of the Space-fleet*. No MPAA rating.

The Woman Vampire/Onna kyuketsuki.
Producer, Mitsuga Okura; Director, Nobuo Nakagawa; Screenplay, Shin Nakazawa, Katsuyoshi Nakatsu; Director of Photography, Yoshimi Hirano.

Cast: Shigeru Amachi (Vampire), Yoko Mihara (Niwako), Keinosuke Wada, Junko Ikeuchi.

A Shintoho Co., Ltd., Production. Western Electric Mirrophonic recording. Black and white. Shintoho-Scope. 78 minutes. Released 1959.

U.S. Version: Distributor, if any, is undetermined. Above is international title. Alternate titles: *The Male Vampire* and *Vampire Man*. *Note:* running time is also given as 98 minutes. No MPAA rating.

Shochiku Company, Ltd.

Black Lizard/Kurotokage (*Black Lizard*). Producer, Akira Oda; Director, Kinji Fukasaku; Screenplay, Masashige Narusawa, based on the play by Yukio Mishima (itself based on the novel by Rampo Edogawa); Director of Photography, Hiroshi Dowaki; Editor, Keiichi Uraoka; Production Manager, Tatsuo Hagiwara; Art Director, Kyohei Morita; Music, Isao Tomita; Song Performance, Akihiro Maruyama; Assistant Director, Hideo Oe; Set Decoration, Keinosuke Ishiwatari; Costumes, Masako Watanabe; Sound, Toshio Tanaka; Sound Effects, Hirobumi Sato.

Cast: Akihiro Maruyama (Midorigawa, aka Kurotokage, the Black Lizard), Isao Kimura (Detective Kogoro Akechi), Kikko Matsuoka (Sanae Iwasa/Yoko Sakurayama),

Junya Usami (Shobei Iwasa), Yusuke Kawazu (Junichi Amamiya), Akira Nishimura (Matoba Keiji), Toshiko Kobayashi (Hina), Sonosuke Oda (Harada), Kinji Hattori (Toyama), Kyoichi Sato (Ohkawa), Isao Kimura (Matsukichi), Jun Kato (Sakai), Ryuji Funakoshi (Kizu), Mitsuko Takera (Show Dancer), Tetsuro Tanba (Kuroki, Akechi's Friend), Yukio Mishima (Living Doll).

A Shochiku Co., Ltd., Production. Fujicolor (processed by Shochiku Laboratory), Shochiku GrandScope. Copyright 1968 by Shochiku Corp. 86 minutes. Released 1968.

U.S. Version: Released by Cinevista in subtitled format. A Rene Ruentes-Chao and John R. Tilley Presentation. Subtitles, Cinetyp, Inc. (Hollywood); Subtitles Editor, H. Eisenman. 83 minutes. No MPAA rating. Released February 1985.

Blood/Oreno chi wa tanin no chi. Executive Producer, Kiyoshi Higuchi; Director, Toshio Senda; Screenplay, Toshio Senda, based on the novel by Yasutaka Tsutsui; Director of Photography, Keiji Maruyama; Editor, Yoshi Sugiwara; Assistant Director, Hidewo Oe; Art Director, Takeshi Machida; Costumes, Shochiku Isho Co., Ltd.; Lighting, Lei Miura; Music, Hiroshi Takada; Sound Recording, Ken Nakamura; Sound Mixing, Kou- Gyo Kowo; Fighting Instructor, Takamitsu Watanabe; Production Manager, Tadashi Shibata; Assistant Production Manager, Junichi Mine.

Cast: Shohei Kano (Ryosuki Kinugawa), Frankie Sakai (Rokusuke Sawamura), Etsuko Nami (Fusako), Wataru Nachi (Ranko), Ichiro Nakaya (Itami), Toru Abe (Toraichiro Yumaga), Isao Hashimoto (Samonji), Yoshiwo Aoki (Ohashi), Kuniyasu Atsumi (Adachi), Kazuo Kato (Fukuda), Takanobu Hozumi (Fori), Housei Komatsu (Chief of Police), Hatsuo Yamatani (Ito), Kin Omae (Hauda).

A Shochiku Co., Ltd., Production, in cooperation with Yokohama Dreamland. Color (processed by Shochiku Laboratory). Panavision (?). 94 minutes. Released October 12, 1974.

U.S. Version: Distributor, if any, is undetermined. Alternate title (?): *My Blood Belongs to Someone Else.*

Curse of the Blood/Kaidan zankoku monogatari (*Cruel Ghost Legend*). Producer, Tsuneo Kosumi; Director, Kazuo Hase; Screenplay, Masahige Narusawa, based on the novel *Kaidan ruigafuchi* by Renzaburo Shibata; Director of Photography, Kenji Maruyama; Production Manager, Hisamune Tamau; Assistant Director, Hideo Oh-e; Art Director, Kyohei Morita; Set Decoration, Shin-ei Bijutsu Kozei; Editor, Kazuo Ohta; Sound Effects, Takashi Matsumoto; Music, Hajime Kaburagi.

Cast: Matsuhiro Tomura [Toura] (Shinzaemon Fukaya), Nobuo Kaneko (Shojun Yasukawa), Masakazu Tamura (Shinichiro), Yunusuke [Yusuke] Kawazu (Shinzo), Hiroko Sakurai (Ohisa), Saeda Kazaguchi (Toyosuga), Masumi Harukawa (Okuma), Yukie Kagawa (Hana), Eizo Kitamura (Sobe Shimofusaya), Genshu Hanayagi (Toyo).

A Shochiku Co., Ltd., Production. Fujicolor (processed by Shochiku Laboratory). Shochiku GrandScope. 88 minutes. Released March 31, 1968.

U.S. Version: Released by Shochiku Films of America, Inc. in the subtitled format. Alternate title: *Cruel Ghost Legend.* *Note:* Phil Hardy says the film is in black and white and runs 126 minutes; credits above are Shochiku's. 88 minutes. No MPAA rating. Released 1969 (?).

Dancing Mistress/Kaidan Iro-Zane-Kyoren onna shisho. Producer, Akira Koito; Director, Ryosuke Kurahashi; Screenplay, Shinichi Yanagawa; Director of Photography, Mikio Hattori.

Cast: Hiroshi Nawa, Yataro Kitagame, Jun Tazaki, Achako Hanabishi, Machiko Mizukara, Michio Saga.

A Shochiku Co., Ltd., Production. Black and white (processed by Shochiku Laboratory). Academy radio. Running time undetermined. Released 1957.

U.S. Version: Distributor, if any, is undetermined.

Demon Pond/Yashagaike. Executive Producers, Shigemi Sugisaki, Yukio Tomizawa, Kanji Nakagawa; Director, Masahiro Shinoda; Screenplay, Takeshi Tamura, Haruhiko Minura, based on the play *Yashanga ike* by Kyoka Izumi; Assistant Producer, Seikichi Iiizumi; Director of Photography, Masao Kosugi; Assistant Director, Isao Kumagai; Second Unit Director, Noritaka Sakamoto; Art Directors, Kiyoshi Awazu, Setsu Asakura, Yutaka Yokoyama; Music, Isao Tomita; Editors, Zen Ikeda, Sachiko Yamachi; Choreography, Rui Takemura; Special Effects Director, Nobuo Yajima.

Cast: Tamasaburo Bando (Yuri/Princess Shirayuki), Go Kato (Akira Hagiwara), Tsutomu Yamazaki (Gaukuen Yamasawa), Koji Nanbara (Priest Shikami), Yatsuko Tanami (Nurse), Hisashi Igawa (The Carp), Norihei Miki (Catfish Messenger), Juro Kara (Denkichi), Ryunosuke Kaneda (Diet Member), Fujio Tokita (The Crab), Jun Hamamura (The Shadow/Yatabei the Bellkeeper), Megumi Ishii (The Camellia), Tadashi Furuta (The Mackerel), Kazuo Sato (Tiger Priest), Kai Ato (The Bone), Hatsuo Yamatani (Yoju the Villager), Maki Takayama (Yoju's Wife), Yumi Nishigami (Yoju's Daughter), Toru Abe (Leader of Village Assembly), Shigeru Yazaki (Village Teacher), Dai Kanai (Village Headman), Toshie Kobayashi (Village Woman), Hitoshi Ohmae (Furosude Kotori), Fudeko Tanaka (Old Woman).

A Shochiku Co., Ltd., Production. Shochikucolor. VistaVision. Four-track stereophonic sound (MagOptical?). 123 minutes. October 20, 1979.

U.S. Version: Released by Shochiku Films of America, Inc., in subtitled format. Reissued by Kino International in 1982, also in subtitled format, as a Myron Bresnick Presentation from Grange Communications, Inc. 123 minutes. No MPAA rating. Released 1980.

Dokuro kyojo. Director, Seiichi Fukuda; Screenplay, I. Nagae; Story, K. Nomura; Director of Photography, K. Kataoda.

Cast: Kokichi Takada, J. Ban, O. Ichikawa.

A Shochiku Co., Ltd., Production. Eastman Color (processed by Shochiku Laboratory). Shochiku GrandScope. 105 minutes. Released 1957.

U.S. Version: Distributor, if any, is undetermined. International title: *Masked Terror.*

Erogami no onryo. Director, Yasujiro Ozu; Screenplay, Kogo Noda; Story, Seizaburo Ishihara; Director of Photography, Hideo Mohara.

Cast: Tatsuo Saito (Kentaro Yumaji), Hikaru Hoshi (Daikuro Ishikawa), Satoko Date (Yumeko), Ichiro Tsukida (Yumeko's Boyfriend).

A Shochidu Kamata Production. Silent. Black and white. Academy ratio. Three reels (approximately 28 minutes). Released July 27, 1930.

U.S. Version: Distributor, if any, is undetermined. International title: *The Revengeful Spirit of Eros.*

Genocide/Konchu daisenso. Producer, Tsuneo Otsuno; Director, Kazui Nihonmatsu; Screenplay, Susumu Takahisa, Based on the story "Konchu daisenso" by Tetsumi Amada; Directors of Photography, Shizuo Hirase, Shozaburo Shinomura; Editor, Akimitsu Terada; Art Director, Tadatake Yoshino; Lighting, Tatsuo Aomoto; Set Decoration, Ryozo Nakamura; Production Manager, Makoto Naito; Assistant Director, Keiji Shiraki; Continuity, Masayuki Fukuyama; Still Photography, Kazumi Kajimoto, Masashi Kaneda; Music, Shunsuke Kikuchi; Sound, Kan Nakamura; Sound Effects, Takashi Matsumoto. Special Effects Unit: Japan Film Special Effects Co., Ltd.; Directors, Keiji Kawakami, Shun Suganuma; Optical Effects, Satohiro Ishikawa.

Cast: Keisuke Sonoi (Dr. Yoshito Nagumo), Yusuke Kawazu (Joji Akiyama), Emi Shindo (Yukari Akiyama), Reiko Hitomi (Junko Komura), Kathy Horan [Cathy Horlan] (Annabelle), Rolf Jessup (Commander Gordon), Toshiyuki Ichimura (Kondo), Tadayuki Ueda (Tsuneo Matsunaga), Hiroshi Aoyama (Yokoi), Chico Roland (Charlie), Eriko Sono (Nagumo's Assistant), Wolfram Pekeshas (Adjutant),

Franz Gruber (Doctor), William Douyuak [Teugel?] (Correspondent), Mike Daning (Aircraft Captain), Raina Gessman (Subpilot), Harold S. Conway (Commander), Hardy Bauman [Happie Barman] (Crewman), Saburo Aonuma (Police Commissioner), Tatsumi Ichiyama, Hideaki Komori, Rainer Gessman.

A Shochiku Co., Ltd., Production. Fujicolor (processed by Shochiku Laboratory; one source says Far East Laboratories, Ltd.). Shochiku GrandScope. Double-billed with *Living Skeleton/Kyuketsu dolurosen*. 84 minutes. Released November 1968.

U.S. Version: Released by Shochiku Films of America, Inc. Advertised as *War of the Insects*. No MPAA rating (?). 84 minutes. Released 1969.

Goke, Bodysnatcher from Hell/Kyuketsuki Gokemidoro (*Vampire Gokemidoro*). Producer, Takashi Inomata; Director, Hajime Sato; Screenplay, Susumu Takaku, Kyuzo Kobayashi; Production Manager, Masayuki Fukuyama; Assistant Director, Keiji Shiraki; Art Director, Tadataka Yoshino; Set Decoration, Shin-ei Bijutsu Kogei; Director of Photography, Shizuo Hirase; Editor, Akimitsu Terada; Sound, Hiroshi Nakamura; Sound Effects, Takashi Matsumoto; Music, Shunsuke Kikuchi.

Cast: Teruo Yoshida (Ei Sugisaka), Tomomi Sato (Kazumi Asakura), Hideo Ko (Hirobumi Teraoka), Eizo Kitamura (Gozo Mano), Masaya Takahashi (Toshiyuki Saga), Cathy Horlan (Mrs. Neal), Kazuo Kato (Momotake), Yuko Kunsunoki (Noriko Tokumatsu), Norihiko Kaneko (Matsumiya), Hiroyuki Nishimoto (Airplane Captain), Andrew Hughes (Ambassador in flashback stills).

A Shochiku Co., Ltd., Production. Fujicolor (processed by Shochiku Laboratory). Shochiku GrandScope. 84 minutes. Released August 14, 1968.

U.S. Version: Released by Shochiku Films of America, Inc., in subtitled format, and possibly released dubbed at this same time. Alternate title: *Goke the Vampire*. Television and home video title: *Body Snatcher from Hell*, listed as a TFC and Pacemaker Films, Inc., Presentation (who may also have distributed the film theatrically) and running 82 minutes. Curiously, the video version retains the Japanese subtitles originally used during Horlan's English dialogue. 84 minutes. No MPAA rating. Released 1969.

The Guyver. Executive Producers, Yutaka Wada, Aki Komine; Producers, Brian Yuzuna, Gary Schmueller; Directors, Screaming Mad George, Steve Wang; Screenplay, Jon Purdy, based on characters created by Yoshiki Takaya; Editors, Andy Horvitch, Joe Woo; Production Designer, Matthew C. Jacobs; Director of Photography, Levie Isaacks; Music, Matthew Morse; First Assistant Director, Tom Milo; Second Assistant Director, Jerry Goldberg; Casting Director, Al Guarino; Production Coordinator, Lorelei; Production Auditor, Bonnie Weis; Production Attorney, Stephen Baron; Assistant Production Coordinator, Victor Garcia; Pre-production Coordinator, Seth Q. Blair; Script Supervisor, Martin Kitrosser; Second Unit Script Supervisor, Elan Papa; Storyboard Artist, Pete von Sholly; Still Photographer, Eric Lasher; First Assistant Editor, Ute Berthold; Second Assistant Editor, Tom Barrett; Apprentice Editors, Trudy Yee, Cindy Fret; Casting Assistant, Cathy Yuzna; Second Second Assistant Director, Paul Kowalczyk; Additional Second Second Assistant Director, Mark Buckles; Key Production Assistant, Doug Patrick; Production Assistants, Garth Grinde, Victoria Halbooth; Second Unit Director, Thomas C. Rainore; Second Unit Director of Photography, Burt Guthrie; Additional Photography, Richard Hutchings, Doyle Smith; First Assistant Camera, Andy Graham; Second Assistant Camera, Bill Roberts, Ted Nutty; Loader, Lisa Guerriero; Set Design, Gilbert Mercer; Set Decoration, Julie Brooke Beattie; On Set Dresser, Madeline Hyman; Prop Masters, Andy Grant, Al Paulson; Assistant Prop Master, Janine Kijner; Lead Person, Nancy Fallace; Swing Man, Chris Grantz; Construction Foreman, Clint DuVall; Art Department Assistant, Mark Isom; Stand-by

Carpenter, Chris Birkhardt; Gaffer, Russ Brandt; Best Boy Electric, Adam Santelli; Electricians, Rob Lewbell, Jeff Journey, Katie Nelson; Key Grip, Daniel "Dano" Adams; Dolly Grip, Mark Pickens; Best Boy Grip, Marcus "Rue" Flowers; Grips, David Salamore, Danny McComas; Production Sound Mixer, Richard Leger; Boom Operator, Paul Coogan; Costumer, Linda "Lulu" Meltzer; Assistant Costumer, Yana Syrkin; Makeup, Jill Bennett; Assistant Makeup and Hair, Janna Denny, Rick Dubov; Transportation Coordinator, Kevin "Hazzard" Hudis; Drivers, Mitch Bergman, Joseph "JC" Coreo, Charles Gaston, Greg Jacobs; Assistant to Mark Hamill, Jay Kelly; Assistant to Vivian Wu, Danielle Cohen; Craft Services, Ted Yonenaka; Sound Editing, Soundbusters; Supervising Sound Editor, Hari Ryatt; Sound Editors, Bob Fitzgerald, Bruce Stubblefield, Fred Wasser, Jon Hohnson, Dick Brass; Rerecording, Patrick Cyccone, Frank Montano; Assistant Sound Editors, Patrick Mullane, Martin Farnum, Michelle Perrone, Joanna Jimezez; Foley Walkers, Alicia Stevenson, Ellen Heuver; Walla Group, Superloopers; Music Editor, Virginia Elsworth; Aikido Consultants, Hauro Matsuoka, Minoru Osaka, Ted Smith, Raman Chamaki; Lighting and Grip Equipment, Cinelease, Inc.; Camera and Lenses, Panavision; Re-recorded at Meridian Studios; ADR and Foley recorded at Directors Sound; Titles-Opticals, Cinema Research Corp.; Special Thanks, New Balance Japan, Inc., Ken Iyadomi, Max Watanabe, Lex Nakashima and Tercel, Inc., Matt Rose, John Criswell, Johnson & Johnson, Coty Perfume, Jolly Ranchers, Tenshin Dojo, Takahiko Mamiya, Tokuma-Shoten; Special Effects Crew, Creature Effects Directors, Steve Wang, Screaming Mad George; Special Effects Supervisor, Michael Deak; SPFX Coordinator, Thomas C. Rainore; Shop Coordinator, Misa Gardner; Shop Supervisors, Motoyoshi Hata, Eddie Wang; Creature Heads, Steve Wang (Guyver), Screaming Mad George (Baleus), Motoyoshi Hata (Max), Eddie Yang (Lisker), James Kagel (Striker), Jordu Schell (Ramsey), Asao Goto (Background Characters Creator); Zoanoid Stunt Coordinator, Brian Simpson; Mechanical Effects, Jake "The Snake" McKinnon, Tim Ralston; Head Lab Technician–Key SPFX Makeup, Wayne Toth; Lab Technicians, Nori Honda, Shawn Patrick Smith, Ted Smith, T. C. Williams, James Slavin, Wyatt Weed, Yoichi Fukuoka, Mike Jolly, Andrew Clement, Aaron Sims, Joey Orosco, Gabe Bartalos, Sally Ray; Additional Mechanical Effects, Yoichi Fukuoka, Wayne Toth; Support Sculptors, Glenn Hanz, Heidi Snyder; Lab Assistants, Koji Hoshi, Yasuko Kudo, Michiko Ishikawwa, Masaaki Fukuda, Chieko Watanabe, Takao Kumaoka, Mika Hagiwara; Production Assistant, Pat Conrad; Visual Effects Director of Photography, Ted Race; Miniature Supervisor, Wyatt Weed; First Assistant Director/UPM Miniatures, Thomas C. Rainore; Camera Assistant, Tom Gleason; Model Makers, Joanne Bloomfield, Carolyn Thorne, Jeanna Crawford, Theodore Van Dooorn; Gaffer, Jeff Cannon; Key Grip, Mark Scholl; Grip, David Stockton; Stop Motion, Ted Rae; Stop Motion Crew, Asao Goto, Robert F. Peppler; Mechanical Effects and Pyrotechnics, Ken Tarallo, FX Concepts, Ltd.; Stooge #1, Howie St. James; Stooge #2, Lloyd McGavin.

Cast: Jack Armstrong (Sean Barker/The Guyver), Mark Hamill (Max Reed), Vivian Wu (Mizsky [Misuki] Segawa), David Gale (Fulton Bakue [Vaulkas]), Greg Paik (Dr. Tetsu Segawa), Jimmy Walker (Striker), Peter Spellos (Ramsey), Michael Berryman (Lisker), Johnnie Saiko (Craig), Deborah Gorman (Ms. Jensen), Danny Gibson (Aikido Instructor's Assistant), Willard Pugh (Colonel Castle), Ted Smith (Ronnie), Doug Simpson (Quinton), Brian Simpson (Gang Member #3), Dennie Madalone (Gang Member #4), Michael Deak (Director), David Wells (Dr. Gordon), Jay Kelley (Lab Scientist), Linnea Quigley (Scream Queen), Jeffrey Combs (Dr. East), Spice Williams, Kenny Ferrugiara, Kim Gyusaki, Tim Trella, Merritt Yohnka, Doug Simpson, Dennis Madalone, Tony Snegoff, Bob Yerkees (Stunts; Ken Lesco, Stunt Coordinator).

A Brian Yuzna Production. A Screaming Mad George and Steve Wang Film. A Shochiku-Fuji Release. Copyright 1991 by The Guyver Productions, Inc. Ultra-Stereo. Color (processed by Foto-Kem). Spherical Panavision. Released 1991.

U.S. Version: Released directly to home video and cable television in 1992 by Imperial Entertainment. MPAA rating: PG-13.

Half a Loaf. . . /Yoku. Director, Heinsuke Gosho.

Cast: J. Ban, Y. Todoroki.

A Shochiku Co., Ltd., Production. Black and white (processed by Shochiku Laboratory). Shochiku GrandScope. 106 minutes. Released 1958.

U.S. Version: Released by Shochiku Films of America, Inc., in subtitled format. No MPAA rating. 106 minutes. Released 1958.

Kaidan ryoko. Executive Producer, Kiyoshi Shimazu; Director, Shoji Segawa; Screenplay, Kazuo Funabashi; Director of Photography, Keiji Maruyama; Art Director, Masao Kumagi; Music, Seitaro Ohmori.

Cast: Frankie Sakai (Shinpei Ohwada), Tomoe Hiiro (Umeko and Satoe), Kensaku Morita (Daisuke Sakaguchi), Yumiko Nogawa (Yumi Okamura), Akane Kawasaki (Chizu), Casey Tamamine (Conductor), Norihei Miki (Shosaku Sakaguchi).

A Shochiku Co., Ltd., Production. Color. Panavision (?). 91 minutes. Released June 10, 1972.

U.S. Version: Distributor, if any, is undetermined. International title (?): *Weird Trip.*

Kurobarano yakata. Director, Kinji Fukasaku.

Cast: Akihiro Maruyama.

A Shochiku Co., Ltd., Production. Color. Shochiku GrandScope. Running time undetermined. Released 1969.

U.S. Version: Distributor, if any, is undetermined. International title: *The Black Rose Inn.*

Kyokanoka musume Dojoji. (no production credits available)

Cast: Utaemon Nakamura.

A Shochiku Co., Ltd., Production. Shochikucolor. Academy ratio. 80 minutes. Released 1956.

U.S. Version: Distributor, if any, is undetermined. International title: *Dojoji Temple.*

Living Skeleton/Kyuketsu dokuro sen. Executive Producer, Shiro Kido; Producer, Takashi Inomata; Director, Hiroki [Hiroshi] Matsuno; Screenplay, Kikuma Shimoizaka, Kyuzo Kobayashi; Production Manager, Yoshinori Ikeda; Assistant Director, Masami Tatesen; Art Director, Kyohei Morita; Director of Photography, Masayuki Kato; Editor, Kazuo Ohta; Music, Noburo Nishiyama; Sound, Hideo Kobayashi; Sound Effects, Hirofumi Sato.

Cast: Kikko Matsuoka (Saeko/Kinuko), Akira Nishimura (Nishizato), Masumi Kaneko (Suetsuga), Yasunori Irikawa (Mochizuki), Asao Koike (Tsuji), Tomoo Uchida (Ejiri), Noriyaki Yamamoto (Ono), Kaoru Yamamoto (Mayumi), Keiko Yanazawa (Sanae Suetsugu), Kaishu Uchida (Uchida), Keijiro Kikyo (First Policeman), Minoru Hirano (Second Policeman).

A Shochiku Co., Ltd., Production. Black and white (processed by Shochiku Laboratory). Shochiku GrandScope. 81 minutes. Released 1968.

U.S. Version: Released by Shochiku Films of America in subtitled format. No MPAA rating. 81 minutes. Released 1969 (?).

The Mask of Destiny/Shuzenji monogatari. Producer, Kiyoshi Takamura; Director, Noboru Nakamura; Screenplay, Kido Okamato, based on his play *Shuzenji monogatari*; Art Director, Kisaku Ito; Director of Photography, Toshio Ubukata; Editor, Toshi Egata; Music, Toshiro Mazazumi.

Cast: Teiji Takahashi, Chikaga Awashima, Minosuke Bando, Keiko Kishi.

A Shochiku Co., Ltd., Production. Western Electric Mirrophonic recording. Eastman Color. Academy ratio. 105 minutes. Released 1955.

U.S. Version: Released by Stratford Pictures Corp., a subsidiary of Allied Artists

Corp. Prints by De Luxe. International title: *The Mask and Destiny*. 105 minutes. No MPAA rating. Released 1957.

Nowhere Man/*Muno no hito*. Executive Producers, Toshiaki Nakazaw, Masaki Sekine; Producers, Kazuyoshi Okuyama, Shozo Ichiyama, Hirotsuyo Yoshida; Director, Naoto Takenaka; Screenplay, Toshiharu Maruchi, based on the comic strip "Muno no hito" by Yoshiharu Tsuge; Production Manager, Noriyuki Takahashi; Assistant Director, Yasu Matsumoto; Production Designer, Iwao Saitoh; Director of Photography, Yasushi Sasakibara; Editor, Yoshiyuki Okuhara; Music, Gontiti; Sound, Mineharu Kitamura.

Cast: Naoto Takenake (Sukezo Sukegawa), Jun Fubuki (Momoko Sukegawa), Kohtaro Santoh (Sansuke Sukegawa).

A KSS/Shochiku Co., Ltd./Daiichi Kogyo Co., Ltd., Production. A Shochiku Co., Ltd., Release. Fujicolor. Widescreen. 107 minutes. Released 1991.

U.S. Version: Distributor, if any, is undetermined. Prints available from Shochiku Films of America, Inc.

Osorezan no onna. Director, Heinosuke Gosho; Screenplay, Hideo Horie; Director of Photography, Shozaburo Shinomura.

Cast: Jitsuko Yoshimura, Kin Sugai, Taiji Tonoyama, Keizo Kawasaki.

A Shochiku Co., Ltd., Production. Black and white (processed by Shochiku Laboratory). Shochiku GrandScope. 98 minutes. Released 1966.

U.S. Version: Distributor, if any, is undetermined. International title: *An Innocent Witch*.

Shinshaku Yotsuya kaidan. Producer, Koichiro Ogura; Director, Keisuke Kinoshita; Screenplay, Eijiro Hisaita, based on the play *Yotsuya kaidan* by Nanboku Tsuruya; Director of Photography, Hiroshi Kusuda.

Cast: Ken Uehara (Iemon), Kinuyo Tanaka (Oiwa/Osode), Hisako Yamane (Oume), Haruko Sugimura, Choko Iida, Osamu Takizawa.

A Shochiku Co., Ltd., Production. Black and white. Academy ratio. 159 minutes (two parts running 86 and 73 minutes). Released 1949.

U.S. Version: Distributor, if any, is undetermined. International title: *New Version of the Ghost of Yotsuya*. Also known as *The Ghost of Yotsuya: New Version*.

Takamuru and Kikumaru. Director, Santaro Marune; Screenplay, Ryuta Mine, Noburo Mizukami; Director of Photography, Kiyomi Kuroda.

Cast: Kinshiro Matsumoto, Kotobuki Hanemoto, Hiroshi Nawa, Kiku Hojo, Kyoko Izumi.

A Shochiku Co., Ltd., Production. Shochikucolor. Academy ratio (?). 144 minutes. Released 1959.

U.S. Version: Released by Shochiku Films of America, Inc. 139 minutes. No MPAA rating. Released 1959.

Vengence Is Mine/*Fukusho suruwa ware ni ari*. Executive Producer, Shohei Imamura; Producer, Kazuo Inoue; Director, Shohei Imamura; Screenplay, Masaru Baba, based on the novel *Fukusho suruwa ware ni ari* by Ryuzo Saki; Director of Photography, Masahisa Himeda; Editor, Keiichi Uraoka; Music, Shinichiro Ikebe.

Cast: Ken Ogata (Iwao Enokizu), Rentaro Mikuni (Shizuo Enokizu), Chocho Mikayo (Kayo Enokizu), Mitsuke Baisho (Kazuko Enokizu), Mayumi Ogawa (Haro Asano), Nijiko Kiyokawa (Hisano Asano).

An Imamura Productions Picture for Shochiku Co., Ltd., Shochikucolor. Widescreen (?). 128 minutes. Released 1979.

U.S. Version: Released by Shochiku Films of America, Inc., in subtitled format. Reissued June 1985 in the United States by Kino International. 128 minutes. No MPAA rating. Released February 7, 1980.

Village of Eight Gravestones/*Yatsu hukamura*. Producers, Yoshitaro Nomura, Shigemi Sugesiaki, Akira Oda; Director, Yoshitaro Nomura; Screenplay, Shinobu Hashimoto, based on the novel *Yatsu hukamura* by Seishi Yokomizo; Art Director,

Kyohei Morita; Director of Photography, Takashi Kawamata; Music, Yasushi Akutagawa.

Cast: Kiyoshi Atsumi (Investigator), Kenichi Hagiware, Mayumi Ogawa, Ryoko Nakano.

A Shochiku Co., Ltd., Production. Shochikucolor. Panavision. 151 minutes. Released October 29, 1977.

U.S. Version: Released by Shochiku Films of America, Inc., in subtitled format. International title: *Village of the Eight Tombs*. 151 minutes. No MPAA rating. Released 1978.

The X from Outer Space/Uchu daikaiju Guirara (*Great Space Monster Guirara*). Producer, Akihiko Shimada; Director, Kazui Nihonmatsu [Nihonmazu]; Screenplay, Kazui Nihonmatsu, Hidemi [Eibi] Motomochi, Moriyoshi Ishida; Art Director, Shigemori Shigeta; Director of Photography, Shizuo Hirase [Hiraze]; Editor, Yoshi Sugihara; Sound, Hiroshi Nakamura; Music, Taku Izumi; Special Effects Director, Hiroshi Ikeda.

Cast: Eiji [Eijii] Okada (Kato), Toshiya Wazaki [Toshinari Kazusaki] (Captian Sano), Peggy Neal (Lisa), Itoko Harada (Michiko), Shinichi Yanagisawa (Miyamoto), Franz Gruber (Dr. Berman), Keisuke Sonoi (Dr. Shioda), Mike Daning (Dr. Stein), Torahiko [Torahike] Hamada (Kimura), Ryuji Kita (Chief of Staff), Takanobu Hozumi (Member of FAFC), Chuji Sato (Guard), Hiroshi Fujioka, Kusanosuke Oda (Moon Station Correspondents), Kamon Kawamura (Substation Clerk), Wataru Nakajima (President of Defense Headquarters), Masaji Hashimoto (Manager of Secretariat), Koji Nakada (President of Police Headquarters).

A Shochiku Co., Ltd., Production. Eastman Color (processed by Shochiku Laboratory). Shochiku GrandScope. 89 minutes. Released 1967.

U.S. Version: Never released theatrically in the United States. Released directly to television by American International Television (AIP-TV) in 1968. A James H. Nicholson and Samuel Z. Arkoff Presentation. Postproduction Supervisor, Salvatore Billitteri; Prints by Perfect. *Note:* Monster's name also given as Guilala, Girara. Copyright 1968 by American International Productions. 88 minutes. No MPAA rating.

Toei Company, Ltd.

Botandoro. Director, Akira Nobuchi.
Cast: Chiyonosuke Azuma, Yuriko Tashiro.
A Toei Co., Ltd., Production. Black and white. Academy ratio. Running time undetermined. Released 1955
U.S. Version: Distributor, if any, is undetermined. International title: *Peonies and Stone Lanterns.*

The Challenging Ghost/Gekko kamen. Dirctor, Shoichi Shimazu.
Cast: Fumitake Omura.
A Toei Co., Ltd., Production. Black and white (processed by Toei Chemistry Co., Ltd.). ToeiScope. Running time undetermined. Released 1959.
U.S. Version: Distributor, if any, is undetermined. (See *The Man in the Moonlight Mask*).

The Claws of Satan/Gekko kamen— Satan no tsume. Director, Eijiro Wakabayashi.
Cast: Fumitake Omura, Tomoko Matsushima.
A Toei Co., Ltd., Production. Black and white (processed by Toei Chemistry Co., Ltd.). ToeiScope. 62 minutes. Released 1959.
U.S. Version. Reportedly released in the United States, distributor undetermined. Also known as *Majin no tsume*. Fifth in a series (see *The Man in the Moonlight Mask*).

The Crescent Moon/Yumihari-zuki. (no credits available).
Cast: Chiyonsuki Azuma, Yumika Hasezawa, K. Yashioji.

A Toei Co., Ltd., Production. Black and white (processed by Toei Chemistry Co., Ltd.). Academy ratio. 55 minutes. Released 1955.

U.S. Version: Distributor, if any, is undetermined. Part two of a trilogy (?).

Curse. Director, Shunya Ito.
Cast: Shunya Owada.
A Toei Co., Ltd., Production. Toeicolor. Panavision (?). Running time undetermined. Released 1977.

U.S. Version: Distributor, if any, is undetermined.

The Final War/Daisanji sekai taisen— yonju-ichi jikan no kyofu (*Great Disaster of the World Waging War: 41 Hours of Fear*). Director, Shigeaki Hidaka; Screenplay, Hisataka Kai; Director of Photography, Tadashi Aramaki [Arakami].

Cast: Tatsuo Umemiya (Shigero), Yoshi [Yoshiko] Mita, Yajoi [Yayoi] Furusato, Noribumi [Nirbumi] Fujishima, Yukiko Nikaido, Michiko Hoshi.

A New Toei Co., Ltd., Production. Black and white (processed by Toei Chemistry Co., Ltd.). ToeiScope. 77 minutes. Released October 19, 1960.

U.S. Version: Released by Sam Lake Enterprises. Also known as *World War III Breaks Out* and *41 jikan no kyofu*. 77 minutes (?). No MPAA rating. Released December 3, 1962.

Ghost of the One-Eyed Man/Kaidan katame no otoko. Producer, Hiroshi Okawa; Director, Tsuneo Kobayashi; Screenplay, Hajime Takaiwa, Ichiro Miyagawa; Director of Photography, Noboru Takanashi.

Cast: Akira Nishimura (Koichiro), Sanae Nakahara, Kikuko Hojo, Masao Mishima, Yusuke Kawazu.

A Toei Co., Ltd., Production. Black and white (processed by Toei Chemistry Co., Ltd.). ToeiScope. 84 minutes. Released 1965.

U.S. Version: Distributor, if any, is unknown. Also known as *Curse of the One-Eyed Corpse.*

Ghost Ship/Yurei-sen. Director, Teija Matsuda; Screenplay, Katsuya Suzaki, based on the novel *Yurei-sen* by Jiro Osaragi; Director of Photography, Shintaro Kawasaki.

Cast: Kinnosuke Nakamura, Ryutaro Otomo, Ryunosuke Tsukigata, Denjiro Okochi, Yumiko Hasegawa, Hiroko Sakuramachi.

A Toei Co., Ltd., Production. Toeicolor. ToeiScope. Running time undetermined. Released 1957.

U.S. Version: Distributor undetermined.

The Green Slime/Gamma sango uchu dai sakusen (*After the Creation of Space Station Gamma: Big Military Operation*). Producers, Ivan Reiner, Walter H. Manley, Kaname Ohgisawa, Koji Ohta; Director, Kinji Fukasada; Screenplay, Charles Sinclair, William Finger, Tom Rowe, Takeo Kaneko; Story, Ivan Reiner; Script Supervisors, Jacqueline Vaanice, Yasuyo Yamanouchi; Story, Ivan Reiner; Associate Producer, William Ross; Music, Toshuaki Tsushima; Title Song and Additional Music, Charles Fox; Director of Photography, Yoshikazu Yamasawa; Sound Recordist, Yoshio Watanabe; Editor, Osama Tanaka; Assistant to the Producer, Michie Ross; Art Director, Shinichi Eno; Costumes, Mami; Lighting, Shigeru Umetani; Set Decoration, Tasaburo Matsumo; Assistant Director, Kazuhiko Yamaguchi; Makeup, Takeshi Ugai; Special Effects, Nihon Special Effects Co., Ltd.; Special Effects Director and Art Director, Akira Watanabe; Special Effects Cameraman, Yukio Manoda.

Cast: Robert Horton (Commander Jack Rankin), Richard Jaeckel (Commander Vince Elliot), Luciana Paluzzi (Dr. Lisa Benson), Bud Widom (Chief of Staff General Jonathan Thompson), Ted Gunther (Station Space [sic] Consultant Dr. Hans Halversen), Robert Dunham (Captain Martin), David Yorston (Lieutenant Curtis), William Ross (Ferguson), Gary Randolf (Cordier), Richard Hylland (Assistant Station Space Consultant Michaels), Jack Morris (Lieutenant Morris), Carl Bengs (Rocket Pilot), Tom Scott (Sergeant Scott), Eugene Vince,

Dan Plante (Technicians), Enver Altenby, Gunther Greve, George Uruf (USNC Technicians), Linda Hardisty, Kathy Horan, Ann Ault, Susan Skersick, Helen Kirkpatrick, Linda Miller, Patricia Elliot (Nurses), Linda Malson (USNC Technician), Strong Ilimaiti (USNC Doctor), Tom Conrad (Sergeant), Arthur Stark (Barnett), David Sentman (Officer), Clarence Howard (Patient), Lynne Frederickson (Thompson's Secretary), Hans Jorgseeberger (Soldier), Bob Morris (Soldier).

A Ram Films, Inc., and Southern Cross Films Production, in association with Toei Co., Ltd., and Lum Film. A Japanese–U.S.–Italian co-production. Filmed at Toei-Tokyo Studios. Westrex Recording System. Fujicolor (processed by Toei Chemistry Co., Ltd.). ToeiScope. 77 minutes. Released December 1968.

U.S. Version: Released by Metro-Goldwyn-Mayer, Inc.; prints by Metrocolor. Widescreen process advertised as Panavision, and in fact Panavision lenses may have been used. Working and international title: *Battle Beyond the Stars*. U.K. Title (?): *Death and the Green Slime*. Copyright December 1, 1969, by Metro-Goldwyn-Mayer, Inc. The fourth in Ivan Reiner's space series, preceded by *Space Devils* (1966), *The Wild, Wild Planet* (1966), and *War between the Planets* (1967), all U.S.-Italian co-productions. 90 minutes. MPAA rating: G. U.S. premiere date: December 1, 1968. General release, May 21, 1969.

Horror of a Deformed Man/Kyofu kikei ningen (*Horror of a Deformed Man*). Producer, Hiroshi Okawa; Director, Teruo Ishii; Screenplay, Teruo Ishii, Masahiro Kakefuda, based on the story "Kyofo nikei ningen" by Rampo Edogawa; Director of Photography, Shigeru Akatsuka; Art Director, Akira Yoshimura; Music, Masao Yagi.

Cast: Teruo Yoshida (Young Kamoda), Minoru Oki (Old Kamoda), Asao Koike (Retainer), Yuki Kagawa (Relative), Mitsuko Aoi (Mrs. Kamoda), Teruko Yumi, Michiko Obata, Tatsumi Hijikata.

A Toei Co., Ltd., Production. Toeicolor. ToeiScope. 99 minutes. Released 1969.

U.S. Version: Distributor undetermined. Alternate title: *Horror of Malformed Men*.

House of Terrors/Kaidan semushi otoko. Producer, Hiroshi Okawa; Director, Hajime Sato; Screenplay, Hajime Takaiwa; Director of Photography, Shoe Nishikawa.

Cast: Akira Nishimura, Yuko Kusunoki, Yoko Hayama, Masumi Harakawa, Shinjiro Ebara.

A Toei Co., Ltd., Production. Black and white (processed by Toei Chemistry Co., Ltd.). ToeiScope. 81 minutes. Released 1965.

U.S. Version: Distributor, if any, undetermined. Also known as *The Ghost of a Hunchback*.

The House Where Evil Dwells. Producer, Martin B. Cohen; Director, Kevin Connor; Screenplay, Robert A. Suhosky, based on the novel by James W. Hardiman; Director of Photography, Jacques Haitkin; Second Unit Director of Photography, Anne Coffey; Editor, Barry Peters; Art Director, Yoshikazu Sano; Wardrobe, Shannon; Music, Kenneth Thorne; Music Director, Richard Kaufman; Sword Choreographer, Ikuo Hiyoshi; Production Manager, Tadashi Noguchi; Special Visual Effects, Cruse & Co.; Visual Effects Supervisor, William Cruse; Lighting, Haruo Nakayama; Sound Recording, Teruhiko Arakawa; Sound Editor, Graham Harris.

Cast: Edward Albert (Ted Fletcher), Susan George (Laura Fletcher), Doug McClure (Alex Curtis), Amy Barrett (Amy Fletcher), Mako Hattori (Otami), Toshiyuki Sasaki (Shugoro), Toshiya Maruyama (Masanori), Tsyako Okajima (Mayjo Witch), Henry Omitowa (Zen Monk), Mayama Umeda (Noriko), Hiroko Takano (Wakado), Shuren Sakura (Noh Mask Maker), Shoji Ohara (Assistant Noh Mask Maker), Jiro Shiraki (Tadashi), Kazuo Yoshida (Editor), Kunihiko Shinjo (Assistant Editor), Gentaro Mori (Yoshio), Tomoko Shimizu (Aiko), Misao Aria (Hayashi), Chiyoko Hardiman (Mama-San), Hideo Shimado (Policeman).

A Martin B. Cohen Productions, Inc.,

Production in association with Toei Co., Ltd. A Japanese–U.S. co-production. Filmed at Toei-Kyoto Studios. Color (processed by Toei Chemistry Co., Ltd.). Widescreen. 88 minutes. Released 1982.

U.S. Version: Released by MGM/UA Entertainment Co. Prints by Technicolor. 88 minutes. MPAA rating: R. Released May 13, 1982.

Image Wife/Riko na oyome-san. Producer, Hiroshi Okawa; Director, Kenjyu Imaizumi; Screenplay, Koreya Senda (!); Art Director, Seigo Shindo; Director of Photography, Nenji Ohyama; Editor, Yoshiki Nagasawa; Music, Hiraku Hayashi.

Cast: Etsudo Ichihara, Kanjiro Taira, Chieko Higashiyama, Sue Mitobe, Kappei Matsumoto, Koreya Senda.

A Toei Co., Ltd., Production. Film processed by Toei Chemistry Co., Ltd. Academy ratio (?). Running time undetermined. Released 1958.

U.S. Version: Distributor undetermined. Released in subtitled format. No MPAA rating. Released 1958.

The Inugamis/Inugamike no ichizoku. Producer, Haruki Kadokawa; Director, Kon Ichikawa; Based on the novel *Inugamike no ichizoku* by Seishi Yokomizo, as published by Kadokawa Publishing Co., Ltd.; Music, Yuji Ohno.

Cast: Koji Ishizada (Detective Kindaichi), Yoko Shimada (Nonomiya), Meiko Takamine (Matsuko Inugami), Teruhiko Aoi (Sukekiyo), Miki Sanjo (Takeko), Mitsuke Kusabue (Umeko), Takeo Chii (Sukatake), Hisashi Kawaguchi (Suketomo), Akira Kawaguchi (Sayoko), Ryunosake Kaneda (Toranosuke), Shoji Kobayashi (Kokichi), Rantaro Mikuni.

A Haruki Kadokawa Films, Inc., Production. A Kon Ichikawa Film. A Toei Co., Ltd., Release. Toeicolor. Spherical Panavision (?). Running time undetermined. Released 1977.

U.S. Version: Distributor undetermined.

Invasion of the Neptune Men/Uchu kaizoku-sen (*Space Pirates Ship*). Producer, Hiroshi Okawa; Director, Koji Ota; Screenplay, Shin Morita; Director of Photography, Shizuka Fuji.

Cast: Shinichi "Sonny" Chiba (Mr. Tabana/Space Chief [Iron Sharp]), Kappei Matsumoto, Mitsue Komiya, Shinjiro Ebara, Kyuko Minakami.

A Toei Co., Ltd., Production. Black and white (processed by Toei Chemistry Co., Ltd.). 1.33:1. Released 1961.

U.S. Version: Release undetermined, but sources indicate it was in 1961 as *Space Greyhound*, possibly subtitled. Alternate titles (?): *Space Chief, Invasion from a Planet*. Released to television by Medallion TV, a division of Medallion Pictures, Inc. (and known today as Walter H. Manley Enterprises, Inc.). English-language version produced by ProPix, Inc. Copyright 1964 by Walter Manley Enterprises, Inc. No MPAA rating.

Jigoku (Hell). Director, Tatsumi Kumashiro; Screenplay, Yozo Tanaka, based on the screenplay by Ichiro Miyagawa and Nobuo Nakagawa for the 1960 production *The Sinners of Hell* (q.v.); Director of Photography, Shigeru Akatsuka; Special Effects Director, Nobuo Yajima; Music, Riichiro Manabe.

Cast: Mieko Harada, Kyoko Kishida, Ryuzo Hayashi, Renji Ishibashi.

A Toei Co., Ltd., Production. Toeicolor. Panavision. 122 minutes. Released 1979.

U.S. Version: Distributor undetermined. International title: *The Inferno*. Released 1981 (?).

The Joys of Torture/Tokugawa onna keibatsushi. Producer, Shigeru Okada; Director, Teruo Ishii; Screenplay, Teruo Ishii and Misao Arai; Director of Photography, Motonari Washio; Art Director, Takatoshi Suzuki; Editor, Tadao Kanda; Sound Recording, Teruhiko Arakawa; Music, Masao Yagi..

Cast: Masumi Tachibana (Mitsu), Teruo Yoshida (Yorimo Yoshioka & Shinzo), Fumio Watanabe (Kazunochi Nanbara), Asao Koike (Horicho), Yukie Kagawa (Reiho), Kinji Nakamura (Yamano Awajinokami),

Akikane Sawa (Gonzo), Kichijiro Ueda (Minosuke), Gannosuke Asiya (Bancho's Teacher), Ryota Monowada (Kanta), Seiji Mori (Sinzo Follower), Miki Obana (Myoshin), Naomi Shiraishi (Rintoku), Reiko Okajima (Shotoku), Keiko Kojima (Gyokei), Mie Hanabusa (Son-ei), Shin-ichiro Hayashi (Shunkai), Reiko Mikasa (Hana), Tamaki Sawa (Kimicho), Toru Yuri (Sanuke), Yuko Namikaze (Restaurant Manageress), Ai Minose (Female Prisoner).

A Toei Co., Ltd. Production. Fujicolor (processed by Toei Chemistry Co., Ltd.). Toeiscope. Filmed at Toei-Kyoto Studios. 96 minutes. Released 1968.

U.S. Version: U.S. distributor undetermined. Also known as *Criminal Women*.

Note: Phil Hardy lists Hiroshi Okawa as producer. Teruo Yoshida is credited with the above two roles by Toei.

Kaibyo Karakuri Tenjo. Director, Kinosuke Fukuda.

Cast: Ryunosuke Tsukigata, Kyonosuke Nango.

A Toei Co., Ltd., Production. Black and white (processed by Toei Chemistry Co., Ltd.). Academy ratio. Running time undetermined. Released 1958.

U.S. Version: Distributor, if any, is undetermined. International title: *Ghost-Cat of Karakuri Tenjo*.

Kaibyo koshinuke daisodo. Director, Torajiro Saito.

Cast: Achako Hanabishi, Michiko Hoshi.

A Toei Co., Ltd., Production. Black and white (processed by Toei Chemistry Co., Ltd.). Academy ratio. Running time undetermined. Released 1954.

U.S. Version: Distributor, if any, is undetermined. International title: *Weak-Kneed from Fear of Ghost-Cat*.

Kaibyo noroi numa. Producers, Shigeru Okada, Norimichi Matsudaira; Writer-Director, Yoshihiro Ishikawa; Director of Photography, Shigeru Aketsuke; Art Director, Tobumichi Igawa; Editor, Kozo Horiike; Music, Isao Tomita; Sound Recording, Yoshibumi Watanabe.

Cast: Ryohei Uchida (Nashige Nabeshima), Kotaro Satomi (Jonosuke Yuki), Kyoko Mikage (Yukiji), Hiroshi Nawa (Shuzen Kuroiwa), Yuriko Mishima (Yuri), Machiko Yashiro (Hyuga no Tsubone), Tatsuo Matsumura (Matauemon Tsuyama), Ryuko Azuma (Sei), Mitsuko Yoshikawa (Kumi), Bunta Sugahara (Ukon Shibayama), Kenji Kusumoto (Hayato Sasaki), Yoichi Numata (Torakichi), Masumi Numata (Torakichi), Masumi Tachibana (Orin no Kata), Hideo Kagawa (Chiyomaru), Misa Toki (Sayo), Yasuko Ogura (Satsuki), Keiko Kojima (Matsushima), Tokuko Mirua (Fujimoto), Keichiro Shimada (Takafusa Tyuzoji), Chiyo Okada (Princess Kiyo), Mie Hayashi (Tsuyama Family Maid), Ichitaro Kuni (Ukon Follower), Kinji Nakamura (Doctor at Castle), Kinya Suzuki (Priest at Zuimiyoji), Takayuki Akutagawa (Narrator).

A Toei Co., Ltd., Production. Black and white (processed by Toei Chemistry Co., Ltd.). ToeiScope. 87 minutes. Released 1968.

U.S. Version: Distributor, if any, is undetermined. International title: *The Cursed Pond*.

Kaidan Bancho saray ashiki. Director, Juichi Kono; based on the play *Yotsuya kaidan* by Nanboku Tsuruya.

Cast: Chiyonosuke Azuma, Hibari Misora.

A Toei Co., Ltd., Production. Black and white (processed by Toei Chemistry Co., Ltd.). Academy ratio. Running time undetermined. Released 1957.

U.S. Version: Distributor, if any, is undetermined. International title: *Ghost Story of Broken Dishes at Bancho Mansion*. Alternate title: *The Ghost of Yotsuya*.

Kaidan hebionna. Producers, Kaname Ohgisawa, Tadayuki Ohkubo; Director, Nobuo Nakagawa; Director of Photography, Yoshikazu Yamasawa; Editor, Yoshiki Nagasawa; Sound Recording, Masanobu Ohtani; Music, Shunsuke Kikuchi.

Cast: Seizaburo Kawazu (Chobei Ohnuma), Shingo Yamashiro (Takeo), Akemi Negishi (Masae), Yukie Kagawa (Kinu), Chiaki Tsukioka (Sue), Yukiko Kuwabara (Asa), Akira Nishimura (Yasuke), Mariko Ko (Saki), Kunio Murai (Sutematsu), Akikane Sawa (Matsugoro), Junzaburo Ban (Fusataro), Hideo Murota (Saiji), Tamae Kiyokawa (Tami), Midori Yamamoto (Yoshi), Hideko Oda (Iku), Asako Hirago (Mino), Keiko Ito (Fuku), Kayo Tauchi (Tome), Shunji Sayama (Kameshichi), Oozo Soma (First Man), Koichi Yamada (Second Man), Nobuo Hara (Third Man), Noboru Aihara (Policeman), Sayoko Tanimoto (First Virgin in Service of Shrine), Michiyo Kozuki (Second Virgin in Service of Shrine), Toshio Ogo (Male Servant), Tetsuro Tanba (Head of Police).

A Toei Co., Ltd., Production. Filmed at Toei-Kyoto Studios. Fujicolor (processed by Toei Chemistry Co., Ltd.). ToeiScope. 83 minutes. Released 1968.

U.S. Version: Distributor, if any, is undetermined. International title: *Fear of the Snake Woman*. Alternate title: *Ghost of the Snake*.

Kaidan hitotsu-me jizo. Director, Kinnosuke Fukuda.

Cast: Tomisaburo Wakayama, S. Chihara.

A Toei Co., Ltd., Production. Black and white (processed by Toei Chemistry Co., Ltd.). Academy ratio. Running time undetermined. Released 1959.

U.S. Version: Distributor, if any, is undetermined. International title: *Ghost from the Pond*.

Kaidan Oiwa no Borei. Director, Tae Kato; based on the play *Yatsuya kaidan* by Nanboku Tsuruya.

Cast: Tomisaburo Wakayama, Miroko Sakuramachi.

A Toei Co., Ltd., Production. Black and white (processec by Toei Chemistry Co., Ltd.). Academy ratio. Running time undetermined. Released 1961.

U.S. Version: Distributor, if any, is undetermined. International title: *Ghost of Oiwa*. Alternate title: *Ghost of Yotsuya*.

Kaidan Shamisen-bori. Director, Kokichi Uchide.

Cast: Ryuji Shinagawa, Noriko Kitazawa.

A Toei Co., Ltd., Production. Black and white (processed by Toei Chemistry Co., Ltd.). Academy ratio. Running time undetermined. Released 1962.

U.S. Version: Distributor, if any, is undetermined. International title: *Ghost Music of Shamisen*.

The Lady Was a Ghost/Kaidan dochu. Director, Tadashi Sawashima; Screenplay, Tadashi Ogawa; Director of Photography, Makoto Tsuboi.

Cast: Kinnosuke Nakamura, Keiko Ohkawa, Kazuo Nakamura, Hibari Misora, Satomi Oka.

A Toei Co., Ltd., Production. Black and white (processed by Toei Chemistry Co., Ltd.). Academy ratio. 85 minutes. Released 1958.

U.S. Version: Distributor undetermined. International titles (?): *A Ghost Story of Passage* and *Ghost Story of Two Travelers*. 85 minutes. No MPAA rating. Released 1959 (?).

The Last Death of the Devil/Gekko kamen. Director, Shoichi Shimazu.

Cast: Fumitake Omura.

A Toei Co., Ltd., Production. Black and white (processed by Toei Chemistry Co., Ltd.). ToeiScope. Running time undetermined. Released 1959.

U.S. Version: Reportedly released in the United States; distributor undetermined. Third in a series (see *The Man in the Moonlight Mask*).

The "Legend of the Dinosaurs"/Kyoryu —kaicho no densetsu (*Legend of Dinosaur and Monster Bird*). Executive Producer, Keiichi Hashimoto; Director, Junji Kurata; Screenplay, Masaru Igami, Isao [Ko] Matsumoto, Ichiro Otsu [Ohzu]; Director of Photography, Sakuji Shiomi [and?] Shigeru Akazuka; Art Director, Yoshimitsu [Yoshiyuru] Amamori; Editor, Isamu Ichida; Music, Masao Yagi; Lighting, Koji Inoie; Sound Recording, Teruhiko Arakawa; Assistant Director, Kazuo Noda; Still Photographer, Takeshi Kimura; Publicity, Takeshi Fijimoto; Special Technical

Adviser/Special Effects Director, Fuminori Chashi [Ohbayashi].

Cast: Tsunehiko Watase (Setsu Serizawa), Nobiko Sawa (Akiko Osano), Shotaro Hayashi (Akira Taniki), Tomoko [Satoko] Kiyoshima (Junko Sonoda), Fuyukichi Maki (Masashira Muku), Hiroshi Nawa, (Masahiko Miyawaki), Kinji [Kinshi] Nakamura (Hideyuki Sakai), Yusuke Tsukasa (Susumu Hirano), So Takizawa (Jiro Shimamoto), Goro Nawata [Oki?] (Hiroshi Sugiyama), Yukari Miyazen (Hiroko Takami), Masashiro Arikawa (Seitaro Shintaku), Tamikashi Karazawa (Uemura), Sachio Miyashiro (Kobayashi), David Freedman, Maureen Peacock, Catherine Laub, Masaraka Iwao, Yukio Miyagi, Akira Moroguchi.

A Toei Co., Ltd., Production. Toeicolor. Panavision (advertised as ToeiScope). 94 minutes. Filmed at Toei Studios and on location at Mt. Fuji. Released April 29, 1977.

U.S. Version: Never released theatrically in the United States. Released to television by King Features Entertainment, a subsidiary of the Hearst Corp., in 1987. Copyright 1983 by Toei Co., Ltd. Onscreen title is as it appears above. English-dubbed version produced by Frontier Enterprises; Dubbing Supervisor, William Ross. International title: *Legend of Dinosaur and Monster Bird*. 94 minutes. No MPAA rating.

Love, Thy Name Be Sorrow/Koiya koi nasuna koi. Director, tomo Uchida; Screenplay, Yoshitaka Yoda; Director of Photography, Teiji [Keiji] Yoshida.

Cast: Hashizo Okawa, Michiko Saga, Sumiko Hidaka.

A Toei Co., Ltd., Production. Toeicolor (processed by Toei Chemistry Co., Ltd.). ToeiScope (?). 109 minutes. Released 1962.

U.S. Version: Distributor undetermined. Alternate titles: *Love Not Again* and *The Mad Fox*. No MPAA rating. Released 1962 (?).

The Magic Serpent/Kai tatsu daikessen (*Decisive Battle of the Giant Magic Dragons*). Producer, Shigeru Okawa; Director, Tetsuya Yamauchi; Screenplay, Masaru Igami, based on an original story by Mokuami Kawatake; Director of Photography, Motonari Washio; Art Director, Seiji Yada; Music, Toshiaki Tsushima.

Cast: Hiroki Matsukata (Ikazuchimaru), Tomoko Ogawa (Tsunate), Ryutaro Otomo (Orochimaru), Bin Amatsu (Yuki), Nobuo Kaneko.

A Toei Co., Ltd., Production. Eastman Color (processed by Toei Chemistry Co., Ltd.). ToeiScope. 86 minutes. Released 1966.

U.S. Version: Never released theatrically in the United States. Released directly to television by American International Television, Inc., in 1968. A James H. Nicholson and Samuel Z. Arkoff Presentation. English-dubbed version produced by Titra Productions, Inc.; Director, Bret Morrison; Editors, Emil Haviv, Eli Haviv. Prints by Perfect. Copyright 1966 by Toei Co., Ltd., and American International Television, Inc. International title: *Grand Duel in Magic*. Alternate title: *Froggo and Droggo*. The sloppily done American titles list producer Okawa twice. 86 minutes. No MPAA rating.

The Magic Sword of Watari. (no credits available)

Cast: Yoshinobu Kaneko (Watari), Pin-Pin Wong.

A Toei Co., Ltd., Production. A Japanese-Taiwanese co-production. Toeicolor. ToeiScope. 100 minutes. Released 1970.

U.S. Version: Released by Transocean; format undetermined. International title: *Watari and the Seven Monsters*. A sequel to *Watari, Ninja Boy* (Toei, 1966) and based on the popular comic strip *Watari*.

Makai tensho. Executive Producer, Haruki Kadokawa; Director, Kinji Fukasaki; Screenplay, Tatsuo Nogami, based on the novel by Hutaro Yamada, as published by Kadokawa Publishing Co., Ltd.; Director of Photography, Kiyoshi Hazagawa; Action Coordinator, Shinichi "Sonny" Chiba.

Cast: Shinichi "Sonny" Chiba, Kenji Sawada, Akiko Kana.

A Haruko Kadokawa Films, Inc./Toei Co., Ltd., Production. Toeicolor. Panavision. 122 minutes. Released 1981.

U.S. Version: Distributor, if any, is undetermined. International title: *Samurai Reincarnation*. Sequels: *Ninja Wars* (Toei, 1982), *Satomi Hakkenda* (Toei, 1983), *Shogun's Ninja* (Toei, 1984).

The Man in the Moonlight Mask/Gekko kamen (*Moonlight Mask*). Director, Tsuneo Kobayashi; Screenplay, Yarunori Kawauchi; Director of Photography, Ichiro Hoshijima.

Cast: Fumitake Omura, Junya Usami, Hiroko Mine, Mitsue Komiya, Yaeko Wakamizu, Yasushi Nagata.

A Toei Co., Ltd., Production. Black and white (processed by Toei Chemistry Co., Ltd.). ToeiScope. 102 minutes. Released April 1, 1959.

U.S. Version: Distributor undetermined. Re-edited from *Dai ichibu* (85 minutes) and *Dai nibu* (51 minutes). First in a series which includes *The Challenging Ghost*, *The Last Death of the Devil*, *The Monster Gorilla* and *The Claws of Satan*. International title: *The Moonbeam Man*. No MPAA rating.

Message from Space/Uchu kara no messeji (*Message from Space*). Director, Kinji Fukasaku; Producers, Banjiro Uemura, Yoshinori Watanabe, Tan Takaiwa; Co-Producers, Ryo Hirayama, Yusuke Okada, Simon Tse, Naoyuki Sugimoto, Akira Ito; Screenplay, Hiro Matsuda [Hiroo Matusda], based on the Toei television series "Uchu kara no messeji" created by Shotaro Ishimori, Masahiro Noda, Hiro Matsuda Kinji Fukasaku; Director of Photography, Toro Nakajima; Music, Ken Ichiro, conducting the Columbia Symphony Orchestra of Japan. Special Effects Unit: Director, Nobuo Yajima; Director of Photography, Noburu Takanaski; Science Fiction Supervisory (?), Masahiro Noda; Space Flying Objects (?), Shotaro Ishimori; Optical Photography, Minoru Nakano; Art Director, Tetsuzo Osawa.

Cast: Vic Morrow (General Garuda), Sonny [Shin-ichi] Chiba (Hans), Philip Casnoff (Aaron), Peggy Lee Brannon (Meia), Sue Shiomi (Esmeralda), Tetsuro Tamba (Noguchi), Mikio Narita (Rockseia XII), Makoto Sato (Urocco), Hiroyuki Sanada (Shiro), Isamu Shimuzu (Robot Beba 2), Masazumi Okabe (Jack), Noburo Mitani (Kamesasa), Hideyo Amamoto (Dark), Junkichi Orimoto (Kido), Harumi Sone (Lazari).

A Toei Co. Ltd./Tohokushinsha Film Co., Ltd., Production; Space Sound 4 (four-track magnetic stereophonic sound); Toeicolor (processed by Toei Chemistry Co., Ltd.); Widescreen. 105 minutes. Released April 29, 1978.

U.S. Version: Released by United Artists Corp.; prints by De Luxe. 105 minutes. MPAA Rating: PG. Released October 30, 1978.

The Monster Gorilla/Gekko kamen. Director, Satoru Ainodu.

Cast: Fumitake Omura, Yaeko Wakamizu.

A Toei Co., Ltd., Production. Black and white (processed by Toei Chemistry Co., Ltd.). ToeiScope. 60 minutes. Released 1959.

U.S. Version: Distributor undetermined. No MPAA rating. Fourth in a series (see *The Man in the Moonlight Mask*). Released 1960 (?).

Ninja Wars. Executive Producer, Haruki Kadokawa; Producers, Masao Sato, Izumi Toyoshima; Director, Mitsumasa Saito; Screenplay, Ei Ogawa, based on the novel by Hutaro Yamada, as published by Kadokawa Publishing Co., Ltd.; Director of Photography, Fujiro Mrita; Art Directors, Norimichi Ikawa, Kazuyoshi Sonoda; Lighting, Yoshiaki Masuda; Editor, Isamu Ichida; Sound Recording, Fumio Hashimoto; Music, Toshiaki Yokota; Action Coordinator, Shinichi "Sonny" Chiba; Assistant Director, Isao Yoshihara; Continuity, Yukiko Morimura; Wardrobe Adviser, Junko Koshino; Choreographer, Toshio Sugawara; Special Effects Director, Hideo Suzuki.

Cast: Henry [Hiroyuki] Sanada, Noriko Watanabe, Jun Miko, Miho Kazamatsuri, Kongo Kobayashi, Gajiro Sato, Noboru Matsuhashi, Akira Hamada, Seizo Fukomoto,

Nodoka Kawai, Sanji Komjima, Hiroshi Tanaka, Syunji Sasmoto, Rentaro Mine, Yoshiji Nakahgashi, Meiko Hoshino, Reiko Tamano, Yasumori Hikita, Yukio Miyagi, Kazuyuki Kosuga, Gentaro Mori.

A Haruki Kadokawa Films, Inc./Toei Co., Ltd., Production. Toeicolor. Panavision. Copyright 1982 by Toei Co., Ltd. 93 minutes. Released 1982.

U.S. Version: Released by American National Enterprises, Inc. A sequel to *Makai tensho* (Toei, 1981). Sequel: *Satomi Hakkenda* (Toei, 1983) 93 minutes. MPAA rating: R. Released 1984.

Ogon Batto. Executive Producer, Yo Aozawa; Director, Hajime Sato; Screenplay, Susumu Takahisa, based on characters created by Takeo Nagamatsu; Director of Photography, Giichi Yamazawa; Music, Shunsuke Kikuchi; Editor, Fumio Soda; Art Dirctor, Shinichi Eno; Production Supervisor, Koji Kuwata; Special Effects, Sadao Uemura.

Cast: Shinichi Chiba (Commander Yamatone), Hiroshisa Nakata (The Golden Bat and Suzuki), Emily Koken (Emily), Wataru Yamakawa (Akira Kazahaya), Andrew Hughes (Dr. Paal), Hisako Tsukuba (Naomi Akiyama), Koji Sekiyama (Nazoh), Yoichi Numata (Keloid), Keiko Kuni (Piranha), Keiichi Kitagawa (Jackal), Kosaku Okano (Nakamura), Yukio Aoshima (Policeman).

A Toei Co., Ltd., Production. Black and white (processed by Toei Chemistry Co., Ltd.). ToeiScope. 73 minutes. Released 1966.

U.S. Version: Distributor, if any, is undetermined. International title: *The Golden Bat.* Includes stock footage from *Invasion of the Neptune Men* (1961). The first entry (originally planned for color production) of a proposed series of films which never materialized.

The Phantom Cat. Director, Masamitsu Igayama.

Cast: Ryunosuke Tsukigata, Shinobu Chihara, H. Tomiya.

A Toei Co., Ltd., Production. Black and white (processed by Toei Chemistry Co., Ltd.). Academy ratio. 73 minutes. Released 1956.

U.S. Version: Distributor undetermined. International title: *Many Ghost-Cats.*

Prince of Space/Yusei oji (*Planet Prince*). Director, Eijiro Wakabayashi; Screenplay, Shin Morita; Director of Photography, Masahiko Iimura [Imura].

Cast: Tatsuo Umemiya [Unemiya] (Prince Planet), Joji [Johji] Oda, Hiroko Mine, Takashi Kanda, Ushui Skashi, Nobu Yatsuna, Ken Sudoh.

A Toei Co., Ltd., Production. A two-chapter serial. Black and white (processed by Toei Chemistry Co., Ltd.). ToeiScope. Chapter 1, 57 minutes; Chapter 2, 64 minutes. Released May 19, 1959.

U.S. Version: Released by Walter H. Manley Enterprises, Inc. Advertised as *Invaders from Space.* Theatrical release in the United States uncertain. English language version produced by Bellucci Productions, Inc.; English dialogue, Joseph Bellucci. Copyright 1964 by Walter Manley Enterprises, Inc. Alternate titles: *Invaders from the Spaceship*, *The Star Prince*, *Prince Planet*, *Planet Prince*. 95 minutes. No MPAA rating. Released 1962.

Satomi Hakkenda. Executive Producer, Haruki Kadokawa; Director, Kinji Fukasaku; Screenplay, Toshio Kamata, based on the novel by Hutaro Yamada, as published by Kadokawa Publishing Co., Ltd.; Action Coordinator, Shinichi "Sonny" Chiba.

Cast: Shinichi "Sonny" Chiba, Henry [Hiroyuki] Sanada.

A Haruki Kadokawa Films, Inc./Toei Co., Ltd., Production. Toeicolor. Panavision. Running time undetermined. Released 1983.

U.S. Version: Distributor, if any, is undetermined. A sequel to *Ninja Wars* (Toei, 1982). Sequel: *Shogun's Ninja* (Toei, 1984).

The Secret of the Fylfot/Shinobi no manji. Producer, Kanji Amao; Director, Norifumi Suzuki; Screenplay, Kan Saji,

Ryunosuke Ono, based on the story "Shinobi no manji" by Futaro Yamada; Art Director, Yoshimitsu Amamori; Director of Photography, Juhei Suzuki; Sound Recording, Hiroo Nozu; Editor, Kozo Horiike; Music, Harumi Ibe.

Cast: Isao Natsuyagi (Shiinoba), Hiroko Sakuramachi (Kagiroi), Tatsuo Endo (Ujin), Kenji Ushio (Senjuro Momo), Yukiko Kuwabara (Yu), Akami Mari (Oei), Shingo Yamashiro (Tadanaga), Kiichi Yamamoto (Uemon Saori), Anne Maroi (Osai), Tomoko Mayama (Obuni), Kantaro Suga (Iemitsu), Akecho Sogamawariya (Doi Ohtanokami), Hosei Komatsu (Torii Tosanokami), Minoru Ohki (Yagui Tajimanokami), Eijiro Sekine (Kiiko), Masao Hori (Owariko), Kinji Nakamura (Mitoko), Kogiku Hanayagi (Lady Kasuga), Yuriko Mishima (Okuni Nokata), Harumi Kiritate (Ofune Nokata), Mariko Ogawa (Okuru), Hitoshi Ohmae (Big Warehousekeeper), Mitsukazu Kawamura (Goro Udai), Takeshi Kumagai (Doctor at Palace), Masaru Shiga (First Ninja), Daisuke Awaji (Second Ninja), Tokuko Miura (Woman in Boat House).

A Toei Co., Ltd., Production. Filmed at Toei-Kyoto Studios. Fujicolor (processed by Toei Chemistry Co., Ltd.). ToeiScope. 89 minutes. Released 1968.

U.S. Version: Never released theatrically in the United States.

Shogun's Ninja. Executive Producer, Haruki Kadokawa; Director, Noribumi Suzuki; Screenplay, Takahiti Ishikawa, Fumio Koyama, Ishiro Otsu; Directors of Photography, Toto Nakamjima, Shin Ogawahara; Associate Producers, Goro Kusakabe, Tatsuo Honda; Lighting, Sakae Kaishi; Sound Recording, Kiyoshige Hirai; Editor, Isamu Ichida; Art Directors, Yoshikazu Sano, Akiyasu Tawarazaka; Script Girl, Teru Ishida; Decoration, Genzo Watanabe; Wardrobe, Mamoru Mori, Masakatsu Suzuki; Music Producer, Masakatsu Suzuki (It is unlikely that Suzuki, also credited with cowardrobe, did both); Shooting Coordinators, Sonny Chiba Enterprises, Japan Action Club.

Cast: Shinichi "Sonny" Chiba, Henry [Hiroyuki] Sanada, Yuki Ninagawa, Shohei Hino Kazuma Hase, Go Awazu, Kumiko Hidaka, Maki Tachibana, Katsumasa Uchida, Issui Lee, Mitishi Sakitsu, Go Iba, Hirofumi Koga, Seiji Koga, Muaisi Sasaki, Iyokazu Nakamuda, Isamu Kaneda, Iamaki Miyagawa, Kenzo Katsuno, Satoru Nabi, Goro Oki, Iyota Minowada, Matsutoshi Akiyama, Aneko Maruhira, Tetsuro Tambia [Tanba?], Yoko Nogima, Masumi Harukawa, Asao Koike, Makoto Sato, Isao Natsuki.

A Toei Co., Ltd., Production. Toeicolor. Panavision. Copyright 1983 by Toei Co., Ltd. 108 minutes. Released 1983.

U.S. Version: Released by American National Enterprises, Inc. MPAA rating: R. 109 minutes. Released 1984. Presumably a sequel to *Satomi Hakkenda* (Toei, 1983).

Shonen tanteidan. Director, Eijiro Wakabayashi.

Cast: (not available)

A Toei Co., Ltd., Production. Toeicolor. ToeiScope. 61 minutes. Released 1959.

U.S. Version: Distributor, if any, is undetermined. A sequel to *20 Faces* (?). International title: *The Boy Detectives.*

The Swamp/Kaidan Chidori-ga-fuchi. Director, Eiichi Koishi.

Cast: Kinnosuke Nakamura, Yoshio Wakamizu.

A Toei Co., Ltd., Production. Black and white (processed by Toei Chemistry Co., Ltd.). Academy ratio. 66 minutes. Released 1956.

U.S. Version: Distributor, if any, is undetermined. International title: *Ghost of Chidori-Ga-Fuchi.* Released 1957 (?).

Swords of the Space Ark. Producers, Kanetake Ochiai (Anb), Keizo Shichijo, Akimasa Ito, Masahide Shinozuka; Director, Minoru Yamada; Teleplay, Masaru Igami; Music, Shunsuke Kikuchi; Special Effects, Nobuo Yajima; Creators, Shotaro Oshimori, Masahiro Noda, Hiroo Matsuda, Kinji Fukasaku.

Cast: Hiroyuki Sanada, others unidentified.

A Japanese teleseries re-edited to feature length for American television and never released theatrically in Japan. A Toei Co., Ltd. Production. 16mm. Toeicolor.

U.S. Version: Never released theatrically in the United States. Released directly to television by New Hope Entertainment in 1981. Producer-Director-Screenplay, Bunker Jenkins; Supervising Editor and Associate Producer, Michael Part; Editor, Floyd Ingram; Additional Effects, George Budd; English Production, 3B Productions; Postproduction, Gomillion Sound, Inc., American Film Factory; Music, Douglas Lackey, Joseph Zappala; Sound Design, Joseph Zappala. Copyright 1981 by New Hope Entertainment. Derived from the teleseries "Uchu-kara no messeji: ginga taisen" ("Message from Space: Galactic Battle"), which ran for 27 episodes in 1978-79 on the NET (TV Asahi) network. International title (?): *Message from Space: Galactic Battle*. Running time of feature version also given at 121 minutes (which seems highly unlikely) and 94 minutes. 70 minutes. No MPAA rating.

Takarajima Ensei. (credits unavailable).
Cast: Kenichi Enomoto, Akira Kishii, Kiiton Masuda, Hibari Misora, Takako Kawada.
A Toei Co., Ltd., Production. Toeicolor (?). Academy ratio (?). 87 minutes. Released 1956.
U.S. Version: Distributor, if any, is undetermined. International title: *Peach Boy.*

Terror Beneath the Sea/Kaitei dai senso (*Battle Beneath the Sea*). Executive Producers, Masafumi Soga, Tokyo First Film Co., Ltd.; Producers, Ivan Reiner, Walter Manley, Kohji [Koji] Kameda, Sei-ichi Yoshino; Associate Producer, William Ross; Director, Hajime Sato [Terence Ford]; Screenplay, Kohichi Ohtsu, based on an original story by Masami Fukushima; Director of Photography, Kazuo Shimomura; Assistant Director, Akira Tateno [Tatemo]; Production Manager, Masatoshi Kohno; Art Director, Shinichi Eno; Lighting Technician, Toshiaki Morisawa; Sound Recording, Kohichi Iwata; Music, Shunsuke Kikuchi; Editor, Fumio Soda; Underwater Photography, Akira Tateishi; Director of Special Effects, Nobuo Yajima.

Cast: Shinichi "Sonny" Chiba (Ken Abe), Peggy Neal (Jennie), Andrew Hughes (Professor Howard), Eric Nielsen [Erick, Erik Nielson] (Dr. Rufus Moore), Mike Daning (Dr. Joseph Heim), Franz Gruber, Gunther Braun, Beverly Kahler, Hideo Murota [Murata], Tsuneji [Tsuneoi] Miemachi, Hans Hornef, John Kleine, Kohsaku Okano, Tadashi Suganuma.

A Toei Co., Ltd./K. Fujita Associates Inc./ Ram Films, Inc., Production. A Japanese-Italian-U.S. co-production. Filmed at Toei Studios. Eastman Color (processed by Toei Chemistry Laboratory Co., Ltd.). ToeiScope (Academy ratio according to some sources). 85 minutes. Released July 1, 1966.

U.S. Version: Never released theatrically in the United States. Released directly to television by Teleworld. Dialogue Continuity, Linda Davies. Copyright 1971 by Regency Productions Corp.

Note: Toei's involvement with this production is uncertain. They may have helped finance the picture, or they may have merely rented studio space. Given credits above, it is included here. Running time is also given by some sources as 95 minutes. International title: *Water Cyborgs.* 78 minutes. No MPAA rating. Released 1967.

Time Slip/Sengoku jieitai. Producer, Haruki Kadokawa; Director, Kosei Saito; Screenplay, Toshio Kaneda, based on the novel *Sengoku jieitai* by Ryo Hanmura; Director of Photography, Iwao Isayama; Shooting Coordinators, Sonny Chiba Enterprises; Music, Kentaro Haneda; Sound Recording, Fumio Hashimoto; Special Effects Director, Hiyoshi Suzuki; Choreographer of Battle Scenes, Sonny Chiba.

Cast: Shinichi "Sonny" Chiba (Lieutenant Iba), Isao Natsuki (Samurai Leader), Miyuki Ono (Village Girl), Jana Okada (Modern Girl).

A Haruki Kadokawa Films, Inc. and Toei Co., Ltd., Production. A Kadokawa Publishing Co., Ltd., Picture. A Toei Co., Ltd., Release. Toeicolor. Panavision. 139 minutes. Released January 30, 1981.

U.S. Version: Released by American National Enterprises, Inc. 94 minutes. No MPAA rating. Released January 1981.

Toki wo kaieru shojo. Executive Producer, Haruki Kadokawa; Producers, Norihiko Yamada, Kyoko Obayashi; Director, Nobuhiko Obayashi; Screenplay, Wataru Kenmotsu; Assistant Director, Shuji Natio; Art Director, Kazuko Satsuya; Director of Photography, Zenshi Sakamoto; Lighting, Akio Watanabe; Sound, Shohei Hayashi; Editor, Nobuhiko Obayashi; Music, Masataka Matsutoya.

Cast: Tomoyo Harada (Yoshiyama), Ryoichi Takayanagi (Fukamachi), Toshinori Oki (Houkawa), Yukari Tsuda (Mariko), Ittoku Kishibe (Fukushima).

A Haruki Kadokawa Films, Inc./Toei Co., Ltd., Production. A Kadokawa Publishing Co., Ltd., Picture. Toeicolor (processed by Toei Chemistry Co., Ltd.). Spherical Panavision. 104 minutes. Released July 15, 1983.

U.S. Version: Distributor, if any, is undetermined. International title: *The Little Gir Who Conquered Time.*

Tokugawa onna keibatsushi. Producer, Shigeru Okada; Director, Teruo Ishii; Screenplay, Terou Ishii, Misao Arai; Director of Photography, Motonari Washio; Art Director, Takatoshi Suzuki; Editor, Tadao Kanda; Sound Recording, Teruhiko Arakawa; Music, Masao Yagi.

Cast: Masumi Tachnibana (Mitsu), Teruo Yoshida (Yorimo Yoshioka/Shinzo), Fumio Watanabe (Kazunochi Nanbara), Asao Koike (Horicho), Yuki Kagawa (Reiho), Kinji Nakamura (Yamano Awajinokami), Akikane Sawa (Gonzo), Kichijiro Ueda (Minosuke), Gannosuke Asiya (Bancho's Teacher), Ryota Monowada (Kanta), Seiji Mori (Sinzo Follower), Miki Obana (Myoshin), Naomi Shiraishi (Tintoku), Raiko Okajima (Shotoku), Keiko Kojima (Gyokei), Mie Hanabusa (Son-ei), Shin-ichiero Hayashi (Shunkai), Reiko Mikasa (Hana), Tamaki Sawa (Kimicho), Toru Yuri (Sanuke), Yuko Namikaze (Restaurant Manageress), Ai Minose (Female Prisoner).

A Toei Co., Ltd., Production. Fujicolor (processed by Toei Chemistry Co., Ltd.). ToeiScope. Filmed at Toei-Kyoto Studios. 96 minutes. Released 1968.

U.S. Version: Distributor, if any, is undetermined. International title: *The Joys of Torture.* Also known as *Criminal Women.* Note: Phil Hardy lists Hiroshi Okawa as producer.

20 Faces/Shonen tanteidan — Kabutomushi no yoki. Director, Hideo Ogawa; Screenplay, Tadashi Edogawa; Story, Ranbo Edogawa, based on a work by Noboru Nezu; Director of Photography, Hiroshi Fukushima.

Cast: Eiji Okada, Jun Usami, Takashi Nakamura, Mitsue Komiya.

A Toei Co., Ltd., Production. Black and white (processed by Toei Chemistry Co., Ltd.). Adademy ratio (?). 43 minutes. Released 1957.

U.S. Version: Distributor undetermined. Also known as *Tetto no kaijin.*

Voyage into Space. Producer, Mitsuru Yokoyama; Director, Minoru Yamada; Head Writer, Masaru Igami; Music, Takeo Yamashita.

Cast: Mitsunobu [Mitsundbu] Kaneko (Johnny Sokko, Unicorn Agent U-7), Akio [Akjo] Ito (Jerry Mono, Unicorn Agent U-3).

A Japanese teleseries re-edited to feature length for American television and never released theatrically in Japan. A Toei Co., Ltd., Production. 16mm. Color (processed by Toei Chemistry Co., Ltd.). 1.37:1 projected screen aspect ratio.

U.S. Version: Never released theatrically in the United States. Released directly to television in 1970 by American International Television, Inc. (AIP-TV). Derived from episodes of "Jiyaianto Robo" ("Giant Robot"), originally broadcast on the NET (TV Asahi) network, which ran 26 thirty-minute episodes in 1967-68. The series was also syndicated in the United States as "Johnny Sokko and His Flying Robot." Producer, Savatore Billitteri. Copyright 1970 by American International Television, Inc. 88 minutes. No MPAA rating.

Watari, Ninja Boy. Producer, Hiroshi Okawa; Director, Sadao Funadoko; Screenplay, Masaru Igami, Shunichi Nishimura, based on the comic strip "Watari"; Directors of Photography, Kunio Kunishida, Shigeru Akatsuka; Special Effects Director, Junji Kurata.
Cast: Yoshinobu Kaneko (Watari), Ryutaro Otomo, Chiyoko Honma, Toshitaka Ito.
A Toei Co., Ltd., Production. Toeicolor. ToeiScope. 83 minutes. Released 1966.
U.S. Version: Released by Toei Co., Ltd., format undetermined. Alternate title: *Ninja Boy.* Sequel: *The Magic World of Watari* (Toei, 1970).

Yoja no maden. Director, Sadaji Matsuda; Screenplay, Shintaro Kawasaki.
Cast: Chiezo Kataoka, Kensaku Hara, Ryunosuke Tsukigata, Kenji Sasukida, Isao Yamagata.

A Toei Co., Ltd., Production. Toeicolor. Academy ratio. 57 minutes. Released 1956.
U.S. Version: Distributor, if any, is undetermined. International title: *Palace of Snakes.*

Yongary, Monster from the Deep/Dai koesu Yongkari. Director, Kiduck Kim; Screenplay, Yunsung Suh; Director of Photography, Kenichi Nakagawa; Special Effects, Inchib Byon.
Cast: Yungil Oh, Chungim Nam, Soonjai Lee, Moon Kang, Kwang Ho Lee.
A Kuk Dong Film Co., Ltd./Toei Co., Ltd., Production. A South Korean–Japanese co-production. Filmed in South Korea. Color. Anamorphic wide screen. 100 minutes. Never released theatrically in Japan.
U.S. Version: Never released theatrically. Released directly to television by American International Productions (AIP-TV). Executive Producers, James H. Nicholson, Samuel Z. Arkoff; Post-production supervisor, Salvatore Billitteri; Re-recording, Titra Sound Studios; Prints by Pathe. Alternate titles: *Monster Yongkari* and *Great Monster Yongkari.* 79 minutes. No MPAA rating.

Toho Company, Ltd.

Adventures of Takla Makan/Kiganjo no boken (*Adventures in Takla Makan*). Executive Producer, Tomoyuki Tanaka; Director, Senkichi Taniguchi; Screenplay, Kaoru Mabuchi (Takeshi Kimura); Director of Photography, Kazuo Yamada; Music, Akira Ifukube; Sound, Toho Recording Centre; Sound Effects, Toho Sound Effects Group.
Cast: Toshiro Mifune, Mie Hama, Tadao Nakamura, Yumi Shirakawa, Tatsuya Mikashi [Mihashi], Makoto Sato.
A Toho Co., Ltd., Production. Black and white (processed by Tokyo Laboratory, Ltd.). TohoScope. Western Electric Mirrophonic recording (encoded with Perspecta stereophonic sound). Filmed in Iran near Isfahan. 105 minutes. Released 1965 (one source says April 1966).

U.S. Version: Apparently released by Toho International Co., Ltd., in subtitled format. Alternate titles: *Adventure of the Strange Stone Castle, Adventure in the Strange Castle* and *Adventure in Taklamakan.* 100 minutes. No MPAA rating. Released 1965 (?).

The Age of Assassins/Satsujin kyo jidai. Producers, Tomoyuki Tanaka, Kenichiro Kakuta; director, Kihachi Okamoto; Screenplay, Ei Ogawa, Tadaski Yamazaki, Kihachi Okamoto, based on the noval *Ueta isan* by Michio Tsuzuki; Art Director, Iwao Akune; Director of Photography, Rokuo Nishigaki; Editor, Yoshitami Kuroiwa; Music, Masaru Sato; Sound Recording, Noboru Tokai; Sound, Toho Recording Centre; Sound Effects, Toho Sound Effects Group.
Cast: Tatsuya Nakadai (Shinji Kikyo),

Reiko Dan (Keiko Tsurumaki), Hideo Tsunazuka (Bill Otomo), Eisei Amamoto (Shogo Mizorogi), Keiichi Taki (Ikeno), Misako Tominaga (Woman with Artificial Eye), Seishiro Hisano (Man with Crutch), Yasuzo Ogawa (Mabuchi), Tatsuya Ehara (Aochi), Atsuko Kawaguchio (Yumie Komatsu), Wataru Omae (Oba-Q), Shin Ibuki (Atom), Hiroshi Hasegawa (Solan), Masanari Nibe (Pappy), Tsutomu Okeura (Hide), Masaji Oki (Yasu), Bruno Luske (Bruckmayer), Ikio Sawamura (Old Murderer), Terumi Oka (Little Woman), Satoko Fukai (Big Woman), Naoya Kusakawa (Chief Editor), Koji Uno (Man with Long Neck), Yutaka Nakamura (Laughing Mad Man), Tamami Urayama (Barking Mad Man), Yaeko Izumo (Hokke Mad Woman), Tomoaki Tsuchiya (Mad Man with Haori).

A Toho Co., Ltd., Production. Westrex recording system. Black and white (processed by Tokyo Laboratory Ltd.) TohoScope. 99 minutes. Released March 1967.

U.S. Version: Released by Toho International Co., Ltd. International title: *Epoch of Murder Madness*. No MPAA rating. 99 minutes. Released 1967.

Atragon/Kaitei gunkan (*Undersea Battleship*) Producer, Tomoyuki Tanaka; Director, Ishiro Honda; Screenplay, Shinichi Sekizawa, based on the novels *Kaitei gunkan* by Shunro Oshikawa and *Kaitei okoku* (*The Undersea Kingdom*) by Shigeru Komatsuzaki; Director of Photography, Hajime Koizumi; Music, Akira Ifukube; Production Designer, Sigeru Komatsuzaki; Sound, Toho Recording Centre; Sound Effects, Toho Sound Effects Group. *Special Effects Unit:* Director, Eiji Tsuburaya; Photography, Teisho Arikawa, Motonari Tomioka; Matte Photography, Hiroshi Mukoyama; Set Decoration, Akira Watanabe; Lighting, Kuichiro Kishida; Assistant to Tsuburaya, Teruyoshi Nakano.

Cast: Jun Tazaki (Captain Shinguji), Tadeo Takashima (Commercial Photographer Susumu Hatanaka), Yoko Fujiyama (Makoto Shinguchi, the Captain's Daughter), Yu Fujiki (Yoshito Nishibe*), Ken Uehara (Retired Admiral Kosumi), Tetsuko Kobayashi (Empress of Mu), Susumu Fujita (Defense Commander), Akihiko Hirata (Mu Agent #23), Kenji Sahara (Journalist/Mu Agent), Yoshibumi Tajima (Amano), Hiroshi Koizumi (Professor), Eisei Amamoto (High Priest of Mu), Akemi Kita.

A Toho Co., Ltd., Production. Eastman Color (processed by Tokyo Laboratories Ltd.). Tohoscope. 96 minutes. Released December 22, 1963.

U.S. Version: Released by American International Pictures. A James H. Nicholson and Samuel Z. Arkoff Presentation. Re-recording, Titra Sound Studios; Prints by Pathe. Wide screen process billed as Colorscope. International title: *Atoragan the Flying Supersub*. Copyrighted at 90 minutes December 23, 1964, by AIP. Actual running time: 79 minutes. Reissued in Japan in 1968, on a double-bill with *Destroy All Monsters*, and in 1983. No MPAA rating. Released March 11, 1965.

Attack of the Mushroom People/Matango. Producer, Tomoyuki Tanaka; Director, Ishiro Honda; Screenplay, Takeshi Kimura, loosely based on the 1907 short story "The Voice of the Night," by W. H. Hodgson; Director of Photography, Hajime Koizumi; Sound, Toho Recording Centre; Sound Effects, Toho Sound Effects Group. Special Effects Unit: Director, Eiji Tsuburaya; Photography, Teisho Arikawa.

Cast: Akira Kubo (Professor Kenji Morrei), Kenji Sahara (Koyama), Yoshio Tsuchiya (Fumio Kessei), Hiroshi Koizumi (Sakeda), Miki Yashiro (Akiko Soma), Kumi Mizuno (Meimi Sekeguchi), Hiroshi Tachikawa (Etsuro Yoshida).

A Toho Co. Ltd., Production. Color (processed by Tokyo Laboratory Ltd.). TohoScope. 89 minutes. Released August 11, 1963.

U.S. Version: Never released theatrically in the United States. Released directly to television by American International Television (AIP-TV) in 1965. A James H. Nicholson

---

*Not Captain Shinguji as listed in some sources!

and Samuel Z. Arkoff Presentation; Re-recording, Titra Sound Studios; prints by Pathe. Copyright 1965 by American International Productions. International Title: *Matango, Fungus of Terror*. 88 minutes. No MPAA rating.

Battle in Outer Space/Uchu daisenso (*Great War in Space*). Producer, Tomoyuki Tanaka; Director, Ishiro Honda; Screenplay, Shinichi Sekizawa; Story, Jotaro Okami; Art Director, Teruaki Abe; Director of Photography, Hajime Koizumi; Editor, Kazuji Taira; Music, Akira Ifukube; Sound Recording, Choshichiro Mikami; Production Manager, Yasuaki Sakamoto; Assistant Director, Koji Kahita; Lighting, Rokuro Ishikawa; Sound, Toho Dubbing Theatre; Sound Effects, Toho Sound Effects Group. *Special Effects Unit:* Director, Eiji Tsuburaya; Art Director, Akira Watanabe; Photography, Teisho Arikawa; Lighting, Kuichiro Kishida; Matte Work, Hiroshi Mukoyama; Optical Photography, Kinsaburo Araki.

Cast: Ryo Ikebe (Major Ichiro Katsumiya), Kyoko Anzai (Etsuko Shiraishi), Minoru Takada (Dr. Adachi), Koreya Senda (Defense Commander), Len Stanford (Dr. Roger Richardson), Harold S. Conway (Dr. Immerman), Elsie Richter (Sylvia), Hisaya Itoh (Koguri), Yoshio Tsuchiya (Iwamura), Kozo Nomura (Rocket Commander), Fuyuki Murakai (Inspector Ariaki of the International Police), George Whyman, Nadao Kirino, Ikio Sawamura, Jiryd Kimagawa, Katsumi Tesuka, Mitsuo Isuda, Tadashi Okabe, Yasuhisa Tsutumi, Kisao Hatamochi, Koichi Sato, Tasuo Araki, Rinsaku Ogata, Keisumi Yamada, Orsan Yuri, Malcom Pearce, Leonard Walsh, Heinz Bolmer, Roma Corlson, Yokikose Kamimera, Yutaka Oka, Snigro Kato, Saburo Kadowaki, Yushihiko Goxoo, Shinjiro Hirota.

A Toho Co., Ltd., Production. A Western Electric Mirrophonic recording (encoded Perspecta Stereophonic Sound). Eastman Color (processed by Far West Laboratories, Ltd.). Tohoscope. 93 minutes. Released December 26, 1959.

U.S. Version: Released by Columbia Pictures Corporation. English-language version production, Bellucci Productions; Dialogue, Joseph Bellucci; prints by Pathe. Copyright June 1, 1960, by Columbia Pictures Corp. Double billed with *Twelve to the Moon* (Columbia, 1960). 90 minutes. No MPAA rating. Released May-June 1960.

Buru kurisumas. Director, Kihachi Okamoto; Music, Masaru Sato; Sound, Toho Recording Centre; Sound Effects, Toho Sound Effects Group.

Cast: Tatsuya Nakadai.

A Toho Co., Ltd., Production. Color (processed by Tokyo Laboratory, Ltd.). Panavision (?). Running time undetermined. Released 1978.

U.S. Version: Distributor, if any, is undetermined. International title: *Blood Type: Blue*.

Computer Free-for-All/Buchamukure daihakken. Executive Producer, Tomoyuki Tanaka; Director, Kengo Furusawa; Screenplay, Yasuo Tanami; Art Director, Kazuo Ogawa; Director of Photography, Senkichi Nagai; Sound, Toho Recording Centre; Sound Effects, Toho Sound Effects Group; Music, Naozumi Yamamoto.

Cast: Hajime Hana (Hanakawado), Kei Tani (Tanii), Hitoshi Ueki (Uemura), Hiroshi Inuzerka, Senri Sakurai, Eitaro Ishibashi, Shin Yasuda.

A Toho Co., Ltd., Production. Westrex recording system. Eastman Color (processed by Tokyo Laboratory, Ltd.). Academy ratio (?). 84 minutes. Released January 1969.

U.S. Version: Released by Toho International Co., Ltd., in subtitled format. 84 minutes. No MPAA rating. Released April 1969.

Dagora, the Space Monster/Uchu daikaiju Dogora (*Giant Space Monster Dogora*). Executive Producer, Tomoyuki Tanaka; Director, Ishiro Honda; Screenplay, Shinichi Sekizawa; Director of Photography, Hajime Koizumi; Music, Akira Ifukube; Sound, Toho Recording Centre; Sound Effects, Hishashi Shimonaga, Toho Sound Recording Centre. *Special Effects*

Unit: Director, Eiji Tsuburaya; Cameraman, Teisho Arikawa, Motonari Tomioka; Art Director, Akira Watanabe; Lighting, Kuichiro Kishida; Optical Photography, Yukio Manoda, Yoshiyuki Tokumasa, Sadao Iizuka; Assistant to Tsuburaya, Teruyoshi Nakano. Scene Manipulation, Fumio Nakadai.

Cast: Yosuke Natsuki (Inspector Kommei), Robert Dunham (Mark Jackson), Hiroshi Koizumi (Korino), Yoko Fujiyama (Musiyo), Jun Tazaki (Chief Inspector), Yoshibumi Tajima (Gangster), Eisei Amamoto (Eiji the Safecracker), Susumu Fujita (General Iwasa), Akiko Wakabayashi, Mie Hama (Women Gangsters), Seizaburo Kawazu (Bearded Bank Robber), Nobuo Nakamuva (Scientist), Keiko Sawai (Scientist's Assistant).

A Toho Co., Ltd., Production. Eastman Color (processed by Tokyo Laboratory, Ltd.). Tohoscope. 83 minutes. Released August 11, 1964.

U.S. Version: Reviewed by *Variety* at the Trieste Sci-Fi Film Festival, but information on its U.S. theatrical release, if any, is undetermined. Possibly released by Toho International, either dubbed or in subtitled format, in July 1965. International Title: *Space Monster Dogora*. Released to television by American International Television (AIP-TV). A James H. Nicholson and Samuel Z. Arkoff Presentation. Executive Producers, James H. Nicholson, Samuel Z. Arkoff; Post-Production Supervisor, Salvatore Billitteri; Re-recording, Titra Sound Studios; prints by Pathe. Copyright 1965 by American International Productions. No MPAA rating. 80 minutes.

Daijoo, mai furendo. Producer, Hidenori Taga; Director-Story-Screenplay, Ryu Murakami; Director of Photography, Kozo Okazaki; Lighting, Kazuo Shimamura; Assistant to the Director, Roichi Nakajima; Art Director, Osamu Yamaguchi; Sound Recordist, Hideo Nizhizaki; Sound, Toho Recording Centre; Sound Effects, Toho Sound Effects Group; Editor, Sachiko Yamaji; Music Direction, Kazuhiko Katoh.

Cast: Peter Fonda (Gonzy Traumerai), Jimpachi Nezu (Doctor), Reana Hirota (Mimimi), Hirayuki Watanabe (Hachi), Yahiyuki Noo (Manika), Kumi Aiochi (Reiko).

A Toho Co., Ltd., Production. A Kitty Films, Inc., Picture. Color (processed by Tokyo Laboratory, Ltd.). Panavision. 119 minutes. Released April 15, 1983.

U.S. Version: Apparently unreleased in the United States. International Title: *All Right, My Friend*. Available through Toho International Co., Ltd.

Daredevil in the Castle/Osaka jo mnogatari. Producer, Tomoyuki Tanaka; Director, Hiroshi Inagaki; Screenplay, Hiroshi Inagaki, Takeshi Kimura; Original Story, Genzo Murakami; Director of Photography, Kazuo Yamada; Music, Yoshio Nishikawa; Sound, Toho Recording Centre; Sound Effects, Toho Sound Effects Group. *Special Effects Unit:* Director, Eiji Tsuburaya; Photography, Teisho Arikawa, Motoyoshi Tomioka; Art Director, Akira Watanabe; Lighting, Kuichiro Kishida; Matte Process, Hiroshi Mukoyama; Optical Photography, Taka Yuki, Yukio Manoda.

Cast: Toshiro Mifune (Mohei), Kyoko Kagawa (Ai), Yurko Hoshi (Senhima), Akihiko Hirata (Hayatonosho Susukida), Isuzu Yamada (Yodogimi), Yoshiko Kawazu, Yu Fujiki, Jun Tazaki, Danko Ichikawa, Yosuke Natsuki, Susumu Fujita.

A Toho Co., Ltd., Production. Western Electric Mirrophonic recording (encoded with Perspecta Stereophonic Sound). Eastman Color (processed by Tokyo Laboratory, Ltd.). 97 minutes. Released January 3, 1961.

U.S. Version: Released by Frank Lee International, Inc., in subtitled format. 97 minutes. No MPAA rating. Released June 6, 1961.

Deathquake. Executive Producer, Tomoyuki Tanaka; *Special Effects Unit:* Director, Teruyoshi Nakano.

Cast: (not available)

A Toho Co., Ltd., Production. Color (processed by Tokyo Laboratory, Ltd.). Panavision. Copyright 1983 by Toho Co., Ltd. 94 minutes (?). Released 1983.

U.S. Version: Never released theatrically in the United States. Released directly to television by UPA Productions of America (?).

Destroy All Monsters/Kaiju soshingeki (*All Monsters Attack*). Producer; Tomoyuki Tanaka; Director, Ishiro Honda; Screenplay, Kaoru Mabuchi (Takeshi Kimura), Ishiro Honda; Director of Photography, Taiichi Kankura [Arikawa]; Music, Akira Ifukube; Editor, Ryohei Fujii; Art Director, Takeo Kita; Sound Recording, Shoichi Yoshizawa; Sound, Toho Recording Centre; Sound Effects, Hisashi Shimonaga, Toho Sound Effects Group; Assistant Director, Seiji Tani. *Special Effects Unit:* Director, Eiji Tsuburaya; Special Photography, Teisho Arikawa; Optical Photography, Yukio Manoda, Sadao Iizuda; Art Director, Akira Watanabe; Lighting, Kyuighiro Kishida; Scene Manipulation, Fumio Nakadai.

Cast: Akira Kubo (SY-3 Flight Captain Katsuo Yamabe), Jun Tazaki (Dr. Yoshido), Yoshio Tsuchiya (Dr. Otani), Kyoko Ai (Queen of the Kilaaks), Yukiko Kobayashi (Kyoto Manaba), Kenji Sahara (Nishikawa), Andrew Hughes (Dr. Stevenson), Chotaro Togane (Okada), Yoshibumi Tajima (General Sugiyama), Hisaya Ito (Tada), Yoshio Katsude (Young Scientist), Henry Ohkawa (Engineer), Kenichiro Maruyama (second Engineer), Ikio Maruyama (Old Farmer), Yutaka Sada (Policeman), Hiroshi Okada (Doctor at Hospital), Hideo Shibuya (First Reporter), Yutaka Oka (second Reporter), Ken Echigo, Yasuhiko Saijo, Seishiro Hisano, Wataru Ohmae (SY-3 Engineers), Hiroo Kirino, Kamayuki Tsubono, Naoya Kusagawa (Detectives), Rinsaku Ogata (First Officer), Haruya Sakamoto (second Officer), Susumu Kurobe, Kazuo Suzuki, Minoru Ito, Toro Ibuki (Control Center Staff), Yukihiko Gondo (Soldier), Michiko Ishii (Kilaaks), Haruo Nakajima (Gojira), Little Man Machan (Minya), Susumu Utsumi (Kingu Ghidorah), Keiko Miyauchi, Atsuko Takahashi, Ari Sagawa, Yoshio Miyata, Kyoko Mori, Midori Uchiyama, Wakako Tanabe, Nadao Kirino, Ikio Sawamura, Kazuo Suzuki. (*Note:* Emi and Yumi Itoh do not appear in the film as is reported in some sources)

A Toho Co., Ltd., Production. Eastman Color (processed by Tokyo Laboratory, Ltd.). TohoScope. Double billed with a reissue of *Atragon* (Toho, 1963). 88 minutes. Released August 1, 1968.

U.S. Version: Released by American International Pictures. A James H. Nicholson and Samuel Z. Arkoff Presentation. Postproduction Supervisor, Salvatore Billitteri; prints by Berkey-Pathe. Wide screen processed billed as ColorScope in the United States. Voice characterization for Akira Kubo, Jack Grimes. Includes brief stock footage from *Ghidrah: The Three-Headed Monster* (1964). Released in the United Kingdom as *Operation Monsterland*. International titles (?): *March of the Monsters, Attack of the Marching Monsters*. Reissued in Japan in 1972 (re-edited to 74 minutes) as *Gojira dengeki taisakusen (Godzilla Electric Battle Masterpiece)*. 86 minutes. MPAA rating: G. Released May 23, 1969.

Dodes'ka-den/Dodesukadan. Executive Producers, Akira Kurosawa, Yoichi Matsue; Producers, Keisuke Kinoshita, Kon Ichikawa, Masaki Kobayashi; Director, Akira Kurosawa; Screenplay, Akira Kurosawa, Hideo Oguni, Shinbu Hashimoto, based on the novel published in English as *The Town Without Seasons* by Shugoro Shugoro; Editor, Reiko Kaneko; Music, Toru Takemitsu; Production Supervisor, Hiroshi Negiu; Assistant Director, Kenjiro Oomori; Art Directors, Yoshiro Muraki, Shinobu Muraki; Directors of Photography, Takao Saito, Yasumichi Fukuzawa; Still Photographer, Naomi Hashiyama; Recording, Fumio Yamaguchi; Hiromitsu Mori; Sound, Toho Recording Centre; Sound Effects, Toho Sound Effects Group.

Cast: Zushi Yoshitaka (Rokuchan), Kin Sugai (Okuni-san), Kazuo Kato (Roadside Painter), Junzaburo Ban (Yukichi Shima), Kiyoko Tange (Shima's Wife), Michio Hino (Okawa), Tatsuhei Shimokawa (Nomoto), Keiji Furuyama (Matsui), Hisashi Igawa (Masuo Masuda), Hideko Okiyama (Tatsu

Masuda), Kunie Tanaka (Hatsuan Kawaguchi), Jitsuko Yoshimura (Yoshi Kawaguchi), Koji Mitsui (Tavern Proprietor), Shinsuke Miname (Tyotaro Sawagami), Yuko Kusunoki (Misao Sawagami), Toshiyuki Tonomura (Taro Sawagami), Satoshi Hasegawa (Jiro Sawagami), Kumiko Ono (Hanako Sawagami), Tatsuhiko Yanashisa (Shiro Sawagami), Mika Oshida (Umeko Sawagami), Tatsuo Matsumura (Kyota Watanaba), Mari Tsuji (Otane Watanaba), Tomoko Yamazaki (Katsuko Watanaba), Masahiko Kametani (Okabe), Minoru Takashima (Policeman), Keiji Sakakida (Sake Shop Proprietor), Noburo Mitani (Beggar), Hiroyuki Kawase (Beggar's Son), Hiroshi Kiyama (Sushi Shop Proprietor), Michiko Araki (Japanese Restaurant Proprietess), Shoichi Kuwayama (Western Style Restaurant Cook), Toki Shiozawa (Waitress), Hiroshi Akutagawa (Mr. Hei), Atsushi Watanabe (Mr. Tamba), Kamatari Fujiwara (Old Man), Masahiko Tanimura (Mr. So), Fujio Jely (Kumanbachi's Wife), Kiyotaka Ishii (Kumanbachi's First Child), Mihoko Kaizuka (Kumanbachi's Second Child), Hideaki Ezumi (Detective), Sanui Kojima (Thief), Akemi Negishi (Attractive Wife), Reiko Niimura (First Wife), Yoshiko Maki (Second Wife), Toshiko Sakurai (Third Wife), Matsue Ono (Fourth Wife), Toriko Takahara (Fifth Wife), Akira Hitoma (First Man Calling Out to Misao), Kanji Ebata (Second Man Calling Out to Misao), Masahiko Ichimura (Third Man Calling Out to Misao), Shin Ibuki (Fifth Man Calling Out to Misao), Tsuji Imura (Mrs. Watanaka), Jerry Fujio (Kumamba), Michiko Araki (Bad Girl).

A Yonki no Kai/Toho Co., Ltd., Production. Westrex recording system. Eastman Color (processed by Tokyo Laboratory, Ltd.). Academy ratio. 244 minutes (later edited to 140 minutes). Released October 1970.

U.S. Version: Released by Janus Films, Inc., in subtitled format. 140 minutes. No MPAA rating. Released November 1974. Although this film is widely available, the fantasy elements are so slight as not to warrent inclusion in the main text.

Don't Call Me a Con Man/Daiboken. Executive Producer, Tomoyuki Tanaka; Director, Kengo Furusawa; Screenplay, Ryozo Kasahara, Yasuo Tanami; Director of Photography, Tadashi Iimura; Sound, Toho Recording Centre; Sound Effects, Toho Sound Effects Group.

Cast: Hitoshi Ueki (Reporter), Reiko Dan, Fubuki Koshiji, Kan Tani, Hajime Hana.

A Toho Co., Ltd., Production. Eastman Color (processed by Tokyo Laboratory, Ltd.). TohoScope. 109 minutes. Released 1966.

U.S. Version: Released by Toho International Co., Ltd., format undetermined. International title: *Crazy Adventure.* 109 minutes. No MPAA rating. Released December 21, 1966.

Drunken Angel/Yoidore tenshi. Producer, Sojiro Motoki; Director-Editor, Akira Kurosawa; Screenplay, Keinosuke Uegusa, Akira Kurosawa; Art Director, So Matsuyama; Director of Photography, Takeo Ito; Still Photographer, Masao Soeda; Lighting, Kinzo Yoshizaa; Music, Fumio Hayasaka; Recording, Wataru Konuma; Sound, Toho Dubbing Theatre.

Cast: Takashi Shimura (Dr. Sanada), Toshiro Mifune (Matsunaga), Reisaburo Yamaoto (Okada), Chieko Nakakita (Nurse Miyo), Michiyo Kogure (Nanae), Noriko Sengoku (Gin), Eitaro Shindo (Takahama), Choko Iida (Old Servant), Taiji Tonoyama (Shop Proprietor), Katao Kawasaki (Flower Shop Proprietor), Sachio Sakai (Young Hoodlum), Yoshike Kuga (Girl), Shizuko Kasagi (Singer), Masao Shimizu (Boss), Sumire Shiroki (Anego).

A Toho Co., Ltd., Production. Western Electric Mirrophonic recording. Black and white (processed by Kinuta Laboratories, Ltd.; prints by Tokyo Laboratory, Ltd.). Academy ratio. 150 minutes (later edited to 102 minutes). Released April 27, 1948.

U.S. Version: Released by Toho International Co., Ltd., in subtitled format. As with *Dodes'ka-den*, the fantasy elements are so slight (virtually nonexistent here) that it doesn't below in the main text, even though it's widely available in the United States. 98

minutes. No MPAA rating. Released December 1959.

Ebirah, Horror of the Deep/Gojira, Ebirah, Mosura: Nankai no dai ketto (*Godzilla, Ebirah, Mothra: Big Duel in the South Sea*) Producer, Tomoyuki Tanaka; Director, Jun Fukuda; Screenplay, Shinichi Sekizawa; Director of Photography, Kazuo Yamada; Music, Masaru Sato; Sound, Toho Recording Centre; Sound Effects, Toho Sound Effects Group; Art Director, Takeo Kita. *Special Effects Unit:* Director, Eiji Tsuburaya; Photography, Teisho Arikawa, Motonari Toioka, Taka Yuki; Optical Photography, Yukio Manoda, Sadao Iizuda; Matte Process, Hiroshi Mukoyama; Art Director, Akira Watanabe; Lighting, Kyuighiro Kishida; Scene Manipulation, Fumio Nakadai; Assistant to Tsuburaya, Teruyoshi Nakano.

Cast: Akira Takarada (Yashi), Toru Watanabe (Ruta), Hideo Sunazuka (Mita), Kumi Mizuno (Daiyo), Jun Tazaki (Base Commander), Toru Ibuki (Yata), Chotaro Togano (Ichiro), Akihiko Hirata (Captain), Eisei Amamoto (Red Bamboo Naval Officer), the Alilena Twins (Mothra's Priestesses), Harou Nakajima (Gojira), Ikio Sawamura (Elderly Slave).

A Toho Co., Ltd., Production. Eastman Color (processed by Tokyo Laboratory, Ltd.). TohoScope. Copyright 1966 by Toho Co., Ltd. 87 minutes. Released December 17, 1966.

U.S. Version: Released to U.S. television by AIP-TV (American International Pictures Television) in 1968. Title was later changed to *Godzilla vs. the Sea Monster*, which is what is on current TV and video prints. Continental Distributing, Inc. may have released the film theatrically (as a Walter Reade, Jr., Presentation), but this has not been confirmed. Prints by Movielab. International title: *Big Duel in the South Sea*.

Reissued in Japan in 1972 (re-edited to 74 minutes). 82 minutes. No MPAA rating.

ESPY. Producers, Tomoyuki Tanaka, Fumio Tanaka; Director, Jun Fukuda; Screenplay, Hideo Ogawa; Story, Sakyo Komatsu; Art Director, Shinobu Muraki; Director of Photography, Seiji Ueda; Music, Masaki Hirano; Recording Mixer, Toshiya Ban; Sound Toho Recording Centre; Sound Effects, Toho Sound Effects Group. *Special Effects Unit:* Director, Teruyoshi Nakano.

Cast: Hiroshi Fujioka (Yoshio Tamura), Kaoru Yumi (Maria Harada), Masao Kusakari (Jiro Miki), Yuzo Kayama (Hojo), Tomisaburo Wakayama (Ulrov), Katsumasa Uchida (Goro Tatsumi), Steve Green (Baltonian Prime Minster), Eiji Okada (Salabad).

A Toho-Eizo Production. A Toho Co., Ltd., Release. Westrex recording system. Color (processed by Tokyo Laboratory, Ltd.). Panavision. 94 minutes. Released December 1974.

U.S. Version: Released by Toho International Co., Ltd., in subtitled format. 94 minutes. No MPAA rating. Released 1975.

Evil of Dracula/Chio o suu bara (*The Vampire's Rose*). Executive Producer, Fumio Tanaka; Director, Michio Yamamoto; Screenplay, Ei Ogawa, Masaru Takasue (based on a character created by Bram Stoker); Director of Photography, Kazutami Hara; Art Director, Kazuo Satsuya; Music, Riichiro Manabe; Editor, Michiko Ikeda; Sound, Toho Recording Centre; Sound Effects, Toho Sound Effects Group; Special Effects Director, Teruyoshi Nakano; Special Effects, Toho Special Effects Group.

Cast: Toshio Kurosawa (Professor Shiraki), Kunie Tanaka (The Principal), Mariko Mochizuki (Kumi?), Katsuhiko Sasaki (Professor Yoshi), Shin Kishida, Hunie Tanaka, Mio Ohta, Mika Katsuragi, Keiko Aramaki, Yunosuke Ito.

A Toho-Eizo Co., Ltd., Production. Color (processed by Tokyo Laboratory, Ltd.). Panavision. Copyright 1974 by Toho Co., Ltd. 87 minutes. Released 1975.

U.S. Version: Never released theatrically in the United States. Released to television by United Productions of America in 1980 (?). A UPA Productions of America

Presentation. Executive Producer, Henry G. Saperstein. International Title: *The Bloodthirsty Roses*. 81 minutes. No MPAA rating.

The Face of Another/Tanin no kao (*The Face of a Stranger*). Executive Producers, Nobuyo Horiba, Kiichi Ichikawa, Tadashi Ohono; Producer-Director, Hiroshi Teshigahara; Screenplay, Kobo Abe (based on his novel, *Tanin no kao*; English translation by E. Dale Saunders); Director of Photography, Hiroshi Segawa; Music, Toru Takemitsu; Editor, Fusako Shuzui; Production Supervisor, Hiroshi Kawazoe; Production Manager, Iwao Yashida; Lighting, Mitsuo Kume; Sound, Keiji Mori; Design, Kiyoshi Awazu; Still Photography, Yasuhiro Yoshioka; Art, Shin Isozaki.

Cast: Tatsuya Nakadai (Mr. Okuyama), Machiko Kyo (Mrs. Okuyama), Kyoko Kishida (His Nurse), Mikijiro Hira (His Doctor), Eiji Okada (The Director), Bibari Maeda ("Mrs."), Miki Irie (Girl), Kunie Tanaka, Minoru Chiaki, Etsuko Ichihara, Hideka Muranatsu, Yoshie Minami, Shinobu Itomi, Hisashi Igawa.

A Teshigahara Production Picture, in association with Tokyo Eiga Co., Ltd. A Toho Co., Ltd., Release. Westrex recording system. Black and white. 1.33:1 projected screen aspect ratio (one sequence presented in cropped wide screen). 124 minutes. Released July 10, 1966.

U.S. Version: Released by Toho International Co., Ltd., in subtitled format. Reissued in the United States in May 1975 by Rising Sun as a Toho Co., Ltd., Presentation. No MPAA rating. Released June 9, 1967.

Frankenstein Conquers the World/Furankenshutain tai chitei kaiju Baragon (*Frankenstein Against the Subterranean Monster Baragon*). Producer, Tomoyuki Tanaka; Director, Ishiro Honda; Screenplay, Kaoru Mabuchi (Takeshi Kimura), from a synopsis (i.e., adaption) by Jerry Sohl, based on a story by Reuben Bercovitch and suggested by characters from Mary Wollstonecraft Shelley's novel *Frankenstein*; Director of Photography, Hajime Koizumi; Color Director (?), Kiyashi Tsurusaki; Music, Akira Ifukube; Editor, Ryohei Fujii; Art Director, Takeo Kita; Makeup, Rika Konna; Casting Assistant, Ai Maeda; Sound Effects, Hisashi Shimonaga, Toho Sound Effects Group; Sound, Toho Recording Centre; Transportation, Yashitomi Transportation. *Special Effects Unit:* Director, Eiji Tsuburaya; Photography, Teisho Arikawa, Motonari Tomioka; Lighting, Kyuighiro Kishida; Art Director, Akira Watanabe; Assistant to Tsuburaya, Teruyoshi Nakano; Optical Photography, Yukio Manoda Sadao Iizuka; Scene Manipulation, Fumio Nakadai.

Cast: Nick Adams (Dr. James Bowen), Tadeo Takashima (Scientist), Kumi Mizuno (Dr. Sueko Togami), Susumu Fujita (Osaka Police Chief), Yoshibumi Tajima (Submarine Commander), Takashi Shimura (Hiroshima Doctor), Jun Tazaki (Military Advisor), Yoshio Tsuchiya (Submarine 1st Officer), Hisaya Ito (Policeman), Kenji Sahara (Soldier), Takashi Shimura (Doctor).

A Toho Co., Ltd. Production, in association with Henry G. Saperstein Enterprises. Eastman Color (processed by Tokyo Laboratory, Ltd.). TohoScope. 95 minutes. Released August 8, 1965.

U.S. Version: Released by American International Pictures. A James H. Nicholson and Samuel Z. Arkoff Presentation, from UPA Productions of America. Executive Producers, Henry G. Saperstein, Reuben Bercovitch; Re-recording Supervisor, Salvatore Billitteri; prints by Pathe. Copyright June 1, 1966, by American International Pictures and UPA Productions of America (Current prints are minus all AIP credits). Double billed with *Tarzan and the Valley of Gold* (AIP, 1966). 87 minutes. No MPAA rating. Released July 8, 1966.

Ganhedo. Executive Producers, Tetsuhisa Yamada, Eiji Yamamura, Tomoyuki Tanaka; Director, Masato Harada; Screenplay, Masato Harada, James Bannon; Music, Toshiyuki Honda; Sound Effects, Toho Sound Effects Group. *Special Effects Unit:* Producer, Yasuo Nishi; Director, Koichi Kawakita; Photography, Kenichi Eguchi;

Optical Photography, Masanori Nakamura; Art Directors, Naoyuki Yoshimura, Tetsuzo Ozawa; Lighting, Kaoru Saito; Wire Manipulation, Koji Matsumoto; Pyrotechnics, Tadaaki Watanabe; Assistant Director, Kiyotaka Matsumoto; Mechanical Design, Shoji Kawamori, Hiwanori Hanyu; Model Construction, Masaharu Ogawa, Ogawa Modeling Group; Special Mechanical Effects, Noburo Watanabe; Animation, Keita Amamiya; Computer Graphics, Fumio Ooi, Yu Tsuchiya; Matte Paintings, Nobuaki Koga; Coordinators, Hiroshi Yamaguchi, Koji Ishihashi.

Cast: Masahiro Takashima (Brooklyn), Brenda Bakke (Texas Air Ranger Nim), Kaori Mizushima (Eleven), Yujin Harada (Seven), Micky Curtis (Bancho), Aya Enjoji (Bebe), Doll Nguyen (Boomerang), James B. Thompson (Barabbas), Jay Kabira (Bombay), Randy Reyes (Voice of Gunhed), Michael Yancy (Narrator).

A Toho Co., Ltd.-Nippon Sunrise Co., Ltd., Production. Dolby Stereo/TKL-Stereo. Color (processed by Tokyo Laboratory, Ltd.). Spherical Wide Screen. Running time undetermined. Released July 22, 1989.

U.S. Version: Unreleased in the United States as this book went to press. International title: *Gunhed*.

Ghidrah: The Three-Headed Monster/ San daikaiju chikyu saidai no kessen (*The Greatest Giant Monster Battle on Earth*). Executive Producer, Tomoyuki Tanaka; Director, Ishiro Honda; Screenplay, Shinichi Sekizawa; Director of Photography, Hajime Koizumi; Music, Akira Ifukube; Song: "Call Happiness," Composer, Hiroshi Miyagawa, Words, Tokiko Iwantani; Editor, Ryohei Fujii; Art Director, Takeo Kita; Lighting Supervisor, Shoshichi Kojima; Sound Recording, Fumio Yanoguchi; Sound Effects, Hishashi Shimonaga, Toho Sound Effects Group; Sound, Toho Recording Centre; Production Manager, Shigeru Nakamura; Assistant to the Director, Ken Sano; Sound Technician, Osamu Chiku; Assistant Manager, Tadashi Koibe. *Special Effects Unit:* Director, Eiji Tsuburaya; Photographers, Teisho Arikawa, Motonari Tomioka; Matte Photography, Yokio Manoda, Taka Yuki; Matte Process Work, Hiroshi Mukoyama; Set Decoration and Suit Design, Akira Watanabe; Lighting, Kyuighiro Kishida; Assistant Director, Teruyoshi Nakano.

Cast: Yosuke Natsuki (Shindo), Yuriko Hoshi (Naoko Shindo), Hiroshi Koizumi (Professor Murai), Takashi Shimura (Dr. Tsukamoto), Emi Ito and Yumi Ito [The Peanuts] (Mothra's Priestesses), Akiko Wakabayashi (Mas Dorina Salno [Princess Selina Salno]), Hisaya Itoh (Malmess [Malness]), Akihiko Hirata (Chief Detective Okita), Kenji Sahara (Chief Editor Kanamaki), Ikio Sawamura (Fisherman), Kenji Sahara (Newspaper Editor), Eiji Okada (Geologist), Yoshibumi Tajima (Ship's Captain), Haruo Nakajima (Gojira), Eisei Amamoto (Woo, the Princess' Aide), Akiro Kurobi, Ietsu Ibuki, Kozo Nomora, Yoshio Kosugi, Minoru Takada, Yuriko Hanabusa, Haruya Kato, Kio Sawamura, Nakatiro Tomita, Shigeki Ishida, Shin Otomo, Yukaka Nakayama, Senkichi Omura, Sensho Matsumoto, Kazuo Suzuki, Senya Aozora, Ichiya Aozora, Shoichi Hiroshi, Henry Okawa, Junickiro Mukai, Yoshiniko Furuta, Shoji Ikeoa, Hideo Shibuya, Kenchiro Katsumoto, Katsumi Tezuka, Koji Uno, Daisuke Inoue, Ooshio Miura, Tamami Urayama, Takuzo Komaga, Mitsuo Isuda, Yoshio Hattori, Kenji Tsubono, Kazoo Imai, Suburo Kadowaki, Kenzo Echigo, Toku Ihara, Bin Furuya, Jun Kuroki, Yotaka Oka, Koji Urugi, Haruya Sakamoto.

A Toho Co., Ltd., Production. Eastman Color (processed by Tokyo Laboratory, Ltd.). TohoScope. 92 minutes. Released December 20, 1964.

U.S. Version: Released by Continental Distributing, Inc. A Walter Reade-Sterling, Inc., Presentation. Americanization by Bellucci Productions; English Dialogue/Dubbing Director, Joseph Bellucci; Additional Music and Sound Effects, Filmsounds, Inc.; Post-Production Consultant, Ray Angus; Additional Optical Photography, Film Cinematics, Inc.; Prints, Movielab. No copyright registered in the United States. Copyright 1964 by Toho Co., Ltd.

81 minutes. Reissued in Japan in 1971 (re-edited to 73 minutes) as *Gojira Mosura Kingughidorah: Chikyu saidai no kessen (Godzilla, Mothra, King Ghidorah: The Greatest Battle on Earth)*. No MPAA rating. Released September 1965.

Gigantis, the Fire Monster/*Gojira no Gyakushu* (*Godzilla's Counterattack*). Producer, Tomoyuki Tanaka; Director, Motoyoshi Oda; Screenplay, Takeo Murata, Sigeaki [Shigeaki] Hidaka; Story, Shigeru Kayama; Art Director, Takeo Kita; Assistant Art Director, Teruaki Abe; Director of Photography, Seiichi Endo; Music, Masaru Sato; Sound, Masanobu Miyazaki; Recording, Toho Dubbing Theatre; Sound Effects, Toho Sound Effects Group; Lighting, Masaki [Masayoshi] Onuma. *Special Effects Unit:* Director, Eiji Tsuburaya; Art Director, Akira Watanabe; Lighting, Masao Shiroda; Optical Photography, Hiroshi Mukoyama.

Cast: Hiroshi Koizumi (Shoichi Tsukioka), Minoru Chiaki (Koji Kobayashi), Setsuko Wakayama (Hidemi Yamaji), Yukio Kasama (Koehi Yamaji, President of the Fishery), Mayuri Mokusho (Radio Operator Yasuko Inouye), Sonosuke Sawamura (Hokkaido Branch Manager Shingo Shibeki), Masao Shimizu (Zoologist Dr. Tadokoro), Takeo Oikawa (Osaka Municipal Police Commisioner), Seijiro Onda (Captain Terasawa of Osaka Defense Corps), Yoshio Tsuchiya (Tajima, Member of Osaka Defense Corps), Minosuke Yamada (Commander of Osaka Defense Corps), Ren Yamamoto (Commander of Landing Craft), Takashi Shimura (Dr. Kyohei Yamane), Haruo Nakajima (Gojira).

A Toho Co., Ltd., Production. Western Electric Mirrophonic soundtrack. Black and white (processed by Kinuta Laboratories, Ltd.). Academy ratio. 82 minutes. Released April 24, 1955.

U.S. Version: Released by Warner Bros. Pictures, Inc. A Paul Schreibman Presentation. Producer, Paul Schreibman; Executive Producer, Harry B. Swerdlon; Associate Producer, Edmund Goldman; Director of Dubbing and Editing, Hugo Grimaldi; Sound Effects Editor, Alvin Sarno; Music Editor, Rex Lipton; Dubbing Cast, Paul Frees, George Takei, Keye Luke, others unidentified; Sound, Ryder Sound Services, Inc. (Westrex Recording System); Additional Music, Paul Sawtell, Bert Shefter (including stock music from *Kronos* [20th Century-Fox, 1957]); Prints by Technicolor. Copyright June 13, 1959, by Harry B. Swerdlon; renewed 1987 by Toho Co., Ltd. Includes footage from *Unknown Island* (Film Classics, 1948). Identity of additional stock footage, possibly outtakes from *The Lost Continent* (Lippert, 1951), the Mexican-made *Adventuras en la Centro del la Tiera* (?) and *One Million B.C.* (United Artists, 1940), is unconfirmed. Cropped wide screen. Double billed with *Teenagers from Outer Space* (Warner Bros., 1959). Released to Japanese-speaking theaters in the United States prior to its dubbed release as *Godzilla Raids Again*, which is also the title of the syndicated television and home video version (though video version credits still read "Gigantis"). 78 minutes. No MPAA rating. Released May 21, 1959.

Godzilla, King of the Monsters!/*Gojira* (*Godzilla*). Producer, Tomoyuki Tanaka; Director, Ishiro Honda; Screenplay, Takeo Murata, Ishiro Honda; Story, Shigeru Kayama; Art Director, Satoshi Chuko; Director of Photography, Masao Tamai; Lighting, Choshiro Ishii; Sound Recording, Hisashi Shimonaga; Sound, Toho Dubbing Theatre; Sound Effects, Toho Sound Effects Group; Music, Akira Ifukube. *Special Effects Unit:* Director, Eiji Tsuburaya; Art Director, Akira Wanatabe; Optical Photography, Hiroshi Mukoyama; Lighting, Kuichiro Kishida; Co-Godzilla Design, Ryosaku Takayama and Iwao Mori.

Cast: Takashi Shimura (Dr. Kyohei Yamane), Momoko Kochi (Emiko Yamane), Akira Takarada (Ogata), Akihiko Hirata (Dr. Daisuke Serizawa), Sachio Sakai (Hagiwara), Fuyuki Murakami (Dr. Tabata), Ren Yamamoto (Masaji Sieji), Toyoaki Suzuki (Shinkichi), Tadashi Okabe (Dr. Tabata's Assistant), Toranosuki Ogawa (President of Shipping Company), Ren Imaaizumi (Chief of Shipping Company's Radio Section), Miki Hayashi (Chairman of Diet Committee), Seijiro Orda, Kin Sugai (Members of Parliment), Katsumi Tezuka (Newspaper Employee), Takao Aikawa (Chief of Emergency Headquarters), Haruo Nakajima (Power Substation Engineer), Haruo Nakajima and Ryosaku Takasugi (Gojira).

A Toho Co., Ltd., Production. Western Electric Mirrophonic soundtrack. Black and white (processed by Kinuta Laboratories, Ltd.). Academy aspect ratio. Copyright 1954 by Toho Co., Ltd. 98 minutes. Released November 3, 1954.

U.S. Version: Released by Godzilla Releasing Company (i.e., Embassy Pictures Corp.). A Jewell Enterprises/ Transworld Presentation. Executive Producers, Terry Turner, Joseph E. Levine; Producers, Richard Kay, Harry Rybnick, Edward B. Barison; Director-Editor, Terrell O. Morse, Sr. [Terry Morse]; Director of Photography, Guy Roe. Academy aspect ratio. Some sources suggest this was released in stereophonic sound; this is unconfirmed. Copyright April 27, 1956, by Jewell Enterprises, Inc. Double billed with *Prehistoric Women* (reissue; Eagle-Lion, 1950). Original version released to Japanese-speaking theaters, possibly with English subtitles, in the U.S. in 1955 as *Gojira*. Reissued minus dubbing and plus subtitles by Toho International in 1982. Dubbed version originally credited Honda, Morse and Burr and title was over black background, not water. Interestingly, the U.S. version was also released theatrically in Japan, as *Kaiju o Godzilla (Monster King Godzilla)*. 81 minutes. No MPAA rating. Released April 1956.

Additional Cast for U.S. Version: Raymond Burr (Steve Martin), Frank Iwanaga (Security Officer Tomo Iwanaga).

Godzilla 1985/Gojira (Godzilla). Executive Producer, Tomoyuki Tanaka; Associate Producer, Fumio Tanaka; Director, Koji Hashimoto; Screenplay, Shuichi Nagahara (based on the original story, "The Resurrection of Godzilla," by Tomoyuki Tanaka); Director of Photography, Kazutami Hara; Production Designer/Art Director, Akira Sakuragi; Music, Reijiro Koroku, performed by the Tokyo Symphony Orchestra; Tokyo Symphony Orchestra Conductor, Katsuaki Nakaya; Sound, Toho Eizo Sound Studio; Recording Mixer, Nobuyuki Tanaka; Sound Effects, Toho Sound Effects Group; Dolby Stereo Consultant, Mikio Mori, Continental Far East, Inc., Tokyo; Lighting, Shiji Kojima; Editor, Yoshitami Kuroiwa; Still Photographer, Yoshinori Ishizuki; Assistant Director, Takao Ogawara; Production Manager, Kischu [Takehide] Morichi; Songs: "Goodbye My Love," Lyrics by Toyohisa Araki, Composed by Takashi Miki and Sung by Yasuko Sawaguchi (Fanhouse Records); "Godzilla," Lyrics by Linda Henrick, Composed by Reijiro Koroku and Sung by the Star Sisters (Warner/Pioneer); Soundtrack available on King Records (K28G-7226); Associate Music Producer, Toho Music Publishing Co., Produced by Tadahiko Maeda; Computer Graphics, Yutaka [Hiroshi] Tsuchiya; Visual Consultant, Toshifumi Sakata; Assistants to the Director, Takashi Wakiya, Takehisa Takarada; Assistant Sound Technician, Noboru Ikeda; Assistant Lighting, Akira Ohba; Lighting Grip, Shunji Yokota; Continuity, Hiroko Kajiyama; Makeup, Fumiko Umezawa; Maintenance, Kazuo Suzuki; Set Construction, Yoshiki Kasahara, Toho Art Co., Ltd.; Set Decoration, Akio Tashiru, Toho Art Co., Ltd.; Electrician, Hideo Inangaki; Special Engineering, Toyoo Tanaka; Assistant Editors, Sae Higashijima, Junko Shirato; Negative Cutter, Fusako Takahashi; Costumes, Kenji Kawasaki, Kyoto Costume Co., Ltd.; Casting Director, Tadao Tanaka; Assistant Producers, Kiyomi Kanazawa, Morio Hayashi; Special Advisors, Hitoshi Takeuchi (Professor Emeritus, Tokyo University), Hideo Aoki (Military Consultant), Yorihiko Ohsaki (Doctor of Engineering), Klein Uberstein (Science Fiction Writer); Cooperation, Mitsubishi Motor Cars, Hattoro Seiko Co., Ltd., Mitsubishi Rayon Co., Ltd., Mitsui Oak Line, Bandal, Inc., International Container Terminal, Ltd., Ogawa Modelling, Inc., Computer Graphic Laboratory, Inc., Tomy Corp., Sohishiro Tahara (Journalist). *Special*

Effects Unit: Director, Teruyoshi Nakano; Cinematography, Takeshi Yamamoto, Toshimitsu Oneda; Production Designer/Art Director, Yasuyuki Inoue; Lighting, Kohei Mikami; Pyrotechnics, Tadaaki Watanabe, Mamoru Kume, Mitsuo Mikakawa; Prosthetics (Suit Construction), Nobuyuki Yasumaru; Wire Works, Koji Matsumoto, Mitsuo Miyakawa; Matte Photography, Takeaki Tsukuda, Yoshio Ishii; Optical Photography, Takeshi Miyanishi, Yoshikazu Manoda; Pyrotechnician, Takeshi Miyanishi; Still Photographer, Takashi Nakao; second Unit Director, Eiichi Asada; Production Manager, Masayuki Ikeda; Cybot Manufacturer, Shunichi Mizuno; Assistant Director, Kyotaka Matsumoto; Assistant Photographer, Toshio Yamaga; Assistant Art Director, Gen Komura; Lighting Assistant, Katsuji Watanabe; Lighting Grip, Tadaaki Ohide; Mantainence, Yoshio Takenaka; Film Editor, Midori Kobayashi; Producer, Shigeo Matsubichi.

Cast: Keiju Kobayashi (Prime Minister Mitamura), Ken Tanaka (Goro Maki), Yasuko Sawaguchi (Naoko Okumura), Shin Takuma (Hiroshi [Ken] Okumura), Yosuke Natsuki (Professor Hayashida), Taketoshi Naito (Chief Cabinet Secretary Takegami), Tetsuya Takeda (Street Bum), Eitaro Ozawa (Finance Minister Kanzaki), Mizuho Suzuki (Foreign Minister Emori), Junkichi Orimoto (Defense Agency Secretary Mori), Shinsuke Mikimoto (Chief of Staff Kakurai), Mikita Mori (Internal Affairs Secretary Okouchi), Nobuo Kaneko (Home Affairs Minister Isomura), Kiyoshi Yamamoto (Science and Technology Agency Director Kajita), Takeshi Kato (Internal Trade and Industry Minister Kasaoka), Yoshibumi Tajima (Environmental Director General Hidaka), Yasuhiko Kono (Maritime Forces Chief of Staff Kishimoto), Eiji Kanai (Ground Forces Chief of Staff Imafuji), Isao Hirano (Air Force Chief of Staff Kiyohara), Kunio Murai (Secretary Henmi), Kenichi Urata (Secretary Ishimaru), Hiroshi Koizumi (Geologist Minami), Kei Sato (Chief Editor Godo), Takenori Emoto (Desk Editor Kitagawa), Takero Morimoto (Newscaster), Takashi Ebata (Number Five Yahata Maru Captain), Shigeo Kato, Sennosuke Tahara (Yahata Maru Crew), Shinpei Hayashiya (Cameraman Kamijo), Sho Hasimoto (*Super X* Commander Hagiyama), Kenji Fukuda (*Super X* Lieutenant), Shin Kazenaka (Uno), Yumiko Tanaka (Akemi), Tetsuya Ushio, Kensui Watanabe (Operators), Walter Nichols (Ambassador Chevsky), Luke Johnston (Captain Kathren), Dennis Falt (Soviet Submarine Captain), Nigel Reed (Soviet Sub Lieutenant), Terry Sonberg (Parasebo Crew Member), Koji Ishizaka (Nuclear Power Plant Technician), Hiroshi Kamayatsu (Shinkansen Passenger), Kenpachiro Satsuma (Gojira).

A Toho Co., Ltd., Production, in association with Toho Eizo Co., Ltd. Dolby Stereo and TKL-Stereo (Dolby in the United States). Color (processed by Tokyo Laboratory, Ltd.). Panavision. 103 minutes. Released December 15, 1984.

U.S. Version: Released by New World Pictures in August 1985. English-language version produced by New World Pictures in association with Toho Co., Ltd. Director, R. J. Kizer; Producer, Anthony Randel; Screenplay, Lisa Tomei; Director of Photography, Steve Dubin; Editor, Michael Spence; Associate Producer, Andrea Barshov Stern; Assistant Director, Lee S. Berger; Camera Assistant, Samuel Buddy Fries; Gaffer, Amy C. Halpern; Best Boy, Lewis A. Weinberg; Key Grip, Tracy Heftzger; Best Boy Grip, Paul S. Isiki; Swingman (i.e., electrician/grip), Richard Kuhn; Sound Mixer, Mark Sheret; Sound Boom Operator, Glenn Berkovitz; Script Supervisor, Veronica Flynn; Hair/Make-Up, Mary Michael George; Art Director and Stylist (i.e., Wardrobe Supervisor), Carol Christine Clements; Assistant Art Director, Greg Lacy; Set Decorator, Pam Moffat; Assistant Wardrobe, Kathryn Sparks; Postproduction Coordinator, James Melkonian; Assistant Editor, Kevin Sewelson; Second Assistant Editor, Mehran Ty Salamati; Production Assistant, Lisa M. Dannenbaum; Production Assistant/Driver, Christopher Ward Trott; Sets, Design Setters; Casting, Danny Goldman; Production Secretary, Anne Marie Trulove; Main Title Design, Ernest D. Farino, Jr.; Computer

Readout Animation, Bert Mixon; Sound Design, Biggert Production Services; Supervising Sound Editor, Bob Briggert; ADR Mixer, Richard Rogers; Postproduction Sound Services, Ryder Sound, Inc.; Sound Director, Leo Chaloukian; Rerecording Mixers, John Keene "Doc" Wilkinson, Charles "Bud" Grenzbach, Joseph Citarella; Additional Music, Chris Young (copyright New World Pictures; Administraters, Chilly D. Music, WB Music Corp. ASCAP); Additional Optical Effects, Ray Mercer and Company; Negative Cutter, Diane Jackson; Special Thanks, The Dr Pepper Bottling Company, Robert Hamlin, David Millheiser, Cynthia T. Clark and Kef Music Publishing, Elliot Chiprut, Stewart Levin, Jill Elliot; processing and prints by Technicolor. Copyright 1985 by Toho Co., Ltd. U.S. footage financed, in part, by Dr Pepper. U.S. credits wrongly bill Takehide Morichi as Prime Minister. Preceded by the animated short subject *Bambi Meets Godzilla* (Marv Newland, 1969). International Title: *The Return of Godzilla*. 91 minutes. MPAA rating: PG. Released August 1985.

Additional Cast for U.S. Version: Raymond Burr (Mr. [Steve] Martin), Warren Kemmerling (General Goodhue), James Hess (Colonel Rascher), Travis Swords (Major McDonough), Crawford Binion (Lieutenant), Justin Gocke (Kyle), Bobby Brown, Patrick Feren, Mark Simon, Shepard Stern, Alan D. Waserman (Extras).

Godzilla on Monster Island/Chikyu kogeki meirei: Gojira tai Gaigan (*The Earth Destruction Directive: Godzilla against Gigan*). Executive Producer, Tomoyuki Tanaka; Director, Jun Fukada; Assistant Director, Fumikatsu Okada; Screenplay, Shinichi Sekizawa; Director of Photography, Kiyoshi Hasegawa; Art Director, Yoshifumi Honda; Music, Akira Ifukube; Theme Song, Toho Records; Songs by Susumu Ishikawa; "Godzilla's March," Lyrics by Shinichi Sekizawa and Jun Fukada, Music by Danro Miyaguchi; Assistant Director, Fumisaka Okada; Film Editor, Yoshio Manoda; Lighting, Kojiro Sato; Mechanical Effects, Takesaburo Watanabe; Sound Recording, Fumio Yanoguchi; Sound, Toho Recording Centre; Production Manager, Takehide Morichi. *Special Effects Unit:* Director, Teruyoshi Nakano; Art Director, Yasuyuki Inoue; Photography, Mototaka Tomioka; Miniature Set Operation, Fumio Nakadai; Optical Printing, Toshiyuki Tokumasa; Sets, Toshiro Aoki; Matte Processing, Saburo Doi.

Cast: Hiroshi Ishikawa (Gengo Kotaka), Yuriko Hishimi (Tomoko Tomoe), Tomoko Umeda (Machiko Shima), Minoru Takashima (Shosaku Takasugi), Kunio Murai (Takashi Shima), Susumu Fujita (The Chairman of World Children's Land), Toshiaki Nishizawa (Secretary Kubota), Wataru Ohmae (Employee), Kuniko Ashiwara (Middle-Aged Woman), Kureyoshi Nakamura (Priest), Akiyo Muto (Editor of *Comics Magazine*), Gan Shimizu (Commander of Defense Forces), Haruo Nakajima (Godzilla), Yukietsu Omiya (Angilas), Kanta Ina (King Ghidorah), Kengo Nakayama (Gigan).

A Toho-Eizo Co., Ltd., Production. A Toho Co., Ltd., Release. Fujicolor (processed by Tokyo Laboratory, Ltd.). Panavision. Copyright 1972 by Toho Co., Ltd. 89 minutes. Released March 12, 1972.

U.S. Version: Released by Downtown Distributing Co., Inc. (i.e., Cinema Shares International) U.K. Title: *War of the Monsters*. Television and home video title: *Godzilla vs. Gigan*. Includes extensive stock footage from *Ghidrah: The Three-Headed Monster* (1964), *Monster Zero* (1965), *War of the Gargantuas* (1966), *Son of Godzilla* (1967), *Destroy All Monsters* (1968) and *Godzilla vs. the Smog Monster* (1971). This was Nakajima's last film as Godzilla. 89 minutes. MPAA rating: G. Released August 1977.

Godzilla's Revenge/Oru kaiju dai shingeki (*All Monsters Attack*). Producer, Tomoyuki Tanaka; Director, Ishiro Honda; Screenplay, Shinichi Sekizawa; Director of Photography, Mototaka Tomioka; Music, Kunio Miyauchi; Editor, Masahima Miyauchi [Mimi]; Art Direction, Takeo Kita; Assistant Director, Masaski Hisumatsu;

Sound Effects, Toho Sound Effects Group; Recording, Toho Recording Centre. *Special Effects Unit:* Director, Eiji Tsuburaya; Photography, Teisho Arikawa, Motonari Tomioka; Optical Photography, Yukio Manoda, Sadao Iizuda; Art Director, Akira Watanabe; Lighting, Kuichiro Kishida; Scene Manipulation, Fumio Nakadai, Assistant Director, Teruyoshi Nakano.

Cast: Kenji Sahara (Ichiro's Father), Eisei Amamoto (Toy Consultant Inami), Yoshibumi Tajima (Detective), Tomonori Yazaki (Ichiro), Sachio Sakai, Kazuo Suzuki (Bank Robbers), Machiko Naka, Chotaro Togin, Ikio Sawamura, Shigeki Ishida, Yutaka Sada, Yutaka Nakayama.

A Toho Co., Ltd., Production. Color (processed by Tokyo Laboratory, Ltd.). Tohoscope. 70 minutes. Double billed with *Kuso tengoku* (*Fancy Paradise*). Released December 20, 1969.

U.S. Version: Released by Maron Films, Ltd. A United Productions of America presentation. Producer, Henry G. Saperstein; Postproduction, Riley Jackson; Theme Song, "March of the Monsters," Crown Records; Sound Recording, Ryder Sound Services, Inc.; Titles and Prints, Consolidated Film Industries. Copyright 1971 by UPA. According to Greg Shoemaker, this was originally released as *Minya, Son of Godzilla*, possibly by Toho International in an English-dubbed version and minus screen credits. The picture was pulled and re-edited to present length and released by Maron as *Godzilla's Revenge*, double billed with *Island of the Burning Damned* (Maron, 1971), also the film's television title. Not to be confused with *Son of Godzilla* (q.v.). Includes extensive stock footage from *Ebirah, Horror of the Deep* (1966) and *Son of Godzilla*, as well as footage from *King Kong Escapes* (1967) and *Destroy All Monsters* (1968). 69 minutes. No MPAA rating. Released 1971.

Godzilla vs. Biollante/Gojira vs. Biorante (*Godzilla vs. Biollante*). Executive Producer, Tomoyuki Tanaka; Associate Producer, Shogo Tomiyama; Director/Screenplay, Kazuki Omori; Based on an original story, "Gojira tai Beollante," by Shinichiro Kobayashi; Assistant Director, Hideyuki Inoue; Assistant Directors, Yutaka Kubo, Kazuhiko Fukami, Isao Kaneko; Director of Photography, Yudai Kato; Camera Operators, Takashi Wakiya, Motonobu Kiyohisa, Hideyuki Yamaguchi; Lighting, Takaeshi Awakibara; Lighting Assistants, Kohei Mikami, Yasuo Watanabe, Kazumi Kawagoe, Shohei Iriguchi, Hiroyuki Futami, Kenya Kato, Takamasa Nakatani; Recording Mixer, Kazuo Miyauchi; Sound Recordists, Sadakazu Saito, Tatsuaki Watanabe, Osamu Kageyama; Special Mechanical Effects, Mitsuo Miyagawa, Kazuo Kayama; Production Design, Shigekazu Ikuno; Art Department, Juichi Ikuno, Osami Tonjo, Fumiko Osada, Hiroto Niigaki; Set Decoration, Akio Tashiro, Osamu Minamizawa, Yuichiro Endo, Masataka Kawara, Toho Art Co., Ltd.; Electrical Set Decoration, Hideo Inagaki, Yoshinao Tanaka; Construction, Eiji Suzuki, Yoshiki Kasahara, Toho Art Co., Ltd.; Still Photographer, Yoshinori Ishizuki; Hair and Makeup, Harumi Ueno; Costumes, Kenji Kawasaki, Kyoto Costume Co., Ltd.; Continuity, Yukiko Eguchi; Casting, Tadeo Tanaka; Editor, Michiko Ikeda; Assistant Editors, Miho Shiga, Mitsuko Saito, Masami Ohashi; Sound Effects, Shinichi Ito; Music Composer, Koichi Sugiyama; Music Arranger and Conductor, David Howell; "Godzilla Themes" by Akira Ifukube; Dolby Stereo Consultant, Mikio Mori, Continental Far East, Inc., Tokyo; Production Manager, Kishu Morichi; Production Runners, Takaya Fukuya, Satoshi Fukushima, Yasuo Kobayashi, Sho Matsue; Publicity Director, Masao Daimon; Publicists, Yuichiro Nakanishi, Minami Ichikawa; Cooperation, New MGC, Reebok, others undetermined. "Thanks to the Defense Agency for their cooperation in the making of this motion picture." *Special Effects Unit:* Director, Koichi Kawakita; Assistant Director, Kyotaka Matsumoto; Assistants to Kawakita, Hideki Chiba, Makoto Kamiya, Yuichi Abe; Director of Photography, Kenichi Eguchi; Miniature Photography, Yoshio

Nozawa, Hiroshi Kidokoro, Masashi Sasaki, Katsumi Arita, Takahide Majio; Lighting, Kaoru Saito; Lighting Assistants, Nobuyuki Seo, Hoya Hayashi, Takhiro Sekino, Masaaki Yokomichi, Shigeru Izumiya, Tsuneo Tanaami; Production Designer, Tetsuzo Osawa; Special Art Department, Takashi Naganuma, Yuji Tsukuba, Isao Takahashi, Masato Matsumura; Prosthetics, Nobuyuki Yasumaru, Tomoki Kobayashi, Yoko Nagata; Wire Works, Koji Matsumoto; Wire Works Assistants, Koshu Katori, Masahiko Shiraishi; Miniature Pyrotechnics, Tadaaki Watanabe, Mamoru Kume; Pyrotechnicians, Yasushi Iwata, Toshitaka Watanabe, Katsumi Nakajo; Miniature Sets, Yasuo Nomura, Sadao Ogasawara; Still Photographer, Takashi Nakao; Editing, Yukari Yaginuma; Continuity, Yoshiko Hori; Production Runners, Taro Kojima, Masaya Kowakura, Isamu Suzuki; Biollante Design, Atsuhiko Sugita, Noritaka Suzuki, Shinji Nishikawa; Mechanical Designs, Kou Yokoyama. Special Optical Effects Unit: Optical Effects; Yoshiyuki Kishimoto, Horiaki Hojo; Motion Control, Ryoji Kinoshita, Kenichi Abe; Video Effects, Kenji Kagiwara; Timing, Maruo Iwata; Effects Animation, Michiaki Hashimoto, Hajime Matsumoto, Masakazu Saito; Animation, Kazuaki Mori, Aki Yamagata, Ryuichi Akahori; Computer Graphics, Tetsuo Obi, Hisashi Kameya, Satoshi Mizuhata; Matte Paintings, Kazunobu Sanbe; Matte Painter, Yoshio Iishi; Coordinators, Toshihiro Ogawa, Masaharu Misawa; Producers, Takashi Yamabe, Mitsuhara Umano.

Cast: Kuniko Mitamura (Kazuhito Kirishima), Yoshiko Tanaka (Asuka Okouchi), Masanobu Takashima (Major Sho Kuroki), Megumi Odaka (Miki Saegusa), Tohru Minegishi (Lieutenant Goro Gondo), Ryunosuke Kaneda (Seido Okouchi), Koji Takahashi (Dr. Genichiro Shiragami), Yasuko Sawaguchi (Erika Shiragami), Toshiyuki Nagashima (Director of Technical Division Seiichi Yamamoto), Yoshiko Kuga (Chief Cabinet Secretary Keiko Owada), Manjhat Beti (SSS9), Koichi Ueda (Self Defense Agency Chairman Yamaji), Isaho Toyohara and Kyoka Suzuki (*Super X2* Operators), Kenji Hunt (John Lee), Derrick Holmes (Michael Low), Hirohisa Nakata (Director General of the Defense Agency), Kusuhiko Sasaki (Director of Science Technology Takeda), Kenzo Hagiwara (Ground Forces Staff Officer), Kazuyuki Senba (Maritime Staff Officer), Koji Yamanaka (Air Force Staff Officer), Iden Yamanrahl (Abdul Saulman), Hiroshi Inoue Kazuma Matsubara, Ryota Yoshimitsu, Tetsu Kawai, Yasunori Yumiya (Self Defense Forces Officials), Shin Tatsuma (Director of Giant Plant Observation Akiyama), Abdula Herahl (Researcher), Curtis Kramer, Brian Wool, Robert Conner (Commandos), Beth Blatt (CCN Newscaster Susan Horn), Makiyo Kuroiwa (Nurse), Haruko Sagara (TVC-TV Reporter), Hiromi Matsukawa (Newscaster), Demon Korgure (Himself), Isao Takeno (Chief of *Super X2* Repair Crew), Kenpachiro Satsuma, Shigeru Shibazaki, Yoshitaka Kimura (Gojira), Masao Takegami (Biorante).

A Toho-Eizo Co., Ltd., Production, in association with Toho Co., Ltd. Dolby Stereo/TKL-Stereo. Color (processed by Tokyo Laboratory, Ltd.). Spherical Wide Screen. 104 minutes. Released December 16, 1989.

U.S. Version: Never released theatrically in the United States. Released directly to home video. Copyright 1989 by Toho Co., Ltd. MPAA Rating: PG. 109 minutes.

Godzilla vs. Megalon/Gojira tai Megaro. (*Godzilla against Megalon*). Producer, Tomoyuki Tanaka; Director, Jun Fukuda; Screenplay, Jun Fukuda, Shinichi Sekizawa; Director of Photography, Yuzuru Aizawa; Music, Riichiro Manabe; Sound, Toho Recording Centre; Sound Effects, Toho Sound Effects Group. *Special Effects Unit:* Director, Teruyoshi Nakano; Mechanical Effects, Takesaburo Watanabe; Optical Effects, Yukio Manoda; Art Director, Yasuyuki Inoue.

Cast: Katsuhiko Sasaki (Goro), Hiroyuki Kawase (Goro's Brother), Yutaka Hayashi, Robert Dunham (Seatopian Leader), Kotaro Tomita, Mori Mikita.

A Toho-Eizo Co., Ltd., Production. A Toho Co., Ltd., Release. Fujicolor (processed by

Tokyo Laboratory, Ltd.). Panavision. 81 minutes. Released March 17, 1973.
U.S. Version: Released by Cinema Shares International Distribution Co., Inc.. Features stock footage from *Ghidrah: The Three-Headed Monster* (1964), *Ebirah, Horror of the Deep* (1966), *War of the Gargantuas* (1966), *Destroy All Monsters* (1968) and *Godzilla on Monster Island* (1972). Cut to 50 minutes for U.S. television network presentation. 80 minutes. MPAA rating: G. Released April 1976.

Godzilla vs. the Cosmic Monster/Gojira tai Mekagojira (*Godzilla Against Mechagodzilla*). Executive Producer, Tomoyuki Tanaka; Director, Jun Fukuda; Assistant Director, Jozaburo Nishikawa; Screenplay, Hiroyasu Yamamura [Yamaura], Jun Fukada, based on an original story by Shinichi Sekizawa and Masami Fukushima; Director of Photography, Yuzuru Aizawa; Art Director, Kazuo Satsuya; Lighting, Masakuni Ikeda; Sound Recording, Fumio Yanoguchi; Music, Masaru Sato; Sound, Toho Recording Centre; Sound Effects, Toho Sound Effects Group. *Special Effects Unit:* Director, Teruyoshi Nakano; Photography, Mototake Tomioka, Takeshi Yamamoto; Optical Photography, Yukio Manoda; Mechanical Effects, Takesaburo Watanabe; Art Director, Yasuyuki Inoue.

Cast: Masaaki Daimon (Keisuke Shimizu), Kazuya Aoyama (Masahiko Shimizu), Akihiko Hirata (Professor Hideto Miyajima), Hiroshi Koizumi (Professor Wagura), Reiko Tajima (Saeko Kaneshiro), Hiromi Matsushita (Iko Miyajima), Masao Imafuku (Azumi Priest), Beru-Bera Lin [Barbara Lynn] (Azumi Princess Nami Kunizu), Mori Kishida (Interpol Agent Namara), Takayasu Torii (Interpol Agent Tamura), Goro Mutsu (Commander of the Alien Attack Force), Daigo Kusano (Kawa Yanagi), Kenji Sahara (Ship's Captain), Yasuzo Ogawa (Construction Workshop Supervisor).

A Toho-Eizo Co., Ltd., Production. A Toho Co., Ltd., Release. Fujicolor (processed by Tokyo Laboratory, Ltd.). Panavision. Copyright 1974 by Toho Co., Ltd. 84 minutes. Released March 21, 1974.

U.S. Version: Released by Downtown Distribution Co., Inc. (i.e., Cinecma Shares). Title changed from *Godzilla vs. the Bionic Monster* after Universal Pictures, the production company behind "The Six Million Dollar Man" and "The Bionic Woman," threatened legal action because of the film's title. Television and home video title: *Godzilla vs. Mechagodzilla*. 84 minutes. MPAA rating: G. Released March 1977.

Godzilla vs. the Smog Monster/Gojira tai Hedora (*Godzilla against Hedora*). Executive Producer, Tomoyuki Tanaka; Director, Yoshimitsu Banno; Screenplay, Yoshimitsu Banno, Kaoru Mabuchi (Takeshi Kimura); Director of Photography, Yoichi Manoda; Music, Riichiro Manabe; Editor, Yoshitami Kuroiwa; Art Director, Taiko [Yasuyuki] Inoue; Sound Effects, Toho Sound Effects Group; Sound, Toho Recording Centre. *Special Effects Unit:* Director, Teruyoshi Nakano; Optical Photography, Yukio Manoda; Mechanical Effects, Takesaburo Wanatabe.

Cast: Akira Yamauchi (Dr. Yano), Hiroyuki Kawase (Ken Yano), Toshie Kimura (Mrs. Yano), Tohio Shibaki (Yukio Keuchi), Keiko Mari (Miki Fujiyama), Harou Nakajima (Gojira), Kenpachiro Satsuma (Hedora).

A Toho Co., Ltd., Production. Color (processed by Tokyo Laboratory, Ltd.). Panavision (possibly advertised as Tohoscope in Japan). Copyright 1971 by Toho Co., Ltd. 85 minutes. Released July 24, 1971.

U.S. Version: Released by American International Pictures. A Samuel Z. Arkoff Presentation. Producer, Samuel Z. Arkoff; Director, Lee Kressel; Postproduction Supervisor, Salvatore Billiteri; (Dialog Replacement) Editor, Eli Haviv; Rerecording, Titan Productions, Inc.; Song, "Save the Earth," English Lyrics and Vocal, Adryan Russ. Guy Hemric is credited with music for the song, but as the number appears in the Japanese cut (in Japanese, of course), his credit is questionable. Wide screen process advertised as Colorscope in the United States. 85 minutes. MPAA rating: G. Released July 1972.

Godzilla vs. the Thing/Mosura tai Gojira (*Mothra Against Godzilla*). Producers, Tomoyuki Tanaka, Sanezumi Fujimoto; Director, Ishiro Honda; Screenplay, Shinichi Sekizawa; Director of Photography, Hajime Koizumi; Music, Akira Ifukube; Editor, Ryohei Fujii; Sound Recording Director, Fumio Yanoguchi; Mixing, Hiroshi Mukoyana; In Charge of Production, Boku Morimoto; Art Director, Takeo Kita; Lighting, Shoshichi Kojima; Sound Technician, Hisashi Shimonaga; Assistant to the Director, Okiji Kajita; Sound Effects, Toho Sound Effects Group; Sound, Toho Recording Centre. *Special Effects Unit:* Director, Eiji Tsuburaya; Cameramen, Teisho Arikawa, Motoyoshi Tomioka; Lighting, Kuichiro [Kyuighiro] Kishida; Art Director, Akira Watanabe; Suit Design, Teizo Toshimitsu; Optical Photography, Yukio Manoda, Sokei Tomioka, Yoshiyuki Tokumasa; Alignment, Hiroshi Mukoyama; Optical Effects Animation, Minoru Nakano; Assistant to Tsuburaya, Teruyoshi Nakano.

Cast: Akira Takarada (News Reporter Ichiro Sakai), Yuriko Hoshi (News Photographer [Yoka] Junko Nakanishi), Hiroshi Koizumi (Professor Miura), Yu Fujiki (Reporter Jiro Nakamura), Emi Ito and Yumi Ito [The Peanuts] (Mothra's Priestesses), Yoshibumi Tajima (Kumayama), Kenji Sahara ([Jiro] Banzo Torahata), Jun Tazaki (Newspaper Editor), Ikio Sawamura (Priest), Kenzo Tadake (Mayor), Susumu Fumita (Public Relations Officer), Yutaka Sada (Old Man), Yoshio Kosugi (Old Man in the Village), Yasuhisa Tsutsumi (Longshoreman), Ren Yamamoto (Sailor), Hauro Nakajima (Gojira).

A Toho Co., Ltd., Production. Eastman Color (processed by Tokyo Laboratory, Ltd.). TohoScope. Copyright 1964 by Toho Co., Ltd. 89 minutes. Released April 29, 1964.

U.S. Version: Released by American International Pictures. A James H. Nicholson and Samuel Z. Arkoff Presentation. Produced by Titra Productions, Inc.; Re-recording, Titra Sound Corp.; prints by Pathe. Copyright August 26, 1964, by American International Productions. Wide screen process advertised as Colorscope in the United States. Double billed with *Voyage to the End of the Universe* (AIP, 1964). Initially released to television by AIP-TV as above; reissued to television by UPA Productions of America and on video as *Godzilla vs. Mothra*. Reissued in Japan in 1970 (re-edited to 74 minutes), 1980 and 1983. 88 minutes. No MPAA rating. Released September 17, 1964.

Gojira vs. Kingughidorah (*Godzilla vs. King Ghidorah*). Executive Producer, Tomoyuki Tanaka; Producer, Shojo Tomiyama; Associate Producer, Tomiya Ban; Director/Screenplay, Kazuki Omori; Director of Photography, Yoshinoru Sakiguchi; Art Director, Ken Sakai; Sound Recording, Katsuo Miyauchi; Lighting Director, Tsuyoshi Awakihara; Editor, Michiko Ikeda; Music, Akira Ifukube; Sound, Toho Recording Centre; Sound Effects, Toho Sound Effects Group; Dolby Stereo Consultant, Mikio Mori, Continental Far East, Inc., Tokyo. *Special Effects Unit:* Director, Koichi Kawakita; Cameramen, Kenichi Eguchi, Toshimitsu Oneda; Art Director, Tetsuzo Osawa; Lighting, Kaoru Saito; Pyrotechnics; Tadashi Watanabe; Wire Works, Koji Matsumoto; Sculpting, Tomoki Kobayashi; Assistant Director, Kenji Suzuki.

Cast: Anna Nakagawa (Emi Kano), Megumi Odaka (Miki Saegusa), Isao Toyohara (Kenichiro Terasawa), Kiwako Harada (Chiaki Morimura), Tokuma Nishioka (Takehito Fujio), Shoji Kobayashi (Yuzo Tsuchiashi), Yoshio Tsuchiya (Yasuaki Shindo), Richard Berger (Grenchiko), Chuck Wilson (Wilson), Kenji Sahara (Prime Minister), Robert Scottfield (M11).

A Toho Pictures Production. Dolby Stereo/TKL-Stereo. Color (processed by Tokyo Laboratory, Ltd.). Spherical Wide Screen. Copyright 1991 by Toho Co., Ltd. Released December 14, 1991.

U.S. Version: Unreleased in the United States as of this writing.

Gojira vs. Mosura (*Godzilla vs. Mothra*). Director, Takao Okawara; Screenplay,

Kazuki Omori; Music, Akira Ifukube and Yuji Koseki and Hiroshi Miyagawa; Additional Music, Arrangements and Conductor, Akira Ifukube; *Special Effects Unit:* Director, Koichi Kawakita.

Cast: Tetsuya Bessho (Takuya Fujita), Satomi Kobayashi (Masako Tezuka), Akira Takarada (Environmental Planning Board Chief Joji Minamino), Keiko Imamura and Sayaka Osawa (The Cosmos), Shoji Kobayashi (Security Chief Ruzo Dobashi), Takehiro Murata (Marutomo Corporation Executive Ando), Makoto Otake (Marutomo Corporation CEO Takeshi Tomokane), Megumi Odaka (Miki Saegusa), Shinya Owada (Ship's Captain), Saburo Shineda (Scientist), Shiori Yonezana (Mideri Tezuka).

A Toho Co., Ltd., Production. Dolby Stereo. Color (processed by Tokyo Laboratory, Ltd.). Spherical Wide Screen. 104 minutes. Released December 12, 1992.

U.S. Version: Unreleased in the United States as of this writing.

Gorath*/*Yosei Gorasu (*Suspicious Star Gorath*). Executive Producer, Tomoyuki Tanaka; Director, Ishiro Honda; Screenplay, Takeshi Kimura, based on an original story by Jojiro Okami; Director of Photography, Hajime Koizumi; Production Manager, Yasuaki Sakamoto; Assistant Directors, Koji Kajita, Masashi Matsumoto, Katsumune Ishida, Shoji Kuroda; Art Directors, Takeo Kita, Teruaki Abe; Music, Kan Ishii; Sound Recording Engineer, Toshiya Ban; Sound Effects, Hisashi Shimonaga, Toho Sound Effects Group; Sound, Toho Recording Centre; Lighting, Toshio Takashima; Editor, Reiko Kaneko; Still Photographer, Tssei Tanaka. *Special Effects Unit:* Director, Eiji Tsuburaya; Directors of Photography, Teisho Arikawa, Motoyoshi Tomioka; Art Director, Akira Wantanabe; Lighting, Kuichiro Kishida; Matte Work, Hiroshi Mukoyama; Optical Effects, Taka Yuki, Yukio Manoda; Production Manager, Kan Narita; Assistant Director, Teruyoshi Nakano.

Cast: Ryo Ikebe (Dr. Tazawa), Yumi Shirakawa (Kiyo [Takiko] Sonoda), Takashi Shimura (Kesuke Sonoda), Kumi Mizuno (Ari [Takiko] Sonoda), Ken Uehara (Dr. Konno), Akira Kubo (Cadet Astronaut Tatsuo Kanai), Akihiko Hirata (Spaceship *Otori* [J-X Eagle] Captain Endo), Jun Tazaki (J-X Hawk [Spaceship *Hayabusa*] Captain Sonoda), Fumio Sakamoto (Sumio Sonoda), Ross Benette (Gibson), George Farness (Huverman), Sachio Sakai (Physician), Shinpei Mitsui (Newspaper Reporter), Ikio Sawamura (Taxi Driver), Eisei Amamoto (Drunk). *J-X Hawk* [Spaceship *Hayabusa*] Crew: Hiroo Kirino (Dr. Manabe), Koji Suzuki (Pilot), Kazuo Imai (Radio Operator), Wataru Ohmae (Mathematician), Yasuo Araki (Navigator), Akira Yamada (Chief Engineer), Tomoo Suzuki (Fuel Checkout). *J-X Eagle* [Spaceship *Otori*] Crew: Kenji Sahara (First Officer Saiki), Hiroshi Tachikawa (Astronaut Wakabayashi), Masanori Jihei (Astronaut Ito), Koichi Sato (Pilot), Yasuhiko Saijo (Radio Operator), Toshihiko Furuta (Navigator), Rinsaku Ogata (Chief Engineer), Tadashi Okabe (Mathematician), Kozo Nomura (Fuel Checkout), Ko Mishima (Engineer Sinda). *The Parliament*: Takamaru Sasaki (Prime Minister Seki), Eitaro Ozawa (Minister of Justice Kinami), Seizaburo Kawazu (Minister of Commerce Tada), Akira Nishimura (Secretary of the Space Agency Murata), Keiko Sata (Murata's Secretary), Haruo Nakajima (Magma, the Giant Walrus), Yasushi Matsubara, Junichiro Mukai, Masayoshi Kawabe, Yoshiyuki Uemura, Koji Uno, Kenichi Maruyama, Yukihiko Gondo, Katsumi Tezuka, Takuya Yuki, Hiroshi Takaki, Ichiro Shioji, Koji Ishikawa, Jiryo Kumagai, Osran Yuri.

A Toho Co., Ltd., Production. Western Electric Mirrophonic recording (encoded with Perspecta Stereophonic sound). Eastman Color (processed by Tokyo Laboratory, Ltd.). Tohoscope. 89 minutes. Released March 21, 1962.

U.S. Version: Released by Brenco Pictures Corp., through Allied Artists Pictures Corp. English-language version, Brenco Pictures Corp. in cooperation with Toho International Co., Ltd.; Executive Producer, Edward L. Alperson; Producer, Stanley

Meyer; Production Coordinator (for Toho), Sanezumi Fujimoto; Sound Recording, Ryder Sound Services, Inc.; Editor, Kenneth Wannberg; Story, John Meredyth Lucas; Postsynchronization Supervisor, Paul Frees; Voices, Paul Frees, William Eidleson, Virginia Craig; Opticals, Pathe. Copyright 1964 by Brenco Pictures Corp. Westrex recording system; Stereo (possibly Perspecta, but this is unconfirmed). Alternate or announced titles: *Gorath, the Mysterious Star* and *Astronaut 1980*. Double billed with *The Human Vapor* (q.v.). 83 minutes. No MPAA rating. Released May 15, 1964.

Half Human: The Story of the Abominable Snowman/Jujin Yukiotako (*Monster Snowman*). Producer, Tomoyuki Tanaka; Associate Producer, Minoru Sakamoto; Director, Ishiro Honda; Screenplay, Takeo Murata; Original Story, Shigeru Kayama; Director of Photography, Tadashi Iimura; Art Director, Takeo Kita; Lighting, Soichi Yokoi; Music, Masaru Sato; Sound, Yoshio Nishikawa; Sound Effects, Toho Sound Effects Group; Recording, Toho Dubbing Theatre. *Special Effects Unit:* Director, Eiji Tsuburaya; Optical Photography, Hiroshi Mukoyama; Art Director, Akira Watanabe; Lighting, Masao Shiroda.

Cast: Akira Takarada (Takeshi Ijima [The Boy]), Akemi Negishi (Chika [The Mountain Girl]), Momoko Kouchi (Machiko Takeno [The Girl]), Kenji Sahara (Shinsuke Takeno), Yoshio Kosuai (Oba [Professor Tanaka?]), Kuninori Kodo (Old Man), Yasuhisa Tsutsumi (Kodama), Sachio Sakai (Norkata), Ren Yamamoto (Shinagawa), Koji Suzuki (Kurihara), Akira Sera (Matsui).

A Toho Co., Ltd., Production. Western Electric Mirrophonic soundtrack (stereophonic sound). Black and white. Academy ratio. 95 minutes. Released August 14, 1955.

U.S. Version: Released by Distributors Corporation of America. Associate Producer, Robert B. Homel; Director-Editor, Kenneth G. Crane; Assistant Director, Hal Klein; Director of Photography, Lucien Andriot; Sound, Jack Wiler; Casting Supervisor, Lynn Stalmaster; Art Director, Nicholai Remisoff; Master of Properties, Sam Heiligman; Script Supervisor, Frances Steene; Wardrobe, Morrie Friedman. Copyright May 22, 1957, by Distributors Corporation of America. "The segments of this picture depicting Japanese peoples and locales were written and filmed in Japan. Special credit is due the artists and technicians there who contributed much to the authenticity of this production." New footage shot for 1.85 x 1 cropping and cut with 1.33:1 Japanese footage. Double billed with *Monster from Green Hell* (DCA, 1958). International title: *Monster Snowman*. 63 minutes (despite some sources' claims that the picture runs 70 and even 78 minutes). No MPAA rating. Released December 1958 (though possibly released on a limited basis in 1957).

Additional Cast for U.S. Version: John Carradine (Dr. John Rayburn), Russell Thorsen (Professor Phillip Osborne), Robert Karnes (Professor Alan Templeton), Morris Ankrum (Dr. Carl Jordan).

Haunted Gold. (no credits available).
Cast: S. Katsu.
A Toho Co., Production. Color (processed by Tokyo Laboratory, Ltd.). Panavision (?). Running time undetermined. Released 1979.
U.S. Version: Distributor, if any, is undetermined.

Hinotori. Executive Producers, Kiichi Ichikawa, Kunihiko Murai; Director, Kon Ichikawa; Screenplay, Shutaro Tanikawa; Story, Osamu Tezuko; Director of Photography, Kiyoshi Hasegawa; Special Effects Director, Teruyoshi Nakano; Animation Director, Osamu Tezuko; Animation, Tezuko Productions; Music, Michel Legrand, Jun Fukamachi; Sound, Toho Recording Centre; Sound Effects, Toho Sound Effects Group.
Cast: Tomisaburo Wakayama, Masao Kusakari, Kaoru Yumi, Reiko Ohara, Mieko Takamine, Tatsuya Nakadai.
A Toho Co., Ltd., Production. Color (processed by Tokyo Laboratory, Ltd.). Panavision. 137 minutes. Released 1978.

U.S. Version: Released by Toho International Co., Ltd., in subtitled format. Advertised as *The Phoenix*. Sequel was the fully animated *Hinotori-2772* (Toho, 1979/U.S. release, July 1982) which is not included in this book. 137 minutes. No MPAA rating. Released October 1980.

The H-Man/Bijo To Ekatai-Ningen (*Beauty and the Liquid People*). Producer, Tomoyuki Tanaka; Director, Ishiro Honda; Screenplay, Takeshi Kimura; Story, Hideo Kaijo; Art Director, Takeo Kita; Director of Photography, Hajime Koizumi; Editor, Ichiji Taira; Music, Masaru Sato; Sound, Choshichiro Mikami, Masanobu Migami; Sound Recording, Toho Dubbing Theatre; Sound Effects, Toho Sound Effects Group; Production Manager, Teruo Maki; Assistant Directors, Koji Murata, Yoshio Nakamura; Lighting, Tsuruzo Nishikawa. *Special Effects Unit:* Director, Eiji Tsuburaya; Photography, Hidesaburo Araki, Teisho Arikawa; Art Director, Akira Wanatabe; Lighting, Kuichiro Kishida; Optical Printing, Hiroshi Mukoyama.

Cast: Yumi Shirakawa (Chikako Arai), Kenji Sahara (Dr. Masada), Akihiko Hirata (Inspector Tominaga), Mitsuru Sato (Uchida), Koreya Senda (Dr. Maki), Yoshio Tsuchiya (Detective Taguchi), Yoshibumi Tajima (Detective Sakata), Eitaro Ozawa (Inspector Miyashita), Ayumi Sonoda (Emi), Toshiko Nakano (Okami), Yosuke Natsuki (Man), Kamayuki Tsubouchi (Detective Ogawa), Minosuke Yamada (Officer Wakasugi), Jun Fujiro (Nishiyama), Akira Sera (Yasukichi), Naomi Shiraishi (Mineko), Yo Kirino (Shimazaki), Hisaya Ito (Misaki), Shin Ohtomo (Hamano), Machiko Kitagawa (Hanae), Tetsu Nakamura (Chinese Gentleman), Yutaka Nakayama (An-chan), Senkichi Ohmura (Oh-chan), Shigeo Kato (Matsu-chan), Ko Mishima (Kishi), Kan Hayashi, Mitsuo Tsuda, Akio Kuama (Police Officers).

A Toho Co., Ltd., Production. Western Electric Mirrophonic soundtrack (encoded with Perspecta Stereophonic Sound). Eastman Color (processed by Far East Laboratories, Ltd.). Tohoscope; 87 minutes. Released June 24, 1958.

U.S. Version: Released by Columbia Pictures Corp. Dubbing Cast, Paul Frees and others unidentified; Perspecta Stereophonic Sound (Westrex recording system); prints by Pathe. Copyright June 6, 1959, by Columbia Pictures Corp. Double billed with *Womaneater* (Columbia, 1959). 79 minutes. No MPAA rating. Released May 28, 1959.

House/Hausu. Producer-Director–Special Effects Director, Nobuhiko [Norihiko] Ohbayashi; Executive Producer, Tomoyuki Tanaka; Screenplay, Chiho Katsura, Nobuhiko Obayashi; Director of Photography, Yoshihisa Sakamoto; Music, Asei Kobayashi, Miki Yoshino, performed by Godiego; Art Direction, Kazuo Satsuya; Editor, Nobuo Ogawa; Assistant Director, Yasuhira Oguri; Sound, Toho Recording Centre; Sound Effects, Toho Sound Effects Group.

Cast: Kimiko Ikegami, Kumiko Oda, Ai Matsubara, Miki Jinbo, Mieko Sato, Masayo Miyako, Enko Tanaka, Saho Sasazawa, Haruko Wanibuchi, Kiyoko Ozaki.

A Toho Co., Ltd., Production. Color (processed by Tokyo Laboratory, Ltd.). Panavision. Also known as *Ie* or *Ei*. 100 minutes (possibly 87 minutes, sources vary). Released August 26, 1977.

U.S. Version: Released by Toho International Co., Ltd., in subtitled format. Also known as *Ie* or *Ei*). No MPAA rating. 87 minutes (?). Released September 1977.

The Human Vapor/Gasu ningen dai ichigo (*Gas Human Being #1*). Executive Producer, Tomoyuki Tanaka; Director, Ishiro Honda; Screenplay, Takeshi Kimura; Director of Photography, Hajime Koizumi; Music, Kunio Miyauchi; Art Direction, Takeo Kita; Production Manager, Yasuaki Sakamoto; Assistant Director, Koji Kahita; Sound Effects, Hisashi Shimonaga, Toho Sound Effects Group; Sound, Toho Dubbing Theatre. *Special Effects Unit:* Director, Eiji Tsuburaya; Art Direction, Teisho Arikawa; Lighting, Kuichiro Kishida; Matte Process, Hiroshi Mukoyama; Optical Photography, Kinsaburo Araki.

Cast: Yoshio Tsuchiya (Mizuno/The Vapor Man), Kaoru Yachigusa (Fujichiyo the Dancer), Tatsuya Mihashi (Detective Okamoto), Keiko Sata (reporter Kyoko), Bokuzen Hidari (Fujichiyo's Guardian).

A Toho Co. Ltd., Production. Western Electric Mirrophonic soundtrack encoded with Perspecta Stereophonic Sound. Eastman Color (processed by Far East Laboratories, Ltd.). Tohoscope. 92 minutes. Released December 11, 1960.

U.S. Version: Released by Brenco Pictures (booked through Allied Artists Pictures Corporation exchanges). An Edward L. Alperson and Stanley D. Meyer Presentation. Executive Producer, Edward L. Alperson; Producer, Stanley D. Meyer; Executive Director in Charge of Production (i.e., coordinator in the United States for Toho), Sanezumi Fujimoto; English Dialog, John Meredyth Lucas; Editor, Kenneth Wannberg; Dubbing Cast, Paul Frees, William Eidleson (?), Virginia Craig (?); Sound, Ryder Sound Services, Inc.; prints by Pathe; Westrex recording system. Advertised as being "In Wide Screen and Stereophonic Sound," but may have been released mono in the United States. Double billed with *Gorath* (q.v.). 79 minutes. No MPAA rating. Released May 20, 1964.

Illusion of Blood/Yotsuya kaidan (*The Yotsuya Ghost Story*). Producer, Ichiro Sato; Director, Shiro Toyoda; Screenplay, Toshio Yasumi [Yamuzi] (based on the Kubuki play, *Tokaido Yotsuya kaidan*, by Namboku Tsuruya); Director of Photography, Hiroshi Murai; Music, Toru Takemitsu.

Cast: Tatsuya Nakadai (Iuemon Tamiya), Mariko Okada (Oiwa), Junko Ikeuchi (Osode), Kanzaburo Nakamura (Gonbei Naosuke), Mayumi Ozora (Oume), Keiko Awaji (Omaki), Yasushi Nagata (Samon Yotsuya), Eitaro Ozawa (Kihei Ito), Masao Mishima (Takuetsu), Kanjiro Taira.

A Tokyo Eiga (Tokyo Movie Co., Ltd.) Production. (Toho may have been involved in this film's production, may have distributed it in Japan, or may have distributed it in the U.S. only, under the Toho International banner, prior to its being picked up by Frank Lee International). Eastman Color. Tohoscope. 107 minutes. Released 1965.

U.S. Version: Released by Frank Lee International. 107 minutes. No MPAA rating. Released March 1966.

Inn of Evil/Inochi bonifuro. Executive Producers, Masayuki Sato, Gin-ichi Kishimoto, Hideyuki Shiino; Director, Masaki Kobayashi; Screenplay, Tomoe Ryu (i.e., Kyoko Miyazaki), based on the novel *Fukagawa anrakutei* by Sugoror Yamamoto; Art Director, Hiroshi Mizutani; Director of Photography, Hideo Nishizaki; Music, Toru Takemitsu; Sound, Toho Recording Centre; Sound Effects, Toho Sound Effects Group.

Cast: Ganemon Nakamura (Ikuzo), Komaki Kurihara (Omitsu), Kei Sato (Yohei), Tatsuya Nakadai (Sadahichi), Shintaro Katsu (Nameless Wanderer), Wakako Sakai (Okiwa), Shigeru Koyama (Officer Kanedo), Ichido Nakaya (Officer Okajima), Kei Yamamoto (Tomijiro), Yusuke Takida (Nadaya Kohei), Yosuke Kondo (Masaji), Daido Kusano (Yunosuke), Hatsuo Yamatani (Suke), Shun Makita (Senkichi), Mori Kishida (Genzo), Masao Mishima (Funayado) Tokubei).

A Haiyuza/Toho Co., Ltd., Production. Westrex recording system. Color (?) (processed by Tokyo Laboratory, Ltd.). Toho-Scope. 121 minutes. Released March 1, 1971.

U.S. Version: Released by Toho International Co., Ltd., in subtitled format. 121 minutes. No MPAA rating. Released March 1972.

Kaiju daifunsen: Daigoro tai Goriasu (*Daigoro Against Goliath*). Producer, Tomoyuki Tanaka (?); Director, Toshihiro Iijima. Special Effects Director, Teruyoshi Nakano.

Cast: (unavailable)

A Toho Co., Ltd., Production. Panavision (?). Color. Running time undetermined. Released 1972.

U.S. Version: Never released theatrically in the United States.

Kigeki ekiame kaidan. Executive Producer, Tomoyuki Tanaka; Director, Kozo

Saeki; Sound, Toho Recording Centre; Sound Effects, Toho Sound Effects Group. Cast: Frankie Sakai, Hisaya Morishige.
A Toho Co., Ltd., Production. Western Electric Mirrophonic recording. Black and white (processed by Tokyo Laboratory, Ltd.). TohoScope (?). Running time undetermined. Released 1964.

U.S. Version: Distributor, if any, is undetermined. International title: *Ghost Story of Funny Act in Front of Train Station.*

King Kong Escapes/KingKong no gyakushu (*King Kong's Counterattack*). Producers, Tomoyuki Tanaka, Arthur Rankin, Jr.; Director, Ishiro Honda; Screenplay, William J. Keenan, Kaoru Mabuchi (Takeshi Kimura), based on the Rankin/Bass Productions animated television series, "King Kong"; The character "King Kong," from the motion picture *King Kong*, used by permission of RKO General, Inc.; Director of Photography, Hajime Koizumi; Music, Akira Ifukube; Art Director, Takeo Kita; Lighting, Shoshichi Kojima; Sound Recordist, Shoichi Yoshizawa; Sound, Toho Recording Centre; Sound Effects, Toho Sound Effects Group; Editor, Ryohei Fujii. *Special Effects Unit:* Director, Eiji Tsburaya; Photography, Teisho Arikawa, Motonaru Tomioka; Art Director, Akira Wanatabe; Optical Photography, Yukio Manoda, Sadeo Iizuda; Scene Manipulation, Fumio Nakadai.

Cast: Rhodes Reason (Commander Carl Nelson), Akira Takarada (Lt. Commander Jiro Nomura), Mie Hama (Madame X [Piranha]), Linda Miller (Lt. Susan Watson), Eisei Amamoto (Dr. Who [Hoo]); Ikio Sawamura (Old Man on Mondo Island); Yoshibumi Tajima, Susumu Kurobe (Who Henchman).

A Rankin-Bass Production. A Toho Co., Ltd., Picture. Westrex recording system. Eastman Color (processed by Tokyo Laboratory, Ltd.). Tohoscope. 104 minutes. Released July 22, 1967.

U.S. Version: Released by Universal Pictures. An Ernest L. Scanlon Presentation. Produced by Rankin/Bass Productions, Inc., at Glen Glenn Sound. Executive Producer, Jules Bass; Producer-Director, Arthur Rankin, Jr.; Screenplay, William J. Keenan; Post-production Supervisor, Riley Jackson; Dubbing Director, Paul Frees; Dubbing Cast, Paul Frees (Dr. Who, misc. characters), others unknown; Titles, National Screen Service; Sound, Glen Glenn; prints by Technicolor. Copyright August 21, 1968, by Universal Pictures. Double billed with *The Shakiest Gun in the West* (Universal, 1968). U.K. Title: *The Revenge of King Kong* (some U.S. prints may have carried this title). Reissued in Japan in 1973. 96 minutes. MPAA rating: G. Released June 19, 1968.

King Kong Vs. Godzilla/King Kong tai Gojira (*King Kong Against Godzilla*). Producer, Tomoyuki Tanaka; Director, Ishiro Honda; Screenplay, Shinichi Sekizawa (based on a screenplay by George Worthing Yates, from "King Kong Versus Prometheus," a story by Willis O'Brien, and characters created by Merian C. Cooper and Shigeru Kayama); Director of Photography, Hajime Koizumi; Music, Akira Ifukube; Art Director, Takeo Kita; Lighting, Shoshichi Kojima; Editor, Echiji Taira; Sound Effects, Hisashi Shimonaga, Toho Sound Effects Group; "King Kong" character and name used by permission of RKO General, Inc. *Special Effects Unit:* Director, Eiji Tsuburaya; Assistant Director, Teruyoshi Nakano; Cameramen, Teisho Arikawa, Motoyoshi Tomioka; Assistant Cameraman, Koichi Kawakita; Lighting, Kuichiro Kishida; Matte Process, Hiroshi Mukoyama; Optical Effects, Taka Yuki, Yukio Manoda; Art Director (including Gojira and King Kong suit designs), Akira Watanabe; Suit Construction, Teizo Toshimitsu.

Cast: Tadeo Takashimi (O. Sakurai), Mie Hama (Fumiko Sakurai), Kenji Sahara (Kazuo Fujita), Yu Fujiki (Kinsaburo Furue), Ichiro Arishima (Mr. Tako), Tatsuo Matsumura (Dr. Markino), Akihiko Hirata (Premier Shigezawa), Akiko Wakabayshi (Tamiye), Senkichi Omura (TTV Translator Konno), Jun Tazaki (General Masami Shinzo), Yoshio Kosugi (Farou Island Chief),

Ikio Sawamura (Witch Doctor), Akemi Negishi (Dancing Girl), Haruo Nakajima (Gojira), Katsumi Tezuka (King Kong), Yoshibumi Tajima (Man Aboard Ship).

A Toho Co., Ltd., Production. Western Electric Mirrophonic recording (encoded with Perspecta Stereophonic Sound). Eastman Color (color by Tokyo Laboratory, Ltd.). Tohoscope. 98 minutes. Released August 11, 1962.

U.S. Version: Released by Universal Pictures Co., Inc., bearing the Universal-International logo. A John Beck Presentation. Director, Thomas Montgomery; Producer, John Beck; Screenwriters, Paul Mason, Bruce Howard; Editor and Music Supervisor, Paul Zinner; stock music from *Creature from the Black Lagoon* and other U-I titles by Henry Mancini, Herman Stein, Milton Rosen, Robert Emmett Dolan, and conducted by Joseph Gershenson; Sound Effects Editor, William Stevenson; prints by Technicolor; Westrex recording system. Copyright July 2, 1963, by RKO General, Inc. RKO's role is uncertain, though it is likely Toho purchased the Far East rights to the picture and use of the Kong character in exchange for the English-language (or Western Hemisphere) rights and all production costs. Michael Hayes suggests RKO probably then took the finished film to Universal, who produced the English-language version, the profits of which were then divided between Universal and RKO. Tajima's role was cut for the U.S. version. Includes stock footage from *The Mysterians* (M-G-M, 1957). Double billed with *The Traitors* (Universal, 1963). International title: *KingKong vs. Godzilla* (sic). Reissued in Japan in 1964, 1970 (re-edited to 73 minutes) 1977, 1979 and 1983. 91 minutes. No MPAA rating. Released June 3, 1963.

Additional Cast for U.S. Version: Michael Keith (Eric Carter), Harry Holcombe (Dr. Arnold Johnson), James Yagi (Yataka Omura), Les Tremayne (Narrator, voice of General, etc.).

Knockout Drops/Tokyo no Tekisasujin. Executive Producer, Tomoyuki Tanaka; Director, Motoyoshi Oda; Screenplay, Shinichi Sekizawa; Director of Photography, Isamu Ashida; Sound, Toho Recording Centre; Sound Effects, Toho Sound Effects Group.

Cast: M. Minami, E. H. Elic.

A Toho Co., Ltd., Production. Western Electric Mirrophonic recording (encoded with Perspecta Stereophonic Sound?). Black and white. TohoScope (?). 59 minutes. Released 1957.

U.S. Version: Released by Toho International Co., Ltd., format undetermined. 59 minutes. No MPAA rating. Released 1957.

Kokusai Himitsu Keisatsu: Zettai zetsumei. Producer, Tomoyuki Tanaka; Director, Senkichi Taniguchi; Screenplay, Shinichi Sekizawa; Story, Michio Tsuzuki; Art Director, Hiroshi Ueda; Director of Photography, Takao Saito; Editor, Yoshitami Kuroiwa; Music, Sadao Wakemiya; Recording, Yoshio Hishikawa; Sound, Toho Recording Centre; Sound Effects, Toho Sound Effects Group.

Cast: Tatsuya Mihashi (Jiro Kitami), Kumi Mizuno (A Girl), Nick Adams (John Carter), Anne Mari (Ayako), Makoto Sato (Kan Hayata), Jun Tazaki (President of Buddabal), Akihiko Hirata (Man with Turkish Hat), Yoshio Tsuchiya (General Rubesa), Tetsu Nakamura (Head of ZZZ Hong Kong Branch Office), Ryuji Kita (Head of Secret Police), Eisei Amamoto (First Murderer), Masaji Oshita (Second Murderer), Kazuo Yokoyama, Kiyoshi Yoshikawa, Jiro Makino (Gang Comedians), Mari Takeno (Dancer), Tatsuo Hasegawa (Man with Rifle).

A Takarazuka Eiga Production for Toho Co., Ltd. Westrex recording system. Eastman Color (processed by Tokyo Laboratory, Ltd.). TohoScope. 93 minutes. Released 1967.

U.S. Version: Distributor, if any, is undetermined. International title: *The Killing Bottle*. Alternate title: *Zettai zetsumei*. Fifth in the Koksai Himitsu Keisatsu ("International Secret Police") series.

Kuroneko/Yabu no naka no kuroneko. Producer, Nichiei Shinsha [Shinska];

Executive Producers, Nobuyo Horiba, Setsuo Noto, Kazuo Kuwahara; Director/Screenwriter, Kaneto Shindo; Director of Photography, Kiyomi Kuroda; Lighting Director, Shoichi Tabata; Music, Hikaru Hayashi; Editor, Hisao [Toshio] Enoki; Art Director, Takashi Marumo; Production Manager, Yasuhiro Kato; Assistant Directors, Hiroshi Matsumoto, Takase Usui, Seijiro Kamiyama, Katsuji Hoshi, Takashi Marumo; Sound Recording, Tetsuo Ohashi; Sound, Toho Recording Centre; Sound Effects, Toho Sound Effects Group; Makeup, Shigeo Kobayashi.

Cast: Kichiemon Nakamura (Gintoki [Ginji] Yabuno), Nobuko Otowa (The Mother), Kiwako Taichi (The Wife), Kei Sato (Raiko), Taiji Tonoyama (The Farmer), Hideo Kanze (The Mikado), Yoshinobu Ogawa (Raiko Follower), Mutsuhiro [Rokko] Toura (A Warlord), Hidsaki Ezumi (First Follower), Masaji Ohki (Second Follower), Kentaro Kaji (Third Follower), Eiju Kaneda (Kumasunehiko), Ikuko Kosai, Kayoko Sebata, Chiyo Okada (Beautiful Girls), Noriyuki Nishiuchi (First Police and Judicial Chief), Masaru Miyata (Second Police and Judicial Chief).

A Nichei Shinsha and Kindai Eiga Kyokai Production. A Toho Co., Ltd., Presentation. Westrex recording system. Black and white (processed by Tokyo Laboratory, Ltd.). TohoScope. 99 minutes. Released February 24, 1968.

U.S. Version: Released by Toho International Co., Ltd., presumably in subtitled format. This film may have been shown in Los Angeles only. Advertised as *The Black Cat*; 99 minutes. No MPAA rating (?). Released July 1968.

Kuso tengoku. Producer, Shin Watanabe; Director, Takeshi "Ken" Matsumori; Screenplay, Yasuo Tanami; Art Director, Yoshifumi Honda; Director of Photography, Rokuro Nishigaki; Editor, Ume Takeda; Music, Tetsuaki Hagiwara; Recording, Fumio Yanoguchi; Sound, Toho Recording Centre; Sound Effects, Toho Sound Effects Group.

Cast: Kei Tani (Keitaro Tamura), Masako Kyozuka (Hisako), Hideo Naka (Gamera), Wakako Sakai (Hiroko Yamamura), Akira Takarada (Takashi Maeno), Akemi Kita (Michiko Akiyama), Takuya Fujioka (Kondo), Yu Fujiki (Kuroda), Yutaka Sada (Chief Guard Yamamura), Yukihiko Gongo, Hiroshi Tanaka, Hirohito Kimura (Followers), Keiko Nishioka, Sakayu Nakagawa, Yuko Yano (Geishas), Keiji Yanoma (Counter Jumper), Ikio Sawamura (Driver), Makoto Fujita (Marathon Runner), Yutaka Nakayama (Policeman), Hajime Hana (First Detective), Senri Sakurai (Second Detective), Jun Tazaki (Boss), Yasuo Araki (First Man), Hans Horneff (Second Man), Hideo Naka, Ultra Trio (Thieves), Masao Komatsu (Jailer), Yoshiko Toyoura (Young Lady with President), Wakako Tanabe (Nurse).

A Toho Co., Ltd., Production. Westrex recording system. Fujicolor (processed by Tokyo Laboratory, Ltd.). TohoScope. 84 minutes. Released 1968.

U.S. Version: Distributor, if any, is undetermined. Alternate title: *Imagery Paradise* and *Fancy Paradise*.

Kwaidan/Kaidan (*Ghost Story*). Executive Producer, Shigeru Wakatsuki; Director, Masaki Kobayashi; Screenplay, Yoko Mizuki (based on the stories "The Reconciliation," "Yuki-onna," "The Story of Mimi-nashi-Hoichi" and "In a Cup of Tea," from the collection *Kwaidan: Stories and Studies of Strange Things* by Lafcadio Hearn); Director of Photography, Yoshio Miyajima; Art Direction, Shigemasa Toda; Lighting, Akira Aomatsu; Color Consultant, Michio Midorikawa; Picture of the Battle of Dan-no-ura, Masayoshi Nakmura [Nakamura?]; Editor, Hisashi Sagara; Main Title written by Sofu Teshigawara; Title Design, Kiyoshi Kuritsh; Music, Toru Takemitsu; Sound Recording, Hideo Nishizaki; Sound, Toho Recording Centre; Sound Effects, Toru Takemitsu, Kuniharu Akiyama, Junosuke Okuyama, Akira Suzuki.

Cast—"The Black Hair" ("Kurokami"): Rentaro Mikuni (Samurai), Michiyo Aratama (first Wife), Misako Watanabe (second Wife), Kenjiro Ishiyama, Ranko Akagi,

Fumie Kitehara, Katsuhei Matsumoto, Yoshiko Ieda, Otome Tsukimiya, Kenzo Taneka, Kiyoshi Nakano.

Cast—"The Woman of the Snow" ("Yuki-onna"): Keiko Kishi (Yuki, The Snow Woman), Tatsuya Nakadai (Minokichi), Mariko Okada (Minokichi's Mother), Yuko Mochizuki, Kin Sugai, Noriko Sengoku, Akiko Momura, Torahiko Hamada, Jun Hamamura.

Cast—"Hoichi-the-Earless" ("Mimi-nashi-Hoichi"): Katsuo [Kazuo] Nakamura (Hoichi), Rentaro Mikuni (Samurai Spirit), Ganjiro Nakamura (Priest), Takashi Shimura (Head Priest), Joichi [Yoichi] Hayashi (Attendant), Tetsuro Tamba (Yoshitsune), Hideko Muramatsu, Kunie Tanaka, Kazuo Kitamura, Ichiro Nakatani, Masanori Tomotake, Tokue Hanazawa, Shin Ryuoka, Makiko Hojo, Shoichi Kuwayama, Mutsuhiko Tsurumaru, Akira Tani.

Cast—"In a Cup of Tea" ("Chawan no naka"): Ganemon [Kan-Emon] Nakamura (Kannai), Noboru Nakaya (Shikibu Heinai), Jun Tazaki (Commander of the Guards), Osamu Takizawa, Haruko Sugimura, Ganjiro Nakamura, Seiji Miyaguchi, Kei Sato, Tomoko Naraoka, Shigeru Kemiyama.

A Ninjin Club/Bungei Production for Toho Co., Ltd., in association with Toyo Kogyo Kabushiki Kaisha. Western Electric Mirrophonic recording (possibly encoded with Perspecta Stereophonic Sound). Eastman Color (processed by Tokyo Laboratory, Ltd.). Prints by Toyo Co., Ltd. Tohoscope. Copyright 1965 by Toho Co., Ltd. 164 minutes. Released 1964.

U.S. Version: Released by Continental Distributing, Inc. in subtitled format. A Walter Reade–Sterling Presentation. Re-edited to 125 minutes (eliminating "The Woman of the Snow") after the film's Los Angeles premiere (when Toho International may have been involved). Most current home video versions have restored the missing episode and are presented in the letterboxed format. International Title: *Ghost Stories*. Alternate title (?): *Weird Tales*. Other Versions include: *Kaidan Yukigoro* (1968) and *Aido* (1969) No MPAA rating. Released July 15, 1965.

Lake of Dracula/Chi o suu me (*Bloodsucking Eyes*). Executive Producer, Fumio Tanaka; Director, Michio Yamamoto; Screenplay, Ei Ogawa, Masaru Takesue, suggested by the novel *Dracula* by Bram Stoker; Director of Photography, Rokuro Nishigaki; Music, Riichiro Manabe; Editor, Hisashi Kondo; Art Director, Shigichi Ikuno; Lighting, Kojiro Sato; Assistant to the Director, Yoshisuke Kawasaki; Sound, Toho Recording Centre; Sound Effects, Toho Sound Effects Group. Special Effects Director, Teruyoshi Nakano; Special Effects, Toho Special Effects Group.

Cast: Midori Fujita (Akiko), Choei Takahashi (Dr. Takashi Saki), Sanae Emi (Natsuoke), Mori Kishida (The Stranger), Kaku Takashina, Suji Ohtaki, Tadao Fumi, Mika Katsuragi, Tatsuo Matsushita, Fusako Tachibana, Yasuzo Ogawa, Wataru Ohmae, Mika Katsuragi, Tadao Futami.

A Toho Co., Ltd., Production. Color (processed by Tokyo Laboratory, Ltd.). Panavision. 82 minutes. Released 1971.

U.S. Version: Released by Toho International Co., Ltd., in subtitled format. Dubbed into English and released directly to television by United Productions of America in 1980. A UPA Productions of America presentation. Executive Producer, Henry G. Saperstein. Television title: *The Lake of Dracula*. The television version was edited to 79 minutes, with the ending substantially cut. Alternate titles include: *Japula*, *Dracula's Lust for Blood*, *The Bloodthirsty Eyes* and *Lake of Death*. 79 minutes. No MPAA rating. Released August 1973.

The Last Days of Planet Earth/Nostradamus no dai yogen (*The Great Prophecies of Nostradamus*). Executive Producers, Tomoyuki Tanaka, Osamu Tanaka; Director, Toshio Masuda; Screenplay, Toshio Yasumi, based on an original story by Tsutomu Goto, loosely based on the writings of Michel de Notredame; Director of Photography, Rokuro Nishigaki; Sound, Toho Recording Centre; Sound effects, Toho Sound Effects Group. *Special Effects Unit:* Director, Teruyoshi Nakano; Photography, Motoyoshi Tomioka; Lighting,

Masakuni Morimoto; Art Director, Yasuyuki Inoue; Matte Processing, Kazunobu Sanpei; Optical Photography, Takeshi Miyanishi.

Cast: Tetsuro Tamba (Dr. Nishiyama), Takashi Shimura (Doctor), Akihiko Hirata, Hiroshi Koizumi (Scientists) Toshio Kurosawa (Akira?), So Yamamura, Kaoru Yumi, Yoko Tsukasa.

A Toho Co., Ltd., Production. Color (processed by Tokyo Laboratory, Ltd.) Panavision. 90 minutes (?). Released 1974.

U.S. Version: Released theatrically in Los Angeles, apparently by Toho International, as *Prophecies of Nostradamus*. Whether it was released dubbed, subtitled or in Japanese only is undetermined, as are any additional bookings. Released to television by United Productions of America, Inc., in 1981. A UPA Productions of America Release. Executive producer, Henry G. Saperstein. Copyright 1981 by Toho Co., Ltd. Also known under its U.K. title: *Catastrophe: 1999*. International title: *Prophecies of Nostradamus*. Features stock footage from *The Last War*. 72 minutes. No MPAA rating. Released July 1979.

The Last War/Sekai daisenso (*The Great World War*). Producer, Tomoyuki Tanaka; Director, Shue Matsubayashi; Screenplay, Toshio Yasumi, Takeshi Kimura; Director of Photography, Rokuro Nishigaki; Sound, Toho Recording Centre; Sound Effects, Toho Sound Effects Group. *Special Effects Unit:* Director, Eiji Tsuburaya; Photography, Teisho Arikawa, Motoyoshi Tomioka; Lighting, Kuichiro Kishida; Art Director, Akira Watanabe; Matte Process, Hiroshi Mukoyama; Optical Photography, Taka Yuki, Yukio Manoda.

Cast: Frankie Sakai (Mokichi), Nobuko Otowa (Oyoshi), Akira Takarada (Takano), Yumi Shirakawa (Seiko), Andrew Hughes (Missile Silo Officer), Yuriko Hoshi.

A Toho Co., Ltd., Production. Western Electric Mirrophonic soundtrack, encoded with Perspecta Stereophonic Sound. Eastman Color (processed by Tokyo Laboratory, Ltd.) Tohoscope. 110 minutes. Released October 8, 1961.

U.S. Version: Theatrical release in the United States uncertain. It may have been released in subtitled form by Toho International, released dubbed by Brenco Pictures Corp. (through Allied Artists exchanges), in association with Toho International Co., Ltd., or released directly to U.S. television. Television version, probably issued in 1964-65, is missing all production credits, but does include the song "It's a Small World," with music and lyrics by Richard M. Sherman and Robert B. Sherman. Brenco Version: Executive Producer, Edward L. Alperson; Producer, Stanley Meyer; Executive Director in Charge of Production, Sanezumi Fujimoto; Story, John Meredyth Lucas (?); Editor, Kenneth Wannberg; Sound, Ryder Sound Services, Inc.; prints by Pathe; Dubbing Cast, Paul Frees, others unknown. Running times according to one source vary between 110- and 80-minute versions. No MPAA rating.

Latitude Zero/Ido zero dai sakusen (*Latitude Zero: Big Military Operation*). Executive Producer, Tomoyuki Tanaka; Producer, Don Sharp; Director, Ishiro Honda; Screenplay, Ted Sherdeman (based on his "Latitude Zero" stories); Screenplay Advisor (i.e., Japanese version), Shinichi Sekizawa; Director of Photography, Taiichi Kankura; Music, Akira Ifukube; Editor, Ume Takeda; Lighting, Kiichi Onda; Editor, Ume Takeda; Set Decoration, Takeo Kita; Costume Designers, Kiichi Ichida, Linda Glazman; Sound Recording Director, Masao Fujiyoshi; Sound Effects, Sadamasa Nishimoto, Toho Sound Effects Group; Mixing, Hisashi Shimonaga; Sound, Toho Recording Centre; Assistant Director, Seiji Tani; Production Manager, Yasuaki Sakamoto; Creative Advisor (additional dialog?), Warren Lewis; *Special Effects Unit:* Director, Eiji Tsuburaya; Photography, Teisho Arikawa; Lighting, Kuichiro [Kyuighiro] Kishida; Set Decoration, Akira Watanabe; Optical Photography, Yukio Manoda, Sadao Iizuda; Scene Manipulation, Fumio Nakadai, Motonari Tomioka.

Cast: Joseph Cotten (Capt. Craig McKenzie), Cesar Romero (Dr. Malic), Richard Jaeckel (Perry Lawton), Patricia Medina

(Lucretia), Linda Haynes (Dr. Anne Barton), Akira Takarada (Dr. Ken Tashiro), Masumi Okada (Dr. Jules Masson), Hikaru Kuroki (Kroiga), Mari Nakayama ("Tsuruko" Okada), Tetsu Nakamura (Dr. Okada), Akihiko Hirata (Dr. Sugata), Susamu Kurobe (Chin), Kin Ohmae.

A Toho Co., Ltd., Production. A Don Sharp Productions Presentation. A Japanese/U.S. co-production. Westrex recording System. Eastman Color (processed by Tokyo Laboratory, Ltd.). Tohoscope. 108 minutes. Released July 26, 1969.

U.S. Version: Released by National General Pictures (a division of National General Corp). Prints by Technicolor. Reissued in Japan in 1974, double billed with *Mothra* (q.v.). 95 minutes (possibly 99 minutes; copyright length 106 minutes). MPAA rating: G. Test-screened in Dallas in July 1969. Released December 1970.

The Lost World of Sinbad/Dai tozoku (The Great Thief). Producers, Tomoyuki Tanaka, Kenichiro Tsunoda; Director, Senkichi Taniguchi; Assistant Director, Susumu Takebayashi; Screenplay, Takeshi Kimura, Shinichi Sekizawa; Story, Kikuo Yasumi; Production Manager, Hiroshi Netsu; Director of Photography, Takao Saito; Music, Masaru Sato; Editor, Yoshitami Kuroiwa; Art Director, Takeo Kita; Set Director, Shiro Yamamoto; Costumes, Shotaro Maki; Sound Recording, Shin Takai; Sound Toho Recording Centre; Sound Effects, Hisashi Shimonaga, Toho Sound Effects Group. *Special Effects Unit:* Director, Eiji Tsuburaya; Lighting, Kiichi Kukuda; Art Director, Akira Watanabe; Photography, Teisho Arikawa, Motoyoshi Tomioka; Lighting, Kuichiro Kishida; Matte Process, Hiroshi Mukoyama; Optical Photography, Taka Yuki, Yukio Manoda, Yuichi Manoda, Ryusei Sachi.

Cast: Toshiro Mifune (Sinbad [Sukezaemon, alias "Luzon"]), Ichiro Arishima (Sennin the Wizard), Mie Hama (Sobei), Kumi Mizuno (Miwa), Akiko Wakabayashi (Princess Yaya), Jun Tazaki (Itaka Tsuzuka of the Royal Guards), Eisei Amamoto (Granny the Witch), Little Man Machan (Dwarf), Takashi Shimura (King), Makoto Sato (The Black Pirate), Jun Funato (The Premier), Takashi Shimura (King Raksha), Tadao Nakamara (Ming), Hideo Sunazuka (Bandit), Satoshi Nakamura (Chief Archer), Masanori Mikame, Masashi Ohki, Yutaka Nakayama, Yoshio Kosugi, Nakajiro Tomita, Ko Korino, Tadanori Kusagawa, Junichiro Mukai, Yasuhisa Tsutsumi, Kozo Nomura, Hiroshi Hasegawa, Hidezu Kane, Haruo Suzuki, Masako Shibaki, Akira Shimada, Rokumaru Furukawa, Chiyoko Tanabe, Shin Ibuki, Shoji Ikeda, Mitsuko Kusabue.

A Toho Co., Ltd., Production. Perspecta Stereophonic Sound. Eastman Color (processed by Tokyo Laboratory, Ltd.). Tohoscope. 97 minutes. Released 1963.

U.S. Version: Released by American International Pictures. A James H. Nicholson and Samuel Z. Arkoff Presentation. English-language version, Titra Sound Studios; prints by Pathe. Wide screen process billed as Colorscope. Copyright March 3, 1965, by AIP. Onscreen credits mis-identify co-screenwriter Sekizawa as director of photography. Retitled *Samurai Pirate* after initial engagements, then switched back to *The Lost World of Sinbad*. Announced by AIP as *7th Wonder of Sinbad*. Double billed with *War of the Zombies* (AIP, 1965). Unreleased in the U.K. until 1976. No MPAA rating. 95 minutes. Released March 1965.

Madame White Snake/Byaku fugin no yoren. Executive Producers, Tomoyuki Tanaka, Sir Run Run Shaw; Director, Shiro Toyoda; Screenplay, Toshio Yasumi, based on the Chinese fairy tale "Pai-she Chuan"; Art Director, R. Mitsubayashi; Director of Photography, Mitsuo Muria; Music, Ikuma Dan; Sound, Toho Recording Centre; Sound Effects, Toho Sound Effects Group; Special Effects Director, Eiji Tsuburaya; Special Effects, Toho Special Effects Group.

Cast: Shirley Yamaguchi (Pai Su-Chen), Ryo Ikebe (Hsui Hsien), Kaoru Yachigusa (Buddhist Monk).

A Toho Co., Ltd./Shaw Brothers (H.K.) Ltd., Production. A Japanese-Cantonese co-production. Filmed at Toho Studios. Western

Electric Mirrophonic recording. Eastman Color (processed by Tokyo Laboratory, Ltd.). Academy ratio. 105 minutes. Released 1956.

U.S. Version: Released by Toho International Co., Ltd., in subtitled format. Released in Hong Kong as *Pai-she Chuan* in 1956. Released internationally by Toho in 1960 as *The Bewitched Love of Madame Pai*. Remade as *Pai-she Chuan* (Shaw Brothers; U.S. release, 1963) and is not to be confused with this production. 105 minutes. No MPAA rating. Released 1965.

Man from Planet Alpha. (no credits available)
Cast: (unavailable)
A Toho Co., Ltd., Production. Westrex recording system? Eastman Color? TohoScope? Released 1966-67?
U.S. Version: Undetermined. Listed in several sources, but the very existence of this film is unconfirmed.

Midare karakuri. Director, Susumu Kodama; Sound, Toho Recording Centre; Sound Effects, Toho Sound Effects Group.
Cast: Yasuke Masuda, Hirako Shiro.
A Toho Co., Ltd., Production. Color (processed by Tokyo Laboratory, Ltd.) Panavision (?). Running time undetermined. Released 1979.
U.S. Version: Distributor undetermined.

Monster Zero/Kaiju daisenso (*The Giant Monster War*). Producer, Tomoyuki Tanaka; Executive Producers, Henry G. Saperstein, Reuben Bercovitch; Director, Ishiro Honda; Screenplay, Shinichi Sekizawa; Director of Photography, Hajime Koizumi; Music, Akira Ifukube; Editor, Ryohei Fujii; Art Director, Takeo Kita; Gaffer, Shoichi Kojima; Sound Recording, Ataru Konuma; Sound Mixing, Hiroshi Mukoyama; Sound Arrangement; Takashi [Hisashi?] Shimonaga; Sound Effects, Sadamasa Nishimoti, Toho Sound Effects Group; Sound, Toho Recording Centre; Assistant Director, Koji Kajita; Production Managers, Masao Suzuki, Tadshi Koike. *Special Effects Unit:* Director, Eiji Tsuburaya; Photography, Teisho Arikawa, Mototaka Tomioka; Optical Photography, Yukio Manoda, Sadeo Iizuda [Izuka]; Assistant to Tsuburaya, Teruyoshi Nakano; Art Direction, Akira Watanabe; Lighting, Kyuighiro Kishida; Scene Manipulation, Fumio Nakadai; Suit Design, Teizo Toshimitsu.

Cast: Akira Takarada (Astronaut K. Fuji), Nick Adams (Astronaut F. Glenn), Kumi Mizuno (Namikawa), Jun Tazaki (Dr. Sakurai), Akira Kubo (Tetsuo), Keiko Sawai (Haruno Fuji), Yoshio Tsuchiya (Controller of Planet X), Yoshibumi Tajima (General), Haruo Nakajima (Gojira), Goro Naya., Takamaru Sasaki, Noriko Sengoku, Toru Ibuki, Kazuo Suzuki, Yasuhida Tsutsumi, Masaaki Taghibana, Kamayuki Tsubono, Somamasa Matsumoto, Takuzo Kumagaya, Yoshizo Tatake, Gen Shimizu, Mitzuo Tsuda, Hirgo Kirino, Hideki Furukawa, Rioji Shimizu, Toki Shiozawa, Yutaka Oka, Shoichi Hirose, Minoru Ito, Rinsaku Ogata, Fuyuki Murakami, Koshi Uno, Tadashi Okabe.

A Toho Co., Ltd./Henry G. Saperstein Enterprises Production. Westrex recording system. Color by Tokyo Developing Labs. Tohoscope. 96 minutes. Released December 19, 1965.

U.S. Version: Distributed by Maron Films Ltd. A United Productions of America Presentation. Postproduction Supervisor, S. Richard Krown; Sound Recording, Glen Glenn Sound; Voice characterizations, Jack Grimes (for Akira Kubo), Marvin Miller (Akira Takarada, many others), additional cast undetermined; prints by Consolidated Film Industries. Copyright 1966 by Benedict Pictures Corporation. Includes stock footage from *Rodan* (1956), *Mothra* (1961) and *Ghidrah: The Three-Headed Monster* (1964). Double billed with *The War of the Gargantuas* (q.v.). International Title: *Invasion of Astro-Monster*. Television and video title: *Godzilla vs. Monster Zero*, with new title credits via video supering. Reissued in Japan in 1971 (re-edited to 74 minutes) as *Kaiju daisenso Kingughidorah tai Gojira (The Giant Monster War: King Ghidorah Against Godzilla)*. 92 minutes. MPAA rating: G. Released July 29, 1970.

Moro no Ichimatsu yurei dochu. Executive Producer, Tomoyuki Tanaka; Director, Kozo Saeki; Sound, Toho Recording Centre; Sound Effects, Toho Sound Effects Group. Cast: Frankie Sakai, Kaoru Yachigusa. A Toho Co., Ltd., Production. Western Electric Mirrophonic recording (encoded with Perspecta Stereophonic Sound). Black and white(?). TohoScope. Running time undetermined. Released 1959.

U.S. Version: Distributor, if any, is undetermined. International title: *Ishimatsu Travels with Ghosts.*

Mothra/Mosura. Producer, Tomoyuki Tanaka; Director, Ishiro Honda; Screenplay, Shinichi Sekizawa; Original Story, Shinichiro Nakamura, Takehido Fukunaga, Yoshi Hotta, as published in *Asahi Shimbun*; Art Directors, Takeo Kita, Kimei Abe; Director of Photography, Hajime Koizumi; Editor, Ichiji Taira; Music, Yuji Koseki; Recording, Shoiehi [Soichi] Fujinawa, Masanobu Miyazaki; Lighting, Toshio Takashima; Production manager, Shin Morita; Assistant Director, Masaji Nanagase [Nonagase]; Sound, Toho Recording Centre; Sound Effects, Toho Sound Effects Group. *Special Effects Unit:* Director, Eiji Tsuburaya; Photography, Teisho Arikawa; Art Direction, Akira Watanabe; Optical Photography, Yukio Manoda; Production Manager, Kan Marita [Narita]; Lighting, Kuichiro Kishida; Matte Work, Hiroshi Mukouyama.

Cast: Frankie Sakai ("Bulldog" Tsinchan [Junichiro Fukuda]), Hiroshi Koizumi (Dr. Chujo [Shinichi] Nakazo), Ken Uehara (Dr. Haradawa), Kyoko Kagawa (Photographer Michi Hanamura), Jerry Ito (Clark Nelson), Emi Ito and Yumi Ito [The Peanuts] (Mothra's Priestesses), Takashi Shimura (News Editor), Akihiko Hirata (Doctor), Yoshibumi Tajima (Military Advisor), Akihiro Tayama (Shiro Nakazo), Andrew Hughes (Roslican Official), Kenji Sahara (Helicopter Pilot), Robert Dunham (Roslican), Tetsu Nakamura (Nelson's Henchman), Haruo Nakajima (Mothra?), Seizaburo Kawazu, Yoshio Kosugi, Yasushi Yamamoto, Haruya Kato, Ko Mishima, Shoichi Hirose, Koro Sakurai, Hiroshi Iwamoto, Mitsuo Tsuda, Masamitsu Tayma, Toshio Miura, Tadashi Okabe, Akira Wakamatsu, Johnny Yuseph, Obel Wyatt, Harold Conway, Akira Yamada, Koji Uno, Wataru Ohmae, Toshihiko Furuta, Keisuke Matsuyama, Yoshiyuki Kamimura, Katsumi Tezuka, Takeo Nagashima, Mitsuo Matsumoto, Shinpei Mitsu, Kazuo Higata, Shigeo Kato, Rinsaku Ogata, Yutaka Okada, Arai Hayamizu, Hiroyuki Satake, Kazuo Imai, Yoshio Hatton, Hiroshi Akitsu, Akio Kusama.

A Toho Co., Ltd., Production. Western Electric Mirrophonic soundtrack, encoded with Perspecta Stereophonic Sound. Eastman Color (processed by Far East Laboratory, Ltd.). Tohoscope. 101 minutes (?). Released July 30, 1961.

U.S. Version: Released by Columbia Pictures Corporation. Producer, David D. Horne; Director, Lee Kressel; English Dialog, Robert Myerson; Sound, Titra Sound Studios; prints by Pathe. Copyright March 1, 1962 (in notice 1961), by Columbia Pictures Corp. Double billed with *The Three Stooges in Orbit* (Columbia, 1962). English-language credits have long misidentified actors to the roles played (Koizumi was listed as playing Michi, Ken Uehara billed in Koizumi's role, etc.). The above credits are correct. Working title: *Daikaiju Masura (Giant Monster Mothra).* In Japan, the Peanuts' characters are billed as "The Little Beauties." Reissued in Japan in 1974 running 62 minutes, and double billed with *Latitude Zero* (q.v.). 88 minutes. No MPAA rating. Released May 10, 1962.

My Friend Death/Yurei Hanjo-ki. Director, Kozo Saheki; Screenplay, Naoshi Izumo; Director of Photography, Hideo Ito; Music, H. Matsui; Sound, Toho Recording Centre; Sound Effects, Toho Sound Effects Group.

Cast: Frankie Sakai, Kyoko Kagawa, Ichiro Arishima, Kingaro Yanagiya.

A Toho Co., Ltd., Production. Western Electric Mirrophonic recording (encoded with Perspecta Stereophonic Sound?). Black and white (processed by Tokyo Laboratory, Ltd.). TohoScope. 95 minutes. Released 1961.

U.S. Version: Released by Toho International Co., Ltd., in subtitled format. 95 minutes. No MPAA rating. Released 1961.

The Mysterians/Chikyu Boeigun (*Earth Defense Force*). Producer, Tomoyuki Tanaka; Director, Ishiro Honda; Screenplay, Takeshi Kimura; Adapter (?), Shigeru Kayama; Original Story, Jojiro Okami; Director of Photography, Hajime Koizumi; Lighting, Kyuichiro [Kuichiro] Kishida; Art Direction, Terukaii Abe; Editor, Hiroichi Iwashita; Music, Akira Ifukube; Sound Recording, Masanobu Myazaki; Sound, Toho Dubbing Theatre; Sound Effects, Ichiro Minawa, Toho Sound Effects Group; Production Manager, Yasuaki Sakamoto; Assistant Director, Koji Kajita. *Special Effects Unit:* Director, Eiji Tsuburaya; Photography, Teisho Arikawa; Art Direction, Akira Watanabe; Optical Photography, Hidesaburo Araki; Matte Process, Hiroshi Mukoyama; Light Effects, Masao Shiroda.

Cast: Kenji Sahara (Joji Atsumi), Yumi Shirakawa (Etsuke Shiraishi), Momoko Kochi (Hiroko), Akihiko Hirata (Ryoichi Shiraishi), Takashi Shimura (Dr. Adachi), Susumu Fujita (Commander Morita), Hisaya Itoh (Captain Seki), Yoshio Kosugi (Commander Sugimoto), Fuyuki Murakami (Dr. Kawanami), Minosuke Yamada (General Hammamoto), Haruo Nakajima (Mogera), Yoshio Tsuchiya (Alien Commander), Harold S. Conway (American Scientist), Tetsu Nakamura, Hehachiro Okawa, Takeo Ikawa, Haruya Kato, Senkichi Omura, Yutaka Sada, Hideo Mihara, Rikie Sanuo, Soji Oikata, Mitsuo Tsuda, Ken Imaizumi, Shin Otomo, Jiro Kumagi, Akio Kusuma, Akio [Shoichi?] Hirose, Tadao Nakamaru, Kaneyuki Tsubono, Rinsaku Ogata, Yasuhiro Sigenobu, George Farness, Katsumi Tezuka.

A Toho Co., Ltd., Production. Western Electric Mirrophonic recording (encoded with Perspecta Stereophonic Sound). Eastman Color (processed by Toyo [sic?] Development, possibly Tokyo Laboratory, Ltd.). Tohoscope. 89 minutes. Released December 28, 1957.

U.S. Version: Released by Metro-Goldwyn-Mayer Pictures. An RKO Radio Pictures, Inc., Presentation. A Loew's, Inc., Release. English Language Supervisor, Jay Bonafield; English Dialog, Peter Riethof, Carlos Montalban; prints by Metrocolor (though possibly Technicolor); Perspecta Stereophonic Sound. Copyright April 30, 1959 (in notice 1958), by RKO Teleradio Pictures, Inc., a division of RKO General, Inc. Originally purchased by RKO, who sold the picture to Loew's Inc. Wide screen process billed as Wide Screen and CinemaScope in the United States. Double billed with *Watusi* (M-G-M, 1959). Reissued in Japan in 1978. 87 minutes. No MPAA rating. Released May 15, 1959.

Onibaba (*The Witch*). Executive Producers, Hisao Itoya, Setsuo Noto, Tamotsu Minato; Producer, Toshio Konya; Director, Screenplay, Art Director, Kaneto Shindo; Director of Photography, Kiyomi Kuroda; Music, Hikaru [Mitsu] Hayashi; Editor, Toshio Enoki.

Cast: Nobuko Otowa (The Mother), Jitsuko Yoshimura (The Daughter-in-Law), Kei Sato (Hachi), Jukichi Uno (The Warrior), Taiji Tonomura (Ushi, the Merchant), Tatsuya Nakadai (Onimasa).

A Kindai Eiga Kyokai (Kindai Movie Co., Ltd.)–Nihon Eiga Shineha (Tokyo Eiga Co.) Production. Distributed by Toho Co., Ltd. Possibly encoded with Perspecta Stereophonic Sound. Black and white. Tohoscope. 104 minutes. Released 1964.

U.S. Version: Released by Toho International Co., Ltd., in subtitled format. Also known as *The Hole*, *The Demon* and *Devil Woman*. The home video version is letterboxed (and slightly squeezed as well). 104 minutes. No MPAA rating. Released February 4, 1965.

Pinku Redei no Katsudoshashin. Director, Tom Kotani.

Cast: Mitsuyo Nemoto, Keiko Masuda.

A Toho Co., Ltd., Production. Westrex recording system. Color (processed by Tokyo Laboratory, Ltd.). Panavision. Running time undetermined. Released 1978.

U.S. Version: Distributor, if any, is undetermined. Also known as *The Pink Ladies Motion Picture*. The characters were later adapted for the U.S. teleseries "The Pink Ladies and Jeff," co-starring Jeff Altman.

Portrait of Hell/Jigokuhen. Executive Producer, Tomoyuki Tanaka; Producer, Tatsuo Matsuoko; Director, Shiro Toyoda; Screenplay, Toshio Yasumi [Yasami] (based on the "Tokyo nichi nichi" serial "Jigokuhen," by Ryunosuke Akutagawa); Director of Photography, Kazuo Yamada; Music, Yasushi Akutagawa; Art Director, Shinobu Muraki; Sound, Toho Recording Centre; Sound Effects, Toho Sound Effects Group.
Cast: Kinnosuke Nakamura (Lord Hosokawa), Tatsuya Nakadai (Yoshihide, the Artist), Yoko Naito (Yoshika, His Daughter), Shun [Toshio] Oide, Hideo Yamamoto, Kichiro Nakamura, Masanobu Okubo, Masao Yamafuki, Ikio Sawamara, Kumeko Otoba.
A Toho Co., Ltd., Production. Westrex recording system. Eastmancolor (processed by Tokyo Laboratory, Ltd.). Panavision. 95 minutes. Released September 1969
U.S. Version: Released by Toho International Co., Ltd., in subtitled format. Reissued in April 1972 by Toho International. Alternate titles: *A Story of Hell* and *The Hell Screen*. 91 minutes. No MPAA rating. Released November 18, 1969.

Rodan/Sora no daikaiaju Radon (*The Sky's Giant Monsters: Rodan*). Producer, Tomoyuki Tanaka; Director, Ishiro Honda; Screenplay, Takeshi Kimura, Takeo Murata; Story, Takashi Kuronomura [Kuronuma]; Director of Photography, Isamu Ashida; Art Direction, Takeo Kita; Sound, Masanobu Miyazaki, Toho Dubbing Theatre; Sound Effects, Toho Sound Effects Group; Lighting, Sigeru Mori; Music, Akira Ifukube. *Special Effects Unit:* Director, Eiji Tsuburaya; Art Direction, Akira Watanabe; Lighting, Masao Shiroda; Optical Photography, Hiroshi Mukoyama.
Cast: Kenji Sahara (Shigeru), Yumi Shirakawa (Kyo), Akihiko Hirata (Dr. Kashiwagi), Akio Kobori (Nishimura), Yasuko Nakata (Young Woman), Monosuke [Minosuke] Yamada (Ohsaki), Yoshibumi Tajima (Izeki), Kiyoharu Ohnaka.
A Toho Co., Ltd., Production. Western Electric Mirrophonic soundtrack (encoded with Perspecta Stereophonic Sound?). Color (processed by Far East Laboratories, Ltd.). Academy ratio. Released December 26, 1956.
U.S. Version: Released by Distributors Corporation of America. A King Brothers Productions, Inc., Presentation. Producers, Frank King, Maurice King; Narration (i.e., English Dialog), David Duncan; Dubbing Cast, Paul Frees, Keye Luke, others unknown; Editor, Robert S. Eisen; Sound Effects Editor, Anthony Carras; Looping Editor, Frank O'Neill; Editorial Assistant, Joyce Sage; Administration, Maurice King; Public Relations, Herman King; prints by Technicolor. Advertised as *Rodan the Flying Monster*, though film's onscreen title is as listed above. Monster footage from *Rodan* appeared in the U.S. production *Valley of the Dragons* (Columbia, 1961). Copyright 1956 by Distributors Corp. of America. 79 minutes. No MPAA rating. Released August 1957.

Sayonara Jiyupeta (*Sayonara Jupiter*). Executive Producers, Tomoyuki Tanaka, Sakyo Komatsu; Associate Producers, Fumio Tanaka, Shiro Fujiwara; Director, Koji Hashimoto; Screenplay and "Chief Director," Sakyo Komatsu, based on his novel; Production Designer, Heio Takanaka; Continuity, Nubuo Ogawa; Editor, Masaji Ohima; Music, Kentaro Haneda; Songs—"Voyager"/"The Blue Ship" by Yumi Matsutoya; Incidental Songs—"Sayonara Jupiter"/"Four Seasons of the Earth" by Jiro Sugita; Soundtrack album available on Toshiba/EMI Records, licensed through Toho Music Publishing Co., Ltd.; Sound, Toho Recording Centre; Sound Effects, Toho Sound Effects Group; Production Manager, Kishu Morichi. *Special Effects Unit:* Director, Koichi Kawakita; Assistant Director, Kyotaka Matsumoto; Assitant to the Director, Kenji Suzuki; Director of Photography, Kenichi Eguchi;

Lighting, Kaoru Saito; Wire Works, Koji Matsumoto; Miniature Pyrotechniques, Tadaaki Watanabe, Mamoru Kume; Production Design, Studio Nue.

Cast: Tomokazu Miura (Eiji Honda), Rachel Hugget (Millicent Wilem), Diane Dangely (Maria Baṣehart), Miyuki Ono (Anita), Akihiko Hirata (Ryutaro Inoue), Hisaya Morishige (President of Earth Federation), Masumi Okada (Mohamed Manshur), Paul Taiga (Peter), Kim Bass (Hooker), Marc Pinonnat (Carlos Arnez), Ron Irwin (Hoger Kinn), William H. Tapier (Edward Webb).

A Toho Co., Ltd., Production. Dolby Stereo. Color (processed by Tokyo Laboratory, Ltd.). Panavision. 140 minutes. Released October 1983.

U.S. Version: Unreleased in the United States as of this writing. International Title: *Bye Bye Jupiter*, released March 1984 by Toho International Co., Ltd.

The Secret of the Telegian/Denso ningen (*The Electrically-Transmitted Man*). Executive Producer, Tomoyuki Tanaka; Director, Jun Fukuda; Screenplay, Shinichi Sekizawa; Director of Photography, Kazuo Yamada; Art Director, Kyoe Hamagami; Lighting, Tsuruzo Nishikawa; Editor, Ichiji Taira; Assistant Producer, Boku Morimoto; Assistant Director, Taku Nagano; Music, Shigeru Ikeno; Sound Recording, Yoshio Nishikawa, Masanobu Miyazaki; Sound, Toho Recording Centre; Sound Effects, Toho Sound Effects Group. *Special Effects Unit:* Director, Eiji Tsuburaya; Art Director, Akira Watanabe; Photography, Teisho Arikawa; Lighting, Kuichiro Kishida; Matte Process, Hiroshi Mukoyama; Optical Photography, Hinsaburo Araki.

Cast: Koji Tsuruta (Kirioka), Tadao Nakamura (Former Corporal Sudo, alias Goro Nakamoto), Akihiko Hirata (Detective Kobayashi), Yumi Shirakawa (Akiko), Seizaburo Kawazu (Onishi), Yoshio Tsuchiya (Detective), Yoshibumi Tajima (Takashi), Senkichi Omura (Fisherman), Eisei Amamoto (Bodyguard), Sachio Sakai, Takamaru Sasaki, Fuyuki Murakami, Ikio Sawamura, Sachio Otomo, Ren Yamamoto, Fumito Matsuo, Kiyomi Mizunoya, Tsuruko Mano, Yutaka Sada, Hiroo Kirino, Shiro Tsuchiya, Tatsuo Matsumura, Kyoro Sakurai.

A Toho Co., Ltd., Production; Western Electric Mirrophonic recording, encoded with Perspecta Stereophonic Sound. Eastman color (processed by Far East Laboratories, Ltd.). Tohoscope. 85 minutes. Released April 10, 1960.

U.S. Version: Never released theatrically in the United States. North American theatrical rights purchased by Herts-Lion International Corp., who released the picture directly to American television instead (with TV prints in black and white). Announced as *The Telegians* and *Secret File of the Telegian*. 75 minutes (some English-language prints run 85 minutes). No MPAA rating. Trade-screened in Los Angeles July 1961.

Secret Scrolls Part I/Yaguy Bugeicho. Producer, Tomoyuki Tanaka; Director, Hiroshi Inagaki; Screenplay, Hiroshi Inagaki, Takeshi Kimura, based on the novel *Yaguy Bugeichi* by Kosuke Gomi; Art Directors, Takeo Kita, Hiroshi Ueda; Director of Photography, Tadashi Iimura; Music, Akira Ifukube; Recording, Yoshio Nishikawa; Sound, Toho Dubbing Theatre; Sound Effects, Toho Sound Effects Group.

Cast: Toshiro Mifune (Tasaburo), Koji Tsuruta (Senshiro), Yoshiko Kuga (Yuhime), Kyoko Kagawa (Oki), Mariko Okada (Rika), Denjiro Okochi (Lord Yagyu), Jotaro Togami (Jubei), Akihiko Hirata (Tomonori), Senjaku Namamura (Matajuro), Hanshiro Iwai (Iyemitsu), Eijiro Tono (Fugetsusai).

A Toho Co., Ltd., Production. Western Electric Mirrophonic recording (encoded with Perspecta Stereophonic Sound). Agfacolor (processed by Tokyo Laboratory, Ltd.). TohoScope. 106 minutes. Released 1957.

U.S. Version: Released by Toho International Co., Ltd., in subtitled format. Sequel: *Secret Scrolls Part II*. Also known as *Yagyu Secret Scrolls*. 106 minutes. No MPAA rating. Released October 11, 1967.

Secret Scrolls Part II/Ninjutsu. Producer, Tomoyuki Tanaka; Director, Hiroshi

Inagaki; Screenplay, Hiroshi Inagaki, Takuhei Wakao, based on the novel *Yagyu Bugeicho* by Kosuke Gomi; Art Directors, Takeo Kita, Hiroshi Ueda; Director of Photography, Asaichi Nakai; Music, Akira Ifukube; Recording, Yoshio Nishikawa; Sound, Toho Dubbing Theatre; Sound Effects, Toho Sound Effects Group.

Cast: Toshiro Mifune (Tasaburo), Koji Tsuruta (Senshiro), Nobuke Otawa (Princess), Jotaro Togami (Jubei), Senjaku Namamura (Matajuro), Hanshiro Iwai (Iyemitsu), Yoshiko Kuga (Yuhime), Marko Ikada (Rika), Denjiro Okochi (Lord Yagyu), Kyoki Kagawa (Oki), Akihiko Hirata (Tomonori).

A Toho Co., Ltd., Production. Western Electric Mirrophonic recording (encoded with Perspecta Stereophonic Sound). Agfacolor (processed by Tokyo Laboratory, Ltd.). TohoScope. 106 minutes. Released 1958.

U.S. Version: Released by Toho International Co., Ltd., in subtitled format. Also released in Japan as *Soryu hiken*. A sequel to *Secret Scrolls Part I* (Toho, 1957). 106 minutes. No MPAA rating. Released May 22, 1968.

Shogun Assassin/Kosure Ookami – Sanzu no Kawa no Ubagurama. Producers, Shintaro Katsu, Hisaharu Matsubara; Director, Kenji Misumi; Screenplay, Kazuo Koike; Story, Kazuo Koike, Goseki Kojima; Director of Photography, Chishi Makiura; Art Director, Akira Naito; Editor, Toskio Taniguchi; Sound, Toho Special Effects Group; Sound, Toho Recording Centre; Sound Effects, Toho Sound Effects Group.

Cast: Tomisaburo Wakayama (Itto [Lone Wolf]), Kayo Matsuo (Supreme Ninja Sayaka), Shin Kishida, Shoji Kabayashi, Minoru Ohki (Masters of Death), Akihiro Tomikawa (Daigaro), Mori Kishida, Shogen Arata, Reiko Kasahara, Yukari Wakayama, Yuriko Mishima.

A Katsu Production Co., Ltd./Toho Co., Ltd., Production. Color (processed by Tokyo Laboratory, Ltd.). Panavision. 86 minutes. Released 1972.

U.S. Version: Released by New World Pictures. A David Weisman and Peter Shanaberg Presentation. Executive Producer, Peter Shanaberg; Producer, David Weisman; Director, Robert Houston; Screenplay, Robert Houston, David Weisman; Associate Producers, Larry Franciose, Michael Maiello, Albert Ellis, Jr., Joseph Ellis; Music, W. Michael Lewis, Mark Lindsay, performed by the Wonderland Philharmonic; Soloists, W. Michael Lewis, Mark Lindsay, Marc Singer, Laine Cook, Robert Houston; Overture Composer and Conductor, Robert Houston; Music Producer, Mark Lindsay; Recording, Mixing and Re-recording, Samuel Goldwyn Studios (Hollywood); First Engineer, Paul McKenny; Second Engineer, Richard Gibbons; Technical Consultant, Ed Romano; Musical Coordinator, Michael Maiello; Psycho-acoustics, Malcom Cecil, courtesy of Centaur Studios; Supervising Sound Editor, Joe Percy; Sound Editor, Steve Nelson; Sound, Tim Holland, Val Kuklowsky; Assistant Sound Editor, Becky Nauert; Dialog Editor, Michael Minkler; Editor, Lee Percy; Sound Effects Recording, Courtney-Courtney Goodin; Budget-Accounting Coordinators, Larry Franciose; Titles, Jim Evans, Bill Evans, Gregory Boone; Production Assistants, Bill Evans, Marguerite Lucas; Opticals, Consolidated Film Industries; Acknowledgments, Andy Kuehn, Tetsuzo Ueda, Steve Corning, Mata Yamamoto, Dan Davis, Kaleidoscope Films, Bob Brent, Masa Tazuki, Igor Dimont, Morrie Eisenmann, Nelson Lyon, David Geffen; Voice Characterizations, Lamont Johnson (Lone Wolf), Gibran Evans (Daigaro), Marshall Efron, Sandra Bernhard, Vic Davis, Lennie Weinrib, Lainie Cook, Sam Weisman, Mark Lindsay, Robert Houston, David Weisman. Copyright 1980 by Baby Cart Productions. Prints by Metrocolor. Dolby Stereo. Includes ten to twelve minutes of stock footage from *Sword of Vengeance* (Toho, 1972). The second in the "Itto" series. The title of the film is sometimes given as *Kozure Ohkmi n. 2* and *Baby Cart at the River Styx*. 90 minutes. MPAA rating: R. Released November 11, 1980.

Silence Has No Wings/Tobenai Chinmoko. Director, Kasuo Kurobi; Screenplay, Kasuo Kurobi, Yasu Matsukawa, Hisaya Iwasa; Director of Photography, Tatsuo Suzuki; Music, Teizo Matsumura; Sound, Toho Recording Centre; Sound Effects, Toho Sound Effects Group.

Cast: Mariko Kaga; Fumio Watanabe, Hiroyuki Nagato.

An Eiga Shinsha Production for Toho Co., Ltd. Westrex recording system. Color (processed by Tokyo Laboratory, Ltd.). TohoScope. 110 minutes. Released 1966.

U.S. Version: Released by Toho International Co., Ltd., format undetermined. 100 minutes. No MPAA rating. Released 1967.

Son of Godzilla/Kaiju shima no kessen: Gojira no musuko (*Monster Island's Decisive Battle: Son of Godzilla*). Producer, Tomoyuki Tanaka; Director, Jun Fukuda; Screenplay, Shinichi Sekizawa, Kazue Shiba; Director of Photography, Kazuo Yamada; Music, Masaru Sato; Art Director, Takeo Kita; Editor, Ryohei Fujii; Sound Recordists, Shin Tokei, Toshinari Ban; Sound, Toho Recording Centre; Sound Effects, Hisashi Shimonaga, Toho Sound Effects Group. *Special Effects Unit:* Director, Eiji Tsuburaya; Photography, Teisho Arikawa, Motonari Tomioka; Optical Photography, Yukio Manoda, Sadao Iizuda; Art Director, Akira Watanabe; Lighting, Kyuighiro Kishida; Scene Manipulation, Fumio Nakadai.

Cast: Tadeo Takashima (Dr. Kusumi), Akira Kubo (Goro Masaki), Beverly [Bibari] Maeda (Reiko [Saeko] Matsumiya), Akihiko Hirata (Fujisaki), Yoshio Tsuchiya (Furukawa), Kenji Sahara (Morio), Kenichiro Maruyama (Ozawa), Seishiro Kuno (Tashiro), Yasuhiko Saijo (Suzuki), Susumu Kurobe (Aircraft Captain), Kazuo Suzuki (Pilot), Wataru Omae (Radio Operator), Chotaro Togane (Surveyor), Kiyoji Onaka and Haruo Nakajima (Gojira), Little Man Machan (Minya).

A Toho Co. Ltd., Production. Eastman Color (processed by Tokyo Laboratory, Ltd.). Tohoscope. 86 minutes. Released December 16, 1967.

U.S. Version: Never released theatrically in the United States. Released to U.S. television by AIP-TV (American International Pictures Television) in 1969. A James H. Nicholson and Samuel Z. Arkoff Presentation. Voice characterizations, Jack Grimes (for Akira Kubo), George Takei? (Tadeo Takashima), Paul Frees (?); prints by Berkey-Pathe. Copyright 1967 by Toho Co., Ltd. Released theatrically in the U.K. running 71 minutes. Reissued in Japan in 1973 (re-edited to 65 minutes). 82 minutes. No MPAA rating.

Submersion of Japan/Tidal Wave/Nippon chiubotsu (*The Submersion of Japan*). Executive Producer, Tomoyuki Tanaka; Associate Producer, Osamu Tanaka; Director, Shiro Moritani; Screenplay, Shinobu Hashimoto (based on the novel by Sakyo Komatsu); Directors of Photography, Hiroshi Murai, Daisaka Kimura; Music, Masaru Sato; Art Director, Yoshiro Muraki; Sound, Toshio Ban, Toho Recording Centre; Sound Effects, Toho Sound Effects Group; Lighting, Kojiro Sato; Assistant Director, Koji Hashimoto; Editor, Michiko Ikeda; Stillman, Yoshinori Ishizuki; Production Manager, Takehide Morichi; Technical Advisers, Hitoshi Takeuchi, Yorihiko Oosaki, Noriyuki Nasu, Akira Suwa. *Special Effects Unit:* Director, Teruyoshi Nakano; Director of Photography, Motoyoshi Tomioka; Set Designer, Yasuyuki Inoue; Lighting, Masakuni Morimoto; Optical Photography, Takeshi Miyanishi; Matte Processing, Kazunobu Sampei; Miniature Set Operation, Fumio Nakadai, Koji Matsumoto; Assistant Director, Yoshio Tabuchi, Tadaaki Watanabe; Stillman, Kazukiyo Tanaka; Unit Manager, Keisuke Shinoda.

Cast: Kenji Kobayashi (Dr. Tanaka Tadokoro), Hiroshi Fujioka (Toshio Onoda), Tetsuro Tamba (Prime Minister Yamoto), Ayumi Ishida (Reiko), Shogo Shimada (Prince Watari), Nubuo Nakamura (Australian Ambassador), Andrew Hughes (Australian Prime Minister), Tadao Nakamura, Yusuke Takita, Isao Natsuyagi, Hideaki Nitiani.

A Toho Co., Ltd., Production. Color

processed by Tokyo Laboratory, Ltd.). Panavision. Westrex Recording System. Copyright 1973 by Toho Co., Ltd. 140 minutes. Released 1973.

U.S. Version: Released by New World Pictures. A New World Pictures and Max E. Youngstein Production, in association with Toho International Co., Ltd. A Roger Corman/Max E. Youngstein Presentation. Executive Producer, Roger Corman; Producer, Max E. Youngstein; Director and Dialogue, Andrew Meyer; Director of Photography, Eric Saarinen; Sound, Ryder Sound Services, Inc. (?); Panavision. Processing and prints by Metrocolor. Released in the United States by New World simultaneously uncut and in subtitled format as *Submersion of Japan* (with no MPAA rating) and in a severely recut, dubbed version with added footage (*Tidal Wave*). An international version was also released by Toho International, running 113 minutes. Copyright 1975 by Toho Co., Ltd. Announced as a Daiei production; property acquired by Toho after the former's bankruptcy., Followed by a Japanese teleseries of the same name, produced by the Tokyo Broadcasting Network (TBS). Running time of recut American edition: 90 minutes. MPAA rating: PG. Released May 1975.

Additional Cast for U.S. Version: Lorne Greene (U.S. Ambassador Warren Richards), Rhonda Leigh Hopkins (Fran), John Fujioka (Narita), Marvin Miller, Susan Sennett, Ralph James, Phil Roth, Cliff Pellow, Joseph J. [Joe] Dante (Voice Characterizations).

Sword of Vengeance/Kosure ookami – ko wo kashi ude kashi tsukatsuru. Executive Producer, Shintaro Katsu; Director, Kenji Misumi; Screenplay, Kazuo Koike; Story, Kazuo Koike, Goyu Kojima; Director of Photography, Chishi Makiura; Art Director, Yoshinobu Nishioka; Lighting, Hiroshi Mima; Editor, Toshio Taniguchi; Music, Eiken Sakurai; Sound Recordist, Tsuchitaro Hayashi; Sound, Toho Recording Centre; Sound Effects, Toho Sound Effects Group; Special Effects, Toho Special Effects Group.

Cast: Tomisaburo Wakayama (Itto), Akihiro Tomikawa (Daigaro), Goh Kato, Yuko Hama, Isao Yamagatu, Michitaro Mizushima, Ichiro Nakaya, Sayoko Kato, Daigo Kusano, Tomoko Mayama, Fumio Watanabe, Shigeru Tsuyuguchi, Yunosuke Ito, Yomiso Kato, Asao Uchida, Keiko Fujita, Sanburo Date.

A Katsu Production Co., Ltd./Toho Co., Ltd., Production. Color (processed by Tokyo Laboratory, Ltd.). Panavision. Copyright 1972 by Katsu Production Co., Ltd. 83 minutes. Released 1972.

U.S. Version: Released by Toho International Co., Ltd., in subtitled format. Reissued in English-dubbed version in August 1983 by Columbia Pictures Industries, Inc., as *Lightning Swords of Death*, with prints by Metrocolor and an MPAA rating of "R." Ten to twelve minutes of footage were later incorporated into the next film in the series, *Shogun Assassin*. 83 minutes. No MPAA rating. Released August 1973.

Tenamonya yurei dochu. Producers, Shin Watanabe, Tadahito Gomyo; Director, Shue Matsubayashi; Screenplay, Ryozu Kasahara, Ryuji Sawada, based on the story by Toshio Kagawa; Art Director, Takashi Matsuyama; Director of Photography, Kiyoshi Hasegawa; Editor, Shuichi Ioihara; Music, Tetsuaki Hagiwara; Recording, Fumio Yanoguchi; Sound, Toho Recording Centre; Sound Effects, Toho Sound Effects Group.

Cast: Makoto Fujita (Anka-ke no Tokijiro), Minoru Shiraki (Chinnem), Yumiko Nogawa (Yuki), Tomoko Kei (Koharu Hakata), Hamime Hana (Shunen), Kei Tani (Masaie Kagami), Senri Sakurai (Jun-an), Ichiro Zaitsu (Takejuro Miki), Ryo Tamura (Seinoshim Kondo), Yu Fujiki (Hyobe Kuroiwa), Toshoiaki Minami (Nezumikozo Jirokichi), Ryoichi Tamagawa (Tadanosuke Moriyama), Chosuke Ikarizy (Doemon Togashi), Cha Kato (Chanosuke Kato), Bu Takagi (Butaro Takagi), Koji Nakamoto (Konin Nakamoto), Chu Arai (Chuzo Arai), Nock Yokoyama (Sukkara Kanbe), Fuck Yokoyama (Kinta), Panch Yokoyama (Hansuke), Tatsuo (Genzo Osugi), Sanpei Taira (Tobe), Ikio Sawamura (Hachirobe), Shozo Nanbu

(Hanpeita Katsuragi), Takashi Akiyama (Call Man), Tetsuo Hara (Pack Horse Driver), Kazuo Kuwabara (Visitor to Theatre).
A Takarazuka Eiga Production. A Toho Co., Ltd., Presentation. Westrex recording system. Eastman Color (processed by Tokyo Laboratory, Ltd.). TohoScope. 90 minutes. Released 1967.
U.S. Version: Distributor, if any, is undetermined. International title: *Tenamonya: Ghost Journey*. Alternate title: *Ghost of Two Travelers at Tenamonya*. Third of a series.

Terror of Mechagodzilla/Mekagojira no gyakushu (*Mechagodzilla's Counterattack*). Executive Producer, Tomoyuki Tanaka; Director, Ishiro Honda; Screenplay, Yukiko Takayama [Yubuko Takazawa]; Director of Photography, Motoyoshi Tomioka; Music, Akira Ifukube; Art Director, Yoshibumi Honda; Production Manager, Keisuke Shinoda; Assistant Director, Sasaki Yamashita; Lighting, Toshio Takashima; Editor, Yoshitami Kuroiwa; Sound Effects, Toho Sound Effects Group; Sound, Toho Recording Centre. *Special Effects Unit:* Director, Teruyoshi Nakano; Optical Photography, Yukio Manoda; Mechanical Effects, Takesaburo Watanabe; Art Director, Yasuyuki Inoue; Assistant Directors, Toshiro Aoki, Kan Komura; Optical Effects, Yoshiichi Manoda; Matte Work, Kazunobu Mikame.
Cast: Katsuhiko Sasaki (Akira Ichinosi [Ichinose]), Tomoko Ai (Katsura Mafune), Akihiko Hirata (Dr. Shinji Mafune), Katsumasa Uchida (Murakoshi), Goro Mutsu (Mugan [Mugal]), Kenji Sahara (Army Commander), Tomoe Mari (Yuri Yamamoto), Shin Roppongi (Wakayama), Tadao Nakamaru (Tagawa), Kotaro Tomita (Tada), Masaaki Damon (Kusagai), Ikio [?] Sawamura (Mafune's Butler), Kazuo Suzuki and Yoshio Kirishima (Aliens), Toru Kawane (Godzilla), Kazunari Mori (Mechagodzilla), Tatsumi Fuyamoto (Titanosaurus), Toru Ibuki, Yasuzo Ogawa, Hiraya Kamita, Taro Yamada, Masaichi H., Haruo Suzuki, Saburo Kadowagi, Shigeo Kato, Kazuo Imagi, Kiyoshi Yoshida, Toshio Hosoi, Masayoshi Kikuchi, H. Ishiya, Shizuko Higashi.

A Henry G. Saperstein/Toho Co., Ltd., Production (one source lists this as a Toho-Eizo Production). Color (processed by Tokyo Laboratory, Ltd.). Panavision. 83 minutes. Released March 15, 1975.
U.S. Version: Released by Bob Conn. Special Material (i.e., English-language version), UPA Productions of America. Executive Producer, Henry G. Saperstein; Production Supervisor, S. Richard Krown; Opening Montage, Richard Bansbach, Michael McCann; Sound, Quality Sound Co.; Titles, Freeze Frame. Copyright 1978 by Toho Co., Ltd. Saperstein's involvement with the original Japanese production is uncertain. Also advertised in the United States as *Terror of Godzilla*. U.K. Title: *Monsters from an Unknown Planet*. Alternate title: *The Escape of Megagodzilla*. Television and home video title: *Terror of Mechagodzilla* (though no actual onscreen title appears on the home video version). Released to television by the Mechagodzilla Releasing Company (i.e., United Productions of America). 83 minutes. Includes footage from *Godzilla vs. the Cosmic Monster* (1974). MPAA rating: G. Released 1978.

The Three Treasures/Nippon Tanjo (*The Birth of Japan*). Producers, Sanezumi Fujimoto, Tomoyuki Tanaka; Director, Hiroshi Inagaki; Screenplay, Toshio Yasumi, Ryuzu Kikushima, based on the legends "Kojiki" and "Nihon Shoki" and the origin of Shinto; Director of Photography, Kazuo Yamada; Sound, Toho Dubbing Theatre; Sound Effects, Toho Sound Effects Group. *Special Effects Unit:* Director, Eiji Tsuburaya; Art Director, Akira Watanabe; Director of Photography, Teisho Arikawa; Lighting, Kuichiro [Kyuighiro] Kishida; Matte Process, Hiroshi Mukoyama; Optical Photography, Kinsaburo Araki.
Cast: Toshiro Mifune (Prince Yamato Takeru), Yoko Tsukasa (Princess Tachibana), Kyoko Kagawa (Princess Miyazu), Koji Tsuruta (Younger Kumaso), Takashi Shimura (Elder Kumaso), Kinyuo Tanaka, Ganjuro Nakamura, Akira Takarada, Eijiro Tono, Misa Uehara, Akihiko Hirata, Jun Tazaki.

A Toho Co., Ltd., Production. Western Electric Mirrophonic recording (encoded with Perspecta Stereophonic Sound). Agfacolor (processed by Far East Laboratories, Ltd.). Tohoscope. 182 minutes. Released November 1, 1959.

U.S. Version: Released by Toho International Company, Ltd., in subtitled format. Some engagements advertised as *Age of the Gods*. 112 minutes. No MPAA rating. Released December 20, 1960.

Throne of Blood/Kumonosu-djo (*Cobweb Castle*). Producer-Editor-Director, Akira Kurosawa; Co-Producer, Shojiro Motoki; Screenplay, Shinobu Hashimoto, Ryuzo Kikushima, Hideo Oguni, Akira Kurosawa (based on the play *Macbeth*, by William Shakespeare); Director of Photography, Asakazu Nakai; Music, Masaru Sato; Art Direction and Costumes, Yoshiro Muraki, Kohei Ezaki; Sound Recordist, Fumio Yanoguchi; Sound, Toho Dubbing Theatre; Sound Effects, Toho Sound Effects Group; Special Effects, Toho Special Effects Group.

Cast: Toshiro Mifune (Taketoki Washizu), Isuzu Yamada (Asaji Washizu), Minoru Chiaki (Yoshiaki Miki), Akira Kubo (Yoshiteru Miki), Takamaru Sasaki (Kuniharu Tsuzuki), Yoichi Tachikawa (Kunimaru Tsuzuki), Takashi Shimura (Noriyasu Odagura), Chieko Naniwa (Witch), Isao Kimura, Seizi Miyaguchi.

A Toho Co., Ltd., Production. Western Electric Mirrophonic recording (encoded with Perspecta Stereophonic Sound). Black and white. 110 minutes. Released January 15, 1957.

U.S. Version: Released by Brandon Films, Inc., in subtitled format. English Subtitles, Donald Richie. Alternate titles include *The Castle of the Spider's Web*, *Cobweb Castle* and *Macbeth*. 105 minutes. No MPAA rating. Released November 22, 1961.

Tomei Ningen. Executive Producer, Tomoyuki Tanaka; Director, Motoyoshi Oda; Based on the novel *The Invisible Man* by H. G. Wells; Sound, Toho Dubbing Theatre; Sound Effects, Toho Sound Effects Group; Special Effects Director, Eiji Tsuburaya; Special Effects, Toho Special Effects Group.

Cast: Seizaburo Kozu, Miki Sanjo, Yoshio Tsuchiya.

A Toho Co., Ltd., Production. Western Electric Mirrophonic Recording. Black and white (processed by Kinuta Laboratories, Ltd.). Academy ratio. Running time undetermined. Released 1954.

U.S. Version: Distributor, if any, is undetermined. International title: *The Invisible Man*.

The Vampire Doll/Chi o suu ningyo (*The Vampire Doll*). Executive Producers, Tomoyuki Tanaka, Fumio Tanaka; Director, Michio Yamamoto; Screenplay, Ei Ogawa, Hiroshi Nagano; Director of Photography, Kazutami Hara; Art Director, Yoshibumi Honda; Music, Riichiro Manabe; Sound, Toho Recording Centre; Sound Effects, Toho Sound Effects Group; Special Effects Director, Teruyoshi Nakano; Special Effects, Toho Special Effects Group.

Cast: Kayo Matsuo (Keiko), Yukiko Kobayashi (Yuko), Yoko Minazake (The Mother), Atsuo Nakamura (Kazuhiko), Junya Usami (Dr. Yamaguchi), Akira Nakao (The Friend), Itaru Takashima, Sachio Sakai, Jun Hamamura, Kinzo Sekiguchi.

A Toho Co., Ltd., Production. Color (processed by Tokyo Laboratory, Ltd.). Panavision. 85 minutes (?). Released 1970.

U.S. Version: Released by Toho International Co., Ltd. Released in subtitled format. International Title: *The Night of the Vampire*. Japanese title also known as *Yureiyashiki no kyofu-chi wo suu ningyo*. 71 minutes (some sources give 85 minutes). No MPAA rating. Released January 1972.

Varan the Unbelievable/Daikaiju Baran (*Giant Monster*). Producer, Tomoyuki Tanaka; Director, Ishiro Honda; Assistant Director, Koji Kajita; Screenplay, Shinichi Sekizawa; Original Story, Takeshi Kuronuma; Director of Photography, Hajime Koizumi; Art Director, Kiyoshi Suzuki; Lighting, Mitsuo Kaneko; Editor,

Ichiji Taira; Production Manager, Shotaro Kawakami; Music, Akira Ifukube; Sound, Wataru Konuma, Masanobu Miyazaki, Toho Dubbing Theatre; Sound Effects, Ichiro Mikame, Toho Sound Effects Group. *Special Effects Unit:* Director, Eiji Tsuburaya; Photography, Teisho Arikawa, Hidezaburo Araki; Art Director, Akira Watanabe; Lighting, Kuichiro Kishida; Optical Photography, Hiroshi Mukoyama; Teizo Toshimitsu (Creature Suits).

Cast: Kozo Nomura (Dr. Kenji Uozaki), Ayumi Sonoda (Yuriko Shinjo), Fumito Matsuo (Motohiko Horiguchi), Koreya Senda (Dr. Sugimoto), Akihiko Hirata (Dr. Fujimura), Fuyuki Murakami (Dr. Umajima), Akira Sera (Priest), Akio Kusama (First Officer Kusama), Yo-shio Tsuchiya (Third Officer Katsumoto), Minosuke Yamada (Secretary of Defense), Hisaya Ito (Ichiro Shinjo), Yoshifumi Tajima (Captain), Nadao Kirino (Yutaka Wada), Akira Yamada (Issaku), Yoshikazu Kawamata (Jiro), Yasuhiro Kasanobu (Sankichi), Takashi Ito (Ken, the Village Boy), Toku Ihara (Village Youth), Fumiko Honma (Mother), Haruo Nakajima and Katsumi Tezuka (Baran), Soji Oikata, Jiro Kumagai, Masaichi Hirose, Keisuke Yamada, Hideo Shibuya, Koji Suzuki, Masaki Shinohara, Toshiko Nomura, Hiroshi Angeizu, Mitsuo Matsumoto, Yasuo Ohnishi, Rinsuke Ogata, Junichiro Mukai, Kakue Ichibanji, Mitoko Taira, Eisuke Nakanishi, Ko Narita, Keiichiro Katsumoto, Anzai Sakamoto, Ryuichi Hosokawa, Sen Hayamizu, Tokio Ohkawa, Hiroko Terazawa, Toriko Takahara.

A Toho Co., Ltd., Production. Western Electric Mirrophonic recording (encoded with Perspecta Stereophonic Sound). Black and white (processed by Tokyo Laboratory, Ltd.). Tohoscope (billed as Toho Pan Scope). 87 minutes. Released October 14, 1958.

U.S. Version: Released by Crown International Pictures, Inc. A Dallas Productions/Cory Productions Picture. Producer-Director, Jerry A Baerwitz; Screenplay, Sid Harris; Director of Photography, Jacques [Jack] Marquette; Special Photographic Effects, Howard A. Anderson Company; Supervising Film Editor, Jack Ruggiero; Assistant Editor, Ralph Cushman; Music Editor, Peter Zinner; Sound Mixer, Victor Appel; Wardrobe, Robert O'Dell; Makeup, Robert Cowan; Assistant Director, Leonard Kunody; Property Master, Sam Harris; Script Supervisor, Margaret Lawrence; Sound Effects Editor, Kurt Hernfeld; Music, Albert Glasser (from *The Amazing Colossal Man*, and possibly other Glasser music and or library music); Sound (mono), Glen Glenn Sound. Copyright 1961 by Dallas Productions, Inc. The new version makes no mention of Toho or any of its production crew in the credits. New footage filmed in Totalscope (2.35 x 1 anamorphic wide screen), using the Westrex recording system. Double billed with *First Spaceship on Venus* (Crown, 1962). Original cut includes stock footage from *Godzilla* and *Godzilla's Counterattack*. 70 minutes. No MPAA rating. Released December 12, 1962.

Additional Cast for U.S. Version: Myron Healey (Commander James Bradley), Tsuruko Kobayashi (Anna Bradley), Clifford Kawada (Captain Kishi), Derick Shimatsu (Matsu), Hideo Imamura, George Sasaki, Hiroshi Hisamune, Yoneo Iguchi, Michael Sung, Roy T. Ogata.

The War in Space/Wakusei Daisenso (Great Planet War). Executive Producers, Tomoyuki Tanaka and Fumio Tanaka; Director, Jun Fukuda; Screenplay, Ryuzo Nakanishi, Hideichi Nagahara, based on an idea by Hachiro Jinguji; Director of Photography, Jo [Yuzuru] Aizawa; Art Director, Kazuo Satsuya; Lighting, Shinji Kojima; Music, Toshiaki Tsushima; Sound Recordist, Toshiya Ban; Sound, Toho Recording Centre; Sound Effects, Toho Sound Effects Group. *Special Effects Unit:* Director, Teruyoshi Nakano; Photography, Takashi Yamamoto, Toshimitsu Ohneda; Art Director, Yasuyuki Inoue; Mechanical Effects, Takesaburo Watanabe; Optical Photography, Yukio Manoda.

Cast: Kensaku Morita (Miyoshi), Ryo Ikebe (Professor Takigawa), William Ross (Dr.

Schmidt/Alien), Akihiko Hirata (Defense Countermeasure Supreme Commander Oshi), David Perin (Jimmy), Yuko Asano (June?), Hiroshi Miyauchi (Morrei?), Masaya Oki, Shuji Otaki, Katsutoshi Atarashi, Goro Mutsu, Isao Hashimoto, Shoji Nakayama.

A Toho Eiga–Toho Eizo Production. A Toho Co., Ltd., Release. Color (processed by Tokyo Laboratory, Ltd.). Panavision. 90 minutes. Released December 17, 1977.

U.S. Version: Never released theatrically. Released to television by Gold Key Entertainment, Inc. International Title: *War of the Planets*. Includes stock footage from *The Last War*, *Submersion of Japan* and *Catastrophe: 1999*. 90 minutes. No MPAA rating.

War of the Gargantuas/Furankenshutain no kaiju – Sanda tai Gairah (*Frankenstein Monsters: Sanda Against Gairah*). Producer, Tomoyuki Tanaka; Executive Producers, Henry G. Saperstein, Reuben Bercovitch; Director, Ishiro Honda; Screenplay, Ishiro Honda, Kaoru Mabuchi (Takeshi Kimura); Story, Reuben Bercovitch; Director of Photography, Hajime Koizumi; Music, Akira Ifukube; Art Director, Takeo Kita; Lighting, Toshio Takashima; Chief Assistant Director, Kohi Kahita; Production Manager, Shoichi Koga; Production Assistant, Kenichiro Tsunoda; Sound Effects, Hisashi Shimonaga, Toho Sound Effects Group; Sound, Toho Recording Centre. *Special Effects Unit:* Director, Eiji Tsuburaya; Photography, Teisho Arikawa, Motonari Tomioka; Production Manager, Yasuaki Sakamoto; Art Director, Arika Wanatabe; Editor, Ryohei Fujii; Assistant to Tsuburaya, Teruyoshi Nakano; Optical Photography, Yukio Manoda, Sadao Iizuka; Scene Manipulation, Fumio Nakadai.

Cast: Russ Tamblyn (Dr. Paul Stewart), Kumi Mizuno (Akemi, His Assistant), Kenji Sahara (Yuzo), Jun Tazaki (General), Kipp Hamilton (Singer), Haruo Nakajima (Sanda), Hisaya Ito (Police Captain), Nobou Nakamura (Scientist), Ikio Sawamura (Fisherman), Yoshibumi Tajima (Policeman), Ren Yamamoto (Sailor), Hiroshi Sekita.

A Toho Co., Ltd., Production. A Henry G. Saperstein Enterprises Presentation. Westrex Recording System. Eastmancolor (processed by Tokyo Laboratory, Ltd.). Tohoscope. 93 minutes. Released July 31, 1966.

U.S. Version: Released by Maron Films Ltd. A United Productions of America Release. Executive Producers, Henry G. Saperstein, Reuben Bercovitch; Editor, Fredric Knudtson; Dialog Supervisor, Riley Jackson; Sound Recording, Glen Glenn Sound Co.; Production Supervisor, S. Richard Krown; Song, "Feel in My Heart"; prints by Consolidated Film Industries. Copyright 1970 by Benedict Pictures Corp. (i.e., Henry G. Saperstein Enterprises). Double billed with *Monster Zero* (q.v.). U.K. Title: *Duel of the Gargantuas*. Working titles: *The Frankenstein Brothers* and *Adventure of the Gargantuas*. Originally intended as a sequel to *Frankenstein Conquers the World* (q.v.), film was allegedly pulled from release by Saperstein and re-edited, removing all references to earlier. A proposed match-up between a gargantua and Godzilla was scripted but never made. 93 minutes. MPAA rating: G. Released July 29, 1970.

Whirlwind/Dai tatsumaki. Executive Producer, Tomoyuki Tanaka; Director, Hiroshi Inagaki; Screenplay, Hiroshi Inangaki, Takeshi Kimura; Director of Photography, Kazuo Yamada; Sound, Toho Recording Centre; Sound Effects, Toho Sound Effects Group; Special Effects Director, Eiji Tsuburaya; Special Effects, Toho Special Effects Group.

Cast: Toshiro Mifune (Lord Akashi), Somegoro Ichikawa (Jubei), Yuriko Hoshi (Kozato), Kumi Mizuno (The Witch), Yosuke Natsuki, Yoshiko Kuga, Makoto Sato.

A Toho Co., Ltd., Production. Western Electric mirrophonic recording (possibly encoded with Perspecta Stereophonic Sound). Eastmancolor (processed by Tokyo Laboratory, Ltd.). Tohoscope. 107 minutes. Released 1964.

U.S. Version: Released by Toho International Co., Ltd., in subtitled format. 107

minutes. No MPAA rating. Released July 26, 1968.

Yog: Monster from Space/Gezora Ganime Kameba Kessen nankai no daikaiju (*Gezora, Ganime, Kameba: Decisive Battle! Giant Monsters of the South Seas*). Producers, Tomoyuki Tanaka, Fumio Tanaka; Director, Ishiro Honda; Production Manager, Yasushi Sakai; Screenplay, Ei Ogawa; Director of Photography, Taaichi Kankura; Music, Akira Ifukube; Editor, Masahisa Himi; Art Director, Takeo Kita; Sound Recording, Kanae Masuo; Sound, Toho Recording Centre; Sound Effects, Toho Sound Effects Group; *Special Effects Unit:* Director, Teruyoshi Nakano, Teisho Arikawa; Optical Photography, Yoichi Manoda, Yoshiyuki Tokumasa.

Cast: Akira Kubo (Taro Kudo), Atsuko Takahashi (Ayako Hoshino), Yoshio Tsuchiya (Dr. Kyoichi Miya), Kenji Sahara (Makoto Obata), Noritake Saito (Rico), Yukiko Kobayasi (Saki), Satoshi Nakamura (Supplicator Ombo), Chotaro Togin (Engineer Yokoyama), Wataru [Mataru] Omae (Sakura), Sachio Sakai (Magazine Editor), Yu Fujiki (Promotion Division Manager), Yuko Sugihara (Stewardess).

A Toho Co., Ltd., Production. Color (processed by Tokyo Laboratory, Ltd.). Panavision. Copyright 1970 by Toho Co., Ltd. 84 minutes. Released August 1, 1970.

U.S. Version: Released by American International Pictures. A Samuel Z. Arkoff Presentation. Postproduction Supervisor, Salvatore Billitteri; prints by Movielab. Wide screen process billed as ColorScope. Copyright 1971 by American International Pictures, Inc. International Title: *The Space Amoeba*. 81 minutes. MPAA rating: G. Released 1971.

The Youth and His Amulet/Gen to Fudo-Myoh (*Gen and Fudo-Myoh*). Executive Producer–Director, Hiroshi Inagaki; Screenplay, Toshiro Ide, Zenzo Matsuyama (based on the story by Shizue Miyaguchi); Director of Photography, Kazuo Yamada; Music, Ikuma Dan. *Special Effects Unit:* Director, Eiji Tsuburaya. Photography, Sadamasa Arikawa, Motonari Tomioka; Matte Photography, Yokio Manoda, Taka Yukio; Matte Process, Hiroshi Mukoyama; Art Director, Akira Watanabe; Lighting, Kuichiro Kishida; Assistant Director, Teruyoshi Nakano.

Cast: Toru Koyanagi (Gen), Hisako Sakabe (His Sister), Toshiro Mifune (Fudo-Myoh), Chishu Ryu, Yosuke Natsuki, Minoru Chiaki, Nobuko Otowa, Mie Hama.

A Toho Co., Ltd., Production. Western Electric Mirrophonic recording (encoded with Perspecta Stereophonic Sound?). Black and white with color insert (processed by Tokyo Laboratory, Ltd.). Tohoscope. 120 minutes. Released 1961 or 1962 (sources vary).

U.S. Version: Released by Toho International Co., Ltd., in subtitled format. 111 minutes. No MPAA rating. Released March 1963.

Zeiramu. Director, Keita Amamiya; Story-Screenplay, Keita Amamiya, Hajime Matsumoto.

Cast: (unavailable).

A Gaga Communications, Inc./Growd, Inc., Production. A Toho Co., Ltd., Release (?) Color. Widescreen (?). Released August 1991.

U.S. Version: Distributor, if any, is undetermined. Alternate title: *Zeiram.*

Tsuburaya Enterprises, Inc.

The Bermuda Depths/Bamyuda no nazo (*Mystery of Bermuda*). Producers, Arthur Rankin, Jr., Jules Bass; Associate Producer, Benni Korzen; Director, Tom Kotani; Screenplay, William Overgard; Story, Arthur Rankin, Jr.; Director of Photography, Jeri Sopanen; Music, Maury Laws; Editor, Barry Walter; Song "Jennie," Music by Maury Laws, Lyrics by Jules Bass, vocals by Claude Carmichael; Director of Underwater Photography, Stanton Waterman; Assistant Underwater Photography (sic), George

Waterman; Diving Consultant, Teddy Tucker; Location Manager, J.A.D. Froud; Sound, Francis Daniels; Boom Man, Keith Gardner; Sound Mixer, Richard Elder; Music Recording, John Richards; Gaffer, Michael Lesser; Best Boy, Jonathan Lumiere; Key Grip, Dustin Smith; Makeup, Fern Buchner; Propman, Peter Polotanoff; Production Supervisor, Barbara Hilsey; Production Assistants, Thomas Bush, Todd Rankin, Linda Wilkinson; Assistant to the Director, Nobuko Oganasofa; first Assistant Cameraman, Douglas Hart; second Assistant Cameraman, Thomas Weston; Still Photographer, Peter Moran; Special Props, Gary Zeller, Jean Vickery, Beverly Welch, Donald Berry; Costumes, Emma Randolph; Sound Effects Editing, Peter Stass; Assistant Editors, Jill Savic, Wendy Warner, Jim Tatum, Jr.; Casting Consultant, Shirley Rich. *Special Effects Unit* (Tsuburaya Enterprises, Inc.): Associate Producers, Kinshiro Okube, Masaki Ilzuki; Director, Mark Segawa; Assistant Director, Akihiko Takahasi; Optical Effects, Minoru Nakani.

Cast: Leigh McCloskey (Magnus Dens), Carl Weathers (Eric), Connie Selleca (Jennie Haniver), Julie Woodson (Doshan), Ruth Attaway (Delia), Burl Ives (Dr. Paulis), Eilse Frick, Nicholas Ingham, Kevin Petty, Nicole Marsh, George Richards, John Instone, Jonathan Ingham, Patricia Rego, Doris Riley, Tracy Anne Sadler.

A Rankin/Bass Productions, Inc., Production, in association with Tsuburaya Enterprises, Inc. An Arthur Rankin, Jr./Jules Bass Film. Distributed by JAD Films International, Inc. A Japanese–U.S. co-production. The producers gratefully acknowledge the valuable cooperation of the Government of Bermuda and its Ministries and the Bermuda Biological Station. Filmed on location in Bermuda, and at Tsuburaya Enterprises, Inc., Studios, Tokyo. Color by Movielab. Spherical Panavision. 90 minutes. July 20, 1979.

U.S. Version: Never released theatrically in the United States. Broadcast on the American Broadcasting Companies, Inc. (ABC) network January 27, 1978. Syndicated by JAD TV. Copyright 1977 by Rankin/Bass Productions, Inc. 95 minutes.

Fugitive Alien. Producers, Noboru Tsuburaya, Jushichi Sano, Akira Tsuburaya; Directors, Kiyosumi Kukazawa, Minoru Kanaya; Teleplay, Keiichi Abe, Bunkou Wakatsuki, Yoshihisa Araki, Hiroyasu Yamaura, Hideyoshi Nagasaka, Toyohiro Andou; Music, Norio Maeda.

Cast: Tatsuya Azuma, Miyuki Tanigawa, Joe Shishido, Choei Takahashi, Tsutomu Yukawa, Hiro Tateyama, Akihiko Hirata.

A Japanese teleseries re-edited to feature length for American television and never released theatrically in Japan. A Tsuburaya Productions, Ltd., Production. 16mm. Color.

U.S. Version: Never released theatrically in the United States. Released directly to television in 1986 by King Features Entertainment, a subsidiary of the Heart Corporation. A Sandy Frank Enterprises Presentation. Concept Editor, William L. Cooper, Jr.; Creative Consultant, Jessie Vogel, Cinemedia, Ltd. Copyright 1986 by Tsuburaya Production, Ltd. Followed by *Star Force: Fugitive Alien II* (q.v.). Derived from the teleseries "Suta-urufu" ("Star Wolf"), which aired in Japan in 1978. 102 minutes. No MPAA rating.

The Ivory Ape. Executive Producer, Jules Bass; Producer, Arthur Rankin, Jr.; Associate Producers, Benni Korzen, Masaki Iizuka; Director, Tom Kotani; Screenplay, William Overgard; Story, William Overgard, Arthur Rankin, Jr.; Director of Photography, Yozo Inagaki; Music, Maury Laws, Bernard Hoffer; Conductor, Bernard Hoffer; Supervising Editor, Barry Walter; Editor, Wendy Mank; Assistant Director, Kaz Kazui; Second Assistant Director, James Bigham; First Assistant Cameraman, Takayoshi Oneda; Second Assistant Cameraman, Akio Inoue; Camera Loader, Peter Spera; Production Designer, Kazuo Satsuya; Art Director and Property Master, Peter Politanoff; Lighting Director, Gengon Nakaoka; Lighting Assistants, Sadao Hasegawa, Koichi Kamada; Key Grip, Zeev Willy Neumann; Sound, Yuji Hiyoshi; Sound Assistant, Osamu Kukuoka; Sound

Mixer, Robert Elder; Stunt Designer, Henry Schrady; Production Coordinator, Lee Dannacher; Sound Effects Editor, Jim Tatum, Jr.; Makeup Artist, Nick Crimi; Wardrobe, Alexandra Layman; Wardrobe Assistants, Sheila Dempster, Elizabeth Wingate; Assistant to the Producer, Barbara Adams; Production Coordinator, Lee Dannacher; Production Assistants, Todd Rankin, Sheena Tucker, Davina Tucker, Sandra Pedro; Still Photographer, Peter Moran; Property Assistants, Beverly Welch, Andrew Outerbridge, Layton Outerbridge, Michael Correia; Location Manager, J.A.D. Froud; Assistant Editor, Gena Hegleman; Dialog Director, David Man; Dialog Supervisor, Frances Herman; Second Unit Photography, Mike Spera, Jeri Sopranen; Transportation, Richard Floyd; Casting, Joy-Todd, Inc.; Location Casting, Richard Morbey; "Rangi" Technicians, Shunichi Mizuno, Masahito Sesaki; Stunt Designer, Henry Schrady; Special Effects, Tsuburaya Enterprises, Inc.

Cast: Jack Palance (Marc Kazarian), Cindy Pickett (Lil Tyler), Celine Lomez (Valerie Lamont Kazarian), Derek Partridge (Aubrey Range), Steven Keats (U.S. Department of Interior Special Agent Baxter Mapes), Earle Hayman (Chief Police Inspector Saint George), Lou David (Roomie Pope), Tricia Sembera (Vita Havermyer), William Horrigan (Ship's Captain), David Man (Dr. Cole), Leonard Daniels (Police Constable Smith), George Rushe (Police Constable Johnny Wilkinson), Daniel Thomas (Taxi Driver), Irving Wilkinson (Kazarian's Butler), Courtney Floyd (Courtney), John Truscott (Police Constable Collins), John Lough (Trot Toomer), Jane Bainbridge (Courtney's Mother), Charles Jeffers (Congo Father), Kevin Dill (Congo Son), Grace Rawlins (Congo Mother), Easton Rawlins (Congo Son), Marlene Butterfield (ZFB-TV Reporter), Barbara Adams (Baxter's Secretary), Duke Soares (Stuntman).

A Rankin/Bass Productions, Inc., Production, in association with Tsuburaya Enterprises, Inc. An Arthur Rankin, Jr./Jules Bass Presentation. A Japanese–U.S. coproduction. Distributed by Worldvision Enterprises, Inc. The producer gratefully acknowledges the valuable cooperation of the Government of Bermuda and its Ministries. Filmed at Tsuburaya Studios, Tokyo, and on location in Bermuda and Japan. Color by Movielab. Widescreen (1.66:1 projected screen aspect ratio). 100 minutes. Released 1980 (?).

U.S. Version: Never released theatrically in the United States. Released directly to television and first broadcast on the American Broadcasting Companies, Inc. (ABC) network April 18, 1980. 96 minutes. Distributed by Worldwide Enterprises, Inc.

The Last Dinosaur/Kyokutei tankensen Pora-Bora ("Polar Probe Ship *Polar-Borer*"). Producers Arthur Rankin, Jr., Jules Bass; Co-producer (for Tsuburaya Productions), Noburo Tsuburaya; Associate Producers, Benni Korzen, Kineshiro Ohkubo [Kinshiro Okube], Masaki Iizuka, Kazuyoshi Kasai; Directors, Alex Grasshoff, Tsugunobu "Tom" Kotani; Screenplay, William Overgard; Director of Photography, Shoji Ueda; Supervising Editor, Barry Walter; Editors, Yatsuji Nakamizu, Minoru Kozono; Art Designer, Kazuniko [Kazumiko] Fujiwara; Production Coordinator, Kiyokama [Keyozama] Ugama; Lighting, Nisaaki Yoneyama; Music, Maury Laws, Arranged and Conducted by Ken Hirose; Song, "He's the Last Dinosaur," Music by Maury Laws, Lyrics by Jules Bass, Arranged and Conducted by Bernard Hoffer, and performed by Nancy Wilson; Assistant Director, Shonei Tojyo; Production Manager, Minoru Kurita; Sound Mixer, Yuji Hiroshi; Sound Studio, Kaino Kai. *Special Effects Unit:* Director, Kazuo Sagawa; Cameraman, Sadao Sato; Lighting, Yasuo Kitayama; Art Director, Tetsueo Ohsawa; Optical Specialist, Morsaki Uematsu; Assistant Director, Yosmimura; Production Manager, Kazuo Onashi.

Cast: Richard Boone (Masten Thrust), Joan Van Ark (Francesca "Frankie" Banks), Luther Rackley (Bunta), Steven Keats (Dr. Charles "Chuck" Wade), Luther Rackley (Bunta), Carl Hansen (Barney), Masumi Sekiya (Prehistoric Girl), Tetsu Nakamura (Dr. Kawamoto), William Ross (Expedition

Captain), Tasso Kamamuda, Nancy Magsig, Don Maloney, Vanessa Cristina, James Dale, Myoe Enoki, Smunsake Karita, Gary Gundersen.

A Rankin/Bass Productions, Inc./Tsuburaya Productions, Ltd., Production. An Arthur Rankin, Jr./Jules Bass Film. A Japanese–U.S. co-production. Filmed at Tsuburaya Studios. Color (processed by Tokyo Laboratory, Ltd.). Widescreen. 100 minutes.

U.S. Version: Slated for theatrical release in New York City on February 11, 1977, but pulled by the American Broadcasting Companies, Inc., network (ABC), which owned the TV rights and elected to telecast it on that date. Copyright 1977 by Rankin/Bass Productions, Inc. Syndicated by Viacom International, Inc. 95 minutes. Japanese title also given as *Saigo no Kyoru*. No MPAA rating.

Mighty Jack. Producers, Eiji Tsuburaya, Yasuji Morita, Yasuhiro Ito; Director, Kazuho Mitsuta; Screenplay, Shinichi Sekizawa, Eizaburou; Editor, Akio Agura; Director of Photography, Yoshihiro Mori; Special Effects Director of Photography, Kazuo Sagawa; Music, Isao Tomita, published by Tsuburaya Music Publishing Co., Ltd.

Cast: Masanori Jihei (Jerry), Hideaki Nitani, Naoko Kobo, Hiroshi Ninami, Eisei Amamoto, Jerry Ito, Wakako Ikeda, Akira Kasuga, Seikou Fukioka, Noriaki Inoue, Yoshitaka Tanaka, Mitsubu Ohya, Eijirou Yanagi.

A Japanese teleseries re-edited to feature length for American television and never released theatrically in Japan. A Tsuburaya Production, Ltd., Production. Copyright 1986 by Tsuburaya Productions, Ltd. 16mm. Color. 1.37:1 ratio.

U.S. Version: Never released theatrically in the United States. Released directly to television in 1988 by King Features Entertainment, a subsidiary of the Hearst Corporation. A Sandy Frank Enterprises Presentation. Derived from the teleseries "Maitei Jiyaku," which ran thirteen one-hour episodes in 1968. This feature was culled from episodes one ("The Man Who Vanished from Paris") and thirteen ("The Mysterious Dirigible").

Space Warriors 2000/Urutora 6-Kyodai tai kaiju gundan (*The Six Ultra Brothers vs. the Monster Army*). Executive Producer, Noburo Tsuburaya; Director, Sompote Sands.

Cast: (unavailable).

A Fuji Eiga/Tsuburaya Productions, Ltd., Production. A Japanese-Thai co-production. Color. Anamorphic wide screen. Running time undetermined. Released 1979.

U.S. Version: Never released theatrically in the United States. Released directly to television by Cinema Shares International Television, Ltd. A Dick Randall and Steve Minasian Presentation. Director, Marc Smith; Director of Photography, Ion Knoller; Music, De Wolf; Dubbing Cast (?), Robert Sessions, Nicholas Curror, Sarah Taunton, Wendy Danvers. Copyright 1985 by Spectacular International Films. Mothra does not appear in the film despite a listing in the opening credits. Released in most of Asia in 1974, but unreleased in Japan until 1979. Thai title unavailable. Both versions contain extensive stock footage from various Tsuburaya-produced "Ultra" teleseries, including "Ultraman." This footage, filmed in 16mm 1.37:1 ratio, was cropped and convereted to 35mm scope. The American television version is presented minus the anamorphic decompression, resulting in an extremely uncomfortable image. 91 minutes. No MPAA rating.

Star Force: Fugitive Alien II. Producers, Noboru Tsuburaya, Jushichi Sano, Akira Tsuburaya; Directors, Kiyosumi Kukazawa, Minoru Kanaya; Teleplay, Keiichi Abe, Bunkou Wakatsuki, Yoshihisa Araki, Hiroyasu Yamaura, Hideyoshi Nagasaka, Toyohiro Andou; Music, Norio Maeda.

Cast: Tatsuya Azuma, Miyuki Tanigawa, Joe Shishido, Choei Takahashi, Tsutomu Yukawa, Hiro Tateyama.

A Japanese teleseries re-edited to feature length for American television and never released theatrically in Japan. A Tsuburaya Productions, Ltd., Production. 16mm. Color.

U.S. Version: Never released theatrically in the United States. Released directly to television in 1986 by King Features Entertainment, a subsidiary of the Heart Corporation. A Sandy Frank Enterprises Presentation. Concept Editor, William L. Cooper, Jr.; Creative Consultant, Jessie Vogel, Cinemedia, Ltd. Copyright 1986 by Tsuburaya Productions, Inc. Preceded by *Fugitive Alien* (q.v.). Derived from the teleseries "Sutaurufu" ("Star Wolf"), which aired in Japan in 1978. 75 minutes. No MPAA rating.

Time of the Apes. Producers, Mataichi Takahashi, Masashi Tadakuma; Directors, Atsuo Okunaka, Kiya Sumi Fukazawa; Screenwriter, Keiiche Abe; Original Story, Sakyo Komatsu, Kouji Tanaka, Aritsume Toyoda; Music, Toshiaki Tsushima; Director of Photography, Yoshihiro Mori.

Cast: Reiko Tokunaga, Hiroko Saito, Masaaki Kaji, Hitoshi Omae, Tetsuya Ushid, Baku Hatakeyama, Kazue Takita, Noboru Nakaya.

A Japanese teleseries re-edited to feature length for American television, and never released theatrically in Japan. A Tsuburaya Productions, Ltd., Production. Color. Filmed in 16mm. 1.37:1 aspect ratio. Copyright 1987 by Tsuburaya Productions, Ltd.

U.S. Version: Never released theatrically in the United States. Released directly to television by Sandy Frank Productions in 1987. Feature Concept and Editing, William L. Cooper, Jr.; Creative Consultants, Jessie Vogel Cinemedia Ltd. 94 minutes. No MPAA rating.

Urutoraman (*Ultraman*). Producers, Toshiaki Ichikawa, Masayoshi Sueyasu; Director, Hajime Tsuburaya; Screenplay, Shinichi Sekizawa, Tetsuo Kinjo, Shozo Uehara, Bunzo Wakatsuki, based on characters created by Eiji Tsuburaya; Director of Photography, Masaharu Utsumi; Art Director, Chikyu Iwasaki; Music, Kunio Miyaguchi; Sound, Kinuta Laboratory, Ltd.

Cast: Susumu Kurobe (Hayata), Shoji Kobayashi (Captin Muramatsu), Ikichi Ishii (Arashi), Hiroko Sakurai (Akiko Fuji), Masanari Nihe (Ide), Toshi Furuya (Urutoraman), Koji Ishizaka, Mitsu Urano (Narrators).

A Tsuburaya Productions, Ltd., Production. A Toho Co., Ltd., Presentation. Blown up to 35mm from 16mm original. Eastman Color (prints by Tokyo Laboratory, Ltd.). 1.37:1 projected screen aspect ratio. Double-billed with *King Kong Escapes*. 79 minutes. Released 1967.

U.S. Version: Never released in the United States. This theatrical feature was derived from the popular 1966-67 Japanese television series "Urutoraman," originally broadcast on the TBS network in Japan. This feature was compiled from several episodes of the series (possibly including newly shot linking footage). International title: *The Ultra Man*. Alternate title: *Ultra Man*. Note: Several episodes from the various "Ultra" series ("Ultraman," "Ultra Seven," "Ultraman Taro," "Ultraman Leo," "Ultraman 80," etc.) have been re-edited and shown theatrically in Japan, usually as shorts, but occasionally as features as well. They include *Urotoruman* (1979), *Urotoruman–Kaiji Daikessen* (1979; released internationally as *Ultraman – Monster Big Battle*) and *The Six Ultra Brothers vs. the Monster Army* (1979), the latter a Japanese-Thai co-production feature derived from the 1974 Tsuburaya series. See below.

Urutoraman Sutori (*The Ultraman Story*). Executive Producers, Noburo Tsuburaya, Kiyotaka Ugawa; Director, Koichi Takano; Creator-Planner, Noburo Tsuburaya; Screenplay, Yasushi Hirano; Director of Photography, Takeshi Yamamoto; Lighting, Kenji Ushiba; Art Director, Shiyun Yamaguchi, Tsuneo Kantake; Assistant Director, Kenichi Uraoka; Research, Koichiro Fujishima, Masumi Kaneda; Music, Toru Fuyuki, Shunsuke Kikuchi, Tsuburaya Music Publishing, Inc.; Music Producers, Shizuka Tamagawa, Kunio Miyaguchi.

Cast: (Unavailable)

A Tsuburaya Productions Picture. A Shochiku/Fuji Co., Ltd., Release. Color.

Academy ratio (?). Running time undetermined. Released July 14, 1984.
U.S. Version: Distributor, if any, is undetermined. Includes stock footage from the various *Ultra* series. However, the majority of the picture is comprised of newly shot footage.

Miscellaneous Productions

Ai no borei. Writer-Producer-Director, Nagisa Oshima; Based on the novel by Itoko Nakamura; Production Coordinators, Shibata Organization, Inc.; Art Director, Jusho Toda; Director of Photography, Yoshio Mujajima; Editor, Keiichu Uraoka; Music, Toru Takemitsu; World Sales, Aros Films.
Cast: Kazuko Yoshiyuki (Seki), Tatsuya Fuji (Toyoji), Takahiro Tamura (Gisaburo), Takuzo Kawatani (Hotta), Akiko Koyama (Boss), Taiji Tonoyama (Toichiro).
An Oshima Productions, Ltd./Argos Films Production. A Japanese-French co-production. Eastman Color. Widescreen. An Oshima Release. 108 minutes. Released 1978.
U.S. Version: Distributor, if any, is undetermined. Released internationally by Argos in May 1978. French title: *Fantom Amour.*

Akira Kurosawa's Dreams/Konna yume wo mita (*I Saw a Dream Like This*). Producers, Hisao Kurosawa, Mike Y. Inoue; Writer-Director, Akira Kurosawa; Creative Consultant, Ishiro Honda; Directors of Photography, Takao Saito, Masaharu Ueda; Art Directors, Yoshiro Muraki, Akira Sakuragi; Music, Shinichiro Ikebe; Sound, Kenichi Benitani; Costume Designer, Emi Wada; Assistant Director, Takashi Koizumi; Production Manager, Teruyo Nogami; Production Coordinator, Izuhiko Suehiro; Associate Producers, Allan H. Liebert, Siekichi Iizumi; Technical Cooperation, Sony; Photography Collaborator, Kazutami Hara; Sound Effects, Ichiro Minawa, Masatoshi Saito; Set Decorator, Koichi Hamamura; Casting Assistant, Yasunori Suzuki; Unit Managers, Kunio Niwa, Masahiko Kumada; Choreographer, Michiyo Hata; Piano Player, Ikudo Endo; Assistant Directors, Okihiro Yoneda, Naohito Sakai, Tsuyoshi Sugino, Kiyoharu Hayano, Toru Tanaka, Vitorio Dalle Ore; Assistant Cameramen, Yoshinori Sekiguchi, Toshio Wattanabe, Hidehiro Igarashi, Hiroyuki Kitazawa, Hiroshi Ishida, Kazushi Watanabe, Shigeo Suzuki, Kosuke Matsushima, Mitsu Kondo, Hiroshi Hattori; Lighting Technicians; Yukio Choya, Tadatoshi Kitagawa, Makoto Sano, Tetsuo Sawada, Miyanobu Inori, Hisanori Furukawa, Isao Yasui, Hideho Ioka, Hiromasa Yonahara; Lighting Rigging, Kenzo Masuda, Yukio Tanaka; Sound Assistants, Soichi Inoue, Masahito Yano, Noriaki Minami; Grips, Isanu Miwano, Satoshi Tsuyuki, Sadanu Takahara, Yuichi Horita; Art Assistants, Kyoko Heya, Nariyuki Kondo, Yasuyoshi Ototake; Set Construction, Ichio Utsuki, Kazuharu Tsuboi; Props, Satoshi Ota, Yuzuru Sakai, Nami Ishida, Yoshiaki Kawai; Wardrobe, Kazuko Kurosawa, Akira Fukuda, Yoko Nagano, Mitsuru Otsuka; Assistant Editors, Rysuke Otsubo, Hideto Aga, Yosuke Yafune; Negative Cutters, Tome Minami, Noriko Meharu; Makeup Artists, Shoshichiro Ueda, Tameyuki Aimi, Norio Sano; Hairdressers, Sakai Nakao, Yumiko Fujii; Still Photographer, Daizaburo Harada; Production Publicity, Yasuhiko Higashi; Mountain Climbing Adviser, Tadao Kanzeki; Dance Instructor, Tokiko Mochizuki; Transportation, Takashi Takei, Kimihiko Tsurugaya, Toru Ikegaki, Keisuke Utsumi, Yasuhisa Serizawa, Masaharu Komatsuki; In Charge of Location Site (Gotemba), Magosaku Osada, Shizuo Osada; Production Accountants, Shuji Matsumoto, Hiroko Idetsu; Production Assistants, Shushin Hosoya, Satoshi Shimozawa, Kazutoshi Wadakura; Recording Studio, Toho Recording Centre; Raw Stock, Kodak Japan; Art Department, Toho E-B; Props, Takatsu Soshoku Bijutsu; Explosives, Ohira Special

Effects; Hair Styles and Wigs, Yauada Katsura; Wardrobe, Tokyo Isho; Sound Effects, Toyo Onkyo Kauove; Music Production, Tokyo Concert; Sound Equipment, Tisman Service; Camera Equipment, Sanwa Cine-Equipment Rental Co., Ltd.; Lighting Equipment, Lee Colortran International; Vehicles, Nippon Shomei, Film Link International; Background Music, Ippolitov-Ivanov "In the Village," from Caucasian Sketches Suite for Orchestra Op. 10; Conducting Moscow Radio Symphony Orchestra, Vladimir Fedoseev; Hi-Definition TV Technology, Sony PCL; Photo-Composite Process, Akio Suzuki, Mikio Inoue, Mutsuhiro Harada, Yoshiya Takahashi; EBR Process, Tonio Onata, Takaya Takizawa; HDTV Coordinator, Tetsuji Maezawa; Composite Technology, Den-Film-Effects; Special Effects Unit (Japan) Visual Effects, Minoru Nakano; Technical Editor, Michihisa Miyashige; Optical Photography, Takashi Kobayashi, Takashi Kawabata; Optical Camera Operators, Makoto Negishi, Takabuni Hirata; Matte Painting, Taksuhiro Miyaguchi; Visual Effects (U.S.), Industrial Light and Magic, a Division of LucasArts Entertainment Company. *ILM Visual Effects Unit*: Supervisors, Ken Ralston, Mark Sullivan; Producer, Peter Takeuchi; Art Director, Claudia Mullaly; Model Supervisor, Barbara Affonso; Optical Supervisor, Bruce Veccitto; Editor, Michael Gleason; Coordinator, Jil Sheree Bergin; Camera Operators, Terry Chostner, Selwyn Eddy III; Assistant Camera Operators, Randy Johnson, John Gazdik, Robert Hill; Matte Camera Operators, Jo Carson, Wade Childress, Paul Huston, Charles Canfield; Assistant Matte Camera Operator, Nancy Morita; Matte Painters, Yusei Useugi, Caroleen Green; Matte Assistant, Jonathan Crowe; Modelmakers, Brian Gernand, E'ven Stromquist, Randy Ottenberg, Wesley Seeds, Marge McMahon; Optical Lineup, Peggy Hunter, Dave Karpman, Lori Nelson, Thomas Tosseter; Optical Camera Operators, Jon Alexander, Jeff Doran; Postproduction Coordinator, Susan Adele Colletta; Rotoscope Artist, Barbara Brennan; Stage Supervisor, Brad Jerrell; Head Electrician, Tim Morgan; Electrician, David Murphy; Chief Pyrotechnician, Charles Ray; Pyrotechnician, Reuben Goldberg; Cloud Tank, Craig Mohegan.

Cast—"Sunshine Through the Rain": Mitsuko Baisho (Mother of "I"), Toshihiko Nakano ("I" as a Young Child). "The Peach Orchard": Mitsunori Isaki ("I" as a Boy), Mie Suzuki ("I's" Sister). "The Blizzard": Mieko Harada (The Snow Fairy), Masayuki Yui Shu Nakajima, Sakae Kimura (Members of the Climbing Team). "The Tunnel": Yoshitaka Zushi (Private Noguchi). "Crows": Akira Terao ("I"), Martin Scorsese (Vincent Van Gogh). "Mt. Fuji in Red": Akira Terao ("I"), Toshie Negishi (Child-Carrying Mother), Hisashi Igawa (Power Station Worker). "The Weeping Demon": Akira Terao ("I"), Chosuke Ikariya (The Demon). "Village of the Watermills": Akira Terao ("I"), Chishu Ryu (103-year-old Man).

Also: Mugita Endo, Ryujiro Oki, Masaru Sakurai, Masaaki Sasaki, Keiki Takenouchi, Kento Toriki, Shu Nakajima, Tokuju Nasuda, Masuo Amada, Sakae Kimura, Shogo Tomomori, Ryo Nagasawa, Akisato Yamada, Tetsu Watanabe, Ken Takemura, Yasuhiro Kajimoto.

Makoto Hasegawa, Nagamitsu Satake, Satoshi Hara, Yasushige Turuoka, Shigeru Edaki, Hideharu Takeda, Katsumi Naito, Masaaki Enomoto, Norio Takei, Eiji Iida, Koji Kanda, Hideto Aota, Kazue Nakanishi, Rika Miyazawa, Mika Edaki, Mayumi Kamimura, Sayuri Yoshioka, Teruko Nakayama, Sachicko Nakayama.

Toshiya Ito, Takashi Ito, Motoyuki Higashimura, Yasuhito Yamanaka, Haruka Sugata, Noriko Hayami, Ayaka Takahashi, Yuko Ishiwa, Sachiko Oguri.

Masayo Mochida, Miki Kado, Ikeya Sakiko Yamamoto, Mayumi Ono Yumiko Miyata, Aya Ikaida, Megumi Hata, Asako Hirano, Chika Nishio, Yuko Harada, Tomomi Yoshizawa, Kunido Ishizuka, Maumi Yoda, Hatsue Nishi, Michiko Kawada, Machiko Ichihashi, Yumi Ezaki, Chika Yanabe, Mayuko Akashi.

Fujio Tokita, Michio Hino, Michio Kida, Ayako Honua, Haruko Togo, Reiko Nanao. Shin Tonomura, Junpei Natsuki, Shigeo

Kato, Saburo Kadowaki, Goichi Nagatani, Shizuko Azuma, Yoshie Kihira, Yukie Shimura, Setsuko Kawaguchi, Kemeko Otowa.

Machiko Terada, Umiko Takahashi, Harumi Fuji, Hiroko Okuno, Mon Ota, Akitokuz Inaba, Kou Ishikawa, Tatsunori Takuhashi.

Yoshiko Maki, Hiroko Maki, Ryoko Kawai, Miyako Kawana, Miyuki Egawa, Megumi Sakai, Yoko Hayashi, Yuko Matsumura, Takashi Odajima, Mitsuru Shibuya, Koichi Imamura, Wasuke Izumi.

Sachio Saki, Torauemon Utazawa, Yukimasa Natori, Tadashi Okumura, Kenzo Shirahana, Masato Goto, Sumimaro Yochini, Juichi Kubozono, Masami Ozeki, Yasuyuki Iwanaga, Akira Tashiro, Koichi Kase, Kenji Fujita, Hiroto Tamura, Osamu Yayama, Yuji Sawayana, Mitsuji Tsuwako, Masatoshi Miya.

Maiko Okamoto, Nana Yanakawa, Yuka Kojima, Shizuka Isami, Mai Watanabe, Sayuri Kobayashi.

Hayakawa Productions, Himawani Theatre Group, Inc., Motoko Inagawa Office, Tanbe Dojo, Kokugakuin University Mizutamakai.

An Akira Kurosawa USA, Inc., Production. A Japanese–U.S. Co-Production. Released by Toho Co., Ltd. (?). Dolby Stereo. Eastman Color (processed by Inagica). Prints by Technicolor. Spherical Panavision. Thanks to the Akira Kurosawa Film Society. Filmed at Kurosawa Film Studio and Toho Studios, Ltd.

U.S. Version: Released by Warner Bros., Inc., in subtitled format. English Subtitles, Donald Richie, Tadashi Shishido. Actors whose roles are not specified are grouped on screen as above. 120 minutes. MPAA rating: PG. Released 1990.

Aru mittsu. "Bi to shu" ("Beauty and Ugliness") Writer-Director, Kan Mukoi; "Shikimu" ("Love Dream") Writer-Director, Shinya Yamamoto; "Kuchibeni" ("Lipstick") Director, Koji Wakamatsu; Screenplay, Jiku Yamatoya.

Cast—"Bi to Shu": Mitsugu Gujii (Old Man), Takako Uchida (Young Girl). "Shikimu": Michiyo Mako (The Beauty), Yuichi Minato (The Man). "Kuchibeni": Hiroshi Nikaido (Newlywed Husband), Yoshiko Ikada (Newlywed Wife), Masayoshi Nogami (Fisherman).

A Nihon Cinema Production. Black and white. Academy ratio. 73 minutes. Released 1967.

U.S. Version: Distributor, if any, is undetermined. International title: *A Certain Adultery.* Only part two has fantastic elements.

The Beast and the Magic Sword. Executive Producer, Sigueiro Amachi; Writer-Producer-Director, Jocinto Molina (Alvarez); Director of Photography, Julio Burgos.

Cast: Paul Naschy [Jocinto Molina Alvarez] (Count Waldemar Daninsky), Julia Saly, Beatriz Escudero, Sigueiro Amachi, Junki Asahina, Violeta Cela, Yoko Fuji, Gerard Tichy, Conrado San Martin.

An Aconito Film (Madrid)/Amachi Films (Tokyo) Production. A Japanese-Spanish co-production. Eastman Color. Wide screen (1.66:1). Running time undetermined. Released 1983.

U.S. Version: Never released theatrically in the United States (?). Sold directly to television (?). Released in Spain in 1983 as *La Bestia y la Espada Magica* (*The Beast and the Magic Sword*), running 118 minutes. Working title: *La Bestia y los samurais* (*The Besat and the Samurais*). Last of the Spanish-made "Count Daninsky the Werewolf" series, preceded, in order, by *Frankenstein's Bloody Terror* (U.S. release, 1972), *Night of the Werewolf* (U.S. release, 1968), *Assignment Terror* (U.S. release, 1970), *The Werewolf and the Vampire Woman* (U.S. release, 1975), *The Fury of the Wolfman* (U.S. release, 1971), *Doctor Jekyll and the Werewolf* (U.S. release, 1974), *Curse of the Devil* (U.S. release, 1977), *Horror of the Werewolf* (U.S. release, 1976) and *Return of the Wolfman* (U.S. release, 1980). 100 minutes. No MPAA rating.

The Beasts' Carnival. Writer-Producer-Director, Jocinto Molina (Alvarez); Director of Photography, Alejandro Ulloa.

Cast: Paul Naschy [Jocinto Molina Alvarez] (The Spaniard), Eiko Nagashima (Mieko), Lautaro Murua, Silvia Aguilar, Azucena Hernandez, Julia Saly, Kogi Maritugu, Mieko Gustanave.

A Dalmata Films (Madrid)/Hori Kikaku Co., Ltd. (Tokyo), Production. A Japanese-

Spanish co-production. Filmed in Japan, Thailand and Spain. Eastman Color. Wide screen (1.66:1). Running time undetermined. Released 1980.

U.S. Version: Distributor, if any, is undetermined. Released in Spain in 1980 as *El Carnaval de los bestias*.

The Big Wave. Executive Producer, Pearl S. Buck; Producer-Director, Tad Danielewski; Screenplay, Pearl S. Buck, Tad Danielewski, based on the novel by Pearl S. Buck; Director of Photograhy, Ichio Yamazeki; Editor, Akikazu Kono; Music, Toshiro Mayuzumi, conducted by Hiroshi Yoshizawa; Song "Be Ready at Dawn," Music by Toshiro Mayuzumi, Lyrics by Tad Danielewski; Production Supervisor, Masayuki Nakajima; Production Manager, Clark Playlow; Assistant Director, Joseph E. Markarof; Dialogue Coach, Sylvia Danielewski; Script Supervisor, Noriko Maebatake; Art Director, Itsuro Hirata; Property Master, Satoru Sango; Special Effects, Kenji Inagawa; Wardrobe, Yoshiaki Murata, Iku Tsuda; Makeup, Haruhiko Yamada; Gaffer, Yokichi Hishinuma; Sound Recording, Hidejiro Yotsie; Sound Mixing, Michio Okazaki; Sound Effects, Toho Sound Effects Group; Sound, Toho Recording Centre.

Cast: Sessue Hayakawa (The Old Gentleman), Ichizo Itami (Toru), Mickey Curtis (Yukio), Kiji Shitara (Toru as a Boy), Hiroyuki Ota (Yukio as a Boy), Rumiko Sasa (Setsu), Judy Ongg (Setsu as a Girl), Reiko Higa (Haruko), Sachiko Atami (Haruko as a Girl), Henry Okawa (Yukio's Father), Cheiko Murata (Yukio's Mother), Tetsu Nakamura (Toru's Father), Frank Tokunaga (Toru's Grandfather), Shigeru Nihonmatsu (Old Servant), Noriko Sengoku (Toru's Mother).

A Stratton Productions, Inc., Production, in cooperation with Toho Co., Ltd. An American-Japanese co-production. Filmed at Toho Studios. Produced in English. Western Electric Mirrophonic recording. Black and white (processed by Tokyo Laboratory, Ltd.). Wide screen. 98 minutes (?). Released 1961 (?).

U.S. Version: Released by Allied Artists Pictures Corporation. U.S. prints by DeLuxe. Copyright April 2, 1962 (in notice 1961), by Allied Artists Pictures Corporation. 73 minutes. No MPAA rating. Released April 2, 1961.

Death by Hanging/Koshikei. Producers, Masayuki Nakajima, Takuji Yamaguchi, Nagisa Oshima; Director, Nagisa Oshima; Screenplay, Tsutomu Tamura, Mamoru Sasaki, Minichiro Fukao, Nagisa Oshima; Supervisor, Teruyoshi Mukae; Assistant Director, Kiyioshi Ogakawara; Art Director, Jusho Toda; Director of Photography, Yasuhiro Yoshioka; Editor, Sueko Shiraishi; Music, Hikaru Hayashi; Sound Recording, Hideo Nishizaki; Sound Effects, Akira Suzuki.

Cast: Kei Sato (Head of Execution Guard), Fumioi Watanabe (Education Officer), Toshio Ishido (Chaplain), Masao Adachi (Security Officer), Mutsuhiro Toura (Doctor), Hosei Komatsu (Prosecutor), Masao Matsuda (Prosecution Official), Akiko Koyama (Girl), Yun-do Yun (R), Yoshio Tsuchiya (Rikichi), Kuninori Kodo (Gisaku), Nagisa Oshima (Commentator).

A Sozosha and Japan Art Theatre Guild Production. Black and white. Vista Vision (possibly cropped wide srcen). 117 minutes. Released 1968.

U.S. Version: Released by New Yorker Films in subtitled format. 117 minutes. No MPAA rating. Released 1971 (?).

Dismembered Ghost/Kaidan barabara yurei. Director, Kinya Ogawa.

Cast: Rieko Akikawa (Masako), Setsu Shimizu (Masako's Stepmother), Miki Hayashi (Surmiko), Kenichiro Masayama (Tsukagoshi), Hiroshi Nikaido (Shinjiro).

An Okura Eiga Production. Black and white. Academy ratio. 71 minutes. Released 1968.

U.S. Version: Distributor undetermined. International title: *A Ghost Story: Barabara Phantom*. Released 1968 (?).

Hikarigoke. Producers, Taketoshi Naito, Tohru Aizawa; Director, Kei Kumai; Screenplay, Taro Ikeda, Kei Kumai, based on the novel by Taijun Takeda; Production Designer, Takeo Kumura; Director of Photography, Masao Tochizawa; Editor, Osamu Inoue; Music, Teizo Matsumura; Sound, Kenichi Benitani.

Cast: Rentaro Mikuni (Captain/Headmaster), Eiji Okada (Nishikawa), Kunie Tanaka (Hachizo), Tetsuta Sugimoto (Gosuke), Taketoshi Naito (Novelist), Hisashi Igawa (Prosecutor), Masane Tsukayama (Defense Attorney), Chisu Tyu (Presiding Judge).

A Film Crescent/Neo-Life Production. Color. Wide screen. 118 minutes. Released 1991.

U.S. Version: Distributor, if any, is undetermined. Released internationally by Herald Ace.

Jasei no in. Director, Thomas Kurihara; Based on the story by Akinari [Shusei] Ueda.

Cast: Tokihiko Okada, Yoko Benizawa.

A Taikatsu Production. Silent. Black and white. Academy ratio. Running time undetermined. Released 1920.

U.S. Version: Distributor, if any, is undetermined. International title: *Obscenity of the Viper, Lasciviousness of the Viper* and *The Maliciousness of the Snake's Evil.* Remade as *Tales of Ugetsu* (Daiei, 1953).

Jotari johatsu. Director, Seiichi Fukuda.

Cast: Midori Enoki (Bar Hostess), Hachiro Tsuruoka (Ejiri), Hiroko Fuji (Ejiri Ex-Wife), Yuri Izumi, Machiko Sakyo, Kemi Ichiboshi.

A Nihon Cinema Production. Black and white. Academy ratio. 83 minutes. Released 1967.

U.S. Version: Distributor, if any, is undetermined. International title: *Woman's Body Vanishes.*

Kaidan Gojusan-tsugi. Director, Kokichi Uchide.

·Cast: Kokichi Takada, Hiromi Hanazono.

Production company undetermined, though likely either Daiei or Toei. Black and white. Running time undetermined. Released 1960.

U.S. Version: Distributor, if any, is undetermined. International title: *Ghost of Gojusan-Tsugi.*

Kaidan ijin yurei. Director, Satoru Kobayashi.

Cast: Miyako Ishijo, Kyoko Ogimachi.

An Okura Eiga Production. Black and white. Academy ratio. Running time undetermined. Released 1963.

U.S. Version: Distributor, if any, is undetermined. International title: *Caucasian Ghost.*

Kyofu no daiuzumaki. Director, Buichi Saito.

Cast: Keiko Natsuo, Toshio Kurosawa.

A Kindai Eiga Kyokai Production. Color. Academy ratio. Running time undetermined. Released 1978.

U.S. Version: Distributor, if any, is undetermined. A Japanese telefeature released theatrically outside Japan. International title: *Horror of the Giant Vortex.*

The Man Who Stole the Sun/*Taiyo o nusunda otoko.* Director, Kazuhiko Hasegawa; Screenplay, Kazuhiko Hasegawa, Leonard Schrader; Director of Photography, Tatsuo Suzuki.

Cast: Kenji Sawada, Bunta Sugawara, Kimiko Ikegemi, Yonosuke Ito.

A Kitty Films Production. Color. 130 minutes. Released 1980.

U.S. Version: Distributor, if any, is undetermined. International release by Kitty Enterprises.

The Manster. Executive Producer, William Shelton; Producer, George P. Breakston; Associate Producers, Robert Perkins, Ryukichi Aimono; Directors, George P. Breakston, Kenneth G. Crane; Screenplay, Walter J. Sheldon, based on an original story by George P. Breakston; Production Supervisor, C. D. Sykes; Production Manager, Yuji Honda; Unit Manager, Richard Herbine; Assistant Director, Dan Takahashi; Continuity, Lynn Cariddi; Art Director, Noboru Miyakuni; Wardrobe, Kazuko Suzuki; Makeup, Fumiko Yamamoto; Director of Photography, David Mason; Special

Effects, Shinpei Takagi; Recording Supervisor, Chisato Ota; Sound, Aoi Studio; Supervising Editor, Kenneth G. Crane; Music, Hirooki Ogawa.

Cast: Peter Dyneley (Larry Stanford), Jane Hylton (Linda Stanford), Tetsu Nakamura (Dr. Robert Suzuki), Terri Zimmern (Tara), Norman Van Hawley (Ian Matthews), Jerry Ito (Police Superintendent Aida), Toyoko Takechi (Emiko Suzuki), Alan Tarlton (Dr. H. B. Jennsen), Kenzo Kuroki, Shinpei Takagi, George Wyman.

A Shaw-Breakston Enterprises Production. A United Artists of Japan, Inc., Picture. A William Shelton Presentation. A Lopert Pictures Corp. Release. RCA Photophone recording. Black and white. Prints by De Luxe. Wide screen (1.66:1 projected aspect ratio). 72 minutes. Released 1961.

U.S. Version: Released by United Artists Corp. Advertised as *The Manster: Half Man, Half Monster*. Working titles: *Nightmare* and *The Two-Headed Monster*. UK title: *The Split*. Double billed with *The Horror Chamber of Dr. Faustus* (Lopert, 1962). 72 minutes. No MPAA rating. Released March 28, 1962.

The Moon Mask Rider/Gekko kamen (?). Executive Producer, Kohan Kawauchi; Producers, Hiromitsu Furukawa, Hisao Masuda; Director, Yukihiro Sawada; Screenplay, Kohan Kawauchi, Yukihiro Sawada, based on a novel by Kohan Kawauchi; Producer's Representative, Michiyo Yoshizaki; Music, Kohan Kawauchi.

Cast: Daisuke Kuwabara, Etsuko Shiomi, Takuya Fujioka, Takeo Chii, Hosei Komatsu.

A Nippon Herald Films, Inc., Production. Color. Panavision (?). Running time undetermined. Released 1981.

U.S. Version: Distributor, if any, is undetermined. Nippon Herald also handled the international release.

Namakubi joshi jiken. Director, Kinya Lgawa [Igawa?]

Cast: Hachiro Tsuruoka (Goro Fujiyama), Kozue Hinotori (Reiko Fujiyama), Junko Kozuki (Junko Arishima), Yoshi Izumida (Dr. Mita), Yuri Izumi (Nurse Machiko).

An Okura Eiga Production. Black and white. Academy ratio. Running time undetermined. Released 1967.

U.S. Version: Distributor, if any, is undetermined. International title: *Love Foolery Case for a Severed Head*.

Okasaretu Byuakui. Producer-Director, Koji Wakamatsu; Screenplay, Koji Wakamatsu, Masao Adachi, Juro Kara; Director of Photography, Hideo Ito; Production Manager, Masayuki Miyama; Special Effects, Fukushima Group; Editor, Fumio Tomita; Sound, Shin Kida; Music, Koji Takamura.

Cast: Jura Kara (The Boy), Michiko Sakamoto (The Girl), Reiko Koyanagi (The Head Nurse), Miki Hayashi, Shoki Kido, Makiko Saegusa, Kyoko Yayoi (Nurses).

A Wakamatsu Productions Production. A Wakamatsu Release. Black and white, with color inserts. CinemaScope. 58 minutes. Released 1967.

U.S. Version: Distributor, if any, is undetermined. International title: *Violated Angels*. Alternate title: *Violated Woman*.

A Page of Madness/Kurutta ippeiji. Producer-Director, Teinosuke Kinugasa; Screenplay, Yasunari Kawabata, Teinosuke Kinugasa; Directors of Photography, Kohei Sugiyama, Eiji Tsuburaya; Music (reissue version), Minoru Muraoka, Toru Kurashima.

Cast: Masao Inoue (Custodian), Yoshi Nakagawa (Wife), Ayako Iijima (Daughter), Hiroshi Nemoto (Young Man), Misao Seki (Doctor), Minoru Takase (First Madman), Kyosuke Takamatsu (Second Madman), Tetsu Tsuboi (Third Madman), Eiko Minami (Dancing Girl).

A Kinugasa Productions/Shin Kankaku-ha Eiga Renmei Production. Silent (musical score on reissue version). Black and white. Academy ratio. 60 minutes. Released 1926.

U.S. Version: Released by New Line Cinema Corp. Reissued in Japan with musical score in 1973. 60 minutes. No MPAA rating. Released January 1975.

The Pitfall/Kashi to kodomo. Executive Producer, Hiroshi Teshigahara; Producers, Kiichi Ichikawa, Tadashi Ohono; Director, Hiroshi Teshigahara; Story-Screenplay, Kobo Abe; Production Supervisor, Hiroshi Kawazoc; Design, Kiyoshi Awazu; Director of Photography, Hiroshi Segawa; Lighting, Mitsuo Kume; Sound, Keiji Mori; Music, Toru Takemitsu; Editor, Fusako Shuzui; Assistant Director, Masuo Ogawa; Production Manager, Iwao Yashida.

Cast: Hisachi Igawa, K. Miyahara.

A Teshigahara Productions Picture. Coproduction company (if any) and distributor undetermined (though likely Toho). Westrex recording system. Black and white. Wide screen (1.66:1) (?). Running time undetermined. Released 1962.

U.S. Version: Distributor undetermined (likely Toho International). Released 1964 (?).

Solar Crisis/Kuraishisu niju-goju nen (*Crisis 2050*?). Executive Producers, Takehito Sadamura, Takeshi Kawate; Producers, Richard Edlund, Tsuneyuki [Morris] Morishima, James Nelson; Associate Producer, Barbara Nelson; Director, Alan Smithee [Richard C. Sarafian]; Screenplay, Joe Gannon, Crispan Bolt, Ted Sarafian, based on the novel by Takeshi Kawata; Director of Photography, Russ Carpenter; Production Design, George Jenson; Art Director, John Bruce; Technical Advisor, Richard J. Terrile; Costume Designer, Robert Turturice; Music, Maurice Jarre; Additional Music, Michael Baddicker. Songs: "Was a Time," Words and Music by Les Hooper, Sung by Sherwood Ball (published by Hooperman Music); "Freedom Sings," Words and Music by Les Hooper, Sung by Carmen Twillie (published by Hooperman Music); "Orlop Piano," Music by Les Hooper; "Travis Rides Again" and "Strip Star Chase," Music by Tedi Sarafian. Casting, Diane Dimeo, C.S.A.; Production Managers, Kim Kurumada, Ronald B. Colby, Robert Anderson; First Assistant Directors, Jerry Ziesmer, Leonid Zisman; Second Assistant Directors, Robert Roda, Michael-McCloud Thompson; Technical Adviser, Richard Terrile, Ph.D.; Art Director, John P. Bruce; Set Decorator, Donna Stamps; Camera Operator, Steven Finestone; Property Masters, Sal Sommatino, Mark Alan Luine; Illustrator, Thomas A. Cranham; Robotruck/Vertol Designs, Simon Murton; Assistant Art Directors, Peter Samishi, Stephen Dane; SPFX Coordinator, Kelly Kerby; Electronic Effects Coodinator, William Klinger, Jr.; Chief Lighting Technician, Reginald F. Lake; Key Grip, Curtiss Bradford; Production Sound Mixer, Dennis W. Carr; Script Supervisor, Connie Barzaghi; Costume Supervisor, Jill M. Ohanneson; Key Makeup Artist, Paula Sutor; Key Hair Stylist, Larry Waggoner; Construction Coordinator, Andrew Hanlen; Transportation Coordinator, Paul Howes; Set Designers, Gina Cranham, Beverly Eagan; First Assistant Cameraman, Mark Jackson; Second Assistant Cameraman, Scott Herring; Still Photographer, Ernest Garza; Assistant SPFX Coordinator, Michael O'Connor; Assistant Chief Lighting Technician, Bob Neville; Best Boy Grip, Cobie Fair; Dolly Grip, Malcolm Doran II; Assistant Property Masters, Anthony DiSalvo, Duff Miller; Leadman, John J. C. Scherer; Set Decorator–Production Buyer, Wilhelm G. Pfau; On-Set Dresser, Tim Van Wormer; Key Costumer, Meg Goodwin; Set Costumer, Scott Barr Tomlinson; Boom Operator, Walter Anderson; Construction Foremen, Jerry Etzler, Bryce Walmsley, Verna Bagby, James Eric; Model Makers, Roderick Schumaker, Phillip Hartman; Transportation Captain, Les Orrison; Picture Car Coordinator, Ken Plumlee; Production Coordinator, Susan Becton; Location Manager, Christopher Ursitti; Production Accountants, Lisa Howard, Ramona Waggoner; Assistant Production Coordinator, Leslie A. Tokunaga; Assistant Production Accountant, Leslie Falkinburg; Accounting Clerk, Michael Vasquez; Art Department Coordinator, Dayle Dodge; Art Department Researcher, John Curtis; DGA Trainee, Robert Scott; Production Assistants, Andrew Flynn, Jonathan Wachtel, Mark Spencer, Patricia O'Reilly; Assistant to the Executive

Producer, Christine Iso; Assistants to Mr. Morishima, Fuyo Arimoto, Rod Findley; Publicist, Ann Strick; First Assistant Camera-Plate, Daniel Dayton; Camera Production Assistants, Morgan Tanaka, Brett Harding, Gary George; Construction, Lexington Scenery and Props, Time and Space, Inc.; Environmental Control Systems, Solex Technologies, Inc. (Houston); Special Props Designer, Ed Eyth; Futuristic Props Creator, Neotek; Strip Star Corvette, Gene Winfield of Rod and Custom; Animals, Hollywood Animal Rentals, Jungle Exotics, Myers and Willis; Catering, Michelson's Food Service; Movie Magic Software, Screenplay Systems; Production Services and Equipment, Keylite PSI; Cranes and Dollies, Chapman; Special Thanks, Titeflex, Inc., Massini, Inc., Mikohn, Inc., Atari Computers, International Game Technology, Inc., Bureau of Land Management, the Westin Bonaventure Hotel, John Wayne Airport (Santa Ana). Additional Production: Producer, Joan McCormick-Cooper; Director of Photography, Steve Finestone; Editor, Charles V. Coleman; Production Manager/First AD, Jerry Sobul; Second AD, Carole Keligian; Set Decorator, Inter World; Set Design and Construction, Time and Space; Special Effects, Howard Jensen; Wardrobe Supervisor, Scott Tomlinson; Key Makeup, Bonita DeHaven; Key Hair Stylist, Susan Mills; Property Master, Tony DiSalvo; Stills, Patrick Bock; Sound Mixer, Bo Harewood; Gaffer, Mike Laviolette; Key Grip, Dyland Shephard; Script Supervisor, Annie Welles; Production Coordinator, Mary Ramirez; Production Accountant, Steve Lazo; Assistant to Arthur Marks, Laurie Foi; Production Secretary, Grace Cobiella; Location Manager, Ron Carr; Casting, Marvin Page; Additional Re-Recording Mixing, William Caughey, CAS, Bob Beemer; Additional Re-Recording Facilities, Skywalker Sound, a division of LucasArts Entertainment Group. Post Production: Editor, Richard Trevor; Earth Sounds Editor, David Baldwin; Space Sounds Editor, Scott Martin Gershwin; Assistant Editor, Hazel Trevor; Second Assistant Editor, Linda Schubell-Sundlin; Apprentice Editor, Dawn Michelle King; Supervising ADR Editor, Greg Baxter, MPSE; Dialogue/Foley Editors, George Fredrick, Kevin Hearst (Raoul), Dan Rich; ADR Editors, Kelly Oxford, Victor Ennis, Michael Hoskinson; Additional Audio, Mark Lanza; Foley Supervisor, Sukey Fontelieu; Foley Artists, Dan O'Connell, Alicia Stevenson; Music Editor, Dan Carlin, Sr.; ADR Group Coordinator, Burton Sharp; Re-Recording Mixers, John Reitz, CAS, David Campbell, CAS, and Gregg Rudloff, CAS; ADR Mixers, Wally Beardon, Chris Tucker; Foley Mixer, Doc Kane; Scoring Mixer, Shawn Murphy; Assistant to Mr. Jarre, Patrick Russ; Negative Cutting, Gary Burritt; Color Timers, Bill Pine, Mike Stanwick; Sound Effects, Soundelux; Re-recorded at Buena Vista Sound; Special Lenses, Meade Industries; Additional Opticals, Howard A. Anderson Company, the Chandler Group; Titles, Howard A. Anderson Company; Computer Generated Main Title Design, Charles McDonald. *Special Visual Effects:* Boss Film Corporation; Producer, Neil Krepela; Director, Richard Edlund; Conceptual Futurist, Syd Mead; Sound Effects Design and Supervisors, Wylie Stateman and Lon E. Bender; (On-Set?) Special Effects, Craig Smith; Chief Lighting Technician, Rob Eyslee; Key Grip, John Donnely; Grip, Pat Van Guken; Pyrotechnician, Joseph Viskocil; Stage Production Assistant, Mark Hartman; Matte Painter, Michael Moen; Matte Camera, Alan Harding; Storyboard Illustrators, John Jensen, Brent Boates; Art Department/Animation Supervisor, Mauro Maressa; Animator, Phil Cummings; Assistant Animator, William Knoll; Animation Production Assistant, Colin Campbell; Technical Animation Supervisor, Holly Hudson; Technical Animator, Maura Alvarez; Assistant Visual Effects Editor, Jim May; Editorial Production Assistnt, Julia Rivas; Post Production Coordinator, Joni Harding; Visual Effects Coordinator, Donna Langston; Computer Graphics Coordinator, Christine Sellin; Camera Equipment Coordinator, Duane Mieliwocki; Stage Coordinator, Donna Lipshin; Production Secretary, Mary Johnston;

Production Assistants, Stephen Ehrensberger, John LaPage; Supervising Model Maker, Pat McClung; Chief Model Maker, Leslie Ekker; Model Makers, Larry De Unger, Kent Gebo, Adam Gelbart, Pete Gerard, Ken Larson, Bruce MacRae, Gerald McClung, Nicholas Seldon; Mechanisms Key Man, Robert Johnson; Mechanisms, Gary Bierent; Head Painter, Ron Gress; Model Shop Production Assistants, Christine Cowan, Roberto DePalma, John Hagen-Brenner, Erik Haraldsted, Doug Miller, Paul Ozzimo, Mike Possert, Scott Schneider, Andy Siegal, Jon Warren; Model Shop Coordinator, Chris Bowler; Model Shop Illustrator, John Eaves; Model Shop Consultant, Ray Shenusay; Machine Shop Foreman, Kan Dudderar; Electronics Technicians, Jeff Platt, Douglass Calli; Controller, Maryjane Zelickovics; Purchasing Agent, Greg Wolff; Special Solar Imaging, Peter Parks of Oxford, Scientific Films, Ltd., assisted by Suzi Parks and Peter Field. Computer Animation: Pacific Data Images, Inc., Carl Rosendahl, President; Executive Producer, Glenn Entis; Producer, David McCullough; Technical Support/Animator, Jamie Dixon; Software/Technical Support, Thad Beier; Animators, Theresa Ellis, Rex Grignon; Technical Assistance, Terry Emmons; Video and Graphic Displays, Video Image (Rhonda C. Gunner, Richard Hollander, Gregory McMurray, John Wash); Video Image Coordinator, Janet Earl; Video Image Crew, Monte Swann, Pete Martinez.

Cast: Tim Matheson (Captain Steve Kelso), Charlton Heston (Admiral "Skeet" Kelso), Annabel Schofield (Alex Noffe), Peter Boyle (Arnold Teague), Tetsuya Bessho (Ken Minami), Corin "Corky" Nemec (Mike Kelso), Jack Palance (Travis James Richards), Paul Koslo (Dr. Haas), Sandy McPeak (Gurney), Scott Alan Campbell (McBride), Frantz Turner (Lamare), Silvano Gallardo (T. C.), Dan Shor (Harvard), Dorian Harewood (Borg), Brenda Blake (Dr. Claire Beeson), Paul Williams (voice of Freddy), David Ursin (Kovac), Scott Allan Campbell (McBride), Frantz Turner (Lamare), Richard S. Scott (Meeks), Eric James (Louisiana), Rhonda Dotson (Waitress), William A. Wallace (Pohl), Michael Berryman (Matthew), Roy Jenson (Bartender), Jimmie F. Skaggs (Biker), Chris Nash ("Corvette" Driver), H. M. Wynant (IXL Executive #1), Paul Carr (IXL Executive #2), Milt Kogan (IXL Man #2 [Baldy]), Arnold Quinn (IXL Man #3 [Ponytail]), Louis Elias (IXL Man #4 [Action Louie]), John Barrymore (Avery), Carole Hemingway (Rhonda), Don Craig (TV Anchorman), Jerry Hauck (Corporal Flynn), John Hugh (Dr. Dufait), Bob Meroff (Camel Rider), Steve Welles (Prophet), Rick Dorio (Bandit #1), Mindy Reid (Astronaut #4), Jimmy Austin (Technician), Sherwood Ball (Little Al's Singer), Carmen Twillie (Army Band Singer), Richard Eden (Medical Technician), Roy T. Fukagaw (Little Al's Cook), Robert Hawkins (Security Officer #1), Jon Tabler (Security Officer #2), Tammy Maples (Mrs. Steve Kelso), Ted Montue (Bridge Officer), Richard Terrile (Hologram Operator), Michael Stanhope (Astronomer), Kathryn Spitz (IXL Receptionist), Ann Fink (VidPhone Operator), Saida Rodrigues Pagan (Correspondent), Stephen R. Kujala (Voice of Robotruck), Tracy Jones Stateman (Voice of Helios Computer), Terrence Beasor (Narrator), Mario Roberts, Vince Deadrick, Larry Duran, Stacy Elias, Eurlyne Epper, Bill Hart (Bandits), Andy Armstrong, David Burton, Steve Lambert, James Lew, Billy Lucas, George Sack, Jr. (Stunts).

A Japan America Picture Company, Inc., Production, in association with Asahi Breweries, Ltd., Toppan Printing Co., Ltd., Yamaichi Securities Co., Ltd., Lotte Co., Inc., Nippon Steel Corp., Mitsui and Co., Ltd., and Nissho Iwai Corporation. A Gakken (Hideto and Hiroshi Furuoka)/NHK Enterprises (Shuji Tanuma) Presentation. A Shochiku-Fuji Release. A Japanese–U.S. co-production. Filmed at Hewitt Street Studios, Harbor Stage, Los Angeles, Baker (California), and Clark County (California). English with Japanese subtitles. Dolby Stereo SR (Spectral Recording). Color by DeLuxe. Panavision. 118 minutes. Released August 1990.

U.S. Version: Never released theatrically in the United States. Released directly to home video in 1993 by Vidmark Entertainment. The laser disc version is letterboxed. A Trimark Pictures Release. U.S. Version copyright 1992 by Gakken NHK Enterprises. International distributor, Inter-Ocean Film Sales, Ltd. International title: *Solar Crisis*. Alternate titles: *Starfire* and *Crisis 2050*. MPAA rating: PG-13. 111 minutes.

Tetsuo: The Iron Man/Tetsuo. Producer, Director, Screenwriter, Co-Director of Photography, Editor, Art Director, Lighting and Special Effects, Shinya Tsukamoto; Co-Director of Photography and Wardrobe, Kei Fujiwara; Music, Chu Ishikawa; Music Operator, Mitsuhiro Ozaki; Insert Music, Akio Okosawa; Sound, Asashi Sound Studio; Assistant Director, Kei Fujiwara; Production Assistants, Nobu Kanaoka, Hiroyuki Kobato, Akiko Ishigami, Akiko Kodaka.

Cast: Tomoroh Taguchi (Salaryman), Kei Fujiwara (Girlfriend), Nobu Kanaoko (Woman in Glasses), Shinya Tsukamoto (Metals Fetishist), Naomasa Musaka (Doctor), Renji Ishibashi (Tramp).

A Kaiju Theatre Production in association with Japan Home Video/K2 Spirit/SEN. 16mm. Black and white. 1.37:1 projected screen ratio. 67 minutes. Released 1988.

U.S. Version: Released by Original Cinema in subtitled format. Subtitles, Kiyo Joo and Tony Rayns. Generally paired with the U.S.-made, 25-minute short *Drum Struck* (Original Cinema, 1991) *Note:* the name Tetsuo as spelled in the Kanji means "iron man." No MPAA rating. Released 1991.

Tetsuo II: Body Hammer. Producers, Fuminori Shishido, Fumio Kurokawa; Executive Producers, Hiroshi Koizumi, Shinya Tsukamoto; Director, Screenwriter, Editor, Art Director and Co-Director of Photography, Shinya Tsukamoto; Co-Directors of Photography, Fumikazu Oda, Katsunori Yokoyama; Music, Chu Ishikawa; Special Makeup Effects, Takashi Oda, Kan Takahama, Akira Fukaya.

Cast: Tomoroh Taguchi (Taniguchi Tomoo), Nobu Kanaoka (Kana), Shinya Tsukamoto (Yatsu "The Guy"), Keinosuke Tomioka (Minori), Sujin Kim (Taniguchi's Father), Min Tanaka (Taniguchi's Mother), Hideaki Tezuka (Big Skinhead), Tomoo Asada (Young Skinhead), Toraemon Utazawa (Mad Scientist).

A Kaiju Theatre Production. A Toshiba/EMI Presentation. Color. Wide screen. 81 minutes. Released 1992.

U.S. Version: Unreleased in the United States as this book was going to press. A sequel (in name only) to *Tetsuo*, though this was filmed in 35mm. Note the executive producer.

Tomeiningen erohakase. Producer, Minoru Suzuki; Director, Koji Seki; Directors of Photography, Hayato Hori, Yugi Go.

Cast: Jun Kitamura (Dr. Ohgari), Lilie Kagawa (Julie), Kako Tachibana (Rila), Reiki Akikawa, Yumiko Matsumoto, Shin Nagaoka.

A Shin Nihon Eiga Production. A Kohuei Release. Black and white. Academy ratio. 67 minutes. Released 1968.

U.S. Version: Distributor, if any, is undetermined. International title: *Invisible Man: Dr. Eros*.

Twilight of the Cockroaches/Gokiburi (*Cockroach*). Executive Producers, Taysumi Watanabe, Mayumi Izumi; Producers, Kauro Kobayashi, Setsuko Karasuma; Writer-Director, Hiroaki Yoshida; Character Design, Hiroshi Kurogane; Music, Morgan Fisher; Sound, Susumu Aketagawa; Director of Photography, Kenji Misumi; Art Director, Kiichi Ichida; Lighting, Masaki Uchida.

Cast: Hiroaki Yoshida, Hidenori Taga.

A TYO (Spirit of Tokyo) Productions, Inc./Kitty Films, Inc., Production. A Kitty Enterprises Release. Dolby Stereo. Panavision. Copyright 1987 by TYO Productions, Inc., and Kitty Films, Inc. Released 1987.

U.S. Version: Released by Streamline Pictures, Ltd., in subtitled format. No MPAA rating. Released 1989 (?).

Violated Angels/Okasaretu Byuakui. Producer/Director, Koji Wakamatsu; Screenplay, Koji Wakamatsu, Masao Adachi and Juro Kara; Director of Photography, Hideo Ito; Production Manager, Masayuki Miyama; Special Effects, Fukushima Group; Editor, Fumio Tomita; Sound, Shin Kida; Music, Koji Takamura.

Cast: Juro Kara (The Boy), Michiko Sakamoto (The Girl), Reiko Koyanagi (The Head Nurse), Miki Hayashi, Shoko Kido, Makiko Saegusa, Kyoko Yayoi (Nurses).

A Wakamatsu Productions Production. A Wakamatsu Release. Black and white, with color inserts. CinemaScope. 58 minutes. Released 1967.

U.S. Version: Distributor, if any, is undetermined. Alternate title: *Violated Women.*

Virus/Fukkatsu no hi (*Resurrection Day*). Producer, Haruki Kadokawa; Associate Producers, Yutaka Okada, Takashi Ohashi; Director, Kinji Fukasaku; Screenplay, Koji Takada, Gregory Knapp, Kinji Fukasaku, based on the novel *Fukkatsu no hi* by Sakyo Komatsu; Director of Photography, Daisaku Kimura; Art Director, Yoshinaga Yokoo; Editor, Akira Suzuki; Music, Teo Macero; Song, "Toujours Gai Mon Cher," Lyrics and Performance, Janis Ian; Music Producer, Teo Macero; Executive Music Producers, PMC International, George Braun, President; Sound Mixer, Kenichi Benitani; Gaffer, Hideki Mochizuki; first Assistant Directors, Junnosuke, J. Anthony Robinow; Script Clerk, Mikiko Koyama; Production Mangers, Isao Nagaoka, Susan A. Lewis, Katsumas Amano; Assistant Directors, Kenichiro Fujiyama, Kazuo Yoshida; second Assistant Director, Jesse Nishihata; Camera Assistants, Masahiro Kishimoto, Toshifumi Nobusaka, Tsutomu Takada; Gaffer, Bob Gallant; Sound Man, Minoru Nobuoka; Boom Man, Brian Richmond; Lighting Technicians, Isao Koyama, Shohei Iriguchi; Key Grip, Jim Craig; Best Boy, Frieder Hochheim; Assistant Grip, Daniel Narduzzi; Assistant Art Directors, Fumio Ogawa, Masumi Suzuki, Lindsay Goddard; Set Dresser, Patricia Gruben; Assistant Set Dresser, Jackie Fields; Set Props, Don Miloyevich; Assistant Set Props, Dawn Tanaka; Special Props, Fernand Durand; Makeup, Kathleen Mifsud; Costumers, Minoru Yamada, Kat Moyer; Wardrobe, Arthur Rowselle; Casting Directors, Shinichi Nakata, Howard Ryshpan, Masayoshi Omodaka; Assistant Casting Director, Arden Ryshpan; Hair Dresser, Tom Booth; Assistant Editor, Akimasa Kawashima; Script Assistant, Nancy Eagles; Director's Interpreter, Toshiko Adilman; Interpreters, Shizuko Kumada, Kazumi Takeshita, Maya Koizumi, John Wales; Special Effects Assistant Director, Ichiro Higa; Special Miniature Consultant, Gregory Jein; Sky Spy Model Design and Matte Paintings, Michael Minor; Special Visual Effects, Coast Productions; Special Visual Effects Supervisor, Phillip Kellison; Still Photographer, Takashi Ikeda; Production Assistant, John Roberts; Production Secretary, Francoise McNeil; Unit Location Manager, Jason Paikowsky; Accountant, Molly Tharyan; Transport Manager, Robert Bartman. *International Version*: Music Post-Production and Creative Sound, Neiman-Tillar Associates, Inc.; Editor, Pieter Hubbard; Associate Editor, Elodie Keene; Music Editors, Jack Tillar, Marty Wereski; Publicity, Guttman and Pam, Ltd.; Assistant Producer, Yoshiaki Tokutome; Supervisors, William R. Kowalchuk, Jr., Kosaku Wada; Special Thanks, Armada de Chile, National Film Board of Canada, Embassy of Canada in Japan, Canadian Armed Forces, Officers and Crew of HMCS *Okanagan*, Cities of Toronto and Halifax, Charles F. Chaplin, I.F.D., Sony of Canada, Ltd., Zodiac, University of Chile (Tsuyoshi Nishimura), Japanese Society of Peru (Eiichi Amamiya), State of Alaska (Toshio Hishimura), Kenwood; Construction, Scenic Productions (Toronto), International Film Studio (Toronto); Canadian Production Services, Marlow Pictures, Inc.; Titles and Opticals, Pacific Title (Hollywood); Re-recording Studios, Nikkatsu Studio (Tokyo), Producers Sound Services (Hollywood); Lenses and Panaflex Cameras, Panavision.

Cast: U.S. Antarctic Wintering Team, George Kennedy (Admiral Conway), Bo

Svenson (Major Carter), Stephanie Faulkner (Sarah), Nicholas Campbell (Radio Operator). Japanese Antarctic Wintering Team, Masao Kusakari (Yoshizumi), Isao Natsuki (Dr. Nakanishi), Tsunchiko Watase (Tatsuno), Shinichi [Sonny] Chiba (Dr. Yamaguchi), Kensaku Morita (Mazawa). Soviet Antarctic Wintering Team, Chris Wiggins (Dr. Borodinov), John Evans (Captain Nevsky). Norwegian Antarctic Wintering Team, Olivia Hussey (Marit). Other Countries' Antarctic Winter Teams, Cec Linder (Dr. Latour), Edward James Olmos (Captain Lopez), Eve Crawford (Irma Ollich), John Granik (Dr. Turowicz), John Bayliss (Major King), Ara Hovanessian (Major Giron), Ted Follows (Major Barnes), Danielle Schneider, Diane Lasko, Laura Pennington, Julie Khaner (Secretaries). United States of America, Glenn Ford (President Richardson), Stuart Gillard (Dr. Meyer), Henry Silva (Chief of Staff Garland), Robert Vaughn (Senator Barkley), George Touliatos (Colonel Rankin), Larry Reynolds (Morrison), David Gardner (Watt), J. Roger Periard (Orderly), Dan Kippy (Reed), William Binney (Simmons), Ron Hartman (Dr. Rogers). East Germany, Ken Pogue (Krause), Wally Bundarenko (Guard), Jim Bearden (Officer). *British Nuclear Submarine Neried* Crew Members, Chuck Conners (Captain McCloud), Ken Camroux (Officer Jones), Gordon Thompson (Radio Operator and Sonar Man), John Rutter (Sailor #1), Alfred Humphreys (Sailor #2), Peter Heppleston (Periscope Operator), Matt Hawthorne (Navigator), Lt. Commander David Griffiths (First Officer), Michael Tough (Young Sailor). Soviet Nuclear Submarine *T232* Crew Members, Jan Muszynski (Ensign Smirnov), Charles Northcote (Sonar Man). *Tokyo, Japan* Yumi Takigawa (Noriko), Ken Ogata (Tsuchiya), Ichiro Kijima (Tadokoro), Takashi Noguchi (Intern #1), Nenji Kobayashi (Intern #2), Tayori Hinatsu, Keiko Ito, Tomoko Igarashi, Sachiko Sato (Nurses), Sanae Nakahara (Young Mother), Yukiko Watanabe (Daughter). Also, Colin Fox (Spy Z), Richard Ayres (Little Man), Jefferson Mappin (Big Man), Dick Grant (Pilot), Tyler Miller (Boy Cossack), Charles L. Campbell (TV Narrator), Terry Martin, George Wilber (Stunts).

A Haruki Kadokawa Films Production in association with the Tokyo Broadcasting System (TBS). A Toho Co., Ltd., Release. Eastman Color (processed by Film House [Toronto], Far East Laboratories, Ltd. [Tokyo], and Consolidated Film Industries [Hollywood]). Spherical Panavision.

U.S. Version: Never released theatrically. Sold directly to cable television. A Broadwood Productions, Inc., Presentation. Copyright 1980 by Haruki Kadokawa. Reviewed at Cannes in May 1980 as "a work-in-progress," running 155 minutes. Current versions are minus footage of Takigawa. Video version: 108 minutes. Current television version: 93 minutes.

World Apartment Horror. Producers, Hiro Osaki, Yasuhiro Kazama; Director, Katsuhiro Otomo; Screenplay, Katsuhiro Otomo, Keiko Nobumoto; Director of Photography, Noboru Shimoda.

Cast: Hiroki Tanaka (Gangster), Yuji Nakamura, Weng Huarong, Kimiko Nakagawa.

An Embodiment Films Production. A Sony Pictures Release. Color. Wide screen. 98 minutes. Released 1991.

U.S. Version: Unreleased as this book went to press.

Yasei no Shomei. Executive Producer, Haruki Kadokawa; Producers, Jun Sakagami, Masaya Endoh, Fumio Matsuda, Simon Tse; Director, Junya Satoh; Screenplay, Koji Takada, based on the novel by Seiichi Norimuma, as published by Kadokawa Publishing Co., Ltd.; Art Director, Horoshi Tokuda; Director of Photography, Mashisa Himeda; Lighting, Hideo Kumagai; Editor, Jun Nabeshima; Music, Kuji Ono.

Cast: Ken Takakura (Ajisawa), Ryoko Nakano (Ochi), Horoko Yakushimaru (Nagai), Isao Natsuki (Detective Kitano), Rentaro Mikuni (Oba), Hajime Hana (Muranaga).

A Haruki Kadokawa Films, Inc., Production. A Kadokawa Publishing Co., Ltd., Picture. A Nippon Herald, Ltd., Release.

Color. Spherical Panavision (?). 143 minutes. Released October 27, 1978.
U.S. Version: Distributor, if any, is undetermined. International title: *Proof of the Wild.*

Yongary, Monster From the Deep/Dai Koesu Yongkari. Director, Kiduck Kim; Screenplay, Yunsung Suh; Director of Photography, Kenishi Nakagawa and Inchib Byon.
Cast: Yungil Oh, Chungim Nam, Soonjai Lee, Moon Kang, Kwang Ho Lee.
A Kuk Dong Film Co., Ltd. Production. A South Korean film. Color, Anamorphic wide screen. 100 minutes. Released in Korea in 1967.
U.S. Version: Never released theatrically. Released directly to television by American International Television (AIP-TV). The picture's South Korean origin disqualifies it from the main text. However, given that a number of Japanese technicians were imported for the film's production, and that most audiences watching the film would think it Japanese anyway, it is included here for the record. 79 minutes. No MPAA rating.

You Only Live Twice. Producers, Albert R. "Cubby" Broccoli, Harry Saltzman; Director, Lewis Gilbert; Screenplay, Roald Dahl; Additional Story Material, Harry Jack Bloom; Based on the novel by Ian Fleming; Director of Photography, Fredrick A. Young; Production Designer, Ken Adam; Music, John Barry; Title Song Lyrics, Leslie Bricusse; Title Song Singer, Nancy Sinatra; Main Title Design, Maurice Binder, Second Unit Director and Supervising Editor, Peter Hunt; Editor, Thelma Connel; Art Director, Harry Pottle; Production Supervisor, David Middlemas; Special Effects, John Stears; Action Sequences, Robert Simmons; Second Unit Cameraman, Robert Huke; Aerial Unit Cameraman, Jonny Jordan, Tony Brown; Underwater Cameraman, Lamar Boren; Assistant Director, William P. Cartlidge; Location Manager, Robert Watts; Camera Operator, Ernest Day; Continuity, Angela Martelli; Makeup, Basil Newall, Paul Rabiger; Dubbing Editors, Norman Wanstall, Harry Miller; Assembly Editor, Robert Richardson; Sound Recordists, John Mitchell, Gordon K. McCallum; Wardrobe Mistress, Eileen Sullivan; Hairdresser, Eileen Warwick; Set Decorator, David Ffolkes; James Bond Theme, Monty Norman; Music Recording, Cine Tele Sound Studios; Technical Adviser, Kikumaru Okuda; Construction Manager, Ronald Udell; Unit Publicist, Tom Carlisle; Autogyro Designer, Ken Wallis; Helicopter Pilot, Gilbert Chomat; Assistant Stunt Arranger, George Leech; Martial Arts Choreographer, Donn Draeger; Martial Arts Instructor, Mas Oyama; Cooperation, Department of Defense, Toho Company Ltd.
Cast: Sean Connery (James Bond), Akiko Wakabayashi (Aki), Tetsuro Tamba ("Tiger" Tanaka), Mie Hama (Kissy Suzuki), Teru Shimada (Osato), Karin Dor (Helga Brandt), Bernard Lee ("M"), Lois Maxwell (Miss Moneypenny), Desmond Llewelyn (Major Boothroyd, aka "Q"), Charles Gray (Dikko Henderson), Donald Pleasence (Ernst Stravo Blofeld), Tsai Chin (Ling), Alexander Knox (President of the United States), Robert Hutton (Presidential Aide), Burt Kwouk (SPECTRE 3), Michael Chow (SPECTRE 4), Patrick Jordan (Policeman), Anthony Ainley (Policeman), Peter Maivia (Wrestler), Ronald Rich (Hans), Diane Cilento (Photo Double), Robert Simmons, George Leech, Ken Wallis, Jenny Le Free (Stunts).
Released by United Artists Corporation. An Albert R. Broccoli and Harry Saltzman Presentation. An Eon Productions, Ltd., Production. A Danjaq, S.A. Picture. A British (Eon), South African (Danjaq) and U.S. (UA) co-production. Filmed at Pinewood Studios, England, Toho Studios, Japan, and on location aboard the HMS *Tenby* off the coast of Gibraltar, in the Bahamas, Japan, Spain (Torremolinos) and Scotland (Finmore). Copyright June 13, 1967, by Danjaq S.A. Westrex Recording System (MagOptical stereophonic sound). Eastman Color (processed by Technicolor, U.S. prints by DeLuxe). Panavision. 116 minutes. No MPAA rating. Released (in the United States) June 12, 1967.

Bibliography

Books

Barrett, Gregory. *Archetypes in Japanese Film: The Religious Significance of the Principal Heroes and Heroines*. London and Toronto: Susquehanna Univeristy Press, no date given (1985?).
Benson, Raymond. *The James Bond Bedside Companion*. New York: Dodd, Mead, 1984.
Bock, Audie. *Japanese Film Directors*. Tokyo, New York and San Francisco: Kodansha International, 1978.
Bronson, John. *Movie Magic: The Story of Special Effects in the Cinema*. New York: Plume, 1976.
Buehrer, Beverley Bare. *Japanese Films: A Filmography and Commentary, 1921–1989*. Jefferson, NC: McFarland, 1990.
Buruma, Ian. *Behind the Mask: On Sexual Demons, Sacred Mothers, Transvestites, Gangsters and other Japanese Cultural Heroes*. New York: Penguin, 1984.
Carr, Robert E., and R. M. Hayes. *Wide Screen Movies: A History and Filmography of Wide Gauge Filmmaking*. Jefferson, NC: McFarland, 1988.
Cotten, Joseph. *Vanity Will Get You Somewhere*. San Francisco: Mercury House, 1987.
Cowie, Peter, general ed. *World Filmography*. London: The Tantivy Press, 1977. Two volumes.
Ebert, Roger. *Roger Ebert's Movie Home Companion*. New York: Andrews, McMeel & Parker, 1985, 1986.
Film Literature Index (volumes 1–19). Albany: State University of New York at Albany, 1973–1991.
Glut, Donald. *Classic Movie Monsters*. Metuchen, NJ: Scarecrow, 1978.
———. *The Frankenstein Legend: A Tribute to Mary Shelley and Boris Karloff*. Metuchen, NJ: Scarecrow, 1973.
Gunji, Masakatsu. *Kabuki*. Palo Alto, CA: Kodansha International, 1969.
Halliwell, Leslie. *The Filmgoer's Companion*; 9th ed. New York: Scribner's, 1988.
Hanson, Patricia King, and Stephen L., eds. *The Film Review Index* (volume 2). Phoenix, AZ: Oryx, 1987.
Hardy, Phil, ed. *The Encyclopedia of Horror Movies*. New York: Harper & Row, 1986.
———, ed. *The Film Encyclopedia: Science Fiction*. New York: William Morrow, 1984.
Katz, Ephraim. *The Film Encyclopedia*. New York: Crowell, 1979.

Krafsur, Richard P., executive ed. *The American Film Institute Catalog of Motion Pictures: Feature Films, 1961-1970.* New York: Bowker, 1976.
Kurosawa, Akira. *Something Like an Autobiography.* New York: Random House, 1982.
Lee, Walt, comp. *Reference Guide to Fantastic Films: Science Fiction, Fantasy & Horror.* Los Angeles: Chelsea-Lee Books, 1972-74. Three volumes.
Lenburg, Jeff. *The Encyclopedia of Animated Cartoons.* New York: Facts on File, 1991.
Lent, John A. *The Asian Film Industry.* London: Christopher Helm, Publishers, 1990.
Lentz, Harris M., III, comp. *Science Fiction, Horror & Fantasy Film and Television Credits.* Jefferson, NC: McFarland, 1983. Two volumes.
Maltin, Leonard, ed. *Leonard Maltin's Movie and Video Guide 1992.* New York, Signet, 1991.
Medved, Harry, with Randy Dreyfuss. *The Fifty Worst Films of All Time (and How They Got That Way).* New York: Popular Library, 1978.
Mellen, Joan. *Voices from the Japanese Cinema.* New York: Liveright, 1975.
_____. *The Waves at Genji's Door: Japan Through Its Cinema.* New York: Pantheon, 1976.
Naha, Ed. *Horrors from Screen to Scream: An Encyclopedic Guide to the Greatest Horror and Fantasy Films of All Time.* New York: Avon, 1975.
_____. *The Science Fictionary: An A-Z Guide to the World of SF Authors, Films & TV Shows.* New York: Seaview Books, 1980.
Nash, Jay Robert, and Stanley Ralph Ross. *The Motion Picture Guide* (1927-1991). Chicago: Cinebooks, Inc., 1986.
New York Times Film Reviews: 1913-1968. The New York Times and Arno Press, 1970.
Ottoson, Robert L. *American International Pictures: A Filmography.* New York: Garland Publishing, 1985.
Peary, Danny. *Cult Movies 2.* New York: Dell, 1983.
_____. *Guide for the Film Fanatic.* New York: Simon & Schuster, 1986.
Richie, Donald. *The Films of Akira Kurogawa.* Berkeley and Los Angeles: University of California, 1965.
Rubin, Steven Jay. *The James Bond Films.* New York: Arlington House, Inc., 1981.
Sato, Tadao. *Currents in Japanese Cinema.* Trans. Gregory Barrett. New York: Harper & Row, 1982.
Slide, Anthony. *The American Film Industry.* Westport, CT: Greenwood, 1986.
_____. *The International Film Industry.* Westport, CT: Greenwood, 1989.
Terrace, Vincent. *The Complete Encyclopedia of Television Programs 1947-1979.* New York: A. S. Barnes, 1976-80.
Tsushinsha, Jiji, ed. *Japanese Motion Picture Almanac 1957.* Tokyo: Promotion Council of Motion Picture Industry of Japan, Inc., 1957.
Tyler, Parker. *Classics of the Foreign Film.* New York: Bonanza Books, 1962.
Vermilye, Jerry, ed. *Five Hundred Best British and Foreign Films to Buy, Rent or Videotape.* New York: William Morrow, 1988.
Warren, Bill. *Keep Watching the Skies.* Jefferson, NC: McFarland, 1982, 1986. Two volumes.
Watson, Elena M. *Television Horror Movie Hosts: Sixty-eight Vampires, Mad Scientists*

and *Other Denizens of the Late-Night Airwaves Examined and Interviewed.* Jefferson, NC: McFarland, 1991.

Weldon, Michael, with Charles Beesley, Bob Martin and Akira Fitton. *The Psychotronic Encyclopedia of Film.* New York: Ballantine, 1983.

Willis, Donald G. *Horror and Science Fiction Films: A Checklist.* Metuchen, NJ: Scarecrow, 1972, 1982, 1987. Three volumes.

Periodicals

Cinefantastique. Oak Park, IL: Fredrick S. Clark. 1970– .
Cult Movies. North Hollywood, CA: Videosonic Arts. 1990– .
Famous Monsters of Filmland. New York: Warren Publishing. 1958–1983.
Fangoria. New York: O'Quinn Studios, 1979– .
Fantastic Films. Chicago: Fantastic Films Magazine, 1978–1985.
Japanese Fantasy Film Journal. Toledo, OH: Greg Shoemaker, 1968–1983.
Japanese Giants. Chicago: Ed Godziszewski, 1974– .
Markalite. Oakland, CA: Pacific Rim, 1990– .
Starlog. New York: O'Quinn Studios, 1976– .
Weekly Variety. New York, 1906– .

Appendix

Additional Godzilla Appearances

Godzilla and the Super 90. Revamped version of *The Godzilla Power Hour* (see below), with 30-minute episodes of "Johnny Quest" added to boast sagging ratings (it didn't work). 13 additional episodes.

The Godzilla Power Hour. Animated teleseries produced for American television. A Hanna-Barbera Productions, Inc., and Benedict Pictures Corporation Production. The character "Godzilla" used by permission of Toho Co., Ltd. and Benedict Pictures. "Godzilla" copyright Toho Co., Ltd. and Benedict Pictures Corp.; all other material copyright Hanna-Barbera Productions.

Voice characterizations: Ted Cassidy (Godzilla), Jeff David (Captain Carl Rogers), Brenda Thompson (Quinn), Al Eisenmann (Pete), Hilly Hicks (Brock), Don Messick (Godzooky).

60 minutes (There were two segments of this short-lived program, "Godzilla" and "Jana of the Jungle," which ran 30 minutes each). Premiered on the National Broadcasting Company (NBC) September 9, 1978. 14 episodes.

The Godzilla Show. Third version of Hanna-Barbera cartoon series, produced in association with Toho and Benedict Pictures, which premiered as *The Godzilla Power Hour.* Series was changed mid-season to *The Godzilla/Globetrotters Adventure Hour*, and later, *The Godzilla/Dynomutt Hour with Funky Phantom*, followed by *The Godzilla/Hong Kong Phooey Hour.* The last show aired in May 1981.

Zone Fighter/Ryusei ningen Zon. ("Zone, The Meteor Man"). Japanese television series. Executive Producer/Creator, Tomoyuki Tanaka; Head Director, Ishiro Honda; Head Writer, Shozo Uehara; Music, Go Nizawa. Cast: Kazuya Aoyama. A Toho Eizo, Co., Ltd. Production for NTV. Godzilla-related episodes are as follows:

"Invasion! The Attack of Garoga's Army Corps"
(episode 4, aired April 23, 1973): Gojira

"The Arrival of King Ghidorah"
(episode 5, aired April 30, 1973): King Ghidorah

"The Revenge of King Ghidorah"
(episode 6, aired May 7, 1973): King Ghidorah

"In the Twinkling of An Eye"
(episode 11, aired June 11, 1973): Gojira, Gigan

"Submersion! Godzilla, You Must Save Tokyo!"
(episode 15, aired July 9, 1973) Gojira

"Invincible! Godzilla Enraged!"
(episode 21, aired August 20, 1973) Gojira

"Gruesome! Zone and Godzilla vs. the Horrible Allies"
(episode 25, aired September 17, 1973) Gojira

StarGodzilla. Producer, Joy Hsu; Director, Futien Hsu; Screenplay, Chris Lee. Cast: Joey Fang, Chang Ching, Charles Woo.

A Hong Kong feature film released by First Distributors (H.K.) Ltd. A StarGodzilla Production. Filmed in Hong Kong. Color, anamorphic wide screen. Not released in the United States. A Hong Kong-made film. Released May 1980.

A redressed Godzilla costume appeared in at least one episode of Tsuburaya Enterprises' "Ultraman" series. Godzilla himself appeared in U.S. commercials for Nike and Dr Pepper, and as a news report in *Airplane II: The Sequel* (1982). Pseudo "behind-the scenes" footage of Toho monster movies appeared in *Hollywood Boulevard* (1976), *Pee Wee's Big Adventure* (1985) and *One Crazy Summer* (1986). Stock footage of Godzilla and other Toho monsters appeared in *Invasion Earth: The Aliens Are Coming! The Aliens Are Here!* Scenes from *Godzilla vs. Megalon* appear in the TV documentary "Hollywood Dinosaur Chronicles." Footage from *The X from Outer Space* and other Japanese genre films appear in *It Came from Hollywood* (1982).

Index

AB-PT Pictures Corporation 16
Abe, Hisayuki 148
Abe, Koko 124, 125
Adam, Ken 27, 156
Adams, Nick 75, 109, 111, 116, 118
Adventuras en el Centro la Terra (195?) 17
Adventure in Taklamakan see *Adventures of Takla Makan*
Adventure in the Strange Castle see *Adventures of Takla Makan*
Adventure of the Strange Stone Castle see *Adventures of Takla Makan*
Adventures of Captain Marvel (1941)
Adventures of Takla Makan 26, 108, 337
"After Japan Sinks" (announced but unproduced feature) 217
Agar, John 43
Age of Assassins, The 337–38
Age of the Gods see *Three Treasures, The*
Kyoko 162
Ai no borei 381
Ai, Tomoko 228
Akatsuki to tsuiseki (1950) 83
Akaza, Miyoko 172
Akira Kurosawa's Dreams 10, 276–9, 381–3
Akiyama, Miyuki 181
"Alfred Hitchcock Presents" (TV series) 171
Alien (1979) 67
Aliens (1986) 171, 281, 288
All Right, My Friend see *Daijoo, mai furendo*
Allen, Woody 56, 212
Along with Ghosts 140, 176, 300
Ama no bakemono yashiki see *Girl Diver of Spook Mansion*
Amachi, Shigeru 47
Amamoto, Eisei 59, 88–89, 90–92, 141, 144
Amatsu, Bin 126
Amazing Colossal Man, The (1957) 44

American Broadcasting Companies, Inc. (ABC) 234
American Film Institute Catalog of Motion Pictures: Feature Films, 1961–1970 (book by Krafsur) xiv, 54
American International Pictures xii, 95, 110, 114, 132, 165, 198, 201
American International Television (AIP-TV) 22, 193, 155, 177
Amicus Films 236
Among the Living (1941) 115
Andrews, Robert ix
"Andy Hardy" (film series) 68
Angilas (aka Angurus; character) 14–17, 43, 209, 217, 219
Angry Red Planet, The (1960) 16
Animated Features xvi, xix
Ankrum, Morris 19–20
Anzai, Kyoko
Aoi shinju (1951) 10
Aoyama, Yoshihiko 130
"Ape Corps" (TV series) 231
Appearance of Supergiant, The see *Supergiant*
Aratama, Michiyo 100
Archer, Eugene (*New York Times* reviewer) 80, 94
Arikawa, Sadamasa see Arikawa, Teisho
Arikawa, Teisho 122, 198
Arishima, Ichiro 77, 80, 88–89
Arishima, Ikumitsu 3
Arkoff, Samuel Z. 11
Armstrong, David 161
Armstrong, Jack 291, 292
Armstrong, Robert 77
Around the World Under the Sea (1966) 134
Art Theatre Guild xvi
Aru mittsu 383
Asano, Yuko 239
Astronaut 1980 see *Gorath*
At the Earth's Core (1976) 236

Atomic Rulers 26–28, 34, 35, 318
Atomic Rulers of the World, The see *Atomic Rulers*
Atoragan the Flying Supersub see *Atragon*
Atragon xxii, 11, 16, 25, 49, 51, 71, 80–84, 92, 119, 161, 174, 210, 239, 240, 241, 275, 338
Attack from Space 28, 34–35, 40, 318
Attack of the Flying Saucers see *Supergiant*
Attack of the Marching Monsters see *Destroy All Monsters*
Attack of the Monsters xi, xix, 192, 166, 181–83, 259, 300
Attack of the Mushroom People xxiii, 16, 56, 75, 84–87, 167, 338–39
Attack of the Puppet People (1958) 72
Attaway, Ruth 243
Azuma, Tatsuya 245, 251

Baby Cart at the River Styx see *Shogun Assassin*
Bad Sleep Well, The (1960) 3, 12
Baisho, Mitsuko 276
Bakke, Brenda 280
Bambi (1942) 284
Bambi Meets Godzilla (1969) 269
Bamyuda no nazo see *Bermuda Depths, The*
Baragon (character) 109, 110, 139
Barry, John 156, 157
Basara: The Princess Goh (1992) 125
Batman (film) 283
Battle Beyond the Stars (1968) see *The Green Slime*
Battle Beyond the Stars (1980) 250
Battle for the Planet of the Apes (1973) 231
Battle in Outer Space xxii, 44–47, 56, 74, 80, 97, 115, 163, 196, 239, 240, 241, 242, 290, 339
"Battlestar Galactica" (TV series) 216, 248
Beast and the Magic Sword, The 383
Beast of Hollow Mountain, The (1956) 189
Beast from 20,000 Fathoms, The (1953) 9, 10, 76
Beasts' Carnival, The 383–84
Beatniks, The (1958) 17
"Beau" (*Variety* reviewer) 157
Beau Geste (1939) 115
Beck, John 77
Beckley, Paul V. (*New York Herald-Tribune* reviewer) 20
Beery, Wallace 236
Beginning of the End, The (1957) 268

"Behind the Glory" (shelved Toho production) 9
Bellucci, Joseph 46
Beneath the Planet of the Apes (1970) 231
Benson, Raymond 155, 157
Berger, Richard 286
Bermuda Depths, The 242–44, 261, 376–77
Bernard, Jami 161
Berryman, Michael 291, 292
Bessho, Tetsuya 280, 293, 296
"Better Tomorrow, A" (film series) 128
Bewitched Love of Madame Pai, The see *Madame White Snake*
Beyond the Poseidon Adventure (1979) 265
Bicycle Thief, The (1949) 5
Big Duel in the North Sea see *Ebirah, Horror of the Deep Big Duel in the South Sea* see *Ebirah, Horror of the Deep*
Big Wave, The 384
Bijo to ekatai-ningen see *H-Man, The*
Billitteri, Salvatore 180
Binder, Maurice 156, 201
Biollante (character) 95, 180
"Bionic Woman, The" (TV series)
Birds, The (1963) 216
Black Cat, The see *Kuroneko*
Black Cat Mansion 315
Black Lizard 157–61, 172, 318–19
Black Rose Inn, The see *Kurobarano yakata*
Blind Beast, The 183, 300
Blind Woman's Curse, The see *Tattooed Swordsman*
Blood 319
Blood Sword of the 99th Virgin see *Bloody Sword of the 99th Virgin, The*
Blood Type: Blue see *Buru kurisumasu*
Bloodthirsty Eyes, The see *Lake of Dracula*
Bloodthirsty Roses, The see *Evil of Dracula*
Bloody Bushido Blade, The (1981) 62
Bloody Sword of the 99th Virgin, The 315
Bloom, Claire 2
Blowen, Michael (*Boston Globe* reviewer) 251
Boat, The (1981) see Boot, Das
Body Snatcher from Hell see *Goke, Bodysnatcher from Hell Bodyguard, The* (1976) 62
"Bonanza" (TV series) 216
Boone, Richard 234, 236
Boot, Das (1981) xiii
Borei kaibyo yashiki see *Black Cat Mansion*

Botandoro (1955) 325
Botandoro (1968) see *Kaidan botandoro*
Boy and His Dog, A (1975) 282
Boy Detectives, The see *Shonen tanteidan*
Boy with Green Hair, The (1948) 138
Boyichi and the Supermonster see *Return of the Giant Monsters*
Boyle, Peter 282
"Brad" (*Variety* reviewer)
Brain from Outer Space see *Supergiant*
Breakston, George 68
Brenco Pictures 75
Bride from Hades, The see *Kaidan botandoro*
Bride from Hell see *Kaidan botandoro*
Bride of the Gorilla (1951) 12
Bronson Canyon 42, 43
Buchamukure daihakken see *Computer Free-for-All*
Buck Rogers (1939) 46
Buddha 13, 301
Burns, Bob 17
Burr, Raymond xiii, 7, 11, 12, 13, 43, 267, 268, 269, 270
Buru kurisumas 339
Bus Stop (1956) 144
Butler, Daws 17
Byaku fugin no yoren see *Madame White Snake*
Bye Bye Jupiter see *Sayonara Jupiter*
Byokuya no yojo see *Temptress, The*
"Byro" (*Variety* reviewer) 114

Canby, Vincent (*New York Times* reviewer) 100, 144, 212–13, 282
"Carmilla" (story by LeFanu) 227
Carr, Robert E. ix
Carradine, John 18–20
Casino Royale (1967) 188
Casnoff, Philip 248
Castle of the Spider's Web, The see *Throne of Blood*
Castastrophe: 1999 see *Last Days of Planet Earth, The*
Cat Murkil and Her Silks (1976) 144
Caucasian Ghost see *Kaidan ijin yurei*
Centuries (book by Nostradamus) 220
Certain Adultery, A see *Aru mittsu*
Challenge, The (1982) 3
Challenging Ghost, The 325
Champion of Death (1977) 62
"Charlie Chan" (film series) 17, 65
Chi o suu me see *Lake of Dracula*

Chi o suu ningyo see *Vampire Doll, The*
Chiaki, Minoru 2, 4, 14, 16, 17, 32 Chiba, Shinichi "Sonny" 60–63, 134, 249
"Chie" (*Variety* reviewer) 108, 123, 125, 133, 140, 150, 166, 173
Chikyu boeigun see *Mysterians, The*
Chikyu kogeki meirei: Gojira tai Gaigan see *Godzilla on Monster Island*
Children of Hiroshima (1952) 13, 65, 107
Chimes at Midnight (1966) 33
Chio o suu bara see *Evil of Dracula*
Chute, David 161
Cinefantastique (magazine) xv, 214, 227
Cinema Shares International 213, 219
CinemaScope xiii
Cirinesi, Andy ix
Citizen Kane (1941) 5
Classic Movie Monsters (book by Glut) 77
Claws of Satan, The 325
Clay, Carl 165
Close Encounters of the Third Kind (1977) 169, 252, 273
Cobweb Castle see *Throne of Blood*
"Code Red" (TV series) 216
Columbia/Tri-Star 297
Combs, Jeffrey 293
Computer Free-for-All 339
Computer Wore Tennis Shoes, The (1970) 189
Concorde: Airport '79, The (1979) 265
Conde Dracula, El (1970) 195
Connery, Sean 155–56, 157, 171
Connors, Chuck 264, 266
Conquest of the Planet of the Apes (1972) 231
Coppola, Francis Ford 276
Corman, Roger 214
Cosmic Man, The (1959) 20
Cosmic Man Appears in Tokyo, The see *Mysterious Satellite, The*
Cosmos, The (characters) 296
Cotten, Joseph 185, 186, 187, 188
Count Dracula see *Conde Dracula, El* (1970)
Count Yorga, Vampire (1970) 195
Countess Dracula (1970) 195
Crane, Kenneth 20
Crazy Adventure see *Don't Call Me a Con Man*
Creature from the Black Lagoon (1954) 79, 134
Creature Walks Among Us, The (1956) 134
Creeping Unknown, The (1956) 115
Crescent Moon, The 325–26

404 Index

Criminal Women see Joys of Torture, The
Crisis 2050? see Solar Crisis
Crown International 41
Crowther, Bosley (*New York Times* reviewer) xi, 4, 6, 13, 33, 105, 157
Cruel Ghost Legend see Curse of the Blood
Cult Movie Stars (book by Peary) 285
Curse 325
Curse of Frankenstein, The (1956) 194, 225
Curse of the Blood 319
Curse of the Fly (1965) 115
Curse of the Ghosts, The 301
Curse of the One-Eyed Corpse see Ghost of the One-Eyed Man
Curse of the Vampire (1970) 195
Cursed Pond, The see Kaibyo noroi numa
Cushing, Peter 194

Daffy Duck (character) 246
Dagora see Dagora, the Space Monster
Dagora, the Space Monster 16, 38, 74, 90–92, 157, 172, 212, 339–40
Dahl, Roald 156, 157
Daiboken see Don't Call Me a Con Man
Daiei Motion Picture Co., Ltd. ix, xvi, 4, 22, 26, 62, 112, 114, 131, 132, 133, 138, 139, 165, 172, 176, 181, 182, 200–1, 258, 300–14
DaieiScope xiii
Daiichibu see Man in the Moonlight Mask, The
Daijoo, mai furendo 340
Daikaiju Baran see Varan the Unbelievable
Daikaiju Gamera see Gammera the Invincible
Daikaiju ketto Gamera tai Barugon see War of the Monsters
Daikaiju kuchusen see Return of the Giant Monsters
Daikaiju kuchusen Gamera tai Gyaosu see Return of the Giant Monsters
Dai Koesu Yongkari see Yongary, Monster from the Deep
Daikyoju Gappa see Monster from a Prehistoric Planet
Daimajin see Majin
Daimajin gyakushu see Majin Strikes Again
Daimajin ikaru see Return of the Giant Majin, The
Daimon, Masaaki 217
Daini no seo (1968) 183

Dai nibu see Man in the Moonlight Mask, The
Dai sanji sekai taisen--yonju-ichi jikan no kyofu see Final War, The
Dai tatsumaki see Whirlwind
Dai tozoku see Lost World of Sinbad, The
Dallas Productions 41
Damnation Alley (1977) 282
Dancing Mistress 319
Dangerous Kiss, The (1961) 12
Daning, Mike xiv, 134, 135, 153
Daredevil in the Castle 52, 340
Daydreamer, The (1966) 141
Deadly Mantis, The (1957) 152
Deak, Michael 293
Death and the Green Slime see Green Slime, The
Death by Hanging 384
Death Race 2000 (1975) 16
Deathquake 340–41
Deerslayer, The (1957) 17
Dekker, Albert 112, 115
De Laurentiis, Dino 235–36
Delta Factor, The (1970) 144
Delta Force 2 (1990) 171
Deming, Lawson J. (aka "Sir Graves Ghastly") 27
Demon, The see Onibaba
Demon Pond 320
Denso ningen see Secret of the Telegian, The
Depths, The 315–6
Dersu Uzala (1975) 276
Destination Inner Space (1966) 134
Destroy All Monsters xi, xii, 16, 25, 26, 33, 44, 56, 83–84, 99, 122, 135, 142, 195, 153, 161–64, 165, 185, 209, 213, 228, 341
Destroy All Planets 140, 165–66, 172, 181, 182, 192, 193, 194, 259, 301–2
Destruction of the Spacefleet, The see Supergiant
Destry Rides Again (1939) 115
Devil Got Angry, The see Majin
Devil Woman see Onibaba
Diamonds Are Forever (1971) 156
Die, Monster, Die (1965) 111
Different Sons (1962)
"Dinosaur Fighting Team Kosheidon" (TV series) 173
"Dinosaur War–Aizenborg" (TV series) 173
Dirty Dozen, The (1967) 171
Dismembered Ghost 384
Distributors Corporation of America (DCA) 18, 21

Divine 160
Dr. Cyclops (1940) 115
Doctor Dolittle (1967) 231
Dr. No (1962) 122, 155
Doctor Zhivago (1965) 283
Dodes 'ka-den 276, 341-42
Dodesukadan see Dodes 'ka-den
Dojoji Temple see Kyokanoka musume Dojoji
Dokuro kyojo 320
Donlevy, Brian 112, 115
Don't Call Me a Con Man 342
Dowling, Tom (*Washington Star* reviewer) 251
Dracula (1957) see Horror of Dracula
Dracula (1979) 225
Dracula vs. Frankenstein (1971) 138
Dracula's Lust for Blood see Lake of Dracula
Dreams see Akira Kurosawa's Dreams
Drum Struck (1991) 272
Drunken Angel 3, 12, 342-43
Duel of the Gargantuas see War of the Gargantuas
Dunham, Robert 90, 172, 210, 212
Duvoli, John R. 189
Dyneley, Peter 66, 68

Earle, Anita (*San Francisco Chronicle* reviewer) 203-4
Early Autumn (1962) 12
Earth in Danger, The see Supergiant
Earth vs. the Flying Saucers (1956) 77
Earth, Wind, and Fire (funk group) 248
Earthquake (1974) 214, 215, 269
Ebert, Roger xii
Ebirah, Horror of the Deep xi, 12, 60, 75, 83, 99, 120-23, 151, 152, 153, 164, 184, 296, 343
Edwards, Blake 258
Ei see House
Elley, Derek 271
Embassy Pictures Corp. 14
Embrace (195?) 11
Emi, Shuntaro 47
Empire of the Ants (1977) 239
Enami, Kyoko 139
Enchanted Princess 302
Encyclopedia of Film: Science Fiction, The (book by Hardy) xx, 31, 51, 54, 60, 66, 67, 76, 81, 84, 87, 99, 135, 138, 145, 153, 157, 164, 169, 185, 189, 194, 198, 204, 210, 213, 222, 242, 251

Encyclopedia of Horror Movies, The (book by Hardy) xx, 49, 105, 129, 132, 195, 173, 176, 183, 206, 227
Endo, Tatsuo 130
Enemy from Space (1957) 115
Epoch of Murder Madness see Age of Assassins, The Eraserhead (1978) 271
Erogami no onryo 320
Escape from the Planet of the Apes (1971) 231
Escape of Mechagodzilla, The see Terror of Mechagodzilla
ESPY 343
Eternity of Love (1961) 80
Evans, Maurice 230, 234
Evil Brain from Outer Space 28, 35-36, 318
Evil Dead, The (1983) 271
Evil of Dracula 195, 225-27, 343-44
Executioner, The (1976) 62
"Executive Suite" (TV series) 244

Face of Another, The 16, 105, 124-26, 344
Falcon Fighters, The (1970) 27
Famous Monsters of Filmland (magazine) 67, 217
Fancy Paradise see Kuso tengoku
Fantastic Voyage (1966) 193, 194
Farewell Rabaul (1953) 9, 11
Farino, Ernest D., Jr. 270
Fear of the Snake Woman see Kaidan hebionna
Female Trouble (1974) 160
Fenton, Roger ix
Feret, Gregory V. 213
Film Encyclopedia, The (book by Katz) 125
Films of Akira Kurosawa, The (book by Richie) Final War, The 54-55, 62-63, 65, 326
"Fireman" (TV series) 173
Flamm, Matthew 272
"Flash Gordon" (serials) 46
Flash Gordon Conquers the Universe (1940) 39
Flight from Ashiya (1964) 135
Fly, The (1958) 59
Fly, The (1986) 271
"Flying High" (TV series) 244
Forbidden Planet (1956) 31
Ford, Glenn 263, 265, 266
41 jikan no kyofu see Final War, The
Frankenstein Conquers the World xii, 9, 12,

56, 75, 80, 83, 109–12, 136, 137, 139, 161, 344
Frankenstein Meets the Wolfman (1943) 111
Frees, Paul ix, 3, 17, 26, 72, 76, 141, 182, 189, 216
Froggo and Droggo see *Magic Serpent, The*
Frogs (1972) 201
From Russia with Love (1963) 155, 156, 157
"Frosty the Snowman" (TV special) 261
Fugitive Alien 177, 244–248, 377
Fujiki, Yu 77, 81, 93, 95, 198
Fujimaki, Jun 130
Fujimura, Shiho 132
Fujioka, Hiroshi 214
Fujioka, John 214–5
Fujita, Midori 204
Fujita, Susumu 92
Fujiwara, Kei 270
Fukasaku, Kinji 160, 172, 250
Fukisuido (release date unknown) 84
Fukkatsu no hi see *Virus*
Fukuda, Jun 55, 60, 120, 123, 150, 210, 213, 219, 242
Fukusho suruwa ware ni ari see *Vengeance Is Mine*
Fumiake, Mach 258
Funakoshi, Eiji 112, 183
Furaibo, Akai Tanima no Sangeki (1961) 160
Furankenshutain no kaiju—Sanda tai Gairah see *War of the Gargantuas*
Furankenshutain tai Baragon see *Frankenstein Conquers the World*
Furankenshutain tai chitei kaiju Baragon see *Frankenstein Conquers the World*
Futureworld (1976) 215

Galaxy Express 999 (1977?) 260
Galbraith, Anne Sharp ix
Gale, David 291, 292
Gamera (aka Gammera; character) xvi, xvii, 26
Gamera see *Gammera the Invincible*
Gamera (film series) 132, 133, 138, 147, 165, 174, 179, 181, 192–94, 198, 200–1
Gamera Super Monster 140, 201, 258–61, 311
Gamera tai Barugon see *War of the Monsters*
Gamera tai daiiaku Guiron see *Attack of the Monsters*
Gamera tai Gaos see *Return of the Giant Monsters*
Gamera tai Guiron see *Attack of the Monsters*
Gamera tai Gyaosu see *Return of the Giant Monsters*
"Gamera tai Leoman" (unproduced feature) 201
Gamera tai shinkai kaiju Jigura see *Gamera vs. Zigra*
Gamera tai uchu kaiju Bairusu see *Destroy All Planets*
Gamera taimaju Jaiga see *Gamera vs. Monster X*
Gamera vs. Barugon see *War of the Monsters*
Gamera vs. Guiron see *Attack of the Monsters*
Gamera vs. Gyaos see *Return of the Giant Monsters*
Gamera vs. Jiger see *Gamera vs. Monster X*
Gamera vs. Monster X 183, 192–94, 259, 302
Gamera vs. the Outer Space Monster Virus see *Destroy All Planets*
Gamera vs. Viras see *Destroy All Planets*
Gamera vs. Zigra 27, 192, 194, 198–201, 259, 302–3
Gamma sango uchu daisakusen see *Green Slime, The*
Gammera the Invincible xxii, 112–5, 138, 140, 149, 165, 182, 303
Ganhedo xx, 344–5
Ganime (character) 197
Gannon, Joe 282
Gappa see *Monster from a Prehistoric Planet*
Gappa: Triphibian Monster see *Monster from a Prehistoric Planet*
Gasu ningen dai ichigo see *Human Vapor, The*
Gate of Hell (1953) xv, 83
Gateway to Glory (1970) 3
Gekko kamen [1959] see *Man in the Moonlight Mask, The*
Gekko kamen [1981] see *Moon Mask Rider, The*
Gekko kamen--Satan no tsume see *Claws of Satan, The*
Gen to Fudo-Myoh see *Youth and His Amulet, The*
Gendaijin soshun (194?) 46
Genocide 320–1
Getaway Glory (1970) 27
Gezora (character) 196, 198
Gezora Ganime Kameba: Kessen nankai no

daikaiju see *Yog: Monster from Space*
Ghidrah (character) see King Ghidorah
Ghidrah: The Three-Headed Monster xii, 16, 25, 92, 96–100, 119, 121, 157, 163, 209, 228, 269, 290, 296, 345–46
Ghost Beauty see *Kaindan botandoro*
Ghost-Cat of Arima Place see *Kaibyo Arima goten*
Ghost-Cat of Gojusan-Tsugi see *Kaibyo Gojusan-tsugi*
Ghost-Cat of Karakuri Tenjo see *Kaibyo Karakuri Tenjo*
Ghost-Cat of Oma-Ga-Tsuji see *Kaibyo Oma-ga-tsuji*
Ghost-Cat of Otam-ag-Ike, The see *Ghost of Otamange-Ike, The*
Ghost-Cat of Yonaki Swamp see *Necromancy*
Ghost-Cat Wall of Hatred see *Kaibyo noroi no kabe*
Ghost from the Pond see *Kaidan hitotsu-me jizo*
Ghost Music of Shamisen see *Kaidan Shamisen-bori*
Ghost of a Hunchback, The see *House of Terrors*
Ghost of Chibusa Enoki see *Kaidan Chibusa Enoki*
Ghost of Chidori-Ga-Fuchi see *Swamp, The*
Ghost of Gojusan-Tsugi see *Kaidan Gojusan-tsugi*
Ghost of Kagami-Ga-Fuchi see *Kaidan Kagami-ga-fuchi*
Ghost of Kasane, The see *Depths, The*
Ghost of Oiwa see *Kaidan Oiwa no Borei*
Ghost of Otamange-Ike 316
Ghost of Saga Mansion see *Kaidan Saga yashiki*
Ghost of the One-Eyed Man xx, 326
Ghost of the Snake see *Kaidan hebionna*
Ghost of the Snow Girl Prostitute see *Snow Woman, The*
Ghost of Two Travelers at Tenamonya see *Tenamonya yurei dochu*
Ghost of Yotsuya (1961) see *Kaidan Oiwa no Borei*
Ghost of Yotsuya, The (1957) see *Kaidan Bancho saray ashiki*
Ghost of Yotsuya, The (1959) 47–49, 316
Ghost of Yotsuya: New Version, The see *Shinshaku Yotsuya kaidan*
Ghost Ship 326
Ghost Stories see *Kwaidan*

Ghost Story: Barabara Phantom, A see *Dismembered Ghost*
Ghost Story of Funny Act in Front of Train Station see *Kigeki ekiame kaidan*
Ghost Story of Booby Trap see *Ghostly Trap, The*
Ghost Story of Broken Dishes at Bancho Mansion see *Kaidan Bancho saray ashiki*
Ghost Story of Devil's Fire Trap see *Kaidan onibi no numa*
Ghost Story of Kakui Street see *Kaidan Kakuidori*
Ghost Story of Passage, A see *Lady Was a Ghost, The*
Ghost Story of Stone Lanterns and Crying in the Night see *Kaidan yonaki-doro*
Ghost Story of Two Travelers see *Lady Was a Ghost, The*
Ghost Story of Wanderer at Honjo see *Seven Mysteries*
Ghost Story of Yotsuda in Tokaido (1959) see *Ghost of Yotsuya, The*
Ghost Story: The Kanane Swamp see *Depths, The*
Ghostly Trap, The 303–4
Ghosts on Parade 304
Gigan (aka Giagan; character) 209
Gigantis the Fire Monster xxii, 4, 12, 14–18, 26, 39, 56, 76, 78, 123, 161, 346
Girl Diver of Spook Mansion 316
Girl with Bamboo Leaves, The 304
"Gilb" (*Variety* reviewer) 13
Gillard, Stuart 263
Glasser, Albert 44
Glut, Donald 111, 113, 153, 185
Godzilla (character) xi, xiv, xv, xvii, xix, xxi–xxiii, 9, 7–14, 15, 29, 43–44, 95–96, 203, 209, 219, 230
Godzilla (film, 1954/1956) see *Godzilla, King of the Monsters!*
Godzilla (film series) 60, 173, 181, 182, 185, 192, 201, 203, 207, 210, 211–12, 217, 227, 229, 268, 296–97, 330
Godzilla (proposed American remake) xxii, xxiii
"Godzilla Fantasia" (laser disc) 108
Godzilla, King of the Monsters! xi, xii, xiii, xv, 3, 7–14, 15, 20, 23, 24, 28, 43, 51, 72, 80, 112, 114, 192, 196, 346–47
Godzilla 1985 xii, 12, 16, 92, 95, 216, 221, 227, 266–70, 272, 274, 275, 296, 347–49
Godzilla on Monster Island 16, 60, 74, 207–10, 211, 212, 217, 219, 290, 349

Godzilla Raids Again see *Gigantis the Fire Monster*
Godzilla vs. Biollante 80, 180, 272–75, 286, 287, 289, 290, 350–51
"Godzilla vs. Charles Barkley" (television commercial) xi
Godzilla vs. Gigan see *Godzilla on Monster Island*
Godzilla vs. King Ghidorah see *Gojira vs. Kingughidorah*
Godzilla vs. Mechagodzilla see *Godzilla vs. The Cosmic Monster*
Godzilla vs. Megalon xii, 60, 209, 210–13, 217, 219, 225, 351–52
Godzilla vs. Monster Zero see *Monster Zero*
Godzilla vs. Mothra (1964) see *Godzilla vs. the Thing*
Godzilla vs. Mothra (1992) see *Gojira vs. Mosura*
Godzilla vs. the Bionic Monster see *Godzilla vs. the Cosmic Monster*
Godzilla vs. the Cosmic Monster xxiii, 16, 60, 123, 143, 217–20, 228, 231, 352
Godzilla vs. the Sea Monster see *Ebirah, Horror of the Deep*
Godzilla vs. the Smog Monster xiv, 25, 36, 201–14, 209, 212, 227, 352
Godzilla vs. the Thing xix, xxiii, 12, 16, 25, 81, 83, 92–96, 97, 99, 152, 198, 269, 295, 296, 353
Godzilla's Revenge 26, 38, 122, 153, 180, 184–85, 203, 229, 259, 349–50
Godziszewski, Ed xv, 14, 84,
Gog (1954) 231
Gojira (1954) see *Godzilla, King of the Monsters!*
Gojira (1984) see *Godzilla 1985*
Gojira dengeki taisakusen see *Destroy All Monsters*
Gojira Ebirah Mosura: Nankai no dai ketto see *Ebirah, Horror of the Deep*
Gojira Mosura Kingughidorah: Chikyu saidai no kessen see *Ghidrah: The Three-Headed Monster*
Gojira no gyakushu see *Gigantis the Fire Monster*
Gojira no musako see *Son of Godzilla*
Gojira tai Gaigan see *Godzilla on Monster Island*
Gojira tai Gigan see *Godzilla on Monster Island*
Gojira tai Megaro see *Godzilla vs. Megalon*
Gojira tai Mekagojira see *Godzilla vs. the Cosmic Monster*

Gojira vs. Biorante see *Godzilla vs. Biollante*
Gojira vs. Kingughidorah 9, 12, 26, 56, 99, 286–90, 293, 295, 296, 353
Gojira vs. Mechagojira (1993) 296–97
Gojira vs. Mosura 13, 293–96, 354–55
Gojirūo (book by Jacobson) xxii
Goke, Bodysnatcher from Hell 166–69, 321
Goke the Vampire see *Goke, Bodysnatcher from Hell*
Gokiburi see *Twilight of the Cockroaches*
Golden Bat, The see *Ogan Batto*
Golden Harvest (H.K.), Ltd. 134
Goldfinger (1964) 155, 157
Golding, William 86
Gomi, Ryutaro 130
Goodbye, Jupiter see *Sayonara Jupiter*
Gorath 12, 25, 26, 46, 56, 71, 72–76, 80, 83, 169, 285, 286, 354–55
Gorath, the Mysterious Star see *Gorath*
Gordon, Alex 11
Gordon, Bert I. 72, 238–39
Gorgo (1961) 44, 146, 147
Gorilla at Large (1954) 12
Graduate, The (1967) 11
Grand Duel in Magic see *Magic Serpent, The*
Grand Prix (1966) 3
Great Expectations (1934) 68
Great McGinty, The (1940) 115
Great Monster Yongkari see *Yongary, Monster from the Deep*
Great Wall, The (1962) 13, 27, 33, 140
Green Slime, The xiv, 135, 144, 160, 169–72, 189, 212, 242, 250, 326–27
Greene, Lorne 215–6
Gross, Linda (*Los Angeles Times* reviewer) 222
Gruber, Franz 153
Gunhed see *Ganhedo*
Gunther, Ted 170, 172
Guyver, The 282, 291–93, 321–23

H-Man, The xv, xxii, 11, 25, 26, 37–39, 41, 55, 59, 60, 123, 196, 356
Hakuja-den (1958) xix
Half a Loaf... 323
Half Human see *Half Human: The Story of the Abominable Snowman*
Half Human: The Story of the Abominable Snowman xiii, 12, 18–21, 25, 355
Hama, Mie 77, 80, 88, 91–92, 108, 141, 144, 155, 157

Hamamura, Jun 113
Hamill, Mark 291, 292
Hamilton, Kipp 136
Hammer Films xii, xv, xxi, 48, 194–95, 204, 206, 225
Hanna-Barbera 17
Harada, Itoko 153
Harada, Kiwako 286
Harada, Mieko 277
Hardy, Phil xx, 23, 39, 108, 155
Harewood, Dorian 280
Harikari (1962) 105, 157
Harp of Burma (19??) 13
Harris, Phil 253
Harris, Sid 43
Harryhausen, Ray 87, 90
Harum Scarum (1965) 100
Harvey, Laurence 2
Hashimoto, Koji 275
Hatsuharu tanuki goten see *Enchanted Princess*
Haunted Castle, The 140, 304–5
Haunted Cave, The see *Girl Diver of Spook Mansion*
Haunted Gold 355
Haunted Life of a Dragon-Tattooed Lass see *Tattooed Swordsman*
Hausu see *House*
Hawley, Norman Van 67
Hayasaka, Fumio 123
Hayes, R. M. ix, 66, 77, 299
Hayman, Earle 262
Haynes, Linda 186
He Had to Die 316
Healy, Myron 41, 42–43
Hearn, Lafcadio 100, 104
Hebimusume to Hakuhatsuki see *Snake Girl and the Silver-Haired Witch, The*
Hedora (aka Hedorah; character) 203
Hell (1960) see *Sinners to Hell, The*
Hell in the Pacific (1969) 3
Hell Screen, The see *Portrait of Hell*
Herrmann, Bernard 13
Herts-Lion 57
Heston, Charlton 230, 231, 234, 279, 280, 281, 282
Hidden Fortress, The (1958) 12, 123, 248
High and Low (1963) 12, 52, 56, 105, 123
Higuchi, Horacio ix, 299
Hikarigoke 384–85
Hiken Yaburi (1969) 129
Hills Have Eyes, The (1977) 291
Hindenburg, The (1975) 115
Hinotori 105, 355–56

Hinson, Hal 279
Hira, Mikijiro 124
Hirata, Akihiko 8, 11–12, 24, 28, 37, 42, 51, 58, 80–81, 83, 99, 121, 123, 187, 189, 217, 219, 220, 228, 229, 239, 242, 246, 247–48
Hiroku kaibyoden see *Haunted Castle, The*
Hiroku onna ro 305
Hiroshima, Mon Amour (1959) xii, 99
Hishimi, Yuriko 207
Hodgson, W.H. 86
"Hogg" (*Variety* reviewer) 99
Holcombe, Harry 77–9
Hole, The see *Onibaba*
Hollywood Boulevard (1976) 212
Homma, Fumiko 2
Honda, Inoshiro see Honda, Ishiro
Honda, Ishiro xxii, 9–10, 11, 25, 41, 57, 60, 70, 75–76, 84, 87, 94, 100, 118, 119, 123, 152, 161, 163, 185, 186, 196, 201, 227, 229, 299
Hongo, Kojiro 132, 139, 140, 147, 165, 172
Horlan, Cathy 168
Horror of a Deformed Man 327
Horror of a Malformed Man see *Horror of a Deformed Man*
Horror of an Ugly Woman see *Masseur's Curse, The*
Horror of Dracula (1957) 194, 206, 225
Horror of the Giant Vortex see *Kyofu no daiuzumaki*
Horton, Robert 169, 171
Hoshi, Yuriko 93, 95–6
House 356
House of Dark Shadows (1970) 195
House of Terrors xx, 327
House of Wax (1953) 157
House That Dripped Blood, The (1970) 195
House Where Evil Dwells, The 327–8
How to Get Ahead in Advertising (1989) 67
Hughes, Andrew xiv, 134, 214
Human Vapor, The 16, 37, 55–57, 75, 290, 356–57
Hundred Ghost Stories, The see *100 Monsters*
Hundred Monsters, The see *100 Monsters*
Hussey, Olivia 264
Huston, John xv
Hylland, Richard 170
Hylton, Jane 66

I Bombed Pearl Harbor (1960) 12, 16, 59, 92

Ibuke, Toru 120
Idiot, The (1951) 3, 12
Ido zero dai sakusen see *Latitude Zero*
Ie see *House*
Ifukube, Akira 13, 31, 44, 46, 79, 84, 94–95, 108, 111, 123, 130, 131, 133, 138, 144, 161, 164, 186, 196, 197, 198, 227, 275, 290, 295, 296, 297
Igawa, Hisashi 277
Ikariya, Chosuke 278
Ikebe, Ryo 9, 44, 46, 73–4, 76, 83, 239, 242
Ikeuchi, Junko 48
Ikiru (1952) xii, 12, 16
Illusion of Blood 105, 357
Image Wife 328
Imagery Paradise see *Kuso tengoku*
Imamura, Keiko 294, 296
Inagaki, Hiroshi 9, 52
Incense for the Damned (1970) 195
Inchon (1982) 3
Incredible Melting Man, The (1977) 43
Incredible Two-Headed Transplant, The (1971) 67
Inferno, The see *Jigoku*
Inheritance, The (19??) 105
Inn of Evil 357
Innocent Witch, An see *Osorezan no onna*
Inochi bonifuro see *Inn of Evil*
Interns, The (1962) 111
Inugamike no ichizoku see *Inugamis, The*
Inugamis, The 328
Invaders from Space (1957) 28, 35, 36, 318
Invaders from Space (1959) see *Prince of Space*
Invaders from the Planets see *Supergiant*
Invaders from the Spaceship see *Prince of Space, The*
Invasion from a Planet see *Invasion of the Neptune Men*
Invasion of Astro-Monster see *Monster Zero*
Invasion of the Body Snatchers (1956) 135, 169, 268
Invasion of the Neptune Men xxii, 60–3, 328
Invisible Invaders, The (1959) 20
Invisible Man, The see *Tomei ningen*
Invisible Man: Dr. Eros see *Tomeiningen erohakase*
Invisible Swordsman, The 305
Invitation to the Enchanged Town see *Sen-nin Buraku*
Isaki, Mitsunori 276

Ishida, Ayumi 214
Ishikawa, Hiroshi 207, 210
Ishimatsu Travels with Ghosts see *Moro no Ichimatsu yurei dochu*
Island, The (1960) 107
Island of Dr. Moreau, The (1977) 135
It Came from Hollywood (1982) 51, 155
It Happened One Night (1934) 68
It's a Mad, Mad, Mad, Mad World (1963) 212
Ito, Akio 177
Ito, Emi 69, 71, 93, 97
Ito, Hisaya 37, 96
Ito, Jerry (Jelly Itoh) 68, 71, 175
Ito, Yumi 69, 71, 93, 97
Ives, Burl 242, 244
Ivory Ape, The 261, 377–78
Iwanaga, Frank 7

"Jac" (*Variety* reviewer)
Jacobs, Arthur P. 230, 231
Jaeckel, Richard 170, 171, 172, 186, 189
Jaiga (aka Jiger; character) 192, 193
"James Bond" (film series) 201
James Bond Bedside Companion, The (book by Benson) 155
James Bond Films, The (book by Rubin) 155
Japanese Fantasy Film Journal, The (magazine) xv, xx, 14, 57, 65, 240, 260
Japanese Giants (magazine) xv, xx, xxii, 14, 83
Japula see *Lake of Dracula*
Jarre, Maurice 283
Jasei no in 385
Jaws (1975) 122, 237, 238, 260
Jenson, George 281, 283
Jet Jaguar (character) 211, 212, 213
Jigoku (1960) see *Sinner of Hell, The*
Jigoku (1979) 244, 328
Jigokuhen see *Portrait of Hell*
Jihei, Masanori 174
"Jiyainto Robo" (TV series) 177
"Johnny Sokko and His Flying Robot" (TV series) 177
Johnson, Bob 175, 225
Johnson, Tor 49
Jotari johatsu 385
Journey Along Tokaido Road see *Along with Ghosts*
Journey of Honor (1992) 3
Journey to the Seventh Planet (1961) 16
Joys of Torture, The 328–29

Jujin yukiotako see *Half Human: The Story of the Abominable Snowman*
"Jumborg Ace" (TV series) 173
Jurassic Park (1993) xxiii
Jyoseini kansuru jyonisho (195?) 16

Kadokawa, Haruki 263
Kadokawa Publishing xvi
Kael, Pauline (*New Yorker* reviewer) 230-1
Kagawa, Kyoko 51, 52, 69, 299
Kagemusha (1980) 10, 12, 105, 276
Kagi no kag see *What's Up, Tiger Lily?* (1966)
Kai tatsu daikessen see *Magic Serpent, The*
Kaibyo Arima goten 305
Kaibyo Gojusan-tsugi 305
Kaibyo Karakuri Tenjo 329
Kaibyo koshinuke daisodo 329
Kaibyo noroi no kabe 305
Kaibyo noroi numa 329
Kaibyo Okazaki sodo 305
Kaibyo Oma-ga-tsuji 305-6
Kaibyo Ota-mange-Ike see *Ghost of Otamange-Ike*
Kaibyo Yonaki numa see *Necromancy*
Kaidan see *Kwaidan*
Kaidan Bancho saray ashiki 329
Kaidan barabara yurei see *Dismembered Ghost*
Kaidan botandoro 172-73, 306
Kaidan Chibusa Enoki 316
Kaidan Chidori-ga-fuchi see *Swamp, The*
Kaidan dochu see *Lady Was a Ghost, The*
Kaidan Fukagawa jowa 306
Kaidan Gojusan-tsugi 385
Kaidan hebionna 329-30
Kaidan hitotsu-me jizo 330
Kaidan Honjo nanfushigi see *Seven Mysteries*
Kaidan ijin yurei 385
Kaidan Iro-Zane-Kyoren onna shisho see *Dancing Mistress*
Kaidan Kagami-ga-fuchi 316
Kaidan Kakuidori 306
Kaidan Kasanegafuchi (1957) see *Depths, The*
Kaidan Kasanegafuchi (1960) 306
Kaidan Kasanegafuchi (1970) see *Masseur's Curse, The*
Kaidan katame no otoko see *Ghost of the One-Eyed Man*
Kaidan noboriryu see *Tattooed Swordsman*
Kaidan Owia no Borei 330

Kaidan onibi no numa 306-7
Kaidan otoshiana see *Ghostly Trap, The*
Kaidan ryoko 323
Kaidan Saga yashiki 307
Kaidan semushi otoko see *House of Terrors*
Kaidan Shamisen-bori 330
Kaidan yonaki-doro 307
Kaidan yukijoro see *Snow Woman, The*
Kaidan zankoku monogatari see *Curse of the Blood*
Kaii Utsunomiya tsuritenjo 317
Kaiju daifunsen: Daigoro tai goriasu 357
Kaiju daisenso see *Monster Zero*
Kaiju daisenso: Kingughidorah tai Gojira see *Monster Zero*
Kaiju Eiga (definition) xiii
Kaiju o Godzilla see *Godzilla, King of the Monsters!*
Kaiju shima no kessen: Gojira no musako see *Son of Godzilla*
Kaiju soshingeki see *Destroy All Monsters*
Kaitei daisenso see *Terror Beneath the Sea*
Kaitei gunkan see *Atragon*
Kameba (character) 197
Kane, Joe 204
Kaneno naru Oka (1948) 75
Karate Killer (1981) 62
Karita, Toyomi 21
Karnes, Robert 18
Kashi to kodomo see *Pitfall, The*
Kato, Daisuke 2
Kato, Kazuo 167
Katsura, Kokan 145
Kawada, Clifford 42
Kawaji, Tamio 145
Kawakita, Koichi 289, 295, 296, 297
Kawase, Hiroyuki 201, 203, 211
Kawata, Takeshi 282
Kawataki, Mokuami 129
Kawazu, Seizaburo 58
Kazima, Nobuhiko 181
Kazusaki, Toshiya 153
Keats, Steven 234, 261, 263
Keep Watching the Skies! American Science Fiction Movies of the Fifties (book by Warren) ix, xv, xx, xxiii, 9, 67, 70
Kemmerling, Warren 267
Kempley, Rita 270
Keneko, Mitsunobu 177
Kennedy, George 264, 266
Keith, Michael 79
Kelly, Gene xv
Kessen nankai no daikaiju see *Yog: Monster from Space*

Kiganjo no boken see *Adventures of Takla Makan*
Kigeki ekiame kaidan 357–58
Killer, The (1989) 128
Killing Bottle, The see *Kokusai Himitsu Keisatsu: Zettai zetsumei*
Kimura, Isao 157, 160–1
Kimura, Takeshi (aka Kaoru Mabuchi) 25, 64, 76
King Features, Inc. 194
King Ghidorah (character) 44, 52, 99, 209
King Kong (character) 213
King Kong (1933) xxiii, 9, 10, 11, 14, 76, 146, 236
King Kong (1976) 213, 235
"King Kong" (TV series) 141
King Kong Escapes 12, 80, 89, 92, 122, 141–45, 157, 161, 164, 172, 209, 219, 234, 290, 358
King Kong vs. Godzilla 9, 25, 63, 76–81, 83, 92, 94–5, 110, 141, 143, 144, 152, 157, 197, 275, 290, 358–9
King Lear (play by Shakespeare) 32
King of the Rocketmen (1949) 26
King Seesar (character) 218–19
KingKong no gyakushu see *King Kong Escapes*
KingKong tai Gojira see *King Kong vs. Godzilla*
KingKong vs. Godzilla see *King Kong vs. Godzilla*
Kinoshita, Keisuke 49, 105
Kinugasa, Teinosuke xv
Kirino, Hiroo 73
Kishi, Keiko 101
Kishida, Kyoko 126
Kishida, Mori 204, 206, 217
Kiss Me Deadly (1955) 115
Kita, Takeo 196
Kitamura, Eizo 167
Kitazawa, Noriko 47
Kitty Films ix
Knievel, Evel 248
Knockout Drops 359
Ko, Hideo 167
Kobal, John 4
Kobayashi, Keiju 269
Kobayashi, Kenji 214, 216, 266
Kobayashi, Masaki 103–5
Kobayashi, Satomi 293, 296
Kobayashi, Setsuo 183
Kobayashi, Shoji 293
Kobayashi, Tetsuko 82–4
Kobayashi, Toshiko 159

Kobayashi, Tsuruko 42
Kobayashi, Yukiko 161, 195, 196
Kochi, Momoko 7, 19, 28
Koiya koi nasuna koi see *Love, Thy Name Be Sorrow*
Koizumi, Hiroshi 14, 16, 17, 68, 71, 85, 90, 93, 95–96, 217, 219, 220, 269, 296
Kojima, Yaeko 258
Kokusai Himitsu Keisatsu: Zettai zetsumei 75, 111, 359
Komatsu, Yoko 258
Konchu daisenso see *Genocide*
Konna yume wo mita see *Akira Kurosawa's Dreams Konyaku samba Garasu* (195?) 16
Koshikei see *Death by Hanging*
Koshoki tomei ningen 314
Koslo, Paul 280
Kosure ookameko wo kashi ude kashi tsukatsuru see *Sword of Vengeance*
Kosure ookami – Sanzu no Kawa no Ubaguruma see *Shogun Assassin*
Kotaka, Yuji 146
Kotetso no kyojin – Supa Jyaiantsu see *Supergiant*
Kotetsu no Kyojin – Supa Jyaiantsu: chikyu metsubo sunzen see *Supergiant*
Kotetsu no Kyojin – Supa Jyaiantsu: Kaiseijin no mayo see *Supergiant*
Kouchi, Momoko see Kochi, Momoko
Kozure Ohkmi n. 2 see *Shogun Assassin*
Kronos (1957) 17
Kubo, Akira xii, 32, 33, 73, 75, 85, 116, 150, 152, 162, 164, 196, 198
Kudo, Keiko 258
Kuhira-gami see *Whale God, The*
Kumonosu-djo see *Throne of Blood*
"Kung Fu" (TV series) 17
Kunsunoki, Yuko 167
Kuraishisu niju-goju nen see *Solar Crisis*
Kurobarano yakata 323
Kuroda, Kiyomi 107
Kuroki, Hikaru 186
Kuroneko 65, 107, 359–60
Kurosawa, Akira xi, xiv, xxiii, 2–4, 6, 9, 10, 16, 32, 52, 56, 105, 118, 123, 160, 248, 299
Kurosawa, Toshio 220, 225
Kurotokage see *Black Lizard*
Kurutta ippeiji see *Page of Madness, A*
Kusakari, Masao 264, 265, 266
Kuso tengoku 360
Kwaidan xxii, xxiii, 12, 83, 100–5, 157, 177, 194, 206, 278, 360–61
Kyo, Machiko 2, 5–6, 124, 125, 126

Kyofu kikei ningen see *Horror of a Deformed Man*
Kyofu no daiuzumaki 385
Kyokanoka musume Dojoji 323
Kyokutei tankensen Pora-Bora see *Last Dinosaur, The*
Kyoren no onna shisho 314
Kyoryukaicho no densetsu see *"Legend of the Dinosaurs, The"*
Kyuju-kyuhonme no kimusume see *Bloody Sword of the 99th Virgin, The*
Kyuketsu dokuro sen see *Living Skeleton*
Kyuketsuki Gokemidoro see *Goke, Bodysnatcher from Hell*

Lady Was a Ghost, The 330
Lahr, Bert 218
Lake of Death see *Lake of Dracula*
Lake of Dracula 195, 204-7, 227, 361
Land That Time Forgot, The (1975) 236
Lasciviousness of the Viper see *Jasei no in*
Last Days of Planet Earth, The 11, 220-22, 239, 361-62
Last Death of the Devil, The 330
Last Dinosaur, The 234-36, 263, 278-79, 290
Last Embrace, The (1955) 12
Last Emperor, The (1987) 292
Last War, The 12, 26, 54-55, 63-66, 74, 216, 220, 222, 239, 362
Latitude Zero 11, 12, 122, 171, 185, 186-89, 241, 296, 362-63
Lawrence of Arabia (1962) 57, 283
Lee, Bruce 134
Lee, Christopher 194
Legend of Dinosaur and Monster Bird see *"Legend of the Dinosaurs, The"*
Legend of Dinosaurs and Monster Birds see *"Legend of the Dinosaurs, The"*
"Legend of the Dinosaurs, The" 236-39, 330-31
Legend of the 7 Golden Vampires, The (1974) 195
Leone, Sergio 219
Let's Go, Young Guy (1967) 12
Levine, Joseph E. 11
Life of Oharu, The (1952) 6, 12
Lightning Swords of Death see *Sword of Vengeance*
Lin, Beru-Bera 217
Little Girl Who Conquered Time, The see *Toki wo kaieru shojo*
Little Shop of Horrors, The (1960) 275

Living Skeleton 323
Lomez, Celine 262
Lord of the Flies (1963) 86
Lord Takes a Bride, The see *Ootori-jo no Hanayume* (1957)
Los Angeles Times 33
"Lost in Space" (TV series) 194
Lost World, The (1925) 236
Lost World of Sinbad, The 3, 75, 87-90, 157, 363
Love at First Bite (1979) 225
Love Foolery Case for a Severed Head see *Namakubi joshi jiken*
Love Not Again see *Love, Thy Name Be Sorrow*
Love, Thy Name Be Sorrow 331
Lovell, Glenn 271
Lower Depths, The (1957) 16, 33, 52, 123
Lucas, George 76, 129, 225, 242, 248, 276
Lucky Dragon No. 5 (1959) 107
Luke, Keye 17, 26
Lust for a Vampire (1970) 195, 227
Lusty Transparent Human see *Koshoki tomei ningen*
Lusty Transparent Man 314
Lynn, Barbara see Lin, Beru-Bera

Mabuchi, Kaoru see Kimura, Takeshi
Macbeth (1948) 32
Macbeth (1971) 32
Macbeth see *Throne of Blood*
McCloskey, Leigh 242, 244
Machida, Masanori 145
Mad Fox, The see *Love, Thy Name Be Sorrow*
Mad Max (1979) 281, 282
Mad Monster Party? (1967) 141
Madadayo (1993) 4, 10, 52
Madame White Snake 363-4
Maeda, Bibari 125, 150, 152
Maeda, Koichi 258
Magic Carpet, The (1951) 189
Magic Serpent, The xx, 87, 126-29, 331
Magic Sword, The (1962) 72
Magic Sword of Watari, The 331
Magma (character) 74-5
Magnificent Seven, The (1960) 250
Mahoney, John 126
Majin (character) xvi
Majin 129-32, 307
Majin Strikes Again 133, 307-8
Majin the Hideous Idol see *Majin*

Majin, the Monster of Terror see *Majin*
Makai tensho 331–32
Male Vampire, The see *Woman Vampire, The*
Maliciousness of the Snake's Evil, The see *Jasei no in*
Man from Planet Alpha 364
Man in the Iron Mask, The (1939) 115
Man in the Moonlight Mask, The xx, 51, 332
Man Who Loved Cat Dancing, The (1973) 283
Man Who Stole the Sun, The 385
Manabe, Riichiro 203, 227
Manda (character) 82, 84
Manji (1964) 183
Manley, Walter 27, 35, 62–63
Mano, Shigeo 183
Manoda, Yukio 172
Manster, The 66–68, 71, 234, 385
Manster: Half Man, Half Monster, The see *Manster, The*
Man Who Stole the Sun, The
Many Ghost-Cats see *Phantom Cat, The*
March of the Monsters see *Destroy All Monsters*
Markalite (magazine) xx, 14, 17, 30, 99, 118, 120, 133, 225, 283
Maruyama, Akihiro 158, 160, 161
Maruyama, Ikio 162
Masamura, Yasuzo 183
Mask and Destiny, The see *Mask of Destiny, The*
Mask of Destiny, The 323–24 *Masked Terror* see *Dokuro kyojo*
Maslin, Janet (*New York Times* reviewer) 279
Masseur's Curse, The 308
Mastermind (1969)
Masuda, Toshio 160
Matango see *Attack of the Mushroom People*
Matango, Fungus of Terror see *Attack of the Mushroom People*
Matheson, Tim 280, 282
Matsumiya, Reiko 152
Matsuo, Kayo 195
Matsuoka, Kikko 158
Matsutaka, Hiroki 126, 129
Maus (graphic novel by Spiegelman) 285
Mechagodzilla (character) 143, 218, 219
Mechani-Kong (character) 219
Medina, Patricia 187, 188
Megalon (character) 210–1
Mekagojira no gyakushu see *Terror of Mechagodzilla*

Melchior, Ib 16
Men Who Tread on the Tiger's Tail, The (1945) 3, 12
Merrick, John 222
Message from Space xiv, 62, 157, 160, 248–51, 283, 332
Message from Space: Galactic Battle see *Swords of the Space Ark*
Metro-Goldwyn-Mayer (M-G-M) xv, 31, 169
Miake, Bontaro 21
Midare karakuri 364
Midori, Mako 183
Midway (1976) 3, 284
Mifune, Toshiro 2–3, 11, 32, 33, 51, 52, 87, 89, 90, 105, 108, 118, 299
Mighty Jack 173–75, 177, 245, 379
"Mighty Jack" (TV series) 174
Mighty Joe Young (1949) 76, 77
Mihashi, Tatsuya 56
Mikuni, Rentaro 100, 101
Miller, Linda 142, 144, 172
Miller, Marvin ix, 17, 189, 216
Milner, David ix, 25, 41, 75, 109, 163, 230, 299
Milstein, Fredric (*Los Angeles Times* reviewer)
Minya, Son of Godzilla see *Godzilla's Revenge*
"Mirrorman" (TV series) 173
Mishima, Yukio 157, 159, 160, 161
"Mission: Impossible" (TV series) 174
Mitamura, Kunihiko 273
Mito, Mitsuke 5–6
Miyaguchi, Kunio 185
Mizoguchi, Kenji xi, xiv, 6, 49
Mizuno, Kumi 73, 85, 88, 109, 111, 116, 118, 121, 136, 137, 138, 152
Moju see *Blind Beast, The*
Monster from a Prehistoric Planet 145–47, 152, 314–15
Monster Gamera, The see *Gammera the Invincible*
Monster Gorilla, The 332
Monster Times, The (magazine) 204
Monster Zero xxii, 12, 56, 75, 83, 99, 111, 115–20, 209, 364
Monsters from an Unknown Planet see *Terror of Mechagodzilla*
Monsters Invade Expo 70 see *Gamera vs. Monster X*
Monthly Film Bulletin (magazine) 46, 68, 90, 198, 210, 219, 230
Moon Mask Rider, The 386

Moonbeam Man, The see *Man in the Moonlight Mask, The*
Mori, Iwao 9
Mori, Masaki 49
Mori, Masayuki 2–3, 5–6
Moricone, Ennio 180
Morita, Kensaku 239
Moro no Ichimatsu yurei dochu 365
Morrow, Vic 248
"Mosk" (*Variety* reviewer) 7, 23, 92, 105, 184, 216–17
Most Beautiful, The (1944) 12
Mostel, Zero 65
Mosura see *Mothra*
Mosura tai Gojira see *Godzilla vs. the Thing*
Mothra (character) 96, 224
Mothra xii, xxii, 16, 49, 51, 52, 63, 65, 68–72, 74, 80, 92, 93, 94, 95, 146, 151, 152, 196, 269, 294, 295, 296, 299, 365
Motion Picture Guide, 1927–1991, The (book by Nash and Ross) xii, xiv, 12, 17–8, 20, 23, 26, 44, 47, 65–6, 68, 81, 87, 90, 96, 100, 105, 108, 112, 114, 119, 123, 138, 140, 150, 153, 169, 172, 185, 213, 286
Muno no hito see *Nowhere Man*
Murai, Kunio 208
Murata, Takehiro 293
Murata, Takeo 9
Murdering Mite, The see *Transparent Man vs. the Fly Man, The*
"Murf" (*Variety* reviewer) 84, 90, 144
Murphy, Christopher 181
Mutsu, Goro 218, 228
My Blood Belongs to Someone Else see *Blood*
My Bride Is a Ghost see *Kaidan botandoro*
My Friend Death 80, 365–66
Mysterians, The xxii, 11, 12, 25, 26, 28–31, 39, 41, 44, 51, 74, 77, 79, 91, 115, 290, 366
Mysterious Island (1961) 122
Mysterious Satellite, The xx, 21–23, 27, 62, 74, 308
Mystery of the Cat-Woman see *Haunted Castle, The*
"Mystery Science Theater 3000" (TV series) 177

Nakadai, Fumio 152
Nakadai, Tatsuya 101, 105, 124, 125
Nakagawa, Anna 286
Nakagawa, Nobuo 49
Nakajima, Haruo 12–3, 74, 137
Nakamura, Atsuo 195
Nakamura, Kan-Emon, 102
Nakamura, Kazuo 101
Nakamura, Masayoshi 103
Nakamura, Nobuo 90, 214
Nakamura, Ryozaburo 47
Nakamura, Tadao 59
Nakamura, Tetsu (aka Satoshi) 66, 68, 187, 234
Nakano, Akiyoshi see Nakano, Teruyoshi
Nakano, Shokei see Nakano, Teruyoshi
Nakano, Teruyoshi 122, 198, 212, 213, 216, 222, 241, 289, 299
Nakano, Toshihiko 276
Nakao, Akira 195
Nakaya, Noboru 102
Nakayama, Mari 187
Namakubi joshi jiken 386
Nanbanji no Semushi-Otoko see *Return to Manhood*
Nanbu, Shozo 21
Naniwa, Cheiko 33
Narita, Mikio 249
Narusawa, Masahige 161
National Lampoon's Animal House (1978) 282
Natsuki, Akira 139, 269
Natsuki, Yosuke 90, 92, 97, 99, 267, 296
Neal, Peggy xiv, 134, 135, 153, 154
Necromancy 308
Negishi, Akemi 19
Negishi, Toru 273
Negishi, Toshie 277
Nemec, Corky 282
New Hope Entertainment 253
New Version of the Ghost of Yotsuya see *Shinshaku Yotsuya kaidan*
New World Pictures 214, 269, 270
Newman, Paul 2
Newsweek (magazine) 13
Night Drum (19??) 13
Night in Hong Kong (1961) 12
Night of the Living Dead (1968) 138
Night of the Vampire, The see *Vampire Doll, The*
Nikkatsu Corporation ix, xvi, 146, 314–5
Ningen no joken see *Human Condition, The*
Ninja Boy see *Watari, Ninja Boy*
Ninja Wars 332–33
Ninjutsu see *Secret Scrolls Part I*
Nippon chiubotsu see *Submersion of Japan*

Nippon tanjo see *Three Treasures, The*
Nishigaki, Rokuro 207
Nishimoto, Hiroyuki 167
Nishimura, Akira 173
Nishizawa, Toshiaki 207
No Regrets for Our Youth (1946) 12
Noche de Walpurgis, La (1970) 195
None but the Brave (1965) 25
Nosferatu: Phantom der Nacht (1979) 225
Nostradamus (Michel de Notredame) 220
Nostradamus no dai yogen see *Last Days of Planet Earth, The*
Now You See Him, Now You Don't (1972) 189
Nowhere Man 324
Nuclear War Films (book by Shaheen) 65

O'Brien, Willis 76-7
Obscenity of the Viper see *Jasei no in*
Odaka, Megumi 273, 287
Oeyama shuten doji see *Ogre of Mount Oe, The*
Ogawa, Ei 196
Ogawa, Tomoku 127
Ogon Batto 333
Ogre of Mount Oe, The 308-9
Oguni, Hideo 22
Ohtsuka, Michiko 172-3
Okabe, Masazumi 248
Okada, Eiji xii, 99, 124, 126
Okada, Manko 101
Okada, Masumi 186
Okada, Shigeru 126
Okasaretsu Byuakui 386-87
Okawara, Takao 297
Okuda, Ted ix
Omae, Mataru 196
Omori, Kazuki 275, 295
Omura, Senkichi 37
On Her Majesty's Secret Service (1969) 156
On the Beach (1959) 62, 265
100 Monsters 131, 176-77, 309
O'Neill, Dick 115
Onibaba xxiii, 65, 105-8, 194, 366
Onna kyuketsuki see *Woman Vampire, The*
Onryo sakura dai-sodo see *He Had to Die*
Onuki, Masayoshi 49
Ootori-jo no Hanayome (1957) xvi
Operation Monsterland see *Destroy All Monsters*
Oppenheimer, Alan 115
Oreno chi wa tanin no chi see *Blood*
Oru kaiju dai shingeki see *Godzilla's Revenge*

Osaka jo monogatari see *Daredevil in the Castle*
Osawa, Sayaka 294, 296
Osorezan no onna 324
Otake, Makoto 294
Othello (1952) 33
Otomo, Jun 48
Otomo, Ryutaro 126
Otowa, Nobuko 106, 108
Otowa, Nobuo 63, 65
Outrage, The (1964)
Oyome in oide (1960) 10
Ozawa, Eitaro 5

Page of Madness, A 386
Paik, Greg 291
Palace of Snakes see *Yoja no maden*
Palance, Jack 262, 280, 281, 282
Paluzzi, Luciana 170, 171-72
Panavision xiii
Paramount Pictures xv
Partridge, Derek 261
Passion of a Woman Teacher see *Kyoren no onna shisho*
Peach Boy see *Takarajima Ensei*
Peanuts, The 71, 96, 99, 296; see also Ito, Emi and Ito, Yumi
Peonies and Stone Lanterns see *Botandoro*
People That Time Forgot, The (1977) 236
"Perry Mason" (TV series) 12
Perspecta Stereophonic Sound 30, 44
Phantom Cat, The 333
Phantom of Rue Morgue, The (1954) 189
Phantom of the Opera (book by Leroux) 55, 59
Phoenix, The see *Hinotori*
Pickett, Cindy 261, 262
Pillow Talk (1959) 111
Pink Ladies Motion Picture, The see *Pinku Redei no Katsudoshashin*
Pinku Redei no Katsudoshashin 366-67
Pit of Death, The see *Ghostly Trap, The*
Pitfall, The 124, 387
Planet of the Apes (book by Boulle) 230
Planet of the Apes (1968) 218, 219, 230-31, 233-34, 280
Planet Prince see *Prince of Space*
Playboy (magazine) 32
Pleasence, Donald 155
Polanski, Roman 32
Portrait of Hell 105, 367
Possessed, The see *Yoba*

Potter, Christopher (*Ann Arbor News* reviewer) 285
"Powe" (*Variety* reviewer) 17
Pretender, The (1948) 115
Prince of Space 49–51, 62, 333
Prince Planet see *Prince of Space*
Princess from the Moon (1987) 3
"Pro Wrestling Star Aztecizer" (TV series) 173
Proof of the Wild see *Yasei no Shomei*
Prophecies of Nostradamus see *Last Days of Planet Earth, The*
Psychotronic Encyclopedia of Film, The (book by Weldon) xx, 23, 28, 31, 36, 63, 67, 81, 84, 87, 99, 105, 112, 135, 138, 145, 164, 169, 172, 194, 210, 213
Pursuit at Dawn (1950) 83

"Quatermass and the Pit" (TV series) 98
Quiet Duel, The (1949) 12
Quigley, Linnea 293

Rackley, Luther 234
Radon see *Rodan*
Ragone, August 96, 118, 225
Ran (1985) 10, 32, 83, 105, 276
Randall, Tony 249
Rankin-Bass Productions, Inc. ix, 17, 141, 144, 173, 234, 236, 242, 261
Rashomon xv, xvi, xxiii, 2–4, 6, 12, 51, 125, 309
Re-Animator (1985) 291, 293
Rear Window (1954) 12
Reason, Rex 144
Reason, Rhodes 141, 144, 172
Rebel Without a Cause (1955) 111
Record of a Living Being (1955) 12, 123
Red Beard (1965) 3, 12, 52, 56, 123
Reeves, George 27
Reich, Howard (*Chicago Tribune* reviewer) 13
Reptilicus (1962) 16, 129, 275
Republic Pictures 16, 35
Rescue from Outer Space see *Supergiant*
Return of Godzilla, The see *Godzilla* 1985
Return of Majin, The see *Majin Strikes Again*
Return of the Giant Majin, The 132–33, 140, 309–10
Return of the Giant Monsters 140, 147–50, 165, 181, 182, 258, 310
Return of the Jedi (1983) 45, 250

Return of the Street Fighter (1976) 62
"Return of Ultraman" (TV series) 173
Return to Manhood 310
Revenge of King Kong, The see *King Kong Escapes*
Revengeful Spirit of Eros see *Erogami no onryo*
Rhapsody in August (1991) 4, 10, 279
Richard III (1956) 33
Richie, Donald 276
Rickey, Carrie (*Village Voice* reviewer) 13
Riko na oyome-san see *Image Wife*
Rikyu (1989) 125
RKO Radio Pictures 2, 77, 251
"Robe" (*Variety* reviewer) 112, 183
Robichaud, Michael ix
Robinson Crusoe on Mars (1964) 16
Robinson, Edward G. 230
Robot Monster (1953) 17
Rodan (character) 23–26, 43–44, 96, 99, 119, 229, 268, 290
Rodan 11, 12, 17, 20, 23–26, 41, 72, 95, 99, 367
Rodan the Flying Monster see *Rodan*
Rogers, Roy xxii
Romero, Cesar 186, 187, 188, 189
"Ron" (*Variety* reviewer) 31, 39
Rosenberg, Scott 272
Ross, Peter 270
Ross, William 239, 242
Rubin, Steven Jay 155
"Rudolph, the Red-Nosed Reindeer" (TV special) 141
Ryu, Chishu 278

Saga of the Vagabonds (1959) 12
Sahara, Kenji 18, 20, 23, 25–26, 28, 30, 31, 37, 78, 80, 82, 83, 85, 93, 95, 96, 99, 136, 152, 164, 196, 198, 219, 290, 296
Saigo no Kyoru see *Last Dinosaur, The*
Saito, Noritake 196
Sakagami, Yusushi 199
Sakai, Frankie 63, 65, 69, 71
Sakai, Sachio 58, 184
Samurai (film series) 52, 55
Samurai (1940) 52
Samurai Part II: Duel at Ichijoji Temple (1955) 11
Samurai Pirate see *Lost World of Sinbad, The*
Samurai Reincarnation see *Makai tensho*
Samurai Saga, The (1959) 12

San daikaiju chikyu saidai no kessen see
   Ghidrah: The Three-Headed Monster
Sanada, Hiroyuki 248, 253
Sandakan 8 (19??) 13
Sands of Iwo Jima (1949) 171
Sandy Frank Enterprises 174, 177, 233, 247
Sanjuro (1962) 11, 12, 56, 105, 123
Sanshiro Sugata (1943) 12, 92
"Santa Claus Is Coming to Town" (TV special) 141
Sarafian, Richard 283
Sarafian, Ted 282
Sasable omon see *Girl with Bamboo Leaves, The*
Sasaki, Katsuhiko 211, 225, 228, 287
Sasaki, Takamuru 58
Sata, Keiko 56
Sato, Kei 106, 108
Sato, Makoto 248
Sato, Masaru 17, 120, 123, 150, 152, 216, 219
Sato, Mitsuru 38
Sato, Tomomi 167
Satomi Hakkenda 333
Satsujin kyo jidai see *Age of Assassins, The*
Saturday Night Fever (1978) 242
"Saturday Night Live" (TV series) 212
Sawada, Kenji 25
Sawaguchi, Yasuko 267, 269, 272, 275
Sawai, Keiko 90, 116
Sawamura, Ikio 97, 142
Sayonara Jiyupeta see *Sayonara Jupiter*
Sayonara Jupiter 11, 367–68
Scandal (1950) 12
Scars of Dracula (1970) 194
Scherman, Tom 139
Schofield, Annabel 283, 285
Scottfield, Robert 287
Scorsese, Martin 277, 279
Secret of the Fylfot, The 333–34
Secret of the Telegian, The 26, 37, 55, 57–60, 368
Secret Scrolls Part I 52, 59, 368
Secret Scrolls Part II 13, 52, 368–69
Segawa, Hiroshi 125
"Sege" (*Variety* reviewer) 285
Sekai daisenso see *Last War, The*
Sekiya, Masumi 235
Sekizawa, Shinichi 25, 59, 70, 94, 98, 118, 120, 122, 150, 184, 210
Selleca, Connie 242, 244
Sellers, Peter 210, 258

Senda, Koreya 42
Sengoku jietai see *Time Slip*
Sengoku, Noriko 183
Sennin Buraku 317
Seven Brides for Seven Brothers (1954) 138
Seven Mysteries 317
7 Faces of Dr. Lao (1963) 249
Seven Samurai (1954) xii, xv, 11, 12, 16, 56, 83, 105, 250
Shadow of the Wolf (1993) 3
Shaka see *Buddha*
Shales, Tom (*Washington Post* reviewer)
Sharp, Don 188
Sheldon, Walter 68
Shiba, Kazue 150
Shibaki, Toshio 202
Shimada, Shogo 214
Shimizu, Isamu 249
Shimura, Takashi xii, 2–3, 7, 12, 13, 17, 28, 30, 31, 32, 33, 51, 71, 73–74, 88, 89, 97, 99, 102, 109, 173, 220, 222
Shindo, Kaneto 107
Shinobi no manji see *Secret of the Fylfot, The*
Shinshaku Yotsuya kaidan 324
Shintoho Co., Ltd. xvi, 26, 47, 62, 315–8
Shirakawa, Yumi 23, 26, 37, 58, 60, 63, 73
Shishido, Joe 245, 251
Shochiku Co., Ltd. ix, xvi, 49, 107, 153, 166, 201, 293, 318–25
Shoemaker, Greg xv, 57, 60, 66, 76, 90, 92, 96, 100, 112, 119, 123, 164, 184, 185, 198, 213, 219, 222, 240, 241
"Shogun" (TV series) 3, 65, 92
Shogun Assassin 369
Shogun's Ninja 334
Shonen tanteidan 334
Shonen tanteidan—Kabutomushi no yoki see *20 Faces*
Shop on Main Street, The (1965) 105
Short, Robert 212
Shuzenji monogatari see *Mask of Destiny, The*
Sight and Sound (magazine) 4
Silence Has No Wings 370
Silva, Henry 263, 266
Sinister Spaceships, The see *Supergiant*
Sinners of Hell, The 317
Sinners to Hell, The see *Sinners of Hell, The*
"Sir Graves Ghastly Presents" (TV series) 27

Siskel, Gene 57
Sister Street Fighter (1976) 62
"Six Million Dollar Man, The" (TV series) 219, 247
Six Ultra Brothers vs. the Monster Army see *Space Warriors 2000*
Skullduggery (1970) 231
Snake Girl and the Silver-Haired Witch, The 310–11
Snow Ghost see *Snow Woman, The Snow White and the Three Stooges* (1961) 189
Snow Woman, The 311
Snowman see *Half-Human: The Story of the Abominable Snowman*
Solar Crisis 279-83, 387–90
Something Weird Video ix
Son of Frankenstein (1939) 19
Son of Godzilla 25, 56, 60, 80, 122, 123, 150–53, 161, 163, 164, 184, 370
Son of Kong (1933) 14, 76
Sonoi, Keisuke 153
Sora no daikaiju Radon see *Rodan*
Soryu hiken see *Secret Scrolls Part II*
Space Amoeba, The see *Yog: Monster from Space*
Space Chief (character) 30
Space Chief see *Invasion of the Neptune Men*
Space Cruiser Yamato (1977?) 261
Space Greyhound see *Invasion of the Neptune Men*
Space Master X-7 (1958) 17
Space Men Appear Over Tokyo see *Mysterious Satellite, The*
Space Monster Dogora see *Dagora, the Space Monster*
Space Warriors 2000 173, 223–25, 379
Spacemen Appear in Tokyo see *Mysterious Satellite, The Spartacus* (1960) 17
"Spectralman" (TV series) 231
"Spectreman" see "Spectralman"
Spellos, Peter 291
Spielberg, Steven 238, 276
Split, The see *Manster, The*
Spook Warfare see *Ghosts on Parade*
Stanford, Len 45
Star! (1968) 231
Star Force: Fugitive Alien II 251–53, 245, 379–80
Star of Hong Kong (1962) 12
Star Prince, The see *Prince of Space*
"Star Trek" (TV series) 281
"Star Trek: The Next Generation" (TV series) 2

Star Wars (1977) 62, 239, 240, 241, 247, 248, 250, 251, 252, 258, 260, 285
Star Wars (film series) 129, 292
Starman (character) 26–28, 30, 63
Starman (film series) 49, 50, 51, 62
"Starwolf" (TV series) 244
Steelman from Outer Space, The see *Supergiant*
Steiner, Max 13
Stinson, Charles (*Los Angeles Times* reviewer) 31
Story of Hell, A see *Portrait of Hell*
Strauss, Bob 271
Stray Dog (1949) 10, 12
Street Fighter, The (1975) 62
Street Fighter's Last Revenge, The (1979) 62
Strongest Man in the World, The (1975) 189
Sturges, Preston xv
Submersion of Japan 123, 157, 289, 370–71; see also *Tidal Wave*
"Submersion of Japan" (TV series) 217
Sugiyama, Koichi 275
Sunazuka, Hideo 120
Supa Jyaiantsu: jinko eisei to jinrui no hametsu see *Supergiant*
Supa Jyaiantsu: uchu kaijin shutsugen see *Supergiant*
Supa Jyaiantsu: uchusen to jinko eisei no gekitotsu see *Supergiant*
Super Monster see *Gamera Super Monster*
Super Monster Gamera see *Supermonster*
Supergiant 317–18; see also *Atomic Rulers, Attack from Space, Evil Brain from Outer Space,* and *Invaders from Space*
Superman (character) 28
Superman (1948) 26
Superman (1978) 22, 260
Suzuki, Kazuo 184
Svenson, Bo 264, 265, 266
Swamp, The 334
Sword of Vengeance 371
Swords, Travis 267, 269
Swords of the Space Ark 253–55, 334–35

Tachikawa, Hiroshi 85
Taguchi, Tomorah 270
Taiyo o nusunda otoko see *Man Who Stole the Sun, The*
Tajima, Reiko 217
Tajima, Yoshibumi 24, 37, 38, 58, 82–83, 90, 93, 95, 117, 142, 162, 269, 296

Tajima, Yoshifumi *see* Tajima, Yoshibumi
Takada, Minoru 44
Takada, Miwa 130, 131
Takada, Toshie 258
Takahashi, Atsuko 196
Takahashi, Koji 272, 275
Takahashi, Masaya 168
Takahashi, Osahide 205
Takaido Yotsuya kaidan (play by Tsuruya) 47
Takaku, Susunu 169
Takamuru and Kikumaru 324
Takarada, Akira 7, 11–12, 19–20, 63, 65, 93, 95, 116, 120, 123, 142, 186, 187, 189, 296
Takarajima Ensei 335
Takashima, Masanobu 80, 273, 275
Takashima, Tadao *see* Takashima, Tadeo
Takashima, Tadeo 77, 80–81, 111, 150, 152, 275
Takasuka, Toru 165
Takechi Toyoko 66
Takei, George 16
Takemitsu, Toru 125
Taking of Pelham One Two Three, The (1974) 115
Takuma, Shin 266
Tale of Peonies and Lanterns, A see Kaidan botandoro
Tales After the Rain see *Tales of Ugetsu*
Tales of Ugetsu xii, xiv, xv, xvi, xvii, xxiii, 3, 4–7, 48, 104, 173, 312
Tamba, Tetsuro 155, 157, 214, 216, 220, 221, 249
Tamblyn, Russ 136, 137, 138
Tanaka, Ken 266
Tanaka, Kinuyo 5–6, 49
Tanaka, Kunie 225
Tanaka, Shigeo 140
Tanaka, Tomoyuki 9, 13, 28, 51, 74, 230, 240, 268, 275, 289
Tanaka, Yoshiko 273
Tanin no kao see *Face of Another, The*
Tarantula (1955) 9
Taste the Blood of Dracula (1970) 194
Tattooed Swordsman 315
Tattooed Swordswoman see *Tattooed Swordsman*
Taxi Driver (1976) 279
Tazaki, Jun 51, 72, 74, 78, 80, 82–83, 88–89, 91, 92, 93, 102, 116, 121, 136, 162, 164
Television Horror Movie Hosts (book by Watson) 27

Temptress, The 315
Temptress and the Monk, The see *Temptress, The*
Ten Commandments, The (1956) 51
Tenamonya: Ghost Journey see *Tenamonya yurei dochu*
Tenamonya yurei dochu 371–72
Terao, Akira 277
Terayama, Shuji 160
Terminator, The (1984) 290, 295
Terminator 2: Judgment Day (1991) 283
Terrible Ghost-Cat of Okazaki see *Kaibyo Okazaki sodo*
Terror Beneath the Sea 62, 134–35, 154, 172, 177, 242, 335
Terror of Godzilla see *Terror of Mechagodzilla*
Terror of Mechagodzilla 26, 143, 227–30, 268, 372
Teshigahara, Hiroshi 105, 124–25, 126
Tetsuka, Katsumi 12
Tetsuo see *Tetsuo: The Iron Man*
Tetsuo: The Iron Man 270–72, 390
Tetsuo II: Body Hammer 271, 390–1
Tetto no kaijin see *20 Faces*
Them! (1954) 9, 23, 24, 77
These Foolish Wives (1946) 3
Thing, The (1982) 67
Thing (From Another World), The (1951) 17, 95, 171
Thing with Two Heads, The (1972) 67
This Island Earth (1955) 45, 144
Thomas, Jason 204
Thomas, Kevin (*Los Angeles Times* reviewer) 126, 251
Thompson, Howard (*New York Times* reviewer) 31, 47, 70, 132, 195
Thorsen, Russell 18
Those Who Make Tomorrow (1946) 12
Three Stooges in Orbit, The (1962) 70
Three Treasures, The 3, 12, 41, 51–52, 83, 87, 99, 372–73
Throne of Blood xii, xiv, xvii, xxiii, 6, 12, 16, 32–33, 75, 123, 373
Thunderball (1965) 155, 156, 171
Thunderbird 6 (1968) 68
Thunderbirds Are Go (1966) 68
Tidal Wave (see also *Submersion of Japan*) 213–17, 219, 239
Time (magazine) 33
Time of the Apes 230–34, 245, 380
Time of Their Lives, The (1946) 43
Time Slip 62, 335–36
Titanosaurus (character) 230

Titra Studios 96
Tobenai Chinmoko see *Silence Has No Wings*
Tobey, Kenneth 43
Toei Co., Ltd. ix, xiii, xvi, 49, 54, 62, 134, 135, 157, 160, 177, 179, 325–337
Togano, Chotaro 120
Togin, Chotaro 196
Togyo (1941) 46
Toho Co., Ltd. xiii, xv, xvi, 9–14, 28, 37, 38, 41, 51, 54, 62, 63, 68, 72, 76, 77, 81, 130, 136, 143, 145, 150, 155, 157, 161, 163, 165, 173, 181, 182, 185, 186, 188, 189, 194, 272, 295, 337–76
Toho International 57
Toho-owned theaters xvi, 11, 51, 52
Tohoscope xiii, 30, 44
Tokaido Yotsuya kaidan (1959) see *Ghost of Yotsuya, The*
Toki wo kaieru shojo 336
Tokugawa onna keibatsushi 336
Tokyo no Tekisasujin see *Knockout Drops*
tom thumb (1958) 138
Tomei Kenshi see *Invisible Swordsman, The*
Tomei ningen 373
Tomei ningen arawaru 312
Tomei ningen erohakase 391
Tomei ningen okase see *Lusty Transparent Man*
Tomei ningen to Hai-Otoko see *Transparent Man vs. the Fly Man*
"Tone" (*Variety* reviewer) 164
Tonomura, Taiji 106
Top 100 Movies, The (book by Kobal) 4
Tora! Tora! Tora! (1970) 56, 160, 269
Tora-san (film series) xvi
Toyohara, Isao (Kohsuke) 286
Tragic Ghost Story of Fukagawa see *Kaidan Fukagawa jowa*
Trail of the Pink Panther (1982) 258
Transparent Man, The see *Tomei ningen arawaru*
Transparent Man vs. the Fly Man 312
Tremayne, Les ix, 182
Tsuburaya, Eiji 9–11, 31, 41, 44, 46, 47, 51, 52, 56, 57, 59, 60, 62, 65–66, 70, 74–5, 76, 81, 84, 87, 89, 92, 94, 110, 118, 122, 137, 140, 146, 172, 173, 174, 185, 186, 198, 201, 290, 296
Tsuburaya Enterprises, Inc. ix, 141, 231, 234, 236, 242, 244, 261, 376–81
Tsuburaya, Hideo 75
Tsuchiya, Yoshio 16, 29, 37, 45, 55, 56, 58, 59, 85, 87, 116, 118, 151, 152, 161, 164, 196, 198, 286, 290, 296
Tsukamoto, Shinya 270, 271, 272
Tsuruta, Koji 58
Tsushima, Toshiaki 241
"Tube" (*Variety* reviewer) 33, 44, 46, 52, 70, 81
Tucker, Guy 96, 118, 283
Turpin, Ben 209
TV Movies (book by Maltin) 123, 134, 137, 138, 172, 222, 244, 263
20th Century-Fox 230–31
20 Faces 336
20 Million Miles to Earth (1957) 9
20,000 Leagues Under the Sea (1954) 9
Twilight of Honor (1963) 111
Twilight of the Cockroaches 283–86, 390
Twilight Zone, The (1983), 282
"Twin Peaks" (TV series) 138
2001: A Space Odyssey (1968) 98, 169, 240, 283

Uchida, Katsumasu 228
Uchu daikaiju Dogora see *Dagora, the Space Monster*
Uchu daikaiju Guirara see *X from Outer Space, The*
Uchu daisenso see *Battle in Outer Space*
Uchu kaiju Gamera see *Gamera Super Monster*
Uchu kaizoku-sen see *Invasion of the Neptune Men*
Uchu kara no messeji see *Message from Space*
Uchujin Tokyo ni arawaru see *Mysterious Satellite, The*
Ueda, Kichijiro 147
Uehara, Ken 49, 69, 71, 73–74, 81, 83
Ugetsu see *Tales of Ugetsu*
Ugetsu Monogatari see *Tales of Ugetsu*
Ultra Man see *Urutoraman*
Ultra Man, The see *Urutoraman*
"Ultra Q" (TV series) 225
"Ultra Seven" (TV series) 173, 225
Ultraman see *Urutoraman*
"Ultraman" (TV series) 173, 177, 180, 225
"Ultraman Ace" (TV series) 173
"Ultraman '80" (TV series) 173
"Ultraman Great" (TV series) 173
"Ultraman Leo" (TV series) 173
Ultraman Story, The see *Urutoraman Sutori*
"Ultraman Taro" (TV series) 173

Umeda, Tomoko 207
Umemiya, Tatsuo 49, 50, 54
Undersea Kingdom, The (1936) 186
Unearthly, The (1957) 43
United Artists xiv, 66
United Productions of America (UPA) ix, 206
Universal-International (U-I) 77, 79
Universal Pictures 144
Universal Television 219
Unknown Island (1948) 17
Unknown Satellite Over Tokyo see *Mysterious Satellite, The*
Uno, Jukichi 106
Urutora 6-Kyodai tai kaiju gundan see *Space Warriors 2000*
Urutoraman 380
Urutoraman Sutori 173, 380-81
Usami, Junya 158, 195
Utsui, Ken 27-28, 39, 35, 36, 50

Vampire de la Autopista, El (1970) 195
Vampire Doll, The 194-5, 373-4
Vampire Lovers, The (1970) 195
Vampire Man see *Woman Vampire, The*
Vampire Moth, The (1956) 46
Vampyros Lesbos (1970) 195
Van Ark, Joan 234
Vanishing Point (1971) 283
Varan (character) 42-44, 161
Varan the Unbelievable xiv, 41-44, 375
Variety (trade paper) 47, 104, 108, 172, 283
Vaughn, Robert 250, 263
Venetian Affair (1967) 172
Vengeance Is Mine 324
Vengeance of the Monster, The see *Majin*
Village of Eight Gravestones 324-25
Village of Eight Tombs see *Village of Eight Gravestones*
Violated Angels see *Okasaretu Byuakui*
Violated Women see *Okasaretu Byuakui*
Virus xvi, 62, 160, 263-66, 391-93
"Voice of the Night" (short story by Hodgson) 86
"Volcano Monsters, The" (unproduced screenplay) 16-17
Voyage into Space 177-80, 336-37
"Voyage to the Bottom of the Sea" (TV series) 174
Vraney, Mike ix

"Wagon Train" (TV series) 171
Wakabayashi, Akiko 88, 96, 155, 156-57
Wakasugi, Kazuko 47
Wakusei daisenso see *War in Space, The*
Walker, Jimmy 291, 292, 293
War in Space, The 11, 46, 60, 239-42, 248, 374-75
War of the Gargantuas xiv, 9, 25, 75, 83, 110, 136-38, 209, 212, 213, 375
War of the Insects see *Genocide*
War of the Monsters (1966) 138-41, 149, 165, 166, 182, 259, 260, 312-13
War of the Monsters (1972) see *Godzilla on Monster Island*
War of the Planets (1977) see *War in Space, The*
War of the Worlds, The (1953) 17, 44
Warehouse see *Blind Beast, The*
Warner Bros. xv, 9, 14, 16
Warning from Space see *Mysterious Satellite, The*
Warren, Bill ix, xv, xx, xxi-xxiii, 9, 17, 26, 29, 31, 39, 44, 47, 68, 70, 137, 214, 216, 217, 227
Watanabe, Akira 80, 146, 172
Watanabe, Misako 100
Watanabe, Toru 120
Watari and the Seven Monsters see *Watari, Ninja Boy*
Watari, Ninja Boy 337
Watasi, Tsunehiko 237
Water Cyborgs see *Terror Beneath the Sea*
Waters, John 160
Watusi (1959) 31
Weak-kneed from Fear of Ghost-Cat see *Kaibyo koshinuke daisodo*
"Wear" (*Variety* reviewer) 108
Weathers, Carl 242
Weed of Crime, The (1964) 60
Weird Tales see *Kwaidan*
Weird Trip see *Kaidan ryoko*
Weldon, Michael xx
Welles, Orson xv, 32
West Side Story (1961) 138
Westworld (1973) 115
Whale God, The 313
What's Up, Tiger Lily? (1966) 56, 75, 89, 144, 157
When a Woman Ascends the Stairs (1963) 3
When Time Ran Out... (1980) 265
When Worlds Collide (1951) 21, 22, 72, 74, 283
Whirlwind 52, 75, 92, 375-76

Index **423**

"Whit" (*Variety* reviewer) 56, 76
White, Tom ix
White Gorilla (1947) 262
"White Hunter" (TV series) 144
White Pongo (1945) 262
White Rose of Hong Kong (1965) 60
Who Framed Roger Rabbit? (1988) 286
Widom, Bud 169
Wild Bunch, The (1969) 115
Wild Strawberries (1957) 5
Wilder, Billy xv
Williams, John 250
Williams, Paul 280
Williams, Peter 165
Williams, Spice 291, 292
Wilson, Chuck 286
Winkler, William 291, 292
Winter Kills (1979) 3
Witch, The see *Yoba*
Wizard of Oz, The (1939) 103
Wolfen (1981) 115
Woman in the Dunes (1964) 124–25, 126
Woman of the Snow see *Snow Woman, The*
Woman Vampire, The 318
Woman's Body Vanishes see *Jotari johatsu*
Women's Cell see *Zoku hiroku onna ro*
Women's Prison see *Hiroku onna ro*
Wonderful World of the Brothers Grimm, The (1962) 129, 138
Wood, Ed, Jr. 247
World Apartment Horror 392
World, the Flesh and the Devil, The (1959) 64
World War III Breaks Out see *Final War, The*
Wu, Vivian 291, 292
Wyant, H.M. 282

X from Outer Space, The 74, 135, 153–55, 325

Yabu no naka no kuroneko see *Kuroneko*
Yachigusa, Kaoru 55
Yada, Seiji 129
Yagi, James 79
Yagyu Bugeicho see *Secret Scrolls Part I*
Yagyu Secret Scrolls see *Secret Scrolls Part I*
Yakuza, The (1975) 299
Yakuza Films xvi

Yamada, Isuzu 32
Yamada, Kazuo 52
Yamada, Minoru 180
Yamagata, Isao 21
Yamamoto, Kajiro 10
Yamamoto, Michio 194, 195, 204
Yamamoto, Yoko 145
Yamashita, Takeo 180
Yamauchi, Akira 201
Yanami, Eiko 199
Yanigasawa, Shinichi 153, 154
Yasei no Shomei 392
Yashagaike see *Demon Pond*
Yashiro, Miki 85
Yasumi, Toshio 64
Yates, George Worthington 77
Yatsu hukamura see *Village of Eight Gravestones*
Yoba 313
Yoda, Yoshitaka 173
Yog: Monster from Space 26, 33, 56, 122, 196–98, 229, 376
Yoidore tenshi see *Drunken Angel*
Yojimbo (1961) 12, 16, 33, 56, 92, 105, 123
Yokai dai senso see *Ghosts on Parade*
Yokai hyaku monogatari see *100 Monsters*
Yoku see *Half a Loaf...*
Yonezawa, Shiori 294
Yongary, Monster from the Deep 393
Yosei Gorasu see *Gorath*
Yoshida, Hiroaki 286
Yoshida, Teruo 167
Yoshimura, Jitsuko 106
Yoshimura, Kazaburo 107
Yotsuya kaidan see *Illusion of Blood*
Yotsuya kaidan: Oiwa no borei see *Curse of the Ghosts, The*
You Nazi Spy (1940) 34
You Only Live Twice 80, 144, 155–57, 393–94
Young, Freddie 156
Young Guy Graduates (1969) 60
Youth and His Amulet 16, 52, 65, 92, 144, 376
Yuasa, Noriaki xxii, 140
Yukioka, Keisuke 145
Yukioona see *Snow Woman, The*
Yumihari-zuki see *Crescent Moon, The*
Yurei Hanjo-ki see *My Friend Death*
Yurei-sen see *Ghost Ship*
Yusei oji see *Prince of Space*
Yureiyashiki no kyofu-chi wo suu ningyo see *Vampire Doll, The*

Zatoichi Meets His Equal 313
Zatoichi Meets the One-Armed Swordsman see *Zatoichi Meets His Equal*
Zatoichi Meets the Yojimbo (1971) 3
Zatoichi: "Yabure! Tojin-ken!" see *Zatoichi Meets His Equal*
Zeiram see *Zeiramu*
Zeiramu 376
Zettai zetsumei see *Killing Bottle, The*
Ziarko, Charles ix

Zigra (character) 199
Zimmern, Terri 67
Zoeller, Arlene 199
Zoku hiroku onna ro 313–4
Zoku kotetsu no kyojin–Supa Jyaiatsu see *Supergiant*
Zoku Supa Jyaiantsu (dai hachibu): akuma no keshin see *Supergiant*
Zoku Supa Jyaiantsu (dai kyubu): dokunga ookoku see *Supergiant*

www.ingramcontent.com/pod-product-compliance
Lightning Source LLC
Chambersburg PA
CBHW051202300426
44116CB00006B/414